Modern Macroeconomics

Modern Macroeconomics

Sanjay K. Chugh

The MIT Press
Cambridge, Massachusetts
London, England

MIT Press books may be purchased at special quantity discounts for business or sales promotional use. For information, please email special_sales@mitpress.mit.edu

This book was set in Times New Roman by Toppan Best-set Premedia Limited. Printed and bound in the United States of America.

Library of Congress Cataloging-in-Publication Data

Chugh, Sanjay K.
  Modern macroeconomics / Sanjay K. Chugh.
  pages   cm
Includes bibliographical references and index.
  ISBN 978-0-262-02937-7 (hardcover : alk. paper) 1. Macroeconomics. 2. Keynesian economics.
 3. Comparative economics.
I. Title.
  HB172.5.C48 2015
  339—dc23

                                                                          2015009283

10 9 8 7 6 5 4 3 2

Contents

Acknowledgments

This textbook began as a collection of notes that I prepared to distribute to undergraduate students more than ten years ago while I was a graduate teaching assistant at the University of Pennsylvania. From the start, I organized the notes in "chapter" form because that made the notes appear coherent in the flow of thoughts and information. Writing these notes also helped me learn what I wanted to discuss with students, and allowed easy communication within the classroom. Or, rather, I think, at least easier than if I were just repeating phrasings and approaches of other textbooks.

Over the years, inevitably, the collection of notes grew, and many students (I hesitate today to even call them "students" because I learned a lot from them) have read various chapters and versions of the text. In reverse chronological order, these students were in classes I taught at Boston College, Boston University, the University of Maryland, Johns Hopkins University, Georgetown University, and the University of Pennsylvania. I thank all the students whose discussions contributed to the early chapters and, occasionally, brand-new drafts of chapters written on the fly.

I also thank all the department chairs at these institutions that permitted me, knowingly or not, to use my "notes" in the classroom rather than a "formal" textbook. Among them all, I owe Frank Weiss at Johns Hopkins an enormous debt of gratitude for his patience and encouragement in developing my notes over the past decade.

I further owe an enormous debt of gratitude to Allan Drazen at the University of Maryland for suggesting my name to Jane Macdonald at the MIT Press in 2011. Without his reference, this textbook would not have come to fruition.

When Jane Macdonald approached me and asked if I would be interested in developing my notes into a textbook, that was the moment I felt that I actually had in hand the makings of a textbook. I can't thank the MIT Press enough, and in particular Jane and Emily Taber for their support and encouragement in my completing the manuscript, for there is no other way my collection of notes could have turned into a textbook I also thank Dana Andrus at MIT Press for her spectacular editing skills, advice, and suggestions.

I have had many teaching assistants over the years who helped students get through various parts and early drafts of notes. There are again way too many to thank, but one really stood out, Dominique Brabant at Boston College. Dominique helped tremendously while I was starting to resume work on the textbook. She went through the draft in early 2014 with a fine-toothed comb, offering lots of suggestions, comments, advice, and ways to maintain consistency across the chapters. It was Dominique's input that finally pushed me to begin rewriting the chapters I wrote at the very start of my teaching career.

Additionally I have had feedback from faculty members who used parts of my notes in their own classes at different universities; I hope this was productive for their students. And then there are the bits and pieces scattered throughout the text based on discussions I have had with fellow researchers, coauthors, friends, colleagues, and members of the economics profession. I thank them all for enriching throughout my thinking experience.

Sanjay K. Chugh
May 18, 2015

Introduction to Modern Macroeconomics

Modern macroeconomics is built explicitly on microeconomic foundations. That is, the modern study and analysis of macroeconomics begins by considering how the microeconomic units, namely consumers and firms, in an economy make their decisions and then considers how the choices of these great many individuals interact with each other to yield economy-wide outcomes. This approach sounds quite reasonable because, after all, it is individuals in a society that ultimately make decisions. However, it may surprise you that macroeconomics was not always studied this way. Indeed much of the evolution of macroeconomic theory occurred without any reference to its microfoundations. We, however, will consider the microeconomic foundations of macroeconomics—as such, our consideration of macroeconomics will mostly be a "modern" one.

The two most fundamental microeconomic units in any economy are consumers and firms. In introductory microeconomics, you studied how these individual units make their decisions. Under economists' usual assumption of rational behavior, the posited goal of consumers is to maximize their utility, and the posited goal of firms is to maximize their economic (as opposed to accounting) profits. Concepts such as marginal utility, marginal revenue, and marginal cost should be familiar to you from your introduction to microeconomics, and they will provide the foundation of our consideration of macroeconomics.

In modern industrialized economies, consumption activity (i.e., purchases of goods and services by individuals) constitutes the largest share of all macroeconomic activity. For example, in the United States, consumption accounts for roughly 70 percent of all economic activity. Understanding how consumers make decisions and the factors, especially government policies, that affect these decisions will be of prime importance in our study of macroeconomics. We thus begin our study of macroeconomics by reviewing the microeconomics of consumer theory in chapter 1. The tools introduced there will be used repeatedly, so it is important to grasp these ideas fully. Following this review of consumer theory, we will develop the macroeconomic theory of consumption, including the impact of various government policies on consumption behavior. After this, we will introduce firms into our theoretical model of the economy, again considering the impact of various government policies on firms' decisions.

We are potentially faced with one daunting task, however. It is obvious that each consumer is different from every other consumer in his preferences for goods and services, and it is equally obvious that firms are very different from one another, both in the goods and services they produce as well as the technologies that they use in producing those goods and services. In short, there is a great deal of heterogeneity in the economy. This poses a potentially intractable theoretical problem because it should strike you as impossible to model theoretically the choices of *every single individual* and *every single firm* in the economy. Quite apart from the fact that there is no way we could know the exact choices of every single microeconomic unit, the point of any theoretical model is to be a simplified description of some complicated phenomenon—if we had to try to determine the choices of every single microeconomic unit, we would not achieve any simplification at all!

One approach, then, is to categorize the individual microeconomic units into broad groups: for example, categorize consumers into "upper class," "middle class," and "lower class" and categorize firms into "goods-producing firms" and "service-producing firms." We could then consider how individuals in these different groups make their decisions, and subsequently "sum up" their choices to yield macroeconomic outcomes. This seems an appealing way of proceeding—it turns out, however, that even doing this becomes quite cumbersome theoretically. The details of the theoretical problems associated with this approach are left to more advanced courses in macroeconomics, but, briefly, the main problems have to do with defining the appropriate broad categories and then determining an appropriate way of "summing up" the individuals' choices.

We will instead adopt what is known as the **representative agent** paradigm. In the representative agent approach, we suppose that there are a great many consumers in the economy *each of whom is identical to all other consumers in every way* and that there are a great many firms in the economy *each of which is identical to all other firms in every way.* This is obviously a gross simplification of reality. However, adopting this approach has the virtue that it becomes much simpler to theoretically model macroeconomic outcomes. Of particular interest for our purposes is that it still allows us to consider the general effects of macroeconomic policies, although we will not be able to say which groups are hurt versus which groups benefit from any given policy (because, by construction, there are no distinct "groups" at all).

A simple example may help illustrate how we will use the representative agent approach. Suppose that there are five different consumers in an economy: in a given year, person A spends $50 on consumption, person B spends $75 on consumption, person C spends $100 on consumption, person D spends $125 on consumption, and person E spends $150 on consumption. The total dollar value of consumption in this economy in this year is thus $500. If we wanted to model every microeconomic unit, we would have to describe how each of persons A, B, C, D, and E made his decisions. However, if our main focus is on studying the total consumption of $500, we could equivalently suppose that there are five individuals in the economy *each of whom spent $100 on consumption.* That is, we could

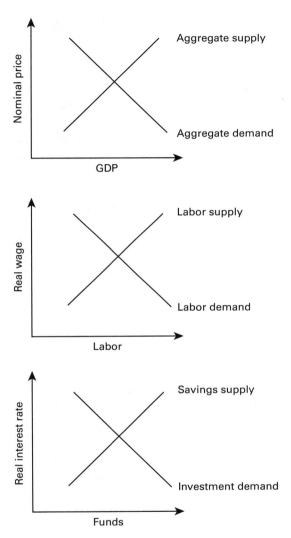

Three macro markets: goods and services markets, labor markets, and financial markets

suppose that each individual simply spent the economy-wide average on consumption. Then our task, at the microeconomic level, is to model just one individual, this "average consumer," because as soon as we know how he made his decisions we know the economy-wide outcome. This average consumer is exactly who the representative agent is. While seemingly a gross simplification of reality (as it is!), we will see that by modeling only this **representative consumer** in the economy we will be able to describe quite well many macroeconomic outcomes and will also be able to consider the effects of macroeconomic policies.

Similarly we will also suppose that there is an "average firm" in the economy—the **representative firm.** This representative firm produces the average level of goods and services in the economy, guided by the usual principle of profit maximization familiar from introductory microeconomics. Once again, the way in which we model this representative firm will allow us to consider how firms respond to various macroeconomic policies.

In all to come, keep the following in mind: our goal is essentially to build a small theoretical model (using the representative agent paradigm) of the entire economy, one that includes consumers, firms, and the government. Putting these components together will allow us to see how they all interact with one another to yield macroeconomic outcomes and allow fairly rich consideration of the effects of macroeconomic policy, both fiscal policy (tax and spending initiatives of Congress) and monetary policy (control of interest rates and the money supply by the Federal Reserve). Throughout, we will be informed by basic microeconomic principles.

Our analysis will be concerned with demand, supply, and equilibrium in the "three macro markets," which are the aggregate goods and services market, the aggregate labor market, and the aggregate financial market depicted in the figure above. All of the demand and supply relationships are sketched as linear only for illustrative purposes.

Exogenous Variables versus Endogenous Variables

Before we begin, a crucial distinction to keep in mind throughout our study is that between **exogenous variables** and **endogenous variables.** In every particular framework and macro market we discuss, the exogenous variables are the *inputs* into the analysis. Exogenous variables are the ones that "are taken as given," as economic language so often puts it. In contrast, the endogenous variables are the *outputs* from the analysis conducted within the particular framework or market we are studying. Stated more mathematically, the endogenous variables are the ones that "need to be solved for," whether we're describing the consumer side of the economy or the firm side of the economy (or, for that matter, the government's role in the macroeconomy).

In each of the three macro markets as depicted in the figure, *prices are endogenously determined at the point at which economy-wide quantities demanded and economy-wide quantities supplied equate.* Of course, "distortions" arise in these perfect markets, and we will discuss many departures from perfect competition, but this diagram provides an important starting point.

Another important starting point is displayed in the next figure. The endogenous prices that arise in this figure are *exogenous ("taken as given") from the point of view of atomistic individuals actively participating in the markets,* be they individual consumers or individual businesses. Keep both figures in mind as we begin to construct our macroeconomic frameworks.

Each atomistic firm and each atomistic individual takes as given prices in markets. Prices are determined in equilibrium, hence are exogenous to atomistic firms and atomistic individuals.

Before we get into the foundations of modern macroeconomics, in chapter 1 we briefly review the microeconomics of consumer theory. Part I next takes us through the various building blocks of modern macro, not just on the consumer side but also with respect of firms and the government.

1

Microeconomics of Consumer Theory

The two broad categories of decision makers in an economy are consumers and firms. Each individual in each of these groups makes its decisions in order to achieve some goal—a consumer seeks to maximize some measure of satisfaction from his consumption decisions while a firm seeks to maximize its profits. We first consider the microeconomics of consumer theory and will later turn to a consideration of firms. The two theoretical tools of consumer theory are utility functions and budget constraints. Out of the interaction of a utility function and a budget constraint emerge the choices that a consumer makes.

Utility Theory

A utility function describes the level of "satisfaction" or "happiness" that a consumer obtains from consuming various goods. A utility function can have any number of arguments, each of which affects the consumer's overall satisfaction level. But it is only when we consider more than one argument can we consider the *trade-offs* that a consumer faces when making consumption decisions. The nature of these trade-offs can be illustrated with a utility function of two arguments, but this case is completely generalizable to the case of any arbitrary number of arguments.[1]

Figure 1.1 illustrates in three dimensions the square-root utility function $u(c_1, c_2) = \sqrt{c_1} + \sqrt{c_2}$, where c_1 and c_2 are two different goods. This utility function displays **diminishing marginal utility** in *each* of the two goods, which means that, holding consumption of one good constant, increases in consumption of the other good increase total utility at ever-decreasing rates. Graphically, diminishing marginal utility means that the slope of the utility function with respect to each of its arguments in isolation is always decreasing.

---

1. An advantage of considering the case of just two goods is that we can analyze it graphically. Graphing a function of two arguments requires three dimensions, graphing a function of three arguments requires four dimensions, and, in general, graphing a function of n arguments requires $n + 1$ dimensions. Obviously we cannot visualize anything more than three dimensions.

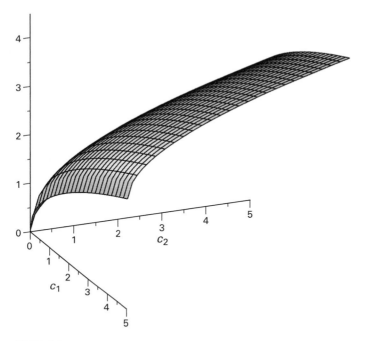

Figure 1.1
Utility surface as a function of two goods, c_1 and c_2. The specific utility function here is the square-root utility function, $u(c_1, c_2) = \sqrt{c_1} + \sqrt{c_2}$. The three axes are the c_1 axis, the c_2 axis, and the utility axis.

The notion of diminishing marginal utility seems to describe consumers' preferences so well that most economic analysis takes it as a fundamental starting point. We will consider diminishing marginal utility a fundamental building block of all our subsequent ideas.

The first row of figure 1.2 displays the same information as in figure 1.1 except as a pair of two-dimensional diagrams. Each diagram is a rotation of the three-dimensional diagram in figure 1.1, which allows for complete loss of depth perspective of either c_2 (the upper left panel) or of c_1 (the upper right panel). The bottom row of figure 1.2 contains the diminishing marginal utility functions with respect to c_1 (c_2), holding constant c_2 (c_1).

Indifference Curves

Figure 1.3 returns to the three-dimensional diagram using the same utility function, with a different emphasis. Each of the solid curves in figure 1.3 corresponds to a particular level of utility. This three-dimensional view shows that a given level of utility corresponds to a given height of the function $u(c_1, c_2)$ above the c_1–c_2 plane.[2]

---

2. Be sure you understand this last point very well.

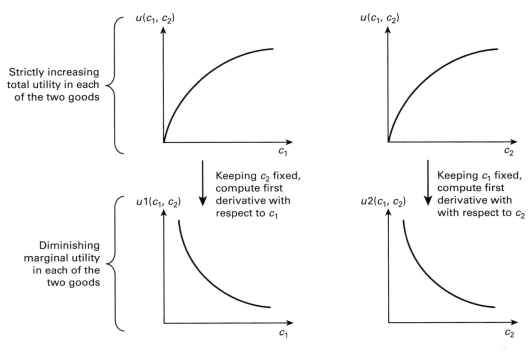

Figure 1.2
Top left: Total utility as a function of c_1, holding fixed c_2. *Top right*: Total utility as a function of c_2, holding fixed c_1. *Bottom left*: (Diminishing) marginal product function of c_1, holding fixed c_2. *Bottom right*: (Diminishing) marginal product function of c_2, holding fixed c_1. For the utility function $u(c_1, c_2) = \sqrt{c_1} + \sqrt{c_2}$, the marginal utility functions are $u_1(c_1, c_2) = (1/2) \cdot \left(1/\sqrt{c_1}\right)$ (*bottom left panel*) and $u_2(c_1, c_2) = (1/2) \cdot \left(1/\sqrt{c_2}\right)$ (*bottom right panel*).

If we were to observe figure 1.3 from directly overhead, so that the utility axis were coming directly at us out of the c_1–c_2 plane, we would observe figure 1.4. Figure 1.4 displays the contours of the utility function. In general, a **contour** is the set of all combinations of function arguments that yield some pre-specified function value. Here in our application to utility theory, each contour is the set of all combinations of the two goods c_1 and c_2 that deliver a given level of utility. The contours of a utility function are called **indifference curves,** so named because each indifference curve shows all combinations (sometimes called "bundles") of goods between which a consumer is *indifferent*—that is, deliver a given amount of satisfaction. For example, suppose that a consumer has chosen 4 units of c_1 and 9 units of c_2. The square-root utility function then tells us that his level of utility is $u(4, 9) = \sqrt{4} + \sqrt{9} = 5$ (utils, which is the fictional measure of utility). There are an infinite number of combinations of c_1 and c_2, however, that deliver this level of utility. For example, had the consumer instead been given 9 units of c_1 and 4 units of c_2, he would have obtained the same level of utility. That is, from the point of view of his overall level of satisfaction,

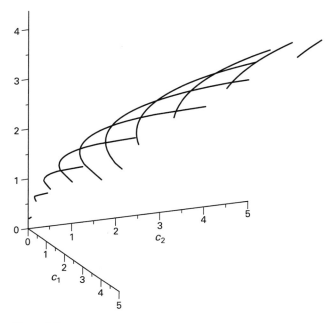

Figure 1.3
Indifference map of the utility function $u(c_1, c_2) = \sqrt{c_1} + \sqrt{c_2}$, where each solid curve represents a given height above the c_1–c_2 plane and hence a particular level of utility. The three axes are the c_1 axis, the c_2 axis, and the utility axis.

the consumer is indifferent between having 4 units of good 1 in combination with 9 units of good 2 and having 9 units of good 1 in combination with 4 units of good 2. Thus these two points in the c_1–c_2 plane lie on the same indifference curve.

A crucial point to understand in comparing figure 1.3 and figure 1.4 is that indifference curves that lie further to the northeast in the latter correspond to higher values of the utility function in the former. That is, although we cannot actually "see" the height of the utility function in figure 1.4, by comparing it to figure 1.3, we can conclude that indifference curves that lie further to the northeast provide higher levels of utility. Intuitively, this means that if a consumer is given more of *both* goods (which is what moving to the northeast in the c_1–c_2 plane means), then his satisfaction is unambiguously higher.[3]

3. You may readily think of examples where consuming more does not always leave a person better off. For example, after consuming a certain number of pizza slices and sodas, you will have likely had enough, to the point where consuming more pizza and soda would decrease your total utility (i.e., it would make you sick). While this may be an important feature of preferences (the technical name for this phenomenon is "satiation"), for the most part we will be concerned with those regions of the utility function where utility is increasing. A way to justify this view is to suppose that the goods that we speak of are very broad categories of goods, not very narrowly defined ones such as pizza or soda.

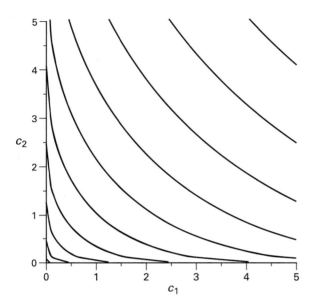

Figure 1.4
Contours of the utility function $u(c_1, c_2) = \sqrt{c_1} + \sqrt{c_2}$ viewed in the two-dimensional c_1–c_2 plane. The utility axis is coming perpendicularly out of the page at you. Each contour of a utility function is called an indifference curve. Indifference curves further to the northeast are associated with higher levels of utility.

Once we understand that figure 1.3 and figure 1.4 are conveying the same information, it is much easier to use the latter diagram because drawing (variations of) figure 1.3 over and over again would be very time-consuming! As such, much of our study of consumer analysis will involve indifference maps such as that illustrated in figure 1.4.

Marginal Rate of Substitution

Each indifference curve in figure 1.4 has a negative slope throughout. This captures the idea that starting from any consumption bundle (i.e., any point in the c_1–c_2 plane), when a consumer gives up some of one good, *in order to maintain his level of utility*, he must be given an additional amount of the other good. The crucial idea is that the consumer is willing to **substitute** one good for another, even though the two goods are not the same. Some reflection should convince you that this is a good description of most people's preferences. For example, a person who consumes two pizzas and five sandwiches in a month may be just as well off (in terms of total utility) had he consumed one pizza and seven sandwiches.[4]

---

4. The key phrase here is "just as well off." Given our assumption above of increasing utility, he would *prefer* to have more pizzas *and* more sandwiches.

The slope of an indifference curve tells us the *maximum number of units of one good the consumer is willing to substitute to get one unit of the other good.* This is an extremely important economic way of understanding what an indifference curve represents. The slope of an indifference curve varies depending on exactly which consumption bundle is under consideration. For example, consider the bundle ($c_1 = 3$, $c_2 = 2$), which yields approximately 3.15 utils using the square-root utility function above. If the consumer were asked how many units of c_2 he would be willing to give up in order to get one more unit of c_1, he would first consider the utility level (3.15 utils) he currently enjoys. Any final bundle that left him with less total utility would be rejected. He would be indifferent between his current bundle and a bundle with 4 units of c_1 that also gave him 3.15 total utils. Simply solving from the utility function, we have that $\sqrt{4} + \sqrt{c_2} = 3.15$, which yields (approximately) $c_2 = 1.32$. Thus, from the initial consumption bundle ($c_1 = 3$, $c_2 = 2$), the consumer is willing to trade at most 0.68 units of c_2 to obtain one more unit of c_1.

What if we repeated this thought experiment starting from the new bundle? That is, with ($c_1 = 4$, $c_2 = 1.32$), what if we again asked the consumer how many units of c_2 that he would be willing to give up to obtain yet another unit of c_1? Proceeding just as above, we learn that he would be willing to give up at most 0.48 units of c_2, giving him the bundle ($c_1 = 5$, $c_2 = 0.84$), which yields total utility of 3.15.[5]

The preceding example shows that the more units of c_1 the consumer has, the fewer units of c_2 the consumer is willing to give up to get *yet another* unit of c_1. The economic idea here is that consumers have preferences for balanced consumption bundles—they do not like "extreme" bundles that feature very many units of one good and very few of another. Some reflection may also convince you that this feature of preferences is a good description of reality.[6] In more mathematical language, this feature of preferences leads to indifference curves that are *convex to the origin.*

Thus the slope of the indifference curve has very important economic meaning. It represents the **marginal rate of substitution** between the two goods—the maximum quantity of one good that the consumer is willing to trade for one more unit of the other. Formally, the marginal rate of substitution at a particular consumption bundle is the negative of the slope of the indifference curve passing through that consumption bundle.

Budget Constraint

The cost side of a consumer's decisions involves the price(s) he must pay to obtain consumption. Again maintaining the assumption that there are only two types of consumption goods, c_1 and c_2, let P_1 and P_2 denote their prices, respectively, in terms of money. For sim-

---

5. Make sure you understand how we arrived at this.

6. When we later consider how consumers make choices across time (as opposed to a specific point in time), we will call this particular feature of preferences the "consumption-smoothing" motive.

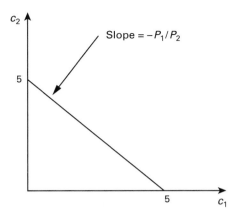

Figure 1.5
Budget constraint, plotted with c_2 as a function of c_1. For this example, the chosen prices are $P_1 = P_2 = 1$, and the chosen income is $Y = 5$.

plicity, we will assume for the moment that each consumer spends all of his income, denoted by Y (more generally, all of his resources, which may also include wealth), on purchasing c_1 and c_2.[7] We further assume (for now) that he has no control over his income—he simply takes it as given.[8] The **budget constraint** the consumer must respect as he makes his choice about how much c_1 and c_2 to purchase is therefore

$$P_1 c_1 + P_2 c_2 = Y.$$

The term $P_1 c_1$ is total expenditure on good 1 and the term $P_2 c_2$ is total expenditure on good 2, the sum of which is equal to income (by our assumption above). If we solve this budget constraint for c_2, we get

$$c_2 = -\frac{P_1}{P_2} c_1 + \frac{Y}{P_2},$$

which, when plotted in the c_1–c_2 plane, gives the straight line in figure 1.5. In this figure, for illustrative purposes, the prices are chosen to both equal one (i.e., $P_1 = P_2 = 1$) so that the slope of the budget line is a negative one, and income is arbitrarily chosen to be $Y = 5$.

7. Assuming this greatly simplifies the analysis and yet does not alter any of the basic lessons to be learned. Indeed, if we allow the consumer to "save for the future" so that he doesn't spend of all of his current income on consumption, the additional choice introduced (consumption vs. savings) would also be analyzed by exactly the same procedure. We will turn to such "intertemporal choice" models of consumer theory shortly.

8. Also very shortly, using the same tools of utility functions and budget constraints, we will study how an individual decides what his optimal level of income is.

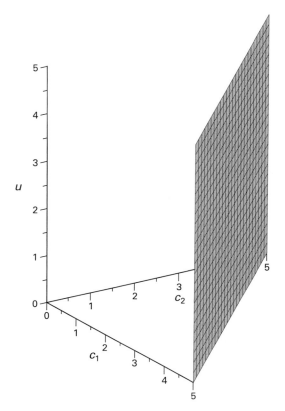

Figure 1.6
Budget constraint drawn in the three-dimensional c_1–c_2–u space. The budget constraint is a plane here because it is independent of utility.

Obviously, when graphing a budget constraint, the particular values of prices and income will determine its exact location.

We discussed in our study of utility functions the idea that we need three dimensions—the c_1 dimension, the c_2 dimension, and the utility dimension—to properly visualize utility. We see here that utility plays no role in the budget constraint, as it should not because the budget constraint only describes expenditures, not the benefits (i.e., utility) a consumer obtains from those expenditures. That is, the budget constraint is a concept completely independent of the concept of a utility function—this is a key point. We could graph the budget constraint in the same three-dimensional space as our utility function—it simply would be independent of utility. The graph of the budget constraint (which we call a budget plane when we construct it in three-dimensional space) in our c_1–c_2–u space is shown in figure 1.6.

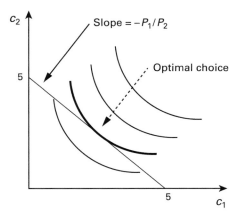

Figure 1.7
Optimal consumption choice displayed as a tangency between the budget line and an indifference curve. The optimal choice must lie on the budget line and attain the highest possible utility for the consumer.

Optimal Choice

We are now ready to consider how consumers make choices. The benefits of consumption are described by the utility function, and the costs of consumption are described by the budget constraint. Graphically, the decision the consumer faces is to choose that bundle (c_1, c_2) that yields the highest utility (i.e., lies on the highest indifference curve) that also satisfies his budget constraint (i.e., lies in the relevant budget plane).

Imagine that both the budget constraint and the utility function were plotted in the three dimensions of figure 1.6—and then imagine that we are observing that figure from directly overhead, so that the utility axis were coming straight out of the c_1–c_2 plane at us, so that we lose perspective of the utility axis. What we would see are an indifference map and a budget line. Figure 1.7 shows that the optimal decision (the one that yields the highest attainable utility) features a tangency between the budget constraint and an indifference curve. Consider what would happen if the optimal choice did not feature such a tangency. In this case it must be that the indifference curve through which the chosen bundle passes also crosses the budget line at another point. Given that indifference curves are convex to the origin, this must mean that there is another consumption bundle that is both affordable and yields strictly higher utility, so a rational consumer would choose it.[9]

At the point of tangency that describes the consumer's optimal choice, the slope of the budget line must equal the slope of the indifference curve. The slope of the budget line, as

9. The assumption of a "rational" consumer must further be augmented by other strong assumptions, some of these being that there is no income uncertainty, prices are fixed, the consumer has no bargaining power, and no uncertainty exists as to the quality of the products. We will discuss some of these strong assumptions later.

we saw above, is simply the price ratio $-P_1 / P_2$. And recall from our discussion of utility functions that the (negative of the) slope of an indifference curve is the marginal rate of substitution—the maximum amount of one good that the consumer is willing to give up in order to obtain one more unit of the other good *such that* his total utility remains the same. These two points lead us to a very important description of a consumer's optimal choice, one that we will refer to as the **consumer's optimality condition:**

$$\frac{P_1}{P_2} = MRS.$$

When markets are functioning well (and we have yet to discuss what "functioning well" means), this optimality condition is what guides the decisions of consumers. When markets are not functioning well, policy discussions at both the microeconomic level and the macroeconomic level can use this optimality condition as a benchmark to strive to achieve when considering intervening in markets.[10]

The economic logic of the optimality condition is as follows. Without regard to prices, the MRS describes the consumer's internal (i.e., utility-based) willingness to trade one good for another. The price ratio describes the market trade-off between the two goods. To understand this last point, suppose that $P_1 = \$3$ per unit of good 1 and $P_2 = \$2$ per unit of good 2.[11] The price ratio therefore, keeping explicit track of units, is

$$\frac{P_1}{P_2} = \frac{\$3 / \text{unit of good 1}}{\$2 / \text{unit of good 2}} = \frac{3 \text{ units of good 2}}{2 \text{ units of good 1}}.$$

Notice the units here—it is units of good 2 per unit of good 1, which is exactly what it must be in our two-dimensional graph with c_1 on the horizontal axis and c_2 on the vertical axis. This demonstrates that the price ratio does indeed describe the market trade-off between the two goods.

Suppose that the consumer had chosen a bundle at which his MRS was higher than the market price ratio. This means that he is willing to give up more units of c_2 for a little more c_1 than the market requires him to—so he should use the markets to trade some of his c_2 for c_1 because he would be made unambiguously better off! Now suppose that he has traded himself in this way all the way to the point where his MRS equals the price ratio. Should he trade yet more units of c_2 to obtain a little more c_1? The answer is no, because doing so would now mean having to give up more units of c_2 than he willing to for a little more c_1.

10. We will have much more to say later about the role of government intervention in markets.

11. It is very easy to lose sight of the fact that prices have units. That is, when a price tag on a T-shirt says "$10," the implicit units attached to this are "10 *per T-shirt*"—because obviously if you want to buy 2 T-shirts you will have to pay $10 \times 2 = \$20$. Unit analysis is often helpful in thinking about how economic variables relate to each other.

Thus, once he has traded his way to the bundle at which his MRS equals the price ratio, he can do no better—he has arrived at his optimal consumption choice, the one that maximizes $u(c_1, c_2)$ subject to his budget constraint.

Lagrange Characterization

Let's now study the optimality condition using our Lagrange tools (described in the mathematical appendix at the end of this book). We can cast the problem we're studying here into mathematical form by way of the Lagrange method: the objective function (i.e., the function that the consumer seeks to maximize) is the utility function $u(c_1, c_2)$, the variables to be chosen are c_1 and c_2, and the maximization of utility is subject to the budget constraint $P_1c_1 + P_2c_2 = Y$. To cast the budget constraint into the form $g(.) = 0$, let's write $g(c_1, c_2) = Y - P_1c_1 - P_2c_2 = 0$.[12] We can thus write the Lagrange function as

$$L(c_1, c_2, \lambda) = u(c_1, c_2) + \lambda[Y - P_1c_1 - P_2c_2],$$

where λ is the Lagrange multiplier. The first-order conditions with respect to c_1, c_2, and λ are, respectively,

$$\frac{\partial u}{\partial c_1} - \lambda P_1 = 0,$$

$$\frac{\partial u}{\partial c_2} - \lambda P_2 = 0,$$

and

$$Y - P_1c_1 - P_2c_2 = 0.$$

From the first two of these expressions, we can obtain the optimality condition we obtained qualitatively/graphically earlier. The first expression immediately above can be solved for the multiplier to give us

$$\lambda = \frac{\partial u / \partial c_1}{P_1}.$$

Next we insert this in the second first-order condition, which gives

$$\frac{\partial u}{\partial c_2} = \frac{P_2 \cdot (\partial u / \partial c_1)}{P_1}.$$

---

12. Alternatively, we could equivalently construct $g(.)$ as $g(c_1, c_2) = P_1c_1 + P_2c_2 - Y = 0$, and we would obtain exactly the same result as we are about to obtain; it would be a good exercise for you to try the subsequent manipulations for yourself using this alternate definition of the function $g(.)$.

Rearranging this result in one more step gives us

$$\frac{P_1}{P_2} = \frac{\partial u / \partial c_1}{\partial u / \partial c_2},$$

which states that when the consumer is making the optimal choice between consumption of the two types of goods, his ratio of marginal utilities (the right-hand side of this last expression) is equal to the ratio of prices of the two goods (the left-hand side of this last expression). We can compare this expression to the expression earlier that we named the optimality condition: inspecting the two reveals that they must be the same and furthermore that *the MRS between two goods is equal to the ratio of marginal utilities.* This latter very important result (that the MRS between any two goods is equal to the ratio of marginal utilities between those two goods) can be derived more rigorously mathematically, but we defer this. Instead, the important idea to understand here is how to apply the Lagrange method to the basic consumer optimization problem and how it yields the same intuitive result that we qualitatively obtained earlier in this chapter.

To link the result here back to our introduction to the Lagrange method, note that if we compute the partial derivatives of the constraint function (the budget constraint in this case) with respect to c_1 and c_2, we have $\partial g / \partial c_1 = -P_1$ and $\partial g / \partial c_2 = -P_2$, which means that the ratio of partial derivatives of the constraint function is $(\partial g / \partial c_1)/(\partial g / \partial c_2) = P_1/P_2$. But this is obviously just the left-hand side of the optimality condition above. Recall that in our introduction to Lagrange theory we noted that a central result was that *at optimal choices, the ratio of partials of the objective function* (here, the utility function) *would be equal to the ratio of partials of the constraint function* (here, the budget constraint): we now have our first specific instance of this important result.

Chapter 1 Problem Set Questions

1. **Sales tax.** Consider the standard consumer problem that we have been studying, in which a consumer has to choose consumption of two goods c_1 and c_2 priced (in money) P_1 and P_2, respectively, before any applicable taxes. Many states charge a sales tax on some goods but not on others—for example, many states charge sales taxes on all goods except food and clothing. Suppose that good 1 carries a per-unit sales tax, while good 2 has no sales tax. Use the variable t_1 to denote this sales tax, where t_1 is a number between 0 and 1 (e.g., so, if the sales tax on good 1 is 15 percent, write $t_1 = 0.15$).

   a. Using sales tax t_1 and consumer income Y, write down the budget constraint of the consumer. Explain economically how/why this budget constraint differs from the standard one we have been considering thus far.

   b. Graphically describe how the imposition of the sales tax on good 1 alters the optimal consumption choice (i.e., how the optimal choice of each good is affected by a policy shift from $t_1 = 0$ to $t_1 > 0$).

    c. Suppose that the consumer's utility function is given by $u(c_1, c_2) = \log c_1 + \log c_2$. Using a Lagrangian, solve algebraically for the consumer's optimal choice of c_1 and c_2 as functions of P_1, P_2, t_1, and Y. Graphically show how, for this particular utility function, the optimal choice changes due to the imposition of the sales tax on good 1.

2. Properties of indifference maps. For the general model of utility functions and indifference maps developed in the chapter, explain why no two indifference curves can ever cross each other. Your answer should include the economic logic that would apply here, and may also include appropriate equations and/or graphs.

3. A canonical utility function. Consider the utility function

$$u(c) = \frac{c^{1-\sigma} - 1}{1 - \sigma},$$

where c denotes consumption of some arbitrary good and σ (Greek lowercase letter "sigma") is known as the "curvature parameter" because its value governs how curved the utility function is. In the following, restrict your attention to the region $c > 0$ (because "negative consumption" is an ill-defined concept). The parameter σ is treated as a constant.

    a. Plot the utility function for $\sigma = 0$. Does this utility function display diminishing marginal utility? Is marginal utility ever negative for this utility function?

    b. Plot the utility function for $\sigma = 1/2$. Does this utility function display diminishing marginal utility? Is marginal utility ever negative for this utility function?

    c. Consider instead the natural-log utility function $u(c) = \ln(c)$. Does this utility function display diminishing marginal utility? Is marginal utility ever negative for this utility function?

    d. Determine the value of σ (if any value exists at all) that makes the general utility function presented above collapse to the natural-log utility function in part c. (Hint: Examine the derivatives of the two functions.)

I
CONSUMER ANALYSIS, FIRM ANALYSIS, FISCAL POLICY, INTRODUCTION TO FINANCE THEORY

Part I introduces the basic building blocks of modern macroeconomic theory, the heart of which is the representative consumer. Chapter 2 describes, in a one-period setting, consumers' optimal choices between spending time in market work and in nonmarket work activities (the consumption–labor framework). Chapters 3 and 4 bring in the time dimension, which is critical for macroeconomic analysis, in the two-period consumption–savings model. Chapter 5 synthesizes the static consumption–labor framework with the two-period consumption–savings framework.

Chapter 6 then introduces firm analysis in the same two-period environment. In chapter 7, the two-period framework is extended to include government taxation and government spending and their potential impact on private-sector outcomes.

Chapter 8 extends the two-period framework to a "many, many, many period" model (technically modeled as an infinite-period economy) and describes the underlying interactions between macroeconomic theory and finance theory.

Chapter 9 introduces the concept of "economic shocks," which lead to fluctuations (recessions and booms) in the overall economy.

2

Static Consumption–Labor Framework

In our review of consumer theory in chapter 1, we simply assumed that an individual has some given amount of "labor income," which we denoted by Y, to spend on consumption goods. Doing so allowed us to focus attention on the tools and principles of consumer theory.

Economics is at its core a set of theories about decision-making, and casual reflection reveals that individuals do have some control over how much labor income they earn. That is, at least to some degree, individuals "choose" how much income they earn just as they choose how much, say, good 1 and good 2 they consume. We now extend our model of consumer theory to incorporate this feature of individual decision-making. As we will see, the tools of analysis and general principles of this extended model are ones with which we are already familiar—simply the tools of indifference curves and budget constraints. To simplify our introduction to this topic, we will use a "one-shot" model in which the individual has no savings decision to make—that is, there is no future, so the only economic decisions to be concerned with are the present. After we understand how the one-period consumption–leisure framework works and we later study the consumption–savings framework, we will bring the two analyses together to complete our analysis of macroeconomic consumer theory.

In addition to considering the structure of the **consumption–labor framework** (alternatively and equivalently referred to as the **consumption–leisure framework**) and to get our feet wet with government policy effects, we will embed within it from the start a consideration of government tax policy. We will have much more to say later about the role of macroeconomic tax policies. As we will see, one of the major schools of tax policy thought to have emerged in the past few years crucially hinges on the main features of the consumption–leisure model.

The Two "Goods": Consumption and Leisure

In our initial look at consumer theory, we supposed that there existed two broad categories of consumption goods, "good 1" and "good 2." We will now condense these two categories into just a single category called "consumption." That is, consumption is any and all "stuff" (goods and services) that individuals might purchase in order to obtain utility (happiness). Thus consumption, which we will denote by c (without any subscripts), is an argument to individuals' utility functions.

Because we are interested in studying how consumers "choose" their income, we must specify how consumers in fact earn their incomes. One seemingly obvious way of proceeding is to suppose that consumers obtain their income by working. An individual can choose to work some number of hours (per day or per week or per month, etc.—we will specify this more carefully below) for which he receives **before-tax pay** of W dollars per hour. That is, W dollars per hour is the individual's gross wage rate, which in general is *not* what the individual actually gets to keep as the result of his efforts. In most countries, individuals are subject to a variety of government taxes—of the many kinds of taxes that exist, the most common type (and certainly the type to which the greatest number of people are subject) is the income tax. Income taxes in the United States and essentially all other countries are specified as some percentage of an individual's total earnings. For example, if the labor tax rate in the United States were 30 percent and an individual earned \$50,000 in a given year, the amount of tax he would have to pay that year is \$50,000 × 0.30 = \$15,000.[1] Thus it is as if the hourly wage W is subject to a 30 percent tax, making the individual's **after-tax wage rate** $0.70W$ dollars per hour. More generally, if we denote the tax rate on labor income by t (where $0 \leq t \leq 1$), then the after-tax wage rate is $(1-t)W$ dollars per hour. Because it is ultimately disposable income that individuals care about, $(1-t)W$ is the relevant wage rate for an individual's decision-making.

Presumably, working is a "bad" for individuals—that is, individuals dislike working because it reduces their total utility. In order to fit our model into standard consumer theory, we can easily recast the "bad" of working into a "good" by defining **leisure** to be the total number of hours an individual has available to him during some relevant period of time *minus* the total number of hours he spends working during that period.

For example, suppose that we were to consider each calendar week as a distinct period of time. If n is the number of hours in a week that an individual spends working, and there are $24 \times 7 = 168$ total hours in a week, then the individual's hours spent in leisure, which we will denote by l, is $l = 168 - n$.[2]

Instead, suppose that we think of a distinct period of time such as one calendar month that has 30 days. Then all of the hours spent in either work or leisure would = 720 hours.

1. The calculation of an individual's tax burden is not nearly so straightforward in reality due to a great many complicating features of tax laws. However, for our purposes this simple example will suffice.

2. Notice that because of our definition, leisure should not be thought of as time spent "having fun." Rather, it is time spent not working. Thus activities like time spent sleeping, time spent watching TV, time spent cooking and cleaning at home, time spend taking care of children, and so on, all count as "leisure." The American Time Use Survey (ATUS), a survey conducted by the US Bureau of Labor Statistics (BLS) provides many more categories of how people spend their 24 hours per day (http://www.bls.gov/tus/).

That is, $n + l = 720$ (= 24×30) hours. Alternatively, if we think in terms of one calendar year, then $n + l = 8,760$ (= 24×365) hours. You get the point.

We could even think of any of these time frames as "one distinct period of time." So instead of writing 168 or 720 or 8,760 (which is itself quite cumbersome to write over and over), we will *normalize the hours available during a given time period to one.* This "one" unit of total hours is a stand-in for 168, 720, 8,760, or whatever frequency of "time" you consider best.

Thus, in our framework, the representative consumer makes optimal choices so that

$n + l = 1$

must be true. Here n should be thought of as the percentage of the one unit of time the individual works, and hence in turn l should be thought of as the percentage of the one unit of time the individual spends in leisure. We will from here on colloquially refer to n and l as "hours spent working" and "hours spent in leisure," respectively.

The above is all about time accounting. Getting back to the framework, leisure is the opposite of working. Because working is a bad, leisure must be a good. We thus postulate leisure to be the second argument to the representative individual's utility function.

Indifference Map for Consumption and Leisure

The two objects in our model from which an individual obtains utility are thus consumption and leisure, giving rise to an abstract utility function $u(c, l)$. We will refer to both consumption and leisure from here on as "goods," even though clearly leisure is not a tangible object. Consumption and leisure, as we have defined them, are very broad categories of goods. As such, it is most useful to think of the general properties of the utility function $u(c, l)$ as being the same as those of the utility function $u(c_1, c_2)$ when we first studied consumer theory. Thus we assume from now on the following properties:

1. Utility is always strictly increasing in consumption (i.e., $\partial u / \partial c > 0$).

2. Utility is always strictly increasing in leisure (i.e., $\partial u / \partial l > 0$).

3. Utility exhibits diminishing marginal utility in consumption (i.e., $\partial^2 u / \partial c^2 < 0$).

4. Utility exhibits diminishing marginal utility in leisure (i.e., $\partial^2 u / \partial l^2 < 0$).

Notice that these are exactly the same properties of the utility function that we have already studied. With these assumptions we can construct an indifference map over consumption and leisure, as illustrated in figure 2.1. Each indifference curve has all the usual properties we initially encountered in our study of consumer theory. Specifically, each indifference curve is downward-sloping, is bowed-in toward the origin, and crosses no other indifference curve.[3]

---

3. At this point this should all be review. Recall especially that these three properties of indifference curves arise precisely because of our four assumptions on the utility function.

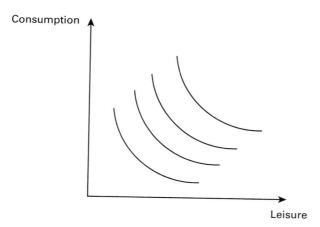

Consumption

Leisure

Figure 2.1
Indifference map defined over consumption and leisure

Although our two goods consumption and leisure are not both "market goods" (i.e., one cannot really "purchase leisure" in a market), there is still a well-defined notion of a *marginal rate of substitution (MRS)* between the two. Again, as is usual, the MRS measures how many units of one good the consumer is willing to give up to get one more unit of the other good. Graphically the MRS is the slope of the indifference curve.

Budget Constraint

Indifference maps alone are, of course, not enough to study an individual's optimal choice. To study optimal decision-making, we need to consider the individual's budget constraint, and it is here where our model of consumption and leisure most differs from the simple model of consumer theory we initially studied. In our simple model of chapter 1, a consumer simply had the income Y to spend on consumption (of good 1 and good 2). In contrast, in the consumption–labor framework the amount of income an individual has to spend on consumption (of the *one* market good) depends on how much he chooses to work. Let's now study formally the budget constraint in this model, reminding ourselves that the length of one period of time in our model is one unit (recall that $n + l = 1$).

We assume that the individual can work as few or as many hours as he wants. Regardless of how many hours he works, he gets paid the before-tax wage W dollars per hour.[4] As

4. Clearly, the assumption of being able to work as few or as many hours as one wants does not capture reality literally. Most workers have some semi-fixed schedule that they must adhere to, at least in some relevant "short run." In a "longer run," workers are freer to move to jobs that better accommodate their lifestyles, and so on. Thus think of our consumption–leisure model as more of an attempt to capture this latter sense rather than the former sense.

mentioned above, though, it is ultimately his after-tax income (his disposable income) that an individual cares about—his after-tax wage rate is $(1-t)W$ dollars per hour. Because he will choose to work n hours per week, his total disposable income is simply

$$Y = (1-t)\cdot W \cdot n.$$

Because $n = 1 - l$, we can write nominal disposable income as a function of leisure,

$$Y = (1-t)\cdot W \cdot (1-l).$$

As in our earlier study, we make the simplifying assumption that the individual spends all his income on consumption and saves nothing for the future. Each unit of consumption c can be purchased at the market price P (the individual is a price-taker). Thus the individual's consumption each period (week) is

$$Pc = Y.$$

Combining the last two expressions yields the budget constraint in the consumption–leisure model

$$Pc = (1-t)\cdot W \cdot (1-l).$$

In this budget constraint the consumer takes as given the nominal price P, the hourly nominal wage rate W, and the tax rate t,[5] and he chooses his level of consumption c and hours of leisure l.

A useful rearrangement of this budget constraint is

$$Pc + (1-t)Wl = (1-t)W.$$

In this version with both the consumption good and leisure on the left-hand side, we see that the "price" of leisure is the after-tax wage rate $(1-t)\cdot W$. Of course, leisure (time off from work) is not directly bought and sold in markets. But the wage is the opportunity cost of leisure—every hour spent in leisure is an hour that could have been spent working. Thus, from an economic point of view, where we explicitly take account of opportunity costs, the after-tax wage is the price of leisure because it is what is being given up for every extra hour of leisure taken.[6]

As always, a budget constraint describes the set of choices that is available to the consumer but does not tell us anything about which point in that set he will choose. To graph this budget constraint in a diagram like figure 2.1, we can rearrange again to get

---

5. That is, the individual is a price-taker in both the consumption-good market as well as the labor market.

6. This is a very general notion of a "price." A price is anything that must be given up in order to obtain something else.

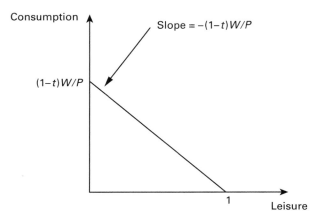

Figure 2.2
Budget line in the consumption–leisure model

$$c = \frac{(1-t)\cdot W}{P} - \frac{(1-t)\cdot W}{P}\cdot l.$$

This budget constraint is a straight line, as shown in figure 2.2, with vertical intercept

$$\frac{(1-t)W}{P}$$

and slope

$$\left(\frac{-(1-t)W}{P}\right).$$

By inserting the value $c = 0$ in the budget constraint, we find that the horizontal intercept is at $l = 1$, which simply states that if the individual wants no consumption, he can use all the hours in a week for leisure.

In our earlier analysis, in which consumers took their income Y as a constant, changes in income led to parallel shifts of the budget line. In the consumption–leisure framework, it is not income that individuals treat as a constant, but rather the after-tax wage rate $(1-t)W$. Notice how the after-tax wage rate enters the budget constraint here. Any change in the after-tax wage rate leads to a rotation of the budget constraint around the horizontal intercept (which is fixed at $l = 1$) because $(1-t)W$ appears in both the vertical intercept and the slope of the budget line.

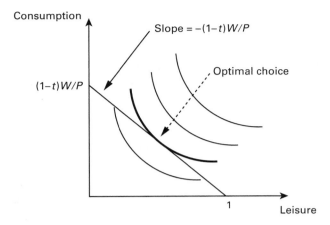

Figure 2.3
At the optimal choice of consumption and leisure, the budget constraint is tangent to an indifference curve

Optimal Choice

As always, to consider optimal choice, we must consider the interaction of the individual's preferences (indifference map) with his budget constraint. Superimposing the budget line and the indifference map, we have that the optimal choice of consumption and leisure is as shown in figure 2.3.

Labor Supply Function

When the individual optimally chooses to spend l hours of his time in leisure, he is, of course, choosing to spend $n = 1 - l$ hours of his time working. He is thus supplying n hours of labor to the labor market. Clearly, the optimal choice of labor in figure 2.3 depends on the after-tax wage $(1-t)W$. A definition is in order before proceeding: the **real after-tax wage** is the after-tax wage in money terms divided by the price of consumption in money terms. With our notation, the real after-tax wage is simply the ratio $(1-t)W/P$,[7] and we see that it is only the real after-tax wage that matters for the vertical intercept and slope of the budget line. For the rest of this section, we will study how the optimal choice of labor varies as the real after-tax wage varies.

7. The term "real after-tax wage" comes from the units of measure associated with $(1-t)W/P$. Because the units of $(1-t)W$ is ($/hour of work) and the units of P is ($/unit of good), the units of $(1-t)W/P$ is (units of goods/hour of work), and hence the terminology: $(1-t)W/P$ measures the number of actual (real) goods a worker earns for each hour of work after he has paid his taxes. This is yet another example of how unit analysis helps us think about the relationships among economic variables.

We begin our analysis by supposing that the initial real after-tax wage is quite low. Denote this initial wage by $((1-t)W/P)_1$. At this low initial real after-tax wage, the optimal choice is labeled point A in figure 2.4. This initial optimal choice has associated with it n_1 hours of work (not shown, of course, because the axes contain c and l, not n). Now suppose that with the price P held constant, the nominal after-tax wage rises to $((1-t)W)_2$, so that the new after-tax real wage is $((1-t)W/P)_2$. Notice that there are two ways the nominal after-tax wage rate can rise: the gross wage W can rise while the tax rate remains constant or the tax rate can fall while the gross wage W remains constant. Regardless of the mechanism by which it occurs, the rise in the real after-tax wage causes the budget line to become steeper by pivoting around the horizontal intercept. With this higher real after-tax wage, the individual's optimal choice is point B. At point B the individual has more consumption than at point A. The individual also enjoys less leisure at point B than at point A—which means that he now works n_2 hours, with $n_2 > n_1$. In other words, n has risen as the real after-tax wage has risen from $((1-t)W/P)_1$ to $((1-t)W/P)_2$.

An important note is in order here. You may be looking at figure 2.4 and wondering why the optimal choice under the higher real after-tax wage did not feature more

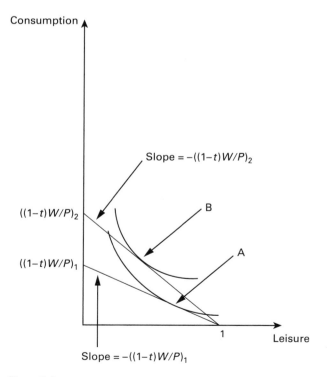

Figure 2.4
Real after-tax wage rises from $((1-t)W/P)_1$ to $((1-t)W/P)_2$ as the individual optimally chooses more consumption and less leisure—the latter implying that he chooses to work more

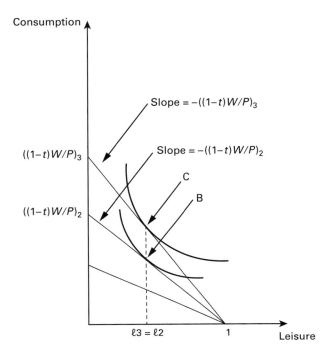

Figure 2.5
Real after-tax wage rises from $((1-t)W/P)_2$ to $((1-t)W/P)_3$ as the individual optimally chooses more consumption but an unchanged amount of leisure—the latter implying that he chooses to not adjust his hours worked

consumption *and* more leisure. In other words, you may be wondering why the indifference map is not such that the new optimal choice lies to the northeast of the original optimal choice, rather than northwest as is drawn. The answer is not at all a theoretical one, but rather one due to evidence about the real world. Much microeconomic and behavioral research has shown that when individuals currently have a low real after-tax wage, an increase in the real after-tax wage induces them to work more (presumably because they simply need the earnings to meet basic expenses). This suggests the partial indifference map in figure 2.4.

Now suppose that with the price P still held constant, the nominal after-tax wage rises again, to $((1-t)W)_3$. Thus, the real after-tax wage has now risen to $((1-t)W/P)_3$. The optimal choice at this new higher real after-tax wage is labeled point C in figure 2.5. Comparing point C to point B, we see that the individual has chosen to not adjust the number of hours he works (and thus also not adjust the amount of leisure time he enjoys) when the real after-tax wage rose from $((1-t)W/P)_2$ to $((1-t)W/P)_3$. Thus, at this higher real after-tax wage, the individual is working n_3 hours, with $n_3 = n_2 > n_1$.

Consider yet another increase in the nominal after-tax wage, to $((1-t)W)_4$, which has associated with it the new real after-tax wage $((1-t)W/P)_4$. At this point the real after-tax

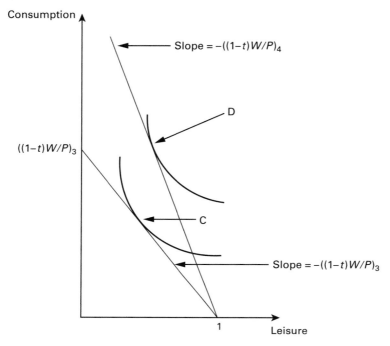

Figure 2.6
Real wage rises from $((1 - t)W/P)_3$ to $((1 - t)W/P)_4$ as the individual optimally chooses more consumption and **more** leisure—the latter implying that he now chooses to work less

wage has gotten quite high, and it may be that the individual simply does not need to spend more time working because his basic expenses (and perhaps even some luxuries) have already been met. At a very high after-tax wage, it may be reasonable to expect that the individual will now choose to spend **less** time working and spend more of his time in leisure. Such a situation is depicted in figure 2.6, in which the rise in the real after-tax wage to $((1-t)W/P)_4$ induces the optimal choice to move from point C to point D. At point D the individual is working fewer hours than at point C. That is, hours worked n_4 given the real after-tax wage $((1-t)W/P)_4$ is smaller than hours worked n_3 given the real after-tax wage $((1-t)W/P)_3$.

To re-emphasize a point made above, notice there is no theoretical reason why the optimal choices of the individual should change in the way depicted in figures 2.4 through 2.6 when the real after-tax wage rate rises. Rather, such a description is justified on the basis of evidence about how individuals do actually seem to respond to changes in their real after-tax wages.

Substitution Effect and Income Effect

We can decompose the effect of the change in the real after-tax wage on the optimal choice of leisure into two separate components: an effect called the substitution effect and an effect called the income effect. Both of these effects have very general meanings in economics and indeed can be applied to any optimal choice problem, not simply the consumption–leisure model. However, for our purpose we will restrict our discussion of these effects to the consumption–leisure model.[8]

Simply put, in the context of our consumption–leisure model, the **substitution effect** of a higher real after-tax wage leads an individual to take less leisure (and hence work more). This is because as the real after-tax wage rises, the opportunity cost of leisure rises (because they are one and the same). As this "price" of leisure rises, an individual would tend to demand less leisure—simply because leisure has become more expensive!

Conversely, the **income effect** of a higher real after-tax wage leads an individual to take more leisure (and hence work less). This is due to the higher income that a higher real after-tax wage tends to bring.[9] With a higher income, an individual would want to consume more of all normal goods.[10] So long as leisure is a normal good, an increase in income would lead an individual to want to take more leisure and thus spend less time working.

The substitution effect and income effect are both always present. From the preceding discussion, it should be clear that they have opposing effects on an individual's optimal choice of leisure (and hence opposing effects on an individual's optimal choice of labor). For any given real after-tax wage and subsequent rise in the real after-tax wage, then, one of two things must occur. Either the substitution effect dominates (is stronger than) the income effect and the rise in the real after-tax wage leads the individual to choose to work more (take less leisure) or the income effect dominates (is stronger than) the substitution effect and the rise in the real after-tax wage leads the individual to choose to work less (take more leisure).

With these notions of substitution and income effects, let's reconsider the events depicted in figures 2.4 through 2.6. The rise in the real after-tax wage from $((1-t)W/P)_1$ to $((1-t)W/P)_2$ led the individual to work more (take less leisure), as illustrated in the move of the optimal choice from point A to point B. Thus it must be that over this range of the real after-tax wage, the substitution effect dominates (is stronger than) the income effect.

When the real after-tax wage rose again from $((1-t)W/P)_2$ to $((1-t)W/P)_3$, the individual decided to not adjust the amount of time he spent working, as illustrated in the move

8. And we defer a more general discussion of substitution effects and income effects to a more advanced course on microeconomic theory.

9. Note the distinction between "wage" and "income." The wage is the hourly rate of pay, while income is the product of the wage and the actual number of hours worked.

10. Recall that this is in fact the definition of a normal (as opposed to an inferior) good.

of the optimal choice from point B to point C. Thus it must be that over this range of the real after-tax wage, the substitution effect exactly cancels with the income effect.

When the real after-tax wage rose yet again from $((1-t)W/P)_3$ to $((1-t)W/P)_4$, the individual decided to work less (take more leisure), as illustrated in the move of the optimal choice from point C to point D. Thus it must be that over this range of the real after-tax wage, the income effect dominates (is stronger than) the substitution effect.

The Backward-Bending Labor Supply Curve

Let's now graph this individual's choice of number of hours worked as a function of the nominal after-tax wage, with the price of consumption held constant at some value P. The resulting graph is the individual's labor supply curve. The following table summarizes the labor supply schedule we found in figures 2.4 through 2.6:

Nominal wage	Number of hours worked
$((1-t)W)_1$	n_1
$((1-t)W)_2$	n_2, with $n_2 > n_1$
$((1-t)W)_3$	n_3, with $n_3 = n_2$
$((1-t)W)_4$	n_4, with $n_4 < n_3$

Graphing these data and passing a smooth curve through the points gives the individual's labor supply curve in figure 2.7. The labor supply curve is said to be "backward-bending" because at high levels of the after-tax wage, the amount of hours worked declines as the after-tax wage rises.

The labor supply curve in figure 2.7 is for a single individual. Every individual in an economy makes a similar labor supply decision, so, in principle, we have backward-bending labor supply curves for each individual. If the positions of every individual's labor supply curve are the same, then summing these individual labor supply curves horizontally yields an economy's labor supply curve (referred to as the **aggregate labor supply curve**), which will also be backward-bending.

Aggregate Labor Supply Curve

Even if every individual an economy has a backward-bending labor supply curve, though, the *aggregate* labor supply curve actually need not be backward-bending. This can occur if the exact positions of each individual's labor supply functions are *not* identical. More precisely, if we are interested only in some "usual" range of macroeconomic outcomes *and* we wish to model events using the representative-agent framework, then our representative agent should *not* have a labor supply curve that is backward-bending. This means that our analysis in figures 2.4 through 2.6 must be modified: the successive optimal choices traced

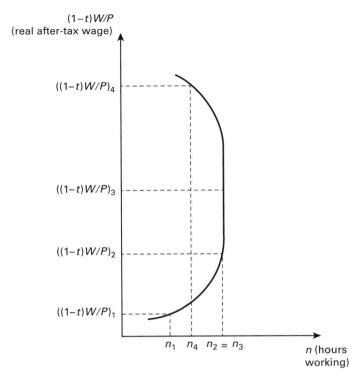

Figure 2.7
Backward-bending labor supply curve. In this diagram, the price of consumption is held constant at some value P. With this, at very low levels of the nominal after-tax wage, the substitution effect outweighs the income effect and thus the labor supply curve has a positive slope. At very high levels of the nominal after-tax wage, the income effect outweighs the substitution effect and thus the labor supply curve has a negative ("backward-bending") slope. At intermediate levels of the nominal after-tax wage, the substitution effect roughly cancels out against the income effect, giving the labor supply curve its vertical region.

out in the progression of these diagrams must feature always decreasing quantities of leisure, which equivalently means always increasing quantities of labor supply. In the terminology of substitution and income effects, we require indifference curves (more fundamentally, a utility function) that feature a substitution effect that is always stronger than the income effect with regard to leisure.[11]

Because in macroeconomic data there is no evidence of a "backward-bending" labor supply curve, the utility functions used in macroeconomic analysis feature just such a property. The particular functional forms for utility that we encounter throughout our studies will exhibit this property.

11. You should be able to trace out for yourself the analogues of figures 2.4 through 2.6 for the labor supply curve to *not* be backward-bending.

Consumption Demand Function

Regardless of whether or not the aggregate labor supply curve is backward-bending, we derived it by considering how the optimal labor choice varied as the real after-tax wage varied. We can use the same analysis in figures 2.4 through 2.6 to consider how the optimal choice of consumption varies as the price P varies, holding the nominal wage W and the tax rate t constant. After all, a change in the real after-tax wage rate can be initiated by any one of P, W, or t changing with the other two held constant. In this section we will suppose that it is the price of consumption that varies and examine how the optimal consumption demand varies.

Begin again at point A in figure 2.4, and suppose that the price of consumption falls. This means that the budget line rotates to become steeper, just as shown in figure 2.4. Point B then shows the new optimal choice of consumption, clearly larger than at point A. Turning to figure 2.5, we see that if the price of consumption falls yet again, the budget line again becomes steeper, leading to a yet higher consumption choice at point C. If the price falls yet again, the budget line becomes even steeper and the optimal consumption choice increases again, as at point D in figure 2.6. The point should by now be clear: a fall in the price leads to rise in optimal consumption, all else being held constant. Indeed this is simply the law of demand that you learned in basic microeconomics. This analysis yields the downward-sloping aggregate consumption function in figure 2.8 (its linearity is for illustrative purposes).

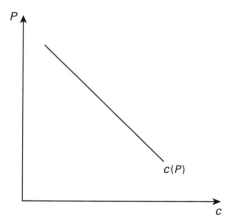

Figure 2.8
Downward-sloping aggregate consumption function, which is derived holding the labor tax rate t fixed and the nominal wage rate W fixed

Lagrange Characterization—The Consumption–Leisure Optimality Condition

Let's now return to the decision problem of the representative agent (i.e., before we aggregated things up to an aggregate labor supply function and an aggregate consumption demand function) and study the optimization problem using our Lagrange tools.

To cast the problem into Lagrange form, we must first identify the objective function (i.e., the function that the consumer seeks to maximize)—which is simply the utility function $u(c, l)$. Then we must identify the constraint(s) on the maximization problem. The only constraint is the budget constraint; to cast it in our general Lagrange form, we write it as $g(c, l) = (1 - t)W - Pc - (1 - t)Wl = 0$. Proceeding as we have a couple of times already now, having identified the objective function and the constraint function(s), we now must construct the Lagrange function; in our problem here, the Lagrange function is

$$L(c, l, \lambda) = u(c, l) + \lambda[(1 - t)W - Pc - (1 - t)Wl].$$

The first-order conditions we thus require are those with respect to c, l, and λ; respectively, they are

$$\frac{\partial u}{\partial c} - \lambda P = 0,$$

$$\frac{\partial u}{\partial l} - \lambda(1 - t)W = 0,$$

$$(1 - t)W - Pc - (1 - t)Wl = 0.$$

The usual second step of the Lagrange method is to eliminate the Lagrange multiplier between the first-order conditions on the main variables of economic interest—here, c and l. Solving the first expression above for the multiplier gives us $\lambda = (\partial u / \partial c)/P$. Inserting this in the second expression above gives us

$$\frac{\partial u}{\partial l} = \frac{\partial u}{\partial c}\frac{(1 - t)W}{P}.$$

Rearranging in one more step gives us

$$\frac{\partial u / \partial l}{\partial u / \partial c} = \frac{(1 - t)W}{P},$$

which is the representative consumer's **consumption–leisure optimality condition.** It states that when consumers are making their utility-maximizing consumption–leisure choices, they choose consumption and leisure such that their MRS between consumption and leisure (the left-hand side of the expression above—recall that the ratio of marginal utilities is the MRS) is equated to the slope of the relevant budget constraint. Graphically, as illustrated in figure 2.8, the slope of the relevant budget line here is the after-tax real wage $(1 - t)W/P$.

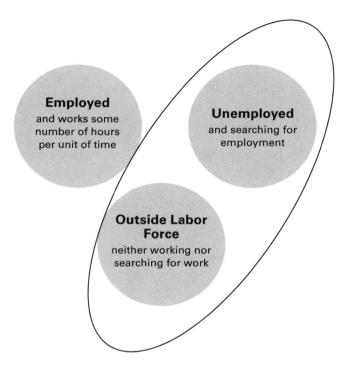

Figure 2.9
Three widely recognized categories of an individual's labor-market status are employment, unemployment but actively seeking a job, and neither working nor searching for a job. The consumption–leisure framework bundles the latter two categories together into "leisure."

Unemployment?

Let's zoom out. In the consumption–leisure framework, is the representative individual employed? Or unemployed?

Given our analysis above of the optimal choice of hours supplied, it should be apparent that our representative individual is employed with 100 percent certainty. Keeping in mind the strict representative-agent framework, this means that every individual is employed with 100 percent certainty. Thus there is no unemployment in this framework, which seems like a major shortcoming.

Clearly, in reality, there are people who would like to work—that is, would like to supply hours—but cannot find a job and hence are unemployed. Broadly, the US Bureau of Labor Statistics (BLS) categorizes individuals into the three groups shown in figure 2.9. As the diagram indicates, the outlined pools of individuals that are unemployed but actively seeking work and those individuals that are outside the labor force are grouped together into "leisure" in the consumption–leisure framework.

Thus, not only is there no notion of "unemployment" in the framework just presented, but there is also no notion of "actively searching" for work. We will later construct an extended version of the consumption–leisure framework that explicitly incorporates time spent searching for work; in that extension it will not be the case that each unit of search activity leads to employment with 100 percent certainty.

Chapter 2 Problem Set Questions

1. **Interaction of consumption tax and wage tax.** A basic idea of President George W. Bush's economic advisers throughout his administration was to try to move the United States further away from a system of investment taxes and more toward a system of consumption taxes. A nationwide consumption tax would essentially be a national sales tax, a system that many Western European countries have in place. You are asked to modify our basic consumption–leisure model to include both a proportional wage tax (which we will now denote by t_n, where, as before, $0 \le t_n < 1$) as well as a proportional consumption tax (which we will denote by t_c, where $0 \le t_c < 1$). A proportional consumption tax means that for every dollar on the price tags of items the consumer buys, the consumer must pay $(1 + t_c)$ dollars. Throughout the following, suppose that economic policy has no effect on wages or prices (i.e., the nominal wage W and the price of consumption P are constant throughout).

   a. Construct the budget constraint in this modified version of the consumption–leisure model. Briefly explain economically how this budget constraint differs from that in the standard consumption–leisure model you studied in class.

   b. Suppose that currently the federal wage tax rate is 20 percent ($t_n = 0.20$) while the federal consumption tax rate is 0 percent ($t_c = 0$), and that the Bush economic team is considering proposing lowering the wage tax rate to 15 percent. However, they wish to leave the representative agent's optimal choice of consumption and leisure unaffected. Can they simultaneously increase the consumption tax rate from its current zero percent to achieve this goal? If so, compute the new associated consumption tax rate, and explain the economic intuition. If not, explain mathematically as well as economically why not.

   c. A tax policy is defined as a particular combination of tax rates. For example, a labor tax rate of 20 percent combined with a consumption tax rate of zero percent is one particular tax policy. A labor tax rate of 5 percent combined with a consumption tax rate of 10 percent is a different tax policy. Based on what you found in parts a and b above, address the following statement: a government can use many different tax policies to induce the same level of consumption by individuals.

d. Consider again the Bush proposal to lower the wage tax rate from 20 to 15 percent. This time, however, policy discussion is focused on trying to boost overall consumption. Is it possible for this goal to be achieved if the consumption tax rate is raised from its current zero percent?

e. Using a Lagrangian, derive the consumer's consumption–leisure optimality condition (for an arbitrary utility function) as a function of the real wage and the consumption and labor tax rates.

2. Non–backward-bending labor supply curve. Consider an economy populated by 100 individuals who have identical preferences over consumption and leisure. In this economy the aggregate labor supply curve is upward-sloping. For simplicity, suppose that throughout this question that the labor tax rate is zero.

a. For such a labor supply curve, how does the substitution effect compare with the income effect?

b. Using indifference curves and budget constraints, show how such a labor supply curve arises.

3. A backward-bending aggregate labor supply curve? Despite our use of the backward-bending labor supply curve as arising from the representative agent's preferences, there is controversy in macroeconomics about whether this is a good representation. Specifically, even though a backward-bending labor supply curve may be a good description of a given individual's decisions, it does *not* immediately follow that the representative agent's preferences should also feature a backward-bending labor supply curve. In this exercise you will uncover for yourself one part of this problem. For simplicity, assume that the labor tax rate is $t = 0$ throughout all that follows.

a. Suppose that the economy is made up of five individuals, person A, person B, person C, person D, and person E, each of whom has the labor supply schedule given below. Using the indicated wage rates, graph each individual's labor supply curve as well as the aggregate labor supply curve.

Nominal wage, W	Person A	Person B	Person C	Person D	Person E
$10	20 hours	0 hours	0 hours	0 hours	0 hours
$15	25	15	0	0	0
$20	30	22	8	0	0
$25	33	27	15	5	0
$30	35	30	20	15	0
$35	37	32	25	20	6
$40	36	31	27	25	21
$45	35	30	26	28	30
$50	33	29	24	25	29

Now suppose that in this economy, the "usual" range of the nominal wage is between $10 and $45.

b. Restricting attention to this range, is the aggregate labor supply curve backward-bending?

c. At a theoretical level, if we want to use the representative-agent paradigm and restrict attention to this usual range of the wage, does a backward-bending labor supply curve make sense?

Explain qualitatively the relationship you find between the individuals' labor supply curves and the aggregate labor supply curve over the range $10 − $45. Especially address the "backward-bending" nature of the curves.

4. **The consumption–leisure framework.** In this question you will use the basic (one-period) consumption–leisure framework to consider some labor market issues.

Suppose that the representative consumer has the following utility function over consumption and labor:

$$u(c,\; l) = \ln c - \frac{A}{1+\phi} n^{1+\phi},$$

where, as usual, c denotes consumption and n denotes the number of hours of labor the consumer chooses to work. The constants A and ϕ are outside the control of the individual, but each is strictly positive. (As usual, $\ln(\cdot)$ is the natural log function.)

Suppose that the budget constraint (expressed in real, rather than in nominal, terms) the individual faces is $c = (1-t)\cdot w\cdot n$, where t is the labor tax rate, w is the real hourly wage rate, and n is the number of hours the individual works.

Recall that $n + l = 1$ must always be true. The Lagrangian for this problem is

$$\ln c - \frac{A}{1+\phi} n^{1+\phi} + \lambda\big[(1-t)wn - c\big],$$

where λ denotes the Lagrange multiplier on the budget constraint.

a. Based on the given Lagrangian, compute the representative consumer's first-order conditions with respect to consumption and with respect to labor. Clearly present the important steps and logic of your analysis.

b. Based on *only* the first-order condition with respect to labor computed in part a, qualitatively sketch two things in a diagram with the real wage on the vertical axis and labor on the horizontal axis. First, the general shape of the relationship between w and n (perfectly vertical, perfectly horizontal, upward-sloping, downward-sloping, or impossible to tell). Second, how changes in t affect the relationship (shift it outward, shift it in inward, or impossible to determine).

Briefly describe the economics of how you obtained your conclusions. (Note: In this question you are *not* to use the first-order condition with respect to consumption nor any other conditions.)

c. Now based on both of the two first-order conditions computed in part a, construct the consumption–leisure optimality condition. Clearly present the important steps and logic of your analysis.

d. Based on both the consumption–leisure optimality condition obtained in part c and on the budget constraint, qualitatively sketch two things in a diagram with the real wage on the vertical axis and labor on the horizontal axis. First, the general shape of the relationship between w and n (perfectly vertical, perfectly horizontal, upward-sloping, downward-sloping, or impossible to tell). Second, how changes in t affect the relationship (shift it outward, shift it inward, or impossible to determine). Briefly describe the economics of how you obtained your conclusions.

e. How do the conclusions in part d compare with those in part b? Are they broadly similar? Are they very different? Is it impossible to compare them? In no more than 60 words, describe as much as you can about the economics (do not simply restate the mathematics you computed above) when comparing the pair of diagrams.

5. **European and US consumption–leisure choices.** Suppose that one unit of time is 168 hours (per week). Europeans work fewer hours than Americans. There are likely very many possible reasons for this, and indeed in reality this fact arises from a combination of many reasons. In this question you will consider two reasons using the simple (one-period) consumption–leisure model.

a. Suppose that both the utility functions and before-tax real wages W / P of American and European individuals are identical. However, the labor income tax rate in Europe is higher than in America. In a single carefully labeled indifference-curve/ budget constraint diagram (with consumption on the vertical axis and leisure on the horizontal axis), show how it can be the case that Europeans work fewer hours than Americans. Provide any explanation of your diagram that is needed.

b. Suppose that both the before-tax real wages W / P and the labor tax rates imposed on American and European individuals are identical. However, the utility function $u^{AMER}(c, l)$ of Americans differs from that of Europeans $u^{EUR}(c, l)$. In a **single** carefully labeled indifference-curve/budget constraint diagram (with consumption on the vertical axis and leisure on the horizontal axis), show how it can be the case that Europeans work fewer hours than Americans. Provide any explanation of your diagram that is needed.

6. **A national service program**. Suppose that one unit of time is 168 hours (per week). Consider the following radical policy proposal: rather than taxes being levied on

individuals and the proceeds of those taxes being used by the government to fund various programs, suppose that every individual pays no taxes of any kind but instead must give ten hours of his time every week to national service. You are to analyze this national service program in the context of the (one-period) consumption–leisure framework. Thus there are now *three* uses of the individual's time: work, leisure, and national service (the mandatory 10 hours). Assume the following:

- Instituting the national service program has no effect on any prices or wages in the economy.

- Any time spent voluntarily performing national service beyond the required 10 hours is considered leisure.

a. Using the notation developed in this chapter (i.e., c to denote consumption, n to denote hours of work per week, l to denote hours of leisure per week, P to denote the nominal price of consumption, and W to denote the nominal hourly wage), construct the representative agent's (weekly) budget constraint in this model with a national service program. Provide brief economic justification for your work.

b. Now recall the baseline consumption–leisure framework with no national service program. Suppose that both the consumption tax rate is zero and the labor tax rate is zero. How does the slope of the budget constraint in this economy compare with the slope of the budget constraint in the economy with the national service program in part a? Provide brief economic explanation.

7. **Quasi-linear utility.** In the static (i.e., one-period) consumption–leisure model, suppose that the representative consumer has the following utility function over consumption and leisure:

$$u(c,\ l) = \ln(c) + A \cdot l,$$

where, as usual, c denotes consumption and l denotes leisure. In this utility function, $\ln(\cdot)$ is the natural log function, and A is a number (a constant) smaller than one that governs how much utility the individual obtains from a given amount of leisure. Suppose that the budget constraint the individual faces is simply $c = (1-t) \cdot w \cdot n$, where t is the labor tax rate, w is the real hourly wage rate, and n is the number of hours the individual works. (Notice that this budget constraint is expressed in real terms, rather than in nominal terms.)

a. Does this utility function display diminishing marginal utility in consumption? Briefly explain.

b. Does this utility function display diminishing marginal utility in leisure? Briefly explain.

c.   The representative agent maximizes utility. For the given utility function, plot the labor supply function (i.e., plot on the vertical axis w and on the horizontal axis the optimal choice of labor), explaining the logic behind your plotted function. Also, how would a decrease in the tax rate t affect the optimal amount of labor supply (i.e., increase it, decrease it, or leave it unchanged)? Briefly explain your logic/derivation. (Note: If you can, try to solve this problem without setting up a Lagrangian)

3

Dynamic Consumption–Savings Framework

We just studied the consumption–leisure model as a "one-shot" model in which individuals had no regard for the future: they simply worked to earn income, all of which they then spent on consumption right away, putting away none of it for the future.

Individuals do, of course, consider their future prospects when making economic decisions about the present. When an individual makes his or her optimal choices about consumption and leisure in the current period, he/she usually recognizes that he/she will make a similar consumption–leisure choice in the future. In effect, then, it seems there are multiple consumption–leisure choices an individual makes over the course of his/her lifetime.

However, these choices are not independent of each other because consumers can save for the future or borrow against future income (borrowing is simply negative savings, also known as **dissaving**). That is, current choices affect future choices, and conversely, (expectations of) future events and choices affect current choices.

In this section we will focus on the study of **intertemporal** (literally, "across time") choices of individuals. The easiest way to understand the basics of intertemporal choice theory is by first ignoring leisure and labor altogether. That is, we will revert to our assumption that an individual has no control over his or her income.

Rather, we will enrich our model of consumer theory by now supposing that each individual plans economic events for two time periods: the "present" period and the "future" period. We will designate the present period as "period 1" and the future period as "period 2." There is no "period 3" in the economic planning horizon, and every individual knows that there is no period 3.[1] This stark division of all time into just two periods will serve to illustrate the basic principles of (macro)economic events unfolding as a sequence over time; after mastering the basics of *dynamic macroeconomics* by using the two-period model, we will eventually extend to consideration of an infinite-period model, which arguably may be more realistic because, after all, when does time "end?" But let's build that up slowly.

---

1. Think of this as meaning that the world (and hence the economy) ends with certainty after two periods.

In the two-period model, our stylized (i.e., representative) individual will receive "labor income" (over which he/she has no control) in each of the two periods, and he has to make a choice about consumption in each of the two periods. Savings or borrowings are allowed during period 1. The notation we will use here, indeed the entire method of analysis, should remind you of our initial study of consumer theory.

A Simple Intertemporal Utility Function

As always, in order to study consumer choice, we need to first specify the individual's utility function. In our present intertemporal context, the two arguments to the utility function are consumption in period 1 and consumption in period 2, which we will denote by c_1 and c_2, respectively.[2] We will assume all the usual properties of utility functions: utility is always strictly increasing in both arguments and always displays diminishing marginal utility in both arguments. In abstract form, we (again!) will write this utility function as $u(c_1, c_2)$, and the utility function can be represented by an indifference map featuring downward-sloping indifference curves that are bowed in toward the origin.

In everything that follows, we will continue to write $u(c_1, c_2)$ to stand for the intertemporal, or lifetime, utility function. To dip our feet a bit into macroeconomics, though, a commonly used intertemporal utility function is

$$u(c_1, c_2) = \ln c_1 + \ln c_2,$$

in which "ln" stands for the natural logarithm. The indifferences curves are plotted in three-dimensional space in figure 3.1 and in two-dimensional coordinates in figure 3.2. Both figure 3.1 and figure 3.2 should remind you of basic micro concepts.

Budget Constraints

The most important way in which the intertemporal consumption model differs from our model of consumer theory heretofore is in the budget constraint(s). Before describing the model further, we need to distinguish between income and wealth, two conceptually different economic ideas.

Income versus Wealth

Income is a receipt of money by an individual during some period of time—the most common forms of income are **labor income** (money earned by working) and **interest income**

---

2. With this choice of notation, you should already start to see the parallels between the intertemporal consumption model and our initial study of consumer theory. Keep in mind the different interpretation here though, that of intertemporal choice.

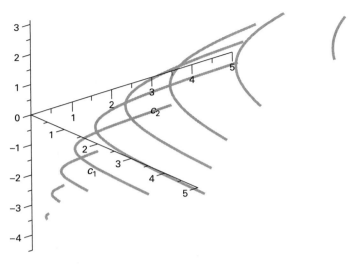

Figure 3.1
Indifference map of the utility function $u(c_1, c_2) = \ln(c_1) + \ln(c_2)$, where each solid curve represents a given (positive or negative) height above the c_1–c_2 plane and hence a particular level of utility. The three axes are the c_1 axis, the c_2 axis, and the utility axis.

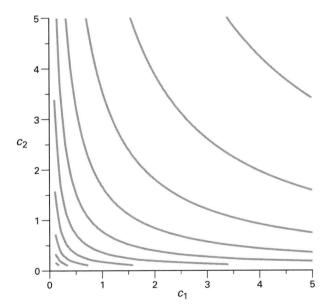

Figure 3.2
Contours of the utility function $u(c_1, c_2) = \ln(c_1) + \ln(c_2)$ viewed in the two-dimensional c_1–c_2 plane. The utility axis is coming perpendicularly out of the page at you. Each contour is called an indifference curve. Indifference curves further to the northeast are associated with higher levels of utility.

(money earned on assets). An individual's **wealth** is the level of assets (cash, checking accounts, savings accounts, stock, bonds, etc.) that an individual has in store. An individual's wealth may be negative, for example, if he is overdrawn on his checking account or otherwise is in debt.

A simple example will illustrate the point. If you currently have $1,000 in your savings account, an economist would say that you have $1,000 in wealth. Say your savings account pays three percent interest per year. If you leave your funds in your savings account alone for the next one year (making neither deposits nor withdrawals), at the end of one year you will have $(1 + 0.03) \cdot \$1,000 = \$1,030$ in your account. This amount can be decomposed into $1,000 of wealth and $30 of interest income. Suppose that during the same year you also earned $10,000 by working—this amount, not surprisingly, we would call your labor income. Thus your total income during the year is the sum of your labor income and interest income, in this case $10,030. The $1,000 still in your savings account is *not* part of your income, although it was the basis of your $30 of interest income.

Period-by-Period Budget Constraints

Returning to the description of the two-period model: individuals receive labor income twice in their lives—once in period 1 and again in period 2. As we said above, for now, the amounts of labor income are outside the control of the individual. Soon we will relax this assumption and allow the individual to have some control over how much labor income he earns. In describing the sequence of economic events, we will need to introduce several elements of notation. The individual receives labor income Y_1 dollars at the beginning of period 1. In addition the individual begins period 1 with some initial wealth (which may be negative), which we denote by A_0—we make no assertion about where this initial wealth came from (perhaps it was bequeathed to him by his ancestors). Regardless of where this initial wealth (or initial debt if A_0 is negative) came from, in period 1 it becomes available to the individual along with some nominal interest income. He chooses consumption c_1 in period 1, each unit of which costs P_1 dollars. He also decides how much wealth to carry into period 2. Denote this level of wealth A_1.

To emphasize, A_1 is chosen in period 1 and is the amount of dollars the individual carries with him (e.g., in a savings account) from period 1 into period 2. Notice that A_1 may be negative, just as A_0 may be negative. A negative A_1 means that the individual is in debt at the beginning of period 2. With this notation, we can write down the **period-1 budget constraint** of the individual as

$$P_1 c_1 + A_1 = (1 + i)A_0 + Y_1, \tag{1}$$

where i denotes the nominal interest rate (we will say more about this shortly). An equivalent version of the period-1 budget constraint is obtained by subtracting $P_1 c_1$ from both sides, which gives

$$A_1 = (1+i)A_0 + Y_1 - P_1 c_1.$$

This equivalent expression of the period-1 budget constraint emphasizes that out of all the resources that were available for the first period, A_1 was *not* spent on period-1 consumption and thus carries over to the next period.

At the beginning of period 2, the individual receives nominal income Y_2. If he chose to carry positive wealth A_1 from period 1 into period 2, he receives back (e.g., from his bank account) the full amount A_1 plus interest earned on that amount. Denote this **nominal interest rate** by i, where $0 \leq i \leq 1$. For our purposes the nominal interest rate is the return on each dollar kept in a bank account from one period to the next.

We need to be very clear about the events occurring here, so to re-emphasize: if, on one hand, the individual chose to carry a positive amount A_1 dollars from period 1 into period 2, he receives at the beginning of period 2 his original A_1 dollars plus another iA_1 dollars in interest. If, on the other hand, the individual chose to carry a negative A_1 into period 2 (i.e., the individual is in debt at the beginning of period 2), he must repay A_1 (e.g., to the bank to whom he is in debt) with an interest rate of i—that is, he would repay $A_1 + iA_1$.[3] This nominal interest rate i is the same interest rate that appears in the period-1 budget constraint in expression (1).

After settling his accounts, the individual then chooses consumption c_2 in period 2, each unit of which costs P_2 dollars. He also decides how much wealth to carry into period 3. Denote this level of wealth by A_2. But the economy ends at the end of period 2, and every individual knows the economy ends at the end of period 2! Thus there is no period 3 to save for, and no rational bank would allow anyone to die in debt to it—so we must have that $A_2 = 0$.

With this notation we can write down the **period-2 budget constraint** of the individual:

$$P_2 c_2 + A_2 = (1+i)A_1 + Y_2, \tag{2}$$

where, as just said, we must have $A_2 = 0$, and A_1 may be positive or negative. This timing of events is depicted by the timeline in figure 3.3, which is crucial to understand.

Before making our next point, we introduce important new terminology. We define an individual's **private savings in a given time period** as the difference between his total income in that period and his total expenditures in that period. The two main categories of expenditures for individuals in any economy are consumption and taxes. We have not yet discussed taxes, but we will soon. Examining the period-1 budget constraint (1) above, we see that the individual's total income in period 1 is $iA_0 + Y_1$ (the sum of his labor income and

---

3. For simplicity, we are supposing that the interest rate at which the individual can save is the same as the interest rate at which the individual can borrow. In general, this need not and usually is not the case. More generally, we can say that there is an interest rate i_s that the individual would receive if he had a positive level of wealth and a different interest rate i_b that the individual would face if he had a negative level of wealth.

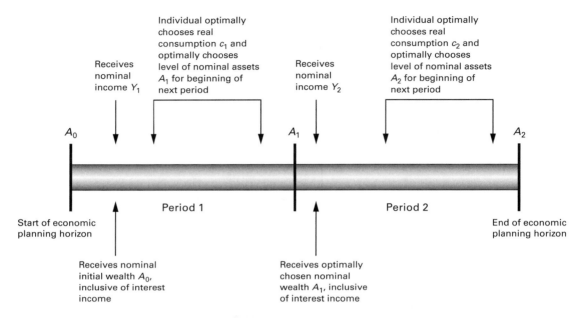

NOTE: Economic planning occurs for the ENTIRE two periods.

Figure 3.3
Timing of events in the two-period consumption framework, stated in nominal units

interest income), and his total expenditure on consumption in period 1 is $P_1 c_1$. Thus we have that the individual's private savings in period 1 is

$$S_1^{priv} = iA_0 + Y_1 - P_1 c_1, \tag{3}$$

where the "priv" superscript indicates that this is the savings of the private individual.[4] If we rearrange expression (1) a bit, we get that

$$A_1 - A_0 = iA_0 + Y_1 - P_1 c_1. \tag{4}$$

Comparing the left-hand sides of expressions (3) and (4), we see that $S_1^{priv} = A_1 - A_0$.

Thus the private individual's savings in period 1 is equal to the change in his wealth during period 1. This is a second useful way of computing an individual's private savings—as the **change in wealth** during the course of a time period. To re-emphasize, this is a *critical* idea to understand, as it is pervasive throughout macroeconomic analysis. At the end of the chapter we will emphasize this point again with rigorous definitions of "stock variables" and "flow variables."

---

4. Later we will also have something called "public savings," in which the government engages—we will denote this by S^{gov}.

To continue the savings account example from above, starting from an initial balance of $1,000, if you withdrew $400 from your savings account during the course of one year (and made no deposits), your savings during the course of the year would be $600 – $1,000 = –$400. That is, you would have *dissaved* during the year.

Similarly the private individual's savings in period 2 is $S_2^{priv} = iA_1 + Y_2 - P_2c_2$, which, using the period-2 budget constraint, can also be expressed as $S_2^{priv} = A_2 - A_1$.

Lifetime Budget Constraint

Examining the period-1 budget constraint and the period-2 budget constraint, we see that they are linked by wealth at the beginning of period 2, A_1. Mathematically, this is the only term that appears in both expressions. The economic interpretation, an important one, is that *an individual's wealth position links economic decisions of the past with economic decisions of the future.* Again continuing the savings account example from above, the $1,000 in your savings account somehow reflects your past income and consumption decisions. Obviously just knowing that you currently have $1,000 in your savings account does not allow anyone to know exactly what or how much "stuff" you bought in the past or how much income you earned in the past. Nonetheless, it is essentially a summary of your past income and consumption behavior, albeit a condensed one. The fact that you have $1,000 in your account now implies some level of interest income for you in the upcoming year, income that is available for your consumption needs over the next year. Thus that $1,000 is a reflection of your past economic behavior and represents part of your future economic opportunities.

This example demonstrates that economic decisions over time are linked by wealth. A useful first approximation to actual economic behavior is to suppose that individuals are completely rational over the course of their lifetimes in the sense that they save and/or borrow appropriately during their whole lifetimes. In the context of our **two-period model** here, such an assumption amounts to an individual deciding on his consumption and savings for his whole life (i.e., both periods 1 and 2) *at the beginning of period 1.* This latter point is an important one for the analysis of the two-period model: *all of our analysis of the two-period model proceeds from the point of view of the very beginning of period 1.* That is, we will consider the very beginning of period 1 as the "moment in time" in which our (and the consumer's) analysis is conducted; hence, in our (and the consumer's) analysis of the two-period world, the entire two periods will always be yet to unfold.

Armed with the assumption of rationality on the part of consumers and the perspective of economic events from the very beginning of period 1, note that it is neither the period-1 budget constraint alone nor the period-2 budget constraint alone that is the relevant one for decision-making, but rather a combination of them both.[5] The way to combine the budget

---

5. Keep this point in mind when we later formulate two different types of Lagrange problems to analyze the two-period framework.

constraints (1) and (2) is to exploit the observation that A_1 is the only term that appears in both. The mathematical strategy to employ is to solve for A_1 from one of the constraints and then substitute the resulting expression into the other constraint. Doing this will yield the individual's **lifetime budget constraint**—which we will abbreviate **LBC** for short.

Let's proceed by first solving for A_1 in expression (2). After a couple of steps of algebra, we get

$$A_1 = \frac{P_2 c_2}{(1+i)} - \frac{Y_2}{(1+i)}, \tag{5}$$

where we have used the fact that $A_2 = 0$ from above.[6] Inserting this resulting expression for A_1 into the period-1 budget constraint in (1) above yields

$$P_1 c_1 + \frac{P_2 c_2}{(1+i)} = Y_1 + \frac{Y_2}{(1+i)} + (1+i)A_0, \tag{6}$$

which is the LBC. The LBC has very important economic meaning. The right-hand side of expression (6) represents the **present discounted value of lifetime resources,** which takes into account both initial wealth as well as all lifetime labor income.[7] The left-hand side of expression (6) represents the **present discounted value of lifetime consumption,** which takes into account consumption in all periods of the individual's life (here, only two periods). Thus, over the course of his lifetime, the individual spends all his lifetime resources on lifetime consumption, leaving nothing behind when he dies (and, indeed, why should he leave anything behind because the world ends with certainty at the end of period 2). It is this LBC that our perfectly rational individual uses in making his choices over time. As such, in order to proceed graphically, we need to represent this LBC in c_1–c_2 space.

Before graphing the LBC, we make one simplifying assumption: $A_0 = 0$, which means the individual begins his economic life with zero initial wealth (equivalently, zero initial debts). None of the qualitative results change if we do not make this assumption—it simply makes the upcoming graphical analysis more straightforward.

To graph the LBC with c_2 on the vertical axis and c_1 on the horizontal axis, we need to solve expression (6) for c_2, which gives us, after a few lines of algebra,

$$c_2 = -\left(\frac{P_1(1+i)}{P_2}\right)c_1 + \left(\frac{1+i}{P_2}\right)Y_1 + \frac{Y_2}{P_2}. \tag{7}$$

---

6. It is a good idea to verify these algebraic manipulations for yourself and the ones that follow.

7. You should be familiar with the notion of present discounted value from introductory economics—if your recollection is a bit hazy on this point, now is the time to refresh yourself because we will use the concept repeatedly.

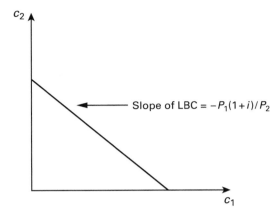

Figure 3.4
Lifetime budget constraint (LBC) of the individual, with the simplifying assumption that $A_0 = 0$

Thus the vertical intercept is the entire term $[(1+i)/P_2]Y_1 + (Y_2/P_2)$, and the slope is the term $-[P_1(1+i)/P_2]$. The graph of the LBC is in figure 3.4.

Optimal Intertemporal Choice—Consumption and Savings

As in all of consumer theory, the individual's actual optimal choice is determined by the interaction of his budget constraint and his indifference map (i.e., his utility function)—the former represents all of the choices available to him and the latter represents his own personal preferences. Figure 3.5 depicts an example, in which the individual's optimal choice is c_1^* in period 1 and c_2^* in period 2.

Also shown in figure 3.5 are the individual's labor incomes in both period 1 and period 2. Actually what are shown are Y_1 / P_1 and Y_2 / P_2, which represent **real labor income** in the two periods, respectively. We will soon discuss exactly what is meant by this term, but for now just think of it as the labor income we have been discussing all along in this two-period model. We see in figure 3.5 that consumption c_1^* in period 1 is higher than real labor income in period 1 Y_1 / P_1. This individual is spending more in period 1 than he earns, which means that the individual must be decumulating wealth (i.e., borrowing) during period 1. We can see this mathematically by looking at the period-1 budget constraint in expression (1) (and recall our simplifying assumption that $A_0 = 0$). Rearranging that expression a bit gives

$$c_1 - \frac{Y_1}{P_1} = -\frac{A_1}{P_1}. \tag{8}$$

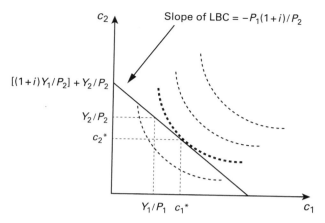

Figure 3.5
Interaction of the individual's LBC and his/her preferences (represented by the indifference map) determine the individual's optimal consumption over time, here c_1^* in period 1 and c_2^* in period 2.

So for the individual in figure 3.5, the left-hand side of expression (8) is positive, which must mean that A_1 for this individual is negative. This individual is in debt at the end of period 1. By similar logic, and using the period-2 budget constraint in expression (2), we have that

$$c_2 - \frac{Y_2}{P_2} = \frac{(1+i)A_1}{P_2}. \tag{9}$$

We already know that A_1 is negative, implying the left-hand side of expression (9) must be negative, as is clearly seen in figure 3.5. The reason why consumption is smaller than income in period 2 is because the individual has to repay the loan obligations he took on during period 1. Thus consumption higher than labor income in one period has to be balanced with consumption lower than income in another period, a result that should strike you as not surprising.

One final point regarding the example in figure 3.5: notice that no mention was made of interest income, only labor income—despite the careful distinction we made earlier between labor income and interest income. The reason for this is that when considering the **lifetime** choices he makes, and as long as asset markets are perfectly functioning (we will discuss in more depth the content of this qualifier), the individual can completely disregard interest income because the only reason for the existence of nonzero wealth at the end of any period is simply to transfer resources across time.

When explicitly considering the lifetime decisions of an individual, as we are here, those "intermediate" wealth positions appear to "completely cancel out." Specifically, notice that from a *mathematical* point of view, A_1 does not appear at all in the LBC in expression (7), and the only relevant income for the individual is that which he receives in period 1 and period 2. However, from an *economic* perspective, the A_1 net wealth term that links activities across time periods is still present. This is a *critical* point to understand about multi-period economic frameworks: there is some "state of economic conditions" that occurred in the past and has implications for current and future outcomes.

Stocks versus Flows

Understanding the two-period model (as figure 3.3 portrays) requires understanding a critical conceptual difference between two different types of variables: **stock variables** (alternative terminology: accumulation variables) and **flow variables.** This conceptual difference arises entirely because of the **dynamic nature** of the two-period framework.

Box 3.1
Stock variables versus flow variables

Flow Variables

Quantity variables whose natural measurement occurs during the course of a given interval of time

Examples:

- Income
- Consumption
- Savings

In our two-period model so far, and as displayed in figure 3.3, the six flow variables are c_1, c_2, Y_1, Y_2, S_1, and S_2.

Stock Variables

Quantity variables whose natural measurement occurs at a particular moment in time

Examples:

- Checking account balance
- Credit card indebtedness
- Mortgage loan payoff
- College loan balance

In our two-period model so far, and as displayed in figure 3.3, the three stock variables (aka accumulation variables) are A_0, A_1, and A_2.

Chapter 3 Problem Set Questions

1. **Wealth effect on consumption.** Consider the two-period consumption–savings model we have been developing in this chapter.

   a. Maintain the simplifying assumption $A_0 = 0$. Show graphically how a rise in the period-1 nominal price of consumption can lead to a decrease in optimal consumption in period 1.

   b. Now suppose that $A_0 \neq 0$. Show graphically how a decrease in A_0 can lead to a decrease in optimal consumption in period 1.

   c. The two effects you analyzed in parts a and b work through seemingly different channels. Actually they are usefully thought of as operating through the same broadly defined channel. Explain this broadly defined channel.

2. **Three-period economy.** Rather than the two-period consumption–savings model economy we have been developing in this chapter, consider a three-period model that is analogous to the two-period model.

   a. Derive the lifetime budget constraint (LBC) for the three-period economy. Define any new notation you introduce, and briefly explain the logic you use in deriving your final expression.

   b. Provide a brief interpretation of the LBC you derive in part a.

   c. In reality there are an "infinite" number of periods. Write down the LBC for an infinite-period economy. (No need to be very mathematical—just use what you've learned in the chapter and what you derived above.)

   d. The Permanent Income Hypothesis states that individuals consider their future lifetime earnings when making their current consumption decision. Discuss briefly how the multi-period models we are considering here (regardless of two-period, three-period, n-period, or infinite-period) are consistent with the Permanent Income Hypothesis.

3. **Mechanics of the consumption–savings model.** Recall that in our two-period consumption–savings model, real labor income in any period is given by nominal labor income divided by the price level (i.e., recall that $y_1 = Y_1 / P_1$ and $y_2 = Y_2 / P_2$). Suppose that nominal labor income in both periods is held constant. Clearly indicating the position of real labor income before and after each change on your diagrams, illustrate how the LBC is affected by the following events. As in the chapter, make the simplifying assumption that the individual has zero initial wealth (i.e., $A_0 = 0$).

   a. The price level in period 1, P_1, rises, while P_2 is held constant.

   b. The price level in period 2, P_2, rises, while P_1 is held constant.

   c. The nominal interest rate i rises, while both P_1 and P_2 are held constant.

4. **Taxes on interest earnings.** In our two-period consumption–savings model (with no leisure), suppose that positive interest income in period 2 is taxed at the rate t_s, where $0 < t_s < 1$. That is, if interest income in period 2 is positive, then the government takes a fraction t_s of the interest income, while if interest income in period 2 is nonpositive, then there is no tax. As in the chapter, make the simplifying assumption that the individual has zero initial wealth (i.e., $A_0 = 0$). Also suppose that the interest tax has no effect on the nominal price level in either period.

   a. In this modified version of the model, algebraically express the period-1 budget constraint and the period-2 budget constraint of the individual.

   b. Using your period-1 and period-2 budget constraints from part a, derive the individual's lifetime budget constraint (LBC). (Hint: Is the slope of this LBC continuous?)

   c. Recall our assumption (based on empirical evidence) that the aggregate private savings function is an increasing function of the real interest rate. Suppose that at the representative agent's current optimal choice, he is choosing to consume exactly his real labor income in period 1.

   i. At his current optimal choice, is his marginal rate of substitution between present consumption and future consumption equal to (one plus) the real interest rate? Explain why or why not.

   ii. President Bush, as part of his first-term economic agenda, lowered the tax rate on interest income from savings (one part of this packages was eliminating the tax on dividends—but there are other elements of this idea in his tax package as well). Part of the rationale is that it will encourage individuals to save more. In this example, would a decrease in the tax rate t_s encourage the representative agent to save more in period 1? Explain why or why not?

4

Inflation and Interest Rates in the Consumption–Savings Framework

The lifetime budget constraint (LBC) from the two-period consumption–savings model is a useful vehicle for introducing and analyzing the important macroeconomic relationships among inflation, nominal interest rates, real interest rates, savings, and debt. Before doing so, we present definitions of these terms and a basic relationship among them.

The Fisher Equation

Inflation is a general rise in an economy's price level over time. Formally, an economy's rate of inflation is defined as the percentage increase in the price level from one period of time to another period of time. In any period t the inflation rate relative to period $t-1$ is defined as

$$\pi_t = \frac{P_t - P_{t-1}}{P_{t-1}},$$

where π denotes the inflation rate.[1] As a matter of terminology, a **deflation** (negative inflation) occurs when $\pi < 0$, and a **disinflation** occurs when π decreases over time (but is still positive at every point in time). For example, if in four consecutive years, inflation was 20 percent, 15 percent, 10 percent, and 5 percent, we say that disinflation is occurring—even though the price level increased in each of the four years.

In our consideration of the consumption–savings model, we defined the nominal interest rate as the return on each dollar kept in a bank account from one period to the next. For example, if your savings account (in which you keep dollars) pays you $3 per year for every $100 you have on balance, the nominal interest rate on your savings account is three percent.

Because of inflation, however, a dollar right now is not the same thing as a dollar one year from now; that is, a dollar one year from now will buy you less (generally) than a dollar right

---

1. Not to be confused with profits, which is what π often represents in microeconomics. The usage is almost always clear from the context.

now because the purchasing power of a dollar changes over time due to inflation. Because it is goods (i.e., consumption) that individuals ultimately care about and not the dollars in their pockets or bank accounts, it is extremely useful to define another kind of interest rate, the **real interest rate.** A real interest rate is a return that is measured in terms of goods rather than in terms of dollars. Understanding the difference between a nominal interest rate and a real interest rate is important. An example will help illustrate the issue.

Example

Consider an economy in which there is only one good—macroeconomics textbooks, say. In the year 2014 the price of a textbook is $100. Wishing to purchase 5 textbooks (because macroeconomics texts are so much fun to read), but having no money with which to buy them, you borrow $500 from a bank. The terms of the loan contract are that you must pay back the principal plus 10 percent interest in one year—in other words, you must pay back $550 in one year. After one year has passed, you repay the bank $550. If there has been zero inflation during the intervening one year, then the purchasing power of that $550 is 5.5 textbooks, because the price of one textbook is still $100. Rather than thinking about the loan and repayment in terms of dollars, however, we can think about it in terms of real goods (textbooks). In 2014, you borrowed 5 textbooks (what $500 in 2014 could be used to purchase), and in 2015, you paid back 5.5 textbooks (what $550 in 2015 could be used to purchase). Thus, in terms of textbooks, you paid back 10 percent more than you borrowed.

However, consider the situation if there *had* been inflation during the course of the intervening year. Say in the year 2015 the price of a textbook had risen to $110, meaning that there had been 10 percent inflation during the year. Then the $550 repayment can be used to purchase only 5 textbooks, rather than 5.5 textbooks. So we can think about this case as if you had borrowed 5 textbooks and repaid 5 textbooks—that is, you did not pay back any additional textbooks, *even though* you repaid more dollars than you had borrowed.

In the zero-inflation case in the example above, the nominal interest rate is 10 percent and the real interest rate is 10 percent. In the 10 percent inflation case, however, the nominal interest rate was still 10 percent but the real interest rate (the extra textbooks you had to pay back) was zero percent. These relationships among the nominal interest rate, the real interest rate, and the inflation rate are captured by the **approximate Fisher equation,**

$$r_t = i_t - \pi_t, \tag{1}$$

where r is the real interest rate, i is the nominal interest rate, and π is the inflation rate. Although almost all interest rates in economic transactions are specified in nominal terms, we will see that it is actually the real interest rate that determines much of macroeconomic activity.

The Fisher equation as stated in expression (1) is a bit of a simplification. The **exact Fisher equation** is

$$(1+i_t) = (1+r_t)(1+\pi_t), \tag{2}$$

the details of which we will not describe yet. This more accurate form of the Fisher equation turns out to be more convenient than its simplification in thinking about our two-period consumption–savings model. Before we analyze the topics of inflation, nominal interest rates, and real interest rates in the consumption–savings model, let's quickly see why expression (1) is in fact an approximation of expression (2). Multiplying out the terms on the right-hand side of expression (2), we get

$$1+i_t = 1+\pi_t + r_t + r_t\pi_t. \tag{3}$$

If both r and π are small, which they usually are in developed economies (United States, Europe, Japan, etc.), then the term $r\pi$ is very close to zero. For example, if $r = 0.02$ and $\pi = 0.02$, then $r\pi = 0.0004$, which is essentially zero. So we may as well ignore this term. Dropping this term and then canceling the ones on both sides of expression (3) immediately yields the "casual" Fisher equation of expression (1). The simplified Fisher equation of (1) is useful for quick analysis, but for our consumption–savings model it will almost always be more useful to think in terms of the exact Fisher equation (2).

For the two-period analysis below, the only economically meaningful inflation rate is that occurs between period 1 and period 2. According to our definition of inflation above, the inflation rate between period 1 and period 2 is

$$\pi_2 = \frac{P_2 - P_1}{P_1}. \tag{4}$$

So π_2 measures the percentage change in the price level (here the nominal price of the consumption basket) between period 1 and period 2. For use below, it is helpful to re-arrange expression (4). First, separate the two terms on the right-hand side to get

$$\pi_2 = \frac{P_2}{P_1} - 1;$$

next, add 1 to both sides, which gives

$$1+\pi_2 = \frac{P_2}{P_1}.$$

Finally, taking the inverses of both sides leads to

$$\frac{1}{1+\pi_2} = \frac{P_1}{P_2}. \tag{5}$$

Consumption–Savings Model in Real Units

Recall the nominal LBC of the two-period model,

$$P_1 c_1 + \frac{P_2 c_2}{1+i} = Y_1 + \frac{Y_2}{1+i} + (1+i)A_0, \tag{6}$$

where the notation is exactly as we have already developed. Each term is in **nominal units** in this expression. As shown in figure 4.2, we can recast the framework into purely *real (goods-denominated) units* and re-do the entire analysis.

Dividing the nominal LBC by P_1 is the first step in re-casting the analysis in real units:

$$c_1 + \frac{P_2}{P_1} \cdot \frac{c_2}{1+i} = \frac{Y_1}{P_1} + \frac{Y_2}{P_1 \cdot (1+i)} + (1+i) \cdot \frac{A_0}{P_1}.$$

The "labor income" terms Y_1 and Y_2 are nominal income. Define **real income** in period 1 and period 2, respectively, as

$$y_1 \equiv \frac{Y_1}{P_1} \tag{7}$$

and

$$y_2 \equiv \frac{Y_2}{P_2}. \tag{8}$$

Notice now we have to be careful in distinguishing uppercase Y from lowercase y!

Substituting y_1 into the LBC gives

$$c_1 + \frac{P_2}{P_1} \cdot \frac{c_2}{1+i} = y_1 + \frac{Y_2}{P_1 \cdot (1+i)} + (1+i) \cdot \frac{A_0}{P_1}.$$

To substitute y_2, observe that we can multiply and divide the second term on the right-hand side by P_2, which gives

$$c_1 + \frac{P_2}{P_1} \cdot \frac{c_2}{1+i} = y_1 + \frac{Y_2}{P_2} \cdot \frac{P_2}{P_1} \cdot \frac{1}{1+i} + (1+i) \cdot \frac{A_0}{P_1}$$

(all we have done is multiply by "1," which is always a valid mathematical operation). Now, using the definition y_2, we have

$$c_1 + \frac{P_2}{P_1} \cdot \frac{c_2}{1+i} = y_1 + y_2 \cdot \frac{P_2}{P_1} \cdot \frac{1}{1+i} + (1+i) \cdot \frac{A_0}{P_1}.$$

The definition of inflation allows us to replace the P_2/P_1 terms to obtain

$$c_1 + c_2 \cdot \left(\frac{1+\pi_2}{1+i} \right) = y_1 + y_2 \cdot \left(\frac{1+\pi_2}{1+i} \right) + (1+i) \cdot \frac{A_0}{P_1}.$$

Next, using the exact Fisher expression $(1+i)/(1+\pi_2) = 1+r$, rewrite the LBC once again as

$$c_1 + \frac{c_2}{1+r} = y_1 + \frac{y_2}{1+r} + (1+i) \cdot \frac{A_0}{P_1}.$$

What's left to deal with is the seemingly complicated term at the far right-hand side. In terms of economics, it represents the **nominal receipts** from the A_0 wealth with which the consumer began period 1, stated in terms of **period-1 purchasing power,** hence the appearance of P_1 in the denominator.

Using the same procedure as before, we can multiply and divide this term by P_0 (the nominal price level in period zero, or more generally stated, the nominal price level "in the past"), which gives us

$$c_1 + \frac{c_2}{1+r} = y_1 + \frac{y_2}{1+r} + (1+i) \cdot \frac{P_0}{P_1} \cdot \frac{A_0}{P_0}.$$

Using the definition of inflation allows us to rewrite this as

$$c_1 + \frac{c_2}{1+r} = y_1 + \frac{y_2}{1+r} + \frac{1+i}{1+\pi_1} \cdot \frac{A_0}{P_0}.$$

Two steps remain. First, invoke the exact Fisher relationship. Second, define $a_0 \equiv A_0/P_0$ as the **real net wealth** of the consumer at the very end of period 0 and hence, equivalently and as shown by the timeline in figure 4.1, at the very start of period 1. Finally, the LBC in **real terms** is

$$c_1 + \frac{c_2}{1+r} = y_1 + \frac{y_2}{1+r} + (1+r) \cdot a_0,$$

which is highly analogous to the LBC in nominal terms. The two results in fact describe the same exact budget restriction on consumer optimization.

The real form of the LBC emphasizes that consumption (which is a real variable! Nobody eats dollar bills or sits down in front of a dollar bill to watch a baseball game!) decisions over time are ultimately dependent on real factors of the economy: the real interest rate and real ("labor") income.

It is true that in modern economies, with developed monetary exchange and financial markets, dollar prices and nominal interest rates are the objects people seem to think in terms of when making consumption and savings decisions. This facet of reality is why our

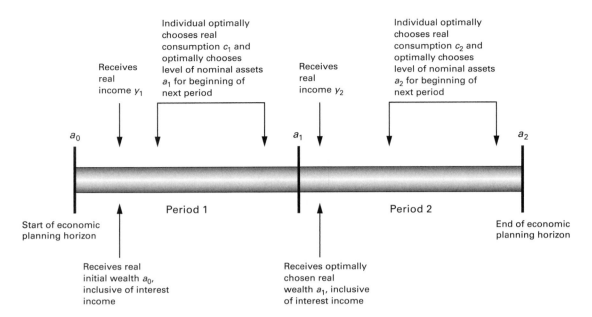

Figure 4.1
Timing of events in two-period consumption–savings framework, stated in real units.

analysis so far has been framed in nominal units. But we can boil these dollar prices and nominal interest rates down to real interest rates and describe much of consumer theory solely in terms of real factors.

None of this is to say, though, that consideration of currencies, dollar prices, and nominal interest rates are unimportant or uninteresting topics. Indeed the whole field of "monetary economics" is primarily concerned with these issues, and we will have a lot to say later about monetary economics. Depending on which issues we are analyzing, we will use either the LBC in real terms or the LBC in nominal terms. If we are considering issues of inflation, for example, then the nominal LBC will typically be more appropriate.

We proceed now with the real LBC. For diagrammatical purposes, it will be, just as before, easier to assume that $a_0 = 0$ (i.e., the individual has no initial wealth). Rearranging the real LBC into the ready to be graphed "slope-intercept" form, we have

$$c_2 = -(1+r)c_1 + (1+r)y_1 + y_2. \tag{9}$$

The utility function $u(c_1, c_2)$ is unaffected by all of these manipulations of the LBC, meaning the indifference map is unaffected—as it must be, since budget constraints and indifference curves are two completely independent concepts.

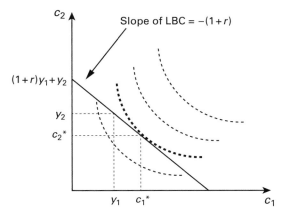

Figure 4.2
Interaction of the individual's LBC (in real terms) and his preferences (represented by the indifference map) determine the individual's optimal consumption over time, c_1* in period 1 and c_2* in period 2. The individual begins period 1 with $a_0 = 0$.

Graphically, then, an example of an individual's optimal choice is shown in figure 4.2 (which takes as given $a_0 = 0$). In this example the individual consumes more than his real income in period 1, leading him to be in debt at the end of period 1; in period 2 he must repay the debt with interest and therefore consume less than his period-2 income. The definition of **real private savings** during the course of period 1 can be stated as

$$s_1^{priv} = ra_0 + y_1 - c_1,$$

which is quite analogous to the definition of **nominal private savings** during the course of period 1 (recall that it was $S_1^{priv} = iA_0 + Y_1 - P_1c_1$).

The Aggregate Private Savings Function

With the aid of figure 4.2 we will now consider how changes in the real interest rate affect savings decisions of individuals. In our two-period model there is only one time junction at which the individual actually makes a decision about saving/borrowing: this is in period 1 when he must decide how much of his period-1 labor income to save for period 2 or how much to borrow so that he can consume more than his period-1 labor income. As such, what we are exactly interested in is how S_1^{priv} (the same notation as before—private savings in period 1) is affected by r. Put more mathematically, what we are interested in is what the **private savings function** looks like.

Let's begin by supposing that the initial situation is as shown in figure 4.2, in which the individual is a debtor at the end of period 1. Consider what happens to his optimal choice

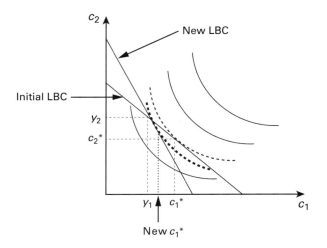

Figure 4.3
If at the initial real interest rate the individual chose to be a debtor at the end of period 1, then a rise in the real interest rate necessarily lowers consumption in period 1, implying that savings during period 1 has increased (or, equivalently, as shown, dissaving has decreased).

if the real interest rate r rises, while his real labor income y_1 and y_2 both remain constant. Such a rise in the real interest rate causes the LBC to both become steeper and have a higher vertical intercept, which we can see by analyzing the LBC (9). Notice that the new LBC must still go through the point (y_1, y_2) because that is still a possible consumption choice for the individual. That is, regardless of what the real interest rate is, it is always possible for the individual to simply not borrow or save in period 1 and simply consume his real labor income in each period. Because this is always possible, the point (y_1, y_2) must always lie on the LBC. Thus the new LBC at the higher real interest rate is as shown in figure 4.3. Also shown in figure 4.3 are the new optimal consumption choices of the individual at the new higher interest rate. Specifically, notice that consumption in period 1 has decreased.

Because labor income in period 1 is unchanged, this means that his savings in period 1 has risen. Recall that private savings in period 1 is

$$S_1^{priv} = Y_1 - P_1 c_1 \tag{10}$$

in nominal terms. We can divide this expression through by P_1 to get savings in real terms,

$$s_1^{priv} = y_1 - c_1. \tag{11}$$

Notice the distinction between lowercase s_1^{priv}, which denotes real savings, and our earlier uppercase S_1^{priv}, which denotes nominal savings. The relationship is simply that

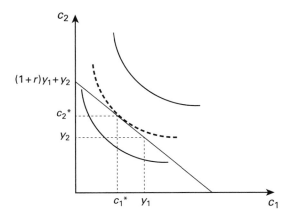

Figure 4.4
At the initial real interest rate the individual's optimal choice may be such that he is *not* a debtor at the end of period 1 but rather a saver. This is because he chooses to consume less in period 1 than his labor income in period 1, which allows him to consume more in period 2 than his labor income in period 2.

$s_1^{priv} = S_1^{priv} / P_1$.[2] Thus, with unchanged y_1 and a decreased c_1^*, s_1^{priv} has increased. Actually, in figure 4.3, savings is still negative after the rise in the real interest rate—but it is less negative, so private savings has increased.

The preceding analysis seems to suggest that there is a positive relationship between the real interest rate and private savings. However, the conclusion is not so straightforward because we need to consider a different possible initial situation. Rather than the initial situation depicted in figure 4.2, suppose instead that figure 4.4 depicted the initial situation of the individual. In figure 4.4 the optimal choice of the individual is such that he consumes less in period 1 than his labor income in period 1, allowing him to accumulate positive wealth for period 2. That is, he saves during period 1.

Now suppose that the real interest rate rises, with labor income y_1 and y_2 both held constant. The budget line again becomes steeper by pivoting around the point (y_1, y_2), as shown in both figure 4.5 and figure 4.6. However, depending on the exact shapes of the individual's indifference curves, the individual's consumption in period 1 may fall (shown in figure 4.5) or rise (shown in figure 4.6). In terms of his savings in period 1, a rise in the real interest rate may induce either a rise in savings (shown in figure 4.5) or a fall in savings (shown in figure 4.6).

Where does this leave us in terms of our ultimate conclusion about how private savings reacts to a rise in the real interest rate? Not very far theoretically, unfortunately. The

---

2. By now, you should be noticing how to convert any nominal variable into its corresponding real variable—simply divide by the price level. The one slight exception is the nominal interest rate—to convert to the real interest rate requires use of the inflation rate (which itself depends on price levels, so the idea is still the same).

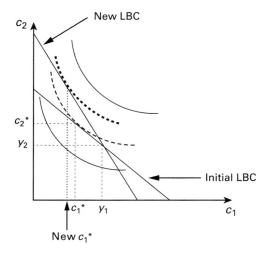

Figure 4.5
If the initial situation is such that the individual optimally chose to be a saver at the end of period 1, then a rise in the real interest rate may cause his savings in period 1 to increase …

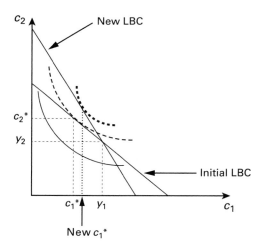

Figure 4.6
… or decrease, depending on the shape of his indifference map (i.e., depending on exactly what functional form his utility function has). Thus, for an individual who optimally initially chooses to be a saver during period 1, it is impossible to determine theoretically in which direction his savings changes if the real interest rate rises.

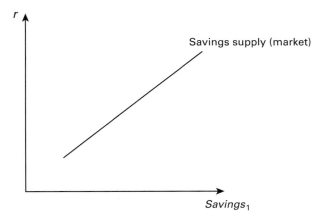

Figure 4.7
Upward-sloping aggregate private savings function

summary of the preceding analysis is as follows. On the one hand, if an individual is initially a debtor at the end of period 1, then a rise in the real interest rate necessarily increases his savings during period 1. On the other hand, if an individual is initially a saver at the end of period 1, then a rise in the real interest rate may increase or decrease his savings during period 1. Yet theory cannot guide us as to how private savings at the macroeconomic level responds to a rise in the real interest rate!

Where theory fails, we can turn to data. Many empirical studies conclude that the real interest rate in fact has a very weak effect, if any effect at all, on private savings behavior. The studies that do show that real interest rates do influence savings almost always conclude that a rise in the real interest rate leads to a rise in savings. The interpretation of such an effect seems straightforward: if all of a sudden the interest rate on your savings account rises (and inflation is held constant), then you may be tempted to put more money in your savings account in order to earn more interest income in the future.

We will adopt the (somewhat weak) empirical conclusion that the real interest rate has a positive effect on private savings—thus we will proceed with our macroeconomic models as if figures 4.3 and 4.5 are correct and figure 4.6 is incorrect.[3] This leads us to graph the upward-sloping aggregate private savings function in figure 4.7.

3. Though the debate among macroeconomists over this issue is not yet settled, this seems to be the most commonly accepted interpretation of the results.

Stocks versus Flows

Let's return to the critical difference between stock variables and flow variables. Stated in terms of real goods (and as figure 4.1 displays), the **stock** (or, equivalently, accumulation) **variables** are a_0, a_1, and a_2, and the **flow variables** are c_1, c_2, y_1, y_2, s_1, and s_2.

It is hard to emphasize how much the distinction between stock variables and flow variables matters for all of macroeconomic analysis! As our multi-period frameworks soon begin to include more and more time periods, the critical concepts of stocks versus flows will continue to help us think about various economic events play out. So you are highly encouraged to understand the difference right away.

Lagrange Characterization—The Consumption–Savings Optimality Condition

As we did with the consumption–leisure model, it is useful to work through the mechanics of analyzing the two-period model using our Lagrange tools. In analyzing multi-period models using Lagrangians, it turns out we have two alternative and distinctly useful ways of proceeding: an approach we will refer to as a **lifetime Lagrange formulation** and an approach we will refer to as a **sequential Lagrange formulation.**

These ideas will hopefully become clear as we describe how to pursue these two different Lagrange approaches, but the advantages and disadvantages of the two approaches can be summarized as follows. For a simple two-period model, the lifetime Lagrange formulation is essentially nothing more than a formal mathematical statement of the graphical analysis we have already conducted. It emphasizes, as the terminology suggests, that consumers can be viewed as making *lifetime* choices. The sequential Lagrange formulation emphasizes the unfolding of economic events and choices over time, rather than starting from an explicitly lifetime view. In the end, the sequential approach will bring us to exactly the same conclusion(s) as the lifetime approach; the sequential approach will thus seem like a more circuitous mode of analysis.

We introduce the sequential Lagrangian approach, however, for two reasons. One reason is that when we soon extend things to an infinite-period model, in which graphical analysis becomes quite infeasible, the lifetime Lagrangian formulation (which, as just stated, is really just a mathematical formulation of analysis that can otherwise be carried out purely graphically) inherently becomes a bit less interesting.

A second, and quite related, reason that sequential Lagrangian analysis is of interest is that it will allow us to explicitly track the dynamics of *asset prices* over time as macroeconomic events unfold over time. In the lifetime view of the two-period model, we effectively end up removing from our analysis the "intermediate asset position" A_1. In the richer infinite-period models to come, we will offer quite specific various interpretations of what A_1 "is," and we will naturally end up being concerned with "its price." Here we have been loosely speaking of A as the "amount of money in the bank." This is a fine enough inter-pretation for now, but we will develop the concept of "A" much further in the chapters ahead, and the sequential Lagrangian approach will prove extremely useful in thinking about specific instantiations of A.

In what follows, we will formulate both the lifetime and sequential Lagrangians in nominal terms, but one could easily pursue either in real terms, as well—a useful exercise for you to try yourself.

Lifetime Lagrangian Formulation

To construct the lifetime Lagrangian for the two-period model, the general strategy is just as we have seen several times already: sum the objective function together with the con-straint function (with a Lagrange multiplier attached to it) to form the Lagrangian, compute first-order conditions, and then conduct relevant analysis using the first-order conditions. The objective function to be maximized is obviously the consumer's lifetime utility func-tion $u(c_1, c_2)$. The relevant constraint—recall we are pursuing the *lifetime* Lagrangian here—is the consumer's LBC. Associating the multiplier λ with the LBC, the lifetime Lagrangian for the two-period model is

$$u(c_1, c_2) + \lambda \left[Y_1 + \frac{Y_2}{1+i} - P_1 c_1 - \frac{P_2 c_2}{1+i} \right].$$

Note that, for simplicity that we have dropped any initial assets, just as we did in our graphical analysis, by assuming $A_0 = 0$; none of the subsequent analysis depends on this simplifying assumption.

It should be clear by now that, apart from the first-order condition on the Lagrange mul-tiplier, the two relevant first-order conditions that we need to compute are those with respect to c_1 and c_2. Indeed these are the formal objects we need to compute. However, before simply proceeding to the mathematics, let's remind ourselves of what it means con-ceptually when we construct these objects. A first-order condition with respect to any par-ticular variable (think in terms of basic calculus here) mathematically describes *how* a maximum is achieved by optimally setting/choosing that particular variable, taking as given the settings/choices for all other variables. In terms of the economics of our model, the consumer is *optimally* choosing *both* c_1 and c_2 (in order to maximize utility), which, from the formal mathematical perspective, requires computing first-order conditions of the Lagrangian with respect to both c_1 and c_2. Keep this discussion in mind when we consider the sequential Lagrangian.

The first-order conditions with respect to c_1 and c_2 (we'll neglect here the first-order condition with respect to λ, which, as should be obvious by now, simply returns to us the LBC) thus are

$$\frac{\partial u}{\partial c_1} - \lambda P_1 = 0$$

and

$$\frac{\partial u}{\partial c_2} - \lambda \frac{P_2}{1+i} = 0.$$

The next step, as usual, is to eliminate λ from these two conditions. From the first expression, we have

$$\lambda = \frac{\partial u / \partial c_1}{P_1};$$

inserting this into the second expression gives us

$$\frac{\partial u}{\partial c_2} = \frac{\partial u}{\partial c_1} \frac{P_2}{P_1(1+i)}.$$

From earlier, we know that

$$\frac{P_2}{P_1(1+i)} = \frac{1+\pi_2}{1+i},$$

which in turn, from the exact Fisher equation, we know is equal to

$$\frac{1}{1+r}.$$

Slightly rearranging the resulting expression

$$\frac{\partial u}{\partial c_2} = \frac{\partial u}{\partial c_1} \frac{1}{1+r}$$

gives us

$$\frac{\partial u / \partial c_1}{\partial u / \partial c_2} = 1+r,$$

which is our two-period model's **consumption–savings optimality condition**. The consumption–savings optimality condition describes what we saw graphically in figure 4.2: when the representative consumer is making his optimal intertemporal choices, he chooses c_1 and c_2 in such a way as to equate his MRS between period-1 consumption and period-2 consumption (the left-hand side of the expression above) to (one plus) the real interest rate (the right-hand side of the expression above). The real interest rate (again, more precisely, one plus the real interest rate) is simply the slope of the consumer's LBC. The two-period model's consumption–savings optimality condition will be present in the richer infinite-period model that we will build soon.

Sequential Lagrangian Formulation

We can alternatively cast the representative consumer's choice problem in the two-period world on a period-by-period basis. That is, rather than take the lifetime view of the consumer's decision-making process, we can take a more explicitly sequential view of events. A bit more precisely, we can think of the consumer as making optimal decisions for period 1 and *then* making optimal decisions for period 2. If there were more than just two periods, we could think of the consumer as *then* making optimal decisions for period 3, and *then* making optimal decisions for period 4, and *then* making optimal decisions for period 5, and so on.

In this explicitly sequential view of events, the consumer, in a given period, *chooses consumption for that period along with an asset position to carry into the subsequent period.* That is, in period t (where, in the two-period model, either $t = 1$ or $t = 2$) the consumer chooses consumption c_t and asset position A_t; note well the time subscripts here. Also, crucially, note that in the sequential formulation, we are thinking explicitly of the consumer as making an optimal choice with regard to intermediate asset positions; in the lifetime formulations of the two-period model, whether graphical or Lagrangian, we effectively removed intermediate asset positions from the analysis, as we have noted a couple of times. In the sequential formulation, we do not remove intermediate asset positions from the analysis; think of this as the consumer deciding how much to put in (or borrow from) the bank.

Formally, in order to construct the sequential Lagangian, we must, as always, determine what the relevant objective function and constraint(s) are. The objective function, as usual, is simply the representative consumer's utility function. In terms of constraints, in the sequential formulation we will impose *all the period-by-period budget constraints,* rather than the LBC. In our two-period model, we obviously have only two budget constraints, one describing choice sets in period 1 and one describing choice sets in period 2.

Almost all of our Lagrangian analyses thus far have used only one constraint function. A review of basic mathematics (see the mathematical appendix at the end of the book) reminds us that it is straightforward to extend the Lagrangian method to handle optimization problems with multiple constraints. All we need to do, once we have identified the appropriate constraints, is associate *distinct* Lagrange multipliers with each constraint and then proceed as usual.

So, to construct the sequential Lagrangian, associate the multiplier λ_1 with the period-1 budget constraint and the multiplier λ_2 with the period-2 budget constraint—*note that λ_1 and λ_2 are distinct multipliers, which, in principle, have nothing to do with each other.* The sequential Lagrangian is thus

$$u(c_1, c_2) + \lambda_1[Y_1 - P_1 c_1 - A_1] + \lambda_2[Y_2 + (1+i)A_1 - P_2 c_2].$$

In writing this Lagrangian, we have used our assumption that $A_0 = 0$ and our result that $A_2 = 0$. The sequential analysis then proceeds as follows. Compute the first-order conditions for the consumer's choice problem in period 1: recall from our discussion above that in period 1, the consumer optimally chooses c_1 and A_1. Mathematically, this requires us to compute the first-order conditions of the Lagrangian with respect to these two variables; they are

$$\frac{\partial u}{\partial c_1} - \lambda_1 P_1 = 0$$

and

$$-\lambda_1 + \lambda_2(1+i) = 0.$$

Next compute the first-order conditions for the consumer's choice problem in period 2: in period 2 the consumer optimally chooses c_2 and A_2. Mathematically, this requires us to compute the first-order conditions of the Lagrangian with respect to these two variables. Of course, in the two-period model we have that $A_2 = 0$, so due solely to the artifice of the two-period model we actually do not need to compute the first-order condition with respect to A_2; only if we had more than two periods in our model would we need to compute it. All we need from the period-2 optimization is the first-order condition with respect to c_2, which is

$$\frac{\partial u}{\partial c_2} - \lambda_2 P_2 = 0.$$

Let's proceed to eliminate multipliers from the three first-order conditions we just obtained (and note that we'll skip considering the first-order conditions with respect to the two multipliers—as should be obvious by now, they simply deliver back to us the period-1 budget constraint and the period-2 budget constraint). Note that we now have *two* multipliers to deal with. From the first-order condition on A_1, we have $\lambda_1 = \lambda_2(1+i)$. We'll have much more to say about this type of relationship between multipliers—that this expression links multipliers across time periods—when we study the infinite-period model; for now let's just exploit the mathematics it provides. Take this expression for λ_1 and insert it in the first-order condition on c_1, to obtain $\partial u / \partial c_1 = \lambda_2(1+i)P_1$. Note that we've gotten rid of the multiplier λ_1 but are still left with λ_2. Fortunately, we can use the first-order condition on c_2 to obtain an expression for the period-2 multiplier: $\lambda_2 = (\partial u / \partial c_2)/P_2$. Now insert this expression into the previously obtained condition to get

$$\frac{\partial u}{\partial c_1} = \frac{\partial u}{\partial c_2} \frac{(1+i)P_1}{P_2},$$

in which we finally have eliminated all multipliers. Rearranging this expression a bit gives us

$$\frac{\partial u / \partial c_1}{\partial u / \partial c_2} = \frac{(1+i)P_1}{P_2}.$$

We have seen the right-hand side of this expression already twice, and we know that we can transform it (using the definition of inflation and the Fisher relationship) into $1 + r$. Thus the last expression becomes

$$\frac{\partial u / \partial c_1}{\partial u / \partial c_2} = 1 + r,$$

which clearly is simply the consumption–savings optimality condition we derived above in the lifetime formulation of the problem. Because we have already derived and discussed it, there is, of course, no reason to discuss the economics of it again.

The idea to really understand and appreciate here is that whether we pursue the lifetime Lagrangian approach or the sequential Lagrangian approach, we arrive at exactly the same prediction regarding how consumers optimally allocate their intertemporal consumption choices: they do so in such a way as to equate the MRS between period-1 consumption and period-2 consumption to (one plus) the real interest rate.

The mathematical difference between the two approaches is that in the sequential approach we had to proceed by explicitly considering the first-order condition on the intermediate asset position A_1, which generated a relationship between Lagrange multipliers over time. Through the optimal decision on A_1, the consumer *does* take into account future period events, even though the mathematics may not make it seem apparent. In the lifetime approach no such relationship had to formally be considered because there was, by construction, only one multiplier.

In the end we should not be surprised that we reached the same conclusion using either approach—this is because they are simply *alternative* approaches to the *same* problem, the problem being the representative consumer's utility maximization problem over time.

Optimal Numerical Choice

Regardless of a lifetime or sequential analysis, the same exact consumption–savings optimality condition arises:

$$\frac{\partial u / \partial c_1}{\partial u / \partial c_2} = 1 + r.$$

This expression is part of the heart of macroeconomic analysis.

However, if we actually wanted to solve for numerical values of the optimal choices of period-1 and period-2 consumption, the consumption–savings optimality condition is not enough. Why? It is because *the consumption–savings optimality condition is one equation in two unknown variables.* A simple way to see this is to take the case of $u(c_1, c_2) = \ln c_1 + \ln c_2$. The consumption–savings optimality condition is thus $c_2/c_1 = 1 + r$ (which at this point you should be able to obtain yourself). Even though the market real interest rate r is taken as given, it is clearly impossible to solve for both c_2 and c_1 from this one equation.

This might be obvious by this point (especially given all of the indifference-curve/budget constraint diagrams in figures 4.3, 4.4, 4.5, and 4.6!), but to complete the numerical solution of the two-period framework requires us to use *both the consumption–savings optimality condition and the budget constraint* to pin down the optimal numerical choices of consumption across time. In other words, there are *two equations in the two unknowns*, period-1 consumption and period-2 consumption. The ensuing example takes us step by step though the analysis, and it also raises an important economic interpretation of the optimal consumption choices that arise across time.

Consumption Smoothing

The concept of **consumption smoothing** is an important underlying theme of the results that emerge from multi-period representative consumer utility maximization. This powerful and intuitive economic result arises not just in the two-period framework but also in the progressively richer models we will construct later.

An example using the two-period model sheds light on the idea of consumption smoothing.

Consumption-Smoothing Example

Suppose that the lifetime utility function is $u(c_1, c_2) = \ln c_1 + \ln c_2$. And also assume that $P_1 = 1$, $P_2 = 1$, $A_0 = 0$, and $r = 0.10$.

Case 1

Suppose that the lifetime stream of nominal income is concentrated in the "later" period of the consumer's economic planning horizon—for example, $Y_1 = 2$ and $Y_2 = 11$.

To solve for the optimal numerical values of c_1 and c_2 requires use of the pair of expressions

$$\left(\frac{\partial u / \partial c_1}{\partial u / \partial c_2} \right) = \frac{c_2}{c_1} = 1 + r$$

and

$$P_1 c_1 + \frac{P_2 c_2}{1+i} = Y_1 + \frac{Y_2}{1+i}.$$

The few steps of algebra are left for you to go through (which is good reinforcement of basics). The numerical values of the optimal choices of consumption across time turn out to be

$c_1^* = 6, \quad c_2^* = 6.6.$

Case 2

Suppose instead that the lifetime stream of nominal income is more evenly spread through the "early" period and the "later" period of the consumer's economic planning horizon— for example, $Y_1 = 7$ and $Y_2 = 5.5$. Once again, the optimal numerical values of consumption are determined by the consumption–savings optimality condition and the budget constraint. And also once again, leaving the few steps of algebra for you to verify, optimal choices of consumption across time turn out to be

$c_1^* = 6, \quad c_2^* = 6.6.$

Clearly, the lifetime path of optimal consumption is the same, despite the large difference between the case 1 lifetime income path ($Y_1 = 2$, $Y_2 = 11$) and the case 2 lifetime income path ($Y_1 = 7$, $Y_2 = 5.5$).

This example demonstrates the two different facets of consumption smoothing. The first aspect is that individuals prefer their consumption across time to not vary very much. This result arises due to strictly increasing and strictly concave lifetime utility, which is part of the **preference** side of the framework.

The second aspect arises from the **constraint** side of the framework. Despite the two very different income scenarios in the example, optimal c_1 and c_2 are identical. The identical optimal consumption streams, despite the very different income streams, is due to the ability of the individual to borrow (in case 1) as much as he or she wants during period 1, and hence be in debt at the very beginning of period 2. This is highlighted in the **negative value** of the A_1 term that arises in case 1:

$$A_1 = Y_1 - P_1 c_1 + (1+i)A_0$$
$$= 2 - 6 + 0$$
$$= -4.$$

If, counter to the example, the individual faced another constraint, in addition to the budget constraints, that allowed no borrowing at all during period 1, the case 1 consumption outcomes would be quite different: we would have $c_1 = 2$ and $c_2 = 11$ as the "credit-constrained" optimal choices for case 1.

Without the credit constraint, the case 1 individual is borrowing (i.e., dissaving) during period 1, and repaying the accumulated debt, inclusive of interest payments, in period 2. In case 2 the individual is saving during period 1, and using the accumulated wealth (inclusive of interest earnings) for consumption in period 2. Using all of the terminology and definitions of the two-period consumption–savings framework, you should be able to verify all of this for yourself.

Chapter 4 Problem Set Questions

1. **Optimal choice in the consumption–savings model with credit constraints: a numerical analysis.** Consider our usual two-period consumption–savings model. Let preferences of the representative consumer be described by the utility function

$$u(c_1, c_2) = \sqrt{c_1} + \beta \sqrt{c_2},$$

where c_1 denotes consumption in period 1 and c_2 denotes consumption in period 2. The parameter β is known as the subjective discount factor and measures the consumer's degree of impatience in the sense that the smaller is β, the higher the weight the consumer assigns to present consumption relative to future consumption. Assume that $\beta = 1/1.1$. For this particular utility specification, the marginal utility functions are given by

$$u_1(c_1, c_2) = \frac{1}{2\sqrt{c_1}}$$

and

$$u_2(c_1, c_2) = \frac{\beta}{2\sqrt{c_2}}.$$

The representative household has initial real financial wealth (including interest) of $a_0 = 1$. The household earns $y_1 = 5$ units of goods in period 1 and $y_2 = 10$ units in period 2. The real interest rate, paid on assets held from period 1 to period 2, equals 10 percent (i.e., $r_1 = 0.1$).

   a. Calculate the equilibrium levels of consumption in periods one and two (Hint: Set up the Lagrangian and solve.)

   b. Suppose now that lenders to this consumer impose credit constraints on the consumer. Specifically, they impose the tightest possible credit constraint—the consumer is not allowed to be in debt at the end of period 1, which implies that the consumer's real wealth at the end of period one must be nonnegative ($a_1 \geq 0$). (Note: a_1 is defined here as being exclusive of interest, in contrast to the definition of a_0 above.) What is the consumer's choice of period-1 and period-2 consumption under this credit constraint? Briefly explain either logically or graphically, or both.

   c. Does the credit constraint described in part b enhance or diminish welfare (i.e., does it increase or decrease lifetime utility)? Specifically, find the level of lifetime utility under the credit constraint and compare it to the level of lifetime utility under no credit constraint.

Suppose now that the consumer experiences a temporary increase in real income in period 1 to $y_1 = 9$, with real income in period 2 unchanged.

d. Calculate the effect of this positive surprise in income on c_1 and c_2, supposing that there is no credit constraint on the consumer.

e. Finally, suppose that the credit constraint described in part b is back in place. Will it be binding? That is, will it affect the consumer's choices?

2. **"Marginal propensity to consume" for various utility functions.** An old (Keynesian) idea in macroeconomics is the "marginal propensity to consume," abbreviated MPC. Briefly, the MPC is the fraction of current-period income that is consumed in the current period. For example, if income in the first period is 2 and consumption in the first period is 1.8, the $MPC = 0.9$.

Consider the standard two-period consumption–savings model in which the representative consumer has no control over his real labor income in periods 1 and 2, denoted by y_1 and y_2, respectively. As usual, denote by r the real interest rate between period 1 and period 2, and assume the individual begins his life with zero initial assets ($a_0 = 0$). Make the additional assumption that in present-discounted-value terms, his real income in each of the two periods is the same—that is, $y_1 = y_2/(1+r)$. Using the LBC and the intertemporal optimality condition, derive for each of the following utility functions the "period-1 MPC"—that is, derive what fraction of period-1 real income the consumer devotes to period-1 consumption. (In other words, derive the coefficient MPC in the expression $c_1 = MPC \cdot y_1 + const.$) Note that not all of these utility functions satisfy the property that utility is strictly concave in both its arguments—but this is irrelevant for the exercise here. (Hint: Set up the Lagrangian in order to solve.)

a. $u(c_1, c_2) = \sqrt{c_1} + \sqrt{c_2}$.

b. $u(c_1, c_2) = \ln(c_1) + c_2$ (no, this is not a typo).

c. $u(c_1, c_2) = c_1^b c_2^{1-b}$, where b is a constant such that $0 < b < 1$ (this type of utility function is called the Cobb–Douglas utility function).

3. **Two-period economy in nominal units.** Consider a two-period economy (with no government and hence no taxes), in which the representative consumer has no control over his income. The lifetime utility function of the representative consumer is $u(c_1, c_2) = \ln c_1 + c_2$, where "ln" stands for the natural logarithm (note that only c_1 is inside the ln(.) function, c_2 is not inside a ln(.) function).

Suppose the following numerical values: the nominal interest rate is $i = 0.05$, the nominal price of period-1 consumption is $P_1 = 100$, the nominal price of period-2 consumption is $P_2 = 105$, and the consumer begins period 1 with zero net assets.

a. Is it possible to numerically compute the *real* interest rate (r) between period 1 and period 2? If so, compute it; if not, explain why not.

b. Set up a sequential Lagrangian formulation of the consumer's problem, in order to answer the following. (i) Is it possible to numerically compute the consumer's optimal choice of consumption in period 1? If so, compute it; if not, explain why not. (ii) Is it possible to numerically compute the consumer's optimal choice of consumption in period 2? If so, compute it; if not, explain why not.

c. The rate of consumption growth between period 1 and period 2 is defined as $(c_2/c_1) - 1$ (completely analogous to how we have defined, say, the rate of growth of prices between period 1 and period 2). Using only the consumption–savings optimality condition for the given utility function, briefly describe/discuss (rambling essays) whether the real interest rate is positively related to, negatively related to, or not at all related to the rate of consumption growth between period 1 and period 2. (Note: No mathematics are especially required for this problem; also note this part can be fully completed even if you were unable to get all the way through part b.)

4. **Two-period economy.** Consider a two-period economy (with no government and hence no taxes at all) in which the representative consumer has no control over his income y_1 and y_2. The lifetime utility function of the representative consumer is $u(c_1, c_2) = \ln c_1 + c_2$, where $\ln(.)$ stands for the natural logarithm (note that only c_1 is inside a $\ln(.)$ function, c_2 is *not* inside a $\ln(.)$ function).

There is only a single asset the consumer trades; and the consumer begins period one with zero assets.

On the asset that consumers trade, the real interest rate is initially $r > 0$. As a mathematical proposition, this is fine, but think of this r as very much larger than zero. In particular, think about the "credit crisis" in the fall of 2008, when certain values of r went to historically large values (and some of them are still very large).

For concreteness, let's think of "period 1" as the fall of 2008 to 2013, and "period 2" to be 2014 through the end of time.

a. Does the lifetime utility function display diminishing marginal utility in c_1? And, does it display diminishing marginal utility in c_2? Briefly explain, in no more than three sentences. (Note the two separate questions here.)

b. The "credit crisis" of the fall of 2008 to 2013 begins, and r shoots way up. From a marginal utility perspective (note this phrase), does the optimal choice of c_1 rise or fall? And, related, does the individual *care* about this rise or fall from a pure (i.e., per-unit) marginal utility perspective? (Note: Your analysis is to be conducted from the perspective of the very beginning of period 1.)

c. The "credit crisis" of the fall of 2008 to 2013 begins, and r shoots way up. From a marginal utility perspective (note this phrase), does the optimal choice of c_2 rise or fall? And, related, does the individual care about this rise or fall from a pure (i.e., per-unit) marginal utility perspective? (Note: Your analysis is to be conducted from the perspective of the very beginning of period 1.)

d. The Federal Reserve notices what's happening. Supposing that the Fed can control both real interest rates and nominal interest rates, it dramatically reduces r. Do the Fed's actions do anything to offset the impact on the pure (i.e., per-unit) marginal utility of c_1? And, do the Fed's actions do anything to offset the impact on the pure (i.e., per-unit) marginal utility of c_2? Explain your answers carefully (whether in mathematical terms, graphical terms, qualitative terms, or some combination of all three). (Note: Your analysis is to be conducted from the perspective of the very beginning of period 1.)

5

Dynamic Consumption–Labor Framework

We have now studied the consumption–leisure model as a "one-shot" model in which individuals had no regard for the future: they simply worked to earn income, all of which they then spent on consumption right away, socking away none of it for the future. Individuals do, of course, consider their future prospects when making economic decisions about the present. We saw this idea in our study of the two-period consumption–savings model. It should not strike you as unusual, then, that when an individual makes his optimal choice about consumption and leisure in the current period, he recognizes that he will make a similar consumption–leisure choice in the future. In effect, then, it seems there are multiple consumption–leisure choices an individual makes over the course of his lifetime. However, these choices are not independent of each other because consumers can save for the future or borrow against future income.

In this section we will bring the consumption–leisure model together with the consumption–savings model. As we will see, doing so in effect is just "gluing" the two models together. The main benefit is that it allows consideration of a broader range of consequences of macroeconomic policies—in particular, it allows us to see that economic policies have their consequences not just in the time period in which they are implemented but also in future time periods.

The dynamic consumption–labor framework is the heart of modern macroeconomic analysis, and it is used for both policy recommendations as well as academic research. We construct the dynamic consumption–labor framework here in the simplest way possible, which is in the two-period context. Later we will enrich the dynamic consumption–labor framework in many dimensions to consider a variety of economic outcomes.

Representative-Consumer Preferences

With two periods, in each of which the individual makes a consumption–leisure choice, there are four objects that determine the individual's lifetime utility: consumption in period 1, leisure in period 1, consumption in period 2, and leisure in period 2. Denote these, respectively, by c_1, l_1, c_2, and l_2, and let the lifetime utility function be $v(c_1, l_1, c_2, l_2)$. We will assume that this lifetime utility function is **additively separable** across time in the following way:

$$v(c_1, l_1, c_2, l_2) = u(c_1, l_1) + u(c_2, l_2).$$

The function $v(c_1, l_1, c_2, l_2)$ is the **lifetime utility function** and the function u is the **sub-utility function** that measures utility over consumption and leisure in each of the two periods. Note especially that the function u is the same function in each of the two periods, meaning that the indifference map over c_1 and l_1 is identical to the indifference map over c_2 and l_2. Furthermore, because consumption in two different periods appears in the lifetime utility function, an indifference map over c_1 and c_2 exists, just as in the two-period model we have already considered.

Lifetime Budget Constraint

The more complicated object to describe in this model is the individual's lifetime budget constraint (LBC). Just as in the simpler two-period model, a budget constraint exists for period 1,

$$P_1 c_1 + A_1 = (1+i)A_0 + (1-t_1)W_1(1-l_1)$$

as well as for period 2,

$$P_2 c_2 + A_2 = (1+i)A_1 + (1-t_2)W_2(1-l_2),$$

where W_1 denotes the hourly wage in period 1, W_2 denotes the hourly wage in period 2, t_1 denotes the labor tax rate in period 1, and t_2 denotes the labor tax rate in period 2. All other notation is the same as in our simple consumption–savings model and our simple consumption–leisure model. The interpretation of these period-by-period budget constraints is the same as before: in each period the individual has some wealth (which may be negative) and some labor income at his disposal, and he must decide how much to consume and how much to save for the future. The difference here versus the simple consumption–savings model is that the individual decides how much labor income he earns.[1]

Because the rational individual considers his entire (two-period) lifetime when making his decisions, the relevant budget constraint is a lifetime budget constraint, which we obtain using the two period-by-period budget constraints above. First, note that because there is no period 3, it must be that $A_2 = 0$, just as before, meaning there is no reason to save for after the end of the world. So we can solve the period-2 budget constraint to get

---

1. If this brief description of these budget constraints, as well as the derivation of the LBC to follow, seems unfamiliar, it is a good idea to review the simple consumption–savings model and the simple consumption–leisure model at this point.

$$A_1 = \frac{P_2 c_2}{(1+i)} - \frac{(1-t_2)W_2(1-l_2)}{(1+i)},$$

which we can in turn substitute into the period-1 budget constraint. After a few steps of algebra, we have

$$P_1 c_1 + \frac{P_2 c_2}{(1+i)} = (1-t_1)W_1(1-l_1) + \frac{(1-t_2)W_2(1-l_2)}{(1+i)} + (1+i)A_0.$$

Finally, as in the consumption–leisure model, we can expand the terms on the right-hand side and then move the terms involving leisure to the left-hand side to get

$$P_1 c_1 + \frac{P_2 c_2}{(1+i)} + (1-t_1)W_1 l_1 + \frac{(1-t_2)W_2 l_2}{(1+i)} = \left((1-t_1)W_1 + \frac{(1-t_2)W_2}{(1+i)} \right) + (1+i)A_0.$$

As always, it is a good idea for you to verify these algebraic manipulations for yourself.

We can now graph the LBC in the previous expression in three different graphs: in c_1–c_2 space, in c_1–l_1 space, and in c_1–l_1 space. As in the simple consumption–savings model, we could assume for graphical simplicity that $A_0 = 0$, but the results that follow in no way depend on this assumption. Solving the previous expression for c_2 gives

$$c_2 = -\left(\frac{P_1(1+i)}{P_2} \right) c_1 + \frac{(1+i)(1-t_1)W_1}{P_2}(1-l_1) + \frac{(1-t_2)W_2}{P_2}(1-l_2).$$

This equation can be usefully viewed in one of two ways: either c_2 as a function of l_2 (in which case we are thinking of the consumption–leisure decision in period 2) or c_2 as a function of c_1 (in which case we are thinking of the consumption–savings decision that spans period 1 and period 2).

If we choose the latter approach (the one that begins as $c_2 = -\ldots$) with c_2 on the vertical axis and c_1 on the horizontal axis, the slope of this function is $-(P_1(1+i)/P_2)$. If $c_1 = 0$, then

$$c_2 = \frac{(1+i)(1-t_1)W_1}{P_2}(1-l_1) + \frac{(1-t_2)W_2}{P_2}(1-l_2)$$

is the vertical intercept, while if $c_2 = 0$

$$c_1 = \frac{(1-t_1)W_1}{P_1(1+i)}(1-l_1) + \frac{(1-t_2)W_2}{P_1(1+i)}(1-l_2),$$

is the horizontal intercept. Notice that these intercepts depend on the choices of leisure in the two periods, l_1 and l_2.

Alternatively, if we graph the same expression with c_2 on the vertical axis and l_2 on the horizontal axis, we see that the slope is $-(1-t_2)W_2 / P_2$, just as in our simple consumption–leisure model. If $l_2 = 0$, then

$$c_2 = -\left(\frac{P_1(1+i)}{P_2}\right)c_1 + \frac{(1+i)(1-t_1)W_1}{P_2}(1-l_1) + \frac{(1-t_2)W_2}{P_2}$$

is the vertical intercept, while if $c_2 = 0$, then

$$l_2 = 1 - \frac{P_1(1+i)c_1}{(1-t_2)W_2} + \frac{(1+i)(1-t_1)W_1}{(1-t_2)W_2}(1-l_1)$$

is the horizontal intercept. Notice that these intercepts depend on the choice of consumption in period 1 and leisure in period 1.

The main point that emerges from the preceding discussion is that all four choices (of consumption in the two periods as well as leisure in the two periods) are interdependent. Essentially we need a five-dimensional graph (which obviously is impossible) in order to visualize the solution to this model. So use of graphical tools here is complicated.

As stated above, we will soon enrich the dynamic consumption–labor framework from two periods all the way up to an "infinite" number of periods, which allows for the study of many relevant economic phenomena: fiscal policy, monetary policy, the interaction of macroeconomic activities and financial market prices, and so on. To get there will require adding further "moving parts" to the dynamic consumption–labor framework.

But let's step back a bit. So far the focus of our study has been only on the consumer side of the economy.

What about the production side?

What about the government side?

The next two chapters, which continue to stick with the two-period framework, bring both firms and the government into our now-expanding model of the economy.

Chapter 5 Problem Set Questions

1. **Intertemporal consumption–labor model—numerical look 1.** Consider the intertemporal consumption–labor model. Suppose that the lifetime utility function is given by $v(B_1c_1, l_1, B_2c_2, l_2) = u(B_1c_1, l_1) + u(B_2c_2, l_2)$, which is a slight modification of the utility function presented in chapter 5. The modification is that preference shifters B_1 and B_2 enter the lifetime utility function, with B_1 the preference shifter in period 1 and B_2 is the preference shifter in period 2. In each of the two periods the function u takes the form

$$u(B_t c_t, l_t) = 2\sqrt{B_t c_t} + 2\sqrt{l_t} \,.$$

Note that the t subscripts whereby $t = 1, 2$ depend on which period we are considering. Labor tax rates, real wages, the real interest rate between periods 1 and 2, and the preference realizations are given by $t_1 = 0.15$, $t_2 = 0.2$, $w_1 = 0.2$, $w_2 = 0.25$, $r = 0.15$, $B_1 = 1$, and $B_2 = 1.2$. Finally, the initial assets of the consumer are zero.

a. Construct the marginal rate of substitution functions between consumption and leisure in each of period one and period two. (Hint: These expressions will be functions of consumption and leisure—you are not being asked to solve for any numerical values yet.) How does the preference shifter affect this intratemporal margin?

b. Construct the marginal rate of substitution function between period-one consumption and period-two consumption. (Hint: Again, you are not being asked to solve for any numerical values yet.) How do the preference shifters affect this intertemporal margin?

c. Using the expressions you developed in parts a and b along with the lifetime budget constraint (expressed in *real* terms, etc.) and the given numerical values, solve numerically for the optimal choices of consumption in each of the two periods and of leisure in the two periods. (Hint: You need to set up and solve the appropriate Lagrangian. Note that the computations here are messy and the final answers do not necessarily work out "nicely." To preserve some numerical accuracy, carry out your computations to at least four decimal places.)

d. Based on your answer in part c, how much (in real terms) does the consumer save in period 1? What is the asset position that the consumer begins period 2 with?

e. Suppose that B_2 were instead higher at 1.6. How are your solutions in parts c and d affected? Provide brief interpretation in terms of "consumer confidence."

2. **Intertemporal consumption–labor model—numerical look 2.** Consider a two-period intertemporal consumption–labor model. Suppose that the representative consumer's lifetime utility function is given by $v(c_1, l_1, c_2, l_2) = \ln(c_1) + l_1 + \ln(c_2) + l_2$. Assume that the representative consumer begins period 1 with zero assets. The period-1, period-2, and lifetime budget constraints in this model, expressed in real terms, are thus given, respectively, by

$$c_1 + a_1 = (1 - t_1) \cdot w_1 \cdot (1 - l_1),$$
$$c_2 + a_2 = (1 + r) \cdot a_1 + (1 - t_2) \cdot w_2 \cdot (1 - l_2),$$
$$c_1 + \frac{c_2}{1 + r} = (1 - t_1) w_1 (1 - l_1) + \frac{(1 - t_2) w_2 (1 - l_2)}{1 + r}.$$

The tax rates in the two periods are $t_1 = t_2 = 0.5$, and the real wages in the two periods are $w_1 = 20$ and $w_2 = 22$. (Note: You are *not* given a numerical value for the real interest rate; you will solve for this in part b below.)

a.   Solve for the representative consumer's optimal choices of consumption in each of the two periods (i.e., solve numerically for the optimal c_1 and optimal c_2). Be clear about any important steps and arguments in your logic/computations. (Note: If you can solve without setting up and solving a Lagrangian, you may do so.)

b.   Using your solution in part a above, solve for the numerical value of the real interest rate r. Show any important steps in your logic/computation. (Note: If you were unable to fully solve part a, you can still work through this part by correctly and fully describing how you would compute r as if you had fully solved part a.)

c.   Can you solve numerically for the optimal choices of leisure in this model? If so, do so, showing any important steps in your logic/computation. If not, briefly describe the economic and/or mathematical issue(s) in this model that prevents you from doing so.

6

Firms

We have studied the static aspect and the dynamic aspect of the demand side (consumers) of the economy. We now study the supply side (firms) of the economy. As with consumers, we could separate our analysis of firms into distinct static and dynamic aspects. However, having become comfortable with static (single time period) versus dynamic (multiple time periods) analysis, we start right away with a version of firm theory that immediately features both dimensions. The basic lessons we will learn are the same as if we studied the two aspects independently.

We first study a small firm making its profit-maximizing decisions. The firm, existing in perfect competition, acts as a price-taker in goods markets, labor markets, and capital markets. Based on its profit function, we can obtain, both intuitively and via formal optimization, its optimality conditions. The profit function is explicitly **dynamic,** though, in a way that is different from the usual microeconomic study of profit functions.

We will then switch our interpretation of the firm to an "aggregate" firm to focus on market prices and market quantities—in this context it is the **representative firm,** exactly analogous to the representative consumer. In terms of market outcomes, the representative firm's decisions provide the foundation for the **demand side of the labor market** and the **demand side of the capital investment market** (an important term yet to be defined). Hence the term "supply side" of the economy mentioned above relates to output markets. Layering the representative firm's optimization choices into a market in which the other side already exists allows us (in subsequent chapters) to finally consider general-equilibrium macroeconomic outcomes.

We adopt a multi-period view of firms because they make fundamentally dynamic (intertemporal) decisions. To keep things as similar as possible to the way we studied intertemporal consumer decisions, we will use the two-period setup that was the basis for the consumption–savings framework. Once we understand the model's setup, its analysis, and the main insights it provides, the entire analysis extends readily beyond two periods.

The discussion proceeds as follows. We begin by introducing some basic concepts regarding firms and production, focusing on how inputs get transformed into outputs. With these basics we construct the dynamic profit function. Using the profit function, we develop the conditions that both formally and intuitively characterize a small firm's profit-maximizing choices of labor and capital. Studying capital decisions inherently requires details about intertemporal markets. We then switch interpretation to a representative firm, which allows us to consider market demand in the two key input markets of labor and capital. We close by returning to the starting point above of "static" versus "dynamic" aspects of firm-level decisions.

Firm Profit Function

Start with a single, atomistic firm (which will often be referred to as a "small firm") that maximizes its profits. The small firm takes prices as given in labor markets, capital markets, and goods markets. The **firm's profit-maximizing decisions** occur at the beginning of period 1, and these decisions encompass economic decisions for both period 1 and period 2. Because of the multi-period (two-period) nature of lifetime profits, the firm must maximize a **dynamic profit function.**

To build up to the dynamic profit function, we establish some basics. First, in each period the small firm uses labor and capital goods in order to produce final output goods.[1] Compressing all the inputs that a firm uses into the two categories of "labor" and "capital" is a useful and nearly universal approach in macroeconomic analysis. Labor should be thought of in exactly the same way as in the static consumption–leisure framework.

Capital goods require more discussion. Capital goods are physical goods such as machines, factories, computers, delivery trucks, and hair dryers that are used by firms in the production of other goods and services. A critical aspect of capital goods is that they are **accumulation (stock) quantities,** which means they take time to build up. If these are, for example, machines or factories, "building" is a very natural view. The way we formalize the "building" idea in the model is to take the simplest view of it: capital goods take one period to build. Which should be contrasted with, for example, labor: labor takes "zero periods" to build.[2]

Let's consider a simple example to illustrate this idea. Suppose that a firm has zero units of capital at the beginning of period 1. If the firm optimally desires a certain strictly positive level of capital for use in production in period 2, it must sink resources into purchasing that capital during period 1. It does so knowing full well that because of the one-period time-to-build aspect of capital, those purchases will not be ready for use until period 2.

---

1. We include only labor costs and capital purchase costs. Any "other" costs that firms incur can typically be counted as either labor costs and/or capital purchase costs, so omitting "other" costs does not change any of the results.

2. In richer applications that feature more than two periods, it is easy to think that the building of certain types of capital itself takes more than one time period. And, once built, the capital will last for multiple time periods. But this is an enrichment of exactly the framework being built here.

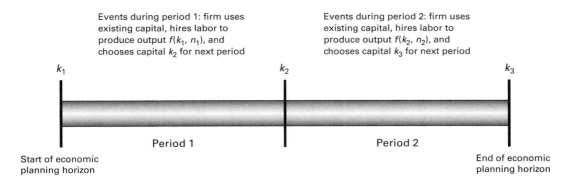

NOTE: Economic planning occurs for the ENTIRE two periods.

Figure 6.1
Timing of events for a firm in the two-period framework. Because capital, k, is an accumulation (stock) quantity, it appears on the junctions between time periods.

The **time-to-build** feature of capital goods is the important point of distinction between capital and labor. The "stock versus flow" differentiation between capital and labor is the main reason behind the nearly universal adoption of these two distinct inputs in macroeconomic analysis. The timeline in figure 6.1 shows capital goods (indicated by k) on the junctions between time periods because capital will not be ready for use until later.

Second, as is common in microeconomic analysis of firms, the small firm uses labor and capital as inputs to a production function in order to produce output. The production function is represented as $y_1 = f(k_1, n_1)$ for period 1 and $y_2 = f(k_2, n_2)$ for period 2.[3] An everyday example is the coffee shop on the corner that uses both workers (labor) and coffee machines (capital) to create, via some production process $f(k, n)$, coffee for its patrons.

Because we are ultimately adopting a macroeconomic view, we make two very important broad assumptions regarding production functions. First, production is assumed strictly increasing in each of the two input arguments. Second, and separately, production displays an ever-decreasing rate of transformation from each input individually into output. Stated in a different way, the latter property simply means: holding the quantity of capital input fixed, increases in labor input increase total output at an ever-decreasing rate; or (switching inputs), holding the quantity of labor input fixed, increases in capital increase total output at an ever-decreasing rate.

---

3. For ease of exposition, both here and elsewhere below, we will sometimes use the subscript notation t, rather than the subscripts "1" and "2," in cases where there is no ambiguity about the time period that is meant. Hence $y_t = f(k_t, n_t)$ is a shortcut representation of the production function in any period t.

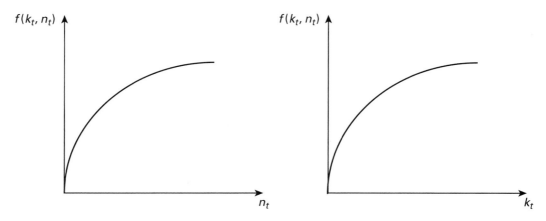

Figure 6.2
Production function $f(k_t, n_t)$ is strictly increasing in each of its two arguments labor and capital, and displays diminishing marginal returns in each of labor and capital individually. The left panel shows that as capital is held constant, increases in labor increase output at a diminishing (ever-decreasing) rate. The right panel shows that as labor is held constant, increases in capital increase output at a diminishing (ever-decreasing) rate.

Formally, the two concepts correspond to a strictly **positive marginal product** in each input individually, and a strictly **diminishing marginal product** in each input individually. The term "marginal product" is important in firm analysis (you perhaps already know its basic definition), but let's leave intuitive description of it until the analysis of first-order conditions below. But the simple idea is that a marginal product describes how much extra (marginal) output is generated by using a little extra (marginal) input.

To continue the formal description of these statements, we can also think via a strict calculus characterization, which is in terms of first derivatives and second derivatives. The strictly positive marginal product corresponds to restrictions on the first derivatives: $f_n(k_t, n_t) > 0$ and $f_k(k_t, n_t) > 0$. And the strictly diminishing marginal product corresponds to restrictions on the second derivatives: $f_{nn}(k_t, n_t) < 0$ and $f_{kk}(k_t, n_t) < 0$. The key words in all of the above are **positive** and **diminishing**, and these effects are shown in figure 6.2. Unless stated otherwise (which could be the case in particular examples), this view of how inputs combine to produce output will be standard.

With these basics established, the small firm's dynamic profit function (sometimes also referred to as the **lifetime profit function** or the **intertemporal profit function)** from the perspective of the beginning of period 1 is

$$\underbrace{P_1 f(k_1, n_1)}_{\text{Period-one revenues}} \underbrace{-P_1(k_2 - k_1) - P_1 w_1 n_1}_{\text{Period-one total costs}} + \underbrace{\frac{P_2 f(k_2, n_2)}{1+i}}_{\text{Period-two revenues}} \underbrace{-\frac{P_2(k_3 - k_2)}{1+i} - \frac{P_2 w_2 n_2}{1+i}}_{\text{Period-two total costs}}.$$

The profit function has the following notation: P_1 is the price of final goods during period 1, P_2 is the price of final goods during period 2, w_1 is the real wage during period 1, w_2 is the real wage during period 2, i is the nominal interest rate between period 1 and period 2, k_1 is the firm's accumulated capital at the very beginning of period 1, k_2 is the firm's accumulated capital at the very beginning of period 2, and k_3 is the firm's accumulated capital at the very beginning of period three. The prices P_1, P_2, w_1, w_2, and i are all taken as given by the small firm.

The profit function is written in nominal terms (each term is denominated in units of currency), which makes the nominal interest rate i the appropriate one to use to discount period-2 revenue and cost terms back to period 1. We could instead represent profits in a purely real form, in which case the real interest rate r would be the relevant discount factor. Regardless of nominal or real, the terms that are discounted by the appropriate interest rate simply adjust for any changes in prices that may occur between period 1 and period 2, all of which is taken as given by the small firm.

Also regardless of nominal or real, we have made the assumption that the market "sticker price" for physical capital in each period is identical to the market "sticker price" for output goods produced and sold by the firm in each period: P_1 in period 1 and P_2 in period 2. Observe that there is *no* price here called, say, P_t^k, that would be the price in period t of a unit of capital goods as distinct from the price, P_t, of a unit of output goods. This assumption makes it appear that the distinction between capital goods and output goods is blurred. To the contrary, as we explain further below when we study the investment demand function, it actually enhances the critical distinction between capital goods and output goods.

The firm's choice variables, which are chosen at the beginning of period 1, are the quantities of labor in periods one and two, n_1 and n_2, and the choice of the quantity of **capital investment** purchases in which to engage during the course of period 1 and during the course of period 2. What we have specified "net investment" in the profit function, which are $k_2 - k_1$ and $k_3 - k_2$, respectively, rather than "gross investment." The details of this are described below, but regardless of net versus gross, the accumulation nature of capital is once again critical. As explained further below, capital investment (net or gross) is the quantity by which the firm desires to change its capital level between consecutive time periods.

Analysis

Formally, the next set of steps is to construct three first-order conditions.

First-Order Conditions
Based on the dynamic profit function, the first-order conditions with respect to n_1 and n_2 are, respectively,

$$P_1 f_n(k_1, n_1) - P_1 w_1 = 0$$

and

$$\frac{P_2 f_n(k_2, n_2)}{1+i} - \frac{P_2 w_2}{1+i} = 0,$$

in which $f_n(k_t, n_t)$ denotes the **marginal product of labor.** We introduced the term "marginal product" above. The marginal product of labor is simply the extra (marginal) quantity of output that results from the hiring and use of an extra (marginal) unit of labor input, holding all else (including capital input usage) constant.

Canceling terms appropriately—in particular, canceling the nominal price of output goods and the nominal interest rate—in each of these expressions gives $w_1 = f_n(k_1, n_1)$ and $w_2 = f_n(k_2, n_2)$.[4] The economic content of this statement is crucial: when the small firm is maximizing profit, it chooses its optimal quantity of labor in such a way that the *(real) marginal product of labor* is exactly equal to the market real wage. Nominal prices and nominal interest rates have nothing to do with this condition, on which we build further below.

Proceeding to the capital purchase decision, the only interesting decision in the two-period framework is with respect to k_2. This is for two reasons. First, as in the two-period framework that was the foundation of consumption–savings decisions, the firm knows that there is no period 3, so it is (trivially) optimal for it to "choose" $k_3 = 0$.[5] Second, given the accumulation nature of capital goods, k_1 cannot be chosen at the beginning of period 1 – k_1 is instead "predetermined" (think of it as reflecting choices that occurred in "period zero," which is outside our analysis). Which thus leaves only k_2 as a firm-level decision.

The first-order condition with respect to k_2 is

$$-P_1 + \frac{P_2 f_k(k_2, n_2)}{1+i} + \frac{P_2}{1+i} = 0,$$

in which $f_k(k_t, n_t)$ denotes the **marginal product of capital.**[6] Similar to the marginal product of labor, the marginal product of capital is simply the extra (marginal) quantity of

---

4. Stated more generally in terms of any period t, the condition that characterizes the optimal choice of labor is $w_t = f_n(k_t, n_t)$.

5. Just as in the two-period consumption framework, the rational individual (here, the rational firm) will always choose to have zero wealth at the end of the economy. The capital (machines, equipment, etc.) is the wealth (i.e., the assets) that a firm owns.

6. To draw attention to a modification of this expression that is made clearer below: once we properly define net investment versus gross investment, another term appears in the first-order condition on k_2 if we formally consider gross investment. This more complete version appears in the appendix, but the simpler case being studied here is just a special case of the more complete version, and none of the economic insights to come are changed by it.

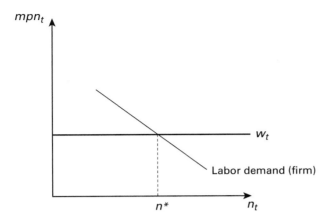

Figure 6.3
From the perspective of a small firm, the marginal product of labor and market real wage w as functions of the firm's own quantity of labor in any period t. The point at which $mpn = w$ is the optimal choice of labor for the small firm, taking all else as given.

output that results from the use of an extra (marginal) unit of capital input, holding all else (including labor input usage) constant.

Labor Demand

From the first-order conditions above and the general properties of the production function $f(k_t, n_t)$, we can establish the **labor demand function,** which is a market-based relationship between the real wage and the optimal choice of labor. Demand for labor is a *derived demand* because it arises due to (is derived from) market demand for the firm's output good.

The expression $w_t = f_n(k_t, n_t)$ characterizes the labor demand function. To see this graphically in a diagram of real wages and labor, consider the right-hand side of the expression. Because the second derivative is, by assumption, strictly negative $(f_{nn}(k_t, n_t) < 0)$, the first derivative $(f_n(k_t, n_t)$, which *is* the marginal product of labor) is strictly decreasing as n increases. This argument is just an application of the properties of the second derivative function to understand something about the behavior of the first derivative function— less technically, this argument simply tells us that the marginal product of labor is becoming strictly smaller as n becomes strictly larger. Hence we have a diminishing marginal product.

Figure 6.3 plots the downward-sloping marginal product of labor schedule (labeled *mpn* in the diagram, a term that will be used interchangeably with $f_n(k_t, n_t)$) as a function of n. Because it emphasizes the qualitative properties on which we are largely interested, a downward-sloping straight line is sketched for the marginal product schedule. In standard macroeconomic applications, though, marginal product functions themselves typically

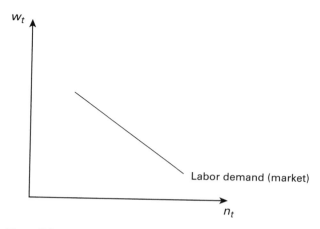

Figure 6.4
Market labor demand function depends negatively on the real wage.

have some convexity (i.e., they are bowed in toward the origin).[7] Figure 6.3 also plots as a horizontal line the market-determined real wage w that the small firm takes as given.

For the small firm, *mpn* represents the marginal benefit of one more worker, and w represents the marginal cost of one more worker. Standard microeconomic results allow us to conclude that the optimal quantity of labor is exactly where marginal benefit equals marginal cost. This optimal quantity is n^* in figure 6.3.

The sketch in figure 6.3 is for a small firm. Moving to an aggregate view requires asking what happens to optimal labor when the market real wage w_t changes. As is clear from figure 6.3, as the market real wage w_t declines, the small firm hires more labor; and, in the opposite direction, hires less labor if w_t increases. This intuitive relationship between movements in the market real wage and optimal labor is the *market labor demand function*, which is shown in figure 6.4.

The two downward-sloping schedules in both figure 6.3 and figure 6.4 are termed "labor demand," which may appear confusing. Standard terminology is that the *mpn* schedule for a small firm is usually referred to as "labor demand," regardless of the market wage (which, note once again, is plotted as a horizontal line in figure 6.3). For macroeconomic purposes, we are interested in market prices and market quantities, so plotting the relationship between the market wage w_t and the market quantity of optimal labor requires moving from

---

7. A typical macroeconomic functional form for production functions is the Cobb–Douglas production function, $f(k_t, n_t) = k_t^\alpha n_t^{1-\alpha}$, in which $\alpha \in (0, 1)$ measures the share (or the "importance") of physical capital in the production process. The parameter $1 - \alpha \in (0, 1)$ thus measures the share of labor in the production process. The share $\alpha \in (0, 1)$ is almost always taken as a parameter, which will also be our view (e.g., in the United States, a standard value is $\alpha \approx 1/3$, based on econometric evidence). The associated marginal product of labor function, which is simply the partial derivative with respect to labor, is $f_n(k_t, n_t) = (1 - \alpha)k_t^\alpha n_t^{-\alpha}$.

the "small firm" view in figure 6.3 to the aggregate view in figure 6.4. Thus figure 6.4 is what we will usually mean when we refer to "the" market labor demand function, and it allows cleaner use of terminology; but many would also consider figure 6.3 as showing the same result.

Building toward Capital Demand

Studying the small firm's decisions about capital purchases proceeds in a similar way as labor demand. As with labor demand, capital purchase decisions are also a derived demand for the firm, hence many big-picture points are very similar. The point at which we will eventually arrive below is that the expression $r = f_k(k_t, n_t)$ characterizes the *capital invest-ment demand function*, which appears very analogous to the $w_t = f_n(k_t, n_t)$ expression that characterizes the labor demand function. However, getting there requires detailing three further issues, which are important.

First, the *macroeconomic notion of investment* is that it measures the change in the quantity of capital between the start of one period and the start of the next.[8] In the context of our two-period model, this change only has interesting meaning between period 1 and period 2 because, as noted above, the "optimal choice" regarding k_3 is that it trivially equals zero.

Net Investment and Gross Investment

First, there are two distinct concepts of investment: net investment and gross investment. We have included the former (net investment) in our dynamic profit function, so we start there. Mathematically, define the variable inv_1 (which will also be referred to as simply *inv* below because there is no ambiguity about time periods in the two-period model) to denote the change in capital between the start of period 1 and the start of period 2,

$$inv = k_2 - k_1 .$$

8. The term "investment" should be properly distinguished from a broader, colloquial usage of the term. Formally, macroeconomic investment is the sum of business purchases of capital goods (goods that businesses use in the production of other goods and services), new homes built, and addition to firms' inventories. In everyday language, we often use the term "investment" to refer to someone's collection of stocks and bonds, as in "I invested in 100 shares of Microsoft stock last week." In formal economics, this latter type of activity is *not* investment. In fact this latter type of activity is termed savings, a topic we have already studied. It is very important, however, to keep this terminology straight, as it is often a source of confusion when discussing matters of savings and investment. As we will see later, there is in fact a deep connection between macroeconomic savings and macroeconomic investment. For now, however, we are only considering the topic of investment. Because it is consumers (for the most part) that purchase homes, we see from the definition of investment that investment encompasses activities of both consumers and firms. However, for convenience of exposition, we will simply speak of investment as being undertaken by firms only.

Formally, this is **net investment,** defined as the change in the level of capital between the start of the subsequent period (period 2) and the start of the current period (period 1). The terms "subsequent" and "current" inherit from the timing of the model: in the two-period model, profit-maximizing decisions, including investment decisions, are made at the beginning of period 1.

Net investment does not include the wearing out of capital goods. Interpreting capital goods as, say, machinery, it is clear that capital goods naturally wear out due to use. **Economic depreciation** is the wearing out of capital goods due to use in the production process.[9] Rates of economic depreciation (often referred to as just "depreciation") are generally thought to vary by country, if we are interested in macroeconomic analysis. US data show that roughly 8 percent of the nation's capital stock depreciates every year, and this numerical value is fairly stable over long periods of time. Let this constant rate of depreciation ("constant" because the rate of depreciation does not vary between one time period and the next) be denoted by δ (Greek lowercase letter "delta"), with the natural restriction that $0 \le \delta \le 1$. In the US example, $\delta = 0.08$. Considering how a US business is affected by depreciation: if it owns k_1 units of capital at the beginning of period 1 and it purchases zero new capital goods during the course of period 1, then it will own $(1 - \delta)k_1$ units of capital at the start of period 2.

While net investment, inv, does not consider economic depreciation, the highly related concept of **gross investment** does. Define gross investment inv^{gross} as

$$inv^{gross} = inv + \delta k_1,$$

which takes into account the replacement of depreciated capital through new investment purchases. Inserting the definition $inv = k_2 - k_1$ from above allows us to rewrite gross investment as

$$inv^{gross} = k_2 - (1 - \delta)k_1 .$$

These two alternative expressions for inv^{gross} measure exactly the same idea: the first casts the relationship between two different notions of investment (gross versus net), and the second casts the relationship in terms of levels of capital.

A simple example illustrates the distinction between net investment and gross investment. Suppose that a hair-drying salon (all they do is dry hair!) uses hairdryers as capital goods (part of their "machines and equipment"). The salon begins period 1 with k_1

---

9. This idea of wearing out of goods is, as the terminology emphasizes, the *economic* notion of depreciation, and it has nothing to do with any types of depreciation rules in business accounting. Accounting standards and regulations are such that sometimes a company has some control over how to *report* its depreciation of capital goods (i.e., accelerated depreciation, straight-line depreciation). Our economic notion of depreciation has only to do with how quickly goods *actually* wear out over time and nothing to do with how a company may choose to *report* how quickly goods wear out.

hairdryers, and it purchases a total of x new hairdryers during period 1. Of the hairdryers with which it began period 1, some of them wore out during the period. At the end of the period, the salon thus has $(1-\delta)k_1 + x$ hairdryers, with which it will begin period 2. Because it replaces the hairdryers that wore out, but also expands the total number of hairdryers, the total quantity x of new hairdryer purchases is gross investment.

If the salon did want to expand the total number of usable hairdryers, the net addition to the number of hairdryers (net investment in hairdryers) during period 1 was smaller than x (gross investment in hairdryers). The reason is simply depreciation. In the example, total depreciation is δk_1, which is the number of hairdryers that wore out. The portion of x that just "replaces" the depreciated capital goods δk_1 does not actually expand the level of capital goods, it simply maintains the number of usable hairdryers. This distinction leads to the definitional relationship between inv and inv^{gross} that appears above.

In quantitative applications, it is gross investment that is most relevant because that is what is measured by the official GDP and GDP-components accounts. However, note that the absolute gap between gross investment and net investment is fairly small, provided that the depreciation rate δ is fairly small, as it is for the United States and other advanced economies.[10] If we are mostly interested in qualitative, rather than quantitative, analysis, and the insights qualitative analysis provides, then a first-pass simplification is to completely ignore the difference. The reason that ignoring depreciation does not change any of the economic reasoning was (implicitly) stated above: the depreciation **rate** is constant over time, and moreover is thought to be outside the control of any firm. Hence it is only **quantitative** results that could be different; none of the economic insights will be different.

Thus, for most of our qualitative analysis and resulting insights, we typically assume that the depreciation rate is $\delta = 0$, in which case there is literally no distinction between inv^{gross} and inv. Indeed $\delta = 0$ was already assumed in everything that has been thus far mathematically formalized. The appendix, however, provides a slightly richer mathematical analysis that includes the δ term; to recover the analysis in the main text from the slightly richer analysis in the appendix simply requires setting $\delta = 0$.

Capital Goods and Output Goods Are Physically Identical

The second issue is that whether analyzing gross investment or net investment, we make an assumption that at first seems an excessive oversimplification. This assumption was

---

10. As noted above, $\delta = 0.08$ at an annual frequency for the United States is a commonly used economy-wide figure. In many macroeconomic applications, quarterly data are studied (simply because many macroeconomic time series are made available at a quarterly frequency), which makes the economic depreciation rate about $\delta = 0.02$, and thus also very small.

pointed out briefly following the dynamic profit function above: the *market sticker prices* for both capital goods and output goods are identical in each period. The underlying economic assumption is that "final goods" (the goods that the firm produces and sells) are exactly identical to "capital goods" (the machines, etc., that firms use to produce final goods). Of course, this cannot literally be true—it is doubtful that the salon in the example above uses hairdryers to produce hairdryers.

But to understand this "identical sticker price" idea, recognize that there are quite a number of goods that have uses both in production of other goods and services, as well as end-user (final good) value in themselves. For example, about 80 percent of households in the United States own a personal computer—these would formally be counted as "consumption goods" in the GDP accounts.[11] But if you walk into any place of business, you are certain to see a computer on virtually every employee's desk—these would formally be counted as "capital goods." To make this even more exact, computer companies use a lot of computers (capital goods) in producing more computers (final goods)! Even if the computers themselves are identical! So there are clearly some indistinguishable goods that are used as both capital goods and consumption goods.

There are, of course, many goods that are usefully thought of partially as final goods and partially as capital goods. And there are also many examples of goods that are either one type or the other but not both. If we want to admit such distinctions in the model (which is certainly possible), we would require a separate price, call it P_t^k, that would denote capital-goods prices in period t, distinct from the price for output goods, P_t.

While obviously realistic, raising such distinctions makes it harder to understand the conceptually most important "price" for capital goods, which is described next. Furthermore, while "realism" of a model is important for quantitative studies, sometimes "departing" from realism actually makes it easier to display the economics of an idea.[12] Thus we simply make the assumption that consumer goods and capital goods are identical goods—for concreteness, the computer example is helpful. Yet this assumption begs the question: What is it that actually is different about capital goods versus output goods?

The Importance of the Real Interest Rate *r*

The answer is the third issue: the conceptually most important price for capital investment goods is the **real interest rate *r*.** This point is critically significant, and it arises because capital investment is a fundamentally intertemporal decision. A firm decides how much

---

11. See http://www.marketingcharts.com/interactive/home-internet-access-in-us-still-room-for-growth-8280/ nielsen-internet-access-household-income-February-2009jpg/.

12. This also is the motivation for considering net investment in the main analysis rather than gross investment. The latter is more "realistic" quantitatively by adding depreciation explicitly into the firm profit function, but doing so does nothing to change the economic insights learned by studying net investment.

capital it would like to have in the future, and the time-to-build nature of capital requires resources to be expended now.[13]

To understand this formally, we can see the "r price aspect" of capital based directly on the first-order condition on k_2. As shown in the appendix, the first-order condition on k_2 can be rewritten as

$$r = f_k(k_2, n_2).$$

This expression appears very different from the one presented above—the appendix shows that getting to this representation simply requires several algebraic steps.[14] But this way of looking at the first-order condition on k_2 clearly displays a tight link with the analysis above of labor demand, in which $w_t = f_n(k_t, n_t)$ characterized the labor demand function. The simple and powerful economic result here, stated as an analogy with labor, is that the *capital investment decision* is governed by a condition that is very similar to the *labor demand condition.*

Digging deeper on the economics of this statement: if the firm is making its optimal choice about capital investment, it does so in a way that the marginal product of capital is exactly equal to something that it takes as given. The economics then reduces to: What is it that the firm takes as given?

When applied to labor, the answer is that the real wage was taken as given. In turn, the real wage is the appropriate notion (measured in real units) of the price of labor.

When applied to capital here, the answer is that the real interest rate is taken as given. By analogy with labor, the real interest rate is thus the appropriate notion (measured in real units) of the price of capital investment. Hence follows the conclusion that the critical price for capital investment goods is the real interest rate r.

If you have followed the arguments this far, it may raise a chain of logic: interest rates are only relevant components of costs if a firm is borrowing in order to purchase capital (capital can be prohibitively costly, in terms of machines and factories). Instead, if we consider a firm that had enough cash on hand to purchase capital outright without any need for borrowing, then the real interest rate seemingly would not be relevant for purchasing capital.

Unfortunately, this logic is incorrect. In terms of a multi-period (two periods or longer, it does not matter) analysis, the correct logic is that it does not matter whether or not the firm is "borrowing" to purchase physical capital investment goods. The real interest rate

13. As we first learned from studying consumption–savings decisions, the real interest rate r is the crucial intertemporal price. Switching to studying firm-level decisions, rather than consumer decisions, does not make the importance of r disappear. Rather, r is vital for the same reasons as it was when studying consumption–savings decisions: the centrality of intertemporal, or dynamic, decisions.

14. Along with the assumption of $\delta = 0$; as the appendix shows, for the more general case of $0 \leq \delta \leq 1$, the condition actually reads $r = f_k(k_2, n_2) - \delta$. But this slightly richer condition including δ blurs the main point being made here.

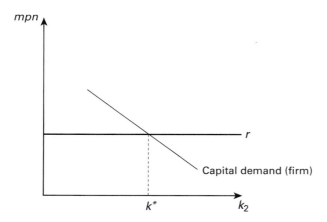

Figure 6.5
From the perspective of a small firm, the marginal product of capital and market real interest rate r as functions of the firm's own period-2 desired capital stock. The point at which $mpk = r$ is the optimal choice of period-2 capital for the small firm, taking all else as given.

r is the relevant price of capital investment goods regardless of financial market arrangements.[15]

For the sake of terminology, it is easier to adopt the point of view of a firm that owns its own capital in both periods, which is what is embodied in the dynamic profit function with which we started.

To recap, the real interest rate r is the central price in capital investment decisions. The centrality of r is true regardless of whether we are considering net investment or gross investment. Gross investment is quantitatively richer because it considers depreciation of capital goods as they are used in the production process. But the economic insights generated by studying net investment, which is the main case in the text, are identical to the ones that emerge from studying gross investment.

From Capital Demand ...

With all of these basics we can turn to the small firm's optimal choice of capital. Figure 6.5 plots the downward-sloping marginal product of capital schedule (*mpk* in the diagram, a term that will be used interchangeably, here and later in the text, with $f_k(k_t, n_t)$) as a function of k_2. As with labor demand, because it emphasizes the qualitative properties on which

---

15. To preview a point of departure later in the text, considering "financing frictions" may alter this result and hence intuition. Even more generally, other market frictions might layer on top of r other prices, taxes, regulations, and so on. But the centrality of r in the capital investment decision is critical in macroeconomic analysis. Thus another way to state the result here, before we get to various models of market imperfections, is that perfect competition in financial markets (even though left unstated) is the basis for the result.

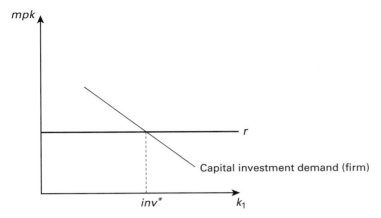

Figure 6.6
From the perspective of a small firm, the marginal product of capital and market real interest rate r as functions of the firm's own quantity of investment between desired period-2 capital and period-1 preexisting capital. The point at which $mpk = r$ is the optimal choice of capital investment for the small firm, taking all else as given

we are mostly interested, a downward-sloping straight line is sketched for the marginal product schedule. Figure 6.5 also plots as a horizontal line the market-determined real interest rate r that the small firm takes as given.

For the small firm, mpk represents the marginal benefit of one more unit of capital, and r represents the marginal (intertemporal) cost of one more unit of capital. Standard microeconomic results allow us to conclude that the optimal quantity of period-2 capital is exactly where marginal benefit equals marginal cost. This optimal quantity is k^* in figure 6.5.

... to Investment Demand (Part I)

We are virtually, but not completely, finished. Figure 6.5 shows the optimal desired quantity of capital, which is an accumulation measure; we are technically interested in the optimal quantity of investment, which is a flow measure. It is easy to make this connection.

At the start of period 1, the firm has k_1 predetermined units of capital that cannot be changed. The firm's optimal desired quantity of capital at the start of period 2 is k_2^*. The definition of (net) investment, $inv = k_2^* - k_1$, shows that there is a one-for-one relationship between quantity of desired future capital and the quantity of current investment. With the assumption that $k_1 < k_2^*$ (because investment is nearly always positive at the macroeconomic level), we have the representation in figure 6.6. Figure 6.6, which plots the optimal investment decision (which is a flow quantity during period 1) of a firm, is qualitatively identical to figure 6.5, which plots the optimal desired quantity of capital (which is an accumulation quantity in period 2). In terms of economic intuition, there is nothing

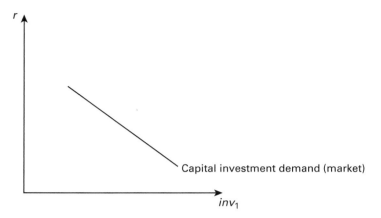

Figure 6.7
Market capital investment demand depends negatively on the real interest rate.

different between figure 6.6 and figure 6.5; but it is figure 6.6 that is more immediately relevant for the subsequent analysis.

The sketch in figure 6.6 depicts a small firm. Switching to an aggregate view requires asking what happens to optimal investment when the market real interest rate r changes. As is clear from figure 6.6, as the market real interest rate r declines, the small firm invests more; and, in the opposite direction, invests less if r increases. This intuitive relationship between movements in the market real interest rate r and optimal investment is the **market capital investment function,** which is shown in figure 6.7.[16]

Investment Demand (Part II)

The market capital investment demand function plotted in figure 6.7 is the properly correct use of the term. Sometimes, though, it is not the figure 6.7 representation but instead a representation of P_1 on the vertical axis and optimal investment on the horizontal axis (and taking all other objects as given, most importantly, P_2 and i) to which people refer as the investment function.

---

16. Similar to labor demand, the two downward-sloping schedules in figure 6.6 and figure 6.7 are both termed "investment demand." Standard terminology is that the *mpk* schedule for a small firm is usually referred to as "investment demand" (or even "capital demand") regardless of the market real interest rate. For macroeconomic purposes, we are interested in market prices and market quantities, so plotting the relationship between the market rate r and the market quantity of optimal investment requires moving from the "small firm" view in figure 6.6 to the aggregate view, or representative firm view, in figure 6.7. Thus figure 6.7 is what we will usually mean when we refer to "the" market investment demand function, and it allows cleaner use of terminology; but many would also consider figure 6.6 as showing the same result.

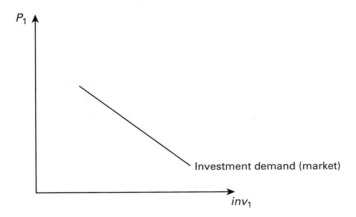

Figure 6.8
Capital investment demand from the perspective of nominal prices in a given time period, rather than from the perspective of the intertemporal price r.

To consider why, the Fisher relation tells us that there is a direct relationship between P_1 and r,

$$1 + r = \frac{1+i}{1+\pi_2} = \left(\frac{P_1}{P_2}\right)(1+i),$$

if we hold P_2 and i fixed. This leads to another graphical view of the investment demand function, shown in figure 6.8.

There is nothing formally incorrect about figure 6.8. But in terms of economic interpretation, it makes it appear that a "static" price leads to a downward-sloping investment demand function. This is somewhat misleading and misses the essence of the effort spent above establishing that it is the **intertemporal price r** that is relevant for investment demand. The Fisher relation does show exactly this—changes in P_1 lead directly to changes in r if P_2 and i are held constant. But it largely mutes the central point above that the intertemporal price r is to be thought of as the most important price when studying changes in investment.

However, the diagram in figure 6.8 is useful because it allows horizontal summation with the consumption demand function derived in (either or both) the consumption–leisure model and the consumption–savings model. With a closed-economy view and leaving government decisions aside, what we thus generate is the aggregate demand function.

Nonetheless, rarely will we imply figure 6.8 when we use the term "investment demand function." Instead, what we will imply is figure 6.7.

Discussion

There are a number of important definitional and conceptual issues that arose as we considered a firm's profit maximization in a multi-period environment. But let's zoom back out to broad issues. The two main results of firm profit-maximization are the labor demand function in any given period and the capital investment demand function across any pair of periods. The labor demand function is depicted in figure 6.4. The capital investment demand function is depicted in figure 6.7.[17]

Returning to the very beginning of the chapter, we can think of labor demand and investment demand in terms of, respectively, static aspects of firm profit maximization versus dynamic aspects of firm profit maximization. To do so, let's depart slightly, but intuitively, from the formal mathematical statements presented earlier about $f(k, n)$.

Suppose that a firm's production process required zero capital inputs, and it required only labor input. This production process is "extremely labor intensive." The firm would hire labor in a profit-maximizing way, and the labor demand function would look identical to the one in figure 6.4. What about investment demand? Investment demand would simply not exist because the extremely labor-intensive firm never needs to own any capital. This extreme type of firm allows the "static" aspect of profit maximization—labor demand—to arise in the same way as analyzed above. But it completely shuts down the "dynamic" aspect of profit maximization—capital investment.

Instead, consider an "extremely capital intensive" firm that requires capital inputs but zero labor inputs in its production process. The firm would invest in capital in a profit-maximizing way, and the capital investment demand function would look identical to the one in figure 6.7. What about labor demand? Labor demand would simply not exist, because the extremely capital-intensive firm never needs any labor. This extreme type of firm allows the "dynamic" aspect of profit maximization—capital investment—to arise in the same way as studied above. But it completely shuts down the "static" aspect of profit maximization—labor demand.

In these extreme examples, labor demand is a "static" phenomenon (at one extreme) because it portrays a relationship between *only* period-t prices and period-t quantities—the real wage and the quantity of labor to hire. There is nothing inherently dynamic about the economic decisions in the model. At the other extreme, investment demand is a "dynamic" phenomenon because it portrays a relationship *only* between the real interest rate **across time periods** and how much investment to purchase across those time periods. There is nothing inherently static about the economic decisions in the model.

As we stated at the beginning, our analysis of firms combines both the static and dynamic aspects into one model, and the model generates the same broad results.

---

17. Rather than in figure 6.8, which technically plots the same function in a different space; to reiterate the point made above, let's consider figure 6.7 the nearly universal way of thinking about the capital investment demand function.

Appendix: Construction of Capital Demand Function

In this appendix we show how to convert the first-order condition on k_2 into a relationship between the real interest rate and the marginal product of capital. This derivation uses the slightly richer version of the model, in which economic depreciation may occur to a firm's capital. This slightly richer analysis does not affect any of the economic intuition described in the text.

With economic depreciation of a firm's capital at the rate $0 \le \delta \le 1$, the dynamic profit function is

$$P_1 f(k_1, n_1) - P_1(k_2 - (1-\delta)k_1) - P_1 w_1 n_1 + \frac{P_2 f(k_2, n_2)}{1+i} - \frac{P_2(k_3 - (1-\delta)k_2)}{1+i} - \frac{P_2 w_2 n_2}{1+i}.$$

Note where the δ term appears: in the investment term of the period-1 component of profits and in the investment term of the period-2 component of profits. The first-order condition on k_2 is

$$-P_1 + \frac{P_2 f_k(k_2, n_2)}{1+i} + \frac{P_2(1-\delta)}{1+i} = 0.$$

The main analysis in the text is recovered by setting $\delta = 0$. The important economic insights remain the same as in the simpler version presented in the main text.

Starting from this richer first-order condition on k_2, divide by P_1, which gives

$$1 = \left(\frac{P_2}{P_1}\right)\left(\frac{1}{1+i}\right) \cdot f_k(k_2, n_2) + \left(\frac{P_2}{P_1}\right)\left(\frac{1-\delta}{1+i}\right),$$

in which we have also pulled the first term on the left-hand side over to the other side of the expression. Regrouping terms obtains

$$1 = \left(\frac{P_2}{P_1}\right)\left(\frac{1}{1+i}\right) \cdot (f_k(k_2, n_2) + 1 - \delta).$$

Next, using the definition of the one-period inflation rate, $1 + \pi_2 \equiv P_2/P_1$, this can be rewritten as

$$1 = \left(\frac{1+\pi_2}{1+i}\right) \cdot (f_k(k_2, n_2) + 1 - \delta).$$

Then, applying the Fisher relation, we have

$$1 = \left(\frac{1}{1+r}\right) \cdot (f_k(k_2, n_2) + 1 - \delta),$$

or multiplying both sides by $1+r$ gives

$$1+r = f_k(k_2, n_2) + 1 - \delta.$$

Canceling the "1" terms on each side gives the final expression,

$$r = f_k(k_2, n_2) - \delta,$$

which can be plotted (provided that the function $f(.)$ has strictly diminishing marginal product in capital) in a diagram with r on the vertical axis and k_2 on the horizontal axis as the **capital demand function.** The capital demand function takes as given a constant value for the depreciation rate δ. The depreciation rate of $\delta = 0$ in the main analysis in the text is just a simpler case.

A common specification in macroeconomic applications is the Cobb–Douglas production function, $f(k, n) = k^\alpha n^{1-\alpha}$, so let's examine it. The parameter $\alpha \in (0, 1)$ measures the capital share of output; hence $1 - \alpha$ (which is also $\in (0, 1)$) measures the labor share of output.

The Cobb–Douglas function has a marginal product of capital function (in period 2, in particular, which is the period of interest here) is $f_k(k_2, n_2) = \alpha k_2^{\alpha-1} n_2^{1-\alpha}$. Substituting this in the previous displayed expression (and maintaining, for sake of completeness of the derivations in the appendix, the parameter $0 \le \delta \le 1$), we have

$$r = \alpha k_2^{\alpha-1} n_2^{1-\alpha} - \delta.$$

Because $\alpha \in (0, 1)$ and recalling the rules of negative exponents (observe that $\alpha - 1 < 0$), we can rewrite this as

$$r = \alpha \left(\frac{n_2}{k_2} \right)^{1-\alpha} - \delta,$$

which simply characterizes the capital demand function for the Cobb–Douglas case.

Without appealing to the Cobb–Douglas or any other functional form, figure 6.9 shows the capital demand function (at the microeconomic level) for the case of $0 < \delta < 1$.

Chapter 6 Problem Set Questions

1. **Lags in labor hiring.** Rather than supposing that the representative firm at the beginning of period t can decide how much labor it would like to hire for use in period t, suppose that labor used in period t must be chosen in period $t - 1$; that is, suppose that n is a stock (aka state) variable. As usual, capital for use in production in period t must be purchased in period $t - 1$ because of the "time to build" surrounding capital goods. With this lag in labor hiring, construct the lifetime (in the two-period model) profit function of the firm, and show that the real interest rate now is a relevant price

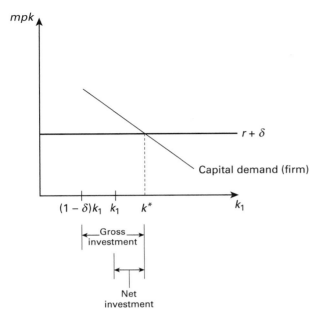

Figure 6.9
Net investment and gross investment as deviations of optimal period-2 capital from, respectively, depreciated period-1 capital and undepreciated period-1 capital.

for labor as well as capital goods. Provide brief economic intuition. (Hint: Make as close an analogy with our model of firm ownership of capital as you can—in particular, think of workers in this model as being "owned" [contractually obligated to] firms.)

2. **Production over the last century.** In any given time period t the representative firm uses the Cobb–Douglas production technology

$$A_t \cdot f(k_t, n_t) = A_t \cdot k_t^{\alpha_t} n_t^{1-\alpha_t}$$

in producing its output of goods and services. As is standard, the exponent $\alpha_t \in (0, 1)$ in every period t—but note here that the exponent could be different in different time periods. The rest of the notation is identical to that used in this chapter.

In the early 20th century US firms used less capital in their production process than they did in the early 21st century. For simplicity, suppose that total factor productivity did not change at all during the century. And further suppose that neither real wages nor real interest rates changed at all during the century.

If the representative firm (which, as per usual economic analysis, maximizes its economic profits) uses a larger ratio of capital to labor (i.e., a larger profit-maximizing ratio k/n) in the early 21st century compared to the early 20th century, what change(s) must have occurred?

Base the analysis on the given production function. Provide brief yet complete mathematical justification, brief economic interpretation, and a simple, qualitative, and clearly labeled pair of graphs that depicts what occurred over the course of the century: one for the demand side of the labor market and one for the demand side of the capital market.

7

Intertemporal Fiscal Policy

An issue that periodically receives much media attention is whether government spending and taxation decisions affect market interest rates. This issue was prominently in the news in the early 2000s when the Bush administration was considering lowering taxes and raising government spending. And it has again been prominent in the United States and in Western Europe as governments are faced with the specter of raising taxes and lowering government spending to reign in fiscal deficits.

The relationship between the government's fiscal position and market interest rates generates much debate among macroeconomists and politicians—some observers claim that there is a strong relationship between the two, while others claim there is no relationship at all.

In this chapter we will study the theory behind this link, using as our basis a two-period framework, which highly resembles the two-period consumption–savings and the two-period investment analyses. Until now, we have neglected government in our two-period models, considering only consumers and firms. After defining some basic terms, we finally introduce a government into the framework. After working through the basic mechanics, we will consider under which circumstances there may be no relationship between the government's fiscal position and private-sector outcomes, as well as under which circumstances there may be.

There are two main "Fiscal Guideposts" that emerge from the analysis that helpfully place intellectual boundaries.

Basic Terminology

You are probably familiar with terms such as a government budget deficit and budget surplus, but we briefly review the concepts. Items affecting the government's budget are termed **fiscal** items, and there are two notions of budget deficits/surpluses: primary and secondary. A **primary budget deficit (surplus)** exists in any given period if the tax revenue collected by the government in that period is smaller than (larger than) the expenditures of the government in that period. Put more mathematically, for any given period t, we compute the difference

Government tax revenue$_t$ − Government expenditure$_t$ (1)

and if this quantity is negative, the primary budget is in deficit in period t, while if this quantity is positive, the primary budget is in surplus in period t. Finally, just to be clear, the primary budget is said to be balanced if this quantity is exactly zero.

Another notion of the government's budget also takes into account interest payments (or interest receipts) on government assets. A **secondary budget deficit (surplus)** exists in any given period if the sum of the tax revenue and interest income collected by the government in that period is smaller than (larger than) the expenditures of the government in that period. Mathematically, if in period t,

Government tax revenue$_t$ + Government interest income$_t$ − Government expenditure$_t$ (2)

is negative, the secondary budget is in deficit in period t, while if it is positive, the secondary budget is in surplus in period t. The secondary budget is said to balanced if this quantity is exactly zero. Comparing expressions (1) and (2) shows that the primary and secondary budgets equal each other only when government interest income is zero.

The secondary budget generally receives less attention in the press in the United States despite the relatively large debt obligations of the federal government. This is because the interest rate on US debt obligations is relatively small compared to the other items in its budget (tax revenue and expenditures), to the effect that the primary budget is usually approximately equal to the secondary budget in the United States. But for other countries, especially for developing nations, this is often not the case.

We define real government savings in period t, which we denote by s_t^{gov}, to be equal to the secondary fiscal balance, so that if there is a secondary fiscal surplus, government savings is positive, whereas if there is a secondary fiscal deficit, government savings is negative.

Government Budget Constraints

The important aspect of the government for studying the issue in which we are interested is the budget constraints of the government.[1] Just like the individual consumer in our two-period world, the government exists for each of the two periods. It has (real) budget constraints in period 1 and period 2, given, respectively, by

$$g_1 + b_1 = (1+r)b_0 + t_1 \tag{3}$$

---

1. We do not attempt to model a utility function for the government, because the welfare incentives of politically elected leaders (who may want to design policy in such a way as to get re-elected) may not align with those the representative consumer's. This is a point of departure between macroeconomic analysis and political economy.

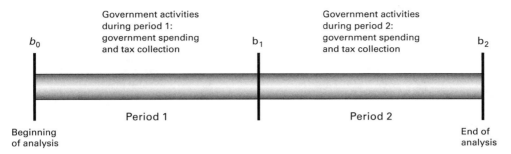

Figure 7.1
Timing of events for the government.

and

$$g_2 + b_2 = (1+r)b_1 + t_2. \tag{4}$$

The notation is as follows: g_1 and g_2 denote real government spending in periods 1 and 2, respectively; t_1 and t_2 denote real tax revenue collected by the government in periods 1 and 2, respectively; and b_0, b_1, and b_2 denote the real asset holdings of the government at the end of periods 0, 1, and 2, respectively. As before, r denotes the real interest rate between one period and the next. Compare these period-by-period budget constraints of the government with those of the individual consumer discussed in our initial look at the two-period model. Inspecting these reveals that they are completely analogous. The right-hand side of expressions (3) and (4) is the income received by the government in each period, and the left-hand side is the expenditure of the government in each period.

Again just like the consumer, the government knows that the economy ends at the end of period 2. Thus there is no period 3 for the government to save for, and no rational institution (e.g., a bank or a foreign country) would allow the economy to end with the government indebted to it—thus we must have that $b_2 = 0$. To further simplify matters, let's also make the assumption that the initial assets of the government are zero, that is, $b_0 = 0$, an assumption that does not impact the main issue we want to consider, which is the relationship between the government's fiscal position and market interest rates.

As with the individual consumer in the two-period model, let's combine the two period-by-period constraints to find the **government lifetime budget constraint (LBC).** Solve equation (4) for b_1: after a couple of algebraic manipulations (and using the result that $b_2 = 0$) we have

$$b_1 = \frac{g_2}{1+r} - \frac{t_2}{1+r}. \tag{5}$$

Now insert this resulting expression into (3)—and note that we are assuming $b_0 = 0$—to get

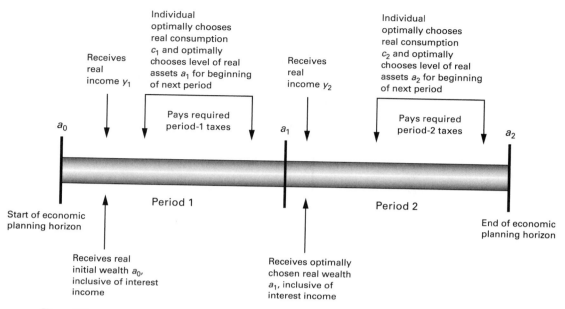

Figure 7.2
Timing of events in consumption–savings framework with taxes.

$$g_1 + \frac{g_2}{1+r} = t_1 + \frac{t_2}{1+r},$$ (6)

which is the government LBC. The government LBC has the usual interpretation of an LBC: it states the present discounted value of all current and future government spending must equal the present discounted value of all current and future tax revenue. In other words, the government must balance its budget in a lifetime sense, even if it does not balance it in any given period. With our definition of government savings above and our assumption of $b_0 = 0$, government savings in period 1 is given by

$$s_1^{gov} = t_1 - g_1.$$ (7)

Consumer Analysis Reconsidered

We also need to modify appropriately the consumer analysis to take into consideration that consumers must now pay taxes to the government. Figure 7.2 generalizes the two-period consumption–savings timeline to include payments of taxes. In real terms, the period-1 and period-2 budget constraints of the representative consumer are now given by

$$c_1 + t_1 + a_1 = (1+r)a_0 + y_1$$ (8)

and

$$c_2 + t_2 + a_2 = (1 + r)a_1 + y_2,$$ (9)

where we have defined the real wealth of the individual as $a = A / P$. That is, real wealth is simply nominal wealth divided by the price level.[2] Thus a_0, a_1, and a_2 denote real wealth of the individual at the ends of periods 0, 1, and 2, respectively. For reasons already discussed in regard to consumption–savings, we have that $a_2 = 0$, and we again assume $a_0 = 0$. The tax terms t_1 and t_2 on the left-hand side represent the fact that taxes are an expenditure item for the consumer.

Proceeding as we have done a couple of times now, we can derive the LBC for the consumer, which at this point you should be able to obtain yourself. After arriving at the consumer LBC,

$$c_1 + t_1 + \frac{c_2}{1+r} + \frac{t_2}{1+r} = y_1 + \frac{y_2}{1+r},$$ (10)

and we move the tax terms to the right-hand side so that

$$c_1 + \frac{c_2}{1+r} = (y_1 - t_1) + \frac{(y_2 - t_2)}{1+r}.$$ (11)

This is the consumer's LBC in real terms, modified to include taxes. The second expression emphasizes that it is the present discounted value of *after-tax* income (i.e., the present value of lifetime *disposable* income) that the consumer has available to spend on lifetime consumption.

We should also extend the definition of private savings to take account of taxes. Real private savings in period 1 is now defined as

$$s_1^{priv} = y_1 - t_1 - c_1;$$ (12)

that is, private savings is disposable income less consumption.

Ricardian Equivalence

We are now ready to begin considering our main issue, whether government spending and taxes affect interest rates, and in particular, whether they affect real interest rates. Throughout our discussion, we have taken the real interest rate r as given from the perspective of the representative consumer, the representative firm, and the government.

Recall from the preview of the representative-agent approach that the intersection of the upward-sloping savings curve (in a graph with r on the vertical axis and savings on the horizontal axis) and the downward-sloping investment curve determines the equilibrium

---

2. Just as any nominal variable is converted into a real variable.

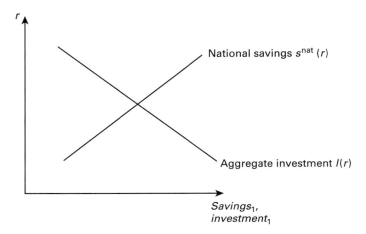

Figure 7.3
Intersection of national savings and investment demand determines the equilibrium real interest rate.

real interest rate in the economy. Technically, it is the interaction of **national savings** and investment that determines the equilibrium r. National savings is defined as the sum of private and government savings,

$$s_t^{nat} = s_t^{priv} + s_t^{gov}. \tag{13}$$

In our earlier analysis without government, s_t^{gov} was implicitly zero, so that national savings coincided with private savings, but with the government in the picture this is no longer the case. Nevertheless—and this is a subtle yet crucial observation for the subsequent analysis—government savings (or dissavings) does not typically depend on market real interest rates. Many politically related issues affect government spending and taxation, which in turn directly affect government savings, regardless of what market interest rates might be. Political economy issues are outside the scope of our analysis.

Now recall that private savings *does* depend on the market real interest rate, through its effect on the slope of the consumer's LBC. As we have already studied, private savings is an increasing function of the real interest rate. Government savings, though, is much less reliant on market real interest rates because spending and taxation legislation can largely reflect other concerns.

Supposing that government savings is independent of the real interest rate, national savings is thus also an increasing function of the real interest rate. Thus the equilibrium real interest rate is determined as shown in figure 7.3, in which both savings and investment are plotted on the horizontal axis.

Next we perform a number of algebraic manipulations to examine the relationship between government savings and the real interest rate. Adding together the consumer's LBC and the government LBC, we get, loosely speaking, the LBC of the economy:

$$c_1 + \frac{c_2}{1+r} = (y_1 - g_1) + \frac{(y_2 - g_2)}{1+r}. \tag{14}$$

From our definitions above we can express national savings as

$$s_1^{nat} = s_1^{priv} + s_1^{gov}$$
$$= y_1 - t_1 - c_1 + t_1 - g_1$$
$$= y_1 - c_1 - g_1.$$

Let's conduct the following thought experiment. Suppose that the government has decided on a particular path for government spending, g_1 and g_2, as well as a path for taxes, t_1 and t_2. It must, of course, be the case that these chosen values for government spending and taxes satisfy the government's LBC, equation (6). Suppose that the government chooses to leave its spending plans unchanged but decides to lower t_1 for some reason (perhaps a new administration has taken over). This necessarily means that t_2 must rise, since the government's present value of lifetime spending is unchanged—if it raises less revenue in the current period, it must raise more revenue in the future to balance its lifetime budget. The question we are interested in is whether this decrease in taxes in period 1 affects national savings in period 1. Examining the expression $s_1^{nat} = y_1 - c_1 - g_1$ suggests that it does not because t_1 seemingly does not appear in this expression. Yet before we can draw this conclusion, we need to determine how, if at all, consumption c_1 changes due to the change in the timing of taxes.

For this part of the analysis, return to the household LBC in real terms (11). The only way that the change in the timing of taxes would affect the optimal consumption choice of the individual is if the consumer's LBC is affected. We are assuming that neither y_1 nor y_2 changed (remember, in our simple two-period consumption–savings model labor income is outside the control of the individual—here we augment this assumption by supposing that it is also outside the control of the government). We can compute by how much taxes in period 2 must change for a given change in taxes in period 1 and given that government spending is assumed to remain unchanged. Because the government has to satisfy its life-time budget constraint, the amount by which taxes in period 2 change is

$$\Delta t_2 = -(1+r)\Delta t_1, \tag{15}$$

which we obtain by inspecting the government LBC (the delta notation stands for "change in"). Specifically, because government spending is assumed to be unchanging, the *change in* the left-hand side of equation (6) is zero, which means that the *change in* the right-hand side must also be zero. But our thought experiment is that the change in taxes in period 1, denoted by Δt_1, is not zero. So the only way that the overall change in the right-hand side of equation (6) is zero is if the change in taxes in period 2, denoted by Δt_2, is also nonzero. The relationship (15) then follows.

Expression (15) formalizes the idea discussed above, that if the path of government spending is held constant, then any change in taxes in period 1 must be met by a change in taxes in period 2 of the opposite sign. Furthermore the change in taxes in period 2 takes into account the interest rate between period 1 and period 2 because of discounting. Finally, it remains to determine how these changes in taxes affect the LBC of the consumer. Computing the *change in* the right-hand side of the consumer LBC (11) (and note that the right-hand side of (11) measures the present value of lifetime disposable income of the consumer—i.e., the lifetime resources the individual has available for consumption purposes) shows that this *change* is exactly zero. If the *change* in the individual's lifetime resources is zero due to the change in the timing of taxes, then the consumer's optimal consumption choice (c_1, c_2) is also unchanged.

Graphically, the position of the representative consumer's LBC is unaffected by changes in the timing of taxes. Finally, we are able to conclude that consumption in period 1 does not in fact change despite the tax cut in period 1. The implication of this timing, based on our analysis is above, is that national savings in period 1 is unaffected by the tax cut of period 1.

More precisely, it is the position of the entire national savings function that is unaffected by this change in the timing of taxes, since the analysis we just conducted holds for any given r. If the national savings function does not shift, and by assumption the investment function is not shifting either, then the equilibrium real interest rate is unchanged. This result is known as Ricardian equivalence.

Ricardian equivalence is the notion that holding fixed a path for government spending, a change in the timing of taxes does not affect the equilibrium real interest rate because it does not affect national savings. It is true that in the thought experiment we just conducted government savings in period 1 declined—in other words, the secondary fiscal budget balance deteriorated (i.e., went further into deficit if it was in deficit to begin with). But private savings increased by exactly the same amount as the decrease in government savings, leaving national savings unaffected, which in turn leaves the equilibrium real interest rate unaffected. Ricardian equivalence thus states that there is no connection between fiscal deficits (induced by changes in the pure timing of taxes) and real interest rates. The intuition for the offsetting rise in private savings is that fully rational consumers understand that because the government must balance its budget in a lifetime sense, if it decreases taxes in the present it will be obliged to raise taxes in the future (which, in the two-period model, is period 2). In order to pay more taxes in the future, then, fully rational consumers will simply save the entire tax cut they receive today—which is what it means to say that private savings increases by exactly the amount that government savings decreases.

Distortionary Taxes and the Failure of Ricardian Equivalence

Let's think a little more carefully about the nature of the taxes that the government collected in the above description. The taxes collected in period 1 and 2 did not depend in any way on any choices that individual consumers made. That is, regardless of a consumer's income or consumption in period 1, say, he has to pay the mandated amount t_1. In reality, though, the total amount of taxes an individual pays is somehow related to some economic choices he makes. For example, total income taxes paid depend on how much an individual earns, which is at least somewhat under the control of an individual, total sales taxes an individual pays depends on how much an individual spends buying things, and total property taxes paid depend on how valuable a house an individual owns, which is at least somewhat of a choice. Suppose that we introduce this type of taxation, taxes that depend on a choice the consumer makes, into our two-period model. In our simple two-period model the only choice the consumer makes is regarding consumption—recall that labor income y_1 and y_2 are outside the individual's control. Let's now suppose that consumption is subject to a sales tax rate of τ_1 in period 1 and τ_2 in period 2. The sales tax rate is a number such that $0 < \tau < 1$. So, for example, if the sales tax rate in period 1 is 6 percent, we would have $\tau_1 = 0.06$.

The consumer's period-by-period budget constraints are now modified as follows:

$$(1+\tau_1)c_1 + a_1 = (1+r)a_0 + y_1 \tag{16}$$

and

$$(1+\tau_2)c_2 + a_2 = (1+r)a_1 + y_2. \tag{17}$$

Again assuming $a_0 = 0$ and using our familiar result that $a_2 = 0$, we can combine these period-by-period budget constraints to obtain the LBC

$$(1+\tau_1)c_1 + \frac{(1+\tau_2)}{(1+r)}c_2 = y_1 + \frac{y_2}{1+r}. \tag{18}$$

If we solve this LBC for c_2, so that we can easily plot it in a graph with c_2 on the vertical axis and c_1 on the horizontal axis, we have

$$c_2 = -\frac{(1+\tau_1)}{(1+\tau_2)}(1+r)c_1 + (1+r)y_1 + y_2. \tag{19}$$

The slope of the LBC now clearly depends on the tax rates τ_1 and τ_2. Now let's conduct a thought experiment analogous to the one above: holding fixed a path for government spending, suppose the government decides to lower the *tax rate* in period 1. To balance its lifetime budget, this obliges the government to raise the *tax rate* in period 2. The question now is whether this change in the timing of *tax rates* changes consumption in period 1.

The answer is that it does because it changes the slope of the consumer's LBC, which in turn generally leads to a new optimal choice of consumption in both periods 1 and 2. Under the initial LBC there is some initial optimal choice of consumption in each period. Following the decline in τ_1 (and attendant rise in τ_2), the LBC flattens (i.e., the absolute value of the slope of the LBC decreases). The optimal choice, in particular, the optimal choice of

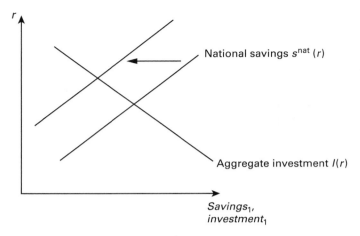

Figure 7.4
With proportional taxes on consumption, a decrease in the tax rate in period 1 raises consumption in period 1, and causes national savings in period 1 to shift inward. The equilibrium real interest rate thus rises.

period-1 consumption, changes, due essentially to substitution effects—purchase less quantity of the more (tax-inclusive) expensive good.

We will continue to assume that the change in period-1 consumption in response to a change in the slope of the LBC is as described when we studied the aggregate private savings function—in particular, optimal period-1 consumption rises when the slope of the LBC decreases.[3]

Returning to our expression $s_1^{nat} = y_1 - c_1 - g_1$, we see that because consumption in period 1 increases, national savings in period 1 decreases. More precisely, the entire national savings function decreases, since the analysis we just conducted holds for any given r. Graphically, the national savings function shifts left, which raises the equilibrium real interest rate, as figure 7.4 shows.

Thus here we have the result that despite an unchanged path of government spending, a change in the timing of taxes does affect the equilibrium real interest rate—that is, Ricardian equivalence does not hold. Clearly, the reason for the difference from the earlier analysis is in how taxes are levied.

In this section the way we have specified taxes is in a proportional, or **distortionary,** way. Total taxes paid in a particular period depend on how much consumption individuals

---

3. It turns out this conclusion does not follow as an immediate consequence of how consumption seems to respond to changes in the slope of the LBC (i.e., the after-tax real interest rate). This is because in addition to the change in the slope of the LBC, a change in the timing of proportional taxes causes a shift in the LBC as well. It turns out that for most practical applications of this model, however, that the induced shift in the LBC is small enough to be negligible in the analysis.

undertake in that period. In turn the tax rate affects, or *distorts*, the consumer's choices because it impacts the slope of the consumer's LBC. In contrast, in our earlier discussion of Ricardian equivalence, taxes were assumed to be lump sum. **Lump-sum taxes** are taxes whose incidence does not depend on any choices individuals make.

Fiscal Guideposts

These two examples together illustrate two crucial guideposts for fiscal policy analysis:

Ricardian Guidepost 1 Lump-sum taxation is an important reason why Ricardian equivalence holds.

Ricardian Guidepost 2 Distortionary taxation is an important reason why Ricardian equivalence disappears.

There are caveats to these guideposts that can arise. But with the disappearance of Ricardian equivalence in the current example, another phenomenon arises. Because the real interest rate rises, investment falls, which follows simply from the fact that investment is a negative function of the real interest rate. The decline in investment due to deterioration in the fiscal balance (which is what happens when tax revenues decline but government spending is unchanged) is termed **crowding out.** The government, because it is competing more heavily with firms for loans in order to fund its government spending, drives out, or "crowds out," some firms that are looking for loans because of the higher interest rates.

Changes in Government Spending

An important point to note from the analysis above is that we were always assuming that government spending is held fixed, regardless of whether taxes are lump sum or distortionary. If government spending changes, then it immediately follows that national savings and hence real interest rates are affected.[4] That is, with a change in government spending— whether or not Ricardian equivalence holds is no longer an issue—the resulting change in the government's fiscal balance will be accompanied by a change in real interest rates.

For example, suppose that g_1 rises and g_2 remains unchanged. For the economy as a whole, the LBC (14) shows that the resources of the economy left over for consumption fall. Graphically, the LBC of the entire economy shifts in due to the rise in g_1. Consumption in period 1 will therefore fall, but not enough to offset the rise in government spending. Thus national savings in period 1 will decline overall due to the rise in g_1. That is, the national savings function will shift inward, causing the equilibrium real interest rate to rise

---

4. More specifically, if the *present value of current and future government spending changes,* then national savings and hence real interest rates are affected.

and resulting in crowding-out of private investment. Thus, if a change in the government's fiscal position is brought about by a change in government spending, then real interest rates are affected.[5]

Lump-Sum versus Distortionary Taxes

At this point you may be wondering why the notion of Ricardian equivalence is important at all considering that it depends crucially on the existence of lump-sum taxes, a type of tax that does not seem prevalent in the real world. That is, it is hard to think of any tax that consumers or firms pay in reality that does not depend *somehow* on some choices they make. As we have seen, as soon as taxes are (even somewhat) distortionary, Ricardian equivalence disappears, meaning that changes in the government's fiscal position likely will be accompanied by changes in the equilibrium real interest rate.[6]

Yet the notion of Ricardian equivalence holds sway among some economists and policy makers. One of the reasons for this may simply be political convenience. For example, if a politician is ideologically committed to lowering taxes and must fend off criticisms that interest rates will rise as a result, using this economic argument could help insulate him from criticism because economic theory predicts that this will not happen. This is true, of course, but only given the specific assumption of lump-sum taxes, which most likely is left out of the political discussion.

Another reason to not simply discard Ricardian equivalence as a possibly important element of policy debates is that at times, macroeconomic data seem to show that total taxes collected by the government are unrelated to major macroeconomic variables, such as GDP or consumption, even though at the microeconomic level they clearly must be. When this happens, lump-sum taxes seem to be not too inaccurate a description of the tax system. In other words, even though taxes are certainly not lump sum when levied on individual consumers and firms, in the aggregate some sort of "cancellation" often seems to occur that makes them appear lump sum at the macroeconomic level. This in part reveals the limitations of the representative-agent approach to macroeconomics—in the representative-agent approach, we cannot see the differing effects of tax policy on different types of individuals that must be occurring for the aggregate cancellations to be taking place because, by assumption, there is only one type of consumer, the representative consumer.

In conclusion, whether or not changes in the government's fiscal position affect market interest rates depend on what the source of the change in the fiscal position is (a change in

---

5. Again, more specifically, it is a change in *the present value of current and future government spending* that is required for an impact to be felt on real interest rates. Try analyzing for yourself the (harder) case in which g_1 and g_2 change in such a way that the present value of all government spending does not change.

6. The "likely" wording is a subtle reminder that there are caveats to the two take-away fiscal guideposts.

taxes or a change in government spending) and on what type of tax system is in place (lump sum or distortionary). These are summarized in the two major "fiscal guideposts" regarding effects of changes in tax policy.

Chapter 7 Problem Set Questions

1. **Government and credit constraints in the two-period economy.** Consider, again, our usual two-period consumption–savings model augmented with a government sector. Each consumer has preferences described by the utility function

    $$u(c_1, c_2) = \ln c_1 + \ln c_2,$$

    where "ln" stands for the natural logarithm, c_1 is consumption in period 1, and c_2 is consumption in period 2.

    Suppose that both households and the government start with zero initial assets (i.e., $A_0 = 0$ and $b_0 = 0$), and that the real interest rate is always 10 percent. Assume that government purchases in the first period are one ($g_1 = 1$) and in the second period are 9.9 ($g_2 = 9.9$). In the first period, the government levies lump-sum taxes in the amount of 8 ($t_1 = 8$). Finally, the real incomes of the consumer in the two periods are $y_1 = 9$ and $y_2 = 23.1$.

    a. What are lump-sum taxes in period two (t_2), given the information above?

    b. Compute the optimal level of consumption in periods one and two, as well as national savings in period one.

    c. Consider a tax cut in the first period of 1 unit, with government purchases left unchanged. What is the change in national savings in period one? Provide intuition for the result you obtain.

    d. Now again suppose that $t_1 = 8$ and also that credit constraints on the consumer are in place, with lenders stipulating that consumers cannot be in debt at the end of period one (i.e., the credit constraint again takes the form $a_1 \geq 0$). Will this credit constraint affect consumers' optimal decisions? Explain why or why not. Is this credit constraint welfare enhancing, welfare diminishing, or welfare neutral?

    e. With the credit constraint described above in place, consider again the tax cut of 1 unit in the first period, with no change in government purchases (i.e., t_1 falls from 8 units to 7 units). What is the change in national savings in period one that arises due to the tax cut? Provide economic intuition for the result you obtain.

2. **An alternative interpretation of Ricardian equivalence?** Consider a modified version of the two-period framework with government studied in the chapter. By "government" here we will mean just the "fiscal authority"; suppose that there is no "monetary authority" at all.

The government and the representative consumer each live for both periods of the economy, and suppose that there are never any credit constraints on the consumer. The government does not have access to lump-sum taxes, only proportional consumption taxes. However (this is different from our baseline framework), the consumption taxes the government collects in a given period are not restricted to be levied on consumption from only in that period.

To be more precise, suppose that total consumption tax revenues the government collects in period 1 are based only on period-1 consumption (e.g., because there was no period zero). However, total consumption tax revenues the government collects in period 2 are based on both period-1 consumption and period-2 consumption. That is, a portion of the revenue collected in period 2 is based on period-1 consumption, and the remaining portion of the revenue collected in period 2 is based on period-2 consumption.

Denote by $\tau_{1,1}$ the tax rate on period-1 consumption that is levied in period 1; denote by $\tau_{1,2}$ the tax rate on period-1 consumption that is levied in period 2; and by $\tau_{2,2}$ the tax rate on period-2 consumption that is levied in period 2. There is no $\tau_{2,3}$ (which would represent the tax rate on period-2 consumption that is levied in period 3) because the economy does not exist in period 3.

With this notation, the government's period-1 and period-2 budget constraints in real terms are

$$g_1 + b_1 = (1+r)b_0 + \tau_{1,1}c_1,$$
$$g_2 + b_2 = (1+r)b_1 + \tau_{1,2}c_1 + \tau_{2,2}c_2.$$

The representative consumer's period-1 and period-2 budget constraints in real terms are

$$(1 + \tau_{1,1})c_1 + a_1 = (1+r)a_0 + y_1,$$
$$\tau_{1,2}c_1 + (1 + \tau_{2,2})c_2 + a_2 = (1+r)a_1 + y_2.$$

For simplicity, suppose that the government and consumer each begin period 1 with zero assets. As usual, you can think of all the tax rates as being numbers between zero and one (but they need not be so restricted). The remainder of the notation is as in the chapter.

Note carefully how the tax rates $\tau_{1,1}$, $\tau_{1,2}$, and $\tau_{2,2}$ appear in these budget constraints.

a.   Construct the government's lifetime budget constraint (LBC), showing important steps. Provide brief economic interpretation.

b.   Construct the consumer's lifetime budget constraint (LBC), showing important steps. Provide brief economic interpretation.

c. The essence of the way we defined Ricardian equivalence was that an economy exhibits Ricardian equivalence if, holding fixed its sequence of government spending—and also assuming no credit constraints and that consumers' planning horizons are the same (in length) as the government's planning horizon—a change in the timing of lump-sum taxes has no effect on consumption or national savings.

In the analysis here, suppose that the government keeps its sequence of g_1 and g_2 unchanged, but decides to cut the tax rate in period 1 on period-1 consumption—that is, it lowers the tax rate $\tau_{1,1}$. Is it possible for this economy to exhibit Ricardian equivalence even though in the framework in this problem taxes are not lump sum (and, as stated in the problem, there are no credit constraints or any mismatches between the planning horizons of consumers or the government)? If so, carefully show how/why and provide brief economic interpretation. If not, precisely explain why not. (Hint: Base the analysis on one or both of the LBCs derived in parts a and b.)

3. **Government debt ceilings.** Just like we extended our two-period analysis of consumer behavior to an infinite number of periods, we can extend our two-period analysis of fiscal policy to an infinite number of periods.

The government's budget constraints (expressed in real terms) for the years 2011 and 2012 are

$$g_{2011} + b_{2011} = t_{2011} + (1+r)b_{2010},$$
$$g_{2012} + b_{2012} = t_{2012} + (1+r)b_{2011},$$

and analogous conditions describe the government's budget constraints in the years 2013, 2014, 2015, and so on. The notation is as in chapter 7: g denotes real government spending during a given time period, t denotes real tax revenue during a given time period (all taxes are assumed to be lump sum here), r denotes the real interest rate, and b denotes the government's asset position (b_{2010} is the government's asset position at the end of the year 2010, b_{2011} is the government's asset position at the end of 2011, etc.).

Describing numerics qualitatively, at the end of 2010, the government's asset position was roughly a debt of $14 trillion (i.e., $b_{2010} = -\$14$ trillion). The fiscal policy plans/projections at the time called for $g_{2011} = \$4$ trillion, $t_{2011} = \$2$ trillion, $g_{2012} = \$3$ trillion, and $t_{2012} = \$2$ trillion.

Finally, given how low interest rates were and how low they were projected to remain for at least the next several years, suppose that the real interest rate is always zero (i.e., $r = 0$ always).

a. Respond to the following in no more than a *total* of 10 words: Assuming that the projections above prove correct, what will be the numerical value of the federal government's asset position at the end of 2011? Explain/justify as needed.

b. Respond to the following in no more than a *total* of 10 words: Assuming that the projections above prove correct, what will be the numerical value of the federal government's asset position at the end of 2012? Explain/justify as needed.

Under federal law at the time, the US government's debt could not be larger than $16 trillion. This limit is known as the "debt ceiling."

c. Respond to the following in no more than a *total* of 20 words: Based on your answer in part a above, does the debt ceiling pose a problem for the government's fiscal policy plans during the course of the year 2011? If it poses a problem, briefly describe the problem; if it poses no problem, briefly describe why it poses no problem.

d. Respond to the following in no more than a *total* of 20 words. Based on your answer in part b above, does the debt ceiling pose a problem for the government's fiscal policy plans during the course of the year 2012? If it poses a problem, briefly describe the problem; if it poses no problem, briefly describe why it poses no problem.

4. **Consumption, taxes, and savings in the two-period economy.** Consider a two-period economy in which the government collects only lump-sum taxes from the representative consumer, and in which the representative consumer has no control over his before-tax income. The lifetime utility function of the representative consumer is $u(c_1, c_2) = \ln c_1 + \ln c_2$, where, as usual, $\ln(.)$ stands for the natural logarithm. We will work here in purely real terms: suppose the consumer's present discounted value of *all* lifetime *real* before-tax income is 26, and the present discounted value of *all* lifetime tax payments is 6. Suppose that the real interest rate between period 1 and period 2 is zero (i.e., $r = 0$), and also suppose that the consumer begins period 1 with zero net assets.

Set up the lifetime Lagrangian formulation of the consumer's problem, in order to answer the following: (a) Is it possible to numerically compute the consumer's optimal choice of consumption in period 1? If so, compute it; if not, explain why not. (b) Is it possible to numerically compute the consumer's optimal choice of consumption in period 2? If so, compute it; if not, explain why not. (c) Is it possible to numerically compute the consumer's real asset position at the end of period 1? If so, compute it; if not, explain why not.

5. **Government in the two-period model.** Consider an economy that lasts for two periods. Neither the representative consumer nor the government starts their lives with any assets (i.e., both $a_0 = 0$ and $b_0 = 0$). All taxes that the government levies are lump

sum. In each period the government has positive government spending (i.e., both $g_1 >$ 0 and $g_2 > 0$). Suppose that the real interest rate between period one and period two is zero (i.e., $r = 0$). Finally, suppose that the government lives for the entire two periods, and until parts d and e below, so does the representative consumer.

a. Briefly (in no more than two sentences/phrases) define/describe what a lump-sum tax is.

b. Suppose that the government is currently planning to collect $t_1 = 3$ and $t_2 = 5$ in taxes in period 1 and period 2, respectively. A policy change is proposed, however, that would reduce period-1 taxes to $t_1 = 2$ without changing either g_1 or g_2. If this policy change is enacted, is it possible to numerically compute the amount of tax collections that the government will require in period 2? If so, compute it; if not, explain why not.

c. If the proposed policy change described in part b is enacted, how will it affect consumers' period-1 optimal choices of consumption? Specifically, will it increase period-1 consumption, decrease it, leave it unchanged, or is it impossible to tell? Briefly discuss/explain.

For the *remainder* of this problem, suppose that instead of living for two periods, each consumer only lives for one period in the two-period economy. Specifically, there is a set of consumers that comes into existence at the beginning of period 1, knowing that at the end of period 1 they will cease to exist. At the beginning of period 2, there is a completely different set of consumers that comes into existence, knowing that at the end of period 2 they (and the entire economy) will cease to exist. The consumers in period 2 have no relation to the consumers in period 1, and the consumers in period 1 do not care at all about the consumers in period 2. The government, however, continues to exist for the entire two periods. Continue to suppose that taxes are lump sum (and furthermore there are no credit constraints).

d. If the proposed policy change described in part b is enacted, is it possible to numerically compute the amount of tax collections that the government will require in period two? If so, compute it; if not, explain why not. Carefully explain your logic.

e. If the proposed policy change described in part b is enacted, how will it affect consumers' period-1 optimal choices of consumption? Specifically, will it increase period-1 consumption, decrease it, leave it unchanged, or is it impossible to tell? Carefully explain your logic.

6. **Government budgets and government asset positions.** Just as we can analyze the economic behavior of consumers over many time periods, we can analyze the economic behavior of the government over many time periods. Suppose that at the beginning of period t, the government has zero net assets. Also assume that the real interest

rate is always $r = 0$. The following table describes the *real* quantities of government spending and *real* tax revenue the government collects starting in period t and for several periods thereafter.

Period	Real government expenditure (g) during the period	Real tax collections during the period	Quantity of net government assets at the end of the period
t	10	12	
$t + 1$	8	14	
$t + 2$	15	10	
$t + 3$	10	10	
$t + 4$	8	12	

a. Complete the last column of the table based on the information given. Briefly explain the logic behind how you calculate these values.

b. Suppose instead that the government ran a balanced budget every period (i.e., every period it collected in taxes exactly the amount of its expenditures that period). In this balanced-budget scenario, what would be the government's net assets at the end of period $t + 4$? Briefly explain/justify.

8

Infinite-Period Framework and Introduction to Asset Pricing

Modern macroeconomic models used in applied research and for policy advice often suppose that there is an infinite number of periods, rather than just two as we have been for the most part assuming. A two-period analysis is usually sufficient for the purpose of illustrating intuition about how consumers make intertemporal choices, but in order to achieve the higher quantitative precision needed for many research and policy questions, moving to an infinite-period model is desirable.

Here we will sketch the problem faced by an infinitely lived representative consumer, describing preferences, budget constraints, and the general characterization of the solution. In sketching the basic model, we will see that in its natural formulation, it easily lends itself to a study of asset pricing. The infinite-period framework indeed lies at the intersection of macroeconomic theory and finance theory and forms the basis of consumption-based asset-pricing theories. We will touch on some of these macro-finance linkages, but we really will only be able to whet our curiosity about more advanced finance theory. For the most part, we will index time by arbitrary indexes $t-1, t, t+1$, and so on, rather than "naming" periods as "period 1," "period 2," and so on. That is, we will simply speak of "period t," "period $t + 1$," "period $t + 2$," and so on, as figure 8.1 displays.

Before we begin, we should again point out that "the consumer" we are modeling is a stand-in for markets or the economy as a whole. In that sense we do not literally mean that a particular individual considers his intertemporal planning horizon to be infinite when making choices. But to the extent that "the economy" outlives any given individual, an infinitely lived representative agent is a simple representation.

Preferences

The utility function that is relevant in the infinite-period model is, in principle, a lifetime utility function just as in our simple two-period model. As before, suppose that time begins in period 1 but now never ends. The lifetime utility function can thus be written as

$$v(c_1, c_2, c_3, c_4, c_5, \ldots).$$

This function describes total utility as a function of consumption in every period 1, 2, 3, …, and is the analog of the utility function $u(c_1, c_2)$ in our two-period model. The function v above is quite intractable mathematically because it takes an infinite number of arguments. In practice, largely for this reason, an **instantaneous utility function** that describes how utility in a given period depends on consumption in a given period is typically used. The easiest formulation to consider is the additively separable function,

$$v(c_1, c_2, c_3, c_4, c_5, ...) = u(c_1) + \beta u(c_2) + \beta^2 u(c_3) + \beta^3 u(c_4) + \beta^4 u(c_5) + ...,$$

where $u(.)$ is the instantaneous utility function. As written, period-t utility depends only on period-t consumption.[1] We discuss below the term β that we have introduced into this utility function.

Remember, there is nothing special about a "period 1." It is just as informative to assume that decisions occur in period t, meaning that decisions about $t - 1$, $t - 2$, …, quantities cannot be undone. Thus, at the beginning of period t, the planning horizon remaining in front of the consumer is t, $t + 1$, $t + 2$, …. In our infinite-period model we will likewise adopt the convention that decision-making in period t is under consideration. Thus the relevant lifetime utility function for the representative consumer when making decisions in period t is

$$u(c_t) + \beta u(c_{t+1}) + \beta^2 u(c_{t+2}) + \beta^3 u(c_{t+3}) + ... = \sum_{s=0}^{\infty} \beta^s u(c_{t+s}).$$

The summation operator on the right-hand side is a useful way of representing the utility function.

Impatience

We introduced in the formulation above a **time discount factor,** denoted β, to represent the idea that utility further out in the future is not as valuable as utility closer in time to the present moment. The discount factor β is a value between zero and one. The way we have written our lifetime utility function is to assume that we are currently in period t, since period-1 utility is not discounted at all by β.

The parameter β is meant to be a crude way of modeling the idea of "impatience." It probably strikes us all as generally reasonable to think of humans as impatient beings: all else equal, most of us (all of us?) would prefer to have x units of goods right this instant rather than one year from now, and we would probably also prefer to have those x units one

---

1. This may strike you as an unnecessary assumption. Indeed it is unnecessary, except that until recently computational limitations made this assumption an often practically necessary one. More recently, time-nonseparable preferences, with an instantaneous utility function of the form $u(c_t, c_{t-1})$, have gained popularity, mostly because they have proved useful in resolving some anomalous predictions of first-generation representative consumer macro models.

year from now rather than two years from now. The time discount factor β gets at this idea: because $\beta < 1$, a given quantity of period-$(t + 1)$ consumption does not generate as much utility as does the same quantity of period-t consumption *when viewed from the perspective of period t.* Furthermore, when viewed from the perspective of period t, a given quantity of period-$(t + 2)$ consumption does not generate as much utility as does the same quantity of period-$(t + 1)$ consumption. To capture this idea, we have introduced the β^2 term in front of $u(c_{t+2})$ so that $\beta < 1$, $\beta^2 < \beta$; this gets at the latter idea. By analogy, we have introduced β^3 in front of $u(c_{t+3})$, β^4 in front of $u(c_{t+4})$, and so on.

Whether the idea of impatience can be modeled simply as a "number between zero and one" remains quite debatable. Furthermore, whether impatience "builds up" over time as we simply raise β to successively higher powers is likewise quite debatable. Crude or not, it does at least allow us to start getting at the idea of impatience. As we will see more often as we build ever-richer models, even making a start on formally modeling an idea is often great progress.

Assets and Budget Constraints

As in the two-period model, the consumer faces period-by-period budget constraints. Rather than just two, though, the consumer here faces an infinite number of budget constraints, one for each period. The infinite-horizon idea, which is meant as a stand-in for a "many, many, many time period" framework, is sketched in figure 8.1. The general idea behind the flow budget constraints is just as in our basic two-period setup.

Besides extending individuals' time horizon to something more realistic, we take a more concrete stand on what the assets are that consumers buy and sell. Rather than just an ambiguous, catch-all A asset as in our two-period model, let's suppose here that the assets that consumers buy and sell are "shares in the stock market"—as in, the Dow or S&P 500.

Arguably, the most salient characteristics of shares of stock (be it Microsoft stock, General Motors stock, or a share of the broad Dow or S&P 500 index) are:

1. stock price, which is the price of one share, and
2. potential dividend, which ownership of one share entitles one to receive.

We will model these particular features of stock ownership. When we later build richer and richer frameworks that include other classes of assets, we will begin by asserting the defining characteristic(s) of the particular category of assets.

Our infinite-period model's period-t **flow budget constraint** is thus

$$P_t c_t + S_t a_t = S_t a_{t-1} + D_t a_{t-1} + Y_t,$$

in which c_t is consumption in period t, P_t is the price level in period t, a_t is the consumer's holdings of real assets—shares of stock—at the end of period t, S_t is the nominal price in

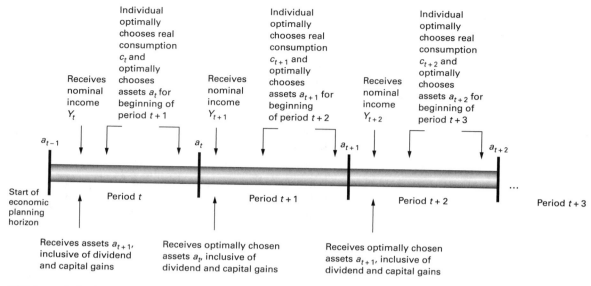

Figure 8.1
Timing of events in infinite-horizon framework

period t of one share, D_t is a nominal dividend paid by each share, and Y_t is nominal income of the consumer in period t, which we will assume the consumer has no control over. Note the terms involving assets. In period t, the consumer begins with asset holdings a_{t-1}. In period t, each unit of these assets has some value S_t, and each unit of these assets carried into t pay a dividend D_t. Each unit of asset (share of stock) the consumer wishes to carry into period $t + 1$, denoted by a_t also has a unit price of S_t. In more formal-sounding language, S_t is an asset price—it is the price of each share of stock.

An analogous flow budget constraint holds in each period $t, t + 1, t + 2, ...$ In principle, we could combine all these flow budget constraints into a single lifetime budget constraint as we did in the two-period model. However, it seems more natural in the infinite-period model to work with the flow budget constraint, which acknowledges that the decision-making happens sequentially (i.e., period by period), rather than once and for all as we implicitly assumed in the two-period model; recall our discussion of the sequential (Lagrangian) approach to the two-period model.

Optimal Choice

In order to consider optimal choices, then, we must formulate a Lagrangian. Specifically, the problem of the representative consumer in period t is to choose consumption c_t and asset holdings a_t to maximize lifetime utility subject to the infinite sequence of flow budget constraints starting with period t, taking as given the nominal price P of consumption for period t and beyond, the nominal price S of assets for period t and beyond, the per-unit nominal dividend D for period t and beyond, and nominal income Y for period t and beyond. The sequential Lagrangian is thus

$$
\begin{aligned}
u(c_t) &+ \beta u(c_{t+1}) + \beta^2 u(c_{t+2}) + \beta^3 u(c_{t+3}) + \ldots \\
&+ \lambda_t \left[Y_t + S_t a_{t-1} + D_t a_{t-1} - P_t c_t - S_t a_t \right] \\
&+ \beta \lambda_{t+1} \left[Y_{t+1} + S_{t+1} a_t + D_{t+1} a_t - P_{t+1} c_{t+1} - S_{t+1} a_{t+1} \right] \\
&+ \beta^2 \lambda_{t+2} \left[Y_{t+2} + S_{t+2} a_{t+1} + D_{t+2} a_{t+1} - P_{t+2} c_{t+2} - S_{t+2} a_{t+2} \right] \\
&+ \beta^3 \lambda_{t+3} \left[Y_{t+3} + S_{t+3} a_{t+2} + D_{t+3} a_{t+2} - P_{t+3} c_{t+3} - S_{t+3} a_{t+3} \right] \\
&+ \ldots,
\end{aligned}
$$

in which λ_t is the *multiplier* on the period-t budget constraint, and the ellipsis indicate that technically the Lagrangian has an infinite number of terms corresponding to the infinite number of future flow budget constraints. As we will see, in the current problem it is sufficient to write out just the t and $t+1$ flow budget constraints.

Also note carefully that the $t+1$ budget constraint in the Lagrangian is discounted by β. This is because *everything* about period $t+1$ is discounted when viewing from the perspective of time t, including income and expenditures. As written above, the period $t+2$ budget constraint in the Lagrangian is discounted by β^2, just as utility in period $t+2$ is discounted by β^2. Recalling our study of the two-period model, each distinct flow budget constraint receives its own distinct Lagrange multiplier.

The objects of choice in period t are c_t and a_t. In line with how a sequential Lagrangian analysis proceeds, the first-order conditions of the Lagrangian with respect to these objects are

$$ u'(c_t) - \lambda_t P_t = 0 $$

and

$$ -\lambda_t S_t + \beta \lambda_{t+1} (S_{t+1} + D_{t+1}) = 0. $$

Likewise the first-order conditions of the Lagrangian with respect to c_{t+1} and a_{t+1} (note carefully the time subscripts!) are

$$ \beta u'(c_{t+1}) - \beta \lambda_{t+1} P_{t+1} = 0 $$

and

$$ -\beta \lambda_{t+1} S_{t+1} + \beta^2 \lambda_{t+2} (S_{t+2} + D_{t+2}) = 0. $$

These two pairs of first-order conditions (especially after canceling the β terms in the second pair) make clear that the first-order conditions with respect to c_t and with respect to c_{t+1}

are identical, except for the time period. The same is true for the first-order conditions with respect to a_t and with respect to a_{t+1}. Logic then tells us that this pattern will repeat for every period into the future, period $t + 2$, period $t + 3$, ..., period $t + 77$, period $t + 78$, ..., and so on. This is an incredibly powerful result, and it relies on the nature of the sequential analysis, so you are urged to understand this point clearly.

Moving on, the (infinite sequence of!) first-order conditions can be combined. When combined, they shed much light on financial market events and macroeconomic fluctuations, both independently of each other and jointly.

From the first-order condition on consumption in period t, we have $\lambda_t = u'(c_t)/P_t$. Also, from the first-order condition on consumption in period $t + 1$ (constructed above, and which you should verify), we have the analogous condition $\lambda_{t+1} = u'(c_{t+1})/P_{t+1}$. Inserting these expressions for both λ_t and λ_{t+1} into the first-order condition on shares of stock, we have the result

$$\frac{u'(c_t)S_t}{P_t} = \beta \frac{u'(c_{t+1})(S_{t+1} + D_{t+1})}{P_{t+1}}.$$

There are two broad, informative ways of interpreting this result: one is geared toward macroeconomic analysis, the other toward financial market analysis.

Macroeconomic Perspective

First, from a macroeconomic perspective, we can rearrange it to highlight the intertemporal marginal rate of substitution:

$$\frac{u'(c_t)}{\beta u'(c_{t+1})} = \frac{S_{t+1} + D_{t+1}}{S_t} \cdot \frac{P_t}{P_{t+1}}.$$

This *is* the consumption–savings optimality condition for the particular framework considered here. The left-hand side is the intertemporal marginal rate of substitution—after all, it is simply a ratio of marginal utilities—between consumption in period t and $t + 1$. This is simply the analogue of our condition u_1/u_2 in the two-period economy.

Turning to the right-hand side of the expression above, the term P_t/P_{t+1} is the inverse of the gross inflation rate between period t and $t + 1$, that is, $1/(1 + \pi_{t+1})$. The term $(S_{t+1} + D_{t+1})/S_t$ is the **holding period return** of the asset a_t—it measures the gain (or loss) of holding the asset from period t to $t + 1$. This gain is higher the higher is the period $t + 1$ price and/or dividend, $S_{t+1} + D_{t+1}$, and is lower the higher is the current (period t) price S_t.

Also note that the discount factor β appears in the denominator of the left-hand side of the consumption–savings optimality condition above. This is because, from the perspective of period t, the marginal utility of period-$t + 1$ consumption is discounted due to impatience.

Analogously, the right-hand side of the consumption–savings optimality condition above is the analogue of the term $(1+r)$ from our two-period model. The reason $(1+r)$ does not appear explicitly is simply because of the assumption about the available assets we have made here. Later, when we study monetary models, we will assume that there are assets in the environment that pay a nominal interest rate, as in our simple two-period model, which will allow us to regenerate that term. To aid us in thinking about some other issues, below, though, sometimes it will be useful to represent the consumption–savings optimality condition above as

$$\frac{u'(c_t)}{\beta u'(c_{t+1})} = 1 + r_t \,,$$

where the term $1 + r_t$ hides all of the details we see in the seemingly more complicated consumption–savings optimality condition; "hiding" (but being aware of) these details can sometimes be useful.

Asset-Pricing Perspective

The consumption–savings optimality condition highlights optimal choices from a macroeconomic perspective, putting things into "MRS equals price ratio" form. Alternatively, and especially given our specific interpretation of a here as shares of stock, we can view things from a more finance-oriented perspective, by focusing on the asset price S_t. More precisely, we can think about what sorts of factors are relevant for determining what the price of a share of stock is in any time period.

Let's return to the first-order condition on assets, which we reproduce here for convenience,

$$-\lambda_t S_t + \beta \lambda_{t+1}(S_{t+1} + D_{t+1}) = 0.$$

From this expression, we can solve for the period-t stock price,

$$S_t = \frac{\beta \lambda_{t+1}}{\lambda_t}(S_{t+1} + D_{t+1}).$$

In finance theory, one would identify two distinct components on the right-hand side of this **asset-pricing expression**: the term $\beta \lambda_{t+1}/\lambda_t$ is the **pricing kernel,** and the term $(S_{t+1} + D_{t+1})$ is the **future return.**[2] Thus, what the asset-price expression states is that the period-t price of a share of stock depends on the future return and a pricing kernel. The future return has two components, arising from any future dividends that buying a share of stock in period t entitles one to and any change in the share price itself between period t and period $t + 1$.

---

2. We will study the "pricing kernel" in much more depth later when we discuss monetary policy.

The pricing kernel seems a bit more esoteric, being a function of the period-t and period-t + 1 Lagrange multipliers. But here is where the link between finance and macroeconomics emerges. We know from our macroeconomic analysis that $\lambda_t = u'(c_t)/P_t$ and $\lambda_{t+1} = u'(c_{t+1})/P_{t+1}$. Inserting these expressions into the asset-pricing expression allows us to express the stock price S_t as

$$S_t = \beta \frac{u'(c_{t+1})}{u'(c_t)}(S_{t+1} + D_{t+1})\frac{P_t}{P_{t+1}}.$$

Furthermore we know that $P_t/P_{t+1} = 1/(1+\pi_{t+1})$, where π_{t+1} is the rate of inflation between period t and period t + 1. Rewriting one more time, we have that the stock price S_t is

$$S_t = \frac{\beta u'(c_{t+1})}{u'(c_t)}\left(\frac{S_{t+1} + D_{t+1}}{1+\pi_{t+1}}\right).$$

Referring to this **stock-pricing expression** allows us to begin to more fully appreciate the linkages between macroeconomic events and asset (stock) prices. The stock-price equation shows that stock prices in period t depend on what the future inflation rate will be and how consumption will change over time. For example, all else equal, the higher is $u'(c_{t+1})/u'(c_t)$, the higher will be S_t. And, all else equal, the higher is π_{t+1}, the lower will be S_t. We will explore such issues in more depth, but the broad point to appreciate here is that things such as monetary policy (which influences what inflation rate occurs in the economy) and how aggregate consumption evolves over time (recall that consumption makes up about 70 percent of total GDP) affect stock prices.

Steady State—A Long-Run Macro-Finance Linkage

Our infinite-period model allows us to explore yet another issue, one that will be important to understand when we study business cycle issues as well as monetary policy issues. We have an infinite number of periods in our model, and in principle, all variables—consumption, interest rates, asset prices, for example—can be moving around over time. Indeed, in a dynamic economy, they inevitably do all move around over time, and understanding how and why certain variables evolve over time as they do is a broadly defined goal of macroeconomics. But suppose, for a moment, that eventually the *real* variables in our infinite-period model "settle down" to some constant values.

Let's formally define a **steady state** of an economy as a situation in which **all *real* variables stop fluctuating over time.** Note the emphasis on the word *real* here. In our infinite-period model, a steady state would involve consumption (which is a *real* variable) becoming constant over time, asset holdings a becoming constant over time, and the real interest rate becoming constant over time. Variables such as S_t, D_t, and P_t, because they are *nominal* variables, need *not* become constant over time in order to fit into our definition of steady state, although they could become constant as well. To introduce more terminology, the steady-state of an economy is often referred to as the **long-run equilibrium** of an economy—think of it, if you will, as the "average" or "potential" performance of the economy (to invoke terms you likely encountered in basic macroeconomics).

To provide ourselves some more notation, suppose that the constant level of consumption to which the sequence of c_t eventually converges is $\bar{c}$; hence we can think of the steady-state as a state of the economy in which $c_t = c_{t+1} = c_{t+2} = \ldots = \bar{c}$. Similarly suppose that the constant level of *real* interest rate to which the sequence of real interest rates eventually converges is $\bar{r}$; hence we can think of the steady state as a state of the economy in which $r_t = r_{t+1} = r_{t+2} = \ldots = \bar{r}$. And so on, for all real variables of our model.

Impatience and the Real Interest Rate

Consider the expression above (repeated here for convenience), $u'(c_t)/\beta u'(c_{t+1}) = 1 + r_t$. This expression is nothing more than the infinite-period model's **consumption–savings optimality condition.** Indeed it is no different from our two-period model's consumption–savings optimality condition, apart from the introduction of the time discount factor. In a steady state the consumption–savings optimality condition can be expressed as

$$\frac{u'(\bar{c})}{\beta u'(\bar{c})} = 1 + \bar{r}.$$

Clearly, the $u'(\bar{c})$ terms cancel, leaving us with

$$\frac{1}{\beta} = 1 + \bar{r}.$$

This expression, which is the *long-run consumption–savings optimality condition,* captures an extremely critical idea embedded in virtually all of modern macroeconomic theory and thus is at the root of a wide range of both academic and policy discussions of macroeconomics.

What this long-run expression states is that in the steady state—alternatively, "in the long run," or "on average"—the real interest rate of the economy is fundamentally tied to the degree of impatience of consumers in the economy. The theoretical upper end of β is $\beta = 1$; if $\beta = 1$, then the long-run consumption-savings condition immediately tells us that the long-run real interest rate equals zero. That is, if consumers are perfectly patient (which is what $\beta = 1$ means), there is no net real return from savings.

Suppose instead, for the sake of numerical illustration, that $\beta = 0.95$, meaning that consumers are somewhat impatient. Long-run consumption–savings optimality then immediately allows us to conclude that the steady-state real interest rate in the economy is roughly $\bar{r} = 0.0526$. Now suppose that $\beta = 0.9$, meaning that consumers are somewhat more impatient. In this case the steady-state real interest rate in the economy is roughly $\bar{r} = 0.11$.

To cast these conclusions in very broad perspective, the most primitive, fundamental source of "interest rates" in the economy is human impatience. If human beings were always infinitely patient creatures ($\beta = 1$), (real) interest rates would be zero. Thus the mere presence of impatience at all ($\beta < 1$) is the fundamental source of positive interest rates in the world. Not Wall Street, not central banks—the primitive reason for the general existence of positive interest rates is human impatience, however crudely we have modeled it. The long-run consumption–savings optimality condition then also shows us that the more impatient consumers are (remember, we are always speaking of the representative consumer) the higher are real interest rates.

This deep connection between interest rates and people's inclination toward impatience cannot be overemphasized in its central importance to macroeconomic theory. It is a deceptively simple idea—the long-run consumption–savings optimality condition obviously looks simple enough, but the idea it captures will continue to be at the root of the richer models we'll continue building. It also is a connection point between short-run business-cycle analysis and long-run growth considerations. As such, it is useful to wrap your mind around this idea as well as possible now.

Overlapping Two-Period Frameworks

It seems a heroic achievement to have stepped seamlessly from a two-period framework to not a three-period framework, nor a four-period framework, not even a five-period framework, but all the way to an *infinite-period* framework.

It's actually not all that heroic.

If we've understood the two-period framework, the **infinite-period framework** is simply an infinite sequence of overlapping two-period frameworks. To see this idea, let's assert that $t = 1$. With $t = 1$, it seems like we're beginning to return to our original two-period framework, in which the first period was indeed period 1 ($= t$).

The upper left-hand side indifference curve/budget constraint diagram in figure 8.2 displays the representative consumer's optimal choice across the two-period span of period 1 and period 2, which ought to look extremely familiar.

Now let's shift our eyes to the first instant of the *second* period displayed in the timeline in figure 8.1 (labeled $t + 1$ in the figure, but here we're supposing it is period 2). *If the beginning of the second period were the point at which "economic planning occurred," and if were thinking in terms of "two-period analysis,"* the upper-right indifference curve/budget constraint diagram in figure 8.2 is how we're viewing consumers' optimal decisions. The upper-right hand side indifference curve/budget constraint diagram in figure 8.2 displays the optimal choice across the two-period span of period 2 and period 3.

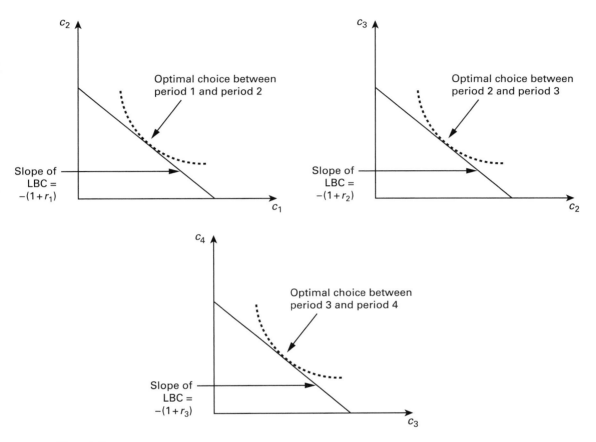

Figure 8.2
Infinite-period framework displayed as a sequence of overlapping two-period frameworks

Let's scroll our eyes further down the timeline in figure 8.1 to the beginning of the *third* period (labeled $t + 2$ in the figure, but here we're supposing it is period 3). If the beginning of the *third* period were the point at which "economic planning occurred," *and* if once again we were thinking in terms of "two-period analysis," the indifference curve/budget constraint diagram of figure 8.2 is how we're viewing consumers' optimal decisions.

Keep on scrolling down the timeline and continue to think in terms of "two-period analysis," and you should be able to understand why the *infinite-period analysis* is simply a collection of overlapping (this is key!) two-period analyses. The "overlap" is clear from this iterative thought process and from figure 8.2. The upper right-hand side and upper left-hand side diagrams in figure 8.2 have only one dimension in common—the period-2 dimension (plotted on the vertical axis of the upper left-hand side diagram and on the horizontal axis of the upper right-hand side diagram).

Similarly the upper right-hand side diagram and the bottom diagram in figure 8.2 have only one dimension in common—the period-3 dimension (plotted on the vertical axis of the upper right diagram and on the horizontal axis of the bottom side diagram). If you repeat this process forward, the idea should be clear.

The powerful idea that figure 8.2 conveys is that the *two-period framework is the starting point for modern macroeconomic analysis* and, as we have seen a glimpse of in our study here, of modern finance theory.

Chapter 8 Problem Set Questions

1. **Infrequent stock transactions.** Consider a representative consumer at time t seeking to maximize the sum of discounted lifetime utility from t on,

$$\sum_{s=0}^{\infty} \beta^s u(c_{t+s})$$

   subject to the infinite sequence of flow budget constraints

   $$P_t c_t + S_t a_t = S_t a_{t-2} + D_t a_{t-2} + Y_t,$$

   where the notation is as in class: a_t is holdings of a real asset (a "stock") at the end of period t, S_t is its nominal price in t, D_t is the nominal dividend that each units of assets carried into t (from period $t - 2$) pays out, Y_t is nominal income in t, c_t is consumption in t, and P_t is the nominal price of each unit of consumption in t. Note well how the budget constraint is written: it is assets accumulated in period $t - 2$ that pay off in period t—thus in this model, stocks (for some reason) must be held for two periods rather than be traded every period. Construct the Lagrangian to compute the stock price S_t in period t. Explain intuitively how and why the stock price differs from that in the model studied in class, in which all shares can be traded every period.

2. **House prices.** With all the talk in the news the past few years of soaring and then crashing house prices, let's see how our simple multi-period model can be used to think of how house prices are determined. Suppose that the instantaneous utility function is $u(c_t, h_t)$, where c_t as usual stands for consumption in period t, and now h_t stands for the level of housing services an individual enjoys in period t (i.e., the "quantity" of house an individual owns). Denote by H_t the nominal price of a house in period t. The quantity of house owned at the beginning of period t is h_{t-1}, and the quantity of house owned at the end of period t is h_t, and assume that the quantity of house can be changed every period (think of this loosely as making additions, repairs, etc., to your house on a regular basis). Thus we can write the flow budget constraint in period t as $P_t c_t + H_t h_t = H_t h_{t-1} + Y_t$, where Y_t is nominal income over which the consumer has

no control. Note that for simplicity, we have omitted other assets from the model, houses are the only assets in this model. Solve for the nominal price of a house in period t, H_t. Discuss qualitatively why the marginal rate of substitution between housing services and consumption appears in the pricing equation. How is the setup of this asset-pricing model different from the setup of our "stock-pricing" model discussed in the chapter? How is it the same?

3. **Habit persistence in consumption.** An increasingly common utility function used in macroeconomic applications is one in which period-t utility depends not only on period-t consumption but also on consumption in periods earlier than period t. This idea is known as "habit persistence," which is meant to indicate that consumers become "habituated" to previous levels of consumption. To simplify things, let's suppose that only period-$(t-1)$ consumption enters the period-t utility function. Thus we can write the instantaneous utility function as $u(c_t, c_{t-1})$. When a consumer arrives in period t, c_{t-1} cannot, of course, be changed (because it happened in the past).

   a. In a model in which stocks (modeled in the way we introduced them in class) can be traded every period, how is the pricing equation for S_t (the nominal stock price) altered due to the assumption of habit persistence? Consumption in which periods affects the period-t stock price under habit persistence? To answer this, derive the pricing equation using a Lagrangian and compare its properties to the standard model's pricing equation developed in the chapter. Without habit persistence (i.e., our baseline model), consumption in which periods affects the stock price in period t?

   b. Based on your solution in part a and the pattern you notice there, if the instantaneous utility function were $u(c_t, c_{t-1}, c_{t-2})$ (i. e., two lags of consumption appear, meaning that period-t utility depends on consumption in periods t, $t-1$, and $t-2$), consumption in which periods would affect the period-t stock price? No need to derive the result very formally here, just draw an analogy with what you found above.

4. **Oil markets.** Displayed below is the price of one barrel of (WTI) oil over the past few decades. A barrel of oil can be thought of as an asset because it is storable. For the sake of simplicity, suppose that this is the only asset via which the infinitely lived representative consumer can accumulate wealth.

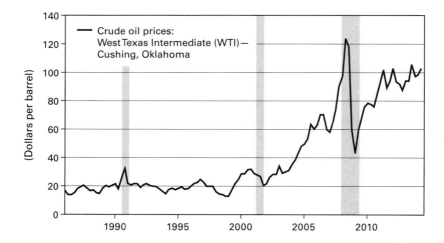

Denote by wti_{t-1} the quantity of barrels owned by the consumer at the start of period t; denote by S_t^{wti} the nominal price during period t of one barrel of oil; as usual, let $0 < \beta < 1$ stand for the consumer's one-period-ahead discount factor, P_t stands for the period-t nominal price of consumption, and Y_t stands for period-t nominal income. Finally, the period-t utility function of the consumer is

$u(c_t, d \cdot wti_t)$

in which $0 < d < 1$ stands for how much "utility" the consumers enjoys from wti_{t-1} (you can think of this as heat for the oven or for the house, etc.)

Thus the consumer's lifetime utility function starting from the beginning of period zero is

$$\sum_{t=0}^{\infty} \beta^t u(c_t, d \cdot wti_t)$$

a.   Using the notation above, construct the period-t budget constraint of the consumer, and provide a *one-sentence* economic comparison of this budget constraint to that in our study of stock-market pricing.

b.   Based on your budget constraint in part a above and the lifetime utility function, construct the Lagrangian for the consumer's optimization *and* compute the FOCs for c_t, c_{t+1}, and wti_t.

c.   Based on the FOCs you obtained in part b above, compute the period-t oil price. That is, construct the expression

$S_t^{wti} = ...$

(the "..." that appears on the right-hand side is for you to construct).

d. You can see in the graph displayed above that oil prices have overall been much higher over the past decade than before. Provide a brief explanation that is just based on how the *d* term in the utility function might have changed over the years. Your explanation should be stated in both mathematical terms *and* in economic terms (i.e., the economic explanation should not simply be a verbal restatement of the mathematics).

5. **"Hyperbolic impatience" and stock prices.** In this problem you will study a slight extension of the infinite-period economy from this chapter. Specifically, suppose thatthe representative consumer has a lifetime utility function given by

$$u(c_t) + \gamma\beta u(c_{t+1}) + \gamma\beta^2 u(c_{t+2}) + \gamma\beta^3 u(c_{t+3}) + \ldots,$$

in which, as usual, $u(.)$ is the consumer's utility function in any period and β is a number between zero and one that measures the "normal" degree of consumer impatience. The number γ (Greek lowercase letter "gamma," which is the new feature of the analysis here) is also a number between zero and one, and it measures an "additional" degree of consumer impatience, but one that only applies between period t and period $t + 1$.[3] This situation occurs when the factor γ is *not* successively raised to higher and higher powers as the summation grows.

The rest of the framework is exactly as studied in the chapter: a_{t-1} is the representative consumer's holdings of stock at the beginning of period t, the nominal price of each unit of stock during period t is S_t, and the nominal dividend payment (per unit of stock) during period t is D_t. Finally, the representative consumer's consumption during period t is c_t and the nominal price of consumption during period t is P_t. As usual, analogous notation describes all these variables in periods $t + 1, t + 2, \ldots$.

The Lagrangian for the representative consumer's utility-maximization problem (starting from the perspective of the beginning of period t) is

$$\begin{aligned}
&u(c_t) + \gamma\beta u(c_{t+1}) + \gamma\beta^2 u(c_{t+2}) + \gamma\beta^3 u(c_{t+3}) + \ldots \\
&+ \lambda_t \left[Y_t + (S_t + D_t)a_{t-1} - P_t c_t - S_t a_t \right] \\
&+ \gamma\beta\lambda_{t+1} \left[Y_{t+1} + (S_{t+1} + D_{t+1})a_t - P_{t+1}c_{t+1} - S_{t+1}a_{t+1} \right] \\
&+ \gamma\beta^2\lambda_{t+2} \left[Y_{t+2} + (S_{t+2} + D_{t+2})a_{t+1} - P_{t+2}c_{t+2} - S_{t+2}a_{t+2} \right] \\
&+ \gamma\beta^3\lambda_{t+3} \left[Y_{t+3} + (S_{t+3} + D_{t+3})a_{t+2} - P_{t+3}c_{t+3} - S_{t+3}a_{t+3} \right] \\
&+ \ldots.
\end{aligned}$$

---

3. The idea here, which goes under the name "hyperbolic impatience," is that in the "very short run" (i.e., between period t and period $t + 1$), individuals' degree of impatience may be different from their degree of impatience in the "slightly longer short run" (e.g., between period $t + 1$ and period $t + 2$). "Hyperbolic impatience" is a phenomenon that routinely recurs in laboratory experiments in experimental economics and psychology, and has many far-reaching economic, financial, policy, and societal implications.

Note carefully where the "additional" impatience factor γ appears in the Lagrangian.

a. Compute the first-order conditions of the Lagrangian above with respect to both a_t and a_{t+1}. (Note: There is no need to compute first-order conditions with respect to any other variables.)

b. Using the first-order conditions you computed in part a, construct two distinct stock-pricing equations, one for the price of stock in period t, and one for the price of stock in period $t + 1$. Your final expressions should be of the form $S_t = \ldots$ and $S_{t+1} = \ldots$ (Note: It's fine if your expressions here contain Lagrange multipliers in them.)

For the remainder of this problem, suppose that it is known that $D_{t+1} = D_{t+2}$, and that $S_{t+1} = S_{t+2}$, and that $\lambda_t = \lambda_{t+1} = \lambda_{t+2}$.

c. Does the information above necessarily imply that the economy is in a steady state? Briefly and carefully explain why or why not; your response should make clear what the definition of a "steady state" is. (Note: To address this question, it's possible, though not necessary, that you may need to compute other first-order conditions besides the ones you have already computed above.)

d. Based on the above information and your stock-price expressions from part b, can you conclude that the period-t stock price (S_t) is higher than S_{t+1}, lower than S_{t+1}, equal to S_{t+1}, or is it impossible to determine? Briefly and carefully explain the economics (i.e., the economic reasoning, not simply the mathematics) of your finding.

Now further suppose that the utility function in every period is $u(c) = \ln c$, and also that the real interest rate is zero in every period.

e. Based on the utility function given, the fact that $r = 0$, and the basic setup of the problem described above, construct two marginal rates of substitution (MRS): the MRS between period-t consumption and period-$t + 1$ consumption, *and* the MRS between period-$t + 1$ consumption and period-$t + 2$ consumption.

f. Based on the two MRS functions you computed in part e and on the fact that $r = 0$ in every period, determine which of the following two consumption growth rates

$$\frac{c_{t+1}}{c_t} \quad \text{or} \quad \frac{c_{t+2}}{c_{t+1}}$$

is larger. That is, is the consumption growth rate between period t and period $t + 1$ (the fraction on the left) expected to be larger than, smaller than, or equal to the consumption growth rate between period $t + 1$ and period $t + 2$ (the fraction on the right), or is it impossible to determine? Carefully explain your logic, and briefly explain the economics (i.e., the economic reasoning, not simply the mathematics) of your finding.

6. **Patience and the dynamics of stock prices and consumption.** Suppose that the economy is in a steady state at the start of the year 2040. The steady-state level of consumption prior to the start of the year 2040 is c^{SS}, and suppose that the economy has been in this steady state for several years. Thus

$$c^{SS} = c_{2039} = c_{2038} = c_{2037} = c_{2036} = ...$$

Furthermore suppose that the steady-state real interest rate in the several years prior to the start of the year 2040 is $r^{SS} > 0$.

Perhaps due to several years of economic tranquility, suppose that at the start of the year 2040, the representative consumer becomes more patient than he used to be before 2040. Furthermore it is not until the start of the year 2040 that the representative consumer understands that he has become more patient (i.e., the consumer never "anticipated" any time prior to 2040 that he would "become more patient" in the year 2040).

Denote the representative consumer's subjective discount factor from the year 2040 onward as β, which, as just described, is a different value than it used to be before 2040; denote the subjective discount factor in the pre-2040 period as β^{PRE}. Despite the change in the representative consumer's patience, both β and β^{PRE} are numbers strictly between zero and one.

In the pre-2040 and post-2040 periods the representative consumer's utility function in each period is $u(c_t) = \ln c_t$. If we view each time period as being one year, then, starting from the beginning of period 2040 (i.e., the year 2040), the representative consumer's lifetime utility function is

$$\ln c_{2040} + \beta \ln c_{2041} + \beta^2 \ln c_{2042} + \beta^3 \ln c_{2043} + ...$$

For simplicity, suppose that the nominal price of consumption is always one in every time period (i.e., $... = P_{2037} = P_{2038} = P_{2039} = P_{2040} = P_{2041} = P_{2042} = ... = 1$ forever), and the nominal dividend paid on each share of stock is always zero in every time period (i.e., $... = D_{2037} = D_{2038} = D_{2039} = D_{2040} = D_{2041} = D_{2042} = ... = 0$ forever). The budget constraints faced by the representative consumer starting from the year 2040 are thus

$$c_{2040} + S_{2040}a_{2040} = Y_{2040} + S_{2040}a_{2039}$$
$$c_{2041} + S_{2041}a_{2041} = Y_{2041} + S_{2041}a_{2040}$$
$$c_{2042} + S_{2042}a_{2042} = Y_{2042} + S_{2042}a_{2041}$$

...,

and so on, in subsequent years. The rest of the notation is as in the chapter: a_t denotes the consumer's stock holdings at the end of a given year t, Y_t denotes the consumer's nominal income during a given year t, and S_t denotes the per-share nominal price of stock during a given year t.

a. In no more than one sentence/phrase, define/describe an economic steady state.

b. Define the rate of stock price growth between the years 2038 and 2039 as $(S_{2039}/S_{2038}) - 1$. Was the rate of stock-price growth between the years 2038 and 2039 positive, negative, zero, or is it impossible to determine? Carefully justify your answer.

c. As described above, the representative consumer is more patient starting in 2040 (and beyond) than before 2040. In terms of the subjective discount factors β and β^{PRE}, does this mean that $\beta < \beta^{PRE}$, $\beta > \beta^{PRE}$, $\beta = \beta^{PRE}$, or is it impossible to tell how β compares to β^{PRE}?

d. Regardless of any events that happen in the year 2040 or the several years following 2040, suppose that many years after the year 2040, the economy is once again in a steady state. In this eventual post-2040 steady state, is the rate of stock price growth from one year to the next positive, negative, zero, or is it impossible to determine? Carefully justify your answer.

e. Is the rate of stock price growth you found in part d larger than, smaller than, or equal to the rate of stock price growth between the years 2038 and 2039 you found in part b? Or is it impossible to determine? Carefully justify your answer.

f. In the eventual post-2040 steady state (i.e., many years after 2040), is consumption larger than, smaller than, or equal to consumption in the steady state prior to the year 2040? Or is it impossible to determine? Carefully justify your answer.

7. Two types of stock. Consider a variation of our usual infinite-period "stock-pricing" model. The variation here is that there are two "types" of stock that the representative consumer can buy: "Dow" stock and "S&P" stock. Denote by a_{t-1}^{DOW} the representative consumer's holdings of Dow stock at the beginning of period t and by a_{t-1}^{SP} the representative consumer's holdings of S&P stock at the beginning of period t. Likewise let S_t^{DOW} and S_t^{SP} denote, respectively, the nominal price of Dow and S&P stock in period t, and D_t^{DOW} and D_t^{SP} denote, respectively, the per-share nominal dividend that Dow and S&P stock pay in period t. The period-t budget constraint of the representative consumer is thus

$$P_t c_t + S_t^{SP} a_t^{SP} + S_t^{DOW} a_t^{DOW} = Y_t + (S_t^{SP} + D_t^{SP}) a_{t-1}^{SP} + (S_t^{DOW} + D_t^{DOW}) a_{t-1}^{DOW},$$

in which all of the other notation is standard: Y_t denotes nominal income (over which the consumer has no control) in period t, c_t is real units of consumption, and P_t is the nominal price of each unit of consumption. Also as usual, the lifetime utility of the consumer starting from period t onward is

$$u(c_t) + \beta u(c_{t+1}) + \beta^2 u(c_{t+2}) + \beta^3 u(c_{t+3}) + \dots,$$

where $\beta \in (0, 1]$ is the usual measure of consumer impatience.

a. Setting up an appropriate Lagrangian, derive period-t stock-pricing expressions for both Dow stock and S&P stock. Your expressions should be of the form $S_t^{DOW} = \dots$ and $S_t^{SP} = \dots$

b. Based on the expressions you obtained in part a above, is it the case that $S_t^{DOW} = S_t^{SP}$? If so, briefly explain why; if not, briefly explain why not; if it's not possible to tell, explain why not.

Assume for the *remainder* of this problem that $\beta = 1$ and that Dow stock always pays *zero* dividends.

c. Suppose that the economy eventually reaches a steady state. In this steady state, Dow stock pays zero dividends (as mentioned immediately above), but S&P stock pays a nominal dividend that is always one-tenth the nominal price of a share of S&P stock. That is, in the steady state, $D_t^{SP} = 0.1 S_t^{SP}$ in every period t. Further suppose that in the steady state, the inflation rate of consumer goods prices between one period and the next is always 10 percent (i.e., $\pi = 0.10$). Compute numerically the steady-state rate at which the nominal price of *each* type of stock grows every period (i.e., what you're being asked to compute is the "inflation" or "appreciation" rates of each of the two types of stock). Justify your answer with any appropriate combination of mathematical, graphical, or qualitative arguments. Also provide brief economic rationale/intuition for your findings.

8. **Effects of tax policy on stock prices.** Consider our infinite-period model with stocks as the only asset. Stocks held at the beginning of period t pay a nominal dividend D_t at the very beginning of period t. Suppose that dividend payments are subject to a proportional tax rate t_t^D in period t, where t_t^D is a number between zero and one. For example, if $t_t^D = 0.20$, then 20 percent of all dividends received by the representative consumer in period t must be paid to the government (we'll disregard here any issues related to what the government does with those revenues).

a. Set up the period-t flow budget constraint, briefly explaining how the dividend tax enters the expression.

b. Using the flow budget constraint you set up above, show algebraically (i.e., using a Lagrangian) how the nominal stock price in period t, denoted as usual by S_t, depends on the dividend tax when the representative consumer is maximizing lifetime utility from period t onward. Also show the dividend tax rate in which period affects the period-t stock price? Provide brief economic interpretation/logic.

c. Suppose that in addition to the dividend tax described above, there is a proportional tax on consumption (a sales tax). The consumption tax rate in period t is t_t^C. Suppose that t_t^C rises, but all other tax rates (including those in the future) remain unchanged. Show algebraically (i.e., using a Lagrangian) how this policy change affects the period-t stock price? Also provide brief economic interpretation/logic for your finding.

9

Shocks

The demand and supply relationships in the frameworks we have studied have been developed from microeconomic foundations, which, in general, are optimizations of some objective function subject to some constraint function(s). The demand and supply relationships can shift (in price-quantity space) if either or both the objective function and constraint function(s) experience some "change." Much of economic analysis concerns the consequences of sudden changes in constraints—for example, prices or taxes in consumer analysis.

But we can also easily imagine that the objective function of whichever framework we are studying may experience sudden changes. This latter idea is the focus of this chapter—in particular, we study here sudden changes in an appropriate utility function if consumer analysis is the focus, and in an appropriate profit function if firm analysis is the focus.

The reason why an objective function might change (apart from examples provided below) will be studied more deeply soon. From an analytical perspective, though, these changes in foundations lead to precise shifts (i.e., a resulting set of changes) in the accompanying demand and/or supply curves.

To introduce formal terminology, the changes that we study here are termed **shocks**. Heuristically, a shock is an unexplained or unexplainable alteration in some basic element of an economic framework, which in turn causes optimal choices to be affected. When taking a supply-and-demand perspective, these alterations manifest themselves in **shifts** of supply and/or demand in appropriate markets.

On the side of consumer analysis, we can study shocks to the consumption–leisure framework, or shocks to the consumption–savings framework, or shocks to both the consumption–leisure and consumption–savings framework (in which case we are considering the intertemporal consumption–leisure framework). For some parsimony, we consider only the consumption–leisure framework below. After discussing shocks to the representative consumer's decision-making, we will discuss shocks to the representative firm's profit-maximizing decisions.

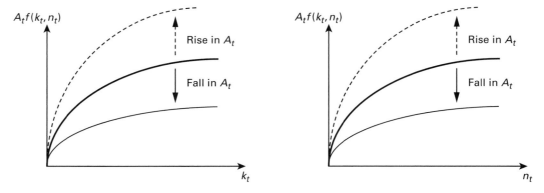

Figure 9.1
An increase (decrease) in A_t causes output to increase (decrease) for any given quantity of capital and labor.

Production Shocks

Just as we can extend our frameworks for consumer analysis by augmenting an individual's utility function with unexpected shocks, we can extend our model of firms to suppose that the aggregate production function sometimes also suffers unexpected shocks.[1] The introduction of a shock to the production function has the effect that for any given amount of both capital and labor, total output depends on the level of the shock. Such a shock is most commonly interpreted as a "technology shock."

The most usual way of introducing production function shocks is to suppose that it simply multiplies the production function. Letting A denote this shock affecting the production function, we would now write the production function as $A \cdot f(k, n)$, where A is simply some constant over which a firm has no control but may change over time. It should be clear that if we set $A = 1$ always, then we recover the basic two-period firm model we have studied.

If A rises or falls, then the production function shifts up or down, shown as in figure 9.1. This technology shock to the production function will be important in our upcoming discussion of real business cycle theory.

Preference Shocks

Recall our usual one-period consumption–leisure model. We now slightly augment the utility function in that framework to be

---

1. TFP shocks are a much more common theoretical modeling device than preference shocks. For reasons beyond the scope of this text, however, this approach has failed to capture at a theoretical level some important features of macroeconomic data, especially regarding the behavior of inflation.

Consumption

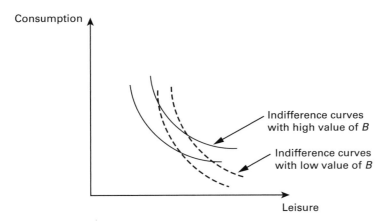

Indifference curves
with high value of B

Indifference curves
with low value of B

Leisure

Figure 9.2
As B falls, the individual's indifference map steepens because the individual is willing to trade more consumption for leisure.

$$u(Bc, l), \tag{1}$$

where B is some given constant over which the individual has no control. The constant B simply multiplies whatever consumption level the individual chooses in the final determination of utility. For example, the utility function may be $u(Bc, l) = \sqrt{Bc} + \sqrt{l}$. With this formulation it is clear that our baseline consumption–leisure model simply had $B = 1$ all the time. For any given value of B then (not only $B = 1$), the indifference map over consumption and leisure is just as before, as illustrated by the solid indifference curves in figure 9.2.

Now suppose that all of a sudden B falls due to some unexplained event. The fact that B multiplies consumption in the utility function means that a lower value of B makes the "consumption utility" component of the utility function stronger for an unchanged level of consumption. For example, if initially $B = 1$ and the consumer were optimally choosing $c^* = 10$, the consumption utility component of the utility function above would be $\sqrt{1 \cdot 10} = \sqrt{10} \approx 3.16$. If all of a sudden B falls, to $B = 0.5$, say, and the consumer did not change his level of consumption, then his consumption component of utility would be $\sqrt{0.5 \cdot 10} = \sqrt{5} \approx 2.23$. This means that each unit of consumption is now less valuable in utility terms.[2]

Because the individual decides both how much consumption and how much leisure he takes, the fact that consumption is now less valuable in utility terms means that he is willing to give up more units of consumption for a given increase in leisure. Thus the indifference curves of the individual steepen in figure 9.2 due to the fall in B.

2. More precisely, in terms familiar from microeconomics, the fall in B means that the marginal utility of consumption has decreased, and at an unchanged price of consumption the individual will optimally choose less consumption.

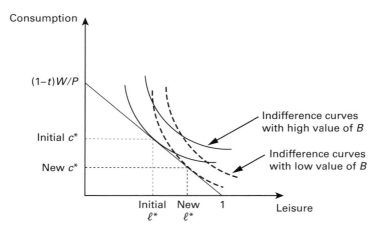

Figure 9.3
Following a decline in B (with the nominal wage W, the nominal price P, and the tax rate t held constant), the new optimal choice features less consumption and more leisure (and hence fewer hours worked).

Now let's think about how the individual's optimal consumption choice changes as a result of the fall in B. The situation is presented in figure 9.3. With the wage rate W, the price P, and the labor tax rate t all held constant, the new optimal choice features less consumption and more leisure—the latter implying that the individual now works fewer hours.

The change in the optimal choice in figure 9.3 occurs with no change in the price P. It should be clear that such a reduction in consumption would occur for any given price P. Thus, for any given price P, optimal consumption is now lower, which is precisely what it means for the consumption demand function to shift inward, as shown in figure 9.4. For convenience, the shift in figure 9.4 is shown to be a parallel shift, but in general, the nature of the shift will depend on the exact shapes of the initial and new indifference curves. But the general point is that the consumption demand curve shifts (and hence the aggregate demand curve shifts) due to changes in consumer tastes.

One further observation follows from this analysis: because the individual chooses to work fewer hours following the fall in B, the entire labor supply curve must shift inward.[3]

Utility function shocks can also be introduced in the consumption–savings model. An important result of doing so is that such shocks would cause the aggregate savings function to shift. The analysis of this effect proceeds completely analogously as the example above, except we would examine the indifference curves in c_1–c_2 space rather than in c–l space. This is left as an exercise for you to work through.

---

3. Verify for yourself that this is true.

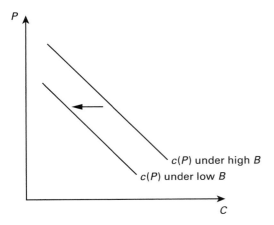

Figure 9.4
Consumption demand function shifts following the preference shock.

Chapter 9 Problem Set Questions

1. **Preference shocks in the consumption–savings model.** In the two-period consumption–savings model (in which the representative consumer has no control over his real labor income y_1 and y_2), suppose that the representative consumer's utility function is $u(c_1, Bc_2)$, where, as usual, c_1 denotes consumption in period 1, c_2 denotes consumption in period 2, and B is a preference parameter.

   a. Use an indifference curve–budget constraint diagram to illustrate the effect of an increase in B on the consumer's optimal choice of period-1 consumption.

   b. Illustrate the effect of an increase in B on the private savings function. Provide economic interpretation for the result you find.

   c. In the months preceding the US invasion of Iraq, data show that consumers decreased their consumption and increased their savings. Is an increase in B and the effects you analyzed in parts a and b above consistent with the idea that consumption fell and savings increased because of a looming war? If so, explain why; if not, explain why not.

   d. Using a Lagrangian and assuming that the utility function is $u(c_1, B \cdot c_2) = \ln(c_1) + \ln(B \cdot c_2)$, show how the representative consumer's MRS depends on B.

   e. How would your analysis in parts a and b change if the consumer's utility function were $u(Dc_1, c_2)$ (instead of $u(c_1, Bc_2)$) and you were told that the value D decreased? (D is simply some other measure of preference shocks.)

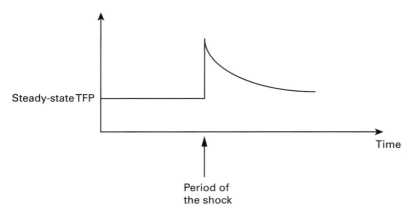

Figure 9.5
Impulse response function and labor supply after a one-time TFP shock occurs for problem 2

2. **Impulse response function and labor supply: part 1.** Suppose that a one-time TFP shock occurs, as shown in figure 9.5.

   As we have studied, an increase in TFP leads to an outward shift in labor demand (recall this from our firm analysis unit), which, as long as the upward-sloping labor supply function does not shift, leads to an increase in the real wages.

   Using an infinite-horizon (recall that this is a heuristic for a "many, many, many time-period" framework) of the combined consumption–savings and consumption–labor framework (which is an extension of the brief two-period framework of chapter 5), qualitatively plot an impulse response function for the representative consumer's optimal labor supply that lines up with the impulse response profile for TFP drawn above.

   Use the lifetime utility function

   $$\ln\left(c_t - \frac{\psi}{1+v}n_t^{1+v}\right) + \beta\ln\left(c_{t+1} - \frac{\psi}{1+v}n_{t+1}^{1+v}\right) + \beta^2\ln\left(c_{t+2} - \frac{\psi}{1+v}n_{t+2}^{1+v}\right)$$
   $$+ \beta^3\ln\left(c_{t+3} - \frac{\psi}{1+v}n_{t+3}^{1+v}\right) + ...$$

   in which the utility parameters $\psi > 0$ (Greek lowercase letter "psi") and $v > 0$ (Greek lowercase letter "nu") are exogenous to the representative consumer. (You should be able to set up the appropriate budget constraints yourself, though you don't need to display them if you don't think you need to.)

   Provide brief justification for the impulse response you have sketched.

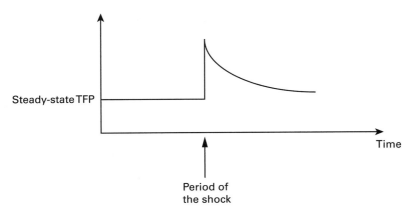

Figure 9.6
Impulse response function and labor supply after a one-time TFP shock occurs for problem 3

3. **Impulse response function and labor supply: part 2.** Suppose that a one-time TFP shock occurs, as shown in figure 9.6.

    As we have studied, an increase in TFP leads to an outward shift in the labor demand function (recall this from our firm analysis unit), which, as long as the upward-sloping labor supply function does not shift, leads to an increase in the real wages.

    Using an infinite-horizon framework of the combined consumption–savings and consumption–labor framework (which is an extension of the brief two-period framework of chapter 5), qualitatively plot an impulse response function for the representative consumer's optimal quantity of labor supply that lines up with the impulse response profile for TFP drawn above.

    Use the lifetime utility function

    $$\ln\left(c_t - \psi \cdot n_t\right) + \beta \ln\left(c_{t+1} - \psi \cdot n_{t+1}\right) + \beta^2 \ln\left(c_{t+2} - \psi \cdot n_{t+2}\right) + \beta^3 \ln\left(c_{t+3} - \psi \cdot n_{t+3}\right) + \dots$$

    in which the utility parameter $\psi > 0$ (Greek lowercase letter "psi") is exogenous to the representative consumer. (You should be able to set up the appropriate budget constraints yourself, though you don't need to display them if you don't think you need to.)

    Provide justification for the impulse response you have sketched.

4. **Preference shocks, production shocks, and general equilibrium.** Suppose that firms and consumers coexist in the static (one-period) consumption–leisure model. The representative firm uses only labor to produce its output good, which the representative consumer uses for consumption. Assume that the production function is linear in labor, so that output of the firm is given by $A \cdot n$, where A is a production function

shock. Also assume that there are no taxes of any kind, and the consumer's utility function is given by $u(Bc, l)$ (the function u satisfies all the usual properties we assume for utility functions). As usual, B denotes a preference shifter. Finally, the real wage is given by $w = A$.

a. Briefly explain why the real wage is given by $w = A$.

For each of the following three questions, clearly sketch your diagrams on a single graph with consumption on the vertical axis and leisure on the horizontal axis.

b. Suppose currently $A = A_0$ and $B = B_0$ (i.e., A_0 and B_0 are some current values for the production shock and preference shock, respectively). On your diagram, clearly (qualitatively) sketch an indifference map, a budget constraint, and associated optimal choices of consumption and leisure.

c. Suppose a negative technology shock occurs, lowering A from A_0 to $A_1 < A_0$. $B = B_0$ still. On your diagram, clearly (qualitatively) sketch an indifference map, a budget constraint, and associated optimal choices of consumption and leisure. Briefly explain any differences between your sketch here and that in part b.

d. Suppose that a preference shock occurs, lowering B from B_0 to $B_1 < B_0$. The level of productivity is still as in part c (i.e., $A = A_1$). On your diagram, clearly (qualitatively) sketch an indifference map, a budget constraint, and associated optimal choices of consumption and leisure. Briefly explain any differences between your sketch here and those in part b and part c as well as any key economic interpretation of your result.

Interlude: General Equilibrium Macroeconomics

Putting together everything we have discussed constitutes **general equilibrium**, which *is* the foundation of modern macroeconomic analysis, as described here.

General Equilibrium Macroeconomics

Why have we developed all of the (at this point) fairly rich economic frameworks? And why do we think these frameworks are the basis of "modern macroeconomics?" We will attempt to answer the first question in the discussion on "History."

To answer the second question, it is crucial to define and understand the concept of general equilibrium. General equilibrium occurs when *all* markets in the economy are simultaneously in equilibrium.[1]

We have seen the accompanying figure before. But now, after all of our discussions, it's worth seeing it again to understand general equilibrium—though with a caveat. The caveat arises from the history of macroeconomic thought over the past century, and we'll discuss that very soon.

But first to fix ideas, general equilibrium contrasts with the idea of **partial equilibrium.** Partial equilibrium occurs when *one* market in the economy achieves equilibrium, regardless of whether or not other markets have reached the point at which quantity supplied equates with quantity demanded.

In hindsight, our analysis thus far has been basically partial equilibrium in nature. But now, by finally putting together all of the partial equilibrium analyses, what emerges *is* (nearly) general equilibrium. General equilibrium is simultaneous clearing in the "three macro markets" that we have been "partially" studying thus far.

How do we "put together" the various demand functions and supply functions we have so far studied? To describe this as clearly as possible, let's suppose that there are no

---

1. The concept of simultaneously clearing markets was pioneered in the 1870s by the French mathematical economist Leon Walras, and developed in the 1950s by Kenneth Arrow and Gerard Debreu. In academic circles, "general equilibrium theory" often goes by the name "Walrasian theory" or "Arrow–Debreu theory."

distortionary taxes (lump-sum taxes, though, are fine). Supposing no distortionary taxes, let's take a look at the following pair of optimality conditions:

$$\frac{u_l(c_t, l_t)}{u_c(c_t, l_t)} = w_t, \quad w_t = mpn_t.$$

The expression on the left is the consumption–labor optimality condition, which (after a few steps of algebra) is the labor supply function. There it is, diagrammed in the accompanying figure. The expression on the right is the firm's optimality condition regarding hiring, which is the labor demand function. It is also diagrammed in the figure.

At what point does equilibrium in the labor market occur? In the diagram it's obviously at the intersection of the labor supply function and the labor demand function, which you know from all of your studies in economics.

But look back at the two analytical expressions above. Putting the *supply side* together with the *demand side* yields

$$\frac{u_l(c_t, l_t)}{u_c(c_t, l_t)} = mpn_t.$$

This condition is labor-market equilibrium! Graphically, this is the intersection. Labor-market equilibrium occurs when the willingness of the consumer side of the economy to trade goods for leisure (which, recall, is the MRS between consumption and leisure) *exactly equates* with the extra (marginal) productivity of an extra unit of time spent in labor.

Let's do the same thing for financial markets, again supposing zero distortionary taxes. Consider the following pair of optimality conditions:

$$\frac{u'(c_t)}{\beta u'(c_{t+1})} = 1 + r_t, \quad r_t = mpk_t.$$

The expression on the left is the consumption–savings optimality condition, which (after a few steps of algebra) yields the (private) savings supply function.[2] There it is, diagrammed in the figure. The expression on the right is the firm's optimality condition regarding investing in new physical capital for the future. There it is, also diagrammed in the figure.

Analytically, putting the supply side of financial markets together with the demand side of financial markets yields

$$\frac{u'(c_t)}{\beta u'(c_{t+1})} = 1 + mpk_t.$$

---

2. Recall the definition of private savings in period t: $s_t^{priv} = a_t - a_{t-1}$, which in turn depends on optimal choices of c_t and c_{t+1}.

This condition is capital-market equilibrium! Graphically, this is the intersection depicted in the funds market in the figure.

To round out the "three macro markets" and get to general equilibrium, we need to also think about the goods market. Back in our study of the static consumption–leisure model, we sketched out the consumption demand (or, more generally, the aggregate demand) function.

What about the "aggregate supply" function? There's the caveat. To think about the caveat of the "aggregate supply" function, let's first take a brief tour of the history of macroeconomics.

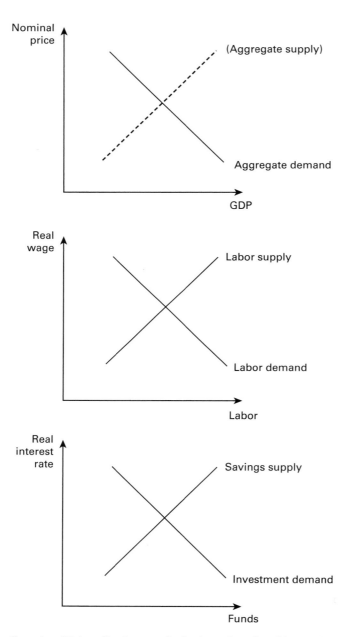

General equilibrium. Simultaneous clearing in goods markets, labor markets, and financial markets

II

A BRIEF (AND PARTIAL) HISTORY OF MACROECONOMIC THOUGHT

A natural question at this point might be how and why did the macroeconomics profession evolve to the point at which it is today. Part II provides a brief history of the subject.

Chapter 10 highlights important events that led to periodic shifts and changes in macroeconomic schools of thought. The remainder of part II describes further, mostly in qualitative terms, some of the shifting points in the history described in chapter 10. Chapter 11 discusses the supply-side view that emerged in the late 1970s and took hold in the 1980s under the Reagan administration—an important element of the supply-side, or "trickle-down," view was the so-called Laffer curve regarding taxation, which is brought up again in the more advanced analysis in part IV.

Chapter 12 describes the classical Phillips curve, which was an important component of the classical Keynesian era in the evolution of macroeconomic thought as discussed in chapter 10. The Phillips curve is also brought up again in more advanced analysis in part V.

Chapter 13 is a primer on the New Keynesian class of models, which builds on the real business cycle framework that emerged in the early 1980s. The real business cycle (RBC) framework, described graphically in chapter 14, has been the general-equilibrium foundation of modern macroeconomic analysis since the early 1980s. Indeed everything we studied in part I essentially *is* the RBC framework.

10

History of Macroeconomics

Macroeconomics as its own distinct branch of economic thought came into widespread existence during the Great Depression of the 1930s. The unemployment rate in the United States reached a record high of 25 percent during that decade, inflation was persistently negative during much of the 1930s (as figure 10.1 shows), and the growth rate of GDP plunged dramatically (as figure 10.2 shows). Neither fiscal policy nor monetary policy was able to do much to mitigate the sharp and widespread impact of the steep and long-lasting downturn. There was indeed not much "fiscal policy" to speak of, as figure 10.3 hints.

What follows is an admittedly brief and partial history of macroeconomics. Other scholars of economics or history might have different interpretations of the events described below. Despite the brevity of the ensuing historical recap, the main point is to provide a glimpse into the evolution of thought about economy-wide events over the past century and, importantly, how chains of thought over the decades have led to the current frameworks used today to provide policy advice and continuing economic research. The taxonomy of this short history is categorized into four phases.

Phase 0: Panics of the 1800s and early 1900s

The Great Depression was by no means the first downturn in US nationwide economic activity. There had been many waves of booms (economic expansions) and busts (economic contractions) prior to the Great Depression. A few examples before the Depression are the Panic of 1873, the Panic of 1893, and the Panic of 1907, which you might have studied in an American History course. As far as historical records indicate, there was very strong GDP growth in between these Panics, but this growth was largely washed away during the sharp, but brief, Panic-induced downturns.

What were the Panics, and how did they arise? To consider this, we have to remember that the US economy was heavily agriculturally based in the mid- to late 1800s. The percentage of workers in the agricultural sector around the turn of the twentieth century was about 50 percent; in contrast, in the 2010s it composes no more than 1 to 2 percent. Another

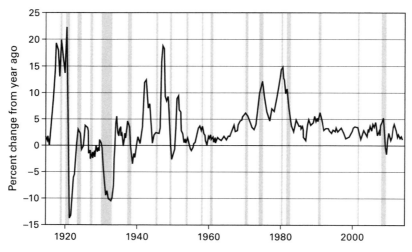

Figure 10.1
US annual inflation rate, 1929 to 2014, as measured by the Consumer Price Index. Source: FRED.

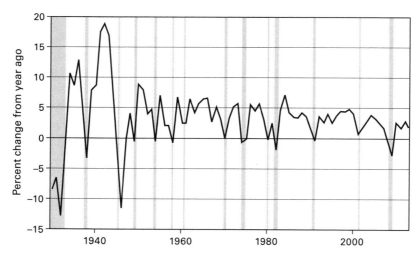

Figure 10.2
US annual GDP growth rate, 1929 to 2013. Source: FRED.

related development after the US Civil War was the rapid rise of the railroad industry. The railroad sector employed the second-largest percentage of US workers, trailing only the agricultural sector.

Given the farming-based US economy, agriculturists often needed to borrow in order to fund themselves during out-of-season periods. This need arose because many crops could only be harvested during particular months or weeks of the year. Even then, the quantity and quality of the crop yield could heavily depend on the weather before harvest season—was it too rainy of a season? Too dry of a season? Were railroads allowed to ship crop?

Regardless, come harvesting time, the bounty of crops was picked and then delivered (think of wheelbarrows and wagons and vendors on the streets) to town or county markets. One reason the developing railroad industry became prominent was because it allowed for faster transportation of wheats and grains. Regardless of mode of transport, this was the *supply* side of that particular crop's market. There were also people and families that wanted to purchase these items, which was the *demand* side of that particular market.

The prices that emerged in these markets depended somehow on the quantity and quality of the items supplied. Nonetheless—and very important—the sale of these crops provided the farmers and their families' revenue—that is, income—which in turn would be available to be spent on households' needs.

However, in out-of-season times of the year, when there were no crops to harvest and sell, some or perhaps many farming families could run short or completely run out of the income they had raised during the previous harvest season. Silos to store food products were not common in the late nineteenth century. What this in turn implied was a natural need for **borrowing:** a family could borrow from willing lenders to meet their expenses during out-of-season times, and then repay their debts, inclusive of interest, when harvested crops were sold on markets. Such a setup is perfectly rational.

More and more willing lenders began sprouting up. Among these were **speculative lenders,** who offered very low interest rates. Although economic historians continue to debate their relative importance, lenders' rationale for offering low-interest rate loans goes along the following two highly related lines.

One is that some fields were left fallow so that the soil and earth would have time to re-fertilize after a crop season. To incentivize farmers to not leave fields fallow, these speculative lenders provided very cheap loans, with the expectation that the fields that should have remained fallow would yield bounty. If this occurred, then lenders would receive a higher total repayment due to the larger revenue raised by the farmers. The second, related, rationale is the decreasing costs to transport harvests to more distant markets, thanks to the quickly rising railroad networks.

From the point of view of agriculture, cultivating fields that should have remained vacant could be considered a risky endeavor. If these "extra harvests" did not eventually materialize, then the farmers who overborrowed would not be able to repay their debts and hence face bankruptcy. If many farming families' extra harvests did not grow—due to, say, inclement weather, which does not affect only one farm but many farms in a particular geographic area—then there would be many bankruptcies. One example is the Dust Bowl of the 1930s in the US prairies caused by severe droughts.

As an aside, from the point of view of economics, however, the overborrowing due to low interest rates need not be viewed as irrational. Why? Because the farmers willingly chose to take on more debt—willingly overborrowed—because of the lower interest rates offered. They were not forced to borrow more but rather were incentivized due to low interest rates.

The various Panics were thus largely tied to big swings in conditions in financial markets, which were heavily dependent, to put it simply, on the quality and quantity of harvests and the rush to invest in easier modes of transportation.

Digging a bit deeper, they were tied to huge ups and downs emanating from newly created banking and lending markets, as well as newly developing (and ultimately short-lived) currencies. One prime example of a short-lived attempt to revive bimetallic currency (gold and silver) was the ill-fated Free Silver Movement of the late 1800s and early 1900s, during which 1896 presidential candidate William Jennings Bryan made his famous "Cross of Gold" speech, advocating the use of silver, in addition to gold and states' own currencies, as a medium of exchange. It was not until after 1913, the year the Federal Reserve System was created, that all the US states shared one unified currency.

Thus the seeds of the idea of sharp swings in economy-wide aggregate outcomes —that is, in *macroeconomic outcomes,* parlance that was little used then—was planted before the largest and longest lasting *PANIC* of all.

Phase 1: Measuring Macroeconomic Activity (1930s to Early 1950s)

It was the very long-lasting and very deep economic Panic of the Great Depression that led to the emergence of the branch of economics that we now know as "macroeconomics." The causes of the Great Depression are typically thought to be financial in nature (indeed Ben Bernanke, the chairman of the Federal Reserve from 2006 to 2014, is one of the leading economic scholars of the Great Depression). It should be noted, however, that virtually all scholars of the Great Depression seem to agree that the cause was not the spectacular stock market crash of 1929.

In the early stages of the Depression, the idea that the national government could and should regulate the periodic ups and downs of the economy rose to prominence. John Maynard Keynes was the most forceful and persuasive proponent of this idea (but by no means the only one), describing it in his tome published in 1936, *The General Theory of Employment, Interest, and Money.* The basic tenet of what soon was dubbed the

"Keynesian view" was that various "rigidities" plague market transactions and lead to potentially long-lasting *disequilibrium* outcomes.

The clearest way to understand Keynesianism (which we will study in more depth later) was that *nominal wages and/or prices* may not adjust quickly enough to clear quantity supplied and quantity demanded. Hence Keynesian logic demands that the government should and is able (the latter because of slowly adjusting nominal prices) to aid the economy.

In order to do so, there needed to be some US-wide measures of the performance of markets; until the Great Depression, there were none. The system of GDP accounting that we more or less still continue to use began during the Great Depression. The concepts and measurements of **aggregate GDP** and **aggregate consumption** and **aggregate investment** that we now take for granted in the typical basic macroeconomics-class GDP accounting equation were essentially invented during the Depression. With only desk calculators, constructing and adding up the national income accounts itself was an agonizingly labor-intensive, time-consuming project. Thousands of economists were hired in Washington, DC, during 1930 to 1938 to work at the newly created New Deal government agencies charged with the task.

The first attempts at the Keynesian policy prescription for the government were to increase national government spending, the G term in the *GDP* accounting equation. It may be surprising to learn, but measured federal government spending pre–Great Depression was essentially zero. Figure 10.3 shows the share of US federal government spending in

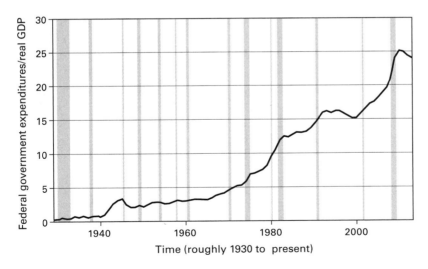

Figure 10.3
Share of government spending, excluding government investment expenditures, as a percentage of aggregate GDP, 1929 to 2013. Source: FRED.

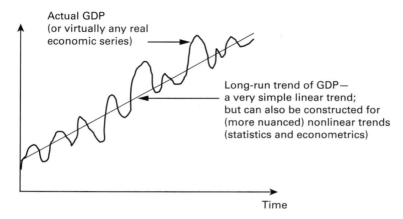

Figure 10.4
Fluctuations across time of real economic outcomes (real GDP)

total GDP—*G/GDP* rose from 0 to about 1 percent during the course of the 1930s, and then spiked higher to about 4 percent when the United States entered World War II.[1]

Perhaps coincidentally, by the mid-1940s, economists had collected and tabulated about 15 years of quarterly data (roughly 60 time periods) on what now are considered "standard macro measures" often used to judge that society's standards of living. Simple sketches, like the illustrative figure 10.4 (which is not based on actual data), convey two basic ideas. First, in the long-time horizon there is a steady upward march of GDP, and hence of individuals' standards of living.[2] But this upward march is not at all smooth—there are many ups and downs along this long-run path.

By no means did this happen immediately, especially because members of society, including economists, were nowhere near as hyperconnected to each other as now. But as the measurements of collected macroeconomic data (not simply the sketch like in figure 10.4, but further statistical measurements of correlations, standard deviations, etc.) seeped into the thinking of many economists and policy makers, a main question emerged. The

1. The percentage has continued to increase over the decades, piercing 20 percent over the last several years. Some of this can be attributed to increases in military spending, and some can be attributed to ever-increased benefits provided by the government to US citizens. Leading examples are the Social Security System, Medicare, and Medicaid—the first began in the New Deal era of President Franklin D. Roosevelt, and the second two began in the Great Society period of President Lyndon B. Johnson. Although, it should be importantly noted, it's not the benefit payments themselves that cause increases in government spending (such benefits are actually accounted for differently); rather, it's the expansion of the infrastructure to maintain and implement the benefits systems (e.g., employees that work for the Social Security Administration who ensure that the people who are eligible to receive Social Security payments do so in a timely fashion).

2. At least for the so-called advanced economies, such as the United States, much of Western Europe, Japan, Canada, and Australia.

question was how to logically, analytically think about economy-wide events, such as depicted in figure 10.4.

More precisely, should there be **one unified framework** to consider both long-run growth and business cycle fluctuations—that is, the ups and downs—of the economy?

Somehow the convention arose that the answer to this question is no. This convention did not have to arise amid all of the discussions and debates among many macroeconomists, but it did. This conventional view has more or less survived to today.

More precisely, the convention arose that economists could study the smoothly growing long-run component of the economy separately from the business cycle fluctuations. Research economists and policy-minded economists to this day essentially continue to consider these as two different branches of economics. Understanding, both empirically and theoretically, the long-run growth component is often referred to as the branch of **economic growth** or **economic development;** understanding the short-run fluctuations of the economy is almost universally referred to as the branch of **macroeconomics.**

The focus of our analysis will be almost entirely on this now more-restricted definition of macroeconomics—the hows and whys of macroeconomic fluctuations in the short-run around the smoother longer run growth trend.

Figure 10.5, which builds directly on figure 10.4, graphically displays the business cycle component of real GDP (which could be generalized to other real quantity measures). The methodology of how to "filter" actual economic time-series data is left to more advanced courses in statistics and econometrics. The takeaway message is that the bottom panel of figure 10.5 explicitly focuses on the business cycle fluctuations and effectively ignores mechanisms that ignite long-run growth.[3]

We've summarized phase 1 (which could be thought of as the "learning how to count" years of the macroeconomics profession) in just a few pages, but this was nearly two decades' worth of effort of many scholars, leaders, and policy-minded economists. Until phase 2, macroeconomics was largely qualitative (the **social** aspect of the growing profession), much more so than today. The mathematized portions (the **scientific** aspect of the growing profession) used fairly simple calculus routines, statistical procedures, and diagrammatic analysis. But the mix of "social" and "science" in the social science of macroeconomics was to soon change.

Phase 2: Keynesian Macroeconometric Approach (Early 1950s to late-1970s)

The end of WWII is often attributed to the powerful engineering and technology the US military rapidly developed. The idea of using advanced mathematics and advanced physics as a foundation for "practical" purposes (in this case, ending the war) captured the

---

3. But more on this later.

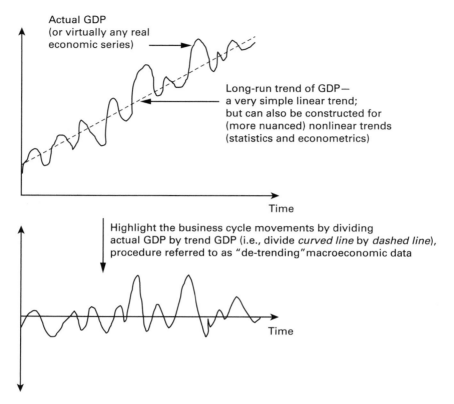

Actual GDP
(or virtually any real
economic series) ——→

Long-run trend of GDP—
a very simple linear trend;
but can also be constructed for
(more nuanced) nonlinear trends
(statistics and econometrics)

Time

Highlight the business cycle movements by dividing
actual GDP by trend GDP (i.e., divide *curved line* by *dashed line*),
procedure referred to as "de-trending" macroeconomic data

Time

Figure 10.5
Business cycle ups and downs of real GDP (bottom panel) and "de-trended" version of the actual measured
GDP (upper panel). The vertical axis of the bottom panel shows the percentage deviation from the long-run
trend.

imagination of many (although surely not of everybody). This was also the period in which
newly developed mainframe computers using punch cards to process computations were
being increasingly put to research use.

These mathematically and computationally based ideas crept—or perhaps, better said,
launched full force—into macroeconomic thinking. Not uncoincidentally, much of the
high-powered technology that aided military efforts was developed at research universities
at which top-notch economists were also housed, so these ideas were only a short skip
away.

Starting in the early 1950s, a heavy dose of mathematics and statistical analytics
using high-powered mainframes quickly became the fashion of macroeconomics, first
in academic circles and then, by the early 1960s, in policy circles. A paramount goal for
these emerging computable statistical descriptions of aggregate economic events—the

Keynesian macroeconometric approach—was to answer an important question hanging over macroeconomics: How can business cycles be "explained"?

In terms of mathematics, the equations that were econometrically tested had the form of several equations that were hypothesized or "believable" descriptions of various interactions among economic variables; and these equations contained several economic price and quantity variables. Depending on the goal of the research, "several" equations and variables could mean just a few to several dozen to several hundred prices and/or quantities. In economics lingo, these are, respectively, *small-scale economic models, medium-scale economic models,* and *large-scale economic models.*

Throughout the 1950s many Keynesian macroeconometric frameworks were developed around the world. One, if not the most, prominent large-scale Keynesian macroeconometric frameworks that quickly took center stage was the **MIT/Penn/Federal Reserve Board** model constructed by a consortium of researchers and policy advisers at these three institutions.

Championing this effort was a group of three prominent economists from academe, all of whom would be future Nobel laureates—Paul Samuelson (Nobel recipient in 1970), James Tobin (Nobel recipient in 1981), and Robert Solow (Nobel recipient in 1987). Samuelson, Tobin, and Solow were not cloistered academics in the Ivory Tower. Each spent significant time in his career serving in various government positions that advised President John F. Kennedy and President Lyndon B. Johnson, including serving on the White House Council of Economic Advisers.[4]

The Keynesian-inspired macroeconometrics models took the form

$$x_{1t} = \alpha_0 x_{2t} + \alpha_1 x_{3t} + \alpha_2 x_{4t} + \ldots$$
$$x_{2t} = \alpha_3 x_{1t} + \alpha_4 x_{3t} + \alpha_5 x_{4t} + \ldots$$

.
.
.

$$x_{136t} = \alpha_{597} x_{1t} + \alpha_{598} x_{13t} + \alpha_{599} x_{69t} + \ldots$$

in which all of the terms denoted $x_{\#t}$ represent *measured economic prices or quantities* in a particular time period t—for example, the CPI-based inflation rate in the fourth quarter of 1952. Coherently measuring macroeconomic outcomes was the significant achievement of phase 1. In phase 2, those interrelationships were being scientifically tested.

---

4. Paul Samuelson's highly acclaimed 1947 graduate-level textbook *Foundations of Economic Analysis* and 1948 undergraduate principles-level textbook *Economics* brought Keynesian ideas into mathematics, physics, and engineering terms. Samuelson popularized Keynesian thought in the classroom, first at Harvard University and then, shortly after, at MIT. Future President Kennedy took a class of Samuelson's at Harvard, and later asked Samuelson to be his economic adviser during his presidential campaign and then a member of the Council of Economic Advisers once he took office.

Each of the equations above represents a hypothesized relationship between some or many of the macroeconomic data. In any given equation, each of the empirically estimated α terms (Greek lowercase letter "alpha") describes the correlation observed in the real world between an economic variable on the right-hand side and the economic variable on the left-hand side. For example, α_{598} was a description of how a one-unit increase in x_{13t} would affect x_{136t}, holding all else constant.[5] Any of the estimated α terms could turn out to be strictly positive, strictly negative, or statistically zero.[6]

This is the "science" component of Keynesian macroeconometrics. The social—or, in Keynes's own words, the "animal spirits"—component of the framework was essentially just the Keynesian idea that nominal wages and nominal prices may not adjust quickly enough over the course of business cycles to clear quantity supplied and quantity demanded. These concepts were embedded into the equations displayed above.

Given the wealth of economic data that was developed between the 1930s and 1950s, not just in the United States but also in other advanced nations, it was possible to estimate the α coefficients fairly tightly. The original intention of the Keynesian macroeconometric paradigm appeared to have been positive one. Not positive in the mathematical sense that the goal was to obtain α coefficients > 0. Rather, positive economics in the sense that the α's could help explain economic phenomena that have already occurred by focusing on the facts.

Some of the x variables in these macroeconometrics frameworks were policy variables over which either fiscal authorities or monetary authorities presumably had good control. For example, suppose that x_{3t} and x_{13t} variables in the set of expressions above were the short-term nominal interest rate and the wage tax rate, respectively. What α_{598} then describes is the amount by which x_{136t}—suppose that it's the quantity of aggregate investment I—changes for a 1 percent increase in the tax rate. In the United States, it is the Congress that has fairly tight legislative control of, and enforcement of collections via the IRS, taxes.

As the macroeconometric approach became widespread, **positive economic** analysis could and did easily slip into **normative economic** analysis. To continue with the example, if politicians wanted to increase aggregate investment, economists could advise them how to achieve this. The advice is revealed in the estimated value of α_{598}. If the facts show that $\alpha_{598} = -0.5$, then to a obtain a 1 percent increase in x_{136t}, the labor tax rate should be decreased by 2 percent, ceteris paribus. Hence the estimated value of α_{598} intended for positive macroeconomic analysis based on past data seemingly could be used to provide normative policy advice to guide future macroeconomic outcomes.

---

5. *Ceteris paribus* (the Latin phrase for "all other things being held constant") analysis in economics, not just macroeconomics, is the usual way to empirically and theoretically understand connections between economic measures.

6. Again, the econometric methodology is left for another course.

And that is indeed what happened in the United States and other advanced countries. Keynesian macroeconometric frameworks were increasingly being used for policy advice, which in turn was intended to improve the standards of living in the country. Referring back to figure 10.2, in the United States the average GDP growth rate between 1950 and 1970 was 4.3 percent per year. In hindsight, economic growth was incredibly strong during the 1950s and 1960s, perhaps in part due to the "great policy tips" provided by the estimated models.

The developers of the Keynesian macroeconometric frameworks in some sense could self-congratulate themselves. Indeed these were the halcyon days, the Golden Age, of the US economy.[7] It came to the point where macroeconomic ups and downs started to be considered a solved problem, even though macroeconomics as a topic of collective thought had just emerged thirty years earlier. To portray the point in its extreme, perhaps there was no longer any need for "judgment" in the conduct of fiscal policy or monetary policy. All that was needed was to conduct policy on autopilot, based on the mechanically constructed α coefficients.

This seemed to be true throughout the 1950s and 1960s—but it then turned out to be no longer true in the stagflationary period of the 1970s and early 1980s. Looking again at figure 10.2, GDP growth between 1970 and 1975 was 2.3 percent per year, down sharply from the 1950s and 1960s. Growth was stronger in the second half of the 1970s, averaging 4.7 percent. But then GDP growth declined precipitously between 1979 and 1983, averaging a paltry 0.5 percent per year.

In terms of price movements, as figure 10.1 shows, inflation was quite tame during the 1950 to 1970 period, averaging about 2.2 percent per year. During the 1970s, however, inflation averaged 7.1 percent per year, meaning nominal prices of goods and services were rising about 3.5 faster per year in the 1970s than in the previous two decades. Inflation was even more extreme between 1979 and 1983, with an average annual rate of 10.4 percent.

Given the events of the 1970s and early 1980s, the term **stagflation** was coined to describe the high-inflation/slow-growth economy. But this characterization arose in hindsight. The stagflationary decade ran counter to the **Phillips curve** idea that was popular in policy circles and economic advisers in the 1960s. You are probably already familiar with the Phillips curve, which describes an inverse relationship between an economy's unemployment rate and inflation rate—the higher is the inflation rate, the smaller is the unemployment rate.[8] Nonetheless, during most of the stagflationary period, policy makers continuously attempted to use Keynesian-based econometric advice to boost GDP growth and lower inflation.

---

7. So much so that a TV show that began in the late 1980s, *The Wonder Years,* garnered rave reviews for its depiction of a family living in suburban United States in the late 1960s.

8. See chapter 12 for further, mostly qualitative, discussion of the "classical" Phillips curve.

But the fiscal policy levers of the airplane on autopilot turned out to no longer work.[9] All of a sudden, the glory decades of macroeconomics of the 1950s and 1960s seemed to have collapsed. If macroeconomics were to remain an organized field of thought, scores of economists figured that the future of macro had to somehow depart from Keynesian macroeconometrics because there was something seemingly inconsistent with economic analysis in these frameworks.

Many researchers struggled to describe the essence of this inconsistency. Finally, in 1976, it was the economist Robert Lucas (future Nobel recipient in 1995) who simply and elegantly described the root of the issue. His (later named) **Lucas critique is** described more fully in box 10.1.

Box 10.1
Lucas critique

The α coefficients in Keynesian macroeconometric frameworks should be thought of as *depending on government policy directly*. The Lucas critique started ringing the death bell for Keynesian macroeconometrics. Why? Because this is not how Keynesian macroeconometric frameworks had been considered previous to the Lucas critique.

The α coefficients multiplied various and many economic measures, including policy instruments, either for positive purposes or normative purposes. But the α coefficients were essentially never seriously thought of as being dependent on policy. Stated mathematically and returning to the earlier example, it was not the case that the macroeconometric models contained terms such as

$$\alpha_{598}(x_{3t})\, x_{3t}$$

in which α_{598} could potentially depend on the wage tax rate x_{3t}. Thus, if the tax rate x_{3t} changed, α_{598} itself would change even though there is no data-based reason for this occur. In principle, this was an econometric and statistical issue, which could be gotten around using higher powered econometrics that would allow the α terms to depend on policy.

But a much larger, much deeper issue arose from the Lucas critique, which is that Keynesian macroeconometric models are not economic models, but rather only **statistical descriptions of economic outcomes.** This then raises the natural question: What is macroeconomics, or indeed, what is economics?

There are alternative ways of "defining" economics, but the theme that runs through them all is that **economics studies how individuals make informed choices given scarce resources.** After the Lucas critique, one could naturally ask: Do the α terms capture these ideas?

The answer was a resounding no. The macro profession was in disrepute by the late 1970s, on the verge of extinction.

---

9. Note the emphasis here on fiscal policy. In 1979 Paul Volcker was appointed chair of the Federal Reserve and adopted a never-before-seen strict monetary policy that is largely credited for the strong economic recovery starting in 1983. Volcker's policies were based on Milton Friedman's ideas that reigning in the growth of money supply will bring down the rate of inflation. More to come on this when we study monetary policy in part III.

Intermezzo Phase 2.5: The Rise of Monetarism

The rise of the monetarist school of thought bridged "phase 2" with "phase 3" of macro-economic though. The outspoken champion of monetarism within the academic community and later in the political community was Milton Friedman.

Milton Friedman was a consultant for Barry Goldwater's (Republican) campaign for President in 1964. Although Goldwater lost to Lyndon Baines Johnson in a landslide, Friedman gained a lot of attention for his debunking of Keynes's views that it was a short-fall of aggregate demand that led to the protracted Great Depression.

Instead, Friedman examined every downturn of the US economy since the mid-1800s and found that they were all accompanied by either an outright decrease in the level of the supply of money or a decrease in the growth rate of the supply of money. As mentioned briefly above in the phase 0 section, the second half of the nineteenth century did not have an economy in which Federal Reserve notes freely circulated because the Federal Reserve was not yet established. Rather, "money" during that period was state-issued or locally issued scripts that were backed by gold and, for a short period, gold and silver (in varying relative prices of the two metals).

Friedman's analysis led to the conclusion that the Federal Reserve should not have clamped down on the nominal money supply in the early stages of the Depression. Friedman sometimes referred to this period as the "Great Contraction" (of the supply of nominal money).

Ronald Reagan was governor of California in the 1960s and a strong proponent of Goldwater's campaign for President. Despite Goldwater's defeat, Reagan found Friedman's descriptions clear. Friedman (who won the Nobel Prize in 1976) was to become, during the end of the 1970s when the United States (along with other developed countries) was in the throes of stagflation, an economic consultant for Reagan's campaign for President in 1980.[10]

Reagan won in a landslide against Jimmy Carter's re-election campaign, and Paul Volcker (the Federal Reserve chair at that time) essentially built directly on the monetarist idea, by clamping down tightly on the issuance of new nominal money. According to monetarist theory, tightening of the nominal money supply ought to bring down the inflation rate—and it did so in spades over the first few years of the 1980s.

Meanwhile, overseas in Britain, Margaret Thatcher had become Prime Minister in June 1979, and she herself held strong views about monetarism (along with balancing the government budget).

In terms of the proper reach of macroeconomic policy and how prescriptive policy should be (especially regarding monetary policy), monetarism (sometimes known by the

---

10. Friedman was also an informal economic adviser to President Richard Nixon.

name "quantity theory of money") ideologically bridged the decline of the Keynesian macroeconometrics phase in the 1970s with the emergence of the microeconomic-based approach of modern macroeconomics of the late 1970s and 1980s.

Phase 3: Modern Macroeconomic Frameworks (late 1970s to Present)

Macroeconomics was resuscitated. There were once again many researchers who postulated many new ideas to consider economy-wide events. The one that stuck, though, and has been the predominant strain of thought for now three decades is what we are calling **modern macroeconomics.**

Modern macroeconomics begins by explicitly studying the **microeconomic** principles of utility maximization, profit maximization, and market clearing. Once all of that is done (we have already spent a lot of effort going through this mathematically and will continue to do so as we further enrich the frameworks), then one can consider the consequences of various fiscal policies or monetary policies on consumers' and firms' informed choices, which then leads to different market-clearing outcomes.

This modern macroeconomic approach quickly captured the attention of the profession through the 1980s for two reasons. First, it actually begins with microeconomic principles, which was a rather attractive idea. Rather than building a framework of economy-wide events from the top down (which macroeconometric models increasingly came to be viewed as), one could build this framework using microeconomic discipline from the bottom up. Figure 10.6 conveys this idea.

Second, it was in the early 1980s that desktop computing started to become widespread. The new breed of modern macroeconomic frameworks could thus be computed directly in one's office, rather than needing to reserve time for use of costly mainframe machines. (Note the parallel between the start of phase 2 and the start of phase 3: in the former, brand-new mainframe computational power was available; in the latter, brand-new desktop computation power was available.[11])

The three distinct types of markets that modern macro was (and continues to be) based on are goods markets, labor markets, and capital markets, as figure 10.6 portrays. Figure 10.6 is all about general equilibrium analysis in which all three macro markets simultaneously clear.

Chapters 11, 12, 13, and 14 discuss in qualitative terms, respectively, the idea of supply-side analysis that emerged first in academe through Lucas's critique, which was then championed in the 1980s under the Reagan presidency; the classic Phillips curve that much of

---

11. Should we chalk that up to innovations in technology? The consensus answer is yes, and we get a short glimpse of this idea later when we get to the growth analysis discussions in part VI.

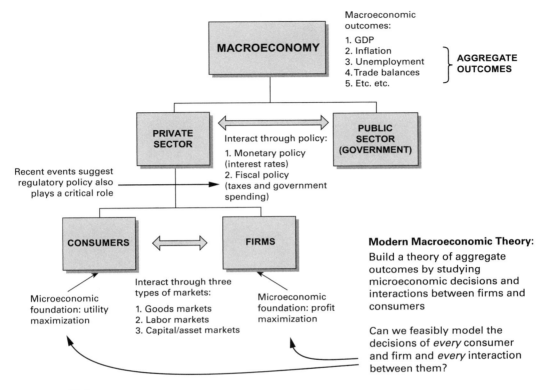

Figure 10.6
Schematic of the overall economy

policy analysis revolved around in the 1960s until its breakdown in the 1970s; the basics of New Keynesian theory, which resuscitates Keynes's ideas of "stickiness" in nominal prices, but in modern general-equilibrium macro form; and a mostly diagrammatical description that walks us through the basics of the "real business cycle framework," which is a phrase often used to characterize the underpinnings of modern macroeconomic frameworks.

11

Supply-Side Economics

The backward-bending labor supply curve of the consumption–leisure model is one basis for a school of macroeconomic policy thought known as "supply-side economics."[1] Its basic premise is that tax cuts would unlock a tremendous increase in the quantity supplied of productive resources (labor and capital) for the economy, thereby dramatically raising GDP. In this chapter we focus on the theoretical mechanism by which it may do so and also discuss the practical problems with such policies.

Taxes and the Backward-Bending Labor Supply Curve

Recall the basic backward-bending labor supply curve of the consumption–leisure model, reproduced in figure 11.1, which we derived in chapter 2 using the underlying indifference curves and budget constraint of the individual. Recall that the labor tax rate t explicitly appears in the budget constraint of the model,

$$Pc + (1-t)W(1-l) = (1-t)W.$$

If we hold the price of consumption P and the before-tax wage rate W constant, then changes in the tax rate t clearly lead to changes in the slope of the budget constraint and hence to changes in the optimal choice of consumption and leisure. Such is the way that we traced out the backward-bending labor supply curve.

The claims of supply-side economics hinges on the assumption that the economy is usually in the upward-sloping portion of the labor supply curve, somewhere near n_1 or n_4, say—the region in which increases in the after-tax wage would lead to a higher quantity of labor supplied. Thus, if the government were to lower the tax rate t, then the real after-tax wage rate $((1-t)W/P)$ would rise (with P held constant).

---

1. This school of thought rose to policy prominence during the Reagan administration and has generally been associated with the Republican Party since then, even though it is sometimes or often viewed as an extreme set of positions. Recently the "Tea Party" faction has been essentially leaning toward supply-side views. For an interesting (and scathing) review of the rise of the supply-siders during the 1970s and 1980s, see *Peddling Prosperity* by Paul Krugman.

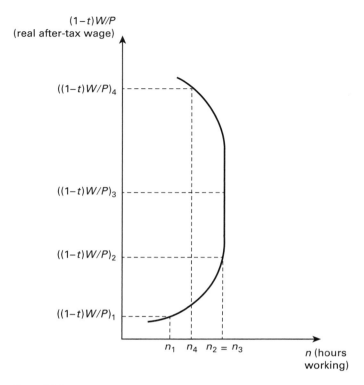

Figure 11.1
Backward-bending aggregate labor supply curve. According to the supply-side view, reductions in tax rates will cause individuals to increase their hours of work—implying that the economy must be in the upward-sloping region of the aggregate labor supply curve.

The resulting increase in quantity of labor supplied[2] would thus shift the aggregate supply function outward because at any given price P firms could now produce more by using more hours of labor. Note carefully that we would get a shift of the entire aggregate supply function rather than just a movement along it, since the tax rate t does not appear on the axes of the aggregate supply graph, as shown in figure 11.2.

Regardless of whether the supply-side claim that the economy is in the upward-sloping region of the labor supply curve is correct, it is the case that the consumption demand function shifts out, and hence the aggregate demand function shifts out, when the tax rate falls. We can see this simply by referring to the underlying indifference curve–budget line

2. For simplicity, the labor demand curve is omitted from Figure 11.1. The more precise mechanism is that at a higher real after-tax wage, individuals demand more consumption. This extra consumption must be produced by firms. To produce more goods, firms will have to hire more labor, causing the labor demand curve (a derived demand) to shift out, which results in a movement along the labor supply curve in figure 11.1.

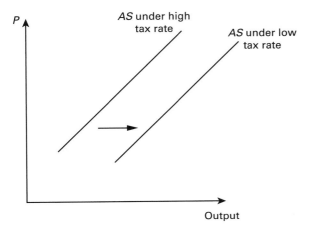

Figure 11.2
According to the supply-side view, reductions in tax rates will shift the aggregate supply function outward as individuals choose to increase their total number of works hours.

diagrams—a fall in t leads to a steeper budget line in the consumption–leisure model, and the new optimal choice features higher consumption. That is, even though P was held constant, a fall in t leads to a rise in the optimal choice of consumption. Thus, at any given price P, consumption is higher—which is precisely what it means for the consumption demand function to shift outward, in turn causing the aggregate demand function to shift out.

The shift out of the consumption demand function is shown in figure 11.3. Note that this effect is not a supply-side effect—this is our familiar result that demand rises when taxes fall. The supply-side effect is that depicted in figure 11.4.

This figure puts together the effects on aggregate demand and aggregate supply of a tax cut in the supply-side view. Clearly, GDP rises more than if aggregate supply did not shift, and the price level rises by less than if aggregate supply did not shift. Thus, under the supply-side view, tax cuts help boost economic growth and dampen inflation—seemingly the best of all possible scenarios.

The Laffer Curve

A potential criticism of supply-side policies is that the tax-cutting they advocate will reduce government tax revenue (the total it collects in taxes), hence causing (or worsening) government budget deficits if the government does not simultaneously reduce its spending. However, the supply-side response is that in fact government tax revenues will *increase* if tax rates are reduced. Again, the backward-bending labor supply curve is used to justify their position.

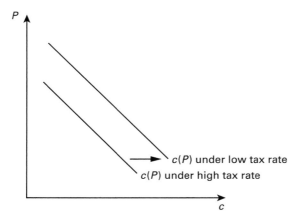

Figure 11.3
Consumption demand (which should be considered as a proxy for aggregate goods demand) shifts outward due to a reduction in the tax rate.

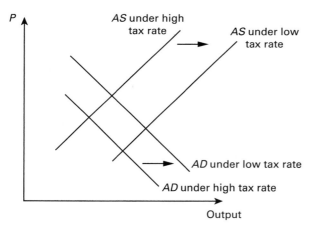

Figure 11.4
As the tax rate falls, the aggregate demand function shifts out. According to the supply-side view, the aggregate supply function also shifts out. The resulting rise in GDP is thus much higher under the supply-side view, while the resulting rise in inflation is lower under the supply-side view.

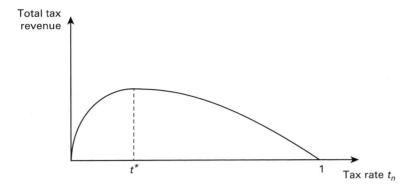

Figure 11.5
Laffer curve showing that total tax revenue is maximized at some tax rate t^*. Beyond t^*, total tax revenue falls as the incentive to work is reduced, to the point where at a tax rate of 100 percent ($t = 1$), there is no incentive to work at all, so that $n = 0$ and total tax revenue equals zero. The supply-side view is that the economy is to the right of t^* on the Laffer curve, so that reductions in tax rates would boost total revenue.

Total tax revenues collected from wage taxes is the multiplicative product of the tax rate, the wage rate, and number of hours worked in total in the economy. That is,

Total tax revenue $= t \cdot w \cdot n$,

so that total revenue is directly proportional to the tax rate.[3] Thus it would seem that as t falls so must total tax revenue. But according to the supply-side view, the economy is in the upward-sloping region of the labor-supply curve. That is, a fall in t induces a rise in n, and obviously if the rise in n is large enough to compensate for the fall in t, then total tax revenue may be unaffected or actually increase when the tax rate falls. This is exactly the argument that supply-siders make. This argument was made famous by Arthur Laffer, President Reagan's first chief economic adviser, in his **Laffer curve,** shown in figure 11.5.

The Laffer curve shows that total tax revenues are zero at two points, at $t = 0$ and $t = 1$. A zero tax rate clearly leads to zero tax revenue because the government is simply not taxing individuals at all. But a 100 percent tax rate also leads to zero tax revenue simply because there would be no incentive to work at all—that is, if the government levied a 100 percent tax rate, then $n = 0$ so that again tax revenues are zero. The fact that this function hits zero at two points and the observation that intermediate tax rates do lead to strictly positive tax revenues indicates that there must be some tax rate, called t^* in the figure, at which total tax revenue is maximized. The argument of supply-siders is that the economy

3. When considering optimal tax policy, we will be more precise about the n term. Technically, as per the consumption–leisure analysis, n—that is, optimal labor supply—*depends* on the tax rate t.

is to the right of $t*$, so cutting tax rates would boost total tax revenues and refuting the argument that the government budget deficit would worsen.

Limitations of Supply-Side Policies

As a theoretical proposition, the supply-side view seems quite appealing: tax cuts for workers, faster economic growth, and lower inflation. A panacea indeed for all macroeconomic ills with little or no cost, if only policy makers were willing to listen to this very simple advice! However, there is a major practical problem with the supply-side claims, and it is purely an empirical one. The argument rests on the economy being on the upward-sloping arm of the aggregate labor supply curve. Moreover the labor supply curve must be quite flat (elastic) in this region so that the quantity of labor supplied increases dramatically when the real after-tax wage rate falls.

The problem is that empirical evidence, and actual policy results, do not support these empirical requirements of supply-side theory. It is true that microeconomic evidence supports the backward-bending labor supply curve at an individual level. Summing horizontally all individuals' labor supply curves suggests that the aggregate labor supply curve is also backward-bending. But at a macroeconomic level, it appears that the economy is usually in the nearly vertical region of the labor supply curve. In terms of figure 11.1, it appears that the economy is generally between $((1-t)W/P)_2$ and $((1-t)W/P)_3$, a region in which total hours worked is simply not very responsive to changes in the real after-tax wage rate and hence not very responsive to tax cuts.[4]

The tax-cutting policies implemented under Reagan did in fact lead to lower tax revenues in the 1980s, suggesting that the economy was on the left side of $t*$ on the Laffer curve. Furthermore there is no evidence that economic growth was faster as a result of such policies. Our final conclusion is that supply-side policies, in theory, seem appealing but, in practice, do not necessarily deliver all they promise. But debate among conservative and liberal economists and politicians continues to rage on this subject.

---

4. This finding suggests that the average person in the United States is middle-class in the sense that he earns a wage that is neither very low nor very high.

12

The Phillips Curve

One recurring stylized feature of short-run macroeconomics is a negative relationship between the inflation rate and the unemployment rate. Despite its seeming regularity in the data, there has been and remains considerable debate in the economics profession about how best to model such an effect at a theoretical level—indeed an important branch of the profession simply dismisses the relationship as an unimportant one and thus not even worthy of serious theoretical modeling. But this inflation–unemployment trade-off seems to still drive much policy discussion, and as such we will adopt the view that it is a potentially important feature of macroeconomics. In this chapter we briefly explore how we can modify our existing theoretical model of the macroeconomy to explain the inflation–unemployment trade-off.

Nominal Wage Rigidity and the Short-Run Phillips Curve

Consider the view of the basic labor market we have developed thus far using the consumption–labor framework and firm analysis; this is depicted in figure 12.1, in which a downward-sloping labor demand function interacts with a backward-bending labor supply function to determine the equilibrium wage in the economy. In such a labor market, where labor supply always equals labor demand, unemployment is, by definition, zero.

Recall that an unemployed person is one who is actively looking for employment, who has not yet found employment. At the equilibrium wage w^* in figure 12.1, no individual wishes to work more hours than he already is. Technically this is zero unemployment—however, we will appeal to our notion from earlier that there is a "natural" rate of unemployment in the economy because of, for example, individuals optimally choosing to leave one job to look for another. With the notion of a natural rate of unemployment in the background of our model, equilibrium in the labor market implies then that the unemployment rate equals the natural rate of unemployment and hence cyclical unemployment is zero. The crucial point to notice is that implicit in our notion of cyclical unemployment is a dependence on the prevailing wage rate.

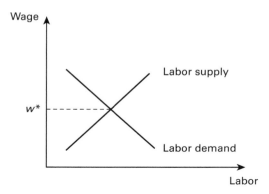

Figure 12.1
Perfectly competitive labor market, whereby the intersection of the labor demand function and labor supply
function determines the equilibrium wage rate

With this view of the labor market, the wage changes due to shifts of labor supply and/
or labor demand. But regardless of these shifts, with a perfectly competitive labor market,
cyclical unemployment is zero. Thus it would seem that it is impossible for us to generate
in our theoretical model a negative relationship between inflation and unemployment
wherein cyclical unemployment never changes!

Impossible, that is, unless we jettison our assumption of perfect competition in the labor
market. The basic premise of perfect competition is that prices adjust quickly and fully to
always match demand with supply. However, there is ample reason to believe that the labor
market is far from perfectly competitive.[1] The strongest evidence is that wages tend to
move very slowly over time, even when other macroeconomic events would tend to suggest
sharp movements in wages. Consider a simple example: suppose that some event causes
the aggregate demand curve to shift inward. This contractionary event on the macroeconomy shifts the labor demand curve in figure 12.1 to the left, which would imply an immediate fall in the wage rate if the labor market were in perfect competition. That is, a fall in the
economy's GDP due to a negative shift of aggregate demand should be accompanied by a
simultaneous fall in the wage rate.

But data show that wages would tend to fall only with a time lag, rather than immediately. However, data also show that the total number of hours worked in the economy does
fall simultaneously. It is impossible to reconcile these three observations (fall in GDP, fall
in total hours worked, no change in wage rate) with a perfectly competitive view of the
labor market.

---

1. No economist believes that any market is perfectly competitive—rather it comes down a matter of degree,
in which we must try to address the question "How far from perfect competition?" for a given market. In many
ways the labor market seems quite far from perfect competition, so we will now, for the upcoming discussion,
abandon the assumption of perfect competition in the labor market while retaining it for other markets.

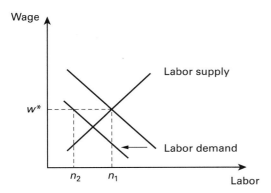

Figure 12.2
With the sticky wage w^*, a fall in demand for labor is accompanied by a fall in total hours worked from n_1 to n_2. But at the wage w^*, the total number of hours individuals would like to work is still n_1—thus unemployment has risen from zero to something strictly larger than zero.

Suppose, however, that there were some institutional features of the labor market that prevented the wage from adjusting immediately to match demand with supply. For example, suppose that a sizable fraction of workers had contracts with their employers that fixed their wages in nominal terms for some period of time, perhaps a year or two. Or suppose that there were laws in effect that prevented firms from cutting the wages of their employees.[2]

If such features are important in the labor market, then a decreased demand for labor, represented in figure 12.2 as the inward shift of the labor demand function, does not change the wage rate, and the wage rate remains stuck at w^*. At the wage rate w^*, the demand for labor is n_2 following the shift of labor demand, while the (desired) supply of labor is n_1, so the actual hours worked in the economy is now n_2. This excess supply of labor is precisely what is meant by the notion of cyclical unemployment: those workers who are willing to work (or, in our case, those hours of work that "want" to be worked) that cannot find employment. Cyclical unemployment has thus risen from zero to something strictly positive due to the **wage rigidity** (also known as a **sticky wage).**

To make our link between unemployment and inflation, we need to consider what happens to inflation in this example. Recall that the initiating event was a fall in aggregate demand, which means that the overall price level of the economy must fall (holding fixed the aggregate supply function). A decline in the price level means, by definition, that inflation has decreased. Thus the rise in unemployment is accompanied by a fall in inflation—precisely the relationship we set out to model. This negative relationship between the

2. Such laws in effect do exist in much of Europe and are an often-cited reason for Europe's persistently higher unemployment rates than in the United States.

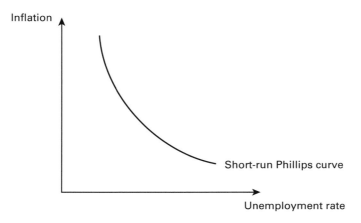

Figure 12.3
Phillips curve depicting the short-run negative relationship between the inflation rate and the unemployment rate.

inflation rate and the unemployment rate is captured by the **Phillips curve,** depicted in figure 12.3

The Long-Run Phillips Curve

Supposing that contracts that specify wages in advance are the primary source of wage rigidity, then if aggregate demand continues to slump for a protracted period, we would expect the new round of labor contracts negotiated when the original labor contracts expire to feature lower wages. Continuing with our example from figure 12.2, suppose that after some period of time with the wage stuck at w^* and unemployment above its natural rate, new rounds of wage negotiation yield the lower nominal wage w^{new} in figure 12.4. At this lower wage, cyclical unemployment is back down to zero, implying that the unemployment rate is back to its natural rate. This occurs even though aggregate demand remains at its depressed level—that is, even though inflation stays low, unemployment will eventually gravitate back to its natural rate.

Thus, in the long-run (i.e., that period of time when all wages can be renegotiated—equivalently, that length of time necessary for nominal wage rigidities to disappear)—the unemployment rate equals the natural rate no matter what the inflation rate. This long-run relationship is embodied in the vertical **long-run Phillips curve** shown in figure 12.5. The main proponents of the idea of the vertical long-run Phillips curve were Milton Friedman and Edmund Phelps in the 1960s, an idea that rose to prominence during the stagflationary decade of the 1970s.

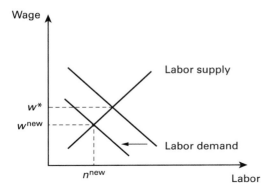

Figure 12.4
After a protracted length of time during which the wage remains stuck above the market-clearing wage, it is likely that firms will win wage reductions (or, at the very least, a threat of layoffs) in the next round of wage negotiations. A decrease in the wage from w^* to w^{new} thus lowers cyclical employment back to zero and hence the unemployment rate down to the natural rate.

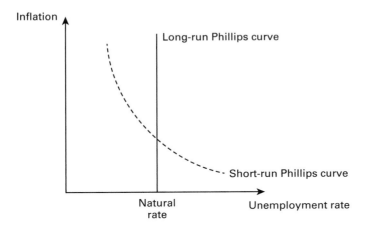

Figure 12.5
Wages adjust in the long run, so there is likely to be no trade-off between inflation and unemployment. This idea is embodied in the vertical long-run Phillips curve.

13

New Keynesian Economics

The two current leading views of business cycles are real business cycle (RBC) theory and New Keynesian economics. Each of these schools of thought has a rich history marked by frequent vigorous debate between them. While a terse summary of their general views does not do them justice, we first briefly highlight the main difference between the two points of view. RBC theory views periodic expansions and recessions as natural, indeed efficient, responses of the economy to the ups and downs of the state of "technology" of the economy.[1] As such, recessions are not dire events for the economy, but rather natural slowdowns that are preceded by an expansion and that will again be followed by future expansions. In terms familiar from microeconomics, pure RBC theory maintains that the aggregate economy operates perfectly competitively on both the demand side and the supply side.[2] An important implication of RBC theory therefore is that the government has no role to play in the macroeconomy—that is, neither fiscal policy nor monetary policy can be used to improve the macroeconomic condition. In contrast, New Keynesian economics adopts the point of view that there are fundamental market failures in the aggregate economy that render business cycle fluctuations inefficient, specifically periods of lower than potential GDP.[3] The important implication of this point of view is that the government may indeed have a role to play in improving macroeconomic conditions.

Here we will consider just one strand of New Keynesian economic theory. As we will see, microeconomic analysis is at the heart of New Keynesian theory. Unlike most of our

1. "Technology" here is broadly defined—specifically, the Solow residual (on which we will have more to say when we study RBC theory) is the most often-used measure of technology.

2. Even the most ardent RBC macroeconomist does not literally believe the economy is perfectly competitive in the pure textbook sense, but rather that in aggregate market failures tend not to be so catastrophic as to make perfect competition a terrible approximation.

3. The notion of "efficiency" you should have in mind throughout our discussion here is exactly that from microeconomics: a market (in our case, the entire macroeconomy) is operating efficiently if there is no deadweight loss, which means that no trades between suppliers and demanders that could increase overall utility go unconsummated. Another familiar characterization of economic efficiency is that price equals marginal cost.

discussion of representative-agent macroeconomics, however, the focus of New Keynesian theory is not on the microeconomics of consumer behavior but rather on the microeconomics of firm behavior.

Differentiated Goods and the Consumption Aggregator

In our study of the representative consumer, we supposed that there was only one object (i.e., "all stuff") that the consumer purchased in order to obtain utility. This was true in both the consumption–leisure model (in which there was literally only one object called "all stuff" that the consumer could purchase) as well as the consumption–savings model (in which there was one object called "all stuff" in each of the time periods of the economy that the consumer could purchase).

The use of a single consumption good is obviously a theoretical simplification. In reality, consumers purchase a vast number of goods and services from which they obtain utility. And in reality, these goods are somewhat substitutable for each other. For example, when making your decision about where to spend your Saturday evening, you may decide to go to the movies or go to a Mets game. Both options are forms of entertainment, but clearly they are not perfect substitutes for each other. Even if you decide to go to the movies, you will have to choose between the latest comedy and the newest action thriller—likewise these two movies are imperfect substitutes for each other.

If we believe that there are available a great many options for consumption, each of which is at least a little different from every other option, then one way to reconcile our previous use of a single consumption good with this fact is to suppose that "all stuff" is composed of these great many differentiated goods. Specifically, we will now suppose that our usual notion of "all stuff" consumption is a function

$$c = c\left(c^1, c^2, c^3, ..., c^N\right) \tag{1}$$

where c^1 denotes the type-1 consumption good (perhaps a movie), c^2 denotes the type-2 consumption good (perhaps a Mets game), c^3 is the type-3 consumption good (perhaps dinner at a fancy restaurant), and so on. If there are N different goods, then we have that "all stuff" consumption is a function of the N different varieties of consumption goods.

Note that we have written this function—formally called the **consumption aggregator function**—in abstract form. Especially note that we do not necessarily mean the simple sum $c = c^1 + c^2 + c^3 + ... + c^N$. In fact, in theoretical New Keynesian models, the function $c(\cdot)$ is usually assumed to satisfy the following two properties: the first partial derivative with respect to consumption of good type i satisfies

$$\frac{\partial c(\cdot)}{\partial c^i} > 0 \tag{2}$$

and the second partial derivative with respect to consumption of good type i satisfies

$$\frac{\partial^2 c(\cdot)}{\partial (c^i)^2} < 0. \tag{3}$$

These two conditions state, respectively, that total consumption c is an increasing function of consumption of type i and that total consumption c increases at an ever-decreasing rate as consumption of type i increases. Think of this simply as (if you're a movie buff) the more movies you see, the more total consumption (not just of movies but of "all stuff") you enjoy—but the more and more movies you see, the less and less extra total consumption you gain. These properties should remind you of the general properties we imposed on the representative consumer's utility function—note well, however, that the consumption aggregator function is not a utility function. Indeed the utility function still takes total consumption c as an argument and continues to have the usual properties we have discussed at length. It is still utility, and not consumption, that is the maximization goal of the representative consumer. A very common functional form assumed for the consumption aggregator in New Keynesian models is

$$c(c^1, c^2, c^3, ..., c^N) = \left[\left(c^1\right)^{1/\varepsilon} + \left(c^2\right)^{1/\varepsilon} + \left(c^3\right)^{1/\varepsilon} + ... + \left(c^N\right)^{1/\varepsilon} \right]^\varepsilon, \tag{4}$$

where $\varepsilon \geq 1$. The value ε (Greek lowercase letter "epsilon") has very important economic meaning in New Keynesian models. It governs how substitutable, from the point of view of the consumer, the different goods are for each other. At one extreme is the value $\varepsilon = 1$. When substituted into the expression above, this value yields the simple sum $c^1 + c^2 + c^3 + ... + c^N$. With $\varepsilon = 1$, each consumption good is just as good as any other from the point of view of the representative consumer—that is, the goods are perfect substitutes for each other. With $\varepsilon > 1$, however, goods are only imperfect substitutes for each other, meaning that they are differentiated to a degree depending on the exact value of ε. A basis for all of New Keynesian economics is the assumption that $\varepsilon > 1$.

Monopolistically Competitive Firms

The heart of New Keynesian economics lies not in the representative consumer but rather with firms. Each of the N differentiated goods is assumed to be produced by a distinct monopolistically competitive firm. Recall from basic microeconomics that a fundamental feature of monopolistic competition is that goods are similar to each other but not completely identical. Continuing the example from above, movies and baseball games are similar goods (forms of entertainment) but obviously not identical.

Also recall from basic microeconomics that a firm that produces a differentiated good possesses market power. In terms of analysis that should be familiar, this market power manifests itself in the fact that the firm faces a downward-sloping demand curve and hence

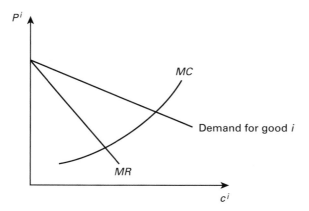

Figure 13.1
A monopolistically competitive firm faces a downward-sloping demand curve for its particular product *i*. The
marginal revenue curve thus lies strictly below the demand curve, and the firm's profit-maximizing choice of
output occurs where $MR = MC$. At this optimal quantity, price exceeds marginal cost.

a marginal revenue curve that lies strictly below its demand curve. This in turn implies that
the firm's profit-maximizing choice features price greater than marginal cost—algebraically,
$P^i > MC^i$, where P^i denotes the nominal profit-maximizing price of the firm that produces
good *i* and MC^i is the nominal marginal cost at the profit-maximizing quantity. These features are summarized in figure 13.1.

Recall from expression (4) above that $\varepsilon = 1$ in the consumption aggregator implies that
the goods are perfect substitutes for each other. The implication for firms of $\varepsilon = 1$ is that
they do not have any market power (and thus face perfectly elastic demand curves). Thus
setting $\varepsilon = 1$ (in New Keynesian models that use this channel to introduce market failures)
is one way of "shutting off" the New Keynesian elements of a New Keynesian model.

For simplicity, in the remainder of our discussion, we will assume that $N = 2$, so that the
representative consumer's total consumption is a function of two differentiated goods, each
of which is produced by a distinct firm. Also we will assume $\varepsilon > 1$ (strictly), except where
noted to highlight some issues, so that the model we are considering is indeed a New
Keynesian model.

The Aggregate Price Level

In our simple models, which featured only one homogenous consumption good, the nominal price level of the economy was a simple object—it was just the nominal price of the
single consumption good. In our New Keynesian model here, however, even specializing
to the case of just $N = 2$ differentiated goods renders the nominal price level of the economy a somewhat more complicated notion to consider. Clearly the aggregate price level,
which we will denote by P, should depend somehow on the nominal prices of the two

distinct goods, which we denote by P^1 and P^2. That is, P is some function of P^1 and P^2. There are many possible ways of aggregating the individual prices into a single measure of the price level of the economy. We will refrain from putting a particular functional form on this **price-level aggregator** (even though New Keynesian models offer a great many from which to choose) and simply use the abstract function

$$P = P(P^1, P^2). \tag{5}$$

To re-emphasize, the unsuperscripted P denotes the nominal price level of the economy (the price of a "market basket" of goods) while P^1 and P^2 denote, respectively, the nominal prices of good type 1 and good type 2. For our purposes the important feature of this function is that P is strictly increasing in each of its arguments. In calculus notation, this means that

$$\frac{\partial P(\cdot)}{\partial P^1} > 0 \tag{6}$$

and

$$\frac{\partial P(\cdot)}{\partial P^2} > 0. \tag{7}$$

The assumption that the price level P is strictly increasing in each of the individual prices should strike you as reasonable. To draw an analogy with the consumer price index (CPI), if the price of any of the goods in the CPI basket rises, the aggregate price level rises even though the relationship between the CPI and the individual price is usually not a straightforward one. Similarly in our New Keynesian model the functional relationship between the price of any individual good and the aggregate price level is, in general, a complicated one, but the aggregate price level depends positively on each individual price in the basket.

Aggregate Consumption Demand

Each of the two firms (in our case where we have specialized to $N = 2$) faces a downward-sloping demand curve for its product. Because there is more than one good, we now need to define aggregate consumption demand. A simple definition of aggregate consumption demand may seem to be that aggregate consumption demand is the sum of the demands for each of the differentiated products. Graphically this latter would mean that aggregate consumption demand is the "horizontal summation" of each individual good's demand curve.[4] However, such a procedure would be incorrect in our New Keynesian model.

---

4. This notion of horizontally summing demand curves should be familiar to you from microeconomics.

Horizontal summation of demand curves is incorrect here because goods that are different cannot be summed. For example if we have 20 apples and 10 bananas, we have—well, 20 apples and 10 bananas. That is, they inherently cannot be summed because they are different objects.[5] More fundamentally, such a procedure turns out to approach the problem of constructing the aggregate consumption demand from the wrong point of view. Recall in our study of the consumption–leisure model that we derived the (aggregate) consumption demand function. This consumption demand function remains the correct notion of consumption demand because it is total consumption, which in turn is the consumption aggregator, that still is the direct argument of the representative consumer's utility function.

The consumption aggregator then shows the relationship between aggregate consumption demand and demand for each of the differentiated goods. Recall from above that total consumption (the "all stuff" object) is an increasing function of each type of differentiated consumption good. This fact is all we need to conclude that there is a positive relationship between total consumption and consumption of each differentiated good. We thus diagram the relationship between the demand for the two goods and aggregate consumption demand in figure 13.2.

The way to interpret the relationship depicted in figure 13.2 is the following: when some event (e.g., preference shocks and government policy shocks) shifts the consumption demand function, the demand functions facing the two individual firms also shift in the same direction. Because the individual firms' demand functions shift, the associated marginal revenue functions shift as well, implying a new profit-maximizing choice of price and quantity for each individual firm.[6]

To preview the comparison of New Keynesian theory and RBC theory that we will make after studying both points of view, notice that the exogenous event (i.e., the "unexplained" event, or shock) that begins the thought experiment is a shift in a component of demand (here, consumption). New Keynesian theory holds that "demand shocks," coupled with the rest of the theoretical apparatus we are describing in this chapter, are the predominant factor that causes macroeconomic fluctuations. In contrast, RBC theory holds that it is "supply shocks" that are the predominant source of macroeconomic fluctuations.

Staggered Price-Setting

Consider the case in which the consumption demand function shifts outward for some reason. As just described, this event in turn causes the demand functions, and hence the associated marginal revenue functions, facing each individual firm to shift outward as well.

---

5. We could then define the term "fruit" to be either a banana or an apple, and assume the conversion one apple = one fruit and one banana = one fruit. With these assumptions (which notice probably come very naturally to you as you think about this example), we would then say we have 30 pieces of fruit.
6. Convince yourself of this last point by diagramming it.

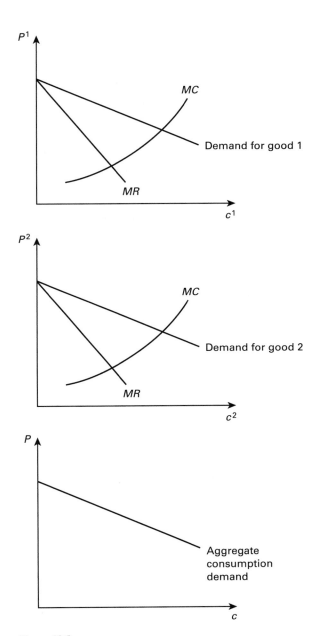

Figure 13.2
There is a positive relationship between aggregate consumption demand and demand for each differentiated good. Aggregate consumption demand is derived by using the consumption–leisure model.

Assuming the marginal cost functions do not shift, these events imply new profit-maximizing choices of price and quantity for each of the two firms in figure 13.2. In particular, both quantity c^i and price P^i rise.[7] Because the price of each good rises, clearly the aggregate price level P rises because of the properties of the price-level aggregator we described above.

However, suppose instead that only one of the two firms can change its price at the time of the event that shifts the aggregate consumption demand curve. Let's suppose it is firm 2 (the firm that produces consumption good c^2) that has the ability to change price. Firm 1 (the firm that produces consumption good c^1), in contrast, cannot change its price at all. The situation facing firm 1 is illustrated in figure 13.3.

Figure 13.3 shows the events facing firm 1 following a rise in consumption demand. Firm 1's demand function and marginal revenue function both shift outward. If Firm 1 were to change its price, it would choose the price labeled "optimal P^1 if no price stickiness" because that price yields the quantity at which marginal cost equals marginal revenue. We can see from the diagram that quantity produced would rise. However, if

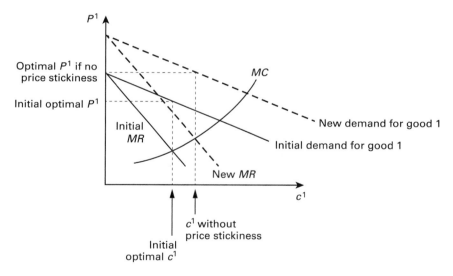

Figure 13.3
With a shift outward of the consumption demand function, the demand function facing firm 1 and hence firm 1's marginal revenue function both shift outward. If firm 1 could change its price, it would raise both its price and quantity produced because the new *MR* function intersects the *MC* function at a higher quantity. Associated with such a price increase is a rise in the quantity produced. However, if firm 1 continues with its initial optimal price, then the quantity of good 1 that it produces rises by even more, as can be read off the new demand function.

7. Again, diagram it to convince yourself.

firm 1 does not change its price and is forced to continue using the initial optimal P^1, then its quantity produced will rise by even more, as can be read off the new demand function.

Firm 2 is assumed to be able to change its price immediately. It thus faces a similar situation as firm 1, except it will raise its price P^2. Consequently its quantity produced also rises, but by less than it would if it were also unable to change its price.

Implications for Government Policy

Now we consider how the macroeconomic effects of policy differ depending on whether or not firm 1 is able to change its price. First, consider the case where firm 1 can change its price. We can conclude that the aggregate price level P rises because the aggregate price level is an increasing function of both P^1 and P^2. Because both P^1 and P^2 rise, P clearly rises. Now, suppose that firm 2 can raise its price but firm 1 does not raise its price. In this case, P^2 still rises by the same amount as in the case where firm 1 could change its price because firm 2's decisions do not depend on firm 1's actions.[8] However, because P^1 does not change, the aggregate price level P does not rise by as much as in the case where firm 1 did change its price. Simultaneously overall consumption c rises by more with firm 1's price held constant because c^1 rises by more in this case.

In the preceding conclusion lie the important implications of New Keynesian theory for government policy. In the presence of staggered price-setting, government policy that raises aggregate consumption demand generates less inflation and a larger increase in production than the same government policy in the absence of staggered price-setting. Thus staggered price-setting gives economic policy makers leverage over real quantities in the economy, more leverage than they would have if all firms could adjust prices simultaneously.

Critique of New Keynesian Theory

A long-standing criticism of the strand of New Keynesian theory that we have developed is the assumption of staggered price-setting. In particular, we have offered no explanation why some subset of firms cannot or does not change its price in the face of an increase in its demand while some other subset does change its price.

One common justification given for staggered price-setting is the presence of asynchronous menu costs. Menu costs are the costs incurred by a firm simply by the act of changing prices.[9] If different sectors of the economy experience menus costs of different magnitudes

---

8. That is, there are no game-theoretic interactions here.

9. The terminology itself implies its meaning: a restaurant that wants to change its prices must print new menus, which itself has a cost associated with it.

at different times during the business cycle, then staggered price-setting may arise. For example, perhaps it is easier (i.e., less costly) for military-equipment producers to raise their prices during wartime than it is for producers of entertainment simply because of the political and/or cultural environment of the time. This example suggests that "menu costs" need not be interpreted as only direct costs of changing prices but also can include more intangible costs such as lost goodwill. While there is little empirical evidence suggesting the magnitude of these intangible menu costs, it is at least a plausible story.

At a more realistic level, it does seem true that firms do not all change prices simultaneously. If we accept this, then staggered price-setting seems less strange of an assumption and perhaps we can accept not having a stronger microeconomic foundation for it.

Finally, strong empirical support for the New Keynesian view comes from data that suggest that government policy, both fiscal and monetary, does have important short-run effects on output. Data generally support the view that government policy is more effective than real business cycle (RBC) theory predicts. This last observation alone may be enough justification for studying New Keynesian theory.

Appendix: Theories of Price Stickiness

During the normal ups and downs of the economy (termed "business cycles," a topic that is usually in the domain of macroeconomics), demand tends to fluctuate—even demand for broadly defined categories of goods. In terms of a supply and demand diagram, this means the demand curve shifts in and out during the "normal" course of economic events. We will consider "good economic times" to be periods of relatively high economy-wide income and "bad economic times" to be periods of relatively low economy-wide income. If we further adopt the simplifying assumption that all goods are normal goods, this means that in good economic times demand curves tend to shift out, while in bad economic times demand curves tend to shift in. With an unshifting supply curve, these shifts of the demand curve imply fluctuations of equilibrium price.

At the other extreme, price fluctuations could arise solely due to changes in costs for firms, holding the demand function constant. Indeed, many industries are subject to such cost "shocks" from time to time. For example, the production costs of manufacturing firms, whose output makes up a sizable fraction of the US economy, generally rise when the price of steel rises.[10] When the general wage level in the economy rises, as occurred during much of the 1990s in the United States, all firms' costs rise. Profit maximization by firms implies that firms would try to pass along most, if not all, of any increase in production costs to consumers in the form of higher prices.

---

10. As occurred, for example, when the Bush administration passed a set of steel tariffs in March 2002.

Thinking then of our usual downward-sloping demand curves and upward-sloping supply curves, these fluctuations in demand and costs should imply that (equilibrium) prices fluctuate a fair amount during the course of business cycles. But much empirical evidence has shown that prices do not in fact fluctuate very much over short periods of time. The phenomenon whereby prices do not fluctuate as much as standard economic theory predicts is known in academic circles as "price stickiness."

Here we will consider five simple theories of price stickiness and also visit some of the real-world evidence surrounding these theories. The discussion follows researchers who have asked and shadowed managers and managerial teams as they go through a periodic review of their firms' and products' pricing targets. The exploration is a very interesting exploration regarding the *micro* origins of price stickiness that proceeds, rather than by simply presenting economic theories in a vacuum, by asking managers of businesses in various industries about the relative importance of various postulated theories of price stickiness.

Theory I: Constant Marginal Cost of Production

Suppose that markets are perfectly competitive and that all firms have constant marginal cost (*MC*) curves over the relevant range of outputs. That is, for a single firm, if the "normal" range of output is between 100 and 500 units, suppose that the *MC* curve is perfectly horizontal over this range. A constant *MC* schedule is not so difficult to rationalize. For example, if a firm has a machine that makes between 100 and 500 units of output and the electricity, water, and so on, necessary to operate the machine has constant per-unit cost (perhaps because the firm has a contract with the utility company), then over the range 100 to 500 units, the extra total cost incurred in producing one more unit could be constant—that is, *MC* is constant. Because the market supply curve is simply the horizontal sum of individual firms' marginal cost curves, this implies that the market supply curve in such an industry is perfectly elastic.

Figure 13.4 illustrates how prices can be constant despite fluctuations in the demand schedule during the course of the business cycle. Thus constant marginal cost is one reason why prices may be sticky.

Evidence about marginal cost curves in US industries provides surprisingly more support for constant marginal cost than many economists may think. According to interview data in the 1990s, 40 percent of US goods and services are produced by firms that report that they have constant marginal cost over "usual" ranges of production. Only 11 percent report rising marginal cost over "usual" ranges of production, while 33 percent report declining marginal costs over "usual" ranges of production (but here there seems to be reason to suspect that respondents were confusing marginal cost with average total cost).[11] This

---

11. Recall that it is possible for marginal cost to be rising even as average total cost is falling—this is true when the *MC* curve is below the *ATC* curve.

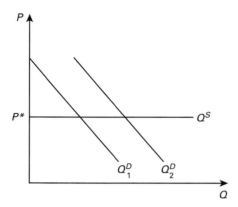

Figure 13.4
If all firms in a perfectly competitive industry have constant marginal cost, then the market supply curve is
perfectly elastic, which in turn implies that fluctuations in the demand curve leave prices unchanged.

evidence seems at odds with the usual textbook assumption that marginal costs rise as
output expands.

Theory II: Variable Elasticity of Demand

Instead of considering perfectly competitive industries, let us think of monopolistically
competitive industries. Recall that in monopolistically competitive industries, each firm,
because it produces a slightly different good than every other firm in the industry, faces a
downward-sloping demand curve.[12] Here we will suppose that each individual firm's MC
curve has the usual upward slope. Profit maximization by the individual firm implies
choosing the quantity such that marginal revenue equals marginal cost ($MR = MC$), as
shown in figure 13.5, in which q^* is the profit-maximizing quantity and P^* the associated
profit-maximizing price.

In good economic times, when incomes are relatively high, the demand curve, and hence
the marginal revenue curve, in figure 13.5 would shift outward. If this shift out is a parallel
shift, the new profit-maximizing quantity and price are as shown in figure 13.6. The profit-
maximizing price rises due to the increase in demand.

The shift out in the demand curve may not be a parallel shift, however. Figure 13.7
shows a shift out of the demand curve in which the entire demand curve becomes more
elastic (i.e., flatter) as economy-wide income rises. Demand curve Q_2^D is shifted out relative
to demand curve Q_1^D but is flatter than Q_1^D. At high prices the demand curve has shifted out
by less than at lower prices. Such a nonparallel shift may seem reasonable on the ground

12. As opposed to the perfectly horizontal demand curve that an individual firm in a perfectly competitive
industry faces.

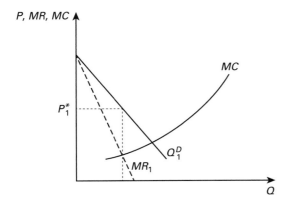

Figure 13.5
A monopolistically competitive firm faces a downward-sloping demand curve, and profit maximization implies producing that quantity that equates marginal revenue to marginal cost.

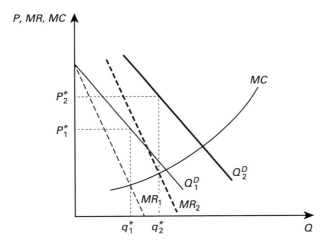

Figure 13.6
When the demand curve facing a monopolistic competitor shifts out (with an associated shift out of the marginal revenue curve) in parallel manner, the profit-maximizing quantity and price both increase, as long as the marginal cost curve remains stable.

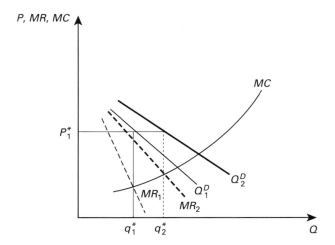

Figure 13.7
If the demand curve facing a monopolistic competitor shifts out in a nonparallel manner, it is possible that the profit-maximizing price may be unchanged.

that as incomes rise, the "newest" units sold in the market are sold to those consumers who have just entered the market. These newest consumers are likely to be the most price-sensitive consumers—that is, the newest consumers are likely to be the ones who have the most elastic demands in the first place. Thus the overall market demand curve becomes more elastic as it shifts out.

The new profit-maximizing quantity in figure 13.7 is q_2^*, the point at which the new MR curve intersects the unchanged MC curve. But the profit-maximizing price, read off of the new demand curve, is unchanged. Of course, the case illustrated is a very special case—the more general point is that because of possibly varying elasticity of demand as demand curves shift, price volatility may be much smaller than would otherwise be the case.

To summarize, the basic idea of this theory of price stickiness is that demand curves becomes less elastic as they shift in and more elastic as they shift out. To operationalize this theory in interview studies, researchers posed the idea as one in which when business turns down a company loses its *least* loyal customers first and retains its *most* loyal customers. Their presumption in stating the theory in this way to business managers was that the most loyal customers are the least price-sensitive ones. When asked whether this phenomenon was an important one in their own pricing decisions, 56 percent responded that it was totally unimportant, 13 percent responded that it was of minor importance, 22 percent responded that it was of moderate importance, and 9 percent responded that it was very important. Thus their survey indicates that while this theory of price stickiness cannot be claimed to be *the* theory of price stickiness, it does not seem completely irrelevant.[13]

Theory III: Kinked Demand Curve

Consider again monopolistically competitive firms, which face downward-sloping demand curves. One classical theory of how an individual monopolistically competitive firm behaves is that it believes any price cut it initiates will be matched by its competitors while any price hike it initiates will not be matched by its competitors. The idea is simple. On one hand, if a firm lowers its price, other firms (which offer similar but not identical products) will find it in their best interest to lower their price as well so as not to lose their customers to the first firm. Thus a lowering price will lead to an increase in quantity demanded, but not a very large increase. On the other hand, if a firm raises its price, other firms will find it in their best interest to keep their prices unchanged, under the belief that customers of the first firm will switch to buying their products instead. Thus, a price increase will lead to a large decrease in quantity demanded. The preceding discussion can be formalized in the demand curve shown in figure 13.8, in which the demand curve above the price P^* is relatively elastic (flat) while below the price P^* is relatively inelastic (steep).

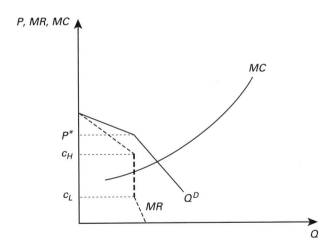

Figure 13.8
In the kinked demand curve model, the *MC* curve could cross the *MR* curve anywhere in the region between c_H and c_L and the profit-maximizing price would be P^* regardless. Thus the price P^* is a "sticky" price for this firm.

13. Notice also that for this theory of price stickiness to be an important one, much of the economy must be characterized by monopolistic competition rather than perfect competition.

This "kinked demand curve" leads to a break in the MR curve. This break is illustrated as a jump down in the MR curve from c_H to c_L in figure 13.8. The reason for the jump in the MR curve is simply the fact that the slope of the total revenue (TR) function changes abruptly at the kink price—and marginal revenue is simply the slope of the total revenue function. Let's understand this a bit more carefully: recall that total revenue is defined as $TR = P \cdot Q$. But from the perspective of a price-setting firm such as a monopolistic competitor, price is related to quantity by the demand function, so we can write the *function* $P(Q)$ to stand for price. With this we have that total revenue is given by $TR(Q) = P(Q) \cdot Q$, where again the functional dependences are emphasized by the notation. When graphing TR versus Q, we have then the slope $TR'(Q) = P'(Q) \cdot Q + P(Q)$, which follows from the chain rule of calculus. But, as mentioned above, marginal revenue is the slope of the total revenue function, so $MR(Q) = TR'(Q) = P'(Q) \cdot Q + P(Q)$. At the kink point in figure 13.8, $P'(Q)$ changes abruptly (i.e., discontinuously), causing a discontinuity in the MR function.

Superimposing an MC curve in the kinked demand curve model, as figure 13.8 does, shows that if the MC curve crosses the MR curve anywhere in the region between c_H and c_L, the profit-maximizing quantity and price remain unchanged. Thus $P*$ is a "sticky" price in the kinked demand curve model because marginal costs can shift over a broad range with no attendant change in price.

In interview studies, the kinked demand curve model was posed to business managers as one of "price leadership." As discussed above, the underlying idea of the kinked demand curve model is that competitors will match price changes in the downward direction but not in the upward direction. Thus, if they could, firms would find it profitable to all agree simultaneously to raise prices.[14] Because such collaboration is usually not feasible, some firms (perhaps the biggest ones, say, or the most popular ones) may naturally emerge as the "price leaders" of the industry: if those leader firms raise prices, that sends a signal to the rest of the firms in the industry that price hikes will be matched. The specific question interviewers posed to business managers concerned "the importance of price coordination failure" as the reason why a firm held back on price changes. A very large 62 percent of firms responded that this factor was a very important one in their pricing decisions. Of thirteen main theories of price stickiness interviewers explored, this one received the most support from business managers, lending support to the importance of the kinked demand curve model as a theory of price stickiness.

Theory IV: Psychological Pricing Points

Casual introspection of your own experiences as a consumer will probably convince you that certain prices occur more often than others. For example, a $999 computer is probably more common than a $1,000 computer. Or a $9.99 pizza pie is probably more common

---

14. Such collaboration on price-setting, called "collusion," is illegal in the United States. A number of laws, including the Sherman Antitrust Act and the Clayton Act, exist to outlaw collusive behavior among firms.

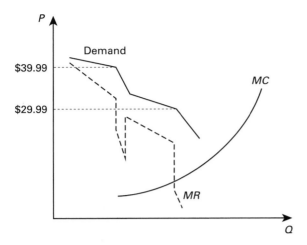

Figure 13.9
With psychological pricing points (here, $39.99 and $29.99), the demand function is very elastic at prices just above those threshold prices and less elastic at prices just below those threshold prices. Thus the monopolistic competitor's marginal revenue function has multiple jumps in it, one corresponding to each kink point on the demand function. Thus the *MC* function can cross through the *MR* function at multiple vertical sections of the *MR* function, giving rise to the "pricing points" as the profit-maximizing prices.

than a $10 pizza pie. Many sellers, especially in the retail business, apparently believe that certain threshold prices have special psychological significance to consumers: a $999 computer may seem "a lot cheaper" than a $1,000 computer, for instance. In terms of our model of supply and demand, the demand curve would be extremely elastic at prices just above these threshold prices, as illustrated in figure 13.9. That is, prices just above the threshold pricing points would cause many consumers to exit the market.

The demand curve in figure 13.9 has multiple kinks and therefore multiple jumps in the *MR* curve. Thus, the analysis here proceeds similar to the case of the kinked demand curve discussed above. As shown in the figure, the *MC* curve can move up and down over a broad range and still cross the *MR* curve at the same quantity, at which the profit-maximizing price is $29.99. The *MC* curve could also shift so far up as to cross the *MR* curve in its leftmost vertical region, at which the associated profit-maximizing price is $39.99. Once the *MC* curve moves into this latter region, it can again move up and down over a broad range in which the profit-maximizing price becomes "stuck" at $39.99.

Interview studies asked business managers several different questions relating to psychological pricing points, the most relevant of which to our discussion here is "How important are psychological price points in deterring price increases in your company?" As with the theories above, the responses yield mixed evidence: 59 percent responded price points were totally unimportant, 16 percent responded they were of minor importance, 15 percent responded they were of moderate importance, and 10 percent responded they were very important. So this is yet another theory of price stickiness that cannot be claimed to be *the* theory of price stickiness but does seem to have some relevance.

Theory V: Menu Costs

The predominant New Keynesian theory of price stickiness is that the very act of changing prices itself entails costs. Indeed this is also the simplest of theories of price stickiness. The basic idea is most easily illustrated with an example. Suppose that a restaurant is considering increasing the prices of some of the items on its menu. Presumably price increases are being considered because they would be in the best interest of the restaurant—that is, the price increases would presumably increase total profit. To make the example concrete, suppose that at current demand conditions, if the restaurant could costlessly change its prices, $1,000 in extra total profit would be generated. However, in order to implement its price changes, the restaurant would have to print new menus. If the restaurant had to pay its printer $2,000 to print new menus, it clearly is not in the interest of the firm to change its prices—indeed changing prices would cause total profit to decrease by $1,000, so the firm instead chooses to hold its prices steady. This example suggests the terminology: a **menu cost** is a cost incurred by a firm due to the price-adjustment process itself—in our example, it is literally the price of printing new menus.

14

Real Business Cycle Theory

Real business cycle (RBC) theory is the other dominant strand of thought in modern macroeconomics. For the most part, RBC theory has held much less sway among policy-makers than has New Keynesian theory. Among theoretical macroeconomists, however, RBC theory is very well-known and well-understood and even provides the foundations for some of New Keynesian theory.[1] Although there are a number of ways in which RBC theory differs from New Keynesian theory, we will focus on two differences. The most important difference by far is that RBC theory eschews the idea of sticky prices, while New Keynesian theory embraces it. RBC theory views prices as fully flexible—that is, all prices can be and are re-set very frequently. Even more precisely, RBC theory supposes that perfect competition in all markets is a good starting point for analyzing the macroeconomy. Second, RBC theory does not view exogenous shifts of consumption demand as a good description of data but rather "shifts in supply" as the predominant reason for macroeconomic fluctuations.

The basic mechanics that we will use to sketch out the main elements of RBC theory are the theory of the representative firm, the simple consumption–savings model, and the static consumption–leisure model. We could instead employ the intertemporal consumption–leisure model, rather than the simple consumption–savings model and the static consumption–leisure model in tandem. As we saw earlier, though, the algebra becomes quite messy and graphical tools become difficult to use. RBC theorists do in fact use the intertemporal consumption–leisure model in their workhorse models, but we will be able to develop the basic results using the two models together.

The RBC Technology Shock

Recall from our discussion of the aggregate production function $f(k,n)$ that we could augment it with a technology parameter A, so that total output is given by $A \cdot f(k,n)$. This

---

1. This is not the staggered price-setting that we emphasized. RBC theory has made important contributions to the understanding of macroeconomics despite never having taken center stage in policy debates. The pioneering work of Ed Prescott and Finn Kydland, widely viewed as the "fathers" of RBC theory, was finally widely recognized in 2004 when they were jointly awarded the Nobel Prize in Economic Sciences.

technology parameter is usually identified with the Solow residual, which is a measure constructed from data on output, capital, and labor. We describe how to compute Solow residuals soon. This way of measuring technology has the virtue that it does not require taking a stand on what constitutes "technology"—that is, it does not require identifying the state of "technology" of an economy with, say, the number of computers it uses or with the number of PhDs it employs or with how many people use wireless Internet connections, or any number of other measurements you might be able to think of that somehow capture how "technologically advanced" an economy is.

The most commonly-used production function in RBC theory (and also in New Keynesian models) is the **Cobb–Douglas production function**

$$f(k, n) = k^\alpha n^{1-\alpha}, \tag{1}$$

in which the parameter α measures the percentage of total GDP that goes toward paying for the costs of capital used in production and the value $1 - \alpha$ measures the percentage of total GDP that goes toward paying for the costs of labor used in production. More common terminology is that "α is capital's share of output" and "$1 - \alpha$ is labor's share of output." Empirical evidence shows that for the United States α is about 0.33. Thus about one-third of the total value of goods and services produced (i.e., GDP) pays for the capital used in production, while the remaining two-thirds pays for labor costs.

To illustrate how to compute Solow residuals (and hence the level of technology), consider the following example. Suppose that it is known (i.e., can be measured) that in the year 2003 the capital stock of the economy was $k = 1,000$ and the quantity of labor used was $n = 8$. Suppose also that the Cobb–Douglas function $k^\alpha n^{1-\alpha}$ describes the economy in question, and it is known (or at least estimated) that $\alpha = 1/3$. Finally, total output (GDP) in the year 2003 was $y = 50$. Using this information, it is possible to compute the level of technology as that amount left "unaccounted for" in the transformation of inputs into outputs. Because we know that $y = A \cdot f(k, n) = A \cdot k^\alpha n^{1-\alpha}$, we can back out the value of A during this period. From the given data it follows that $A = 1.2$. Now suppose that in the year 2004, the capital stock, the quantity of labor used, and the production function (including capital's share α) all remained unchanged but total output was $y = 60$. Again, using the production function, we can conclude that in 2004, $A = 1.5$, meaning technology improved between 2003 and 2004. This notion of "technology" is a very broad and in some sense vague one—it simply identifies "technology" as some unexplained factor that changes the nature of the production process. In our simple example, the capital stock and quantity of labor did not change between 2003 and 2004, yet output increased. The reason for this may be manifold: the quality of computers and machines used in production might have improved; decreased government regulation might have removed hindrances on companies' practices; the state of knowledge of workers in the economy might have advanced (i.e., people become more educated), and so on. As this list suggests, this macroeconomic notion of "technology" need not correspond literally to the usual notion of technology, that of computers and the Internet, for example.[2]

Technology Shocks and Aggregate Fluctuations: An Overview

Unexplained variations in the technology parameter A should be viewed as supply shocks because they affect the production function, which ultimately determines the supply function of an economy. This stands in contrast to New Keynesian theory, which holds that shocks to aggregate demand—in the form of shocks to government policy or consumer preferences—provide the important impetus for business cycles. In the influential study that effectively launched the RBC school of thought, Kydland and Prescott (1982) found that fluctuations in the Solow residual accounted for well over half of fluctuations in GDP, leading them to conclude that a theory of business cycles could be built with technology as its centerpiece.

Before we study in more depth how RBC theory works, we sketch the basic outline of the theory. With perfect competition, the real wage rate and the real rental rate of capital in the economy respond to technology shocks immediately.[3] For simplicity, assume that it is consumers rather than firms that own the capital that is used in production and that consumers rent their capital on a period-by-period basis to firms, in addition to supplying labor to firms.[4] Consider a temporary positive rise in productivity. In terms of total output for a given quantity of k and n, the rise in A causes the production function to rotate upward around the origin when viewed in both y–n space and in y–k space, as we saw in our earlier study of the theory of the representative firm and investment demand. The marginal product of each factor of production is thus larger, holding all else constant. With perfectly competitive factor markets this means that the price of each factor rises (in this case, the wage and rental rate). Intuitively, the usual notion of the "law of supply" tells us that when price increases, supply will increase. The rise in capital and labor, coupled with the initial rise in A unambiguously causes total output to rise both in the present *and* the future.

In what follows we use w to denote the real wage and r to denote the real rental rate of capital. Also, for simplicity, we assume that the labor tax rate is always zero, so that $t = 0$.

---

2. Indeed, when Nobel Prize winning economist Robert Solow first proposed this way of measuring technology, he likened it to "a measure of ignorance," since ultimately it is simply an unexplained (a "residual") aspect of the production process, one that we do not understand. At the time it was effectively just an accounting exercise. But RBC theory re-cast the Solow residual as the centerpiece of a new view of macroeconomics.

3. That is, no prices—and the real wage and the real rental rate are, after all, prices—are "sticky" at all.

4. You may not think this is a simplification at all, given that in reality firms are usually thought of as "owning" their capital. Ultimately, however, it is the stakeholders of the firms that own the firm and hence the capital—in our theoretical model, this reduces to the representative consumer.

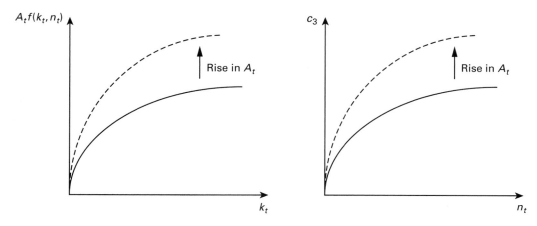

Figure 14.1
A rise in A_t causes output to rise for any given quantity of capital and labor

Technology, Factor Prices, and Output

With the production function $A \cdot f(k, n)$, the marginal product with respect to capital is given by $A \cdot f_k(k, n)$ and the marginal product of labor is given by $A \cdot f_n(k, n)$. Here $f_k(k, n)$ and $f_n(k, n)$ denote the derivatives of the function f with respect to k and n, respectively. Notice that these derivatives are in general themselves functions of both k and n, as suggested by the notation. From our study of firms we know that these marginal product functions determine the demand functions for labor and capital. The important feature now to consider is that changes in A shift these demand functions.

Suppose that A rises suddenly. Then, for any given quantity of labor and capital, the output function becomes steeper (i.e., the slope increases)—which graphically is what it means for the marginal product to rise. This situation is depicted in figure 14.1.

Figure 14.2 illustrates the effect on the marginal product of labor from a different perspective, plotting the marginal product directly on the vertical axis, rather than leaving it implied by a plot of the output function as in figure 14.1. The rise in A shifts the marginal product of labor outward. A profit-maximizing firm will hire labor only to the point at which the marginal product equals the wage. For a given wage, a rise in A raises the profit-maximizing quantity of labor any given individual firm desires. But the wage itself will rise, as figure 14.3 illustrates. Figure 14.3 shows the aggregate labor market. The labor demand function is a horizontal summation of each individual firm's demand function (which in turn is simply the marginal product function), and the labor supply function is that derived from the consumption–leisure model. Note that here we are assuming that the representative consumer is in the upward-sloping portion of the labor supply curve. As figure 14.3 shows, the equilibrium real wage rises, and the aggregate quantity of labor

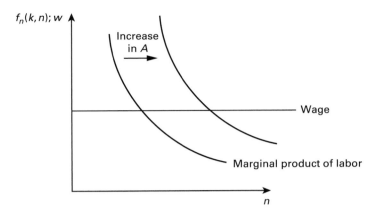

Figure 14.2
Marginal product of labor rises when A rises. For a given wage, the optimal quantity of labor demanded by a firm rises.

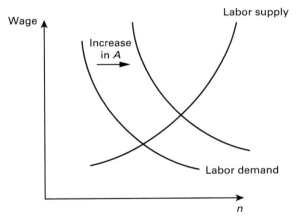

Figure 14.3
Equilibrium real wage rises in the aggregate labor market when technology improves

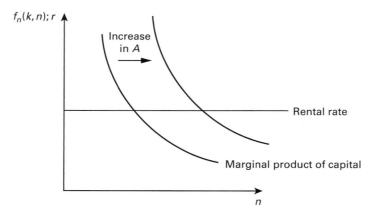

Figure 14.4
Marginal product of capital rises when A rises. For a given rental rate, the optimal quantity of (future) capital demanded by a firm rises.

hired increases. Thus, returning to figure 14.2, we see that the wage from the perspective of the price-taking representative firm also rises but not enough to prevent it from, on net, hiring more labor than before the increase in A.

The effects on the market for capital are qualitatively similar. Figure 14.4 shows that the marginal product of capital shifts out due to the rise in A. A profit-maximizing firm will hire (future) capital only to the point at which the marginal product equals the rental rate. For a given rental rate, a rise in A raises the profit-maximizing quantity of (future) capital any given individual firm desires. But the rental rate itself will rise, as figure 14.5 illustrates. Figure 14.5 shows the aggregate market for savings and investment.[5] As figure 14.5 shows, the equilibrium rental rate rises, and the aggregate quantity of investment undertaken increases. Thus, returning to figure 14.4, we see that the rental rate from the perspective of the price-taking representative firm also rises but not enough to prevent it from, on net, undertaking more investment than before the increase in A. Figure 14.5 also shows that in funds-market equilibrium, the representative consumer saves more due to the rise in A.

Given all the effects of an increase in A that we have traced out, the effect on total output y is clear. The increase in A led to an increase in both *future* k and current n through its effects on factor prices. The function $k^{\alpha}n^{1-\alpha}$ is strictly increasing in both arguments, so total output $y = A \cdot k^{\alpha}n^{1-\alpha}$ unambiguously increases in both the current period as well as the future.

---

5. Because there is an increasing relationship (in fact linear in the way that we studied firm behavior) between demand for future capital and current investment, we can make the jump from the market for (future) capital to the funds market of figure 14.5.

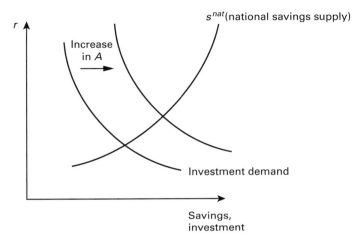

Figure 14.5
Equilibrium rental rate rises in the aggregate funds market when the technology improves.

Now that we have traced out the aggregate effects, we examine the representative consumer's response along both the static consumption–leisure margin and the consumption–savings margin. This analysis actually becomes simple because we already know what the aggregate effects are—in this sense the rest of the analysis is simply "looking under the hood."

Effects on Consumption–Leisure Margin

The effects on the consumer's optimal choice along the consumption–leisure margin are particularly simple to describe—indeed they are identical to what we have already studied. Recall from above that we are assuming that the economy is in the upward-sloping portion of the labor supply curve. This means that as the real wage rises and the budget constraint steepens as a result, the new optimal choice of (c, l) in the current period features higher consumption and *less* leisure.[6]

Effects on Consumption–Savings Margin

The effects on the consumer's optimal choice along the consumption–savings margin are more subtle than we presented earlier because, unlike in our earlier analysis, the consumer's

---

6. The slope of the budget constraint in the static consumption–leisure model is, recall, $-(1 - t)(W/P)$. In our discussion here, we have assumed that the labor tax rate is zero; recall that the real wage is simply the nominal wage divided by the aggregate price level W/P. Thus a rise in the real wage causes the budget line to steepen.

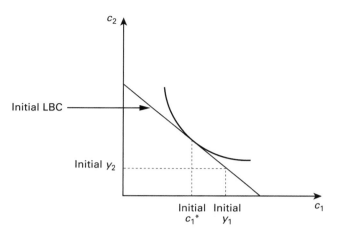

Figure 14.6
Initial optimal choice, before the rise in A. The slope of the LBC is $-(1 + r)$ in the case where there are no distortionary taxes.

income y (which equals GDP if consumers are the owners of both labor *and capital*) does not remain constant when the real rental rate increases.[7] We will frame our discussion here in terms of the real LBC of the consumer.

Figure 14.6 shows the consumer's initial consumption–savings decision before the improvement in technology that raises the rental rate. We assume no distortionary taxes, so the slope of the LBC is $-(1+r)$. As we have already traced out, the rise in A causes the rental rate r to rise. We know that this causes the LBC to steepen. However, rather than pivoting around the point marked (y_1, y_2) in figure 14.6, the ordinates y_1 and y_2 both increase because total output increases due to the rise in A.

Let's make this idea more precise. We've already seen above how and why a rise in A leads to a rise in total output. Suppose that the rise in A is purely temporary—it occurs unexpectedly in period 1, and then in period 2 A reverts to its normal value. Even though the rise in A occurs only for period 1, its effects on total output are felt in both periods 1 and 2 due to the effect on investment.

With consumers owning both labor *and* capital, total output in any given time period is paid to consumers. Total output is higher in period 1 due to improved technology *and* the rise in labor supplied, so the representative consumer's income in period 1, y_1, rises. In period 2, total output, and hence the consumer's income, is higher as well. The reason that total output is higher in period 2, even though by then A has reverted to its previous value, is that the increased investment in period 1 means that the capital stock in period 2 is higher

---

7. Recall from our earlier presentation of the simple consumption–savings model that the consumer had no control over his income—that is no longer the case here.

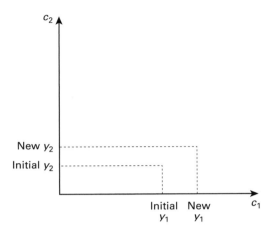

Figure 14.7
Temporary rise in A in period 1 leads to higher income for the consumer in both period 1 and period 2

than it otherwise would have been. The increase in the capital stock means that period-2 output will rise as well. Graphically the point through which the consumer's LBC must pass moves as shown in figure 14.7.

Figure 14.8 then adds the LBCs to the diagram in figure 14.7. Note that the new LBC is steeper because r is larger and passes through the point marked (new y_1, new y_2) rather than the point marked (initial y_1, initial y_2). That is, the LBC both shifts and rotates, rather than just rotating as in the simple consumption–savings model.

Finally, figure 14.9 illustrates how the optimal choice of consumption across time changes. We see that consumption rises in both period 1 and period 2. However, consumption in period 1 does not rise by as much as income rises in period 1—we can conclude this because the horizontal distance between the new c_1^* and the initial c_1^* is smaller than the distance between the new y_1 and the initial y_1.[8] The consumer thus optimally spends only part of the gain in period-1 income and saves the rest for period 2, when he can again consume more than originally planned. The consumer thus smooths the gain in period-1 income over time—this illustrates the important principle of *consumption-smoothing*. The intuition for this result is reasonable—when faced with a rise in current income, individuals typically increase their current spending less than one for one with the rise in current income.[9] With consumption-smoothing, private savings in period 1 rises—which we

8. This need not always be the case—it actually depends critically on the shape of the indifference curves (i.e., it depends critically on the exact functional form of the utility function). We've illustrated here the most usual assumption made in modern macroeconomics models, however.

9. Another way to state this result, which should be familiar from introductory macroeconomics, is that the marginal propensity to consume (out of current income) is typically taken to be less than one. A one-dollar rise in current income thus leads to a less than one-dollar rise in current consumption.

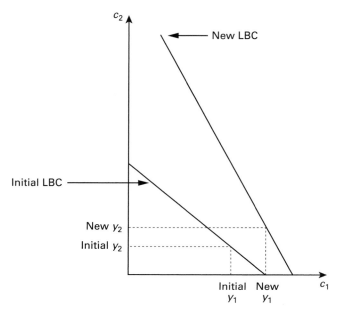

Figure 14.8
Following the rise in A and the resulting rise in r, the consumer's income rises in both period 1 and period 2. The new LBC is steeper than the initial LBC and passes through the new income point.

already knew from our analysis of the aggregate funds market above. Now we have also analyzed the same effect from the representative consumer's perspective.

Putting It Together—Business Cycle Fluctuations

With the foregoing descriptions of the effects of a change in technology, we are ready to understand how fluctuations in technology lead to the periodic ups and downs, termed business cycles, of the economy. A temporary rise in A causes the two factors of production, labor and capital, to be more productive on the margin. The increased productivity leads to increases in the real wage and the real rental rate, which induces both increased labor supply and increased private savings. In equilibrium in the funds market, increased savings means increased investment, which in turn means a higher *future* (i.e., period 2) capital stock. Thus output (equivalently, income) rises in both period 1 and 2—in the parlance of the RBC literature, the temporary (i.e., for only one period) technology shock leads to a persistent (i.e., for more than one period) change in output and consumption. To test your understanding of the basics of RBC theory, it is useful for you to trace out for yourself the effects of a temporary decline in A.

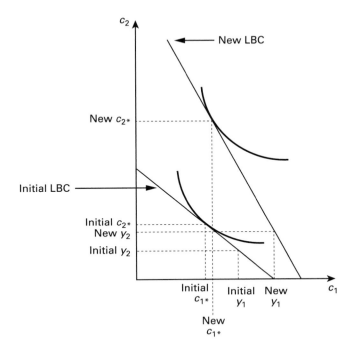

Figure 14.9
Optimal consumption in both period 1 and period 2 rises following the temporary rise in A

III
POLICY ANALYSIS

Based on the macroeconomic frameworks constructed in part I, and with some historical context provided in part II, part III takes up two important policy applications.

Chapter 15 describes an application of our frameworks to monetary policy, in a positive sense (we will consider normative issues for monetary policy in parts IV and V). After a recap of the interaction between money markets and bond markets, the main objectives are to understand the central bank's control of money supply and interest rates both in the short run (as business cycle fluctuations of the economy are occurring) and in the long run (when the economy is at its steady state).

Chapter 16 takes us through an application to both fiscal policy and monetary policy, with a focus on the interactions between congressional authority on the fiscal budget and the central bank's (supposed?) control of monetary and interest rate matters.

15

Monetary Policy in the Intertemporal Framework

We have for the most part ignored the role of money and thus monetary policy in our study so far. This is because the main issues we have been considering—in particular, the idea of optimal decision-making by representative agents, which lead to the benchmark consumption–leisure and consumption–savings optimality conditions—turn out to not require explicit consideration of money.

Our lack of meaningful inclusion of "money" is also in part due to the fact that it has proved somewhat difficult to construct a simple framework for the three distinct roles that "money" plays in modern society. For centuries (or perhaps millennia) those three distinct roles have been thought to be:

1. Medium of exchange (which circumvents the problems of barter exchange, which is nearly impossible in developed economies)

2. Unit of account (e.g., if you spend US dollars at a US store, the price tags will be denoted in numbers of US dollars, rather than in, say, numbers of ballpoint pens)

3. Store of value (if a piece of fruit were used to make payments, one piece of fruit would obviously decay very quickly, within days or weeks at best—which implies that its value erodes quickly—whereas one piece of fibrous and secure paper that displays George Washington's portrait is likely to last for decades)

Despite the theoretical difficulty of incorporating the "hows" and "whys" of particular societies or countries or eras settling on a commonly understood definition of "money," it is virtually entirely about money around which the divide between the RBC school of thought and the New Keynesian school of thought emerges. To illustrate the fundamental difference between the two theories and hence the fundamental split in modern macroeconomic theory, we need to develop a concept of **money market equilibrium**, which in turn requires both money demand and money supply. We will take a shortcut, and widely used approach, which is the **money-in-the-utility (MIU) function** framework to generate demand for money.

Simply put, the MIU approach simply inserts (real) money—that is, the purchasing power of monetary units—as an argument to the representative consumer's utility function.

Before getting to the economics of and short-run and long-run policy recommendations that emerge from the MIU framework, though, let's refresh ourselves on the linkages between monetary markets and bond markets.

Government Bond Market

You should already be familiar with the concepts briefly presented in this section. But because the connection between monetary markets and bond markets is crucial for understanding how monetary policy operates, a brief recap seems appropriate.

We assume that the bonds are all government bonds.[1] In "conventional" times, the Federal Reserve implements its policy decisions via open market purchases or sales of US government bonds. Moreover we assume all bonds are nominal bonds, meaning that each unit of a bond pays back a fixed amount of currency.

We will speak of a single government bond market within a country, even though there are many different types of bonds issued by governments, distinguished primarily by their maturity length and face value. A bond's **maturity length** is the time from issuance until the full value of the bond is repaid to the bondholder, while a bond's **face value** is the full value that is repaid upon maturity. For example, the US government issues one-month Treasury bills, three-month Treasury bills, six-month Treasury bills, two-year Treasury notes, three-year Treasury notes, five-year Treasury notes, and ten-year Treasury notes of various face values.[2]

Bonds are simply loans, a point that is often misunderstood. Regardless of a bond's maturity length and face value, a government bond is simply a loan that a bondholder provides to the government to be repaid at a later date with interest. The amount to be repaid at the pre-specified date is the bond's face value.

Because the face value is not repaid until some future time period, the amount that a bondholder would be willing to pay *in the current period* for a bond of face value FV dollars is something less than FV dollars. The reason for this is simply the time-discounting of future values. For example, $100 one year from now is likely worth less than $100 to you right now—in other words, you are likely to be willing to accept something less than $100 at this instant in lieu of receiving nothing now and $100 one year from today.

Because of time-discounting, the period-t price (denoted P_t^b) of a one-period maturity bond is related to its face value FV_{t+1} and the nominal interest rate i_t, which represents the interest component between period t and period $t + 1$. The relationship between these three objects is

---

1. There exist also corporate bonds (bonds issued by companies) and hence markets for corporate bonds, which are important markets. However, for standard, or "conventional," monetary policy purposes, it is fairly irrelevant which types of bonds exist, so we will ignore corporate bond markets.

2. There are also many other maturity lengths of US government bonds.

$$P_t^b = \frac{FV_{t+1}}{1+i_t}.$$

The way this expression is written makes it seem that it defines the price of a bond. But a common interpretation of this expression is that it instead defines the nominal interest rate i_t because at any point in time a bond's face value and the amount bond demanders are willing to pay are known. Thus knowledge of P_t^b and FV_{t+1} can be thought of as defining i_t.

Algebraically we can emphasize this relationship by simply rearranging the expression above to isolate for the nominal interest rate, which is

$$i_t = \frac{FV_{t+1}}{P_t^b} - 1.$$

These two equations are obviously equivalent to each other.

We also include three other simplifying points for the sake of ease of the ensuing analysis.

1. The face value is always equal to $FV = 1$; hence we can drop the time subscript and the tedious-to-write FV.

2. In practice, there are two main types of bonds—coupon bonds and zero-coupon bonds. A coupon bond is one that makes interest payments (called "coupon payments") to the bondholder at specified times before a final payment of the face value at the maturity date, while a zero-coupon bond offers no intermediate payments before the payment of the face value at the maturity date. For convenience, we will suppose that all bonds are zero-coupon bonds because it does not matter for either the short-run or long-run analysis.

3. Nominal bond repayments are always fully repaid on time.

The last point says the government never defaults on its nominal bond obligations, which, if we zoom in on the US government, is true.

Money-in-the-Utility (MIU) Function and Money Demand

Next let's bring in the infinite-horizon framework. The particular financial asset application when we first considered the infinite-horizon framework was stock-market pricing. But a broader theme that emerges from the previous analysis is about *asset pricing* in general, regardless of the particular type of financial asset under consideration. In the expanded infinite-period framework here, there will be three distinct types of assets: stocks, money, and bonds. Figure 15.1 portrays this richer class of financial assets and the timing of events.

Mathematically, we augment the representative consumer's period-t utility function to now include **money demand** as an argument—in particular, the demanded quantity of

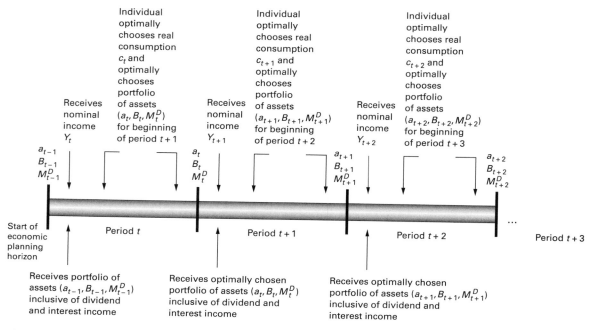

Figure 15.1
Timeline of events in infinite-period monetary framework

money, which is the essence of the MIU model. Suppose that the representative consumer's period-t utility function is

$$u\left(c_t, \frac{M_t^D}{P_t}\right),$$

in which M_t^D / P_t is the consumer's demand for **real** money balances—that is, for the **purchasing power** that a **given nominal demand** M_t^D holdings provides. Overall, the real money demand argument is a stand-in for the various roles that money plays in different time periods, as described earlier.

Because of the subjective discount factor $\beta \in (0,1)$ (which carries over from our earlier analysis of the infinite-period framework), the **lifetime discounted utility** from the perspective of the very beginning of period t can be stated as

$$u\left(c_t, \frac{M_t^D}{P_t}\right) + \beta u\left(c_{t+1}, \frac{M_{t+1}^D}{P_{t+1}}\right) + \beta^2 u\left(c_{t+2}, \frac{M_{t+2}^D}{P_{t+2}}\right) + \beta^3 u\left(c_{t+2}, \frac{M_{t+3}^D}{P_{t+3}}\right) + \dots$$

$$= \sum_{s=0}^{\infty} \beta^s u\left(c_{t+s}, \frac{M_{t+s}^D}{P_{t+s}}\right);$$

the second line writes the present-value lifetime utility function compactly using the summation operator Σ.

During every time period, an optimal "rebalancing" among the three assets in the portfolio occurs. This is described in the period-t budget constraint of the consumer,

$$P_t c_t + P_t^b B_t + M_t^D + S_t a_t = Y_t + M_{t-1}^D + B_{t-1} + (S_t + D_t) a_{t-1},$$

in which, as in the basic asset-pricing framework, P_t is the nominal price of consumption, S_t is the nominal price of a unit of stock in period t, and D_t is the nominal dividend per share in period t. Notice the timing of the budget constraint: in period t, the consumer chooses nominal money holdings to carry into period $t + 1$.[3] (And see also figure 15.1.)

In turn is implied that the period $t + 1$ flow budget constraint is

$$P_{t+1} c_{t+1} + P_{t+1}^b B_{t+1} + M_{t+1}^D + S_{t+1} a_{t+1} = Y_{t+1} + M_t^D + B_t + (S_{t+1} + D_{t+1}) a_t,$$

the period $t + 2$ flow budget constraint is

$$P_{t+2} c_{t+2} + P_{t+2}^b B_{t+2} + M_{t+2}^D + S_{t+2} a_{t+2} = Y_{t+2} + M_{t+1}^D + B_{t+1} + (S_{t+2} + D_{t+2}) a_{t+1},$$

and so on, for periods $t + 3$, $t + 4$, $t + 5$, ….

Optimal Choice

The sequential Lagrange problem stated in nominal terms is

$$
\begin{aligned}
u\left(c_t, \frac{M_t^D}{P_t}\right) &+ \beta u\left(c_{t+1}, \frac{M_{t+1}^D}{P_{t+1}}\right) + \beta^2 u\left(c_{t+2}, \frac{M_{t+2}^D}{P_{t+2}}\right) + \beta^3 u\left(c_{t+2}, \frac{M_{t+3}^D}{P_{t+3}}\right) + \dots \\
&+ \lambda_t \cdot \left[Y_t + M_{t-1}^D + B_{t-1} + (S_t + D_t) a_{t-1} - P_t c_t - P_t^b B_t - M_t^D - S_t a_t\right] \\
&+ \beta \lambda_{t+1} \cdot \left[Y_{t+1} + M_t^D + B_t + (S_{t+1} + D_{t+1}) a_t - P_{t+1} c_{t+1} - P_{t+1}^b B_{t+1} - M_{t+1}^D - S_{t+1} a_{t+1}\right] \\
&+ \beta^2 \lambda_{t+2} \cdot \left[Y_{t+2} + M_{t+1}^D + B_{t+1} + (S_{t+2} + D_{t+2}) a_{t+1} - P_{t+2} c_{t+2} - P_{t+2}^b B_{t+2} - M_{t+2}^D - S_{t+2} a_{t+2}\right] \\
&+ \dots,
\end{aligned}
$$

which should look familiar to you—it is simply an extension of the sequential Lagrange function in our earlier study of stock-market pricing.

The first-order conditions with respect to c_t, a_t, B_t, and M_t^D are, respectively,

$$u_1\left(c_t, \frac{M_t^D}{P_t}\right) - \lambda_t P_t = 0,$$

$$-\lambda_t S_t + \beta \lambda_{t+1} (S_{t+1} + D_{t+1}) = 0,$$

$$-\lambda_t P_t^b + \beta \lambda_{t+1} = 0,$$

---

3. Mechanically, we know this because it is M_t^D, rather than M_{t-1}^D, that appears on the left-hand side of the budget constraint, and the left-hand side represents "outlays" in period t.

and

$$u_2\left(c_t, \frac{M_t^D}{P_t}\right) \cdot \frac{1}{P_t} - \lambda_t + \beta\lambda_{t+1} = 0.$$

The first condition states the usual result that the marginal utility of consumption equals the Lagrange multiplier (scaled by the price level P_t). The second first-order condition is our familiar stock-pricing equation. The third first-order condition is that on bond holdings. In the fourth first-order condition, the $1/P_t$ term arises because each individual can choose his/ her nominal money holdings, but takes the aggregate price level P_t as given. Because real, not nominal, money demand is the second argument of the utility function, the chain rule is required, which generates the $1/P_t$ term.

These four first-order conditions taken together generate many rich insights about link-ages between bonds markets and stock markets, between bond markets and monetary markets, and are the foundation of possible ideological divides between whether or not changes in monetary policy affect short-run macroeconomic conditions or long-run macro-economic conditions, or both. The following sections describe these insights in turn. As you will see, we will go back and forth between "macroeconomic theory" and "finance theory"—given the richness of the framework, the "intersection" between the two appar-ently different strands of thought turns out to be a very clear intersection.

Pricing Kernel and Asset Prices

Delving back into a bit of finance theory, we can rearrange the first-order condition on bond holdings to get

$$P_t^b = \frac{\beta\lambda_{t+1}}{\lambda_t}.$$

This already sheds a lot of light on the intersection of macro and finance! Recall from our study of stock-pricing that $\beta\lambda_{t+1} / \lambda_t$ was defined as the "pricing kernel" of the economy.

> Here it is! The price of a nominal bond equals the pricing kernel times one.[4] Or, stated from the opposite perspective, the pricing kernel of an economy equals the price of a short-term riskless nominal bond.[5]

---

4. The "one" here is simply the payoff of the nominal bond in our model—that is, we assumed that the face value, hence the payoff, of the bond is $FV = 1$.

5. The "riskless" component was mentioned above, so we can think of these nominal bonds as US government nominal bonds.

Note that P_t^b in the expression above is of the same general form as the stock-pricing equation we encountered earlier—the price of an asset (P_t^b) depends on a pricing kernel and a future payoff (which is simply $FV = 1$). Bonds are thus priced using the general type of asset-pricing equation we used to price stocks.

Continuing, the first-order condition on a_t gives us

$$S_t = \frac{\beta \lambda_{t+1}}{\lambda_t}(S_{t+1} + D_{t+1}),$$

which is our usual stock price condition. From what we now know, we can alternatively express the stock price as

$$S_t = P_t^b(S_{t+1} + D_{t+1}),$$

which explicitly shows a crucial linkage between bond prices and stock prices. Stock prices can thus be said to be keyed (partially) off of bonds prices.

The big-picture, finance-theoretic, lesson to take away here is that asset-pricing equations invariably have the same general form, regardless of what specific type of asset is being considered. That general form is

Price of asset in current period
= (Pricing kernel)×(Asset-appropriate future returns)

Fisher Equation

We can obtain the exact Fisher equation as an implication of optimal choices in this model, rather than as a relationship which we so far have seemingly "assumed" to be true.

To see this, begin with the last expression, $S_t = P_t^b(S_{t+1} + D_{t+1})$. Divide this expression through by the nominal price level P_t (which is distinct from the nominal price of a bond P_t^b) to get

$$\frac{S_t}{P_t} = P_t^b \frac{(S_{t+1} + D_{t+1})}{P_t}.$$

Next, on the right-hand side, multiply and divide by P_{t+1} / P_{t+1} (which is, of course, just multiplying by one, which is always a valid operation to conduct…) to arrive at

$$\frac{S_t}{P_t} = P_t^b \frac{(S_{t+1} + D_{t+1})}{P_{t+1}} \cdot \frac{P_{t+1}}{P_t}.$$

The real price of stock purchased in period t is S_t / P_t (because it is divided by the current price level), while the real payoff in period $t + 1$ of the stock purchased in period $t + 1$ is $(S_{t+1} + D_{t+1}) / P_{t+1}$ (because it is divided by the future price level). The period-($t + 1$) real payoff divided by the period-t real price is defined as the **real return** on the asset—that is, it is the object we have heretofore been calling the real interest rate.[6]

Letting r_t denote the real interest rate between period t and period $t + 1$, we therefore have that

$$1 + r_t = \frac{(S_{t+1} + D_{t+1}) / P_{t+1}}{S_t / P_t}.$$

With this, we can write the previous expression as

$$\frac{1}{P_t^b} = (1 + r_t) \cdot \frac{P_{t+1}}{P_t}.$$

Only one more step remains in obtaining the exact Fisher relation from first principles. To finish the algebra, note that, by construction and based on our definitions, $1 / P_t^b = 1 + i_t$, and $P_{t+1} / P_t = 1 + \pi_{t+1}$.

The previous expression can thus be rewritten as

$$1 + i_t = (1 + r_t)(1 + \pi_{t+1}),$$

which *is the exact Fisher relation.*

The economic intuition behind the Fisher equation is that it links the returns available on nominal assets (nominal bonds) and the returns available on real assets (stocks). The linkage is through inflation; once the nominal returns of bonds are adjusted by inflation, *the returns on nominal bonds are exactly equal to the returns on stocks,* provided that financial markets are "operating well."

This type of idea—that, once returns are converted into comparable units, they are equalized when markets are behaving rationally—goes by the terminology of **no-arbitrage** in finance theory. No-arbitrage relationships are key building blocks of more advanced finance theory; we defer richer consideration of issues stemming from such relationships to a more advanced course on finance theory.

The exact Fisher equation emerges naturally in any model featuring both nominal assets and any type of real asset, not just stocks. This brings us back full circle to our initial study of the two-period consumption–savings model, in which we asserted the exact Fisher equation.

---

6. Stocks are considered to be "real" assets because their payoff is generally not fixed in currency terms, whereas bonds are considered to be "nominal" assets because their payoff is generally fixed in currency terms (nonindexed bonds, at least).

Nominal Interest Rates and Money Demand

Next let's consider how the nominal interest rate i_t affects macroeconomic conditions. So far we have not exploited the information contained in the first-order conditions with respect to consumption or money holdings, but now we finally will.

Rewrite the first-order condition on nominal money holdings from above as

$$\frac{u_2\left(c_t, M_t^D/P_t\right)}{P_t} - \lambda_t = -\beta\lambda_{t+1}.$$

We know from the first-order condition on bond holdings that $\beta\lambda_{t+1} = \lambda_t P_t^b$; inserting this in the previous expression gives

$$\frac{u_2\left(c_t, M_t^D/P_t\right)}{P_t} - \lambda_t = -\lambda_t P_t^b.$$

Dividing through by λ_t,

$$\frac{u_2\left(c_t, M_t^D/P_t\right)}{\lambda_t P_t} - 1 = -P_t^b.$$

Next we can use the first-order condition on consumption to replace the $\lambda_t P_t$ term on the left-hand side, giving us

$$\frac{u_2\left(c_t, M_t^D/P_t\right)}{u_1\left(c_t, M_t^D/P_t\right)} = 1 - P_t^b.$$

The term on the left-hand side now is just the MRS between real money demand and consumption—that is, it is the ratio of the marginal utility of (real) money to the marginal utility of consumption.

As for the right-hand side of this expression, because $P_t^b = 1/(1+i_t)$, it can be stated as

$$\frac{u_2\left(c_t, M_t^D/P_t\right)}{u_1\left(c_t, M_t^D/P_t\right)} = 1 - \frac{1}{1+i_t}.$$

One final algebraic simplification gives us the **consumption–money optimality condition**

$$\frac{u_2\left(c_t, M_t^D/P_t\right)}{u_1\left(c_t, M_t^D/P_t\right)} = \frac{i_t}{1+i_t},$$

which states that the MRS between period-t real money and period-t consumption equals a function of the nominal interest rate at the representative agent's optimal choice. This optimality condition is completely analogous to the consumption–leisure optimality condition

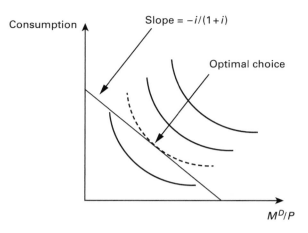

Figure 15.2
Consumption–money demand optimality condition

and the consumption–savings optimality condition with which we have become familiar. The consumption–money optimality condition states that when consumers are making their optimal choices, they choose consumption and *real* money holdings in such a way as to equate their MRS between consumption and money demand to a function of the *nominal* interest rate.

Except for interpretation, the indifference curve–budget constraint diagram in figure 15.2 ought to look familiar by now.

Also as in, say, the consumption–leisure analysis we can translate the optimal choices for any particular nominal interest rate i in the indifference curve–budget constraint diagram in figure 15.2 to a market diagram. Figure 15.3 traces the quantity of money demanded as a function of its price i. To get from figure 15.2 to figure 15.3, conduct the following thought experiment: successively lower the nominal interest rate i in figure 15.2. Along the money demand axis, it seems to be the case that M^D successively increases. If this is true, this generates the clear downward-sloping portion of the money demand function in the money-market space of figure 15.3.

Continuing the thought experiment, suppose i is extremely small—for example, $i = 0.0125$. It is apparent from the consumption–money optimality condition that the budget line is extremely flat. If i were to hit exactly zero or turn strictly negative, the optimality condition would make no sense at all. Because of the strict equality sign in the consumption–money optimality condition, it would imply that the MRS between consumption and real money demand was negative, which violates (at least 99.9999 percent of the time) basic microeconomic principles. Casual inspection of figure 15.2, which has the "usually shaped indifference curves" that are strictly convex to the origin, also visually confirms this.

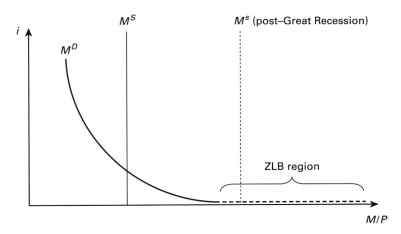

Figure 15.3
Money market whereby money demand (M^D) increases as nominal interest rate i decreases. Nominal interest rates can never fall below zero.

Hence emerges the **"zero lower bound" (ZLB) restriction** on nominal interest rates, which states exactly what we concluded: nominal interest rates can never fall below zero. The ZLB restriction is clear in the money-market space in figure 15.3.

Functional Form for Preferences

To facilitate both the short-run and long-run monetary policy analysis, as well as to formalize what was seemingly casually concluded immediately above, let's specialize our utility function to

$$u\left(c_t, \frac{M_t^D}{P_t}\right) = \ln c_t + \ln \frac{M_t^D}{P_t}.$$

This functional form displays strictly convex to the origin indifference curves in the indifference curve space of figure 15.2. And none of the policy conclusions we reach below depend on this particular functional form, but it allows for ease of algebraic manipulations to come.

The marginal utility functions associated with this utility form are obviously[7]

$$u_1\left(c_t, \frac{M_t^D}{P_t}\right) = \frac{1}{c_t}$$

---

7. Verify this for yourself. Also note well that there is no use of the chain rule here—the chain rule was already used to obtain the consumption–money optimality condition, regardless of the precise utility functional form.

and

$$u_2\left(c_t, \frac{M_t^D}{P_t}\right) = \frac{1}{M_t^D / P_t}.$$

This means that the period-t consumption–money optimality condition can be written as

$$\frac{c_t}{M_t^D / P_t} = \frac{i_t}{1+i_t},$$

which is diagrammable in figure 15.2. Or, recasting it in money-market space,

$$\frac{M_t^D}{P_t} = \left(\frac{1+i_t}{i_t}\right)c_t,$$

which is diagrammable in figure 15.3.

With all of this now in place, we are ready to examine two long-standing questions in monetary analysis, one a short-run issue, the other a long-run issue. Both the long-run and short-run issues center on the question of whether or not monetary policy is neutral.

Monetary policy is said to be **neutral** with respect to the economy if changes in monetary policy *do not* affect real aggregate outcomes in the economy. Symmetrically, monetary policy is said to be **nonneutral** with respect to the economy if changes in monetary policy *do* affect real aggregate outcomes in the economy.

Monetary Policy I: The Short Run

To consider neutrality and nonneutrality in the short run, we first have to define more rigorously what the short run is, and then look at the ordering of events within that short run.

A natural interpretation of "short run" in our multiple-period model is *one period of time,* which we label "period t."

What about the "ordering of events" within that one period of time? Figure 15.4 zooms in on period t and diagrams one example. The two main aspects around which the short-run neutrality debate revolves are whether or not an "unexpected change" in Federal Reserve monetary has occurred and the fact that money markets almost universally clear quickly.[8] Figure 15.4 contains both of these aspects.

Suppose that a monetary policy "shock" has occurred. For the sake of concreteness, suppose that the money supply in period t, M_t^S, unexpectedly turns out to be larger than markets had earlier (earlier within the short-run period t, to be more precise, and as figure 15.4 shows) anticipated. The motivation is likely meant to "boost aggregate demand."

---

8. The vastly liquid and continuously operating money market fund (which directly corresponds to the money market in our analysis) had failed to clear only three times in their 37-year history up until the 2008 financial crisis.

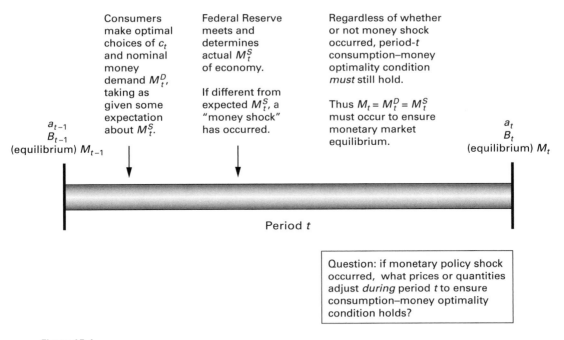

Figure 15.4
Timing of events within a given period. Second half of timeline emphasizes that money-market equilibrium is achieved in every period time of time.

Regardless of policy motivation, by definition of money market equilibrium,

$$\frac{M_t}{P_t} = \frac{M_t^D}{P_t} = \frac{M_t^S}{P_t}$$

must be true, regardless of whether a policy shock has occurred.[9] In turn the (equilibrium) money demand function (based on the particular functional form described above) requires that

$$\frac{M_t}{P_t} = \left(\frac{1+i_t}{i_t}\right) c_t.$$

For this expression to hold with equality, a nominal money supply shock requires that P_t adjusts or c_t adjusts or i_t adjusts, or any combination thereof. Notice that whatever it is that adjusts to maintain money-market equilibrium, it all occurs in the short run. That is, all of these prices and quantities are dated period t.

9. Note that in equilibrium, we drop the S and D superscripts because the very definition of equilibrium is that supply = demand.

To simplify the analysis, and because it has been empirically true in the United States from late 2008 until at least 2015, suppose the short-term nominal rate is $i_t = 0$. In terms of figure 15.3, the economy has hit the zero lower bound. The unanticipated monetary stimulus then has to affect nominal prices P_t in the short run or consumption quantity demand c_t in the short run, or both.

Let's paint the two polar extreme cases, first the strict Keynesian sticky price view, and then the strict RBC flexible price view. In the strict Keynesian case, nominal prices do not adjust in the short run. Thus, feeling flush with unexpectedly large quantities of cash, consumers will raise their demand for goods in the short run. "Monetary stimulus" has succeeded in that real quantity demanded has increased, at least in the short run. *Monetary policy is thus nonneutral in the Keynesian school of thought.*

In the strict flexible-price RBC case, nominal prices adjust very quickly. Provided that "very quickly" is shorter than the length of period t, the unexpected increase in consumption demand is quickly **neutralized**—the terminology is not coincidental—by a rapid increase in P_t. In this case, all "monetary stimulus" has created is a burst of inflation. *Monetary policy is thus neutral in the RBC school of thought.*

Figure 15.5 illustrates these two extreme cases from the perspective of the period-t goods market. The aggregate goods demand function necessarily shifts outwards due to an unexpected increase in the nominal supply—the (equilibrium) money demand expression

$$\frac{M_t}{P_t} = \left(\frac{1+i_t}{i_t}\right)c_t$$

shows this.

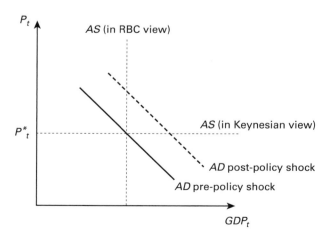

Figure 15.5
Following a positive shock to monetary policy, aggregate demand shifts outward

Whether or not this leads to a temporary increase in equilibrium GDP depends entirely on the shape of the "short-run aggregate supply function." For macro-relevant lengths of period t (which is typically quarterly because GDP accounts are compiled and referenced for the January–March quarter, April–June quarter, the July–September quarter, and the October–December quarter), data suggest that an empirically relevant slope of aggregate supply is strictly positive—somewhere between the extremely flat Keynesian AS function and the extremely vertical RBC-style AS function. For modern macroeconomists, this begs the question: What are the microeconomic reasons for "partial" nominal price stickiness?

We sidestep this issue for now, and return to it later in the more advanced New Keynesian theory in chapters 22 through 24. For the remainder of the analysis here, we consider the effects of monetary policy in the long run.

Monetary Policy II: The Long Run

We have been considering an infinite-period framework. As we were able to do in our earlier, simpler, infinite-period model absent money, it is useful to consider steady states. In our explicitly monetary model here, considering the steady state will starkly reveal a relationship important to all of monetary theory, a relationship between inflation and the rate of growth of the nominal money supply of the economy. This way of thinking about inflation commonly goes under the name of "monetarism" or the "quantity theory of money."[10]

Let's continue to use the utility function

$$u\left(c_t, \frac{M_t^D}{P_t}\right) = \ln c_t + \ln \frac{M_t^D}{P_t},$$

but, just as in the consideration of short-run effects above, none of the conclusions we reach depend on this particular functional form.

For the sake of not having to turn back several pages, recall that the money demand expression is

$$\frac{M_t^D}{P_t} = \left(\frac{1+i_t}{i_t}\right)c_t.$$

10. One of the most-often quoted sayings by the late Milton Friedman, the 1976 Nobel laureate in economics, is that "inflation is everywhere and always a monetary phenomenon," which has commonly been interpreted to mean that it is the actions of the central bank of an economy (in particular, how the central bank manages the money supply of an economy) that alone determine the rate of inflation in the economy. As we are about to see, more precisely, only in the steady state (i.e., in the "long run" or "on average") is inflation a purely monetary phenomenon.

A completely analogous condition holds in period $t - 1$ (or period $t - 2$, or period $t + 1$, etc.):

$$\frac{M_{t-1}^D}{P_{t-1}} = \left(\frac{1+i_{t-1}}{i_{t-1}}\right) c_{t-1}.$$

Let's combine these time-t and time-$(t - 1)$ versions of the consumption–money optimality condition by dividing the former by the latter; doing so gives us

$$\frac{M_t^D / P_t}{M_{t-1}^D / P_{t-1}} = \frac{c_t}{c_{t-1}} \left(\frac{1+i_t}{i_t}\right) \left(\frac{i_{t-1}}{1+i_{t-1}}\right).$$

Reorganizing terms a bit, we have

$$\frac{M_t}{M_{t-1}} \frac{P_{t-1}}{P_t} = \frac{c_t}{c_{t-1}} \left(\frac{1+i_t}{i_t}\right) \left(\frac{i_{t-1}}{1+i_{t-1}}\right).$$

From our usual definition of inflation, we have

$$\frac{P_{t-1}}{P_t} = \frac{1}{1+\pi_t}.$$

Now define the **growth rate of nominal money** in an analogous way. Specifically, define

$$\mu_t = \frac{M_t}{M_{t-1}} - 1$$

as the growth rate μ of the nominal money stock of the economy between period $t - 1$ and period t. As an example, if the nominal money supply does not change between period $t - 1$ and period t, the nominal money growth rate is $\mu_t = 0$.

Using our definitions of the inflation rate and the money growth rate, we can rewrite the money growth rate equation as

$$\frac{1+\mu_t}{1+\pi_t} = \frac{c_t}{c_{t-1}} \left(\frac{1+i_t}{i_t}\right) \left(\frac{i_{t-1}}{1+i_{t-1}}\right).$$

Now let's consider the steady state. Recall our definition of a steady state as a state of the economy when all real variables settle down to constant values over time, but nominal variables need not. Let's make the latter part of this concept a bit more precise than we did earlier: it is only nominal *level* variables that need not settle down to constant values in the long run. For example, the nominal price *level* of the economy need not settle down to a constant value in the long run. The same is true of the *level* of the nominal money supply of the economy.

Yet nominal *growth rate* variables *do* settle down to constant values in the long run. That is, the **growth rate of a nominal variable** is considered to be a real variable. Moreover interest rates, regardless of real or nominal, also settle down to constant values in the steady state.

Applying this more precise concept of a steady state to the previous expression above, we see that *all* of the variables contained in it settle down to constant values in the long-run: that is, $c_{t-1} = c_t = \bar{c}$, $i_{t-1} = i_t = \bar{i}$, $\mu_{t-1} = \mu_t = \bar{\mu}$, and $\pi_{t-1} = \pi_t = \bar{\pi}$. Imposing these steady-state values and canceling terms, we obtain

$$\frac{1+\bar{\mu}}{1+\bar{\pi}} = 1,$$

or more simply,

$$\bar{\pi} = \bar{\mu}. \tag{1}$$

Expression (1) captures the essence of the **monetarist school of thought** within macroeconomics, stating that (in the long run—i.e., in the steady state) the inflation rate of the economy is governed by the rate of growth of the money supply.

The rate of growth of the money supply is controlled by an economy's central bank because it is ultimately the economy's sole (legal) supplier of money. The higher is the growth rate of money in an economy, the higher is (in the long run) the economy's inflation rate.

Hence **monetary policy is nonneutral in the long run.** This long-run monetarist perspective is universally accepted by modern-day RBC oriented macroeconomists and modern-day New Keynesian oriented macroeconomists—both camps acknowledge that in the long run, nominal prices do adjust.[11] The neutrality debate is entirely about the short run.

We will next examine even further the causes and consequences of monetary policy in both the short run and the long run, with a special focus on the interactions between monetary policy and fiscal policy. This monetarist linkage will be in the background of many of the causes and effects we discuss there.

Chapter 15 Problem Set Questions

1. **Deriving a money demand function.** Denote by $\phi(c_t, i_t)$ the real money demand function. Here you will generate particular functional forms for $\phi(\cdot)$ using the MIU model we have studied.

---

11. This view apparently would not have been shared by Keynes himself, to whom the famous phrase "In the long run, we're all dead!" is attributed.

In an MIU model, recall that the consumption–money optimality condition can be expressed as

$$\frac{u_{m_t}}{u_{c_t}} = \frac{i_t}{1+i_t},$$

where u_{m_t} denotes marginal utility with respect to real money balances (what was named u_2 in our look at the MIU model) and u_{c_t} denotes marginal utility with respect to consumption (what was named u_1 in our look at the MIU model). In each of the following, you are given a utility function and its associated marginal utility functions. For each case, construct the consumption–money optimality condition and use it to generate the function $\phi(\cdot)$. In each case, your money demand function should end up being an increasing function of c_t and a decreasing function of i_t. (Note: Be careful to make the distinction between real money holdings and nominal money holdings. The marginal utility function u_{m_t} is marginal utility with respect to real money holdings.)

a. $u\left(c_t, \frac{M_t}{P_t}\right) = \ln c_t + \ln\left(\frac{M_t}{P_t}\right).$

b. $u\left(c_t, \frac{M_t}{P_t}\right) = 2\sqrt{c_t} + 2\sqrt{\frac{M_t}{P_t}}.$

c. $u\left(c_t, \frac{M_t}{P_t}\right) = c_t^\sigma \cdot \left(\frac{M_t}{P_t}\right)^{1-\sigma}.$

2. **M1 money and M2 money.** Consider an extended version of the infinite-period MIU framework. In addition to stocks and nominal bonds, suppose that there are two forms of money: M1 and M2. M1 money (which we will denote by M_t^1) and M2 money (which we will denote by M_t^2), both of which directly affect the representative consumer's utility. The period-t utility function is assumed to be

$$u\left(c_t, \frac{M_t^1}{P_r}, \frac{M_t^2}{P_t}\right) = \ln c_t + \ln\frac{M_t^1}{P_t} + \kappa \ln\frac{M_t^2}{P_t},$$

which has three arguments. The Greek lowercase letter "kappa" (κ) in the utility function is a number between zero and one, $0 \le \kappa \le 1$, over which the representative consumer has no control. The period-t budget constraint of the consumer is

$$P_t c_t + M_t^1 + M_t^2 + B_t + S_t a_t = Y_t + M_{t-1}^1 + (1+i_{t-1}^M)M_{t-1}^2 + (1+i_{t-1})B_{t-1} + (S_t + D_t)a_{t-1},$$

where i_t denotes the nominal interest rate on bonds held between period t and $t+1$ (and hence i_{t-1} on bonds held between $t-1$ and t) and i_t^M denotes the nominal interest rate on M2 money held between period t and $t+1$ (and hence i_{t-1}^M on M2 money held between $t-1$ and t). Thus note that M2 money potentially pays interest, in contrast to M1 money, which pays zero interest.

As always, assume the representative consumer maximizes lifetime utility by optimally choosing consumption and assets (i.e., in this case choosing all four assets optimally).

a. Using the functional form for utility given in this problem, what is the marginal rate of substitution between real M1 money and real M2 money? (Hint: You do not need to solve a Lagrangian to answer this—all that is required is using the utility function.) Explain the important steps in your argument.

b. A sudden, unexplained change in the value of κ would be interpretable as which of the following: a preference shock, a technology shock, or a monetary policy shock? Briefly explain.

Let $\phi^2(c_t, i_t, i_t^M)$ denote the real money demand function for M2 money. Note the three arguments to the function $\phi^2(.)$. Using the first-order conditions of the representative consumer's Lagrangian, generate the function $\phi^2(c_t, i_t, i_t^M)$ (i.e., solve for real M2 money demand as a function of c_t, i_t, and i_t^M). Briefly explain (economically) why i_t^M appears in this money demand function. (Note: You must determine yourself which are the relevant first-order conditions needed to create this money demand function.)

3. **The yield curve.** An important indicator of markets' beliefs/expectations about the future path of the macroeconomy is the "yield curve," which, simply put, describes the relationship between the maturity length of a particular bond (recall that bonds come in various maturity lengths) and the per-year interest rate on that bond. A bond's "yield" is alternative terminology for its interest rate. A sample yield curve is shown in the following diagram:

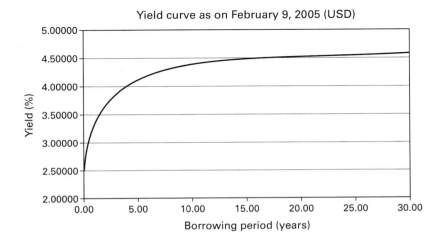

This diagram plots the yield curve for US Treasury bonds that existed in markets on February 9, 2005: as it shows, a 5-year Treasury bond on that date carried an interest rate of about 4 percent, a 10-year Treasury bond on that date carried an interest rate of about 4.4 percent, and a 30-year Treasury bond on that date carried an interest rate of about 4.52 percent.

Recall from our study of bond markets that prices of bonds and nominal interest rates on bonds are negatively related to each other. The yield curve is typically discussed in terms of nominal interest rates (as in the graph above). However, because of the inverse relationship between interest rates on bonds and prices of bonds, the yield curve could equivalently be discussed in terms of the prices of bonds.

In this problem, you will use an enriched version of our infinite-period monetary framework from this chapter to study how the yield curve is determined. Specifically, rather than assuming the representative consumer has only one type of bond (a one-period bond) he can purchase, we will assume the representative consumer has several types of bonds he can purchase—a one-period bond, a two-period bond, and, in the later parts of the problem, a three-period bond.

Let's start just with two-period bonds. We will model the two-period bond in the simplest possible way: in period t, the consumer purchases B_t^{TWO} units of two-period bonds, each of which has a market price $P_t^{b,TWO}$ and a face value of one (i.e., when the two-period bond pays off, it pays back one dollar). The defining feature of a two-period bond is that it pays back its face value *two* periods after purchase (hence the term "two-period bond"). Mathematically, then, suppose that the representative consumer has a lifetime utility function starting from period t:

$$\ln c_t + \ln\left(\frac{M_t}{P_t}\right) + \beta \ln c_{t+1} + \beta \ln\left(\frac{M_{t+1}}{P_{t+1}}\right) + \beta^2 \ln c_{t+2} + \beta^2 \ln\left(\frac{M_{t+2}}{P_{t+2}}\right)$$
$$+ \beta^3 \ln c_{t+3} + \beta^3 \ln\left(\frac{M_{t+3}}{P_{t+3}}\right)...,$$

and his period-t budget constraint is given by

$$P_t c_t + P_t^b B_t + P_t^{b,TWO} B_t^{TWO} + M_t + S_t a_t = Y_t + M_{t-1} + B_{t-1} + B_{t-2}^{TWO} + (S_t + D_t)a_{t-1}.$$

(Based on this, you should know what the period $t + 1$ and period $t + 2$ and period $t + 3$, etc., budget constraints look like.) This budget constraint is identical to that discussed in the chapter, except for the terms regarding two-period bonds. Note carefully the timing on the right-hand side—in accordance with the defining feature of a two-period bond, in period t, it is B_{t-2}^{TWO} that pays back its face value. The rest of the notation is just as discussed in the chapter, including the fact that the subjective discount factor (i.e., the measure of impatience) is $\beta < 1$.

a. Qualitatively represent the yield curve shown in the diagram above in terms of prices of bonds rather than interest rates on bonds. That is, with the same maturity lengths on the horizontal axis, plot (qualitatively) on the vertical axis the prices associated with these bonds.

b. Based on the utility function and budget constraint given above, set up an appropriate Lagrangian in order to derive the representative consumer's first-order conditions with respect to both B_t and B_t^{TWO} (as usual, the analysis is being conducted from the perspective of the very beginning of period t). Define any auxiliary notation that you need in order to conduct your analysis.

c. Using the two first-order conditions you obtained in part b, construct a relationship between the price of a two-period bond and the price of a one-period bond. Your final relationship should be of the form $P_t^{b,TWO} = ...$, and on the right-hand-side of this expression should appear (potentially among other things), P_t^b. (Hint: In order to get P_t^b into this expression, you may have to multiply and/or divide your first-order conditions by appropriately chosen variables.)

d. Suppose that the optimal nominal expenditure on consumption (Pc) is equal to 1 in every period. Using this fact, is the price of a two-period bond greater than, smaller than, or equal to the price of a one-year bond? If it is impossible to tell, explain why; if you can tell, be as precise as you can be about the relationship between the prices of the two bonds. (Hint: You may need to invoke the consumer's first-order condition on consumption.)

e. Now suppose there is also a three-period bond. A three-period bond purchased in any given period does not repay its face value (also assumed to be 1) until *three* periods after it is purchased. The period-t budget constraint, now including one-, two-, and three-period bonds, is given by

$$P_t c_t + P_t^b B_t + P_t^{b,TWO} B_t^{TWO} + P_t^{b,THREE} B_t^{THREE} + M_t + S_t a_t$$
$$= Y_t + M_{t-1} + B_{t-1} + B_{t-2}^{TWO} + B_{t-3}^{THREE} + (S_t + D_t) a_{t-1},$$

where B_t^{THREE} is the quantity of three-period bonds purchased in period t and $P_t^{b,THREE}$ its associated price. Following the same logical steps as in parts b, c, and d above (and continuing to assume that nominal expenditure on consumption (Pc) is equal to one in period every period), is the price of a three-year bond greater than, smaller than, or equal to the price of a two-year bond? If it is impossible to tell, explain why; if you can tell, be as precise as you can be about the relationship between the prices of the two bonds. (Hint: You may need to invoke the consumer's first-order condition on consumption).

f. Suppose $\beta = 0.95$. Using your conclusions from parts d and e, plot a yield curve in terms of bond prices (obviously, you can plot only three different maturity lengths here).

g. What is the single most important reason (economically, that is) for the shape of the yield curve you found in part f? (This requires only a brief, qualitative/conceptual response.)

4. **The cash-in-advance (CIA) framework.** A popular alternative to the money in the utility function (MIU) framework is one in which money holdings directly facilitate transactions—that is, provide a medium of exchange role, one of the basic functions of "money" that the MIU framework captures in only a shortcut form.

Suppose that in any given time period, there are two types of consumption goods: cash goods and credit goods. "Cash goods," denoted by c_{1t}, are goods whose purchase in period t requires money, while "credit goods," denoted by c_{2t}, are goods whose purchase in period t does not require money (i.e., they can be bought "on credit"). The market nominal price of each type of good is identical, P_t.

The representative consumer consumes both cash and credit goods. Specifically, suppose the period-t utility function is $u(c_{1t}, c_{2t}, n_t)$, with n_t denoting the individual's labor during period t. (Suppose that total hours available in any given time period is 168 hours per week and that the only possible uses of time are labor or leisure.)

The consumer's period-t budget constraint is

$$P_t c_{1t} + P_t c_{2t} + M_t + P_t^b B_t = P_t w_t n_t + M_{t-1} + B_{t-1},$$

Income is earned from labor supply (with w_t denoting the market determined real wage in period t, which is taken as given by the individual), and for simplicity, suppose that there are no stock markets (hence one-period riskless bonds and money markets are the only two asset markets). The consumer's bond and money holdings at the start of period t are B_{t-1} and M_{t-1}, and at the end of period t are B_t and M_t. The individual's budget constraints for period $t + 1$, $t + 2$, …, are identical to the above, with the time subscripts appropriately updated. As always, suppose that the representative consumer's subjective discount factor between any pair of consecutive time periods is $\beta \in (0, 1)$.

In addition to the budget constraint, in each time period the representative consumer also has a cash-in-advance constraint,

$$P_t c_{1t} = M_t.$$

The cash-in-advance (CIA) constraint captures the idea that in order to purchase some goods, a certain amount of money (or more generally, "liquidity" such as checkable deposits) has to be held. In principle, the CIA constraint is an inequality constraint (specifically, $P_t c_{1t} \leq M_t$), but in analyzing this problem, you are to assume that it always holds with equality, as written above. From the standpoint of the analysis, you will conduct, because the CIA is technically an inequality constraint, you may *not* substitute the CIA constraint into the budget constraint.

The consumer's budget constraints and CIA constraints for period $t + 1, t + 2, \ldots$, are identical to the above, with the time subscripts appropriately updated.

a. Set up an appropriate sequential Lagrangian from the perspective of the beginning of period t. Define any new notation you introduce.

b. Based on the Lagrangian constructed in part a, derive the first-order conditions (FOCs) with respect to period-t choices, c_{1t}, c_{2t}, n_t, B_t, and M_t. Define any new notation you introduce.

c. Using the FOCs from above, derive the cash good/credit good optimality condition, which should have a final form $u_1(c_{1t}, c_{2t}, n_t)/u_2(c_{1t}, c_{2t}, n_t) = f(i_t)$. Note that $f(i_t)$ is a function that depends *only* on the nominal interest rate. You are to determine $f(i_t)$ as part of this problem; there should be no other variables or parameters at all on the right-hand side of the cash good/credit good optimality condition you derive. Show clearly the important steps in the algebra.

d. Suppose now that the utility function is $u(c_{1t}, c_{2t}, n_t) = \ln c_{1t} + \ln c_{2t} + v(n_t)$, in which $v(n_t)$ is some unspecified function of labor. Taking into account the fact that the CIA constraint holds with equality at the optimal choice, derive, based on this utility function and your work above, the real money demand function,

$$\frac{M_t}{P_t} = \ldots$$

e. Recall that in the MIU framework, the consumption–money optimality condition was

$$\frac{\text{Marginal utility of real money holdings}}{\text{Marginal utility of consumption}} = \frac{i_t}{1 + i_t}.$$

Compare, in terms of economics, this optimality condition to the optimality condition you obtained in part c above for the CIA framework by briefly commenting on the similarities and differences between the results predicted by the two frameworks. (Note: This does not mean restate in words the mathematics; rather, offer two or three thoughts/critiques/etc., on how and why the two frameworks do or not capture the same ideas, how and why the two frameworks perhaps are or are not essentially identical to each other, etc.)

5. **Monetary policy in the MIU model.** In this question you will analyze, using indifference curve–budget constraint diagrams, the implications of alternative nominal interest rates on the representative consumer's choices of consumption and real money balances.

Recall that, with an instantaneous utility function $u(c_t, M_t / P_t)$ (where, as usual, c_t denotes consumption and M_t / P_t denotes real money balances), the consumption–money optimality condition (which we derived in this chapter) can be expressed as

$$\frac{u_{m_t}(c_t, M_t / P_t)}{u_{c_t}(c_t, M_t / P_t)} = \frac{i_t}{1+i_t},$$

where, again as usual, i_t is the nominal interest rate, $u_c(.)$ denotes the marginal utility of consumption, and $u_m(.)$ denotes the marginal utility of real money balances.

a. Suppose that the central bank is considering setting one of two (and only two) positive nominal interest rates: i_t^1 and i_t^2, with $i_t^2 > i_t^1$. On the indifference map shown above, qualitatively (and clearly) sketch relevant budget lines and show the consumer's optimal choices of consumption and real money under the two alternative policies. Note in the diagram the point on the vertical axis marked "fixed"—this denotes a point that must lie on every budget constraint. Clearly label your diagram, including the slopes of the budget lines.

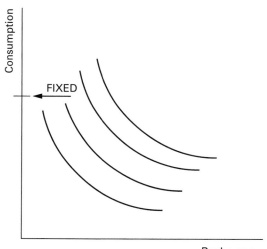

b. You are a policy adviser to the central bank, and any advice you give is based only on the goal of maximizing the utility of the representative consumer. The central bank asks you to help it choose between the two nominal interest rates i_t^1 and i_t^2 (and only these two). Referring to your work in the diagram above, which nominal interest rate would you recommend implementing? Briefly explain.

c. Suppose instead that the central bank is willing to consider setting any nominal interest rate, not just either i_t^1 or i_t^2. What would your policy recommendation be? Briefly justify your recommendation, and also in the diagram (of part a) sketch and clearly label a new budget line consistent with your policy recommendation.

16

Monetary–Fiscal Interactions

In this chapter we briefly explore some issues surrounding the interactions between monetary policy and fiscal policy. In developed countries, monetary policy-setting is effectively "independent" from fiscal policy-setting, in the sense that separate authorities control the two types of policies. For example, Federal Reserve policy makers are not the same as congressional policy makers. Even in a country where institutional arrangements seemingly insulate monetary and fiscal policy from each other, however, the conduct of each has bearing on the optimal choices of the other. Casual observation makes this point seem relatively obvious—for instance, it is not rare to hear a central bank worry about the implications of fiscal deficits for inflation and its consequences for its own policy-setting.

There are potentially very many ways in which monetary and fiscal policy interact with each other. One way in which interactions between the two are thought about is using game-theoretic tools. In such an approach fiscal authorities and monetary authorities are viewed as playing a "game" against each other. Microeconomists have developed rich game-theoretic tools to analyze various aspects of such interactions. Another approach to thinking about monetary–fiscal interactions in recent years has its grounding in the dynamic equilibrium models that have become a staple of macroeconomic theory since the RBC evolution. The focus on the analysis in this approach is on a government budget constraint that involves both fiscal and monetary interactions. We sketch the basic idea behind this second way of considering monetary–fiscal interactions. Before even beginning, we point out that using the dynamic equilibrium approach to studying monetary–fiscal interactions is in its infancy. The model we touch on here is likely only the beginning of a large field of research to be developed in coming years.

In the model there are two agents: a fiscal authority that controls government spending and taxes, and a monetary authority that controls the money supply. We describe each agent in turn and then examine how and why they interact with each other, including how which authority gets to "set policy first" has an important effect on the policy choice of the other authority.

Fiscal Authority's Budget Constraint

To describe the fiscal authority, all we need do is specify its flow budget constraint. In period t the fiscal authority has a flow budget constraint

$$P_t g_t + B_{t-1}^T = T_t + P_t^b B_t^T + RCB_t . \tag{1}$$

From left to right, the terms in this expression are the nominal amount of government spending (g_t is the real amount of spending), the nominal quantity of government bonds that must be redeemed (i.e., paid back) in period t (which is simply the value of bonds outstanding at the beginning of period t), the lump-sum taxes collected by the government, the nominal value of new bonds sold to the public in period t (each unit of which has nominal price P_t^b), and nominal receipts from the central bank, RCB_t which are the profits earned by the central bank and transferred to the fiscal authority. The notation used is as we've developed throughout the book, except for the slight modification that we denote using B_t^T the *total government bonds* outstanding at the end of period t. We assume, as before, that the face value of each bond is $FV = 1$.

In developed countries, even though the monetary authorities and fiscal authorities are distinct institutions, "profits" earned by the central bank (from its normal operations as well as from the act of printing money, over which the central bank has control) are turned over to the fiscal authority on a regular basis (on the grounds that the central bank is a nonprofit organization and is ultimately chartered by the fiscal authority). These profits that the fiscal authority receives from the monetary authority are captured by the term in RCB_t in the budget constraint equation above. The left-hand side of the equation represents outlays for the fiscal authority in period t, and the right-hand side represents income items for the fiscal authority in period t.

Monetary Authority's Budget Constraint

There also exists a budget constraint for a monetary authority (a central bank). Its purpose is essentially to control the nominal supply of money in the economy. In the United States the system that has evolved by which the Federal Reserve changes the money supply in the economy is by conducting open-market operations, which requires the Fed to trade some of its holdings of government (i.e., fiscal-issued) bonds for money. For example, if the Fed wants to increase the supply of money in circulation, it buys some government bonds from the so-called open market (hence the term "open-market operations"), for which it exchanges money, thereby increasing the quantity of money in circulation. If the Fed wants to decrease the supply of money in circulation, it does the opposite: it sells some of the government bonds it holds in its asset holdings to the open market, in exchange receiving money from the counterparties to the transactions. The money the Fed thus receives is no longer in circulation.

Denote by B_t^M the monetary authority's holdings of government bonds (as distinct from B_t^T above). The flow budget constraint of the monetary authority is thus

$$P_t^b B_t^M + RCB_t = B_{t-1}^M + M_t - M_{t-1}.$$

The left-hand side represents outlays of the monetary authority, which consist of purchases of government bonds (i.e., even the monetary authority must pay the market price P_t^b to purchase bonds—it is not simply given bonds by the fiscal authority) and the profits that must be turned over the fiscal authority. The right-hand side represents income for the monetary authority, which consists of maturing bonds B_{t-1}^M, and the printing of new money, which is the term $M_t - M_{t-1}$. As per our usual notation, M_{t-1} is the quantity of money outstanding in the economy at the end of period $t-1$ (equivalently, at the beginning of period t) and M_t is the quantity of money outstanding in the economy at the end of period t. Thus $M_t - M_{t-1}$ is the amount by which the nominal money supply changes *during* period t. If $M_t - M_{t-1} > 0$, the central bank printed money during period t, and if $M_t - M_{t-1} < 0$, the central bank removed money from circulation in period t. Changes in the money supply show up on a central bank's balance sheet; as such, they represent income items for the central bank, which thus need to be accounted for in the budget constraint.

From the money authority's budget constraint, it is easy to see that

$$RCB_t = B_{t-1}^M - P_t^b B_t^M + M_t - M_{t-1}$$

is the amount that the monetary authority ends up turning over to the fiscal authority.

Consolidated Government Budget Constraint

Combining the last way of expressing the monetary authority budget constraint with the fiscal authority budget constraint, we have

$$P_t g_t + B_{t-1}^T = T_t + P_t^b B_t^T + B_{t-1}^M - P_t^b B_t^M + M_t - M_{t-1}.$$

Next let's define the difference between the total bond issue of the fiscal authority, B_t^T, and the bond holdings of the monetary authority, B_t^M, as the quantity of bonds held by the private sector (denoted by B_t, without superscript). That is, $B_t = B_t^T - B_t^M$ is the quantity of fiscal-issued bonds not held by the central bank. B_t represents the net government debt held by the private sector, since bond repayments by the fiscal authority to the monetary authority do not "enter" the private sector. This B_t is what we considered when we studied the MIU model.

With the definition $B_t = B_t^T - B_t^M$, the preceding expression can be rearranged to give

$$P_t g_t + B_{t-1} = T_t + P_t^b B_t + M_t - M_{t-1},$$

which we refer to as the **consolidated government budget constraint** (consolidated GBC). This budget constraint links the activities of the fiscal authority—taxing, spending, and issuing bonds—with the activities of the monetary authority—changing the supply of money. The link fundamentally comes through the *RCB* that the central bank is required to turn over to the fiscal authority.

The consolidated GBC is a condition that must always hold in the economy. It thus makes clear that fiscal policy and monetary policy must be "consistent" with each other, an issue to which we now turn.

Active Fiscal Policy/Passive Monetary Policy

Suppose that when period t begins, the fiscal authority is able to commit to a particular choice of g_t, T_t, and B_t—that is, it "picks" a particular combination of spending, taxes, and debt. Suppose further that the fiscal authority makes these choices without heed to the consolidated GBC. Can it simply "ignore" the consolidated GBC when choosing its policy? The answer is yes, because there is another "free variable" in the consolidated GBC: the amount of money outstanding in the economy at the end of period t, M_t, which is under the monetary authority's control. After committing to its particular fiscal policy, the onus is then on the central bank to make the consolidated GBC hold by printing some appropriate quantity of money.

Recall that in the introduction we said game-theoretic concepts are often used to study monetary–fiscal interactions. We can apply a game-theoretic idea to the scenario above: suppose that the fiscal authority gets to "move first" (i.e., before the central bank) in that it can choose taxes, spending, and debt before the central bank chooses the money supply. As we just saw, the fiscal authority is then able to force the monetary authority into a particular action because the monetary authority must see to it that the consolidated GBC is satisfied. In the language that has developed in the field, the scenario just outlined is one in which **fiscal policy is active** (because it gets to move first and thus is not constrained in any of its choices) and **monetary policy is passive** (because it moves second and its choice is bound by the consolidated GBC). Monetary policy here is essentially just reactive (passive) to fiscal policy.

Active Monetary Policy/Passive Fiscal Policy

Suppose that the opposite scenario were true. Suppose that it is the monetary authority that gets to "move first" in that it can set whatever money supply M_t it wants (e.g., motivated by some inflation stabilization goal). In this case the fiscal authority must "react" by setting some appropriate combination of g_t, T_t, and B_t. Here we say that **monetary policy is active** (because it gets to move first and thus is not constrained in its choice) and **fiscal policy is passive** (because it moves second and *one of its choices is bound by the consolidated GBC*).

It may seem that because the fiscal authority has three instruments at its disposal (spending, taxation, and debt issuance), the fiscal authority is not all that constrained in its decisions. It is constrained, however, compared to the active fiscal policy case considered above. In the active fiscal policy case, the fiscal authority is able to choose all three of the instruments g_t, T_t, and B_t freely, knowing that the monetary authority will have to "pick up the slack" by printing some appropriate quantity of money. In contrast, when monetary policy is active, the fiscal authority is able to freely choose only two out of the three instruments g_t, T_t, and B_t: once it has fixed two of them, the third is pinned down by the consolidated GBC.

Intertemporal Government Budget Constraint

To continue our analysis of fiscal–monetary interactions, let us turn to the consolidated GBC above, which is actually a flow budget constraint, into the lifetime (or intertemporal) government budget constraint, which is the more typical form of the government budget constraint used in analyzing dynamic fiscal–monetary interactions. In transforming the flow GBC into an intertemporal one, we will also along the way introduce important terminology and ideas.

First, take the flow GBC above and divide through by the period-t price level, which gives

$$g_t + \frac{B_{t-1}}{P_t} = \frac{T_t}{P_t} + \frac{P_t^b B_t}{P_t} + \frac{M_t - M_{t-1}}{P_t}.$$

The last term on the right-hand side, $(M_t - M_{t-1})/P_t$, measures the real resources, in units of period-t goods, accruing to the government from the act of money creation: the amount of money created (which could be a negative number, whereby money is destroyed—i.e., taken out of circulation) during period t is $M_t - M_{t-1}$, and dividing by P_t, which has algebraic units of (time-t dollars/time-t goods), yields the amount of period-t goods the government earns by expanding the money supply (or loses if it contracts the money supply). These real resources are known as **seignorage revenue,** and we will often abbreviate it as sr_t. Formally,

$$sr_t = \frac{M_t - M_{t-1}}{P_t}.$$

Now to continue rearranging the GBC, we can move terms around to arrive at

$$\frac{B_{t-1}}{P_t} = \left(\frac{T_t}{P_t} - g_t + \frac{P_t^b B_t}{P_t} \right) + sr_t.$$

The left-hand side is the real amount of government debt that comes due at the start of period t, and the right-hand side is the real amount of (net) revenue the government has. This net revenue comes from monetary sources (the seignorage revenue) and fiscal sources (the difference between tax revenue plus proceeds of new bond sales and government spending).

Defining $t_t \equiv T_t / P_t$ as real tax collections in period t, and $b_t \equiv B_t / P_t$ as the real amount of government debt outstanding at the end of period t, we can express the preceding as

$$\frac{B_{t-1}}{P_t} = sr_t + \left(t_t - g_t + P_t^b b_t \right).$$

This expression is, of course, simply still the period-t GBC. The period-$(t + 1)$ GBC is analogous,

$$\frac{B_t}{P_{t+1}} = sr_{t+1} + \left(t_{t+1} - g_{t+1} + P_{t+1}^b b_{t+1} \right).$$

The objective of the next several algebraic rearrangements that we will go through is to replace the b_t term in the period-t GBC using the period-$(t + 1)$ GBC. First, multiply both sides of the latter by P_{t+1} to obtain

$$B_t = P_{t+1} sr_{t+1} + \left(P_{t+1} t_{t+1} - P_{t+1} g_{t+1} + P_{t+1}^b P_{t+1} b_{t+1} \right).$$

Next divide both sides by P_t:

$$\frac{B_t}{P_t} = \frac{P_{t+1} sr_{t+1}}{P_t} + \left(\frac{P_{t+1} t_{t+1}}{P_t} - \frac{P_{t+1} g_{t+1}}{P_t} + \frac{P_{t+1}^b P_{t+1} b_{t+1}}{P_t} \right).$$

The left-hand side, by our definition, is simply b_t. Now recall from our earlier study of dynamic models that inflation between periods t and $t + 1$ is defined by $\pi_{t+1} \equiv (P_{t+1} - P_t)/P_t$, which means that $1 + \pi_{t+1} = P_{t+1}/P_t$. Using these definitions in the last expression, we have

$$b_t = (1 + \pi_{t+1}) sr_{t+1} + \left((1 + \pi_{t+1}) t_{t+1} - (1 + \pi_{t+1}) g_{t+1} + P_{t+1}^b (1 + \pi_{t+1}) b_{t+1} \right),$$

which, despite all the algebraic manipulations, is still just the period-$(t + 1)$ GBC. Finally, we are ready to insert this into the period-t flow GBC from several steps ago; doing so gives us

$$\frac{B_{t-1}}{P_t} = sr_t + \left[t_t - g_t + P_t^b \left((1 + \pi_{t+1}) sr_{t+1} + \left((1 + \pi_{t+1}) t_{t+1} - (1 + \pi_{t+1}) g_{t+1} + P_{t+1}^b (1 + \pi_{t+1}) b_{t+1} \right) \right) \right].$$

Pulling the $(1 + \pi_{t+1})$ terms together, we have

$$\frac{B_{t-1}}{P_t} = sr_t + \left[t_t - g_t + P_t^b (1 + \pi_{t+1}) \left(sr_{t+1} + \left(t_{t+1} - g_{t+1} + P_{t+1}^b b_{t+1} \right) \right) \right],$$

and then cleverly grouping the seignorage terms together and the fiscal terms together gives us

$$\frac{B_{t-1}}{P_t} = \left[sr_t + P_t^b(1+\pi_{t+1})sr_{t+1} \right] + \left[(t_t - g_t) + P_t^b(1+\pi_{t+1})(t_{t+1} - g_{t+1}) \right] + P_t^b(1+\pi_{t+1})P_{t+1}^b b_{t+1}.$$

Recall from the MIU model (or from any monetary model) the relation between the nominal price of a bond and the nominal interest rate,

$$P_t^b = \frac{1}{1+i_t};$$

also recall the Fisher equation,

$$1 + r_t = \frac{1+i_t}{1+\pi_{t+1}}.$$

These two facts imply that

$$P_t^b(1+\pi_{t+1}) = \frac{1+\pi_{t+1}}{1+i_t} = \frac{1}{1+r_t}.$$

Using this expression for $P_t^b(1+\pi_{t+1})$ write the period-t GBC as

$$\frac{B_{t-1}}{P_t} = \left[sr_t + \frac{sr_{t+1}}{1+r_t} \right] + \left[(t_t - g_t) + \left(\frac{t_{t+1} - g_{t+1}}{1+r_t} \right) \right] + \frac{P_{t+1}^b b_{t+1}}{1+r_t}.$$

Notice that in this representation of the period-t GBC, seignorage revenue, tax revenue, and government spending in both periods t and $t + 1$ appear. If we were to substitute out the b_{t+1} term on the far right of the last expression using the period-$(t + 2)$ GBC, we would have

$$\frac{B_{t-1}}{P_t} = \left[sr_t + \frac{sr_{t+1}}{1+r_t} + \frac{sr_{t+2}}{(1+r_t)(1+r_{t+1})} \right]$$
$$+ \left[(t_t - g_t) + \left(\frac{t_{t+1} - g_{t+1}}{1+r_t} \right) + \left(\frac{t_{t+2} - g_{t+2}}{(1+r_t)(1+r_{t+1})} \right) \right] + \frac{P_{t+2}^b b_{t+2}}{(1+r_t)(1+r_{t+1})}$$

after going through a similar set of algebraic rearrangements.[1] If we then substituted out b_{t+2} using the period-$(t + 3)$ GBC, and then continued successively substituting out future

---

1. Tedious, yes, but perhaps worthwhile for you to trace through yourself to convince yourself that this is in fact correct.

real bond terms using successive flow GBCs, we would ultimately arrive at the infinite-period version of the GBC:

$$\frac{B_{t-1}}{P_t} = \sum_{s=0}^{\infty} \left[\frac{sr_{t+s}}{\prod_{s=0}^{\infty}(1+r_{t+s})} + \frac{t_{t+s} - g_{t+s}}{\prod_{s=0}^{\infty}(1+r_{t+s})} \right],$$

which, note well, involves both an infinite product and an infinite summation.[2] The successively growing products—the first term of which is $1/(1+r_t)$, the second term of which is $1/[(1+r_t)(1+r_{t+1})]$, the third term of which is $1/[(1+r_t)(1+r_{t+1})(1+r_{t+2})]$, and so on—are discount factors.[3] We will refer to this last expression as the **intertemporal government budget constraint,** which is an infinite-period version of the flow GBC obtained by chaining together *all* of the flow GBCs from period *t* into the infinite future.

Note that the right-hand side of the intertemporal GBC is a function of all current (period-*t*) and future seignorage revenue (which stems from money creation, which is in the province of the monetary authority) as well as all current and future **primary budget surpluses** (which is the difference between tax collections and government spending and is in the province of the fiscal authority). There are a host of macroeconomic implications of the intertemporal GBC, a few of which we turn to now. In the following, we essentially just take alternative views on the intertemporal GBC, in the sense that we treat some parts of it as "fixed" and ask what other parts of it "must adjust" in order to make it hold with equality.

---

2. Technically, if you do several steps of the forward substitutions and let time go to infinity, you will see that there is actually another term on the right-hand side:

$$\lim_{s \to \infty} \left[\frac{P_{t+s}^b b_{t+s}}{\prod_{s=0}^{\infty}(1+r_{t+s})} \right].$$

A technical condition that must be imposed in any well-specified dynamic macro model (including ours) is that this limit is zero; hence the infinite-period GBC above is correct. This limit being zero is the infinite-period analogue of the restriction from our very simple two-period model that $A_2 = 0$. Whether in the two-period case or the infinite-period case here, this so-called No-Ponzi condition just states, essentially, that the value of assets at the end of the economy are zero (whether the end is at the end of period 2 or at the end of "period infinity"). Analyzing this No-Ponzi restriction further is outside our scope and is better left to a more advanced course in macroeconomic theory.

3. Recall from our infinite-period model that in steady state

$$\frac{1}{\beta} = 1 + r \, ,$$

which means that

$$\beta = \frac{1}{1+r} \, .$$

Our interpretation of β was that it was consumers' discount factor (i.e., a measure of their impatience), hence the terminology here.

Before proceeding, we define one more notion: **non-Ricardian fiscal policy,** which is a policy by the fiscal authority (again, that controls taxation and government spending) in which the current and future path of "regular" fiscal instruments (i.e., taxes and spending) is *not* adjusted to ensure that the intertemporal GBC holds (or, in the terminology common in macroeconomics, to ensure that "intertemporal solvency holds"). Loosely speaking, if the fiscal authority is running a non-Ricardian fiscal policy, it does not "care" about or pay heed to the needs of intertemporal solvency when setting its current and future policy instruments.

By contrast, a **Ricardian fiscal policy** is then one in which the fiscal authority does pay heed to the intertemporal GBC when setting current and future policy. Under a Ricardian fiscal policy, the fiscal authority views itself as being constrained by the intertemporal GBC (i.e., it believes that its actions must be consistent with it), while non-Ricardian fiscal policy is unconstrained by the intertemporal GBC. Whether or not the fiscal authority believes it must satisfy its budget constraint is likely an issue we cannot resolve, since in the end, as we will now see, the (intertemporal) government budget constraint *is* satisfied—the bite comes in *which prices and/or quantities must adjust to ensure that it is satisfied.*

In all that follows the analysis is based on the intertemporal government budget constraint, which is reproduced here for convenience:

$$\frac{B_{t-1}}{P_t} = \sum_{s=0}^{\infty}\left[\frac{sr_{t+s}}{\prod_{s=0}^{\infty}(1+r_{t+s})} + \frac{t_{t+s} - g_{t+s}}{\prod_{s=0}^{\infty}(1+r_{t+s})} \right].$$

A Fiscal Theory of Inflation

Entering period t, the nominal debt stock B_{t-1} is fixed—that is, it cannot be changed (assuming no default), and hence that B_{t-1} is the nominal debt the government must repay at the start of period t. Suppose that the monetary authority, through its control of the money supply, is perfectly able to control and commit to a path through time of seignorage revenue starting from date t onward. That is, suppose the monetary authority is able to credibly commit itself to a sequence of seignorage revenue into the infinite future $(sr_t, sr_{t+1}, sr_{t+2}, sr_{t+3}, ...)$. Further suppose that it is monetary factors that (effectively) determine the price level in period t so that, once the central bank has "announced" its monetary policy (which here takes the form of the "announcement" of its path of seignorage), the price level P_t becomes fixed.

With these policy and market arrangements in place, fiscal policy, through its sequence of current and future primary fiscal surpluses (which, after all, is what the sequence of $(t_t - g_t)$ terms represents) must be set so as to satisfy the intertemporal government budget constraint. Relating this to the notions developed above, fiscal policy here can be viewed as passive: any changes in what the monetary authority is doing in terms of generating seignorage and/or any changes in the price level P_t must be met by a reaction by fiscal authorities to ensure intertemporal solvency.

Yet the active power could reside with the fiscal authority; the fiscal authority could "independently" (in our earlier terminology, "actively") set its path of $t_t - g_t$. If it is still the case that P_t is determined by factors other than the intertemporal government budget constraint, then active fiscal policy requires that the path of seignorage revenue adjusts to ensure intertemporal government solvency. Note that as viewed through the lens of the intertemporal government budget constraint, it is not necessarily the case that *current* (period-t) money creation must change if there is a change in period-t primary fiscal policy but rather that *current and/or future* seignorage generation must change.[4]

Current or future seignorage generation—which is fueled by money creation—ultimately means (higher or lower) inflation, so long as we believe that a quantity-theoretic link operates between money growth and inflation—the MIU model, to take one example, builds in the view that such a link exists, at least in the long run. Hence, with active fiscal policy and a fixed period-t nominal price level P_t, the intertemporal government budget constraint articulates a **fiscal theory of inflation.** This is nothing more than a slightly more careful restatement of our earlier active/passive distinctions: if the fiscal authority does not balance the government budget constraint, then it falls on the monetary authority to do so. Monetary policy actions in turn have consequences for inflation, but because these actions themselves were induced by fiscal policy, the outcome is ultimately a *fiscal* theory of inflation, even though the proximate cause of the inflation was "money creation."

A Fiscal Theory of the Price Level

What if in the scenario just outlined of an active fiscal policy, the monetary authority did not "blink?" What if the central bank was instead strong enough/credible enough/committed enough to its own "independent" monetary policy (presumably guided by some welfare maximization ideas in the background) that it refuses to be induced to money creation/ destruction by fiscal policies. The intertemporal government budget constraint *must* be satisfied *somehow.* But how, if neither authority "reacts" to make it hold?

The answer lies in the market-determined price level P_t. In our preceding discussion of the *fiscal theory of inflation,* we took the stand that P_t is determined by factors other than the intertemporal government budget constraint. But if neither regular fiscal policy nor monetary policy adjusts appropriately, then it must be that P_t (which, after all, is not set in

---

4. If it is not the case that current-period seignorage changes, it must be that the government debt position between t and $t + 1$ absorbs the change—though, of course, as in any intertemporal budget constraint, "intermediate" asset positions do not appear, only initial asset positions.

stone at the beginning of period t unless prices are "completely sticky") adjusts to satisfy the intertemporal budget constraint, for a given B_{t-1}.[5]

To make the discussion a bit more concrete, suppose that relative to its original plans for the sequence of $(t_{t+s} - g_{t+s})_{s=0}^{\infty}$, the fiscal authority decides to lower $(t_t - g_t)$ but leaves $(t_{t+s} - g_{t+s})_{s=1}^{\infty}$ unchanged (note carefully the time indexes here!). That is, suppose that the government decides to lower the primary fiscal surplus in period t but leave all future surpluses unchanged. Further suppose that the "independent" central bank remains committed to its plan for the money stock, which means it will not be induced to deviate from its plan for the sequence sr_{t+s}, $s = 0, 1, 2, ..., \infty$.

The government cannot/does not default on its nominal debt repayment obligation B_{t-1}. The only way, then, for the intertemporal GBC to hold is for the period-t price level P_t to rise; it must rise because the right-hand side of the intertemporal GBC has fallen (due to the reduced primary fiscal surplus in period t), which requires that the left-hand side falls, too. With B_{t-1} fixed, this requires a rise in the price level in the current period. This mechanism, by which a change in fiscal policy translates into a direct change in P_t is termed the **fiscal theory of the price level.**

We might want to say that in this case a change in fiscal policy resulted in inflation because it caused a rise in P_t. Viewed this way, there seems to be little difference between the *fiscal theory of the price level* and the *fiscal theory of inflation*. The distinction is subtle, yet important. Under the fiscal theory of the price level, any "fiscal shock" (i.e., a change in fiscal policy unanticipated by markets) translates *immediately and fully* into a *one-time* change in the nominal price level. If fiscal policy never changes again, there need be no future unanticipated changed in the nominal price level. However, under the fiscal theory of inflation, the period-t price level has nothing to do with fiscal policy from period-t onward; instead, a change in current or future fiscal policy translates into a change in money creation *at some time in the present or future,* implying *additional inflation in the future.*

In some sense the fiscal theory of inflation and the fiscal theory of the price level are polar opposite theories. The former effectively states that surprise changes in fiscal policy lead *only to future changes in inflation, but current inflation is unaffected.* The latter effectively states that surprise changes in fiscal policy lead *only to changes in current inflation, but future inflation is unaffected.* In reality, one might (probably naturally) expect that fiscal pressures are relieved through both channels—that surprise changes in fiscal policy lead to changes in both current and future inflation. Such a division of fiscal pressure on nominal prices into current pressure versus future pressure is, in practice, hard to disentangle, and indeed it probably plays out in different ways in different countries and in

---

5. There is indeed another option, one alluded to above: it could be that the government reneges on the promised B_{t-1}, which is to say, it could be that the government defaults on (part of) its nominal debt. Such an adjustment would be a very relevant one to consider for developing countries, in which debt defaults are not that uncommon. For the government of a country such as the United States, however, which has never defaulted on its debt, this situation would be a less relevant description of reality.

different time periods. It is good to understand, though, the underlying tensions present; the tensions are articulated in the fiscal theory of inflation and the fiscal theory of the price level.

Chapter 16 Problem Set Questions

1. **Unpleasant monetarist arithmetic**[6]. Consider a finite-period economy, the final period of which is period T (so that there is no period $T+1$)—every agent in the economy knows that period T is the final period of the economy. In this economy the government conducts both fiscal policy (engaging in government spending and collecting taxes) and monetary policy (expanding or contracting the money supply). The timing of fiscal policy and monetary policy will be described further below.

   The economy has now arrived at the very beginning of period T, and the period-T consolidated government budget constraint is

   $$M_T - M_{T-1} + B_T + P_T t_T = (1 + i_{T-1})B_{T-1} + P_T g_T,$$

   where the notation is as follows:

   - M_t is the nominal money supply at the end of period t.

   - B_t is the nominal quantity of government debt outstanding at the end of period t (i.e., a positive value of B_t here means that the government is in debt at the end of period t).

   - t_t is the real amount of lump-sum taxes the government collects in period t (and there are no distortionary taxes).

   - i_{t-1} is the nominal interest rate on government assets held between period $t-1$ and t, and it is known with certainty in period $t-1$.

   - g_t is the real amount of government spending in period t.

   - P_t is the nominal price level of the economy in period t.

   Once period T begins, the economic objects yet to be determined are t_T, g_T, M_T, and B_T. How P_T is set is described more fully in part a.

   a. Compute the numerical value of B_T? Show any important steps in your computations/logic.

   The remainder of this question is independent of part a. For the remainder of this question, suppose that for some reason $B_T = 0$—the fiscal authority is committed to this

---

6. This problem is based on a classic work in macroeconomic theory by Thomas Sargent and Neil Wallace (1981: "Some Unpleasant Monetarist Arithmetic," Federal Reserve Bank of Minneapolis *Quarterly Review* 5).

decision about bonds and will never deviate from it. Also suppose for the remainder of this question that $i_{T-1} = 0.10$, $B_{T-1} = 10$ (i.e., the government is in debt at the beginning of period T, given the definition of B_t), $P_{T-1} = 1$ (notice the time subscript here), and $M_{T-1} = 10$. The timing of fiscal policy and monetary policy is as follows: at the beginning of any period t, the monetary authority and the fiscal authority independently decide on monetary policy (the choice of M_t) and fiscal policy (the choices of t_t and g_t), respectively.

In parts b and c, suppose that the nominal price level is flexible (i.e., it is not at all "sticky").

b. Suppose that the fiscal side of the government decides to run a primary real fiscal surplus of $t_T - g_T = 9$ in period T. Also suppose that the monetary authority chooses a value for M_T which when coupled with this fiscal policy implies that there is zero inflation between period $T-1$ and period T. Compute numerically the real value of seignorage revenue the government earns in period T, clearly explaining the key steps in your computations/logic. Also provide brief economic intuition for why the government needs to generate this amount of seignorage revenue in period T?

c. Suppose that the monetary authority sticks to its monetary policy (i.e., its choice of M_T) you found in part b above. However, the fiscal authority decides instead to run a primary real fiscal surplus of $t_T - g_T = 8$. Compute numerically the real value of seignorage revenue the government must earn in period T as well as the inflation rate between period $T-1$ and period T. Clearly explain the key steps in your computations/logic. In particular, why is real seignorage revenue here different or not different from what you computed in part b?

In part d, assume the nominal price level is "completely sticky"—that is, the nominal price level never varies from one period to the next.

d. With "complete stickiness" of the price level, is a monetary policy that sets the level of M_T you found in part b consistent with a fiscal policy that sets a real fiscal surplus of $t_T - g_T = 8$ as in part c? In other words, can those policies work simultaneously? Explain carefully why or why not, using any appropriate mathematical or logical arguments.

e. Reviewing the scenarios posed in parts b, c, and d, address the following question in a brief discussion: what is the role of fiscal policy in determining the inflation rate and/or the nominal price level in the economy? If possible, connect your remarks to the debate between the RBC view and the New Keynesian view. (Note: There is no single correct answer here, but if you conducted the analysis above correctly, there is a generally correct theme that emerges. Also note that you are not simply being asked to summarize the results above but rather to try to draw some bigger-picture insight.)

2.   **The dynamics of fiscal policy.** President Obama and his primary economic advis-
     ers put in place large fiscal stimuli in early 2009. In early 2009, the precise details of
     the fiscal stimulus were still to be worked out, but they included tax cuts as well as
     increased government spending in the next few years.

     It is early 2009 and the new administration has just recently been seated. At the begin-
     ning of 2009 the lifetime consolidated budget constraint of the government is

$$\frac{B_{2008}}{P_{2009}} = (t_{2009} - g_{2009}) + \frac{t_{2010} - g_{2010}}{1 + r_{2010}} + \frac{t_{2011} - g_{2011}}{(1 + r_{2010})(1 + r_{2011})} + \frac{t_{2012} - g_{2012}}{(1 + r_{2010})(1 + r_{2011})(1 + r_{2012})} + \dots$$

$$+ sr_{2009} + \frac{sr_{2010}}{1 + r_{2010}} + \frac{sr_{2011}}{(1 + r_{2010})(1 + r_{2011})} + \frac{sr_{2012}}{(1 + r_{2010})(1 + r_{2011})(1 + r_{2012})} + \dots$$

     Line 1: Present discounted value (PDV) of fiscal deficits

     Line 2: PDV of seignorage

     The notation here is as follows: t denotes real lump-sum tax collections, g denotes real
     government spending, sr denotes real seignorage revenue, r denotes the real interest
     rate, B denotes nominal (one-period) government bonds, and P denotes the nominal
     price level of the economy (i.e., the nominal price of one basket of consumption).
     Subscripts indicate time periods, which we will consider to be calendar years. Note the
     ellipsis (…) in each line of the equation above.

     As indicated above, the first line of the right-hand side is the present discounted value
     of all fiscal deficits the government will ever run starting from 2009 onward, and the
     second line of the right-hand side is the present discounted value of all seignorage
     revenue that will ever result from the monetary policy actions of the Federal Reserve
     starting from 2009 onward.

     The primary economic advisers to President Obama are Treasury Secretary Timothy
     Geithner, National Economic Council Chairman Lawrence Summers, and Council of
     Economic Advisers Chairwoman Christina Romer.

     In addressing each of the following issues, no quantitative work is required at all; the
     following questions all require only conceptual analysis. Each issue should be
     addressed in no more than three or four sentences.

     a.   Geithner, because of his background as president of the New York Federal
          Reserve, implicitly advocates that no matter what fiscal policy actions the new
          administration takes, they should be designed in such a way as to have no effects
          on the conduct of monetary policy whatsoever. If this is so, what type of fiscal
          policy—a Ricardian fiscal policy or a non-Ricardian fiscal policy—does Geithner
          advocate? Briefly explain.

b. The less even-keeled that he is, Summers' comments sometimes seem to imply that the fiscal stimulus measures should not take into account any consequences they may have for the conduct of monetary policy. If the combination of tax cuts and government spending that ultimately pan out over the next few years follow Summers' advice, what are likely to be the consequences for the Federal Reserve's monetary policy in 2009 and beyond? In particular, will the Fed likely have to expand or contract the nominal money supply? Briefly explain.

c. The objective academic macroeconomist that she is, Romer typically points outs in her remarks that because fiscal policy plans (for both taxes and government spending) will almost surely be revised as the years unfold (i.e., fiscal policy plans adopted in 2009 can be revised in later years), it may be impossible to know beforehand what the eventual consequences for monetary policy of a particular fiscal policy action adopted at the start of 2009 might be. Use the government budget constraint presented above to interpret what Romer's statements mean.

d. If, later in 2009 after the new fiscal plans are (supposedly) clarified further, the nominal price level of the economy behaves as shown in the following diagram (the price level, P, is plotted on the vertical axis), which of the following is the most relevant explanation: the fiscal theory of the price level or the fiscal theory of inflation? Briefly justify your answer.

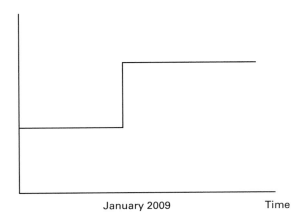

January 2009   Time

3. **Greece and long-run fiscal (in)solvency.** The recent European economic and sovereign debt crisis has put into sharp focus one of the main challenges of enacting a single currency zone (the eurozone, or the euro area, as it is officially called) and hence a single monetary policy among many sovereign countries, but without enacting a single fiscal policy across those countries. Consider specifically the case of Greece, which is the most highly indebted country (in terms of percentage of its GDP—the Greek government's debt is roughly 150 percent of Greek GDP) in the euro area. (Throughout the rest of this problem, the terms "single-currency zone," "eurozone," and "euro area" are used interchangeably.)

In this problem you will apply the fiscal theory of the price level (FTPL) studied in this chapter to the analysis of fiscal policy in a single-currency zone. In studying or applying the FTPL, the condition around which the analysis revolves is the present-value (lifetime) consolidated government budget constraint (GBC). Recall that starting from the beginning of period t, the present-value consolidated GBC is

$$\frac{B_{t-1}}{P_t} = \sum_{s=0}^{\infty} \frac{t_{t+s} - g_{t+s}}{\prod_{x=1}^{s}(1 + r_{t+x-1})} + \sum_{s=0}^{\infty} \frac{sr_{t+s}}{\prod_{x=1}^{s}(1 + r_{t+x-1})},$$

in which all of the notation is just as in this chapter.

You are given three numerical values. First, suppose that B_{t-1} = €340 billion (which roughly corresponds to what the Greek government's total nominal debt is at present). Second, assume that $t_t - g_t$ = – €20 billion (note the minus sign—this value roughly corresponds to Greece's fiscal balance in the third quarter of 2011). Third, the Greek nominal price level in period $t - 1$ is P_{t-1} = 1 (which is a normalization).

Due to its high indebtedness, Greece was under the specter of default and possible exit from the single-currency zone. To avoid these dramatic adverse consequences, Greece was compelled (by other European governments) to make strict fiscal adjustments as well as other reforms to stabilize the rapid increase in government debt.

(Note: In some of the analysis below, you will need to make use of the geometric summation result from basic mathematics.) A brief description of the geometric summation result: suppose that a variable x is successively raised to higher and higher powers, and the infinite sequence of these terms is summed together, as in

$$x^0 + x^1 + x^2 + x^3 + x^4 + \ldots$$

$$= \sum_{s=0}^{\infty} x^s,$$

in which the second line compactly expresses the infinite summation using the summation notation Σ. This sum can be computed in a simple way according to

$$\sum_{s=0}^{\infty} x^s = \frac{1}{1-x}.$$

This expression is the geometric summation result (which you studied in a pre-calculus or basic calculus course), which you will need to apply in some of the analysis below.

a. In a single-currency zone (e.g., the euro area) monetary policy is carried out by a "common" central bank (which is the European Central Bank in the euro area). A consequence of this is that individual countries—in particular, Greece—cannot print their own money (despite the fact that there is a Bank of Greece). What is the implication of this for Greece's seignorage revenue? And how would this impact Greece's present-value GBC? Explain as clearly as possible, including, if needed, any mathematical analysis.

b. Suppose that Greece commits to stay in the single-currency zone and to carry out all necessary fiscal adjustments to ensure its present-value GBC is satisfied. Suppose that the real interest rate is constant in every period at 5 percent ($r = 0.05$) and that the nominal price level in period t will remain $P_t = 1$ (note this is the period-t price level, not the period $t - 1$ price level).[7] Suppose that Greece carries out its fiscal adjustments in period t, and (to simplify things a bit) Greece will keep the new fiscal surplus (or fiscal deficit) constant at that level in all subsequent time periods. What is the numerical value of the fiscal surplus (or fiscal deficit) in order to ensure that the present-value consolidated GBC from part a is satisfied? That is, what is the numerical value of $(t - g)$? Be clear about the sign and the numerical magnitude of $(t - g)$. Present your economic and/or mathematical logic; and provide brief economic explanation.

c. Re-do the analysis in part b, assuming instead that $r = 0.025$. Compare the conclusion here with the conclusion in part b, providing brief economic explanation for why the conclusions do or do not differ.

d. Under a more realistic view, suppose that Greece still commits to stay in the single-currency zone and to make some, but not all, of the required fiscal adjustments that you computed in part b (perhaps because of "political constraints" that we are leaving outside the analysis). To make it concrete, suppose that Greece is able to run a fiscal surplus of only €5 billion in every period (i.e., $t - g =$ €5 in every time period). If the real interest rate is 5 percent ($r = 0.05$), compute the numerical value of P_t to ensure that the present-value consolidated GBC is satisfied. Be clear about your logic and computation to arrive at the result, and provide brief economic explanation.

e. Re-do the analysis in part d, assuming instead that $r = 0.025$. Compare the conclusion here with the conclusion in part d, providing brief economic explanation for why the conclusions do or do not differ.

---

7. And note that what is relevant here is the real interest rate, not the nominal interest rate, which had shot up in Greece to about 25 percent in October 2011. The reason why real interest rates, not nominal rates, matter most directly is that markets' expectations of inflation for Greece (if Greece did indeed exit from the eurozone) was near 20 percent.

f. Assume that Greece decides (against the collective wisdom of other European governments) to leave the single-currency zone. Once having left the eurozone, instead of making a serious fiscal adjustment, Greece prefers to cover its debt burden through seignorage revenue, while keeping the fiscal balance unchanged (in every time period into the future) at $t - g = -€20$ billion (note the minus sign). Suppose that the required seignorage revenue is kept at the same level in all subsequent years, and assume that $r = 0.05$ (which suppose cannot be affected by monetary policy). Address the following three questions:

    i. How much (per-period) seignorage revenue would Greece need to generate in order to keep its prices at $P = 1$ in period t and for every period beyond t?

    ii. What are the implications of this particular monetary and fiscal (and, ultimately, political) policy on Greece's own future (i.e., period t and beyond) inflation rate?

    iii. What is the theoretical difference between the analysis in this question and the analysis conducted in parts b and c, and with the analysis conducted in parts d and e?

4. **Inflationary finance and long-run fiscal solvency in the United States (circa 2010).** In studying the fiscal theory of inflation (FTI) and the fiscal theory of the price level (FTPL), the condition around which the analysis revolves is the present-value (lifetime) consolidated government budget constraint (GBC). As studied in this chapter, starting from the beginning of period t, the present-value consolidated GBC is

$$\frac{B_{t-1}}{P_t} = \sum_{s=0}^{\infty} \frac{t_{t+s} - g_{t+s}}{\prod_{s=1}^{\infty}(1 + r_{t+s})} + \sum_{s=0}^{\infty} \frac{sr_{t+s}}{\prod_{s=1}^{\infty}(1 + r_{t+s})},$$

in which all of the notation is just as in the chapter.

Let's leave aside the FTPL, which makes a very sharp prediction about when the inflationary consequences of government indebtedness may occur (the FTPL predicts these consequences occur "immediately"). That leaves us with the FTI if we are concerned about understanding the inflationary consequences of government indebtedness. Unfortunately, the FTI makes no sharp prediction whatsoever about when any inflationary consequences of government indebtedness may occur, only predicting that it must occur at some time if the fiscal side of the government does not conduct tax policy and government spending policy appropriately.

In this problem, you will study a "steady-state" version of the FTI, which enables the FTI to generate some "long-run" predictions about the inflationary consequences of government indebtedness. To operationalize the steady-state version of the FTI, suppose the following:

- The real interest rate is constant at the same value from period t onward. That is, $r_t = r_{t+1} = r_{t+2} = r_{t+3} = \ldots = r > 0$ (i.e., steady state). However, the numerical value of r is left unspecified here.

- The fiscal side of the government (i.e., Congress/Treasury) always has the same fiscal surplus/deficit from period t onward. That is, $t_t - g_t = t_{t+1} - g_{t+1} = t_{t+2} - g_{t+2} = t_{t+3} - g_{t+3} = \ldots = t - g$ (i.e., steady state). However, the numerical value of $t - g$ (and even whether $t - g$ is zero, positive, or negative) is left unspecified here.

- The monetary side of the government (i.e., the Federal Reserve) always collects the same seignorage revenue from period t onward. That is, $sr_t = sr_{t+1} = sr_{t+2} = sr_{t+3} = \ldots = sr$ (i.e., steady state). However, the numerical value of sr (and even whether sr is zero, positive, or negative) is left unspecified here.

- The monetary side of the government (i.e., the Federal Reserve) always expands the nominal money supply at the same rate from period t onward. That is, $\mu_t = \mu_{t+1} = \mu_{t+2} = \mu_{t+3} = \ldots = \mu$ (i.e., steady state). However, the numerical value of μ (and even whether μ is zero, positive, or negative) is left unspecified here.

- Suppose $P_t = 1$ and does not change under any circumstances (this assumption effectively allows us to leave aside the FTPL, as stated above). (Note: This assumption does not necessarily imply that P_{t+1} or P_{t+2} or P_{t+3}, etc., are equal to one.)

With these steady-state assumptions, the present-value consolidated GBC from above simplifies considerably to

$$B_{t-1} = \sum_{s=0}^{\infty} \frac{t-g}{(1+r)^s} + \sum_{s=0}^{\infty} \frac{sr}{(1+r)^s}.$$

You are given two numerical values. First, suppose that $B_{t-1} = \$14$ trillion (which roughly corresponds to what the US government's total nominal debt is at present). Second, the steady-state value of real money balances equals $2 trillion in every time period. That is,

$$\frac{M_t}{P_t} = \frac{M_{t+1}}{P_{t+1}} = \frac{M_{t+2}}{P_{t+2}} = \frac{M_{t+3}}{P_{t+3}} = \ldots = \$2 \text{ trillion}$$

(which roughly corresponds to what the value of M1 money in the US economy was at the end of the year 2010).

Finally, in some of the analysis below, you will need to make use of the geometric summation result from basic mathematics. A brief description of the geometric summation result: suppose that a variable x is successively raised to higher and higher powers, and the infinite sequence of these terms is summed together, as in

$$x^0 + x^1 + x^2 + x^3 + x^4 + \dots$$

$$= \sum_{s=0}^{\infty} x^s$$

(in which the second line compactly expresses the infinite summation using the summation notation Σ). This sum can be computed in a simple way according to

$$\sum_{s=0}^{\infty} x^s = \frac{1}{1-x}.$$

This expression is the geometric summation result (which you studied in a pre-calculus or basic calculus course), which you will need to apply in some of the analysis below.

a. Suppose that seignorage revenue will be always be zero ($sr = 0$ in every time period). If the real interest rate is 5 percent ($r = 0.05$), compute the numerical value of $(t - g)$ that the fiscal side of the government must set in every time period to ensure the present-value consolidated GBC is satisfied. Be clear about the sign and the magnitude. Present your logic, and provide brief economic explanation.

b. Re-do the analysis in part a, assuming instead that $r = 0.025$. Compare the conclusion here with the conclusion in part a, providing brief economic explanation for why the conclusions do or do not differ.

c. Suppose that the fiscal side of the government is able to balance its budget in every period ($t - g = 0$ in every time period) but (perhaps because of political considerations) is never able to run a surplus (but also never runs a deficit). If the real interest rate is 5 percent ($r = 0.05$), and assuming that r cannot be affected by monetary policy, compute the numerical value of sr that the monetary side of the government must generate in every time period to ensure the present-value consolidated GBC is satisfied. Be clear about the sign and the magnitude. Present your logic, and provide brief economic explanation.

d. Re-do the analysis in part c, assuming instead that $r = 0.025$. Compare the conclusion here with the conclusion in part c, providing brief economic explanation for why the conclusions do or do not differ.

e. In order to generate the amount of seignorage revenue you computed in part c, what money growth rate μ will the Federal Reserve have to set? And, as a consequence, what will the inflation rate be? Present your logic, and provide brief economic explanation.

f. In order to generate the amount of seignorage revenue you computed in part d, what money growth rate μ will the Federal Reserve have to set? And, as a consequence, what will the inflation rate be? Present your logic, and provide brief economic explanation.

g. Unlike some countries' central banks, in 2010 the US Federal Reserve did not have an inflation rate that they "officially" were "required" to conduct policy with a goal toward attaining. However, the "informal" inflation goal of the Federal Reserve at the time seemed to be 2 percent a year. If the real interest rate is 5 percent ($r = 0.05$) and assuming that r cannot be affected by monetary policy, compute the numerical value of $(t - g)$ that the fiscal side of the government must set in every time period to ensure the present-value consolidated GBC is satisfied provided that the Fed will always attain its 2 percent inflation target. Be clear about the sign and the magnitude. Present your logic, and provide brief economic explanation.

h. Re-do the analysis in part g, assuming instead that $r = 0.025$. Compare the conclusion here with the conclusion in part g, providing brief economic explanation for why the conclusions do or do not differ.

IV

OPTIMAL POLICY ANALYSIS I: THE FLEXIBLE-PRICE CASE

Whereas part III tilted toward positive analysis of both monetary policy and fiscal policy, part IV is more about normative analysis. That is, we address here how a "benevolent" central bank and a "benevolent" Congress would conduct, or perhaps even coordinate, their policy actions to achieve the highest welfare (the maximum level of utility) for the citizens of the economy.

Chapter 17 gets us started by going through the details of optimal monetary policy. Chapter 18 describes what it means for policy makers to be "benevolent" by rigorously characterizing economic efficiency.

Building on chapter 18, chapter 19 and chapter 20 bring us into the domain of "macro public finance," in which the government must raise revenues via taxation, but lump-sum taxation is ruled out. Hence the government has to raise revenue through distortionary taxation, which will lead to inefficient outcomes in the economy. Chapter 19 discusses optimal fiscal policy (and brings back in rigorous form the idea of the Laffer curve discussed heuristically in part II). Chapter 20 describes jointly optimal fiscal policy and monetary policy.

Chapter 21 introduces us to the "financial accelerator" framework. After describing the basic model, we discuss how "regulatory policies" could mitigate the consequences of events like the Great Recession, in which financial-market disruptions led to a large-scale downturn in the overall economy.

17

Optimal Monetary Policy

We now begin thinking about optimal monetary policy. Our notion of "optimality" will be from the perspective of the representative consumer's utility function. That is, we will suppose that the monetary authority's objective in setting policy is to maximize the utility of the representative consumer. This seems like a natural notion of optimality—it builds in the idea that the "government," here in the guise of a central bank, exists to try to make people as well off as possible. There may be other notions of optimality one might want to consider, as well. For example, perhaps central bankers are primarily interested in being re-appointed by the government, and perhaps being re-appointed involves different incentives than simply maximizing the utility of the consumers in the economy. Such political considerations are interesting ones to think about when studying the determination of policy, but given our focus thus far, we will only consider the first notion of optimality—that of maximizing the utility of the representative consumer.

This look at optimal policy is an introductory look. Two of the limitations we impose on our analysis here is that we only consider steady-state optimal monetary policy, and we do not consider fiscal policy and its possible impacts on the conduct of monetary policy. Limiting our scope this way will allow us to hone in on core principles of monetary policy; it will also allow us to develop the basic mode of analysis for all optimal policy problems without too many extraneous issues. After we have developed the basic results and intuition, we will study to what extent the lessons learned here carry over to richer environments that include both dynamically optimal (as opposed to just steady-state) policy and interactions between fiscal and monetary policy.

The structure of any optimal policy problem is the following. We must first specify how households make optimal choices (including, as a preliminary step, what sorts of assets are available to consumers). We must also specify how production occurs and how firms make optimal choices. We must then consider *simultaneously* the optimal choices of both households and firms *along with* the resource constraint of the economy; together, all of these elements comprise the equilibrium of the economy. The way we will think of policy makers (whether monetary policy makers or fiscal policy makers) is that they sit "above" the economy, watching how equilibrium unfolds. Policy makers understand that for any given policy they choose, the private sector (consumers and firms) will make optimal choices that will result in *some* equilibrium. The various equilibria that result for any given arbitrary policy can be welfare-ranked according to the representative-agent utility function. That is, we can evaluate the welfare of any given policy by simply inserting the resulting equilibrium levels of consumption (and leisure, if we allow for leisure in our model) into consumers' utility functions. We can think of *optimal policy problems* as problems of choosing the *best* equilibrium, meaning the equilibrium that maximizes the utility of the representative consumer.

We will develop the details of the analysis using the basic cash-in-advance model. The basic results and intuition carry over to other typical monetary models as well, including the MIU model (with which we are familiar and is highly-related to the cash-in-advance model).

Firms

The way in which we model firms here is the simplest possible way: the representative firm simply hires labor each period in perfectly competitive labor markets and sells its output. The production technology we assume here is also as simple as possible, linear in labor: $y_t = f(n_t) = n_t$. Firms' profits in period t (in nominal terms) are thus simply $P_t y_t - W_t n_t$, in which the notation is standard: P_t is the nominal price of goods, W_t is the nominal wage, and n_t is the quantity of labor. When the firm is maximizing profits, we assume it takes as given both the nominal price P and the nominal wage W.[1]

Substituting the linear production technology into the profit function and optimizing with respect to n_t (the only thing the firm decides here is how many units of labor to hire on a period-by-period basis) yields the firm first-order condition $P_t - W_t = 0$. If we define, as usual, the real wage as $w_t = W_t / P_t$, the result of firm profit maximization is

$$w_t = 1. \tag{1}$$

Condition (1) is one of the equilibrium conditions of the simple model we are developing, and is the only one that arises from the firm (supply) side of the model.

Consumers

We will model consumers using a cash-in-advance (CIA) specification. The representative consumer begins period t with nominal money holdings M_{t-1}, nominal bond holdings B_{t-1}, and stock (a real asset) holdings a_{t-1}. The period-t budget constraint of the consumer is

$$P_t c_t + P_t^b B_t + M_t + S_t a_t = W_t n_t + M_{t-1} + B_{t-1} + (S_t + D_t) a_{t-1} + \tau_t, \tag{2}$$

where the notation is as in the MIU framework studied earlier: S_t is the nominal price of a unit of stock, D_t is the nominal dividend paid by each unit of stock, and P_t^b is the nominal

---

1. Nothing more than our usual assumption of price-taking behavior; here price-taking describes the firm's behavior in both output markets and input markets.

price of a one-period nominal bond with face value $1. Because we continue to assume that all bonds are one-period bonds and the face value of each bond is $FV = 1$, we have that $P_t^b = 1/(1+i_t)$ (which you should recall), where i_t is the net nominal interest rate on a nominal bond held from period t to period $t + 1$. Note the term $W_t n_t$ in the budget constraint: it represents total labor income in period t.[2] The consumer takes the market-determined nominal wage W_t as given.[3]

The term τ_t in the budget constraint is a lump-sum amount that consumers receive from (or must pay to) the central bank. This τ_t is the means by which the monetary authority achieves changes in the money supply: a positive value of τ_t means the government is expanding the money supply in period t, and a negative value of τ_t means the government is contracting the money supply in period t. We return to how τ_t is set when we discuss below what the monetary authority does.

The consumer also faces in each period the CIA constraint

$$P_t c_t = M_t. \tag{3}$$

The instantaneous utility function of the consumer is $u(c_t, 1-n_t)$.[4] Note that the second argument is indeed *leisure* (as in our basic consumption–leisure model), which equals the total time endowment minus the amount of time spent working. Therefore, with subjective discount factor β, the consumer's lifetime utility function beginning from period t is given, as usual, by $\sum_{s=0}^{\infty} \beta^s u(c_{t+s}, 1-n_{t+s})$.

We will use the sequential Lagrangian approach to solve the consumer's utility maximization problem. Let λ_t be the Lagrange multiplier on the period-t budget constraint, and let μ_t be the Lagrange multiplier on the period-t CIA constraint. Writing out the first couple of terms of the Lagrangian,[5] we have

$$
\begin{aligned}
&u(c_t, 1-n_t) + \beta u(c_{t+1}, 1-n_{t+1}) + \beta^2 u(c_{t+2}, 1-n_{t+2}) + \dots \\
&+ \lambda_t \left[W_t n_t + M_{t-1} + B_{t-1} + (S_t + D_t) a_{t-1} + \tau_t - P_t c_t - P_t^b B_t - M_t - S_t a_t \right] \\
&+ \mu_t \left[M_t - P_t c_t \right] \\
&+ \beta \lambda_{t+1} \left[W_{t+1} n_{t+1} + M_t + B_t + (S_{t+1} + D_{t+1}) a_t + \tau_{t+1} - P_{t+1} c_{t+1} - P_{t+1}^b B_{t+1} - M_{t+1} - S_{t+1} a_{t+1} \right] \\
&+ \mu_{t+1} \left[M_{t+1} - P_{t+1} c_{t+1} \right] \\
&+ \dots
\end{aligned}
\tag{4}
$$

2. Thus what we have here on the consumer side (demand side) of the model is the "intertemporal consumption–leisure model" studied earlier, in the form of an infinite-period model. That is, we have a dynamic setting in which consumers repeatedly (sequentially) make consumption–leisure decisions along with consumption–savings decisions. By now, this sort of idea should be straightforward.

3. We, "the modeler," know from the firm optimality condition (1) that it will (in equilibrium) be the case that $W_t = P_t$; however, the consumer need not "understand" this; all the consumer does is take *whatever that market-determined W_t is* as given.

4. Recall from the basic consumption–leisure model that total time available in a period is "one unit."

5. By now, formulating the Lagrangian should be essentially automatic. If it is not, now is certainly the time to go back and review this type of formulation.

In period t the consumer chooses $(c_t, n_t, M_t, B_t, a_t)$. Proceeding mechanically, we can write the first-order-conditions with respect to each of these five choice variables, respectively, as

$$u_1(c_t, 1 - n_t) - \lambda_t P_t - \mu_t W_t = 0, \tag{5}$$

$$-u_2(c_t, 1 - n_t) + \lambda_t W_t = 0, \tag{6}$$

$$-\lambda_t + \mu_t + \beta \lambda_{t+1} = 0, \tag{7}$$

$$-\lambda_t P_t^b + \beta \lambda_{t+1} = 0, \tag{8}$$

$$-\lambda_t S_t + \beta \lambda_{t+1}(S_{t+1} + D_{t+1}) = 0. \tag{9}$$

You should be able to recognize that these first-order conditions are essentially identical to those from our study of the infinite-period MIU model, though with the exception that there we ignored the consumption leisure dimension.[6]

Conditions (5) through (9) describe how consumers make optimal choices; as such, they represent equilibrium conditions. However, it is instructive to not work with these raw first-order conditions directly, but instead combine them into interpretable expressions of the form "MRS equals a price ratio," which are the cornerstone of consumer theory. Begin by rewriting the FOC on consumption as

$$\frac{u_1(c_t, 1 - n_t)}{P_t} = \lambda_t + \mu_t. \tag{10}$$

Next, note that (7) and (8) can be combined to give $\mu_t = \lambda_t(1 - P_t^b)$, a relationship between Lagrange multipliers. For the most part, we have tried to avoid thinking directly in terms of multipliers, but for optimal policy issues, it turns out to often be useful to think directly in terms of multipliers.

Very briefly (and somewhat informally), a Lagrange multiplier measures the marginal utility value of relaxing a particular constraint by a small (marginal) amount. Take the budget constraint, for example. If somehow we (the modeler or, more pertinently, the policy maker) could add a little extra income or wealth (which could be in the form of money but need not be) to the consumer's budget, the multiplier ends up measuring the marginal utility of those extra resources to the consumer. Similarly, if we (the modeler or

---

6. Indeed comparing these FOCs with the FOCs in our discussion of monetary policy shows that the FOCs on consumption, stock, and bonds are very similar; the FOC on money is identical once one recognizes that the multiplier μ_t in our CIA model here is effectively just the term

$$\frac{u_2(c_t, M_t/P_t)}{P_t}$$

(which involves the marginal utility of real money balances) from the MIU model.

the policy maker) could hand a little *money* (actual money in this case) to the consumer, *both* of the multipliers λ_t *and* μ_t would somehow be involved in determining the marginal utility of this extra cash to the consumer.[7]

Regardless, using $\mu_t = \lambda_t(1 - P_t^b)$ in condition (10) gives us

$$\frac{u_1(c_t, 1 - n_t)}{P_t} = \lambda_t + \lambda_t(1 - P_t^b). \tag{11}$$

Next, because

$$P_t^b = \frac{1}{1 + i_t},$$

we can rewrite the previous expression as

$$\frac{u_1(c_t, 1 - n_t)}{P_t} = \lambda_t + \lambda_t \left(\frac{i_t}{1 + i_t} \right). \tag{12}$$

Note that condition (6) yields $\lambda_t = u_2(c_t, 1 - n_t)/W_t$; inserting this equation in (12) gives

$$\frac{u_1(c_t, 1 - n_t)}{P_t} = \frac{u_2(c_t, 1 - n_t)}{W_t} + \left(\frac{u_2(c_t, 1 - n_t)}{W_t} \right) \cdot \left(\frac{i_t}{1 + i_t} \right). \tag{13}$$

Divide this result through by $u_1(c_t, 1 - n_t)$ and then multiply through by W_t to arrive at

$$\frac{u_2(c_t, 1 - n_t)}{u_1(c_t, 1 - n_t)} + \left(\frac{u_2(c_t, 1 - n_t)}{u_1(c_t, 1 - n_t)} \right) \cdot \left(\frac{i_t}{1 + i_t} \right) = \frac{W_t}{P_t}. \tag{14}$$

The right-hand side is then simply the real wage, w_t. The left-hand side resembles the MRS between consumption and leisure. Indeed, if the nominal interest rate were zero ($i_t = 0$), it would be exactly that MRS, and condition (14) would be exactly the consumption–leisure optimality condition we have already studied, which would state, as usual, that at the consumer's optimal choice, the MRS between consumption and leisure (which, again, is what $1 - n$ is) equals the real wage.[8]

Combining the terms on the left-hand side and rearranging slightly, we can write this optimality condition as

$$\frac{u_2(c_t, 1 - n_t)}{u_1(c_t, 1 - n_t)} = w_t \cdot \left[1 + \frac{i_t}{1 + i_t} \right]^{-1}, \tag{15}$$

7. You may have encountered this notion of multipliers measuring marginal utility in an intermediate microeconomics course; any more advanced study of this idea, however, we leave for a more advanced course in economic theory.

8. Here, with no taxes, which we allowed for in the basic consumption–leisure model. We will re-introduce taxation in our second, more in-depth study of optimal policy when we consider the joint effects of fiscal and monetary policy.

which shows exactly how, at the optimal choice, the MRS between consumption and leisure depends on the real wage and the nominal interest rate.

The nominal interest rate is linked to the multipliers μ_t and λ_t via

$$\mu_t = \lambda_t \cdot \left(\frac{i_t}{1 + i_t} \right), \tag{16}$$

which, recall, comes from combining (7) and (8) and using the relationship between the nominal price of bonds and the nominal interest rate. We could thus alternatively express the optimality condition (14) as

$$\frac{u_2(c_t, 1 - n_t)}{u_1(c_t, 1 - n_t)} + \left(\frac{u_2(c_t, 1 - n_t)}{u_1(c_t, 1 - n_t)} \right) \cdot \left(\frac{\mu_t}{\lambda_t} \right) = w_t. \tag{17}$$

What condition (15), or equivalently (17), reveals is that the presence of money in this economy somehow throws a "wedge" (think of it as a deadweight loss) into the consumption–leisure optimality condition. If the nominal interest rate were zero, condition (15) tells us the consumption–leisure margin would be set according to just the real wage. Condition (16) tells us that if the nominal interest rate were zero, then the multiplier μ_t would be zero; condition (17) tells us (again) that the consumption–leisure margin would be set according to just the real wage.

The wedge being thrown into the consumption–leisure margin stems from the CIA constraint itself. Indeed one way of thinking about an economy *without a CIA constraint* is to assume that $\mu_t = 0$ always, in which case clearly (17) shows us that the consumption–leisure optimality condition would depend on just the real wage. Apparently, though, the presence of this CIA wedge means that at the consumer's optimal choice, the MRS between consumption and leisure depends on *both the real wage and the nominal interest rate.*

Thinking of money, and more generally, government policy variables, as throwing "wedges" into consumer optimality conditions is an important way of understanding the effects of (both monetary and fiscal) policy, as well as understanding how to design *optimal* policies. We already know from our study of the basic consumption–leisure model that labor taxes throw a wedge (in the form of one minus the labor tax rate) into the consumption–leisure optimality condition. We now have encountered another policy variable that potentially throws a wedge into this margin: money.

Next, as usual, the asset a_t in our model allows us to construct an intertemporal optimality condition, linking the real interest rate to consumers' intertemporal marginal rate of substitution. We can rewrite condition (9) as

$$\frac{\lambda_t}{\lambda_{t+1}} = \beta \left(\frac{S_{t+1} + D_{t+1}}{S_t} \right).$$

We can multiply and divide the numerator by P_{t+1}, and multiply and divide the denominator by P_t, to get

$$\frac{\lambda_t}{\lambda_{t+1}} = \beta \left(\frac{(S_{t+1} + D_{t+1})/P_{t+1}}{S_t/P_t} \right) \cdot \frac{P_{t+1}}{P_t}. \tag{18}$$

Recall from our earlier study of monetary policy in chapter 15 that we can define the real interest rate as

$$1 + r_t = \frac{(S_{t+1} + D_{t+1})/P_{t+1}}{S_t/P_t}; \tag{19}$$

using this in the previous expression yields

$$\frac{\lambda_t}{\lambda_{t+1}} = \beta(1 + r_t) \cdot \frac{P_{t+1}}{P_t}. \tag{20}$$

Next recall that the first-order condition on labor can be written $\lambda_t = u_2(c_t, 1 - n_t)/W_t$; using this along with the time $t + 1$ version in (20) allows us to express the consumption–savings condition as

$$\frac{u_2(c_t, 1 - n_t)}{u_2(c_{t+1}, 1 - n_{t+1})} = \beta(1 + r_t) \frac{W_t}{W_{t+1}} \frac{P_{t+1}}{P_t}. \tag{21}$$

This is one way of expressing consumption–savings optimality in this model; note that on the left-hand side, the intertemporal MRS (note the different t and $t + 1$ subscripts!) is expressed in terms of the marginal utility of leisure rather than in terms of the marginal utility of consumption, but this is no problem. The interpretation is the same as any "standard" consumption–savings optimality condition: it describes the consumer's optimal trade-off *over time*.

Conditions (15) and (21)—or equivalently, condition (17)—summarize the optimization problem of the representative consumer; understand well that (15) condenses conditions (5) through (8). Condition (15) is the model's consumption–leisure (intratemporal) optimality condition, and condition (21) is the model's consumption–savings (intertemporal) optimality condition.[9] Also the CIA constraint itself, condition (3), is a description of the household's choices. Thus condition (3), condition (15), and condition (21) are equilibrium conditions of the model we are developing.

9. Recall from our brief consideration of the intertemporal consumption–leisure model that *both* a consumption–leisure and a consumption–savings trade-off arises in a dynamic model once we "glue together" the simple consumption–savings and the simple consumption–leisure models; although couched inside a more complicated model, this idea underpins things here as well.

Government

When studying optimal (government) policy, we need to specify what the government does. In the model here the only thing the government, which is just a monetary authority thus far, does is print money and hand it to consumers (or, if shrinking the money supply, "ask for money back from consumers").[10] This handing over of (or "asking to return") money occurs via the τ_t introduced above. The government's (monetary authority's) budget constraint is thus simply

$$M_t = M_{t-1} + \tau_t. \tag{22}$$

If $\tau_t > 0$, the central bank is expanding the nominal money supply in period t, while if $\tau_t < 0$, the central bank is contracting the nominal money supply in period t.

We can express this transfer τ_t in terms of the growth rate of money. Letting g_t be the net growth rate of nominal money during period t, we can write $\tau_t = g_t M_{t-1}$. For example, if the central bank expands the money supply by 10 percent in period 16, we would write $g_{16} = 0.10$. Based on this example, the government budget constraint can be written as

$$M_t = (1 + g_t)M_{t-1}. \tag{23}$$

This government budget constraint seems trivial here, but conceptually it will be crucial when, a few chapters from now, we consider the interactions of fiscal and monetary policy.

Resource Constraint

The resource constraint of the economy describes all of the different uses of total output (GDP) of the economy. In our economy, output is produced by the linear-in-labor production technology, and there is no other use for output other than consumption. Hence the resource constraint is simply

$$c_t = n_t. \tag{24}$$

In richer models that we will develop, government spending and investment will also be components of the resource constraint. Informally, you should think of the resource constraint as the "GDP accounting equation" from basic macroeconomics.[11]

---

10. Obviously this is not literally true. Remember from basic macroeconomics and from the review in chapter 15 that in practice central banks use open market operations to expand or contract the money supply. Open-market operations are conducted with the banking (financial) sector; in our model here, we do not include a banking sector, hence our metaphor that the central bank deals directly with consumers. In reality, the banking sector effectively just acts as an intermediary between the central bank and consumers (and firms) in the conduct of monetary policy. Given that our model is already quite large (and will soon become even larger as we continue to enrich the scope of issues we want to consider), it seems worthwhile to not try to model a banking sector.

11. As on the first day of basic macroeconomics, the GDP accounting identity states that $GDP = C + I + G + NX$. In our model here, $I = G = NX = 0$, hence all output is simply consumed by consumers.

Equilibrium and Steady-State Equilibrium

Any (well-specified) macroeconomic model must have a notion of *general equilibrium*. General equilibrium is a collection of prices and quantities that in concert make all markets clear, given that both demand (consumer choices) and supply (firm choices) decisions in the economy are made optimally. When constructing a macroeconomic model, making sure to identify properly the equilibrium conditions is crucial, and this step can only be done after setting up and solving the household and firm optimization problems. In our model, equilibrium is described by the firm optimality condition (1); the household optimality conditions, which, recall, we were able to condense into (3), (15), and (21); and the resource constraint (24).

Because conditions (1) and (24) are so simple, let's simply substitute the w_t and n_t terms in the other equilibrium conditions, in which case we can represent the equilibrium conditions of the model as

$$c_t = \frac{M_t}{P_t},\tag{25}$$

$$\frac{u_2(c_t,1-n_t)}{u_1(c_t,1-n_t)} = \left[1+\frac{i_t}{1+i_t}\right]^{-1},\tag{26}$$

and

$$\frac{u_2(c_t,1-c_t)}{u_2(c_{t+1},1-c_{t+1})} = \beta\cdot(1+r_t).\tag{27}$$

Note that in writing (27) we are using the fact that in equilibrium,

$$\frac{W_t}{W_{t+1}}\frac{P_{t+1}}{P_t} = \frac{w_t}{w_{t+1}} = \frac{1}{1}.$$

Next, if we take the time $t-1$ version of (25) and divide (25) by it, we have

$$\frac{M_t/M_{t-1}}{P_t/P_{t-1}} = \frac{c_t}{c_{t-1}}.\tag{28}$$

Because, by assumption, $M_t = (1+g_t)M_{t-1}$ and, by earlier definition, inflation between periods $t-1$ and t is given by $1+\pi_t = P_t/P_{t-1}$, we can express this as

$$\frac{1+g_t}{1+\pi_t} = \frac{c_t}{c_{t-1}},\tag{29}$$

which shows that the inflation rate between $t-1$ and t is linked to *both* the rate of money growth between $t-1$ and t *and* by how much consumption grows between $t-1$ and t.

Condition (29) is not a new equilibrium condition of the model; rather it arose from combining the t and $t-1$ versions of (25) with the money supply rule being followed by the government.

Recall the notion of steady-state equilibrium: a steady state is a condition in which all real quantity variables are constant. In terms of the preceding two expressions, steady state would involve constant c and constant i over time.[12] Imposing steady state on (29) immediately shows us that in *steady state* (i.e., in the long run), *the rate of inflation is equal to the rate of money growth*. That is, in this economy, the *quantity-theoretic prediction that inflation is governed by money growth **in the long run*** shines through. But note well that *outside* a steady state (i.e., when business cycles swing away from the steady state are occurring), condition (29) shows that inflation and the money growth rate *need not be identical*.

Next, the steady-state version of the consumption–savings optimality condition reveals that, in a steady-state equilibrium, $1 + r = 1/\beta$, a condition we have encountered before: in steady state (again, read this as "in the long run" or "on average"), the real interest rate is determined by the representative consumer's discount factor. Furthermore, because we know the Fisher relation also exists in the background the steady-state version of (27) can also be written as

$$1 + \pi = \beta(1 + i). \tag{30}$$

Continuing to link the conditions we are deriving: we just concluded that in steady state, $\pi = g$. That is, the inflation rate equals the money growth rate. Thus the last expression can be written yet again to

$$1 + g = \beta(1 + i). \tag{31}$$

This of course means that $1 + i = (1 + g)/\beta$, or if we isolate the nominal interest rate, $i = (1 + g - \beta)/\beta$.

Finally, using these expressions in the steady-state version of the consumption–leisure optimality condition as expressed in (26), we have that

$$\frac{u_2(\overline{c}, 1 - \overline{c})}{u_1(\overline{c}, 1 - \overline{c})} = \frac{1 + g}{1 + g + 1 + g - \beta}, \tag{32}$$

in which $\overline{c}$ denotes the quantity of steady-state private consumption.

Let's take stock of where we've arrived. After setting up and solving the firm profit-maximization problem and the consumer utility-maximization problem, as well as specifying how monetary policy is conducted (a simple money growth rule), we defined

---

12. Note that even though i is the *nominal* interest rate, it is not a *quantity* variable; it is more akin to a price (i.e., the opportunity cost of holding money).

equilibrium. We then condensed the equilibrium conditions into a more compact set of conditions. Next we imposed steady state on the equilibrium conditions, which in turn allowed us to express the steady-state equilibrium *of the entire private sector of the model* in the single, compact form of equation (32).

What condition (32) describes is *how the steady-state equilibrium quantity of consumption depends on the steady-state rate of growth of the nominal money supply.* Even though we've seemingly shrunken down the entire model (i.e., its setup and solution) into a single expression, there is no (reliable) shortcut for all of the analysis we have done. One *must* go through the entire solution of the demand and supply sides of the model, description of the equilibrium, and then (*and only then*) can one impose steady state. For the purpose of what we now (finally!) turn to, the optimal (steady-state) policy problem, condition (32) is crucial.

Formulation of Optimal Policy Problem

The reason condition (32) is crucial is that *it describes how the private sector of the economy responds (in steady state) to monetary policy.* That is, it encapsulates the decision-making of consumers and firms, who all *take monetary policy as given.* Recall our heuristic description at the outset of how to think of the optimal policy maker (or, at least, what one useful way of thinking about policy makers might be): policy makers understand how the economy responds to various policy settings, and (if they are benevolent) set policy to bring about the highest possible welfare for the economy.

In our model, welfare is naturally measured by the representative consumer's utility, and the idea of "how the economy responds to various policy settings" is captured by the equilibrium of the model, which in turn we have been able (after quite some effort) to condense down to the single restriction (32). In the parlance of optimal policy analysis, we will say that policy makers respect the equilibrium of the economy when choosing policy.

Note also the game-theoretic undertones here: it is as if the private sector (both firms and consumers) "moves second," after policy has been set. The "first move" belongs to the policy maker, who takes into account the "optimal response" of the private sector when deciding its "move" (its policy-setting). If you have studied the idea of Bertrand or Cournot competition in intermediate microeconomics, there is some similarity in idea here: the policy maker takes into account the response function of the entire economy when choosing the optimal policy. This idea is an important one, one that will carry over into the richer optimal policy questions we consider later (chapters 19, 20, and 24).

In terms of setting up the optimal policy problem, condition (32) defines the steady-state equilibrium $\bar{c}$ *as a function of g.* To emphasize this **functional** dependence, let's from now on write $\bar{c}(g)$; this expression defines the function $\bar{c}(g)$. If you were given a particular utility function, you could (after a number of steps of algebra) solve for the function $\bar{c}(g)$.

Finally, then the optimal (steady-state) policy problem is to choose a (constant) growth rate of money g that maximizes consumer's (steady-state) utility subject to the equilibrium of the economy described by (32). In a steady-state equilibrium, consumers' lifetime utility (formally, still starting at date t, but "dates" have less meaning once the economy has arrived in steady state—nonetheless, we will keep this formalism) is given by

$$\sum_{s=0}^{\infty} \beta^s u\left(\overline{c}(g), 1-\overline{c}(g)\right) = \frac{u\left(\overline{c}(g), 1-\overline{c}(g)\right)}{1-\beta}. \tag{33}$$

So the optimal policy problem boils down to choosing a constant growth rate of money that maximizes (33); mathematically, no constraints are required on this optimization problem *because we have already built all constraints imposed by equilibrium into* (33).

Solution of Optimal Policy Problem

Being careful in using the chain rule of calculus, the first-order condition of (33) with respect to g is

$$u_1\left(\overline{c}(g), 1-\overline{c}(g)\right) \cdot \overline{c}'(g) - u_2\left(\overline{c}(g), 1-\overline{c}(g)\right) \cdot \overline{c}'(g) = 0, \tag{34}$$

where $\overline{c}'(g)$ describes how steady-state equilibrium consumption responds to a marginal change in the money growth rate (i.e., it is the derivative of the function $\overline{c}(g)$ with respect to g).[13]

As it stands, this condition may not seem particularly illuminating, but it is the solution to the policy problem: the value of g that solves (34) *is* the optimal steady-state money growth rate, the one that maximizes consumers' utility, taking into account how the private sector responds to monetary policy.

Notice that we can cancel the $\overline{c}'(g)$ terms from (34); doing so and rearranging terms gives us that under the optimal policy,

$$\frac{u_2\left(\overline{c}(g), 1-\overline{c}(g)\right)}{u_1\left(\overline{c}(g), 1-\overline{c}(g)\right)} = 1. \tag{35}$$

This condition states that *when policy is chosen optimally,* the representative consumer's MRS between consumption and leisure equals one.

Our final task (and most important task conceptually) is to compare (35) with (32): they look very similar, but they have importantly different interpretations. Condition (32) describes, *for any arbitrary money growth rate,* how steady-state equilibrium consumption responds. Condition (35) instead describes how the marginal utilities of consumption and

---

13. Note that we've canceled the $1 - \beta$ term from this first-order condition because it does not affect the solution of the policy problem.

leisure should relate to each other *when policy is set optimally,* in the sense we have defined. Clearly, the two conditions coincide only if $g = \beta - 1$. Thus the optimal steady-state growth rate of money is $\beta - 1$; this is the final solution of the optimal policy problem. *Note that this conclusion has absolutely nothing to do with the precise functional form of the utility function—we have made absolutely no assumptions about what the utility function is.*

With this steady-state optimal growth rate of the money supply in hand, we can also determine what the optimal steady-state nominal interest rate is. To do so, return to the steady-state equilibrium condition (31), which, recall, is the Fisher equation with the steady-state version of the CIA constraint imposed on it. From this condition and the result $g = \beta - 1$ if policy is set optimally, it immediately follows that

$$i = 0 \tag{36}$$

when monetary policy is set optimally. That is, the optimal nominal interest rate is zero. This result, originally due to Friedman (1969), is a hallmark result in the theory of optimal policy and has come to be known as the **Friedman rule.** Because of the steady-state equilibrium relationship, $1 + g = \beta(1 + i)$, we can think alternatively (and equivalently) of the Friedman rule as $i = 0$ and/or $g = \beta - 1$.

The Friedman Rule

The Friedman rule is a celebrated result in monetary theory. Let's first explicitly note the implication of what it states: with $g = \beta - 1$ and with $\beta \in (0,1)$, clearly the Friedman rule means $g < 0$. The *optimal money growth rate is negative*—the central bank should steadily *contract* the nominal money supply. In turn, because in steady state $g = \pi$, if the central bank is running the Friedman rule, *the optimal inflation rate is negative as well.*

There are a few alternative (and ultimately interrelated) ways to think about this result. One way to think about it is to think about what purpose money serves in this model. The CIA constraint is meant to represent some transactions motive for holding money; it is intended as a way of capturing money's medium of exchange function. Let's step back from the CIA model for a moment, though. The consumers (the representative consumer) in the dynamic macro model we had been building *before* we introduced the topic of money demand were perfectly well able to acquire consumption goods. In the basic dynamic macro model we had built *without* the CIA constraint, consumers were not clamoring for a body called a "central bank" to provide them with an object called "money." In introducing the CIA or MIU structure, we as the modelers are *forcing* the consumers in our model to hold and use money. But they didn't need it in the first place. So the optimal thing for the central bank to do is to remove it.

Here is another way to think about the Friedman rule. There are two nominal assets in the model, money and bonds. Stocks, as we have mentioned before, are fundamentally a real asset. Bonds potentially pay interest at a nominal rate i, but they do not (by assumption) serve a medium of exchange function. Money pays no interest, but consumers must carry it in order to purchase goods. Every dollar of his resources that the consumer holds as money is a dollar he cannot hold in the form of an interest-bearing bond.

Thus there is an opportunity cost of holding money, which is the forgone interest earnings on nominal bonds. The benevolent central bank, realizing that consumers *must* hold money (due to the CIA constraint, which was *not* put into place by the central bank) seeks to make it as costless as possible for them to do so. Making money costless to hold means making the opportunity cost of holding money zero, hence conducting monetary policy in such a way as to make, at least in the long run, $i = 0$.

Yet another way of considering the optimality of the Friedman rule is using the basic tools of consumer theory. Recall from our study of the simple consumption–leisure model that at the consumer's optimal choice, the MRS between consumption and leisure is equated to the real wage.[14] Yet, here in the CIA model, we see that the consumer's optimal choice depends not only on the real wage but also on the nominal interest rate—condition (15) shows us this.

Condition (15) is the consumption–leisure optimality condition of this model: a positive nominal interest rate is interfering with the (unfettered) optimal choice along the consumption–leisure margin. That is, a positive nominal interest rate introduces a wedge in consumers' work–leisure choice, a wedge that, from the point of view of optimality, shouldn't be there: work/leisure choices "should" be made (again, from the point of view of economy-wide optimality) according to *only* the real wage.[15] The benevolent central bank does not want there to be such a wedge in consumers' decisions; hence it conducts monetary policy in such a way as to make $i = 0$. Once the government chooses to conduct policy in such a way as to make $i = 0$, the steady-state version of the Fisher equation immediately tells us that the way to do so is to make the inflation rate equal to $\beta - 1$; but because $\pi = g$ in steady state, this means a gradual withdrawal of money from the economy.

The optimal rate of money contraction depends on β. Suppose that consumers were completely patient, meaning $\beta = 1$ (i.e., no discounting of future utility at all). Then the Friedman rule (which, note, is still optimal) means that $g = 0$—the central bank should not change the money supply at all.

The reason why results depend so critically on β is that every unit of money held means one less unit of an interest-bearing bond that is held. If the consumer *had* held that bond, he would have waited one period before receiving the principal plus interest on the bond back. Waiting one period entails an "impatience cost" measured by β. So the higher is β,

---

14. More precisely, it is equated to the after-tax real wage. Here we ignore labor taxes, so the prescription from the basic consumption–leisure model is that consumers choose consumption and leisure to set their MRS equal to the real wage.

15. We will study in more depth the content of this statement that work–leisure choices "should" be made only according to the real wage; the issue has to do with social efficiency/Pareto optimality.

the less "bad" from a welfare perspective is *not* removing money and its attendant wedge from the economy.

Thus in steady state the Friedman rule can either be stated as $i = 0$ or $g = \beta - 1$. This is *not* true when we consider things outside of steady state. When we later turn to dynamically optimal monetary policy, the correct notion of the Friedman rule is as $i_t = 0$, which does *not* necessarily translate into $g_t = \beta - 1$.

Chapter 17 Problem Set Questions

1. **Evaluating the welfare of various policies.** In our cash-in-advance model, recall that we were able to condense the description of the entire equilibrium of the economy to the single expression

$$\frac{u_2(\overline{c}, 1 - \overline{c})}{u_1(\overline{c}, 1 - \overline{c})} = \frac{1 + g}{1 + g + 1 + g - \beta}.$$

The notation is just as we studied: β is the representative consumer's subjective discount factor, $\overline{c}$ is the steady-state equilibrium consumption, and g is the (steady state, hence constant) net growth rate of the nominal money supply.

Suppose that consumers' annual discount factor is $\beta = 0.96$ (which corresponds to a net steady-state real interest rate of about 4 percent).

   a. Suppose the instantaneous utility function is $u(c, 1 - n) = \ln c + \ln(1 - n)$. Rank, in terms of steady-state utility, the following money growth rates: $g = -0.04$, $g = 0$, $g = 0.04$. To ensure accuracy, carry your computations to at least five decimal places.)

   b. In part a, how does steady-state consumption change as g rises (i.e., does it rise, fall, or remain the same)? Briefly discuss the economic intuition behind this result.

2. **Optimal monetary policy in the simple MIU model.** Consider the MIU model from chapter 15. There are no firms in this model, hence no labor (or capital); the consumer's nominal income Y_t is simply an endowment (i.e., it "falls from the sky"), hence the resource constraint of this economy is the trivial relationship, $c_t = y_t$ (where $y = Y / P$ is the real endowment). The central bank has no control over the real endowment. As in our study of optimal policy in the CIA model, suppose that the central bank uses a lump-sum transfer τ_t to achieve money expansions or contractions, and $\tau_t = g_t M_{t-1}$. In a steady-state equilibrium of the MIU model, consumption, *real* money balances, the nominal interest rate, the inflation rate, and the money growth rate are all constant.

a. For an arbitrary utility function

$$u\left(c_t, \frac{M_t}{P_t}\right),$$

proceed as far as you can in determining the optimal steady-state rate of money growth? Show the key steps and logic in your arguments. (Hint: Try to proceed in as close analogy as possible with our optimal policy analysis in the CIA model; in particular, condense the description of the entire equilibrium down to one expression, and then ask, using that expression, what the optimal policy is.)

b. Using what you learned/derived in part a, describe what the optimal steady-state policy is if the instantaneous utility function is

$$u\left(c_t, \frac{M_t}{P_t}\right) = \ln c_t + A \cdot \frac{M_t}{P_t},$$

where $A \geq 0$ is some positive constant, which the central bank has no control over.

3. **Consumption as a function of the money growth rate.** In our study of optimal policy in the CIA model, we had that steady-state consumption depended on the money growth rate according to the condition,

$$\frac{u_2(\overline{c}, 1-\overline{c})}{u_1(\overline{c}, 1-\overline{c})} = \frac{1+g}{1+g+1+g-\beta};$$

that is, this condition defines the function $\overline{c}(g)$. In the optimal policy problem, we concluded that the optimal growth rate of money should satisfy the condition

$$u_1\left(\overline{c}(g), 1-\overline{c}(g)\right) \cdot \overline{c}'(g) - u_2\left(\overline{c}(g), 1-\overline{c}(g)\right) \cdot \overline{c}'(g) = 0.$$

We proceeded to simply cancel the $\overline{c}'(g)$ terms and then conducted the analysis that led to our conclusion that the Friedman rule was optimal. What if we did not cancel these terms? Clearly, if somehow $\overline{c}'(g) = 0$, then that also would satisfy the FOC of the optimal policy problem. Suppose the instantaneous utility function is $u(c_t, 1-n_t) = \ln c_t + \ln(1-n_t)$. Is it ever possible for this utility function that $\overline{c}'(g) = 0$ can occur?

4. **A cash–credit economy.** Consider a variation of the basic CIA model we have studied. Suppose that there are two "types" of consumption goods, "cash goods" and "credit goods." Cash goods, denoted by c_{1t}, are goods whose purchase requires money, while credit goods, denoted by c_{2t}, are goods whose purchase does not require money (i.e., they can be bought "on credit.").

The representative consumer wants to consume both cash and credit goods: his instantaneous utility function is $u(c_{1t}, c_{2t})$. Note that there is no leisure in this utility function: the economy is an endowment economy, in which the real endowment y_t in each period t is outside the control of anyone in the economy. The resource constraint of the economy is $c_{1t} + c_{2t} = y_t$. Furthermore the nominal price of each type of good is the same, P_t.

The only asset that consumers have to accumulate is money (no bonds, no stock), and let M_{t-1} be the nominal amount of money that consumers begin period t with. Hence the period-t budget constraint of the consumer is $P_t c_{1t} + P_t c_{2t} + M_t = P_t y_t + M_{t-1} + \tau_t$, where, as always, τ_t is a lump-sum transfer from (or to) the central bank. The cash-in-advance constraint in this economy *applies only to* c_{1t}: in period t, the cash-in-advance constraint is $P_t c_{1t} = M_t$ (note the subscript!). Finally, as usual, the transfer depends on some growth rate of money, $\tau_t = g_t M_{t-1}$.

In period t the consumer chooses c_{1t}, c_{2t}, and M_t.

a. Setting up an appropriate Lagrangian, obtain the consumer's first-order conditions with respect to c_{1t}, c_{2t}, and M_t.

b. Combine the three FOCs you derived in part a in a single condition that involves only marginal utilities and inflation, *and then* do the following: impose steady state, and express the final steady-state condition in terms of

$$\frac{u_1(\overline{c}_1, \overline{c}_2)}{u_2(\overline{c}_1, \overline{c}_2)} = ...,$$

where the (...) is for you to figure out. (Note the order in which you should do things here.)

c. For this cash–credit model, solve for the optimal g, showing the important steps in your work.

18

Economic Efficiency

The benchmark for any notion of optimal policy, be it optimal monetary policy or optimal fiscal policy, is the economically efficient outcome. In diagrammatical form, macroeconomic efficiency occurs when all markets simultaneously clear; figure 18.1, which we have seen a few times already, displays economic efficiency.

Once we know what the efficient outcome is for any economy, we can ask "how good" the optimal policy is (note that optimal policy need not achieve economic efficiency—we will have much more to say about this later). In a representative agent context, there is one essential condition describing economic efficiency: *social marginal rates of substitution are equated to their respective social marginal rates of transformation.*[1]

We already know what a marginal rate of substitution (MRS) is: it is a measure of the maximal willingness of a consumer to trade *consumption* of one good for *consumption* of one more unit of another good. Mathematically, the MRS is the ratio of marginal utilities of two distinct goods.[2] The MRS is an aspect of the demand side of the economy. The **marginal rate of transformation (MRT)** is an analogous concept from the production side (firm side) of the economy: it measures how much *production* of one good must be given up for *production* of one more unit of another good. Very simply put, the economy is said to be operating efficiently if and only if the consumers' MRS between any (and *all*) pairs of goods is equal to the MRT between those goods. MRS is a statement about consumers' preferences: indeed, because it is the ratio of marginal utilities between a pair of goods, clearly it is related to consumer preferences (utility). MRT is a statement about the production technology of the economy.

---

1. We qualify this statement with "in a representative-agent context" because if we consider heterogeneous agents (both heterogeneous consumers as well as heterogeneous firms), there are two additional conditions that are components of the definition of economic efficiency: marginal rates of substitution between any two goods are equated across all consumers; and marginal rates of transformations between any two inputs are equated across all firms. Clearly (and trivially), with a representative (single) consumer, marginal rates of substitution are equated across "all" consumers, and with a representative (single) firm, marginal rates of transformation are equated across "all" firms.

2. Review these basic ideas if you need to.

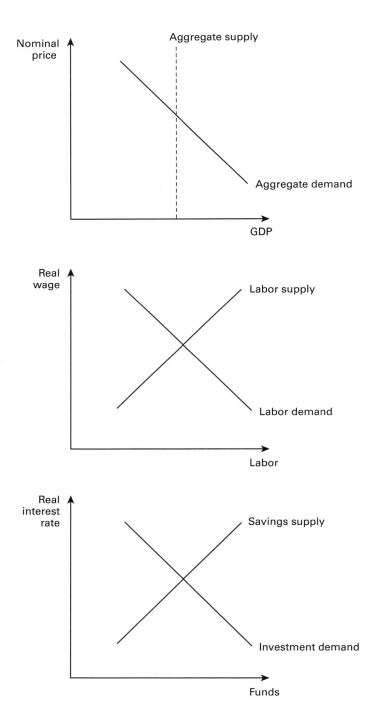

Figure 18.1
Market clearing in all macro markets (goods, labor, and financial).

To illustrate further the notion of economic efficiency, we proceed in two simple steps. First, we use the simple one-period consumption–leisure model to understand economic efficiency in a static setting. Then we use the simple two-period consumption–savings model to understand the dynamic analogue. Before proceeding in these two steps, we introduce a device that is useful for determining efficient allocations.

The Social Planner

It is quite easy to characterize, in terms of the solution to an optimization problem, economically efficient outcomes. To do so, we introduce the concept of a **Social Planner.** The Social Planner is an all-knowing "individual" or "institution" that is able to perfectly control and allocate the resources of an economy.[3] The Social Planner is a "dictator," but a benevolent one. The Social Planner is able to simply take, by order or decree, any resources it needs from any parties it sees fit. The Social Planner does not need to resort to "taxes" in order to achieve this. Thus we should not think of the Social Planner as a "government" in the sense we typically have in mind in capitalist societies. Rather, the Social Planner is able to directly command how production in the economy occurs and how the fruits of that production get distributed to consumers. Most important, the Social Planner does *not* have any need for markets or prices (or, as alluded to already, taxes). The Social Planner does not care if "markets" (and hence market prices) exist—because it *directly and independently* chooses what happens, markets are irrelevant for the Social Planner.[4]

Economic Efficiency in the Static Consumption–Leisure Model

So what does the Social Planner do? Consider the one-period consumption–leisure model we have studied. The representative consumer has preferences over consumption and leisure, described by the utility function $u(c, 1-n)$, where, as usual, c denotes consumption, and $1-n$ denotes leisure (with n being labor and the total time available is normalized to one; i.e., if l denotes leisure $n + l = 1$ here).

Suppose that the production technology is simple: linear in labor. One unit of labor always yields one unit of output, with no diminishing marginal product in labor. We have used this simple production technology for illustrative purposes before. The resource constraint of the economy is thus given by

$$c = n. \tag{1}$$

The Social Planner understands the economy's resource frontier—it embodies the production technology of the economy. The Social Planner understands consumers' utility

3. The Social Planner is also often referred to as a "central planner."
4. This will not be true of another type of planner—the Ramsey Planner—that we encounter soon.

functions—it embodies consumers' preferences. The optimization problem of the benevolent Social Planner is to *maximize (one-period) consumer utility with respect to the resource frontier*. Pay close attention to the economic content of this maximization statement: there is an institution in the economy (the Social Planner) that is choosing how to satisfy demand in the economy (which consumers' utility functions give rise to) with *direct* regard for the supply constraints (which the resource constraint/production function gives rise to) of the economy. This is something that does not occur in modern capitalist economies: consumers maximize their utility *with regard to market prices and their budget constraints,* and separately, firms maximize their profits *with regard to market prices and their production technologies.* Note the intermediary in market-based transactions: market prices mediate the exchange between suppliers and demanders. In contrast, the Social Planner ignores markets, examines consumers' preferences, examines firm's production technologies, and simply *commands* both consumers and firms to do what it decides.

The formal maximization that the Social Planner subsequently performs is to choose c and n to maximize $u(c, 1-n)$ subject to the resource constraint (1). Clearly, we can simplify the problem by inserting (1) into the utility function, avoiding the need to set up a Lagrangian.

Doing so, we can then write the representative consumer's one-period utility function simply as $u(c, 1-c)$. The Social Planner chooses c to maximize this; the first-order condition with respect to c (which by now should be trivial to compute) is likewise simply

$$u_1(c, 1-c) + u_2(c, 1-c)(-1) = 0. \tag{2}$$

Note the "−1" term in the second term on the left-hand side, which arises from using the chain rule to differentiate with respect to c. Clearly, (2) states that if the Social Planner gets to choose c (and hence n) for this economy, it would choose it in such a way that

$$\frac{u_1(c, 1-c)}{u_2(c, 1-c)} = 1. \tag{3}$$

We have seen this condition before: it was part of the characterization of optimal monetary policy that we studied. With our brief review of the notion of economic efficiency and the idea of the Social Planner, we can now understand a bit better the (deep) idea behind this condition.

The left-hand side of (3) is, as we know by now, the MRS between consumption and leisure (because, as usual, $u_1(.)$ is the marginal utility of consumption and $u_2(.)$ is the marginal utility of leisure). What we did not emphasize before was the right-hand side of (3): in the simple economy we are studying here, it is the economy's *marginal rate of transformation* between consumption and leisure.

To understand why "1" is the economy's marginal rate of transformation (MRT, for short) between consumption and leisure in this example, return to the resource frontier shown in (1). If as a whole the economy takes—"produces"—one *less* unit of leisure, clearly it works one *more* unit of time. But the resource constraint tells us that that means there is one *more* unit of consumption produced in the economy. Hence, in order for the economy to produce one more unit of consumption, it must "produce" one less unit of leisure—but this means, by the definition of MRT, that the MRT between consumption and leisure is one.

Condition (3) thus states that if the Social Planner makes choices for the economy, it makes sure that the MRS between consumption and leisure is equated to the MRT between consumption and leisure—but this means, by the definition of economic efficiency, that the Social Planner's choice is economically efficient.[5] Condition (3) characterizes economic efficiency along the consumption–leisure dimension. The importance of this efficiency condition is evident when studying optimal monetary policy (as we have already seen) and when studying optimal labor taxation (which we will soon see).

Economic Efficiency in the Two-Period Consumption–Savings Model

We just studied economic efficiency along the (intratemporal) consumption–leisure margin. Let's turn to economic efficiency along the (intertemporal) consumption–savings margin. To think about this issue, let's return to our simple two-period model, before we started to think about monetary issues.

The lifetime (here, of course, lifetime means only two periods) utility function of the representative consumer is

$$v(c_1) + \beta v(c_2), \tag{4}$$

where $v(.)$ is the single-period utility function and $\beta \in (0,1)$ is the subjective discount factor.[6] Note that we are assuming additive-separability across time—this, of course, is nothing new; we have been doing this all along in our infinite-period models whenever we write $u(c_t) + \beta u(c_{t+1}) + \beta^2 u(c_{t+2}) + \beta^3 u(c_{t+3}) + \ldots$.

The production technology of the economy is the following. In each period there is a *diminishing-returns* production technology that transforms capital into output, all of which is consumed.

In period 1 the production function is $f(k_1)$, and in period 2, the production function is $f(k_2)$. As before, the notational convention we are adopting is that k_1 is the capital used *for production in period* 1, which was *decided in period* 0; likewise k_2 is the capital used

---

5. Return now to our study of optimal monetary policy. Was the benevolent central bank, through its control of the (steady-state) rate of money growth, able to achieve economic efficiency?

6. We use the notation $v(.)$ only to avoid confusion with the notation $u(.)$ we used in the previous section. Of course, as always, the names of utility functions don't matter: we could just as well call the function $Bob(c)$ or anything else we care to.

for production in period 2, which was *decided in period* 1. Thus even the Social Planner has to respect that fact that machines "take time" to build—the Social Planner cannot create machines by magic. If the Social Planner wants there to be a certain quantity of machines (capital) available for use in period 2, it must plan for that in period 1 by appropriately choosing how many machines it wants available the next period.

To describe the resource frontier of the economy, we actually need to proceed period by period. In period 1 the resource frontier is

$$c_1 + k_2 - (1 - \delta)k_1 = f(k_1),$$ (5)

and in period 2, the resource frontier is

$$c_2 + k_3 - (1 - \delta)k_2 = f(k_2).$$ (6)

The term $\delta \in (0,1)$ is the depreciation rate of capital (that portion of the machines that get "used up" or "worn out" by the act of production); hence the term $k_2 - (1 - \delta)k_1$ is gross investment in period 1, and $k_3 - (1 - \delta)k_2$ is gross investment in period 2.

As in our earlier study of the two-period model, there is no reason ever for the economy to have positive assets left over at the end of period 2 (and it is not feasible to have negative assets left over at the end of period 2), which immediately tells us that $k_3 = 0$. By our "time-to-build" assumption regarding capital, at the beginning of period 1 (which is where our analysis is focused), it is too late for the Social Planner to alter k_1; remaining to be chosen, though, is k_2.

The Social Planner's objective is to maximize consumers' lifetime utility subject to the pair of resource constraints (5) and (6), which will yield the economically efficient outcome in this two-period model. To proceed, let's first formulate the sequential, two-period Lagrangian for the Social Planner's problem,

$$v(c_1) + \beta v(c_2)$$
$$+ \lambda_1 [f(k_1) - c_1 - (k_2 - (1 - \delta)k_1)]$$
$$+ \beta \lambda_2 [f(k_2) - c_2 - (k_3 - (1 - \delta)k_2)],$$

where, as usual, λ_1 is the multiplier on the period-1 resource constraint and λ_2 is the multiplier on the period-2 resource constraint. The maximization here is from the perspective of the very beginning of period 1, and the objects of choice are c_1, c_2, and k_2; the three first-order conditions are, respectively,

$$v'(c_1) - \lambda_1 = 0,$$ (7)

$$\beta v'(c_2) - \beta \lambda_2 = 0,$$ (8)

and

$$-\lambda_1 + \beta \lambda_2 [f'(k_2) + 1 - \delta] = 0.$$ (9)

To emphasize again, by the time the beginning of period 1 arrives, k_1 has already been chosen, so there can be no first-order condition regarding k_1. Regarding k_3, it must be equal to zero because, in the two-period framework, there is no "production" that occurs in period 3. Any expenditure on k_3 would therefore be wasteful (so no first-order condition with respect to k_3 is needed).

Conditions (7), (8), and (9) describe the economically efficient outcome in this two-period economy. We can rearrange these three conditions to emphasize what is happening along the consumption–savings (intertemporal) margin. Condition (7) tells us that $\lambda_1 = v'(c_1)$; condition (8) tells us that $\lambda_2 = v'(c_2)$. If we insert both of these in condition (9) and rearrange a bit, we have

$$\frac{v'(c_1)}{\beta v'(c_2)} = f'(k_2) + 1 - \delta. \tag{10}$$

The left-hand side of (10) is nothing but the consumer's MRS between period-1 consumption and period-2 consumption (the β appears because it accounts for the consumer's impatience between the two periods).

The right-hand side of condition (10) is the economy's MRT between period-1 output and period-2 output. How can we understand the economic rationale behind the MRT term $f'(k_2) + 1 - \delta$?

Recall that the MRT measures how much production of one good must be forgone in order to have production of one more unit of another good. In our simple two-period economy, there are only two goods being produced: period-1 consumption and period-2 consumption.

Conduct the following thought experiment. Suppose that the economy wants to forgo one unit of period-1 consumption—meaning the economy needs to produce one less unit of period-1 output. Forgoing one unit of period-1 consumption means the economy (controlled, as it is here, by the Social Planner) can have one more unit of capital available for production in period 2. We can see this fact by examining the period-1 resource constraint, (5): recalling that k_1 is fixed, a one-unit reduction in c_1 means a one-unit rise in k_2. Qualitatively, forgoing one unit of consumption in a given period means one extra unit of *savings* (which is, at the economy-wide level, investment in capital accumulation) available for the next period.

Next we must consider what that one extra unit of k_2 implies for production in period 2. The extra unit of k_2 means a little extra production can take place in period 2. How much extra production is measured by the marginal product $f'(k_2)$—after all, the marginal product is *defined* as the extra production resulting from a one-unit increase in input.

However, during the wear and tear of the production process in period 2, a fraction δ of the one extra unit of k_2 will disappear in the form of depreciation. Thus, of the one extra unit of k_2, only the fraction $(1 - \delta)$ of it will remain intact. So, on net, the total extra resources that are *available* to the economy *in period 2* as a result of the economy forgoing one unit of consumption in period 1 is $f'(k_2)+1-\delta$, and this extra $f'(k_2)+1-\delta$ is available for period-2 consumption. Hence the economy's MRT between period-1 consumption and period-2 consumption is $f'(k_2)+1-\delta$.

Condition (10) tells us, as we know by now it should, that if the Social Planner makes choices for the two-period economy, it makes sure that the MRS between period-1 consumption and period-2 consumption is equated to the MRT between period-1 consumption and period-2 consumption. Condition (10) characterizes economic efficiency along the consumption–savings dimension. The importance of this efficiency condition is evident when studying the optimal tax rate on savings. An interesting point to note is that optimal *monetary* policy has nothing to do with the consumption–savings efficiency condition; even though *money* and *interest rates* are commonly thought of as being "intertemporal" features of the economy (i.e., money and interest rates "link" together different periods), the basic consideration of optimal monetary policy only has to do with efficiency along the consumption–leisure (a *static*, aka *intratemporal*) dimension, an idea that we saw in our first look at optimal monetary policy.

Chapter 18 Problem Set Questions

1. **Graphical representation of economic efficiency.** In the static (i.e., one-period) consumption–leisure model, the resource constraint is given by $c = n$, and consumers' (one-period) utility is given by $u(c, 1-n)$. In a plot with *leisure* on the horizontal axis and consumption on the vertical axis, represent (qualitatively) the resource constraint of the economy along with the economically efficient outcome.

2. **Economic efficiency in the two-period consumption–leisure model.** Recall the two-period consumption–leisure model (chapter 5). Suppose that the representative consumer's lifetime utility (two-period) function is given by $v(c_1, 1-n_1) + \beta v(c_2, 1-n_2)$, where c_t is consumption in period t, n_t is labor in period t, and thus $1-n_t$ is *leisure* in period t. The period-1 resource constraint of the economy is $c_1 + k_2 - (1-\delta)k_1 = f(k_1, n_1)$, and the period-2 resource constraint is $c_2 + k_3 + (1-\delta)k_2 = f(k_2, n_2)$. Note here that the production function depends on *both* capital and labor; the rest of the timing of events and notation are as in chapter 18.

   a. Combine the period-1 resource constraint and period-2 resource constraint into a lifetime resource constraint for the economy. (Hint: If you need to recall how to combine period-by-period constraints into a lifetime constraint, refer back to chapter 3.)

   b. Using the lifetime resource constraint you derived in part a, set up a lifetime Lagrangian for the Social Planner's problem in this two-period economy and characterize the economically efficient choices of consumption and labor (leisure) in each of the two periods—that is, derive the first-order conditions of the Social Planner's problem that describe the economically efficient choices of c_1, c_2, n_1, and n_2 and combine them into appropriate optimality conditions. (Hint: You should obtain two consumption–leisure optimality conditions and one consumption–savings condition here. Note that you won't actually be able to solve for these objects, though, because you are not given a utility function.)

19

Optimal Fiscal Policy

We now proceed to study optimal fiscal policy. We should make clear at the outset what we mean by this. In general, "fiscal policy" entails the government choosing its spending (how much to spend on building roads, bridges, wars, etc.) and some combination of taxes that finance that spending.[1] The convention in most macroeconomic analysis of fiscal policy is to *take as given* government spending; we will adopt this convention. That is, we will not think about *why* the government is choosing a particular level of spending, but rather just focus on, given some amount of spending, the optimal way for the government to pay for that spending. The reasons why the government chooses a particular level of spending are surely interesting to study, but they probably take us too far afield into the realms of political economy, the provision of public goods, and political science. Thus we confine ourselves here to the narrower topic of just the *optimal financing* of a pre-set amount of government spending.

Even given this limitation, we still have a lot to think about. One issue we need to take a stand on right away is what *types* of tax instruments we will assume the government has available to use in order to pay for its spending. For example, the government may be able to levy a labor income tax, it may be able to levy consumption taxes (sales taxes), and it may be able to levy taxes on savings or interest income. As our starting point, we will consider optimal fiscal policy in the context of the one-period consumption–leisure model; as such, a tax on savings or interest income has no meaning because, recall, the basic consumption–leisure model abstracts from time altogether and hence abstracts from

---

1. We are already being a bit loose about the elements of fiscal policy: another component is how much debt to issue. In any given period of time, a government can pay for its spending by either collecting taxes or issuing debt (bonds)—by borrowing. For our discussion of fiscal policy, we will assume that a government must always run a balanced budget; this assumption can indeed be justified given our restriction (discussed immediately below) here to a one-period setting. Debt only becomes interesting to think about in an explicitly dynamic (multi-period) setting. When we turn to the consideration of *jointly optimal* fiscal and monetary policy, we will do so in an explicitly dynamic setting and allow the government to issue debt. As we will see (even before turning to that topic), government debt plays a critical role in the *interaction* between fiscal policy and monetary policy; the basic idea behind this comes through in the *consolidated government budget constraint*.

savings and interest income. However, we will, once we have developed the core principles of optimal fiscal policy, see to what extent the lessons learned extend to a multi-period economy and what role, if any, taxes on savings or interest income play in the optimal conduct of fiscal policy.

Given our starting point of the one-period consumption–leisure model, it seems we still must decide whether we want to allow our government to have access to a labor income tax, a consumption tax, or both. It turns out that in our simple model, it does not matter which one we allow it to have, and in fact if we allow it to have both, we run into problems in figuring out what the optimal *mix* of consumption taxes and labor taxes is. Thus we will assume that it is only labor income taxes that the government has available in order to finance its spending.

As we proceed, the structure of the optimal policy problem should strike you as very familiar. When we studied optimal monetary policy, we laid out a framework that is applicable for *any* optimal policy problem, not just optimal monetary policy. Specifically, we (as the modelers) must specify how consumers make optimal choices. We must specify how production occurs and how firms make optimal (profit-maximizing) choices. We must then consider *simultaneously* the optimal choices of both consumers and firms *along with* the resource constraint of the economy. All of this so far should sound familiar.[2]

In studying optimal fiscal policy, there is one more element that becomes critical: the *government budget constraint.* This is not a new aspect of studying optimal policy problems: indeed it was present in our study of optimal monetary policy, but there it was not really at center stage.[3] There, it was easy to subsume it into the consumer and firm optimality conditions; here, it is not so easy to subsume it in that way, so it will play a more central role in our analysis. The simultaneous optimal choices of firms, consumers, *along with the government budget constraint,* comprise the *equilibrium* of the economy.

Just as before, we will assume the policy makers (here, fiscal policy makers) sit "above" the economy, watching how equilibrium unfolds. Fiscal policy makers understand that for any *given* policy they choose, the private sector (consumers and firms) will make optimal choices that result in *some* equilibrium. The various equilibria that result for any given, arbitrary, policy can be welfare-ranked according to the representative consumer's utility function. The *optimal policy problem* is thus once again a matter of choosing the *best* equilibrium, by choosing some appropriate policy.

---

2. If not, take a look back at our study of optimal monetary policy.

3. In our earlier study of optimal monetary policy, there was a government budget constraint (recall that it was $\tau_t = g_t M_{t-1}$, where τ was a lump-sum transfer and g was the growth rate of the nominal money supply). But this fiscal budget constraint did not play a very prominent role earlier for two reasons: (1) the tax was lump-sum in nature and (2) the only task for "fiscal policy" was to simply transfer nominal currency from (to) the central bank to (from) the private sector. The fiscal authority in that case had no decisions to make. In contrast, what we have in mind in this chapter by a "government budget constraint" is how a government can/does finance its own fiscal spending via non–lump-sum taxes.

We now proceed through the elements of the model, define equilibrium, develop the optimal policy problem, and then consider the results. Because here we are not concerned with monetary issues *at all*, we will not even bother to write things in nominal terms; all prices, quantities, and the like, will be written in real terms.

Firms

In this one-period economy, firms hire labor in a perfectly competitive labor market in order to produce output according the simple linear-in-labor production technology $f(n) = n$.[4] The (real) wage w is taken as given by the firm. The firm maximizes its profit, $f(n) - wn$, by choosing n. Substituting the linear production technology into the profit function and optimizing with respect to n, the result of the firm profit-maximization problem is

$$w = 1. \tag{1}$$

Condition (1) is one of the equilibrium conditions of the model, and is the only one that arises from the firm (supply) side of the model.

Notice the similarity of the representative firm's environment with our previous study of optimal monetary policy: in both cases the firm's problem is static and not affected by any tax.

Consumers

The representative consumer has a (one-period) utility function $u(c, 1 - n)$, in which c denotes consumption, n stands for labor, and $1 - n$ is leisure (thus, as we have done before, total time available for all activities is arbitrarily chosen to be one). The utility function thus depends on consumption and *leisure.*

The budget constraint of the representative consumer (again, we are expressing things in purely real terms here) is

$$c = (1 - t)wn, \tag{2}$$

in which the labor tax rate $t \in (0, 1)$ is taken as given, along with the real wage w, by the consumer. That is, one atomistic (i.e., small compared to the market) consumer has control over neither the market-determined (before-tax) real wage w nor the labor tax rate the government levies.[5]

---

4. Note there are no time subscripts here because we considering a one-period model—there are no distinct time periods.

5. This part of the model should be familiar from the basic consumption–leisure framework.

The consumer maximizes utility subject to the budget constraint (2). We know from our study of this model that at the optimal choice of the representative consumer, the condition

$$\frac{u_2(c, 1-n)}{u_1(c, 1-n)} = (1-t)w, \tag{3}$$

holds, where, as always, $u_1(.)$ is the marginal utility of consumption and $u_2(.)$ is the marginal utility of leisure. This completely standard consumption–leisure optimality condition states, as usual, that if the consumer is making utility-maximizing choices, the MRS between consumption and leisure is equated to the after-tax real wage rate.[6] Condition (3) is one of the equilibrium conditions of the model, and is the only one that arises from the consumer (demand) side of the model.

Government

As we mentioned, the government budget constraint plays a central role here. Denote government spending by the (sort of self-explanatory) variable *govt*. The government must pay for all of its spending through labor income taxes. The total amount of revenue generated by the labor income tax is total wages earned by the consumers in the economy times the tax rate: hence total labor tax revenue is $t \cdot w \cdot n$. The government budget constraint is thus

$$t \cdot w \cdot n = govt, \tag{4}$$

which simply states that total government spending must be covered by total tax revenues. Thus we assume that the government cannot/does not fail to pay for its spending.

Resource Constraint

As always, the resource constraint describes all of the different uses of total output (GDP) of the economy. In the model here, output is produced by the linear-in-labor production technology and there are *two* uses for output: private consumption (by consumers) and *public consumption* (i.e., government expenditures). Hence the resource constraint here is

$$c + govt = n. \tag{5}$$

Despite the supposition of a one-period economy, you should, as always, think of the resource constraint as the "GDP accounting equation" from basic macroeconomics.[7]

---

6. And, of course, the graphical analysis of this statement is also familiar to you from the basic consumption–leisure framework.

7. Because we have neither capital (thus no investment) nor net exports here, all of the output of the economy is used by either consumers or the government, which is what (5) states.

Private-Sector Equilibrium

Having described the actions of firms, consumers, the government, and the resource constraint, the next step, as always, is to consider *equilibrium.* Specifically, the equilibrium that we describe is the *private-sector equilibrium.* The private sector, which is composed of consumers and firms, of course, does not set fiscal policy—that is, agents in the private sector choose neither government spending nor tax rates. Rather, private-sector agents take as given both government spending and tax rates when making their optimal choices. Specifically, firms make profit-maximizing decisions that lead to their optimality condition (1); consumers make utility-maximizing decisions that lead to their optimality condition (3); and all markets clear, including goods markets, which means the resource constraint (5) must be satisfied. Thus conditions (1), (3), and (5) describe the *private-sector equilibrium* of the economy (again, the equilibrium that results for *any* arbitrarily chosen policy by the government).

In our study of optimal monetary policy we next proceeded to condense the private-sector equilibrium conditions into a single condition before proceeding to the optimal policy problem. We will do something similar here, but before we do, it turns out that in studying optimal *fiscal* policy, it is convenient from a mathematical standpoint to describe the private-sector equilibrium in a slightly different (but completely equivalent) way. Rather than saying the private-sector equilibrium is described by (1), (3), and (5), let's say that the private-sector equilibrium is described by (1), (2), and (3). That is, let's replace in our definition of equilibrium the resource constraint (5) with the representative consumer's budget constraint (2). We'll return below to why we do so, and why this is justified. For now, let's just proceed to analyze the optimal policy problem by supposing that conditions (1), (2), and (3) describe the private-sector equilibrium.

As we did in our study of optimal monetary policy, let's then try to condense as far as possible these private-sector equilibrium conditions. It is easy to substitute (1) into (3); the expression

$$\frac{u_2(c, 1-n)}{u_1(c, 1-n)} = (1-t) \tag{6}$$

condenses these conditions. Next we can substitute the consumer budget constraint (2) (with $w = 1$ substituted into it...) into (6) to eliminate the c, which gives us

$$\frac{u_2((1-t)n, 1-n)}{u_1((1-t)n, 1-n)} = (1-t). \tag{7}$$

Condition (7) condenses the entire description of the private-sector equilibrium of the economy down to a single expression—we will provide below the reason why it is valid in our analysis here to replace condition (5) with condition (2). In terms of prices and quantities being determined by the interaction of consumers and firms in markets, the only unknown in (7) is labor, n.

We can think of condition (7) as defining a function $n(t)$.[8] Condition (7) is further crucial for the optimal policy problem; it characterizes the *equilibrium* quantity of labor for any given tax rate t.

Formulation and Solution of Optimal Policy Problem

In terms of setting up the optimal policy problem, condition (7) defines the equilibrium quantity of labor in the economy *as a function of the labor tax rate t.* To emphasize this functional dependence, we will continue to write $n(t)$ to summarize the content of expression (7).

The policy problem is to choose such a tax rate that maximizes the representative consumer's utility, taking into account the $n(t)$ function *and* the government budget constraint. The government budget constraint was presented in expression (4). As has always been the case in our consideration of optimal policy problems, the government understands everything about the private-sector equilibrium of the economy: specifically, it understands that $w = 1$ and that the function $n(t)$ describes how equilibrium labor in the economy responds to tax rates.

Then, in the government budget constraint (4), because we are now at the stage of formulating the **optimal policy problem,** we can substitute these two conditions. Doing so allows us to now re-express the government budget constraint as

$$t \cdot n(t) = govt. \tag{8}$$

Note that here (to re-emphasize, we are *at the stage of formulating the optimal policy problem*), the labor tax rate appears *twice* in the government budget constraint: once directly and once through its influence on the private-sector equilibrium quantity of labor.

The government's policy problem thus boils down to the government choosing a tax rate t that maximizes the representative consumer's utility $u((1-t) \cdot n(t), 1 - n(t))$ subject to its (the government's) budget constraint (8). Here we must seemingly formulate a Lagrangian for the optimal policy problem. The Lagrangian for the optimal policy problem is

$$u((1-t) \cdot n(t), 1 - n(t)) + \lambda \cdot [govt - t \cdot n(t)], \tag{9}$$

in which λ is the Lagrange multiplier for the government budget constraint. As already stated, we are assuming here that $govt$ is predetermined, so the only policy choice the government must make is that of the optimal labor tax rate.

---

8. This idea is completely analogous to the idea that the consumer's optimality condition implicitly defined a function $c(g)$ when we studied optimal monetary policy.

Thus far we have been proceeding in very close analogy with our analysis of optimal monetary policy. However, at this point we depart from this close analogy. In the monetary policy problem, there was no government budget constraint to consider because there was no government spending that needed to be financed. In contrast, in the analysis here, there is a government budget constraint.

The *equilibrium version* (emphasis on equilibrium here) of the government budget constraint, (8), has only one unknown in it—the labor tax rate t. We have one equation (the government budget constraint) with one unknown (the tax rate t) to be chosen. The emphasis on equilibrium here is due to the fact that we already know, at this stage of the analysis, the equilibrium $n(t)$ function!

Hence, at this stage of the analysis, *there is no need to set up a Lagrangian for the optimal policy problem.* That is, we can simply solve condition (8) for the labor tax rate *given that $n(t)$* already appears in it!

Before doing so, first suppose that *govt* $= 0$. In this case there would obviously be no need to levy taxes (there is no expenditure that the government needs to finance), and indeed the government budget constraint immediately tells us that the government should levy $t = 0$. With $t = 0$, the consumer ends up choosing consumption and leisure in such a way as to make the MRS between consumption and leisure equal to one—this follows simply from plugging in $t = 0$ (along with $w = 1$) in condition (6).

Having studied economic efficiency in chapter 18, we can draw some further conclusions. We saw in chapter 18 in the one-period consumption–leisure model that *economic efficiency* requires the MRS between consumption and leisure to equal one. That is *exactly* the same outcome that we have here in the optimal policy problem with *govt* $= 0$. The government we have been thinking about here is *not* a Social Planner that gets to direct all the resources of the economy by fiat. The government we have been thinking about here *does,* in contrast to the Social Planner, explicitly consider markets and prices and equilibrium when making the optimal policy choice. Yet, if *govt* $= 0$, the government ends up choosing a policy that implements the economically efficient outcome, which is the beneficent Social Planning outcome.

Things are different when *govt* > 0, in which case the government necessarily has to levy $t > 0$. The question before us is: what is the t the government should pick? We just answered this question above in very general terms: the government must pick a t that satisfies (8)—there is no need to formulate a Lagrangian given that we have already obtained the private-sector's "reaction function" $n(t)$. However, we cannot make any more progress on computing the optimal labor tax rate without making some particular assumptions about the utility function. That is, without any knowledge of the function $n(t)$ (and ultimately it is the utility function that pins down the function $n(t)$), there is nothing further to say than that "the government should pick a t that satisfies expression (8)." We will assume a particular functional form for utility in a moment.

The Laffer Curve

Before we zoom in on a special case, let's generalize our analysis a bit. The government budget constraint equates tax revenues with government expenditures. The two objects are conceptually distinct from each other—that is, in concept, tax revenues and government expenditures need not have anything to do with each other. It is only the fact that governments try to make their revenues roughly line up with their expenditures that the two end up being related.

So let's define total tax revenue as a function of the tax rate, $TR(t)$. The left-hand side of the equilibrium version of the government budget constraint, expression (8), reveals that

$$TR(t) \equiv t \cdot n(t), \tag{10}$$

meaning total tax revenue collected depends not only on the tax rate directly but also on the equilibrium labor supply induced by a particular tax rate. Thus there are two effects of any given tax rate t on tax revenues, TR. These two effects are revealed by differentiating TR with respect to t; using the chain rule,

$$TR'(t) = n(t) + t \cdot n'(t), \tag{11}$$

which states that any *change* in the tax rate has two effects on tax revenue: it directly raises revenue—the first term on the right-hand side of (11)—and it also leads to a *fall* in revenue provided that $n'(t) < 0$—the second term on the right-hand side of (11).

That is, if the equilibrium quantity of labor in the economy falls when the tax rate rises (which is what $n'(t) < 0$ means), then a rise in the tax rate has a depressing effect on total tax revenue. Overall, whether tax revenues rise or fall when the tax rate increases (i.e., whether $TR'(t) > 0$ or $TR'(t) < 0$) depends on which of the two effects on the right-hand side of (11) is larger. For some (but not all) utility functions—and hence specifications of the function $n(t)$—the first effect dominates for small values of t and the second effect dominates for large values of t. For such utility functions the behavior of $TR(t)$ as a function of t is as depicted in figure 19.1.

The labor tax rate naturally takes on values only between zero and one; hence we limit the horizontal axis to this range. As figure 19.1 shows, total tax revenue rises until some threshold tax rate and then falls. This concept, known as the **Laffer curve,** is one you may be familiar with from basic macroeconomics.

For history buffs, the idea of the Laffer curve was popularized during the Reagan years. The Laffer curve fell under the umbrella of the casual, catch-all phrase "supply-side economics" that President Reagan promoted in the 1980s. The next section describes the numerical example that underlies figure 19.1.

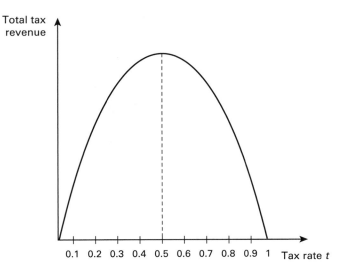

Total tax revenue

0.1 0.2 0.3 0.4 0.5 0.6 0.7 0.8 0.9 1   Tax rate t

Figure 19.1
Laffer curve, with total tax revenue (which in turn equals government spending, as per the GBC), plotted on the vertical axis and the labor tax rate plotted on the horizontal axis

A Numerical Example

To take a concrete example, suppose that the utility function is $u(c, 1-n) = 2\sqrt{c} + 2\sqrt{1-n}$. This means the marginal utility functions are $u_1 = 1/\sqrt{c}$ and $u_2 = 1/\sqrt{1-n}$. With this functional form for utility, we next need to determine the function $n(t)$. Recall from our definition of the private-sector equilibrium that it is condition (7) that we must use to figure out the function $n(t)$. With our assumed utility function, condition (7) takes on the form

$$\frac{\sqrt{1-t} \cdot \sqrt{n}}{\sqrt{1-n}} = 1-t, \tag{12}$$

which you should verify. Going through the few steps of algebra to solve (12) for n, we have that the function $n(t)$ for this particular utility function is

$$n(t) = \frac{(1-t)^2}{1-t+(1-t)^2}. \tag{13}$$

A plot of this result is shown in figure 19.2. Thus, for the assumed utility function, the equilibrium quantity of labor does indeed fall as the labor tax rises. That is, $n'(t) < 0$ in this example, meaning that a Laffer curve could potentially arise.

Using expression (13), we can in turn rewrite the government budget constraint as

$$\frac{t \cdot (1-t)^2}{1-t+(1-t)^2} = govt, \tag{14}$$

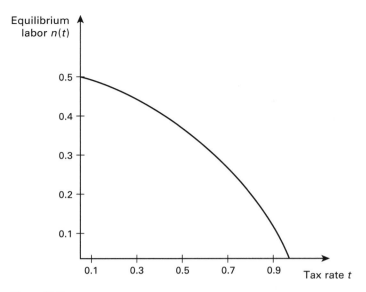

Figure 19.2
For the given utility function, equilibrium labor supply (plotted on vertical axis) as a function of the labor tax rate (plotted on the horizontal axis)

which, of course, is simply $t \cdot n(t) = govt$ with (13) substituted in. The left-hand side of (14) is the function $TR(t)$—that is, it shows total tax revenue as a function of the tax rate. If we plot the $TR(t)$ function, we have exactly what is plotted in figure 19.1. Thus a Laffer curve does indeed arise for this particular utility function.[9]

Now let's conclude our analysis—that is, let's finally determine the optimal tax rate that finances a given amount of government spending. Suppose that $govt = 0.1$ is the amount of spending that needs to be financed via taxes. Figure 19.1 shows us that there are *two* tax rates that raise this amount of total revenue: $t = 0.22984$ and $t = 0.87015$ both raise 0.1 units of total revenue. So is the government indifferent about which one it chooses? Or is there still a meaningful decision for the *optimal* policy maker to make?

To answer the question, we (i.e., the policy maker) must evaluate the representative consumer's utility under the two possible choices of tax rates—after all, the policy maker is trying to maximize the consumer's utility, albeit subject to the need to raise a given amount of revenue through taxation. If the government chooses the higher tax rate, $t = 0.87015$, then expression (13) tells us that $n = 0.1149$, meaning $1 - n = 0.8851$.

The consumer budget constraint (2) then reveals that $c = (1 - 0.87015) \cdot 1 \cdot 0.1149 = 0.01492$. This means that the representative consumer's utility is

---

9. A Laffer curve does not arise for every utility function; thus one needs to begin from the basics in order to determine whether a Laffer curve arises for any particular utility function under consideration.

$u(0.01492, 1-0.1149) = 2\sqrt{0.01492} + 2\sqrt{1-0.1149} = 2.12589$. If the government instead chooses the lower tax rate $t = 0.22984$, the same analysis reveals that $n = 0.43508$, $1 - n = 0.56492$, $c = (1-0.22984) \cdot 1 \cdot 0.43508 = 0.33806$, and thus $u(0.33806, 1-0.43508) = 2.66608$. The objective of maximizing utility then dictates that the government should choose the lower tax rate; it raises the same amount of total revenue and allows the representative consumer to achieve higher total utility.

It may seem, from the latter part of our analysis, that we used only the government budget constraint to obtain the optimal tax rate. This is not true. In the government budget constraint (8), we needed to know the *private-sector function* $n(t)$. We could not obtain this equilibrium "reaction function" that the government needs to know without *first* solving for the private-sector equilibrium; once we solved for the private-sector equilibrium, then and only then were we able to proceed to the formulation and solution of the policy problem.

The first part of our analysis—solving for the private-sector equilibrium—was exactly the same (with one caveat that we return to below) as in our study of optimal monetary policy. The second part of the analysis differed a bit because of the presence of the government budget constraint. In particular, we did not need to formulate a Lagrangian because in essence the policy problem boiled down to solving one equation (the government budget constraint) in one unknown. The twist was that two solutions arose, so that we had to compare the two solutions to see which delivered higher utility. But in both our earlier study of optimal monetary policy and our study here of optimal fiscal policy, the idea and approach are similar: *first solve for the private-sector equilibrium, from which we need to glean a private-sector equilibrium reaction function*; then formulate and solve the policy problem.

The only caveat in our formulation of the private-sector equilibrium here, recall, was that we used the household budget constraint (2) rather than the economy's resource constraint (5). The reason using either turns out to be equivalent in our analysis here is that we knew that we were ultimately going to use (had to use ...) the government budget constraint in the optimal policy problem. Any two of the three—the household budget constraint, the government budget constraint, and the resource constraint—imply that the third holds as well. For example, if we sum the household budget constraint and the government budget constraint (and use the equilibrium condition $w = 1$), we immediately have the resource constraint. Thus, as long two of the three conditions are satisfied, the third is satisfied as well. It turns out to be more convenient in the formulation of an optimal fiscal policy problem to use the household budget constraint rather than the resource constraint in the specification of the private-sector equilibrium.

Chapter 19 Problem Set Questions

1. **The Laffer curve.** Consider the model of optimal labor income taxation we studied in chapter 19. All the notation and ideas are as developed there. For each of the following utility functions, first derive the function $n(t)$ (i.e., the function relating the equilibrium quantity of labor supply to the labor tax rate), then express total tax revenue as a function of the labor tax rate $TR(t)$, then determine whether a Laffer curve arises.

   a. $u(c, 1-n) = 2\sqrt{c} + (1-n)$.

   b. $u(c, 1-n) = \ln c + \ln(1-n)$.

2. **A consumption tax.** In the one-period model from chapter 19, suppose that instead of having access to labor income taxes, the government can levy only a consumption tax (i.e., a sales tax) in order to pay for its expenditures. The household budget constraint is thus $(1 + t^C)c = w \cdot n$, where $t^C \geq 0$ is the consumption tax rate (e.g., in Washington, DC, $t^C = 0.0575$). The government budget constraint is thus $t^c \cdot c = govt$. For each of the following utility functions, first derive a function $c(t^C)$ (which is a function relating the equilibrium quantity of consumption to the consumption tax rate), then express total tax revenue as a function of the consumption tax rate $TR(t^c)$, then determine whether a Laffer curve for consumption tax revenue arises. You should proceed in as close an analogy as possible with the analysis we conducted in chapter 19. Furthermore continue to assume that firm-optimization leads to the condition $w = 1$ and the resource constraint of the economy is $c + govt = n$.

   a. $u(c, 1-n) = 2\sqrt{c} + (1-n)$

   b. $u(c, 1-n) = \ln c + \ln(1-n)$

3. **Optimal tax policy.** Consider our static (i.e., one-period) consumption–leisure framework from chapter 2. In this problem you will use this framework as a basis for offering guidance regarding optimal (i.e., the "best") labor income tax policy.

   Recall the basic consumption–leisure optimality condition

   $$\frac{u_l(c, l)}{u_c(c, l)} = (1 - t)w,$$

   in which all of the notation is as in chapter 2: t denotes the labor income tax rate, w denotes the real wage, c denotes consumption, l denotes leisure, u_c denotes the marginal utility of consumption, and u_l denotes the marginal utility of leisure.

Suppose that firms are monopolistically competitive (rather than perfectly competitive). It can be shown in this case that when firms are making their profit-maximizing choice regarding labor hiring, the following condition is true:

$mpn = w(1 - monpol)$.

Here mpn denotes the marginal product of labor and $monpol$ is a measure of the degree of monopoly power that firms wield. For example, if $monpol = 0$, then firms wield no monopoly power whatsoever, in which case we are back to our perfectly competitive framework of firm profit maximization from chapter 6.

If instead $monpol > 0$, then firms do wield some monopoly power. (Note: The variable $monpol$ can never be less than zero. You also do not need to be concerned here with how the expression above is derived—just take it as given. Further note that there are no financing constraint issues here whatsoever.)

Assume the following:

1. The only goal policy makers have in choosing a labor tax rate t is to ensure that the perfectly competitive outcome in labor markets is attained.

2. Any monopoly power that firms have cannot be directly eliminated by policy makers. That is, if $monpol > 0$, the government cannot do anything about that; all the government can do is choose a tax rate t.

Based on both of the assumptions above, derive a relationship between the optimal (i.e., in the sense that it attains the goal of policy makers described in assumption 1) labor income tax rate and the degree of firms' monopoly power. Very carefully explain all your logic and arguments, including any mathematical derivations involved. (Note: There are a number of logical steps to the argument, which are left to you to determine.)

4. **Two-period Ramsey optimal taxation.** Consider a two-period economy in which the government must collect taxes in order to finance government purchases g_1 and g_2. Suppose that the government *cannot* levy lump-sum taxes; instead, all taxes are in the form of proportional consumption taxes (i.e., sales taxes). When taxes are proportional, one general lesson we've seen is that the timing of taxes *does* matter (for consumption and national savings).[10]

What it means that the timing of taxes "matters" is that consumption decisions of the economy are affected by the tax rates that the government levies. In order to raise the revenue needed to pay for g_1 and g_2, the government does have to levy some taxes: an interesting question is what is the optimal tax rates for the government to set. Here we

---

10. Let's ignore the result we saw on the midterm exam that if the government can collect taxes on period-1 consumption in period 2, then the timing of taxes does not matter.

mean "optimal" in the sense that the government ultimately cares about the representative consumer's lifetime utility, which is known as a "Ramsey government problem."

The Ramsey government problem essentially tries to answer the following question: What tax rates should the government set?

Assume the following:

a. The real interest rate between period 1 and period 2 is zero (i.e., $r_1 = 0$).

b. The representative agent has no control over his real income y_1 or y_2.

c. The consumption tax rates in the two periods are denoted t_1^C and t_2^C.

d. The representative consumer starts with zero initial assets ($a_0 = 0$); thus the LBC of the consumer is $(1 + t_1^C)c_1 + (1 + t_2^C)c_2 = y_1 + y_2$.

e. The government starts with zero initial assets ($b_0 = 0$); thus the LBC of the government is $g_1 + g_2 = t_1^C c_1 + t_2^C c_2$.

f. The lifetime utility function of the consumer is $u(c_1, c_2) = \ln c_1 + \ln c_2$.

There are three steps to computing the Ramsey-optimal tax rates.

a. The first step is to determine the consumer's optimal choices of c_1 and c_2 as functions of y_1, y_2, t_c^1, and t_2^C. In setting up the appropriate Lagrangian, solve for the optimal choices of consumption in period 1 and consumption in period 2 as a function of these four objects.

Next, for a moment, suppose that the government did have the ability to levy lump-sum taxes. If it could levy lump-sum taxes, then the government's LBC would be $g_1 + g_2 = T_1 + T_2$ (i.e., these are the *same* g_1 and g_2 as above) and the consumer's LBC would be $c_1 + T_1 + c_2 + T_2 = y_1 + y_2$, where T_1 and T_2 denote lump-sum taxes in periods 1 and 2.

b. In the case of lump-sum taxes, what would be the consumer's optimal choices of consumption in period 1 and period 2? (Set up a Lagrangian here if you need, but if you are able to logically determine the optimal quantities of consumption here, you may do so.)

c. Compare your solutions for optimal period-1 consumption and optimal period-2 consumption in parts a and b above. Solve for the tax rates t_1^C and t_2^C that equate these two different sets of choices. These tax rates you find, which are the optimal tax rates, should be functions of y_1, y_2, g_1, and g_2 and no other variables. How do the two tax rates compare to each other?

5. Welfare losses from distortionary taxation. A central question behind many policy proposals in macroeconomics and public finance is the potential welfare consequences of distortionary tax systems. Here you will consider the welfare consequences associated with labor income taxation in the context of the static consumption–leisure model.

Specifically, we will consider how much consumers "lose" due to a labor income tax rate of 20 percent as compared to a labor income tax rate of 0 (zero) percent. (To connect with ideas you know from basic economics, what you will formally compute is the "deadweight loss" of a system with 20 percent labor income taxation compared to a system with zero percent labor income taxation.)

A typical welfare analysis proceeds in the following three steps:

1. Solve for the representative consumer's optimal choices under the proposed tax policy (in our case, a labor income tax rate of 20 percent).

2. Solve for the representative consumer's optimal choices under the alternative tax policy (in our case, a labor income tax rate of zero percent).

3. Compute the *additional percentage of consumption* that the representative consumer would need under the proposed tax policy to be equally happy in terms of utility as under the alternative tax policy.

How to implement step 3 is described in detail after part b below. If the units of time are 168 hours (per week), the representative consumer's budget constraint in the static consumption–leisure model can be expressed in real terms as $c + (1-t)wl = 168(1-t)w$; for simplicity, suppose throughout the analysis that the real wage is $w = 1$ no matter what tax policy is in place. A critical component to the answer to welfare questions could be the precise functional form that the (representative consumer's) utility function takes.

a. Suppose that the representative consumer's utility function over consumption and leisure is $u(c, l) = \ln c + \ln l$. Numerically solve for the optimal choices of consumption and leisure under both the proposed policy (20 percent labor tax) and the alternative policy (zero labor tax)—that is, conduct steps 1 and 2 of the analysis for this utility function.

b. Suppose that the representative consumer's utility function over consumption and leisure is $u(c, l) = 2\sqrt{c} + 2\sqrt{l}$. Numerically solve for the optimal choices of consumption and leisure under both the proposed policy (20 percent labor tax) and the alternative policy (zero labor tax)—that is, conduct steps1 and 2 of the analysis for this utility function. (Note: The remainder of this question is more difficult.)

Implementing step 3 of the welfare analysis means first comparing the total number of utils under the proposed policy with the total number of utils under the alternative tax policy and then determining how much additional consumption (measured in percent) would be required under the proposed policy to make the total number of utils the same under both policies. For example, suppose that the total number of utils (when consumers are making their optimal consumption–leisure choices) under the proposed policy were 5, while the total number of utils (when consumers are making their optimal consumption–leisure choices) under the alternative policy were 7. If policy makers implemented the proposed policy and also could somehow just "hand" to consumers an extra X percent of consumption that would make them equally well off (in utility terms) as under the alternative policy, the number X would measure the welfare loss of the proposed policy compared to the alternative policy. The reason why welfare losses are computed this way is because utils in and of themselves are meaningless numbers.

Mathematically, the welfare measure X solves the equation

$$u\left((1+X)c^{*}_{PROPOSED\ POLICY}, l^{*}_{PROPOSED\ POLICY}\right) = u\left(c^{*}_{ALTERNATIVE\ POLICY}, l^{*}_{ALTERNATIVE\ POLICY}\right);$$

note carefully how the variable X enters this expression.

c. Based on your work in part a, compute, for the utility function $u(c,l) = \ln c + \ln l$, how much extra consumption X (as defined above) is required under the tax policy of 20 percent as compared to the tax policy of zero percent? Show all important steps/logic in your work. (Note: The number X will not necessarily be a nice "round" number and may require use of a calculator.)

d. Based on your work in part a, compute, for the utility function $u(c,l) = 2\sqrt{c} + 2\sqrt{l}$, how much extra consumption X (as defined above) is required under the tax policy of 20 percent as compared to the tax policy of zero percent? Show all important steps/logic in your work. (Note: The number X will not necessarily be a nice "round" number and may require use of a calculator.)

20

Optimal Fiscal and Monetary Policy

We now proceed to study jointly optimal monetary and fiscal policy. The motivation behind this topic stems directly from observations regarding the consolidated government budget constraint. Specifically, a broad lesson emerging from our study of fiscal–monetary interactions is that *money creation* and thus inflation potentially helps the *fiscal authority* to pay for its government spending. Alternatively, a broad interpretation we made when we studied optimal monetary policy in chapter 17 was that steady-state inflation (more precisely, any steady-state deviation from the Friedman rule) acted as a *tax* on consumers. At that stage we did not note that a deviation from the Friedman rule, acting as a "tax," potentially *raised revenue* for the government; now, with our notion of a consolidated budget constraint, we are in a position to understand this latter idea.

Here the question that we take up is: If *both* monetary *and* fiscal policies are conducted optimally, what is the *optimal steady-state mix* of labor taxes and inflation needed to finance some fixed amount of government spending? Our approach to answering this question will hew very closely to the methods of analysis we have already developed in our separate looks at optimal monetary policy in chapter 17 (without regard for fiscal policy) and optimal fiscal policy in chapter 19 (without regard for monetary policy).

The model we use to answer this question mostly combines elements we have already seen. To overview the key elements of the model, we will use to try to think about our main question, our model will:

- feature an infinite number of periods,
- model money using the money-in-the-utility function (MIU) approach,
- feature labor income taxes as the only direct fiscal instrument (i.e., no consumption taxes and no taxes on savings),
- feature a consolidated government budget constraint,
- feature a simple linear-in-labor production technology,
- focus on the steady state.

Because by now most of these model elements are familiar to us, we will not spend much time developing the details of the basic model; rather we will spend most of our time analyzing the optimal policy problem and its solution.

Firms

The way in which we model firms is as we have often done: the representative firm simply hires labor each period in perfectly competitive labor markets and sells its output. The production technology we assume here is also as simple as possible, linear in labor: $y_t = f(n_t) = n_t$. Firms' profits in period t (in nominal terms) are thus simply $P_t y_t - W_t n_t$, where the notation is standard: P_t is the nominal price of goods, W_t is the nominal wage, and n_t is the quantity of labor. When the firm is maximizing profits, we assume that it takes as given both the nominal price P and the nominal wage W.[1] Substituting the linear production technology into the profit function and optimizing with respect to n_t (the only item the firm decides here is how many units of labor to hire on a period-by-period basis) yields the firm first-order condition $P_t - W_t = 0$. If we define, as usual, the real wage as $w_t = W_t/P_t$, the result of firm profit maximization is

$$w_t = 1. \tag{1}$$

Condition (1) is one of the equilibrium conditions of the simple model we are developing, and is the only one that arises from the firm (supply) side of the model.

Consumers

As mentioned above, we will model consumers using our money-in-the-utility function (MIU) specification. The representative consumer begins period t with nominal money holdings M_{t-1}, nominal bond holdings B_{t-1}, and stock (a real asset) holdings a_{t-1}. The period-t budget constraint of the consumer is

$$P_t c_t + P_t^b B_t + M_t + S_t a_t = (1 - t_t)W_t n_t + M_{t-1} + B_{t-1} + (S_t + D_t)a_{t-1}, \tag{2}$$

where the notation again is as in the MIU model presented earlier: S_t is the nominal price of a unit of stock, D_t is the nominal dividend paid by each unit of stock, and P_t^b is the nominal price of a one-period nominal bond with face value \$1. Because we continue to assume that all bonds are one-period bonds and the face value of each bond is $FV = 1$, we have that

$$P_t^b = \frac{1}{1 + i_t}$$

---

1. Nothing more than our usual assumption of price-taking behavior; here price-taking describes the firm's behavior in both output markets and input markets.

(which you should recall), where i_t is the net nominal interest rate on a nominal bond held from period t to period $t + 1$. Note the term $(1 - t_t)W_t n_t$ in the budget constraint: it represents total after-tax labor income in period t. The consumer takes both the wage W_t and the fiscal tax rate t_t as given.[2]

Note the *absence* in the consumer budget constraint of the lump-sum amount of transfer from the government that was present in our chapter 17 study of optimal monetary policy. This is one subtle, but crucial, difference in the model we are using here to study *jointly optimal* fiscal and monetary policy.

The present value of lifetime utility of the consumer is, as expected, given by

$$u\left(c_t, \frac{M_t}{P_t}, 1 - n_t\right) + \beta u\left(c_{t+1}, \frac{M_{t+1}}{P_{t+1}}, 1 - n_{t+1}\right) + \beta^2 u\left(c_{t+2}, \frac{M_{t+2}}{P_{t+2}}, 1 - n_{t+2}\right) + ..., \tag{3}$$

in which each period's utility depends on consumption c, real money balances M / P, and leisure $1 - n$ and also, as is standard by now, future utility is discounted by the factor β.

Setting up a sequential Lagrangian (with λ_t as the multiplier on the consumer's time-t budget constraint) obtains

$$u\left(c_t, \frac{M_t}{P_t}, 1 - n_t\right) + \beta u\left(c_{t+1}, \frac{M_{t+1}}{P_{t+1}}, 1 - n_{t+1}\right) + \beta^2 u\left(c_{t+2}, \frac{M_{t+2}}{P_{t+2}}, 1 - n_{t+2}\right) + ...$$
$$+ \lambda_t\left[(1 - t_t)W_t n_t + M_{t-1} + B_{t-1} + (S_t + D_t)a_{t-1} - P_t c_t - P_t^b B_t - M_t - S_t a_t\right]$$
$$+ \beta\lambda_{t+1}\left[(1 - t_{t+1})W_{t+1} n_{t+1} + M_t + B_t + (S_{t+1} + D_{t+1})a_t - P_{t+1} c_{t+1} - P_{t+1}^b B_{t+1} - M_{t+1} - S_{t+1} a_{t+1}\right]$$
$$+ .... \tag{4}$$

In period t, the consumer optimally chooses $(c_t, n_t, M_t, B_t, a_t)$. Proceeding mechanically, we write the first-order-conditions with respect to each of these five choice variables, respectively, as

$$u_1\left(c_t, \frac{M_t}{P_t}, 1 - n_t\right) - \lambda_t P_t = 0, \tag{5}$$

$$-u_3\left(c_t, \frac{M_t}{P_t}, 1 - n_t\right) + \lambda_t(1 - t_t)W_t = 0, \tag{6}$$

$$\frac{u_2\left(c_t, \frac{M_t}{P_t}, 1 - n_t\right)}{P_t} - \lambda_t + \beta\lambda_{t+1} = 0, \tag{7}$$

$$-\lambda_t P_t^b + \beta\lambda_{t+1} = 0, \tag{8}$$

$$-\lambda_t S_t + \beta\lambda_{t+1}(S_{t+1} + D_{t+1}) = 0. \tag{9}$$

---

2. As before, we "the modeler" know from the firm optimality condition (1) that it will (in equilibrium) be the case that $W_t = P_t$. However, the consumer need not "understand" this; all the consumer does is take W_t is as given.

Conditions (5) through (9) describe how consumers make optimal choices; as such, they represent equilibrium conditions. As usual, though, it is instructive to not work with these raw first-order conditions directly but instead to combine them into interpretable expressions of the form "MRS equals a price ratio," which is the cornerstone of consumer theory. From here on, to save on notation, we will adopt the following convention regarding arguments of functions. Rather than write, for example,

$$u_1\left(c_t, \frac{M_t}{P_t}, 1-n_t\right)$$

to stand for the marginal utility of consumption in period t, we will simply write u_{1t}, and it will be understood that the second subscript t indicates time-t arguments (specifically, c_t, M_t/P_t, and $1-n_t$) that are arguments of the marginal utility function. Thus u_{2t} stands for the marginal utility of real money balances in period t, u_{3t} stands for the marginal utility of leisure in period t, u_{1t+1} stands for the marginal utility of consumption in period $t+1$, u_{2t+1} stands for the marginal utility of real money balances in period $t+1$, and so on.

With this notational convention, condition (5) implies that

$$\lambda_t = \frac{u_{1t}}{P_t}.$$

Inserting this in condition (6) and rearranging, we have

$$\frac{u_{3t}}{u_{1t}} = (1-t_t)w_t, \tag{10}$$

where, as usual, $w_t = W_t/P_t$, stands for the *real* wage in period t. We have seen condition (10) countless times by now: it is simply the consumer's consumption–leisure optimality condition, stating that the MRS between consumption and leisure (the left-hand side) equals the after-tax real wage. Condition (10) is an equilibrium condition of the model, and it describes how consumers make optimal consumption–leisure trade-offs.

Next condition (8) tells us $\beta\lambda_{t+1} = \lambda_t P_t^b$. Using this fact in condition (7), we can write

$$\frac{u_{2t}}{P_t} - \lambda_t + \lambda_t P_t^b = 0,$$

or equivalently,

$$\frac{u_{2t}}{P_t} = \lambda_t\left[1 - P_t^b\right].$$

But recall that with bonds that always have a face value of one,

$$P_t^b = \frac{1}{1+i_t},$$

we can write the previous expression as

$$\frac{u_{2t}}{P_t} = \lambda_t \left[1 - \frac{1}{1+i_t} \right],$$

which can be further simplified to

$$\frac{u_{2t}}{P_t} = \lambda_t \left[\frac{i_t}{1+i_t} \right].$$

Recalling from above that

$$\lambda_t = \frac{u_{1t}}{P_t},$$

we can therefore write

$$\frac{u_{2t}}{u_{1t}} = \frac{i_t}{1+i_t}, \tag{11}$$

which states that when consumers are making optimal choices, the MRS between consumption and real money holdings (the left-hand side) depends on the nominal interest rate.[3] Condition (11) is the *consumption–money optimality condition* of this model, in analogy with the consumption–leisure optimality condition, and is an equilibrium condition of the model.

Finally, the first-order condition on stock holding, equation (9), can be algebraically re-arranged—along with condition (8) and the time-$t + 1$ version of condition(5)—to yield a consumption–savings optimality condition,

$$\frac{u_{1t}}{u_{1t+1}} = \beta(1+r_t). \tag{12}$$

To recall details, refer back to the analysis of the consumer's optimization problem in chapter 17.

Resource Constraint

As always, the resource constraint describes all of the different uses of total output (GDP) of the economy. In the model here, output is produced by the linear-in-labor production

---

3. Don't be misled by the notation: here, u_2 stands for the marginal utility *of real money balances* because real money balances is the second argument of the utility function. In much of what we've done before, the second argument of the utility function was leisure, meaning that in previous models u_2 stood for the marginal utility *of leisure;* in the model we are studying here, the marginal utility of leisure is u_3 because leisure is the *third* argument of the utility function. This is simply a notational choice, however; we could have just as readily chosen to make leisure the second argument and real money balances the third argument.

technology, and as in the model we used to study just fiscal policy, there are *two* uses for output: private consumption (by consumers) and *public consumption* (i.e., government expenditures). Hence the resource constraint in any arbitrary period t is

$$c_t + govt_t = n_t. \tag{13}$$

Government

The government is a consolidated fiscal–monetary authority, as in our study of fiscal–monetary interactions. The period-t budget constraint of the consolidated government is

$$t_t \cdot W_t \cdot n_t + P_t^b B_t + M_t - M_{t-1} = P_t \cdot govt_t + B_{t-1}, \tag{14}$$

which is an adaptation of the consolidated period-t government budget constraint we encountered in chapter 16; the only difference is that rather than fiscal tax revenue being specified arbitrarily as T_t, here we have $t_t \cdot W_t \cdot n_t$. The consolidated government budget constraint (GBC) has the same interpretation as in chapter 16: the GBC states that government spending on goods and services as well as repayments of maturing government debt—the right-hand side of (14)—can be covered by three sources—the left-hand side of (14): labor income tax revenue, issuance/sales of new government bonds, and money creation.

Equilibrium and Steady-State Equilibrium

The next step, as usual, is to describe the private-sector equilibrium. Because the general idea is the same as in our earlier (separate) studies of optimal monetary policy and optimal fiscal policy, we do not discuss this in detail here. Rather, we simply proceed to list the equilibrium conditions and then condense things down to a small set of steady-state equilibrium conditions.

The firm optimality condition (1) is the only equilibrium condition arising from the supply (of goods) side of the model. On the demand side of the model, expressions (10), (11), and (12) describe, respectively, the representative consumer's consumption–leisure optimality condition, consumption–money optimality condition, and consumption–savings optimality condition. As such, all three are also equilibrium conditions of our model.

In principle, the resource constraint is an equilibrium condition of the model, as well. But, as we were able to do in our study of optimal fiscal policy in chapter 19, we can use the consumer's budget constraint, given by expression (2), in place of the resource constraint. Hence expression (2) is the final condition describing the private-sector equilibrium.

We are concerned with steady states, so we must impose steady state on all of the equilibrium conditions. At this stage imposing steady state should be a relatively straightforward exercise. Let's analyze in some detail, though, the steady-state version of the consumer budget constraint.

For reasons that will become a bit clearer when we formulate the optimal policy problem below, let's assume that $B = 0$ always. Also it turns out that for our purpose (studying jointly optimal fiscal and monetary policy), the steady-state quantity of stock holdings the consumer has is irrelevant, thus let's also assume (without further proof of its irrelevance) that $a = 0$ always.[4] With these simplifying assumptions, we can rewrite (2) in real terms (i.e., dividing through by P_t) as

$$c_t + \frac{M_t}{P_t} = (1 - t_t)w_t n_t + \frac{M_{t-1}}{P_t},$$ (15)

or by putting both terms involving money on the same side of the equation, as

$$c_t = (1 - t_t)w_t n_t + \frac{M_{t-1}}{P_t} - \frac{M_t}{P_t}.$$ (16)

Defining $m_t \equiv M_t / P_t$ as real money balances, and using the manipulation

$$\frac{M_{t-1}}{P_t} = \frac{M_{t-1}}{P_{t-1}} \frac{P_{t-1}}{P_t} = \frac{m_{t-1}}{1 + \pi_t},$$

we can rewrite (16) as

$$c_t = (1 - t_t)w_t n_t + \frac{m_{t-1}}{1 + \pi_t} - m_t.$$ (17)

Imposing steady state results in

$$c = (1 - t)wn + m\left[\frac{1}{1 + \pi} - 1\right].$$ (18)

We already know that in steady state, the inflation rate equals the money growth rate; if it did not, then real money balances could not be constant in the steady state.[5] Re-adopting our notation from before, let g be the steady-state growth rate of the nominal money supply. Then

$$c = (1 - t)wn - m\left[\frac{g}{1 + g}\right];$$ (19)

4. Note that we are making these assertions *after* we have already obtained the consumer's FOCs. If we had made these assumptions *before* computing FOCs, the structure of the entire model would be drastically different; as it stands, it is relatively innocuous, but for reasons that we leave for a more advanced course in macroeconomic theory.

5. In other words, having already asserted that real money balances become constant in the steady state, it must be, by the definition of real money balances, that M/P is constant. The only way for M/P to be constant is for the numerator and the denominator to both be changing at the same exact rate. This is nothing more than our usual monetarist/quantity-theoretic notion that in the long run (i.e., in steady state), the money growth rate is equal to the inflation rate.

notice the appearance of the minus sign on the right-hand side. Substituting $w = 1$, we have that the consumer's choice of consumption depends on his choice of labor supply and real money holdings,

$$c = (1-t)n - m\left[\frac{g}{1+g}\right]. \tag{20}$$

As we did in our analysis in purely optimal fiscal policy, we can substitute this expression for steady-state equilibrium consumption into the remaining private-sector equilibrium conditions, which are the (steady-state version of the) consumption–leisure optimality condition (10) and the (steady-state version of the) consumption–money optimality condition (11). Note that we do *not* need to make this substitution into the (steady-state version of the) consumption–savings optimality condition because if we impose steady state on equation (12), we find, as always, that $1/\beta = 1+r$. Of course, by the exact Fisher equation and the fact that $\pi = g$ in steady state, this can in turn be expressed as

$$\frac{1}{\beta} = \frac{1+i}{1+\pi} = \frac{1+i}{1+g},$$

which reveals that in steady-state equilibrium,

$$1+i = \frac{1+g}{\beta}, \tag{21}$$

which was also true in our discussion of purely optimal monetary policy in chapter 17.

Making the substitution for c in the consumption–leisure and consumption–money optimality conditions thus give us

$$\frac{u_3\left((1-t)n - m\left[\frac{g}{1+g}\right], m, 1-n\right)}{u_1\left((1-t)n - m\left[\frac{g}{1+g}\right], m, 1-n\right)} = 1-t \tag{22}$$

and

$$\frac{u_2\left((1-t)n - m\left[\frac{g}{1+g}\right], m, 1-n\right)}{u_1\left((1-t)n - m\left[\frac{g}{1+g}\right], m, 1-n\right)} = \frac{1+g-\beta}{1+g}. \tag{23}$$

In writing these two expressions, we have (intentionally) re-introduced the arguments to the marginal utility functions and also used the relationship in (21) to eliminate the nominal interest rate.

Conditions (22) and (23) condense the entire description of the private-sector equilibrium of the economy down to two conditions. Jointly, these two conditions should be thought of as defining *a pair of functions* $n(t, g)$ and $m(t, g)$.[6]

Formulation of Optimal Policy Problem

Our objective is to study *jointly optimal steady-state* fiscal and monetary policies. The policy problem is to choose a tax rate t and a monetary growth rate g that maximizes the representative consumer's utility taking into account the equilibrium function $n(t, g)$, the equilibrium function $m(t, g)$, and the government budget constraint.

Because we are only concerned with steady-state policy, to move toward this goal, let's first rearrange the government budget constraint (14) and turn it into a steady-state expression. First recognize, as usual, that $P_t^b = 1/(1+i_t)$, and divide through by P_t to put everything in real terms:

$$t_t w_t n_t + \frac{1}{1+i_t} \frac{B_t}{P_t} + \frac{M_t - M_{t-1}}{P_t} = govt_t + \frac{B_{t-1}}{P_t}. \tag{24}$$

On the right-hand side, notice, as is always the case in a consolidated fiscal–monetary budget constraint, the appearance of seignorage revenues, $sr_t = (M_t - M_{t-1})/P_t$. As above and in chapter 16, define $b_t \equiv B_t / P_t$ as the real amount of government debt outstanding at the end of period t. Also break up the seignorage revenue term as

$$\frac{M_t - M_{t-1}}{P_t} = \frac{M_t}{P_t} - \frac{M_{t-1}}{P_t} = \frac{M_t}{P_t} - \frac{M_{t-1}}{P_{t-1}} \frac{P_{t-1}}{P_t}.$$

Recalling that $m_t \equiv M_t / P_t$ is real money balances and recalling that $P_{t-1} / P_t = 1/(1+\pi_t)$, we can rearrange (24) further to get

$$t_t w_t n_t + \frac{1}{1+i_t} b_t + m_t - \frac{m_{t-1}}{1+\pi_t} = govt_t + \frac{B_{t-1}}{P_{t-1}} \frac{P_{t-1}}{P_t}, \tag{25}$$

or a little more compactly,

$$t_t w_t n_t + \frac{1}{1+i_t} b_t + m_t - \frac{m_{t-1}}{1+\pi_t} = govt_t + \frac{b_{t-1}}{1+\pi_t}, \tag{26}$$

6. You should think of this analogously as the equilibrium "reaction function" $c(g)$ in our consideration of purely optimal monetary policy and $n(t)$ in our consideration of purely optimal fiscal policy. The technical difference here is that the government has *two* policy instruments (the labor tax rate and the money growth rate) and there are *two* steady-state equilibrium objects to be determined. However, for a wide class of utility functions used in quantitative macroeconomic models, it can be shown (in a more advanced treatment of monetary theory) that labor will depend only on the labor tax rate and money balances will depend only on the money growth rate.

where, in the last step, we used the expression

$$\frac{B_{t-1}}{P_t} = \frac{B_{t-1}}{P_{t-1}} \frac{P_{t-1}}{P_t} = \frac{b_{t-1}}{1+\pi_t}.$$

Our next step is to impose steady state on expression (26); doing so and combining terms, we have

$$twn + b\left[\frac{1}{1+i} - \frac{1}{1+\pi}\right] + m\left[1 - \frac{1}{1+\pi}\right] = govt. \tag{27}$$

Because $\pi = g$ in steady state, we can write the previous expression as

$$twn + b\left[\frac{1}{1+i} - \frac{1}{1+g}\right] + m\left[1 - \frac{1}{1+g}\right] = govt. \tag{28}$$

We can condense this expression even further. The Fisher equation tells us that $1+i = (1+r)(1+\pi)$, which in turn can be expressed as $1+i = (1+r)(1+g)$. We know from our consumption–savings optimality condition (12) that in steady state $1+r = 1/\beta$. Thus in steady-state, $1+i = (1+g)/\beta$, which we saw in expression (21). Inserting all of this on the left-hand side of (28), we have

$$twn + b\left[\frac{\beta-1}{1+g}\right] + m\left[\frac{g}{1+g}\right] = govt. \tag{29}$$

After several algebraic rearrangements, we have arrived at a very useful intermediate form of the steady-state equilibrium version of the government budget constraint.[7] Expression (29) shows that government spending must be financed in the long run (i.e., in the steady state) by a combination of labor income taxes (the first term on the left-hand side), seignorage revenue (the third term on the left-hand side), and *deflation of government debt* (the second term on the left-hand side).

This last "revenue source," deflation of government debt, can be thought of as a steady-state version of the ideas of the fiscal theory of the price level and the fiscal theory of inflation that we studied earlier. In that analysis, recall that the two ideas were distinct, and the distinction between them lay in *when* the inflation wrought by an active fiscal policy was going to occur: the fiscal theory of the price level stated that it would occur *now,* while the fiscal theory of inflation stated that it would occur *at some time in the current period or future periods, or perhaps spread out over multiple periods.* In steady state, however,

---

7. Note that in our study of the FTPL and the FTI in chapter 16, we were not focused on the *steady-state* version of the government budget constraint; there, we were explicitly concerned with the *dynamics* (of inflation and seignorage revenue) implied by the intertemporal government budget constraint.

which is what we are focused on here, the very notions of "now" and "later" disappear: in steady state, time "disappears," thus "now" and "later" are blurred. Hence in steady state we cannot distinguish between the fiscal theory of the price level and the fiscal theory of inflation; the two roll into what we are here calling *deflation of government debt.*[8]

It turns out that for the purpose at hand (studying the optimal steady-state *mix* of money growth/seignorage and labor taxes) the deflation of government debt channel is not important.[9] Thus from now on we will assume $b = 0$ (i.e., the government has no debt obligations), which also justifies why we assumed above that $B = 0$ when we were describing the private-sector equilibrium. The GBC can thus now be written as

$$twn + m\left[\frac{g}{1+g}\right] = govt.$$

(30)

Recall our mode of analysis of optimal policy problems: at the stage of determining the optimal policy, the government (in this case, the consolidated fiscal–monetary government) *takes into account all equilibrium conditions,* including functions that describe how the private sector responds to *any arbitrary* policy that it sets. Thus there are three more things to do with (30): insert the equilibrium steady-state real wage rate $w = 1$ (recall equilibrium condition (1)), insert the equilibrium function $n(t, g)$, and insert the equilibrium function $m(t, g)$. After making these insertions, we have

$$t \cdot n(t,g) + m(t,g) \cdot \left[\frac{g}{1+g}\right] = govt.$$

(31)

So the government's policy problem boils down to the government choosing the tax rate t and the growth rate of money g to satisfy its budget constraint (31). The reason that the optimal policy problem has just one constraint—the government budget constraint—is just as it was in our study of optimal fiscal policy: the functions $n(t, g)$ and $m(t, g)$ already capture how the private sector responds to a given policy the government chooses.

There are, in principle, an infinite number of combinations of (t, g) pairs that satisfy (31). In chapter 19, when we arrived at the analogous place in the analysis, what we had was one equation (the government budget constraint) in one unknown (the tax rate); here we have one equation in *two* unknowns. Clearly, if we knew either t or g, then we would know the other as well—that is, if we somehow pick either t or g, then equation (31) would reduce to one equation in one unknown.

8. In yet other words, both the fiscal theory of the price level and the fiscal theory of inflation are inherently *dynamic* concepts.

9. We leave the precise reasons behind the *steady-state* irrelevance of the debt-deflation mechanism for a more advanced course in monetary theory.

In order to pin down one of the policies, let's proceed to compute the first-order conditions of (31) with respect to t and g; using the product and quotient rules, they are, respectively,

$$n(t, g) + t \cdot \frac{\partial n}{\partial t} + \frac{\partial m}{\partial t} \cdot \left[\frac{g}{1+g} \right] = 0 \tag{32}$$

and

$$t \cdot \frac{\partial n}{\partial g} + \frac{\partial m}{\partial g} \cdot \left[\frac{g}{1+g} \right] + \frac{m(t, g)}{(1+g)^2} = 0. \tag{33}$$

Conditions (32) and (33) define *either* the optimal labor tax rate *or* the optimal growth rate of the money supply; they do *not* define both. We will make this point more clear through an example in the next section, but when free to "choose" two variables (here, policy variables) to satisfy one equation, one is, of course, not really free to "choose" both of them. As was the case in chapter 19, we cannot make any more analytical progress computing the optimal values of t and g without making some assumptions about the utility function.[10] This is the task we take up in the next section. In the next section we first assume a conventional form for the utility function, make some progress toward analyzing the jointly optimal policy, and draw on lessons we have learned previously to reach some general conclusions.

A Workhorse Utility Function

A utility function that is a staple in modern macroeconomic models and one that we have had many occasions to work with already is the additively separable utility function. For the rest of our analysis, we thus assume that the utility function is

$$u(c, m, 1-n) = \ln c + \ln m + \ln(1-n), \tag{34}$$

which means the marginal utility functions are $u_1 = 1/c$, $u_2 = 1/m$, and $u_3 = 1/(1-n)$. Before we can use equations (32) and (33) to figure out what *either* the optimal tax rate *or* the optimal money growth rates is given this utility function, we must first determine what the functions $n(t, g)$ and $m(t, g)$ are for this utility function because we need to reuse these functions.

---

10. Note that in the analysis of *only* optimal monetary policy, we *were* able to completely solve for optimal monetary policy (in isolation from fiscal policy) *without* making any assumptions about the utility function. Things are different in the analysis of *only* optimal fiscal policy and the joint analysis because of the presence of the government budget constraint—that is, the presence of a *financing* concern (i.e., how should the government raise revenue?) makes things much more complicated, and the level of generality of proofs/results that we can obtain is not as high as it was in in the case of *only* optimal monetary policy.

In order to determine the functions $n(t, g)$ and $m(t, g)$, recall that we must use conditions (22) and (23). Using the marginal utility functions associated with our assumed utility function in these two conditions, respectively, we have

$$\frac{(1-t)n - m\left[\dfrac{g}{1+g}\right]}{1-n} = 1 - t \tag{35}$$

and

$$\frac{(1-t)n - m\left[\dfrac{g}{1+g}\right]}{m} = \frac{1+g-\beta}{1+g}. \tag{36}$$

The task is to solve equations (35) and (36) for n and m. There are obviously a number of ways one can attack this problem, but all that is required is some brute-force (though tedious) algebra. Let's first solve (36) for m. After a couple of steps of algebra and rearrangement, we have

$$m = \frac{(1-t)n(1+g)}{1+2g-\beta}. \tag{37}$$

Next take this expression for m and insert it in equation (35); doing so, we have

$$\frac{(1-t)n}{1-n} - \left[\frac{g}{1+g}\right] \cdot \left[\frac{(1-t)(1+g)}{1+2g-\beta}\right] \cdot \left[\frac{n}{1-n}\right] = 1 - t. \tag{38}$$

Canceling some terms gives us

$$\frac{n}{1-n} - \frac{n}{1-n} \cdot \left[\frac{g}{1+2g-\beta}\right] = 1, \tag{39}$$

or even more compactly,

$$\frac{n}{1-n} \cdot \left[\frac{1+g-\beta}{1+2g-\beta}\right] = 1. \tag{40}$$

Solving this for n, we find that

$$n(g) = \frac{1+2g-\beta}{2+3g-2\beta}, \tag{41}$$

which shows that n is a function of g *but not a function of the tax rate t.* This is not a general statement, of course, but rather simply a property of the utility function we are using here; nonetheless, it is an interesting property to note.[11]

---

11. With log utility, optimal labor supply is not a function of the labor tax rate due to issues regarding long-run growth (which are left to a more advanced macroeconomics class).

Now we need the function $m(t, g)$. To compute it, insert (41) into (37) to obtain

$$m(t, g) = \frac{(1-t)(1+g)}{2+3g-2\beta}. \tag{42}$$

Neither expression (41) nor expression (42) may appear to be particularly informative—indeed they really are not. But they are the intermediates that we require to take us to our next step, which is to insert these functions *and their partial derivatives* into expressions (32) and (33).

Solution of Optimal Policy Problem

It is impossible to compute the solution for the optimal labor tax rate and money growth rate by hand here. As is often the case in ever-more complicated macro models, we instead resort to computational methods to solve for optimal policy using the given equilibrium functions $n(g)$ and $m(t, g)$.

Using a standard software package such as Matlab or Maple, the optimal money growth rate turns out to be…. $g = \beta - 1$! Recall from chapter 17 that this is the *Friedman rule*, which is part of the *optimal mix* of fiscal and monetary policy when both the fiscal authority and monetary authority *jointly* are charged with financing government spending. So this is quite an interesting result: it states that even though the government *could* use seignorage revenue to finance its spending, the optimal *mix* of fiscal and monetary policy dictates that it *shouldn't*. Furthermore, because the Friedman rule calls for *shrinking* the nominal money supply, seignorage revenues are actually negative, meaning there is a seignorage *expenditure* that the government must pay for in addition to its "normal" spending *govt*.

The last step is then to solve for the labor tax rate. With the Friedman rule $g = \beta - 1$ describing the optimal money growth rate, the government budget constraint informs us that the labor tax rate must satisfy

$$t \cdot n(\beta - 1) + m(t, \beta - 1) \cdot \left[\frac{\beta - 1}{\beta}\right] = govt,$$

in which, note carefully, we have substituted in $g = \beta - 1$. This expression for the GBC is now one equation in one unknown, which can be solved (computationally) for the optimal labor tax rate. At this stage the analysis is quite similar to that conducted in chapter 19.

Taken together, these results suggest that despite the need to raise government revenue in non–lump-sum manner, obtaining economic efficiency along the consumption–money margin is a goal more important in optimal macroeconomic policy, more so than achieving efficiency along the consumption–leisure margin.

21

Financial Accelerator and Role of Regulatory Policy

Starting in 2007, and becoming much more pronounced in 2008, macro-financial events took center stage in the macroeconomic landscape. The "financial collapse," as many have termed it, had its proximate cause in the United States, as several financial-sector institutions experienced severe or catastrophic downturns in the values of their financial assets. Various and large-scale policy efforts were implemented very quickly in the United States to try to contain possible consequences.

The motivation behind these policy efforts was not to save the financial sector for its own sake. Instead, the rationale for policy responses was that severe financial downturns often lead to contraction in *real macroeconomic* markets (e.g., think in terms of goods markets). Despite a raft of policy measures to try to prevent such effects, the severe financial disruption did cause a sharp contraction of economic activity in real markets: GDP declined by nearly 4 percent in the third quarter of 2008, the time period during which financial disruptions were at their most severe. This quarterly decline was the largest in the United States since the early 1980s, and GDP continued declining for the next three quarters.

But the reason this pullback in GDP was especially worrisome was something history shows is common. When a recession is triggered by financial turbulence, *a contraction in real economic activity can further exacerbate the financial downturn.* This downstream effect was the real fear of policy makers. If this downstream effect occurred, the now-steeper financial downturn then could *even further* worsen the macro downturn, which in turn could *even further* worsen the financial downturn, which in turn could *even further* worsen the macro downturn, and on and on. If this chain of events is set in motion, then it can become extremely difficult for anyone, policy officials or others, to do anything about it.

This type of adverse feedback dynamic between financial activity and macroeconomic activity is referred to by different terms. In media portrayals, terms such as the "financial accelerator," "financial feedback loops," and "loan spirals" quickly came into use to describe exactly this scenario as both financial and macro conditions deteriorated.

This chapter studies the **financial accelerator** framework, and its broad purpose is to study general properties of events like the one just described. The accelerator model is not a new framework, despite its sharp popularity in macroeconomics since 2008. It actually dates back to Irving Fisher and other economists in the 1930s, as they attempted to understand the adverse linkages between macroeconomic activity and financial markets during the Great Depression. In the 1980s and 1990s Ben Bernanke became one of the world's leading scholars of the Great Depression, and he, first on his own and then later with academic colleague Mark Gertler and others, built quantitatively richer versions of the accelerator. The framework has been a staple in macroeconomic research since then but, until 2007 and 2008, had not been used for much practical policy-making.

But its appeal as a foundation for macro-finance issues has exploded since 2008, as many policy officials (including Bernanke himself as chair of the Federal Reserve at the time!) and researchers have actively developed the model further. The goals have been to both inform policy advice and to simply learn more about the interconnections between macroeconomic markets and financial markets.

To be clear, our study of the accelerator framework is meant as neither a history of the recent financial collapse nor of the Great Recession in the United States that it precipitated. When scholars such as Fisher, Bernanke, Gertler, and others, developed the framework, they did not have these very recent events in mind. Rather, they were interested in learning more about the general properties of adverse feedback loops. Recent events have cast a spotlight on thinking more deeply about how financial fluctuations and macroeconomic fluctuations interact with each other through feedback effects when certain shocks affect the economy, and the accelerator framework has once again been viewed as a good starting point.

The accelerator model developed below builds on the multi-period firm analysis of chapter 6; but it could just as easily be developed in the context of multi-period consumer analysis. To make things as simple as possible, yet rich enough to study the accelerator and related effects, we work with the two-period firm model from chapter 6, but the ideas extend readily beyond two periods.

There are four building blocks of the accelerator model: (1) a multi-period view of firm profit maximization, (2) a financing constraint that captures how financial assets can be important for loans that are used to back physical capital investment purchases, (3) a notion of "government regulation" that operates through financing constraints, and (4) a relationship between firm profits and dividends.

While introducing the building blocks, extended discussion describes fundamentally new ideas that we have thus far not encountered. We then formally work through several results and insights that the framework delivers, including the "accelerator" effect itself. We conclude with some bigger-picture discussion about the framework. But even before describing the building blocks, we have to consider an aspect about the nature of assets that is crucial for the accelerator model.

Risk Properties of Assets

Even before introducing the four building blocks of the accelerator model, we need to describe the natures of the two fundamentally different types of assets that are central for the model. The fundamental difference between assets is in their **risk properties.** At one end of the economic risk spectrum are **riskless assets.** In the model, short-term government bonds are to be thought of as the riskless asset (although we will also consider the marginal product of capital to be a riskless asset when we get into the model's details). At the other end of the economic risk spectrum are **risky assets.** In the model, we will consider stocks (defined exactly as in the infinite-horizon model of chapter 8) as the risky asset.

For all of our analysis, **risk** is defined to mean the "guarantee" about the value of an asset's payoff at some point in the future. More precisely, at a fixed date in the future, a riskless asset is one whose value is known for sure by market participants, whereas a risky asset is one whose value is not known for sure by market participants.[1] The latter, risky, asset is the one whose value has less guarantee.

No asset is truly riskless. But what matters for the definition is a relative notion of risk. As an example, US aggregate stock returns vary more sharply over time than do US short-term government bond returns.[2] US bond returns do vary, in sometimes unexpected ways— hence one may want to call them "risky." But stock returns are even more risky than US short-term government bond returns. For the purposes of economic analysis, it is thus sufficient to identify stocks as risky and US short-term bonds as riskless,[3] which is helpful taxonomy. Several further aspects about risk and asset returns are worth describing.

First, we should recognize that financial assets that are not bonds (even more precisely, that are not short-term government bonds), by definition, do not guarantee, based on purely economic incentives, any payment(s). In practice, any "guarantee" provided by risky assets is conferred on them by legal precedents, government decrees, social norms, and so on, which have various degrees of social value—but they are *not* conferred by pure economic incentives. Thus, if stocks carry some "guarantees" of payment(s), they should be thought of as arising for "noneconomic" reasons.

Second, there is no reason why "stocks" had to be selected as the model's risky asset. In principle, *any* financial asset that is more risky than US short-term government bonds serves the goals of the model equally well, especially because our analysis, while couched

---

1. In terms of probability and statistics, a riskless asset has a known expected value (the first central moment) and zero variance (the second central moment) around that expected value. A risky asset has a known expected value and a *positive* variance around that expected value. "Risk" is implied by the positive variance.

2. As in chapter 6, we should think of stocks as something like the S&P 500, which is representative of stock-market aggregates.

3. Recall the discussion in chapter 6 that US short-term government bonds have long been considered the riskless asset in markets. Of course, it is possible that some (adverse and large) negative shock could prevent the US government from making its next short-term bond repayment. But, in practice, this has never happened in over 200 years of US history.

in a formal optimization problem, is ultimately qualitative. A few examples of other financial assets include foreign stock, shares in oil companies, and holdings of financial products based on housing mortgages—the last example, in particular, is relevant for the recent US financial and economic downturn. But the accelerator framework, developed as it was originally in the 1930s and then re-developed in the 1980s and 1990s, captures much broader ideas than the events of just the past few years. A bit further discussion appears when we describe the first building block of the model, but the broad notion of "stocks" captures the crucial risk idea for the accelerator.[4]

Third, for either riskless or risky assets, one can always define the "interest rate" on that asset. For short-term bonds (which sometimes will be referred to from here on simply as "bonds"), the nominal interest rate is defined by $1 + i = 1/P_1^b$ (in which we are continuing with our maintained assumption of unit face value of bonds ($FV = 1$) upon payoff, and the "1" subscript on the price of a bond (P_1^b) is the period in which that price is being paid). For stocks, the nominal "interest rate," or nominal "rate of return," is defined by

$$1 + i^{STOCK} = \frac{S_2 + D_2}{S_1},$$

in which the notation is exactly as in our earlier study of stock prices: S_t is the nominal price of a share of stock in period t, and D_t is the nominal dividend payment per share of stock in period t. In the accelerator model, any gap between i and i^{STOCK} drives critical results.

Fourth, as a point of terminology, we will refer interchangeably to both i and i^{STOCK} as "interest rates" or "rates of return." For nonbond assets, "interest rates" is unconventional language (rate of return is usually preferred). But from a presentation perspective, using the same terminology for different types of assets emphasizes that there are economic relationships between them and consequences implied by them that matter for some types of transactions. These relationships emerge in detail below.

Fifth, regardless of risk properties, we can measure an asset's rate of return in either nominal terms, as shown above, or in real terms (in which we measure the returns by r and r^{STOCK}), the latter by appropriate application of the Fisher relation. For consistency with earlier analyses, we begin with a nominal view as we now turn to the building blocks of the model.

Building Block 1: Firm Profit Function

The first building block is the firm's dynamic profit function. As stated above, we limit ourselves to a two-period time horizon, with optimization conducted at the start of period

---

4. We should also note that assets whose risk properties lie between "purely riskless" and "extremely risky" also exist. For the purposes of this chapter, we do not need to consider such "intermediate" risk levels; the two we have of "riskless" versus "risky" is sufficient.

1. But note that all of the analysis and results can be readily extended to more than two periods.

Given that stock is the risky financial asset in the model, it appears in the first building block of the framework, the **dynamic profit function,**

$$P_1 f(k_1, n_1) + (S_1 + D_1)a_0 - P_1(k_2 - k_1) - P_1 w_1 n_1 - S_1 a_1$$
$$+ \frac{P_2 f(k_2, n_2)}{1+i} + \frac{(S_2 + D_2)a_1}{1+i} - \frac{P_2(k_3 - k_2)}{1+i} - \frac{P_2 w_2 n_2}{1+i} - \frac{S_2 a_2}{1+i},$$

which is an extension of the profit function studied earlier. The extension is simply that stocks are accumulated by the firm, for the purpose described in the next subsection. As in our earlier study, because the analysis is being conducted from the perspective of the start of period 1, the period-2 components of profits are discounted by a (gross) nominal interest rate $1+i$.

Two important points are useful to clarify. First, a natural question may be: Where are the short-term riskless bonds? The answer is that the interest rate i that appears in the discounting is exactly the one on short-term bonds. Thus, even though it superficially appears that bonds are not present in the profit function—they actually do appear. Hence both the riskless interest rate and the risky interest rate appear in the profit function.

Second, an important distinction to make in reading the profit function is that between the optimization problem faced by *a single (small) firm* versus aggregate market variables. Although we will take the representative-firm approach in analyzing the results of the optimization, at this stage of the analysis, the firm is to be viewed as one of the small, atomistic firms in the overall economy. Thus the terms involving stock in the profit function are *not*, at this stage of the analysis, this particular firm's own stock. If they were this particular firm's own shares, it would be hard to understand why (in the ensuing analysis) stock prices and dividends would be taken as given. Stock prices and stock dividends are to be thought of in their usual aggregate terms, and they are taken as given until we get to the first-order conditions. This distinction is exactly the one between partial-partial equilibrium, partial equilibrium, and general equilibrium that we have drawn several times.

From an analytical perspective (and as always in considering the two-period framework) the firm needs neither physical capital at the start of the nonexistent "period three"—hence $k_3 = 0$—nor financial assets at the start of the nonexistent "period 3"—hence $a_2 = 0$.[5]

Building Block 2: Financing Constraint

The second building block of the accelerator framework is its critical conceptual idea. All of the analysis ultimately revolves around it, so it is important that we clearly understand it, both technically and conceptually.

---

5. Nor any other assets, if there were other assets in the formal framework.

An important practical issue for many firms is that in order to purchase physical assets (think large-scale expenditures for investment in machinery, equipment, computers, etc.), they require a sufficient (market) value of **financial assets,** which facilitates the borrowing that is needed in order to finance their purchase. The "market value" nature of financial assets is important: it indicates that *both the price and the quantity of financial assets* held by a firm matter for its ability to borrow.

This raises a question: Why does a firm need to borrow at all? In chapter 6, firms simply demanded as much labor and as much capital as was maximizing profit: there was nothing formal within the framework that concerned borrowing. In certain situations, however, a firm may need to borrow for large-scale investment purchases. In these cases a particular type of market imperfection, which is viewed as central in financial theory, necessitates that a firm "back" a loan, or "pledge collateral against" procurement of a loan. The proceeds of the loan are then used for physical capital expenditures. By inherent properties of assets, it is "risky assets" that must be used to back the loans obtained for capital expenditures (which are to be interpreted as "riskless" assets).[6] These points are expanded below. But a critical connection with the basic firm analysis of chapter 6 is that all of the ideas to be presented below could indeed have been present there as well; for a reason to be made very precise, though, they can all be thought of as zeroing out in chapter 6.

To make progress with the mathematics of the model, the expression that forms the centerpiece of the second building block is $P_1 \cdot inv_1 = S_1 \cdot a_1$ (in which $inv_1 = k_2 - k_1$ is physical capital investment). Or, to instead express things in terms of only k, simply substitute the definition of investment. This allows the **financing constraint** to be written a bit more explicitly as

$$P_1(k_2 - k_1) = S_1 \cdot a_1.$$

This financing constraint will be modified in a slight, but important, way in the next subsection. So this will not be the exact way we use it in the analysis later. Nonetheless, if this constraint did not exist, *none* of the rest of the framework matters, a point that will be established rigorously when we study the model's insights.

Regarding the formal expression of the financing constraint as written so far, the left-hand side is the nominal value of physical investment expenditures, $P_1(k_2 - k_1)$, the firm plans to undertake in period 1. On the right-hand side, the term $S_1 a_1$ is the firm's **market value of collateral** for the loan. The market value of collateral is the backing pledged by the firm in order to obtain the loan, whose proceeds in turn will be used to purchase physical assets. Even though the financing constraint is not yet in its technical final form, it is

---

6. We are using "stock" as the risky asset, but an appropriate interpretation is that any financial asset(s) could be held by firms to back borrowing that will be used for physical capital purchases. The details of exactly which financial assets are collateralizable are country-specific and/or market-specific and/or industry-specific, and they are governed by various private-market arrangements and government regulations. The details of such institutional setups are beyond the scope of our study.

close enough to its final form that three important points are worth discussing (the first two of which are highly related, but we disentangle them to make them conceptually easier to understand).

In financial theory, one of the most important market imperfections is **informational asymmetries.** We distinguish two aspects of informational asymmetries: those arising between potential borrowers and potential lenders, and those arising between the pair and the overall economic environment as time evolves. For both aspects, a simple illustrative example is the case of an individual seeking a mortgage loan in order to purchase a house.

First, no matter how many credit references, income verifications, and other means testing a potential lender conducts, a potential borrower fundamentally knows more about his own personal circumstances when the time for (long-lived) loan repayments begins. This informational asymmetry provides the potential lender an incentive to not make a loan in the first place, even if the loan would be beneficial to both the lender and the borrower. The incentive driving the lender is fear that he will not be repaid.

Private markets have developed a way to manage some of the consequences of this aspect of informational asymmetries: lenders require borrowers to "put some skin in the game" at the time a loan is originated. If the potential borrower puts down, say, 20 percent of the total value of the house, this affects the lender's incentives to loan the remaining 80 percent[7] The lender now effectively knows that if the borrower does "walk away" from the loan repayments very quickly, the borrower would at the very least have lost 20 percent of the value of the house. And that cost may be large enough that it would induce the potential borrower to not approach the lender in the first place, unless he was serious about making a steady stream of repayments.

Such "down payment" requirements affect not only consumers but also firms when they are making large-scale purchases. The intuitive way to think about the market value of assets on the right-hand side of the financing constraint is thus as a down payment that is being used to back a loan for use on purchases of capital goods. The firm then makes a steady stream of repayments that slowly repays the loan.

The "steady stream of repayments" raises the second of the two aspects of informational asymmetries: there is inherently a **maturity mismatch** between the financial asset being used as a down payment, and the physical asset for which the loan is being made. This aspect does not involve any "malicious" informational asymmetry between borrower and lender. Instead, the asymmetry is between the perfectly aligned goals of the borrower–lender pair and the overall economic environment—the latter naturally changes over time even if the aligned borrower–lender goals do not.

The maturity mismatch is captured in the model in a simple way by including a_1, not a_0, on the right-hand side of the financing constraint. The reason for a_1 appearing on the

---

7. In the United States 20 percent down payments for home mortgages was a long-standing norm, until the several years before the events of 2007 and 2008, when down payment requirements sharply declined.

collateral side can be described in purely technical terms: a_0 is predetermined at the start of period 1, implying there is no choice by the firm about its value. In order for the framework to make testable predictions, the firm should have some choice about the right-hand side of the collateral constraint, hence the inclusion of a_1.

But to understand this conceptually, it is helpful to continue the example of an individual person pursuing a mortgage loan in order to purchase a house. Obtaining a mortgage loan typically requires a down payment (e.g., as above, 20 percent of the market value of the house). In the process of completing the loan, the individual has to make several decisions about his own personal finances. These decisions are intended to obtain the 20 percent down payment in a liquid form to pass on to the lender.[8] Regardless of the precise decisions, the key aspect is that there are some decisions that the potential borrower had to make in the process of going to the bank, withdrawing funds from certain accounts, depositing extra funds in other accounts if necessary, obtaining a certified check, and so on.

In contrast, the very nature of a house, which is the ultimate reason for borrowing in this example, makes it a much longer term asset: the average house can last for decades. So the "maturity mismatch" is that the financial asset used to collateralize the loan on which the house is actually purchased is much shorter in time horizon than the long-lived physical asset being bought. The long-lived nature of the physical asset is the source of the long-lived "steady stream of repayments" by the borrower back to the lender.

The same maturity mismatch idea applies to firms' financing of physical capital purchases collateralized by loans secured by stock. New machines, new factories, new delivery vehicles, and so on, last for much longer periods of time than the financial assets being used to collateralize loans for their purchase. Their long-lived nature provides part of the source of profits for many periods, which in turn is the source of the long-lived steady stream of repayments by the firm back to the lender.

In the two-period setup the end of the second period makes things rather stark because there is no more need for either physical capital or financial assets. Extending the analysis beyond two periods and, importantly, allowing capital to be productive and therefore

---

8. For example, the borrower might have to withdraw funds from a protected savings account against which checks cannot be written and then transfer it to his own checking account. Regarding passing on the down payment to the lender, it is convenient to think of a "down payment" on a home-mortgage application as being "in cash." But it is technically not cash. Technically the down payment is a type of "short-term bond." The bond nature of a down payment arises because (given the magnitude of resources involved) a potential lender inevitably asks for a "certified check" from an individual's bank. The certified check is a verification provided by the individual's personal bank that the funds are actually in his bank account, and that the funds are being held for the explicit purpose of payment to the lender. These details are unlike the case of an individual handing over literally cash, or of providing an uncertified check. The uncertified check provides no verification of the availability of funds when the lender tries to redeem it (which again raises the consequences of the first, "malicious," aspect of informational asymmetries); whereas hard cash is generally not accepted (partly for legal reasons) for such large transactions. The individual's own financial institution essentially has issued a "short-term bond," which will be repaid (out of the borrower's funds) when the lender redeems the certified check. From an operational standpoint, these "bank-issued short-term bonds" are equivalent to a reliable government's short-term bonds—the key aspect is that they are both short term.

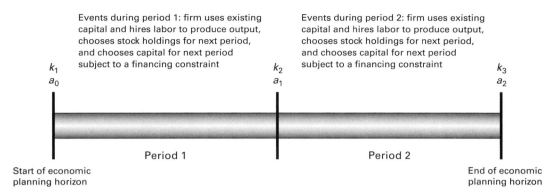

Figure 21.1
Timing of events in financial accelerator framework

profit-generating for many periods, brings the maturity mismatch idea squarely into view in the model.[9] While the starkness of the two-period framework mutes the maturity mismatch idea a bit, it does capture it in a simplified form and it does not obscure the economic insights provided by the accelerator framework.

The third point is more technical. The financing constraint should properly be considered an *inequality* constraint: $P_1(k_2 - k_1) \leq S_1 \cdot a_1$. The fully correct analysis of inequality-constrained optimization problems requires the use of Kuhn–Tucker optimization tools, which is a generalization of the Lagrange optimization tools we have been using (the Lagrange method formally applies only to *equality* constrained problems). To keep things in line with our Lagrange-based methodology, we will formally assume that the financing constraint always holds with strict equality—or, in more technical language, that the financing constraint "always binds."

However, when we briefly discuss the consequences of ever-increasing financial market returns (which will not be our main analytical experiment), we will have to move away from the Lagrange-based predictions. The richer Kuhn–Tucker analysis would allow us to rigorously establish what happens in this particular case; but we will simply approach it qualitatively. More details are provided when we get to that point, but the important idea is that *a borrower cannot be compelled to borrow more than he wants to borrow, even though he can be compelled to borrow less than he wants to borrow.* This asymmetry is important, one that will be reflected in the permissible values of the Lagrange optimization, which we discuss when we begin considering first-order conditions.

---

9. To see this, suppose that we take a weekly view of time periods. If new physical capital takes 52 weeks to build and be ready for use by a firm, and it takes only one week to arrange financing-related decisions, then the financial constraint would intuitively read as $P_1(k_{52} - k_1) = S_1 \cdot a_1$.

To recap, the financing constraint is the central building block of the accelerator framework. It arises due to fundamental informational asymmetries that affect the borrowing–lending transaction. Although there are other crucial elements of the model, if the financing friction were not present, the entire analysis below would collapse, and the predictions would literally return to those of the baseline firm analysis, as we will point out in key places. The constraint is a summary way of portraying markets' mechanisms for trying to mitigate the consequences of informational asymmetries that are impossible to avoid in any interesting financial transaction. From a more analytical perspective, the constraint also captures the idea that a firm (more generally, any potential borrower) has to make purposeful decisions about both the value of collateralizable financial assets and about the quantity of physical investment it wants to purchase using loans backed by those financial assets.

Building Block 3: Government Regulation

The financing constraint is to be viewed as a primitive feature of private-market transactions, ones plagued by important informational asymmetries, that arises directly from private parties' incentives. Given the existence of this constraint, it permits the government a channel by which it can possibly regulate market transactions in which informational asymmetries are present.

Specifically, let's layer into the financing constraint above a catch-all "government regulatory measure" $R > 0$, so that the financing constraint with which we will actually work is

$$P_1(k_2 - k_1) = R \cdot S_1 \cdot a_1.$$

Although this form of the financing constraint looks nearly identical to the one introduced above (it would be exactly identical if $R = 1$), it is useful to think of this expression as distinct from the "basic" financing constraint that arose directly in the private sector. Thus, despite their formal near-similarity, it is very useful to keep the second and third building blocks conceptually separate.

The measure $R > 0$ (more precisely, its inclusion in the financing constraint as written above—we will sometimes simply say "$R > 0$" as a shorthand way of describing the entire idea) is the third building block of the accelerator framework. Except for brief discussion immediately below regarding the nature of R, we will stick with the very general interpretation that it is controlled by the government. Extra precision about R is not critical for analysis of the accelerator.

If we do interpret R as reflecting only government regulation, or government oversight, it is easy to imagine that it consists of various components. For example, suppose that the US Securities and Exchange Commission (SEC) and the US Treasury are the only two government agencies that have any role in the process of setting R. For certain applied questions, it may be useful to think of R as being decomposed into $R = R^{TREAS} \cdot R^{SEC}$, which is the multiplicative product of each agency's own regulatory scheme. If the Federal Reserve System is also involved in providing such regulation, then it may also be helpful to think in terms of $R = R^{TREAS} \cdot R^{SEC} \cdot R^{FED}$. Decompositions of this type may be useful in considering the details of government regulatory policy and its implementation.

One could instead think of R as being set by both government regulation (by one or many underlying institutions) and by private-sector "norms" regarding borrowing and lending. In this case, it can be useful to decompose R into $R = R^{GOV} \cdot R^{PRIV}$, which emphasizes the private-sector/government spectrum. Then, just as above, one could decompose R^{GOV} into finer subcategories if needed; by analogy, one could also decompose R^{PRIV} into finer subcategories if needed.

However, in the basic analysis we will simply consider $R > 0$, since R is taken as given from the perspective of private-market participants in a financial transaction. Our analysis has nothing concrete to say about how different groups might organize to "lobby" various government agencies and/or private-market organizations to change (components of) R. While interesting as talking points, this more advanced analysis requires bringing in additional constraints that describe the organizing process, the lobbying process, and so on. For the general analysis of the accelerator framework, though, it is overkill. In the interest of keeping things as simple as possible, and to fix some language for the rest of the analysis and discussion, let's return to describing $R > 0$ as a catch-all government regulation measure that affects private-market financial transactions.

Given this interpretation, what exactly is R? Some examples include institutions such as rules regarding filing of proper documentation, full disclosure ("truth in lending") laws, regulations that provide for direct lending in some markets and/or geographic regions, or regulators looking favorably at some submarkets. But these are all talking points, since, once again, the model makes no statements about the sources of R.

Regardless of the interpretation of R, it plays an important role in markets. To see this directly, examine again the financing constraint that contains R. Now including $R > 0$, its literal statement is that for a given market value of collateralizable assets $S_1 a_1$, the amount that can be used as the backing for a loan to be used for physical investment is **R times that market value.**

In financial analysis, R is referred to as the **leverage ratio,** which measures the **multiple** of the market value of collateralizable assets up to which borrowing can occur for the purchase of physical assets. Intuitively, a very high value of R indicates "fragility" (which need not be, but could be, excessive) on the part of a borrower, a point that has been brought up frequently in discussing the US financial and economic situation starting in 2007. Finally, if R is set solely by government regulation, purposeful changes in R, holding $S_1 a_1$ constant, imply that the amount that can be borrowed scales directly with R.

To recap, $R > 0$, as embedded in the financing constraint, is the third building block of the accelerator framework. In the analysis below, this version of the financing constraint will appear in the formal problem, *not* the primitive form $P_1(k_2 - k_1) = S_1 \cdot a_1$ described earlier. The primitive form should be thought of as a mechanism originated solely by private-market participants in order to manage the consequences of informational asymmetries. Given the existence of the basic constraint, the government can impose some "regulation" on financial transactions through it. The financing constraint in its final form is thus written as $P_1(k_2 - k_1) = R \cdot S_1 \cdot a_1$ (a special case of which is obviously $R = 1$). But, to be clear, the regulatory aspect could not even manifest itself if not for the existence of the constraint in the first place. It is important to keep these two ideas distinct, even though the third building block builds directly on the second building block.

Building Block 4: Profits and Dividends

Dividends are the payments made by publicly traded companies to their shareholders, who are ultimately the owners of public companies. Corporate dividend policies naturally differ among countries, among industries within a country, among subindustries within industries, and so on. Differences reflect different economic structures, different governing institutions, and various degrees of social and cultural norms regarding acceptability.

Adopting a US-centered representative (publicly traded) firm approach, it is instructive to examine the share of total corporate profits paid out as dividends. Figure 21.2 plots the S&P 500 dividend payout rate, which is simply the fraction of total corporate profits of the S&P 500 firms that are paid out as dividends.

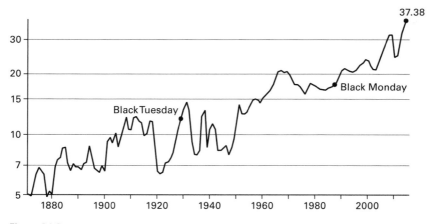

Figure 21.2
S&P 500 dividend yield, 1873 to 2014. Sources: Standard and Poor's and Robert Shiller's book *Irrational Exuberance*.

While the dividend rate has clearly increased over time, a stark point to note is that there was *not* much of a change in the rate as the financial turmoil and ensuing US Great Recession occurred.

The fourth building block closes the macro-finance link with the statement that the percentage ρ (Greek lowercase letter "rho") of profits paid out as dividends is constant over time. Formally, the nominal quantity of per-share dividends relates to ρ, P_2, and real profits according to

$$D_2 = \rho \cdot P_2 \cdot profit_2,$$

in which $profit_2$ is real per-share profits, and in which attention is limited to just period 2 because of the two-period framework being studied. If we extend the framework beyond two periods, this relationship simply generalizes to $D_2 = \rho \cdot P_2 \cdot profit_2$. For simplicity in the upcoming analysis, suppose that $\rho = 1$.

Analysis Part I: Basics

Having established the four building blocks of the model, we can now begin studying its predictions. In terms of formal optimization, the Lagrangian for the problem is

$$P_1 f(k_1, n_1) + (S_1 + D_1)a_0 - P_1(k_2 - k_1) - P_1 w_1 n_1 - S_1 a_1$$
$$+ \frac{P_2 f(k_2, n_2)}{1+i} + \frac{(S_2 + D_2)a_1}{1+i} - \frac{P_2(k_3 - k_2)}{1+i} - \frac{P_2 w_2 n_2}{1+i} - \frac{S_2 a_2}{1+i}$$
$$+ \lambda \cdot [R \cdot S_1 \cdot a_1 - P_1 \cdot (k_2 - k_1)],$$

in which λ is the Lagrange multiplier on the financing constraint. The next step would be to compute first-order conditions. But it is very helpful to discuss important economic intuition about the multiplier λ.

When presenting the second building block, we asserted that the financing constraint will be assumed to always hold with equality in the formal analysis. However, it need not hold with equality in practice. A consequence of the *possibility* that it holds with equality is that the Lagrange multiplier must be (weakly) positive at the optimal choice—that is, $\lambda \geq 0$ must hold at the optimal choice. The multiplier λ cannot be a strictly negative value at the optimal choice. The nonnegativity of λ is a condition we have not at all encountered before, and its meaning is important.

The nonnegativity of λ may seem a somewhat technical point, but it is actually easy to describe in terms of economic insight. Note that the nonnegativity of λ is simply an *asymmetry* regarding λ. The reason this mathematical asymmetry about λ arises as part of the optimal solution of the accelerator framework is that it reflects the conceptual asymmetry about borrowing that is an input into the framework. If the firm optimally chooses not to borrow at all for the purpose of physical capital purchases, then it optimally decides that there is no need for it to rely on the financing restriction. There is nothing that compels a firm to find a lender to procure a loan if it optimally chooses to not borrow. If the firm optimally chooses to not borrow, then $\lambda = 0$.[10] Important here is the repeated use of the term *optimal.*

This intuition is a very general and powerful one in optimization analysis, regardless of whether it is an economics application, an engineering application, a physics application, or any application: if asymmetries inherently exist in the inputs to the optimization problem, then multipliers must themselves display asymmetries at the optimal solution. Once again, important here is the use of the term *optimal.*

The housing example is again useful for further illustrative intuition; for simplicity, let $R = 2$ throughout the rest of this example. Suppose that the optimal level of spending for (the total value of) a house is $100,000, and an individual has, say, $200,000 in funds in his personal bank account that have been optimally chosen for the sole purpose of backing a loan for the house. Then there is optimally no reason for the individual to obtain a loan at all! He can simply pay $100,000 directly for the purchase of the house with his own available funds, without any need for borrowing. Optimally choosing to not rely on the financing constraint exactly implies $\lambda = 0$ at the optimal choice.[11]

The Kuhn–Tucker analysis (which, to reiterate, we are not employing) properly rules out strictly negative values of λ and, intuitively, inserts $\lambda = 0$ when this situation arises. In the context of the examples above, Kuhn–Tucker thus mathematically delivers the correct result.

Instead, the straightforward Lagrangian analysis leads to the conclusion that the value of λ, in the same examples, is strictly negative. This is despite the logical conclusions above that λ cannot be strictly negative due to the optimal lack of reliance on the financing constraint. The incorrect conclusion that $\lambda < 0$ in turn leads to other downstream conclusions that, unfortunately, are also incorrect. The bottom line is that in cases where the financing constraint simply "does not bind" (i.e., is optimally ignored), the formal Lagrange analysis leads to incorrect results.

The opposite case, however—that is, when $\lambda \geq 0$ turns out as part of the result—works just fine from the perspective of both Lagrange and Kuhn–Tucker analyses. The opposite case is that of a borrower being compelled to borrow because his pledgeable funds are insufficient to pay for the optimally chosen spending. In the housing example (and with R

---

10. This result can be stated more powerfully, given the structures built into the accelerator model, as will become clear through the first-order conditions and ensuing analysis below: even if a firm does have to borrow, if borrowing interest rates are identical to our standard notion of interest rates—that is, if $i = i^{STOCK}$, then $\lambda = 0$.

11. A more everyday example is a personal favorite. I enjoy driving fast. What if speed limits everywhere were 300 miles per hour? You are allowed to drive as fast as you want, but your speed cannot exceed 300 miles per hour. In principle, this is a constraint imposed on my optimal speed. But, in practice, it is one that is irrelevant for my optimal choice because I cannot purchase a car that drives that fast. The constraint exists, but it does not affect my behavior, hence the multiplier on it at the solution of my optimization problem about how fast to drive is zero.

= 2) from above, suppose that the individual has only $50,000 in his personal bank account to optimally pledge against a loan for the purpose of buying the $100,000 house. In this case he must collateralize his funds in order to borrow enough to pay for the house. In this simple example, he can take out a loan of $50,000 with his own personal $50,000 pledged as collateral, and then use the resulting $100,000 to purchase the house. This result is reflected technically in a positive value of λ, which both the Kuhn–Tucker and Lagrange analyses correctly deliver.

This discussion regarding numerical values of multipliers at the optimal choice should strike you as intuitive—read it over several times, though, to allow it to sink in. Also think of similar personal situations, like purchasing a car or paying to attend college, which are also events that may or may not have required obtaining a loan.

In none of the models studied thus far have nonnegativity issues regarding multipliers arisen. This is because asymmetry has fundamentally not appeared in our models thus far. In such cases the value of multipliers at the optimal choice could be positive or negative—there is no asymmetry conditions regarding values of the multiplier. But asymmetries do (easily) arise in the accelerator framework, due to the basic economic asymmetry in the need for borrowing.

In all of the formal analysis of the accelerator, we will limit attention to cases in which $\lambda \geq 0$ turns out to be part of the optimal solution. The discussion regarding asymmetries is nonetheless raised here because one may wonder why situations like the financial collapse of 2007 and 2008 and associated downstream events do not occur "all the time." The basic reason is simply the asymmetry regarding borrowing, which is reflected in the asymmetry regarding λ.

Given the setup of the accelerator framework and limiting attention in the formal analysis to cases in which $\lambda \geq 0$ is part of the optimal solution, we could in fact re-interpret the analysis of chapter 6 as being the special case of $\lambda = 0$ (which is intuitively the knife-edge case between the Kuhn–Tucker and Lagrange cases). What $\lambda = 0$ at the optimal choice means is that despite the existence of informational asymmetries that require a financing constraint, they turn out to not at all matter for the results of chapter 6. More precisely, the financing constraint ends up not at all affecting either the capital demand or the labor demand functions if $\lambda = 0$ is in place. We will see these points formally below.

However, by allowing $\lambda \geq 0$ and not assuming $\lambda = 0$ (note this distinction), the richer accelerator analysis allows us to study a crucial issue (besides that of the accelerator effect itself): the market and/or regulatory settings that allow for $\lambda = 0$ to arise as an *outcome,* rather than being imposed as an *assumption.* Stated more technically, the accelerator allows us to consider how or why $\lambda = 0$ can emerge *endogenously,* rather than simply being assumed *exogenously.* We will revisit this important economic question after obtaining first-order conditions and doing some other preliminary analysis.

First-Order Conditions

Based on the Lagrangian above, the first-order conditions with respect to n_1 and n_2 are

$$P_1 f_n(k_1, n_1) - P_1 w_1 = 0$$

and

$$\frac{P_2 f_n(k_2, n_2)}{1+i} - \frac{P_2 w_2}{1+i} = 0.$$

Canceling terms appropriately in each of these expressions gives $w_1 = f_n(k_1, n_1)$ and $w_2 = f_n(k_2, n_2)$. If the analysis is extended beyond two periods, the first-order condition on labor is $w_t = f_n(k_t, n_t)$, for every time period t. Regardless of whether the time horizon is two periods or longer, these labor demand conditions are identical in functional form to those from chapter 6. Thus, up to first order, there is no shift of the labor demand functions; but further discussion about labor demand appears below.

Given the particular setup of the framework, in which it is only physical capital purchases that are subject to financing constraint (which is the most common form of the accelerator model), it is only physical capital investment in period 1 that is (potentially!) directly affected by financing issues. The first-order conditions with respect to k_2 and a_1 are thus the heart of the analysis. These conditions are, respectively,

$$-P_1 + \frac{P_2 f_k(k_2, n_2)}{1+i} + \frac{P_2}{1+i} - \lambda \cdot P_1 = 0$$

and

$$-S_1 + \frac{S_2 + D_2}{1+i} + \lambda \cdot R \cdot S_1 = 0.$$

Zooming in again on the multiplier $\lambda \geq 0$, its appearance is what differentiates the first-order condition on k_2 from the simpler one that appears in basic firm analysis. The basic firm analysis is to be thought of as the special case of $\lambda = 0$. In order to work out the implications of the more general case in which $\lambda \geq 0$ is part of the optimal solution, a joint analysis of both of the immediately preceding first-order conditions is required.

The ensuing analysis takes up two distinct, but related, questions: first, what economic and/or regulatory conditions cause $\lambda \geq 0$ to emerge as an *outcome* (rather than being assumed); and second, how, in the case of $\lambda \geq 0$, the capital demand function modifies. The first issue requires analysis of only the first-order condition on stock; the second issue requires joint analysis of both the first-order condition on stock and the first-order condition on physical capital. Once we have the modified capital demand function in place, we can then directly study the accelerator effect itself.

When Does $\lambda = 0$?

An important question is the conditions (if any exist) under which $\lambda = 0$ emerges as an outcome as part of the optimal choice. Studying this question requires only the first-order condition on stock. Because doing so spotlights the insights, isolating the λ term from this first-order condition is helpful. Simultaneously emphasizing the real (as opposed to nominal) nature of the accelerator, although not required, is also helpful.

The full set of algebraic rearrangements (which is simply several steps of algebra) appears in the appendix; proceeding here directly to the resulting expression, the multiplier λ that emerges is

$$\lambda = \left[\frac{r - r^{STOCK}}{1 + r} \right] \cdot \frac{1}{R} .$$

Based on earlier discussion, we know that $\lambda < 0$ cannot occur. The fact that it seems that $\lambda < 0$ can occur reflects the use of purely Lagrange tools. Thus we can formally ignore the case of $\lambda < 0$ because the Kuhn–Tucker analysis would properly insert $\lambda = 0$ in its place. In terms of rates of return, we can thus ignore the case of $r - r^{STOCK} < 0$.

Discarding the case of $\lambda < 0$, the expression states that two basic conditions determine whether or not $\lambda = 0$ (or, more precisely, whether or not λ is such a small positive number that it is tantamount to zero).

First, if $r - r^{STOCK} = 0$, then $\lambda = 0$ emerges as an outcome of the analysis. This result is irrespective of the precise numerical value of $R > 0$. Intuitively, if the real returns on riskless assets are aligned with the real returns on risky assets, then, despite the presence of informational asymmetries and the attendant financing constraint, they turn out to simply not matter at the optimal choice. This is all captured by $\lambda = 0$. An exactly analogous result ($i - i^{STOCK} = 0$) emerges if we prefer thinking in terms of nominal rates of return.

If instead $r - r^{STOCK} > 0$, then the expression states (again, given the maintained assumption $R > 0$) that $\lambda > 0$ strictly. We have already discussed the interpretation of the strict positivity of the multiplier: the firm must actually rely on the constraint to obtain a loan, due to financial assets that are insufficiently large to purchase the physical capital outright without a loan.

But consider also the case of $r - r^{STOCK} > 0$ simultaneously with a regulatory measure R so large that it can be effectively interpreted as $R = \infty$ (more properly, think in terms of mathematical limits, $\lim_{R \to \infty}$). If R is extremely large, then a very small market value of financial assets can be leveraged up to a very large loan for the purpose of physical capital purchases. An extreme example again using housing markets illustrates this: suppose that \$1 of financial assets could be leveraged up to obtain a loan that can pay for a \$1,000,000 house. In this case, $R = 1,000,000$. If R is only government regulation, it is quite lax regulation! To also use other language introduced earlier, the marginal borrower in this case has a lot of "fragility" in the sense that if some shock (either personal or aggregate) affects his ability to repay the remainder of his loan, he may be more hard-pressed to do so than if he were compelled, at his optimal choice, to put up more collateral to obtain the loan (which is tantamount to a lower, finite, value of $R > 0$). The example makes the point that whether it is controlled just by the government or by some combination of government and private-market conditions, an extremely high R effectively renders moot the financing constraint even if $r - r^{STOCK} > 0$.

Stated more formally, the mathematical limit

$$\lim_{R \to \infty} \left[\frac{r - r^{STOCK}}{1 + r} \right] \cdot \frac{1}{R} = 0$$

shows the result that $\lambda \to 0$ as $R \to \infty$. Financial markets or submarkets sometimes seem to be characterized by very lax regulation for one reason or another; some economists and policy officials interpret the events in housing and housing-mortgage markets in the years leading up to 2007 and 2008 as being excessively lax.

Capital Demand Function

With the condition $\lambda = \left[(r - r^{STOCK})/(1 + r)\right]/R \cdot$ (which, recall, is nothing but the first-order condition on stock), the next step we can take is to jointly analyze it simultaneously with the first-order condition on k_2. The resulting condition characterizes the capital demand function. To obtain the capital demand function, we do not have to proceed this way. We could instead directly analyze the first-order condition on k_2 above because it does contain the critical object λ, and it is shifts in the capital demand function induced by changes in λ that is the economic issue of interest. But, combining the first-order condition on k_2 with the first-order condition on a_1 in order to eliminate λ allows us, in this case, to think more directly in terms of economics.

As in our initial study of firm profit maximization, let's specialize attention to the Cobb–Douglas production function, $f(k, n) = k^\alpha n^{1-\alpha}$, which has associated marginal product of capital $f_k(k_2, n_2) = \alpha k_2^{\alpha-1} n_2^{1-\alpha}$.[12] Some algebra is again involved in obtaining an analytic form for the capital demand function, and the derivations appear in the Appendix. Proceeding here directly to the resulting expression, the capital demand function is characterized by

$$r = \left[\frac{R}{R+1} \right] \cdot \alpha k_2^{\alpha-1} n_2^{1-\alpha} + \frac{r^{STOCK}}{R+1},$$

12. Note that we are abstracting from total factor productivity (TFP), for the sake of some parsimony in the notation. But TFP could easily be introduced in exactly the same way as in the basic firm analysis.

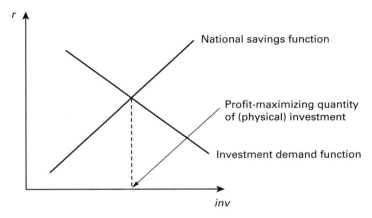

Figure 21.3
Equilibrium in the physical investment market, in the case of financing constraints not affecting capital demand at all, due to $r - r^{STOCK} = 0$

which is a generalization of the simpler capital demand function that appeared in chapter 6. The formal way to see this is to again consider the mathematical limit as regulation R becomes very lax,

$$\lim_{R \to \infty} \left\{ \left[\frac{R}{R+1} \right] \cdot \alpha k_2^{\alpha-1} n_2^{1-\alpha} + \frac{r^{STOCK}}{R+1} \right\} = \alpha k_2^{\alpha-1} n_2^{1-\alpha}.$$

The right-hand side is simply the marginal product of capital for the Cobb–Douglas production function, in which case the standard condition $r = f_k(k_2, n_2)$ emerges.

For the accelerator analysis below, we will consider the case in which R is strictly positive, but is not so large that it can be considered to be infinite. That is, our benchmark for the rest of the analysis will be a finite positive R, $(0 < R < \infty)$. The interest is then on how changes in the $r - r^{STOCK}$ term affect the capital investment demand function.

All of the analysis up to now can be thought of as firm-specific (i.e., one small, atomistic firm) in nature. For the rest of the analysis, we switch to an equilibrium viewpoint because we will be describing the stages through which, among other effects, the equilibrium quantity of investment is affected. Because it allows intuition to be described in a clear way, a good starting point is exactly the capital demand function from chapter 6. The downward-sloping capital demand function qualitatively plotted in figure 21.3 represents the basic capital demand function (i.e., when $\lambda = 0$, which results if $r - r^{STOCK} = 0$).[13] Also indicated

13. Just as in our basic firm analysis, the diagram is qualitative because it uses linear functions, even though the Cobb–Douglas function implies strictly convex functions. For our qualitative purposes, this is sufficient.

is the profit-maximizing quantity of physical capital investment, which is simply the equilibrium in figure 21.3; this is a key point for the subsequent analysis.

Labor Demand Function

Before proceeding to the accelerator effect itself, let's briefly consider labor demand. The first-order conditions on n (regardless of time period) do not directly contain λ. The financing constraint thus apparently does not directly shift the labor demand conditions at all.

The result is more nuanced, however, and it depends on the depth of analysis we are considering. If we take functional forms and the values of k (in particular, it is k_2 that is important for the accelerator effect in the formal model) as given, then we arrive at exactly the conclusion reached above: the financing constraint does not affect the labor demand functions. Intuitively, this (non)effect arises from the fact that nothing regarding n appears in the financing constraint.

However, in doing a complete joint analysis of the firm's optimal decisions for both labor and capital, the optimal value of k_2 in principle can be different from the one that is optimal in the basic firm analysis of chapter 6. Inserting this possibly new value of the optimal k_2 into the first-order condition on n shows that the labor demand function would, in principle, be "shifted" after all.

This complete joint solution is not difficult to obtain, but it requires a little more algebra than just examining whether, conditional on functional form and a particular value of k (whether or not it is the optimal k), the labor demand function shifts. In terms of vocabulary that we have used earlier, the former corresponds to the case of *zero first-order effects* on the labor demand function; the latter corresponds to the case of examining *higher order effects* on the labor demand function. Zero first-order effects are simple to analyze graphically; the presence of higher order effects are harder to analyze graphically, and they are instead more amenable to solving the model jointly for both the optimal k and the optimal n (i.e., in general equilibrium).

Moving away from the details of the particular way in which we have constructed the accelerator framework, a broader reason that labor demand can be affected directly by financing constraints is if some aspect about labor expenditures directly appeared in the financing constraint. Such a setup is also admissible. In this case the first-order conditions on n *would* directly contain terms arising from the constraint (in particular, would contain terms that involve λ). The labor demand functions would then directly—that is, to first order—be affected by the financing constraint. But our baseline accelerator model is not set up this way.

Analysis Part II: The Accelerator Effect

We now proceed to the accelerator effect itself. The starting point is figure 21.3 which is drawn for the case of $r - r^{STOCK} = 0$. Figure 21.3 displays equilibrium in the investment market when the physical investment demand function is exactly the one studied in chapter 6. While we do not have to begin exactly here, this point of departure makes it simple to describe the ultimate economic insights; but the economics is the same if we start at some other equilibrium.

Several points are worth clarifying before conducting the main analytical experiment. First, given $(0 < R < \infty)$, the main interest is in how changes in the interest rate gap $r - r^{STOCK}$ affect the investment demand function. An important observation is that the accelerator model does not explain why the interest rate gap itself might change. Changes in the interest gap are thus viewed from the perspective of the model as shocks, in the way we studied in chapter 9. The accelerator instead primarily focuses on understanding macro-finance dynamics following such financial shocks.

Second, regarding directionality of shocks, the relevant experiment in the formal analysis is any shock that causes returns on risky financial assets to *decline* compared to returns on riskless assets. That is, the relevant experiment is any shock that causes the gap $r - r^{STOCK}$ to become larger. Consideration of the other direction for shocks is briefly discussed later, but is only qualitative due to the asymmetry of borrowing at the heart of the model.

Third, the analysis is mostly graphical. This is partly because the basic results are fairly intuitive, given the effort introducing the building blocks and the analysis already conducted. A truly complete analysis would require much more numerical precision through computer simulations, which is beyond the scope of our analysis. Rather, the goal here is to describe the insight of the accelerator effect, which is easy. The analysis is also graphical because we will adopt an equilibrium-centered view, which requires both the demand and supply sides of the market, as shown in figure 21.3.

Fourth, to simplify the analysis even further, suppose that r is constant as r^{STOCK} declines. As we will see as we work through the stages of the experiment, r itself will also decline (in equilibrium). But the quantitative decline in r will not be as large as the (possibly very sharp) declines in r^{STOCK} (which again raises the issue of numerical general-equilibrium solutions). This simplification thus also does not obscure the economic insight.

With these several points in mind, start from figure 21.3 and consider a negative shock to r^{STOCK} that causes $r - r^{STOCK} > 0$. Our analysis of the capital demand function above shows that the widening of the interest gap $r - r^{STOCK}$ shifts it leftward. This is plotted in figure 21.4. The adverse development in the rate of return on financial assets means that it is now more expensive for a firm to use a given quantity of financial assets to back a loan to use for physical capital investment. Starting from any point on the investment demand function, fewer capital goods can thus be purchased.

Next, focusing on an equilibrium-centric view, the equilibrium quantity of investment declines. The pullback in investment in turn means that profits decline. This effect on profits occurs because the starting point in figure 21.3 was one in which profits were at a maximum. Any other point thus necessarily implies smaller profits, including the new equilibrium level of profits in figure 21.4.

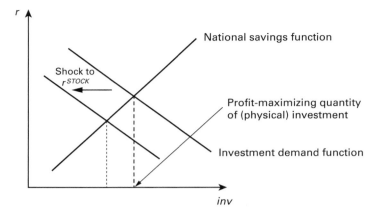

Figure 21.4
After a decline in r^{STOCK} relative to r, $r - r^{STOCK} > 0$, which shifts the physical capital investment function inward

It is this stage at which the "accelerator" part of the framework kicks in. The fourth building block of the model, which describes the fairly stable relationship between profits and dividends, means that dividends decline. The return on risky assets is

$$1 + i^{STOCK} = \frac{S_2 + D_2}{S_1}$$

(or, to express it in real terms, $1 + r^{STOCK}$, divide $1 + i^{STOCK}$ by the gross goods inflation rate $1 + \pi_2$). The decline in dividends thus means that the *return on risky assets declines even further.* Note the very stark nature of this conclusion.

The analysis began with an adverse shock to r^{STOCK}. The background reason is unknown, due to its very nature as a shock, but it sets into motion some events. One of the conclusions that the model then predicts is that r^{STOCK} *declines even further.* Stated very bluntly, the input to the analysis is a negative shock to r^{STOCK}—and one of the outputs of the analysis is that r^{STOCK} declines even further. In more technical terms, *an exogenous negative shock to* r^{STOCK} leads to the *endogenous result that* r^{STOCK} *declines even further.*

You should stop and re-read the last few paragraphs again. This is a very dramatic conclusion. Its nature is not something we have seen before.

This now predicted (endogenous) decline in r^{STOCK} causes the investment demand function to shift in even further than the shift illustrated in figure 21.4. Figure 21.5 illustrates this further shift.

Again, taking an equilibrium-centric view, the equilibrium quantity of investment falls even further. The decline in investment thus means that profits fall even further, because the market quantity has moved even further away from its starting point in figure 21.3. The stable relationship between profits and dividends (the fourth building block) then predicts

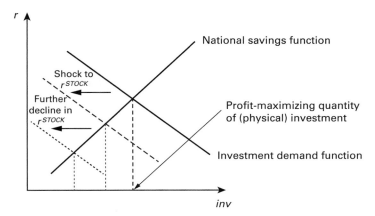

Figure 21.5
With a further endogenous decline in r^{STOCK} relative to r, $r - r^{STOCK}$ even more strictly positive, which shifts the physical capital investment function even further inward

that dividends fall *even further*. In turn the return on risky assets falls even further—that is, by even more than illustrated in figure 21.5.

But this now predicted *EVEN* sharper decline in r^{STOCK} causes the investment demand function to shift inwards *even further* than the shift illustrated in figure 21.5. But this means that equilibrium investment falls *even further*, which in turn means that profits decline *even further*, which in turn means that dividends fall *even further*. But this means that the returns on risky assets fall *EVEN* further. And the effects continue on and on.

For parsimony, we will not sketch any further diagrams. But it should be clear where things are heading from the point of view of the framework. They are heading toward a very severe and jointly connected downward spiral in macroeconomic outcomes and financial outcomes. This is exactly the accelerator effect: once a financial downturn (captured in this analysis by a decline in r^{STOCK}) begins, if it is sufficiently widespread, then the adverse feedback loop kicks in. Intuitively, the adverse feedback loop arises due to the linkage between profits, and this reflects fundamentally macro outcomes, and dividends, which are a fundamental aspect of finance.

Discussion

This chain of logic returns us to the very beginning of the chapter: what are policy authorities to do in the face of such events? In a short and almost, but not quite, facetious sense—who knows. In a slightly less short, and slightly more serious, sense—increase R.

If we are thinking specifically about the events that occurred in the United States in 2007 and 2008, the Federal Reserve, the US Treasury, and many other regulatory agencies were trying to do exactly this—increase R. What exactly was the nature by which R was increased, if it was successfully increased at all? Thinking back to the events of that period, some assorted slices of policy were "quantitative easing," "high-quality financial injections," and some changes in the literal regulatory structure, which, along with other things, required some firms to hold on to larger quantities of financial assets on their balance sheets. But these are all talking points, because the accelerator model does not take a stand on any of this. As discussed when introducing the third building block, the model makes no prediction regarding R; rather, R is simply taken as given by the framework.

What about the opposite of the situation analyzed above, in which r^{STOCK} increases relative to r? It is again helpful to start this analysis with the case drawn in figure 21.3 in which $r - r^{STOCK} = 0$. If r^{STOCK} rises relative to r, then it is clear that $r - r^{STOCK} < 0$. If we follow the chain of logic and the exact analytical expressions of the arguments laid out above, then we would claim that $\lambda < 0$.

But we know from our earlier discussion about the Lagrange multiplier that $\lambda < 0$ cannot occur at the optimal choice! The smallest possible value of λ is $\lambda = 0$, at which point there is no need for the firm to use loans backed by financial assets to help pay for physical capital purchases. The accelerator effect by its very nature does not work in the opposite direction, and this follows from the asymmetry regarding borrowing already studied. Or, stated in terms of figure 21.3, there is an optimal, profit-maximizing, quantity of physical capital investment. If the firm is given the chance to invest more in physical assets for a given market value of financial assets—that is, for the physical capital demand function to shift outwards at every r—it would optimally choose to not invest any further. There is no "acceleration" on the upside.[14]

The financial accelerator model has been in existence for decades. In the United States, events described by it do not occur very often—in the past roughly 100 years, the Great Depression and the Great Recession of 2007 to 2009 are really the only events that can be classified as accelerator periods. But when they do occur, the adverse effects, or possible adverse effects, can be very pronounced. The interpretation of many policy authorities and academic researchers is that the after-effects of the events of 2007 to −2009 are not yet over.

Appendix A: Isolating λ from the First-Order Condition on Financial Assets

The following presents the algebra that isolates the Lagrange multiplier λ from the first-order condition on a_1. Repeated here for convenience is the first-order condition on a_1:

$$-S_1 + \frac{S_2 + D_2}{1 + i} + \lambda \cdot R \cdot S_1 = 0.$$

---

14. Stated more subtly, there could be acceleration for a while, but it would eventually choke off. The point at which it would choke off is as soon equilibrium investment reaches the point at which it is truly profit maximizing, which was the highlighted point in figure 21.3.

To isolate the λ term, first rearrange this expression to get

$$\lambda = \left[S_1 - \frac{S_2 + D_2}{1+i} \right] \cdot \frac{1}{R \cdot S_1}.$$

Next pull the S_1 term outside the square brackets inside the square brackets, which gives

$$\lambda = \left[1 - \frac{S_2 + D_2}{S_1} \cdot \frac{1}{1+i} \right] \cdot \frac{1}{R}.$$

Then multiply and divide the second term in parentheses by P_1 and P_2, which gives

$$\lambda = \left[1 - \frac{S_2 + D_2}{S_1} \cdot \frac{P_1}{P_2} \cdot \frac{P_2}{P_1} \cdot \frac{1}{1+i} \right] \cdot \frac{1}{R}.$$

Using the definition of goods-price inflation between period 1 and period 2,

$$1 + \pi_2 = \frac{P_2}{P_1},$$

in both the numerator in denominator of the previous expression gives

$$\lambda = \left[1 - \frac{S_2 + D_2}{S_1} \cdot \frac{1}{1+\pi_2} \cdot \frac{1+\pi_2}{1+i} \right] \cdot \frac{1}{R}.$$

Now insert the definition of the interest rate (or rate of return) on stock, $1 + i^{STOCK} = (S_2 + D_2)/S_1$, to replace the term involving nominal prices and dividends of stock, which gives

$$\lambda = \left[1 - \frac{1 + i^{STOCK}}{1+\pi_2} \cdot \frac{1+\pi_2}{1+i} \right] \cdot \frac{1}{R}.$$

Use of the usual Fisher relation allows us to express the rates of return in real units (rather than in nominal units),

$$\lambda = \left[1 - \frac{1 + r^{STOCK}}{1+r} \right] \cdot \frac{1}{R}.$$

A final algebraic step inside the square brackets yields

$$\lambda = \left[\frac{r - r^{STOCK}}{1+r} \right] \cdot \frac{1}{R}.$$

This final expression is what is used in the analysis in the main text. Despite several steps of rearrangement, note that it fundamentally is the same first-order condition on a_1 based on the Lagrangian.

Appendix B: Construction of the Capital Demand Function

The following shows how to combine the first-order conditions on a_1 and on k_2 to obtain predictions about the capital demand function. The reason both conditions are required is that the multiplier λ appears in each. Start with the expression for λ obtained above (which is simply a re-expressed version of the first-order condition on a_1)

$$\lambda = \left[\frac{r - r^{STOCK}}{1+r} \right] \cdot \frac{1}{R},$$

and insert it in the first-order condition on k_2 (which, repeated for convenience, is

$$-P_1 + \frac{P_2 f_k(k_2, n_2)}{1+i} + \frac{P_2}{1+i} - \lambda \cdot P_1 = 0).$$

This gives the single expression

$$-P_1 + \frac{P_2 f_k(k_2, n_2)}{1+i} + \frac{P_2}{1+i} - \left[\frac{r - r^{STOCK}}{1+r} \right] \cdot \frac{1}{R} \cdot P_1 = 0,$$

which will now be rearranged in several steps. While there are several steps, keep in mind this is just algebra.

First divide the entire expression by P_1, which gives

$$\frac{P_2 f_k(k_2, n_2)}{P_1 \cdot (1+i)} + \frac{P_2}{P_1 \cdot (1+i)} - \left[\frac{r - r^{STOCK}}{1+r} \right] \cdot \frac{1}{R} = 1$$

(in which we have also moved the $-P_1$ term over to the other side of the expression in the same step). Then, using the definition of inflation between period 1 and period 2,

$$1 + \pi_2 = \frac{P_2}{P_1},$$

rewrite the expression as

$$\left(\frac{1+\pi_2}{1+i} \right) \cdot f_k(k_2, n_2) + \frac{1+\pi_2}{1+i} - \left[\frac{r - r^{STOCK}}{1+r} \right] \cdot \frac{1}{R} = 1.$$

Next apply the Fisher relation, which gives

$$\frac{f_k(k_2, n_2)}{1+r} + \frac{1}{1+r} - \left[\frac{r - r^{STOCK}}{1+r} \right] \cdot \frac{1}{R} = 1.$$

This expression is helpful because it shows that if $r = r^{STOCK}$ or if $R \to \infty$, then the capital demand function obtained in basic firm analysis, characterized by $f_k(k_2, n_2) = r$, emerges.

Going further is useful, though, if $r - r^{STOCK} > 0$ (which in turn implies $\lambda > 0$). Multiplying the previous expression by $1 + r$ gives

$$f_k(k_2, n_2) + 1 - \left[\frac{r - r^{STOCK}}{R} \right] = 1 + r,$$

or, after canceling the 1's on each side,

$$f_k(k_2, n_2) - \left[\frac{r - r^{STOCK}}{R} \right] = r.$$

As in basic firm analysis, let's focus on the Cobb–Douglas production function, $f(k, n) = k^\alpha n^{1-\alpha}$, for the rest of the analysis. This is simply because virtually all practical studies in macroeconomics use this particular form because it is empirically relevant; however, any production function that displays a constant elasticity of substitution between k and n (the Cobb–Douglas case is just one example) works.

The Cobb–Douglas function implies that the marginal product of capital (in period 2, in particular, which is the period of interest regarding the capital stock in the formal model, due to the fact that k_1 is fixed at the beginning of period 1) is $f_k(k_2, n_2) = \alpha k_2^{\alpha-1} n_2^{1-\alpha}$. Substituting this in the previous displayed expression gives

$$\alpha k_2^{\alpha-1} n_2^{1-\alpha} - \left[\frac{r - r^{STOCK}}{R} \right] = r.$$

As in basic firm analysis, this expression defines the capital demand function, and we want to represent it in $r - k_2$ space. To get there, there is a bit more algebra to do because we need to isolate the r terms on one side of the expression.

Proceeding with this part of the algebra, first open up the term in square brackets, which gives

$$r = \alpha k_2^{\alpha-1} n_2^{1-\alpha} - \frac{r}{R} + \frac{r^{STOCK}}{R}$$

(and also interchanges the left-hand and right-hand sides of the expression for clarity). Then combine terms involving the riskless rate r on the left-hand side, which gives

$$\left[1 + \frac{1}{R} \right] \cdot r = \alpha k_2^{\alpha-1} n_2^{1-\alpha} + \frac{r^{STOCK}}{R},$$

or, after combining terms in the square brackets on the left-hand side,

$$\left[\frac{R+1}{R} \right] \cdot r = \alpha k_2^{\alpha-1} n_2^{1-\alpha} + \frac{r^{STOCK}}{R}.$$

Finally, multiply both sides by $R/(R+1)$ to get the final form

$$r = \left[\frac{R}{R+1}\right] \cdot \alpha k_2^{\alpha-1} n_2^{1-\alpha} + \frac{r^{STOCK}}{R+1},$$

which is the modified version of the capital demand function that appears in the main text. As noted in the main discussion,

$$\lim_{R\to\infty}\left\{\left[\frac{R}{R+1}\right] \cdot \alpha k_2^{\alpha-1} n_2^{1-\alpha} + \frac{r^{STOCK}}{R+1}\right\} = \alpha k_2^{\alpha-1} n_2^{1-\alpha},$$

the right-hand side of which is simply the marginal product of capital from the Cobb–Douglas production specification. Thus, as $R \to \infty$, the relation above converges to $r = \alpha k_2^{\alpha-1} n_2^{1-\alpha}$, which is exactly the condition that characterizes the capital demand function in basic firm analysis.

Chapter 21 Problem Set Questions

1. **Stock, bonds, "bills," and the financial accelerator.** In this problem you will encounter an enriched version of the accelerator framework we studied in the chapter. As in our basic analysis, we continue to use the two-period theory of firm profit maximization as our vehicle for studying the effects of financial-market developments on macroeconomic activity. However, rather than supposing it is just "stock" that is the financial asset at firms' disposal for facilitating physical capital purchases, we now suppose that both "stock" and "bonds" are at firms' disposal for facilitating physical capital purchases.

   Before describing more precisely the analysis you are to conduct, a deeper understanding of "bond markets" is required. In "normal economic conditions" (i.e., in or near a "steady state," in the sense we first discussed in chapter 8), it is usually sufficient to think of all bonds of various maturity lengths in a highly simplified way: by supposing that they are all simply one-period face-value = 1 bonds with the same nominal interest rate. Recall that this is in fact how our basic discussion of monetary policy proceeded. In "unusual" (i.e., far away from steady-state) financial market conditions, however, it can become important to distinguish between different types of bonds and hence different types of nominal interest rates on those bonds.

   You might have seen discussion in the press about central banks, such as the US Federal Reserve, considering whether or not to "begin buying bonds" as a way of conducting policy. Viewed through the standard lens of how to understand open-market operations, this discussion makes no sense because in the standard view, central banks *already do* buy (and sell) "bonds" as the mechanism by which they conduct open-market operations!

A difference that becomes important to understand during unusual financial market conditions is that open-market operations are conducted using the shortest maturity "bonds" that the Treasury sells, of duration one month or shorter. In the lingo of finance, this type of bond is called a "Treasury bill." The term "Treasury bond" is usually used to refer to longer maturity Treasury securities—those that have maturities of one, two, five, or more years. These longer maturity Treasury "bonds" have typically *not* been assets that the Federal Reserve buys and sells as regular practice; buying such longer maturity bonds is/has not been the usual way of conducting monetary policy.

In the ensuing analysis, part of the goal will be to understand/explain why policy makers are currently considering this option. Before beginning this analysis, though, there is more to understand.

In private-market borrower/lender relationships, longer maturity Treasury bonds ("bonds") are typically allowed to be used just like stocks in financing firms' physical capital purchases.[15] We can capture this idea by enriching the financing constraint in our financial accelerator framework to read:

$$P_1 \cdot (k_2 - k_1) = R^S \cdot S_1 \cdot a_1 + R^B \cdot P_1^b \cdot B_1.$$

The left-hand side of this richer financing constraint is the same as the left-hand side of the financing constraint that we considered in our basic theory (and the notation is identical, as well—refer to your notes for the notational definitions).

The right-hand side of the financing constraint is richer than in our basic theory, however. The market value of "stock," $S_1 a_1$, still affects how much physical investment firms can do, scaled by the government regulation R^S. In addition the market value of a firm's "bond holdings" (which, again, means long-maturity government bonds) now also affects how much physical investment firms can do, scaled by the government regulation R^B. The notation here is that B_1 is a firm's holdings of nominal bonds ("long-maturity") at the end of period 1, and P_1^b is the nominal price of that bond during period 1. Note that R^B and R^S need not be equal to each other.

In the context of the two-period framework, the firm's two-period discounted profit function now reads:

---

15. Whereas, for various institutional and regulatory reasons, very short-term Treasury assets ("T-bills") are typically not allowed to be used in financing firms' physical capital purchases.

$$P_1 f(k_1, n_1) + P_1 k_1 + (S_1 + D_1)a_0 + B_0 - P_1 w_1 n_1 - P_1 k_2 - S_1 a_1 - P_1^b B_1$$

$$+ \frac{P_2 f(k_2, n_2)}{1+i} + \frac{P_2 k_2}{1+i} + \frac{(S_2 + D_2)a_1}{1+i} + \frac{B_1}{1+i} - \frac{P_2 w_2 n_2}{1+i} - \frac{P_2 k_3}{1+i} - \frac{S_2 a_2}{1+i} - \frac{P_2^b B_2}{1+i}.$$

The new notation compared to our study of the basic accelerator mechanism is the following: B_0 is the firm's holdings of nominal bonds (which have face value $= 1$) at the start of period 1, B_1 is the firm's holdings of nominal bonds (which have face value $= 1$) at the end of period 1, and B_2 is the firm's holdings of nominal bonds (which have face value $= 1$) at the end of period 2.

Note that period-2 profits are being discounted by the nominal interest rate i: in this problem, we will consider i to be the Treasury bill interest rate (as opposed to the Treasury bond interest rate). The Treasury bill interest rate is the one the Federal Reserve usually (i.e., in "normal times") controls. We can define the nominal interest rate on Treasury bonds as

$$i^{BOND} = \frac{1}{P_1^b} - 1 \left(\Leftrightarrow P_1^b = \frac{1}{1 + i^{BOND}} \right).$$

Thus note that i^{BOND} and i need not equal each other.

The rest of the notation above is just as in our study of the basic financial accelerator framework. Finally, because the economy ends at the end of period 2, we can conclude (as usual) that $k_3 = 0$, $a_2 = 0$, and $B_2 = 0$.

With this background in place, you are to analyze a number of issues.

a. Using λ as your notation for the Lagrange multiplier on the financing constraint, construct the Lagrangian for the representative firm's (two-period) profit-maximization problem.

b. Based on this Lagrangian, compute the first-order condition with respect to nominal bond holdings at the end of period 1 (i.e., compute the FOC with respect to B_1). (Note: This FOC is critical for much of the analysis that follows, so you should make sure that your work here is absolutely correct.)

c. Recall that in this enriched version of the accelerator framework, the nominal interest rate on Treasury bills, i, and the nominal interest rate on Treasury bonds, i^{BOND}, are potentially different from each other. If financing constraints do *not* at all affect firms' investment in physical capital, how does i^{BOND} compare to i? Specifically, is i^{BOND} equal to i, is i^{BOND} smaller than i, is i^{BOND} larger than i, or is it impossible to determine? Be as thorough in your analysis and conclusions as possible. Your analysis here should be based on the FOC on B_1 computed in part b above. (Hint: If financing constraints "don't matter," what is the value of the Lagrange multiplier λ?)

d. If financing constraints DO affect firms' investment in physical capital, how does i^{BOND} compare to i? Specifically, is i^{BOND} equal to i, is i^{BOND} smaller than i, is i^{BOND} larger than i, or is it impossible to determine? Furthermore, if possible, use your solution here as a basis for justifying whether or not it is appropriate in "normal economic conditions" to consider both Treasury bills and Treasury bonds as the same asset. Be as thorough in your analysis and conclusions as possible. Once again, your analysis here should be based on the FOC on B_1 computed in part b above. (Note: The government regulatory variables R^S and R^B are both strictly positive—i.e., neither can be zero or less than zero).

The analysis above was framed in terms of nominal interest rates; the remainder of the analysis is framed in terms of real interest rates.

e. By computing the first-order condition on firms' stock holdings at the end of period 1, a_1, and following exactly the same algebra as presented in class, we can express the Lagrange multiplier λ as

$$\lambda = \left[\frac{r - r^{STOCK}}{1+r} \right] \cdot \frac{1}{R^S}. \text{ (P.1)}$$

Use the first-order condition on B_1 you computed in part b above to derive an analogous expression for λ except in terms of the real interest rate on bonds (i.e., r^{BOND}) and R^B (rather than R^S). (Hint: Use the FOC on B_1 you computed in part b above and follow a very similar set of algebraic manipulations as we followed in class.)

f. Compare the expression you just derived in part e with expression (P.1). Suppose that $r = r^{STOCK}$. If this is the case, is r^{BOND} equal to r, is r^{BOND} smaller than r, is r^{BOND} larger than r, or is it impossible to determine? Furthermore, in this case, does the financing constraint affect firms' physical investment decisions? Briefly justify your conclusions and provide brief explanation.

g. Through late 2008, suppose that $r = r^{STOCK}$ was a reasonable description of the US economy for the preceding 20+ years. In late 2008, r^{STOCK} fell dramatically below r, which, as we studied in the chapter, would cause the financial accelerator effect to begin. Suppose that policy makers, both fiscal policy makers and monetary policy makers, decide that they need to intervene in order to choke off the accelerator effect. Furthermore suppose that there is no way to change either R^S or R^B (because of coordination delays among various government agencies, perhaps). Using all of your preceding analysis as well as drawing on what we studied in the chapter, explain why "buying bonds" (which, again, means long-maturity bonds in the sense described above) might be a sound strategy to pursue. (Note: The analysis here is largely *not* mathematical. Rather, what is required is a careful logical progression of thought that explains why buying bonds might be a good idea.)

2. **Financing constraints and housing markets.** Consider an enriched version of the two-period consumption-savings framework from chapters 3 and 4, in which the representative individual not only makes decisions about consumption and savings but also housing purchases. For this particular application, it is useful to interpret period 1 as the "young period" of the individual's life, and interpret period 2 as the "old period" of the individual's life.

In the young period of an individual's life, utility depends only on period-1 consumption c_1. In the old period of an individual's life, utility depends both on period-2 consumption c_2, as well as his/her "quantity" of housing (denoted h).[16] From the perspective of the beginning of period 1, the individual's lifetime utility function is

$$\ln c_1 + \ln c_2 + \ln h,$$

where $\ln(.)$ stands for the natural log function; the term $\ln h$ indicates that people directly obtain happiness from their housing.

Due to the "time-to-build" nature of housing (i.e., it takes time to build a housing unit), the representative individual has to incur expenses in his/her young period to purchase housing for his/her old period. The *real* price in period 1 (i.e., measured in terms of period-1 consumption) of a "unit" of housing (again, think of a unit of housing as square footage) is p_1^H, and the *real* price in period 2 (i.e., measured in terms of period-2 consumption) of a unit of housing is p_2^H.

In addition to housing decisions, the representative individual makes stock purchase decisions. The individual begins period 1 with zero stock holdings ($a_0 = 0$), and ends period 2 with zero stock holdings ($a_2 = 0$). How many shares of stock the individual ends period 1 with, and hence begins period 2 with, is to be optimally chosen. The real price in period 1 (i.e., measured in terms of period-1 consumption) of each share of stock is s_1, and the real price in period 2 (i.e., measured in terms of period-2 consumption) of each share of stock is s_2. For simplicity, suppose that stock never pays any dividends (i.e., dividends = 0 always).

Because housing is a big-ticket item, the representative individual has to accumulate financial assets (stock) while young to overcome the informational asymmetry

---

16. For concreteness, you can think of "quantity" of housing as the square footage and/or the "quality" of the housing space.

problem and be able to purchase housing. Suppose that the financing constraint that governs the purchase of housing is

$$\frac{p_1^H h}{R^H} = s_2 a_1$$

(technically an inequality constraint, but we will assume it always holds with strict equality). In the financing constraint, $R^H > 0$ is a government-controlled "leverage ratio" for housing. Note well the subscripts on variables that appear in the financing constraint.

Finally, the *real* quantities of income in the young period and the old period are y_1 and y_2, over which the individual has no choice.

The sequential Lagrangian for the representative individual's problem lifetime utility maximization problem is

$$\text{Lagrangian} = \ln c_1 + \ln c_2 + \ln h + \lambda_1 [y_1 - c_1 - s_1 a_1 - p_1^H h]$$
$$+ \lambda_2 \left[y_2 + s_2 a_1 + p_2^H h - c_2 \right] + \mu \left[s_2 a_1 - \frac{p_1^H h}{R^H} \right],$$

where μ is the Lagrange multiplier on the financing constraint, and λ_1 and λ_2 are, respectively, the Lagrange multipliers on the period-1 and period-2 budget constraints.

a. In no more than two brief sentences/phrases, qualitatively describe what an informational asymmetry is, and why it can be a serious problem in financial transactions.

b. In no more than three brief sentences/phrases, qualitatively describe the role that the leverage ratio R^H plays in the "housing finance" market. In particular, briefly describe/discuss what higher leverage ratios imply for the individual's ability to finance a house purchase (i.e., "obtain a mortgage").

c. Based on the sequential Lagrangian presented above, compute the two first-order conditions: with respect to a_1 and h. (You can safely ignore any other first-order conditions.)

d. Based on the first-order condition with respect to h computed in part c, solve for the period-1 real price of housing p_1^H (that is, your final expression should be of the form $p_1^H = ...$ where the term on the right hand side is for you to determine). (Note: you do *not* have to eliminate Lagrange multipliers from the final expression.)

e. Based on the expression for p_1^H computed in part d, and assuming that the Lagrange multiplier $\mu > 0$ (recall also that $R^H > 0$), answer the following: is the period-1 price of housing larger than or smaller than what it would be if financing constraints for housing were not at all an issue? Or is it impossible to determine? Carefully explain the logic of your argument/analysis, and provide brief economic interpretation of your conclusion.

For the remainder of this problem (i.e., for parts f, g, and h), suppose that $\lambda_1 = \lambda_2 = 1$.

f. Consider the period-1 housing market, with the quantity h of housing drawn on the horizontal axis and the period-1 price, p_1^H, of housing drawn on the vertical axis. Using the house-price expression computed in part d, qualitatively sketch the relationship between h and p_1^H that it implies. Your sketch should make clear whether the relationship is upward-sloping, downward-sloping, perfectly horizontal, or perfectly vertical. Clearly present the algebraic/logical steps that lead to your sketch, and clearly label your sketch.

g. In the same sketch in part f, clearly show and label what happens if p_2^H rises. (Examples of what could "happen" are that the relationship you sketched rotates, or shifts, or both rotates and shifts, etc.) Explain the logic behind your conclusion, and provide brief economic interpretation of your conclusion.

h. In the same sketch in part f, clearly show and label what happens if R^H rises. (Examples of what could "happen" are that the relationship you sketched rotates, or shifts, or both rotates and shifts, etc.) Explain the logic behind your conclusion, and provide brief economic interpretation of your conclusion.

3. **Long-run real interest rate.** In this problem you will analyze the steady state of an infinite-period consumer analysis in which a "credit crunch" is occurring. Specifically, consider a *real* (and simplified) version of the infinite-period consumer framework in which, in each period of time, a budget constraint affects the consumer's optimization, and a credit restriction also affects the consumer's optimization. In period t the credit restriction has the form

$$c_t = y_t + (1+r_t)a_{t-1}$$

(hence the restriction in period $t + 1$ is $c_{t+1} = y_{t+1} + (1+r_{t+1})a_t$, in period $t + 2$ is $c_{t+2} = y_{t+2} + (1+r_{t+2})a_{t+1}$, etc.). The consumer's budget constraint in period t is

$$c_t + a_t - a_{t-1} = y_t + r_t a_{t-1}$$

(hence the restriction in period $t + 1$ is $c_{t+1} + a_{t+1} - a_t = y_{t+1} + r_{t+1}a_t$, in period $t + 2$ is $c_{t+2} + a_{t+2} - a_{t+1} = y_{t+2} + r_{t+2}a_{t+1}$, etc.). In the equations above the notation for period t is the following: c_t denotes consumption in period t, r_t denotes the real interest rate between period $t - 1$ and t, a_{t-1} denotes the quantity of assets held at the beginning of period t, a_t denotes the quantity of assets held at the end of period t, and y_t is the consumer's real income during period t. (Similar notation with updated time subscripts describes prices and quantities beyond period t.)

Denote by $\beta \in (0, 1)$ the subjective discount factor, by $u(c_t)$ the utility function in period t, by λ_t the Lagrange multiplier on the period t budget constraint, and by ϕ_t (Greek lowercase letter "phi") the Lagrange multiplier on the period t credit restriction. (Similar notation with updated time subscripts describes prices, quantities, and multipliers beyond period t.)

The Lagrangian of the consumer lifetime utility maximization problem is

$$u(c_t) + \beta u(c_{t+1}) + \beta^2 u(c_{t+2}) + \beta^3 u(c_{t+3}) + ...$$
$$+ \lambda_t \left[y_t + r_t a_{t-1} - c_t - (a_t - a_{t-1}) \right] + \phi_t \left[y_t + (1 + r_t) a_{t-1} - c_t \right]$$
$$+ \beta \lambda_{t+1} \left[y_{t+1} + r_{t+1} a_t - c_{t+1} - (a_{t+1} - a_t) \right] + \beta \phi_{t+1} \left[y_{t+1} + (1 + r_{t+1}) a_t - c_{t+1} \right]$$
$$+ \beta^2 \lambda_{t+2} \left[y_{t+2} + r_{t+2} a_{t+1} - c_{t+2} - (a_{t+2} - a_{t+1}) \right] + \beta^2 \phi_{t+2} \left[y_{t+2} + (1 + r_{t+2}) a_{t+1} - c_{t+2} \right]$$
$$+ \beta^3 \lambda_{t+3} \left[y_{t+3} + r_{t+3} a_{t+2} - c_{t+3} - (a_{t+3} - a_{t+2}) \right] + \beta^3 \phi_{t+3} \left[y_{t+3} + (1 + r_{t+3}) a_{t+2} - c_{t+3} \right] + ...$$

a. Based on the Lagrangian as written above, construct the first-order conditions with respect to c_t, c_{t+1}, and a_t.

b. In no more than two brief sentences/phrases, describe/define (in general terms, not necessarily just for this problem) an economic steady state.

c. Use just the first-order condition on a_t you obtained in part a above to answer the following: in the steady state does the conclusion

$$\frac{1}{\beta} = 1 + r$$

hold? Or is it impossible to determine? Carefully develop the logic that leads to your conclusion, including showing any key mathematical steps. Also briefly, but thoroughly, provide the economic interpretation of your conclusion (i.e., something beyond what is simply apparent from the mathematics).

d. Suppose that the consumer begins period t with zero assets (i.e., $a_{t-1} = 0$). Further suppose that the credit restriction holds with equality in every period. Is the consumer's savings positive, negative, or zero in the steady state? Or is it impossible to determine? In answering this question, also briefly define the economic concept of "savings."

4. **Financing constraints and labor demand.** In the chapter discussion on the way in which financing constraints affect firms' profit-maximization decisions, we focused on the effects on firms' physical capital investment. In reality most firms spend twice as much on their wage costs (i.e., their labor costs) than on their physical investment

costs. (In other words, for most firms roughly two-thirds of their total costs are wages and salaries, while roughly one-third of their total costs are devoted to maintaining or expanding their physical capital.)

For many firms, payment of wages must be made before the receipt of revenues within any given period. (For example, imagine a firm that has to pay its employees to build a computer; the revenues from the sale of this computer typically don't arrive for many weeks or months later because of inherent lags in the shipping process, the retail process, etc.) For this reason firms typically need to borrow to pay for their payroll costs.[17] But, because of asymmetric information problems, lenders typically require that the firm put up some financial collateral to secure loans for this purpose.

You are asked to analyze the consequences of financing constraints on firms' wage payments using a variation of the accelerator framework we studied in the chapter. For simplicity, suppose that the representative firm, which operates in a two-period economy, must borrow in order to finance only period-1 wage costs; for some unspecified reason, suppose that period-2 wage costs are not subject to a financing constraint.

As in our study of the accelerator framework in class, the representative firm's two-period discounted profit function is

$$P_1 f(k_1, n_1) + P_1 k_1 + (S_1 + D_1) a_0 - P_1 w_1 n_1 - P_1 k_2 - S_1 a_1$$
$$+ \frac{P_2 f(k_2, n_2)}{1+i} + \frac{P_2 k_2}{1+i} + \frac{(S_2 + D_2) a_1}{1+i} - \frac{P_2 w_2 n_2}{1+i} - \frac{P_2 k_3}{1+i} - \frac{S_2 a_2}{1+i},$$

and suppose now that the financing constraint relevant for firm profit maximization is

$$P_1 w_1 n_1 = S_1 a_1.$$

The notation is as always: P denotes the nominal price of the output the firm produces and sells; S denotes the nominal price of stock; D denotes the nominal dividend paid by each unit of stock; n denotes the quantity of labor the firm hires; w is the real wage; a_0, a_1, and a_2 are, respectively, the firm's holdings of stock at the end of period 0, period 1, and period 2; k_1, k_2, and k_3 are, respectively, the firm's ownership of physical capital at the end of period 0, period 1, and period 2; i denotes the nominal interest rate between period 1 and period 2; and the production function is denoted by $f(.)$. Also as usual, subscripts on variables denote the time period of reference for that variable. Finally, because this is a two-period framework, we know that $a_2 = 0$ and $k_3 = 0$.

---

17. This is a reality of the commercial paper market, about which much has been discussed in the news.

a. Based on the information provided, construct the Lagrangian for the firm's profit maximization problem. Define any new notation you introduce.

b. Based on the Lagrangian you constructed in part a, compute the first-order conditions with respect to k_2 and a_1.

c. Based on the Lagrangian you constructed in part a, compute the first-order conditions with respect to n_1 and n_2.

Suppose that immediately after firm profit maximizing decisions have been made, the real return on STOCK, r^{STOCK}, all of a sudden falls below r, the real return on riskless ("safe") assets. Suppose that before this shock occurred, it was the case that $r = r^{STOCK}$.

d. Consider the investment (capital) market in period 1. Does the adverse shock to r^{STOCK} shift either the investment demand and/or the savings supply function? If so, explain how, in what direction, and why.

e. Consider the labor market in period 1. Does the adverse shock to r^{STOCK} shift either the labor demand and/or the labor supply function? If so, explain how, in what direction, and why.

V

OPTIMAL POLICY ANALYSIS II: THE RIGID PRICE CASE

Part V continues considering optimal policy, except now with rigidities (aka stickiness) in nominal prices. The New Keynesian sticky-price model is constructed in chapter 22 and chapter 23. Chapter 24 then uses the New Keynesian framework to study optimal monetary policy (and, in a subtle yet important way, optimal fiscal policy) with sticky prices, using all the tools and techniques developed in part IV.

22

Monopolistic Competition: The Dixit–Stiglitz Framework

The real business cycle (RBC) view of the macroeconomy is premised on perfect competition in all three macro markets (goods markets, labor markets, and financial markets). For the seminal issue of the degree of (goods) price stickiness, it is goods markets on which we need to focus, so we limit our attention to goods markets from here on.

In perfect competition there is a sense in which no supplier makes any purposeful, meaningful decision regarding the price that *it* sets. Rather, because of perfect substitutability between all products (recall the assumption of *homogeneous goods* in a perfectly competitive market), firms are all *price-takers*. A view of firms as price-takers is incompatible with the notion that we would now like to entertain, that of *firms only infrequently setting their prices*. Thus the most basic step we must take in order to even begin to conceptually understand the idea of (possibly sticky) price-setting is to assert that firms are indeed price-*setters* rather than pure price-*takers*.

As you should recall from basic microeconomics, the market structure of *monopoly* offers a relatively easy analytical framework in which firms are indeed price-*setters*. However, from the point of view of macroeconomics, pure monopoly seems an untenable view to adopt. After all, it is implausible, at the aggregate level, to assert that there is *one* producer of *all* the goods that are produced and sold in the economy. A more realistic view should admit the simple fact that there are many producers of goods as well as the fact that these goods are not all identical to each other. That is, there is some *imperfect substitutability* among the many goods an economy produces.

The concept of **monopolistic competition** offers an intermediate theoretical ground between pure monopoly and perfect competition. Indeed the terminology itself suggests that the concept is an intermediate one between pure monopoly and perfect competition. Modern New Keynesian models are based on a monopolistically competitive view of goods markets, in contrast to the RBC framework's perfectly competitive view. The basic economic idea underlying a monopolistically competitive view of goods markets is that there are many varieties of goods that consumers purchase and that they all are, to some degree, imperfect substitutes for each other.

In what follows, we will lay out the basic theoretical structure of macroeconomic models based on monopolistic competition. Before beginning, though, we define an important concept for the analysis of models employing or based on monopolistic competition.

Markup

We will often want to speak of by how much a firm's (presumably, optimally) chosen price, on a per-unit basis, exceeds the cost of production of a given unit of the good. As you should recall from basic microeconomics, a firm's cost of producing a given (i.e., the marginal) unit of output is measured by its **marginal cost.**

A firm's **gross markup** is defined as the (per-unit) price it charges divided by its marginal cost. Denoting by p the unit price chosen by a firm, by mc the firm's marginal cost of production, and by μ the gross markup, we thus have that

$$\mu = \frac{p}{mc}.$$

Recall from basic microeconomics that *in a perfectly competitive market, market forces dictate that $p = mc$.* Thus we have that $\mu = 1$ in a perfectly competitive market.[1] The interpretation of this is that a firm operating under the conditions of perfect competition has no scope whatsoever to earn a (marginal) profit on the goods it sells. Again recalling results and ideas from basic microeconomics, zero marginal profits is consistent with the idea that in perfect competition, firms earn zero (economic, as distinct from accounting) total profits.

As we will see below, a firm operating in a monopolistically competitive market will earn positive (marginal) profits, and thus will be able to achieve a gross markup of $\mu > 1$.

Retail Firms

From an aggregate perspective, monopolistic competition forces us, among other things, to confront the fact consumers purchase a wide variety of goods. For theoretical modeling purposes, however, it turns out to be convenient to assume a structure in which consumers purchase just *one* (type of) good, just as in the RBC view. Our objective here is to continue using the concept of the "consumption basket" purchased by the representative consumer (i.e., we will still be able to speak of "all stuff" consumption). However, we will slightly relabel some of our concepts.

---

1. We can also define the concept of a firm's net markup, which is the percentage by which price exceeds marginal cost. In the case of perfect competition, clearly the net markup is zero percent. For many applications, gross markup is an easier concept with which to work, so we will almost solely rely on it rather than net markup.

We will call the (homogeneous) good (the consumption basket) that consumers purchase **retail goods.** Retail goods are assumed to be sold by **retail-goods producing firms** in a perfectly competitive market. That is, we will assume that a given retail firm is completely identical in every respect, including in what good it sells, to every other retail firm. The implication of this is that we can suppose that there is a representative retail firm.

Denote by y_t the quantity of retail goods that the representative retail firm sells, and by P_t the nominal price of a unit of those retail goods. Because we are assuming that retailers sell their output in a perfectly competitive goods market, there thus far is nothing different, apart from some relabeling of concepts, from the RBC-style view.

Here is where we layer in monopolistic competition. In order to produce the retail good, a retailer must purchase a great many **wholesale goods.** That is, the inputs into the "production process" of a retail firm are themselves goods.[2] As a heuristic, think of a large department store that purchases items (clothes, furniture, electronics, jewelry, etc.) from a great many manufacturers and puts them "on display" in its retail outlets. In this example, the "wholesale goods" would be the great many clothes, electronics, and the like, that the retailer purchases, and the "retail good" is the "basket of goods" that the store offers to its customers.

How many is a "great many" wholesale goods? Casual introspection about the world suggests *a lot* of goods and services comprise the aggregate "consumption basket." While consumers do not face literally an *infinite* number of possible goods they can purchase, clearly the number is somewhat beyond our comprehension, especially when one takes into account the fact that there are various sizes, colors, styles, and the like, for many seemingly identical goods. For this reason and because it is convenient mathematically, we will assert that "many" means "infinite." Specifically, we will assume that there is a *continuum* of wholesale goods and that each good is indexed on the unit interval [0, 1]. Note that we will work with a *continuous* number of wholesale goods rather than with a *discrete* number of goods.[3]

To be a bit more concrete, suppose that every point on the unit interval [0, 1] represents a particular wholesale good. Each of these goods is imperceptible—infinitesimally small—when compared to the entire spectrum of goods available, which seems like a plausible representation of the reality described above. We will assume that each good that lies on the unit interval is produced by a unique **wholesale goods producer** and is *imperfectly substitutable* with any other of these goods. Thus these goods that lie on the unit interval—wholesale goods—are differentiated products, which, as stated above, allows us to admit the possibility of some monopoly power. We will describe wholesale goods producers in the next section.

2. For simplicity, we will abstract from other types of inputs (e.g., capital and labor) that retailers might require. That is, we are assuming that it is *only* wholesale goods that are required for the production of retail goods.

3. Because applying the tools of calculus typically requires continuous, as opposed to discrete, objects.

First, though, we must describe the "production technology" and profit-maximization problem that retail-goods firms solve. In very general terms, we can describe the activities in which a retail-goods firm engages as the following: it must purchase (via markets) each of the wholesale goods, apply some "packaging" or "transformation" technology to them (i.e., provide "retail services" that allow consumers to purchase the final "consumption basket"), and then sell the resulting retail good.

Since the incorporation of the idea of monopolistic competition into mainstream macro-economics in the 1980s and 1990s, the most commonly employed functional specification for the "packaging technology" of retail firms is the **Dixit–Stiglitz aggregator,**

$$y_t = \left[\int_0^1 y_{it}^{1/\varepsilon} di \right]^{\varepsilon}.$$

In this expression y_t is the output, in period t, of the retailers, and y_{it}, for $i \in [0,1]$ (note well this notation) is wholesale good i, of which, recall, there is an infinite number.[4] The parameter ε measures the curvature of this aggregation (aka packaging, aka transformation) technology.

Basic monopoly theory requires that $\varepsilon > 1$. In the limit, as $\varepsilon \to 1$, obviously we would have $y_t = \int_0^1 y_{it} di$. With $\varepsilon = 1$, the resulting *linear* aggregation technology implies that each of the wholesale goods is a *perfect* substitute for another, which undermines our whole analytical objective.

In the context of our theoretical model, allowing for curvature (i.e., $\varepsilon > 1$) in the aggregation technology is the basis for the existence of monopolistic competition. What curvature achieves for us is that retail firms *must* purchase some of every type of wholesale good. To continue the department store example from above, this means that a retailer wants to purchase some TVs, some shirts, some pants, some watches, some men's shoes, and so on—it wants to have some of every variety of product on hand to put on display for the customers that it sells to. As will become clear below when we study wholesale goods firms, the parameter ε will also denotes the gross markup that they (the wholesale goods firms) charge.

Denote by P_t the nominal price of the retail good (i.e., the per-unit price of the retail good) and by P_{it} the nominal price of wholesale good i, $i \in [0,1]$. The price of any wholesale good is taken as given by the retail firm—thus we assume that there are no "negotiations" between retail firms and wholesale firms.[5] The profit function of the representative retailer is thus

$$P_t y_t - \int_0^1 P_{it} y_{it} di,$$

---

4. See Avinash K. Dixit and Joseph E. Stiglitz, "Monopolistic Competition and Optimum Product Diversity," *American Economic Review* 67 (1977): 297–308.

5. A more nuanced view of the world probably would want to admit that because they both often can be large players, retailers and wholesalers do "negotiate" with each, and thus neither necessarily needs to be thought of as a price-taker. This is a topic for a more advanced course in macroeconomic theory, game theory, and/or industrial organization.

which is simply its total revenue net of its total costs (recall the assumption we made above that purchases of wholesale goods are the only cost item for a retailer). Inserting the aggregator technology from above, we can re-express the profit function as

$$P_t \left[\int_0^1 y_{it}^{1/\varepsilon} di \right] - \int_0^1 P_{it} y_{it} di .$$

As we just stated, the retail firm takes as given the price P_{it} of any given wholesale good i. Because we have assumed that retail goods are sold to consumers in perfectly competitive product markets, it also takes as given the price P_t of the (retail) goods that it sells. Hence the only objects of choice in the profit function given above are the individual y_{it}'s, for each $i \in [0,1]$. That is, given the input and output prices it faces, the retail firm makes an optimal choice with respect to each wholesale good in order to maximize its profits, which are given by the previous expression.

Let's focus on good j within the unit interval $[0, 1]$.[6] Taking the first-order condition of the profit function (with the Dixit–Stiglitz aggregator substituted in, as in the second expression of profits presented above) with respect to y_{jt}, we have

$$\varepsilon \cdot P_t \left[\int_0^1 y_{it}^{1/\varepsilon} di \right]^{\varepsilon-1} \cdot \frac{1}{\varepsilon} \cdot y_{jt}^{(1/\varepsilon)-1} - P_{jt} = 0 .$$

Note carefully how the first term of this first-order condition arises—it arises by use of the chain rule of calculus, realizing that differentiation can be performed underneath an integration, and being careful about the distinction between product j and the arbitrary index of integration i.[7] We can simplify this expression to a very useful and interpretable form. In the several steps that follow, what we will do is rearrange this expression into an expression that is easily understandable as the **demand function for wholesale good j.**

First we cancel the ε terms. Next we can dramatically simplify the term in square brackets. To do this, note that by appropriately manipulating exponents, the Dixit–Stiglitz aggregator can be rewritten as

$$y_t^{1/\varepsilon} = \int_0^1 y_{it}^{1/\varepsilon} di .$$

Then, raising both sides of this expression to the power $\varepsilon - 1$, we have

$$y_t^{(\varepsilon-1)/\varepsilon} = \left[\int_0^1 y_{it}^{1/\varepsilon} di \right]^{\varepsilon-1} .$$

---

6. Keep straight the use of the indexes i and j. In the integrals we have so far written down, i is a dummy index of integration—we know this from the fact that di appears in each integral we have written down. Thus i is simply keeping track of goods as we "loop through" the integral; i in these integrals is not referring to any particular good within $[0, 1]$.

7. A technical point you may recall from basic calculus is that integration and differentiation are both linear operators. Linear operators are commutative; hence their order of operations can be interchanged freely. This property is what allows us to differentiate in a very straightforward way with respect to y_{jt} inside the integral.

The right-hand side is exactly the term we wanted to eliminate from the retail firm's first-order condition. Now making this substitution, we find that the retail firm's first-order condition can be expressed as

$$P_t \cdot y_t^{(\varepsilon-1)/\varepsilon} \cdot y_{jt}^{(1/\varepsilon)-1} = P_{jt}.$$

We want to now isolate the y_{jt} term. Combining exponents and rearranging, we have

$$y_{jt}^{(1-\varepsilon)/\varepsilon} = \left(\frac{P_{jt}}{P_t} \right) \cdot y_t^{(1-\varepsilon)/\varepsilon}.$$

Finally, raising both sides to the power $\varepsilon/(1-\varepsilon)$, we have

$$y_{jt} = \left(\frac{P_{jt}}{P_t} \right)^{\varepsilon/(1-\varepsilon)} \cdot y_t.$$

This expression is the *demand function for wholesale good j*. Note that it has the basic properties required of any demand function: it articulates an inverse relationship between the price P_{jt} of wholesale good j and the demand for it, y_{jt} (holding everything else, i.e., P_t and y_t, constant).[8] This demand function is an important building block for our description of a wholesale goods firm's profit-maximization problem, which we provide next.

The demand function we have derived is for good j. Clearly, we would obtain an identical-looking demand function for any other wholesale good, say, good k. That is, we could have started this entire analysis by taking the retail firm's first-order condition with respect to wholesale good k; apart from replacing j by k everywhere in our analysis, nothing would be substantively different.

Wholesale Firms

Now we turn to a description of the activities of wholesale firms. As described above, wholesale firms (of which, recall again, there is a continuum) sell their differentiated output to retailers in a perfectly competitive market. Due to the differentiated nature of wholesale products, wholesale firms have some market power and thus are explicitly price-*setters*.

We make two additional auxiliary assumptions regarding wholesale firms (relaxing these would not substantively change the conclusions of our analysis; the expense of doing so is some more cumbersome mathematics). First, suppose that there are no fixed costs of production. As you should recall from basic microeconomics, this means that the average variable cost of production is equal to the average total cost of production. Second, suppose

---

8. Recall from above that we must have, consistent with monopoly theory, $\varepsilon > 1$. This means that the exponent to which the term (P_{jt}/P_t) is raised is a negative number.

that the per-unit production cost of each unit of wholesale output is identical *regardless of the scale of production*. In the language of basic microeconomics, this means we are assuming that wholesale firms have production technologies that exhibit *constant returns to scale*, which has the consequence that the wholesale firm's *marginal cost of production is invariant to the quantity that it chooses to produce*.

Coupled together, these two assumptions lead to the mathematically convenient consequence that the marginal cost function coincides with the average total cost function. In turn this means that total costs of production can be expressed simply as the quantity produced times the marginal cost of production.[9]

Let's continue to focus on the particular wholesale good j. Given our assumptions, the profit function of wholesale firm j in period t can be expressed as

$$P_{jt} \cdot y_{jt} - P_t \cdot mc_{jt} \cdot y_{jt}.$$

We have expressed profits in nominal terms. The first term $P_{jt}y_{jt}$, which is wholesaler j's total revenues, is clearly in nominal terms. In the cost term, $mc_{jt}y_{jt}$ denotes the *real* total cost to wholesaler j of producing y_{jt} units of output. Thus the way we will denote things is that mc measures the *real* (not the nominal) marginal cost of production.[10] To then turn this into a nominal object, we multiply by P_t, which is the economy-wide nominal price level, which, in our environment, is simply the price of the "bundled" retail good. Note carefully that we are multiplying by P_t, not by P_{jt}, to convert into nominal units here.

A monopolist (in our environment, monopolistic competitor j) **takes as given the demand function it faces** when making its profit-maximizing choices. This is where the demand function for wholesale good j that we derived above comes into use. Substituting in the demand function for good j (alternatively, we could express it as a constraint on the optimization problem and introduce a Lagrange multiplier), we can express wholesale firm j's profit function as

$$P_{jt} \cdot \left(\frac{P_{jt}}{P_t}\right)^{\varepsilon/(1-\varepsilon)} \cdot y_t - P_t \cdot mc_t \cdot \left(\frac{P_{jt}}{P_t}\right)^{\varepsilon/(1-\varepsilon)} \cdot y_t.$$

This term looks quite messy at first glance, but the path of the rest of our analysis is now clear: the only object in this expression over which wholesaler j has any control is the price P_{jt} it charges (it does, after all, have monopoly power). So the next step is to compute the

9. There is a lot of basic microeconomics underlying these results and conclusions. It's probably worthwhile to convince yourself or review that all this is correct from the point of view of first principles of microeconomics.

10. We have also allowed for the wholesaler-specific index j in the specification of marginal cost, though we will not actually make use of this. That is, we will only consider cases in which mc is identical between any two wholesalers j and k, $j \neq k$. This is tantamount to assuming that not only does each wholesaler use a constant-returns-to-scale production technology but that each wholesaler uses *the same* constant-returns-to-scale production technology. Thus, from here on, we drop the firm-specific index on marginal costs.

first-order condition of profits with respect to P_{jt} and then analyze the resulting optimal price.

To make our algebra a bit more transparent, we can combine the relevant P_{jt} terms in the profit expression. We can combine the above to

$$P_{jt}^{1/(1-\varepsilon)} \cdot P_t^{\varepsilon/(\varepsilon-1)} \cdot y_t - P_{jt}^{\varepsilon/(1-\varepsilon)} \cdot P_t^{(2\varepsilon-1)/(\varepsilon-1)} \cdot mc_t \cdot y_t = 0.$$

The first-order condition of this expression (which is still simply wholesaler j's profits in period t) with respect to P_{jt} is

$$\frac{1}{1-\varepsilon} \cdot P_{jt}^{\varepsilon/(1-\varepsilon)} \cdot P_t^{\varepsilon/(\varepsilon-1)} \cdot y_t - \frac{\varepsilon}{1-\varepsilon} \cdot P_{jt}^{(2\varepsilon-1)/(1-\varepsilon)} \cdot P_t^{(2\varepsilon-1)/(\varepsilon-1)} \cdot mc_t \cdot y_t = 0.$$

We can now obviously cancel the y_t terms as well as the $1/(1-\varepsilon)$ terms; doing so leaves us with the slightly easier expression

$$P_{jt}^{\varepsilon/(1-\varepsilon)} \cdot P_t^{\varepsilon/(\varepsilon-1)} - \varepsilon \cdot P_{jt}^{(2\varepsilon-1)/(1-\varepsilon)} \cdot P_t^{(2\varepsilon-1)/(\varepsilon-1)} \cdot mc_t = 0.$$

Let's continue to simplify this expression. Multiply the entire expression by $P_{jt}^{-\varepsilon/(\varepsilon-1)}$, which yields

$$P_t^{\varepsilon/(\varepsilon-1)} - \varepsilon \cdot P_{jt}^{-1} \cdot P_t^{(2\varepsilon-1)/(\varepsilon-1)} \cdot mc_t = 0.$$

Next, multiply this expression by $P_t^{-\varepsilon/(\varepsilon-1)}$, which leaves us with

$$1 - \varepsilon \cdot P_{jt}^{-1} \cdot P_t \cdot mc_t = 0.$$

Finally, solving for the profit-maximizing price of wholesale good j, we obtain

$$P_{jt} = \varepsilon \cdot P_t \cdot mc_t.$$

If we define wholesale firm j's **relative price** as $p_{jt} = P_{jt}/P_t$ (note the distinction between lowercase and uppercase notation!), which is the *real* (in units of retail goods—as opposed to in units of currency) price charged by wholesaler j, we can instead express the profit-maximizing price as

$$p_{jt} = \varepsilon \cdot mc_t.$$

Regardless of which way we prefer to view things (the profit-maximizing price chosen by wholesaler j in nominal terms or in real terms), a very important result emerges here: *the profit-maximizing choice is a simple markup over marginal cost.* Moreover *the markup is time-invariant*: regardless of any shocks hitting the economy, in *every* period t, the wholesale firm sets its price as a constant markup over marginal cost. The markup is given by ε (which we noted above it would), which controls the curvature of our Dixit–Stiglitz aggregator. Recall that in a monopolistic (or monopolistically competitive) environment, it must be the case that $\varepsilon > 1$. This means that wholesale firms here are earning positive marginal profits (and indeed due to our assumption of zero fixed costs, positive total profits as well). Given our precise definition of gross markup, it is clear that the (optimal) markup here turns out to be

$$\mu = \frac{p_{jt}}{mc_t} = \varepsilon$$

in every period.

Discussion

As with any theoretical structure (whether in economics or any field), the pure Dixit–Stiglitz based view, which implies (among other things) that firms never alter their markups, taken too literally is an untenable view of the world. Lots of empirical evidence suggests that firms *do* purposefully change their markups, sometimes in very specific, predictable ways (i.e., firms holding seasonal "sales" can be interpreted in terms of a strategic change in the markup that it changes). Even at the aggregate level, evidence suggests that markups fluctuate at business cycle frequencies.[11] A great deal of research attempts to uncover why markups fluctuate over the course of the business cycle, but there really is no compelling explanation (which is another way of saying that there are a great many possible explanations, but none of them so far has stood out as obviously *the* main reason).

Nevertheless, being quite tractable, the Dixit–Stiglitz structure has become ubiquitous as a foundation of modern New Keynesian models. All of our analysis thus far has presumed completely flexible prices—that is, we have nowhere asserted that price adjustment entails any "menu costs" or are "sticky" in any way. And yet, as we mentioned at the outset, a theory that asserts that firms only infrequently (re-)set their prices or incur costs of setting prices requires, as a prerequisite, adopting a view in which firms are price-*setters* in the first place. The Dixit–Stiglitz structure at least makes progress on this front. Next we turn to the most basic sticky-price New Keynesian model based on the Dixit–Stiglitz structure.

---

11. That is, if one constructed a series of markups at the aggregate level and performed any number of usual de-trending procedures, one typically finds clear cyclical patterns in markups. Moreover markups are generally found to be *countercyclical* with respect to GDP—that is, periods of lower than usual GDP growth tend to be associated with high markups, and vice versa. An important problem behind any empirical analysis of markups, however, is the appropriate measurement of marginal costs. In our theoretical model, the concept of marginal cost is clear. In an empirical implementation, due to the presence of (sometimes large) fixed costs and nonconstancy of returns to scale, marginal cost and average total cost are easy to conflate with each other. The theory clearly tells us that marginal cost, not average total cost, is relevant for optimal markups. It is often unclear whether empirical measures of marginal cost are measuring true *marginal* cost or measuring average costs instead.

Chapter 22 Problem Set Questions

1. **Equilibrium real wages and optimal** *fiscal* **policy in the Dixit–Stiglitz model.** Consider the Dixit–Stiglitz model of monopolistic competition exactly as we laid out in this chapter. Wholesale firms are assumed to operate a constant returns to scale (CRS) production technology, which simply means that if all inputs are scaled by the factor k, total output is scaled by the same factor k. Suppose that the production technology that any given wholesale firm (e.g., wholesale firm j, as in this chapter) operates is simply linear in labor,

   $$y_j = f(n_j) = n_j,$$

   which you should be able to easily verify is CRS (let's assume everything is static here, hence the lack of time subscripts).

   The representative consumer has (static) utility function $u(c, 1-n)$, with total time available normalized to one (i.e., $n + l = 1$). With a real wage of w and, as in chapter 2, a labor income tax rate of t, the consumption–leisure optimality condition is of course simply

   $$\frac{u_2(c, 1-n)}{u_1(c, 1-n)} = (1-t)w.$$

   Finally, the resource constraint of the economy is $c = n$.

   a. What is the economy's marginal rate of transformation (MRT) between consumption and leisure?

   b. If wholesale firm j (and indeed every wholesale firm) hires labor in a perfectly competitive market at the real wage w, how does its real marginal cost of production (mc) relate to w? (You should be able to make an extremely precise statement here, not simply a qualitative one.)

   c. (Hard) Consider a symmetric equilibrium, in which every wholesale firm charges the same exact nominal price as every other wholesale firm, and, moreover, the same exact nominal price as the nominal price of retail goods. (We will discuss the idea of symmetric equilibrium in more detail in chapter 23; here, just take this concept at face value.) In a symmetric equilibrium, provide an exact analytical expression for the value of the real wage w. (Again, you should be able to make an extremely precise statement here, not simply a qualitative one.) (Hint: Start with the constant-markup-pricing outcome for wholesale firm j.)

   d. If the labor income tax rate were zero ($t = 0$), does the private-sector equilibrium achieve economic efficiency? Explain why or why not. (Note: You must draw on your conclusions in parts a, b, and c to analyze this question.)

If you concluded "no" in part d, provide an exact analytical expression for the labor income tax rate that *would* achieve economic efficiency. Explain.

2. **Monopolistic competition and optimal fiscal policy.** In the static (i.e., one-period) consumption–leisure model, suppose that the representative consumer has utility function over consumption and leisure, $u(c, 1-n)$, where, as usual, c denotes consumption and n denotes labor (and so $1-n$ is leisure). The budget constraint the individual faces is $c = (1-t) \cdot w \cdot n + profit$, where t is the labor tax rate, w is the real hourly wage rate, n is the number of hours the individual works, and $profit$ is the profit earnings of the firm (described below) which are "earned" by the representative consumer (e.g., because the consumer "owns" the firm). Notice that this budget constraint is expressed in real terms, rather than in nominal terms.

    There is a large number of monopolistically competitive firms, and each firm hires labor to produce its output good according to the production function $y_i = n_i$ (the index i refers to the ith firm). Total output of the economy y (note the lack of subscript) is related to the output of the ith firm by the function

    $$y_i = p_i^{-\theta} y \ (= c_i),$$

    where p_i is the real price charged by firm i and $\theta > 1$ governs how substitutable different goods are for each other (this setup is essentially just like we studied in the chapter).

    The ith monopolistic producer's profit function is given by

    $$(p_i - w) p_i^{-\theta} y,$$

    and the goal of the monopolistic producer is to maximize profits by choosing its own price p_i. Prices are not sticky in this economy (since there is no money and no nominal variables at all in this economy). In equilibrium, prices are all the same, $p = 1$, but this is only in equilibrium: from the perspective of a single firm, it *does* choose its own price p_i.

    Finally, the resource constraint of the economy is $c = n$.

    a. For the given utility function, state (in the expression begun for you below) the consumer's consumption–leisure optimality condition.

    $$\frac{u_l}{u_c} =$$

    (Note: If you can, try to solve this problem without setting up a Lagrangian.)

b. If the i th firm chooses its price p_i to maximize its profits, what is the equilibrium real wage in the economy? Show the important steps in your logic/arguments. (Note: In equilibrium, $p_i = p = 1$, but only in equilibrium.)

c. Suppose that there is zero government spending and $\theta = 10$. In order to achieve economic efficiency, what (qualitatively) labor tax rate t should the government set: $t < 0$, $t = 0$, or $t > 0$. Your answer here should draw on what you found in parts a and b above. Show the important steps in your logic/argument, and briefly provide an economic interpretation for your result.

23

A New Keynesian View of Sticky Prices: The Rotemberg Framework

Modern New Keynesian sticky-price models are built on a foundation of monopolistic competition. With the basic Dixit–Stiglitz based framework of monopolistic competition now in our toolkit, we are ready to sketch one of the simplest, yet quantitatively serious, modern sticky-price macroeconomic models.

Our starting point will be exactly the monopolistically competitive model we just laid out: namely we will continue assuming that consumers purchase a "retail good" from retail firms, retail firms transform a continuum [0, 1] of differentiated wholesale products into the retail good by operating a Dixit–Stiglitz aggregation technology, and each producer of a differentiated wholesale product wields some monopoly power over its output, which renders it a price-setter instead of a price-taker. However, rather than assuming that price-setting is costless, as we did in our introduction to monopolistic competition, we will now assume that there are some *costs associated directly with the act of price-setting*. In particular, when a wholesale firm in period t decides to set a (nominal) price different from the one it charged in period $t - 1$, it must pay a cost of resetting its price. This cost is completely independent of any costs associated with the physical production process itself. That is, this cost is completely unrelated to any wage costs or capital investment costs that a wholesale firm pays. In the language used in the field, this pure cost of price-adjustment is a **menu cost**.

At both an empirical level and a theoretical level, the nature of these menu costs deserves some discussion. As such, we begin there; we then proceed to sketch one of the most commonly used (and simplest) versions of a sticky-price model featuring menu costs and analyze some of its implications.

Menu Costs

The predominant core of any modern theory of price stickiness is that the very act of changing prices itself entails costs. Indeed, this is also the simplest of theories of price stickiness. The basic idea is most easily illustrated with an example. Suppose a restaurant is considering increasing the prices of some or all of the items on its menu. Presumably price increases are being considered because they would be in the best interest of the restaurant—that is, the price increases would presumably increase total profit. To make the example concrete, suppose that at current demand conditions, if the restaurant could cost-lessly change its prices, $1,000 in extra total profit would be generated. However, in order to implement its price changes, the restaurant would have to print new menus. If the restaurant had to pay its printer $2,000 to print new menus, it clearly is not in the interest of the firm to change its prices—indeed changing prices would cause total profit to decrease by $1,000, so the firm instead chooses to hold its prices steady.[1] This example suggests the general terminology: a menu cost is a cost incurred by a firm due to the price-adjustment process itself—in our example, it is literally the price of printing new menus. This is an example of a fixed menu cost—it costs $2,000 to print new menus regardless of by how much the optimal new price would be compared to the current price.

Adopting a bit broader notion of what a "menu cost" is, though, might lead us to think that "costs of price adjustment" might sometimes depend on the magnitude of the price change itself. For example, if the "costs of price adjustment" include things such as concerns about upsetting customers, it is likely that these costs are larger the larger is the price change. This aspect of menu costs is admittedly a softer notion than the physical cost of "printing a menu," but it is often implicit in what macroeconomists have meant and continue to mean by the term.[2]

For this reason we will adopt not a discrete (fixed) view of menu costs, but rather a continuous (variable) view of menu costs. It also turns out that a continuous view of menu costs is much more tractable in the context of macroeconomic analysis (for the usual reason that continuous functions are readily amenable to standard calculus tools). A simple, continuous, specification of menu costs is to assert that a firm's total cost of price adjustment depends in a convex—specifically, a quadratic—manner on the magnitude of the price change it implements.

In all of what follows, we will suppose that the *real* costs to wholesale firm j of changing the nominal price it charges is

$$\frac{\psi}{2}\left(\frac{P_{jt}}{P_{jt-1}}-1\right)^2.$$

1. To illustrate the basic issues at stake here, we are purposely ignoring the timing of "when" these potential extra profits would accrue. The answer to the question "Is it worth it to pay the menu cost?" depends on whether the $1,000 in total extra profit is a present-discounted value of *all current and future* profits the firm will ever earn after the price change or whether the $1,000 is the increase in *per-period profits* the firm will enjoy after the price change.

2. The profession has only lately begun to try to more seriously grapple with the issue of what some of these softer, more social "costs" of changing prices might be. Thus far empirical evidence regarding this (limited though it still is) leads the development of theoretical frameworks with which to think about this.

This **quadratic price-adjustment cost function** is quite common in modern New Keynesian models.[3] If wholesaler j decides to set $P_{jt} = P_{jt-1}$, clearly it pays no menu cost (because the quadratic term disappears). Instead, if it chooses to set a P_{jt} different from P_{jt-1}, it does incur a menu cost; moreover the cost is larger the further from the "reference level" P_{jt-1} it chooses to set P_{jt}. Due to the quadratic nature of the cost function, price-adjustment costs are symmetric with respect to both price increases and price decreases.[4] The parameter $\psi > 0$ is simply a scale parameter; it is particularly convenient to include because if we set $\psi = 0$, we return exactly to the flexible-price (i.e., zero menu cost) case.

Finally, note that we emphasized that the total price-adjustment cost

$$\frac{\psi}{2}\left(\frac{P_{jt}}{P_{jt-1}} - 1\right)^2$$

is a *real* cost—that is, it is denominated in terms of real consumption baskets (here the consumption "basket" is the "retail good" that consumers purchase). If we wish to express the total price adjustment cost in nominal units, we must multiply by the nominal price of the retail consumption basket, which is P_t. Hence the total price-adjustment cost incurred by wholesale firm j in nominal terms is

$$\frac{\psi}{2}\left(\frac{P_{jt}}{P_{jt-1}} - 1\right)^2 \cdot P_t;$$

note carefully the subscripts on the various P's.

Our main task in what follows is to embed into our previous model of monopolistic competition these quadratic costs of price adjustment.

Retail Firms

The representative retail goods firm is identical to that described in our introduction to monopolistic competition in chapter 22; refer there for a review of the details. Most important to keep in mind for what follows is that we are continuing to assume that nominal prices of retail goods are determined in a perfectly competitive environment, which means, among other things, that there are no menu costs associated with price changes of retail goods.

---

3. It was first proposed as a tractable way of incorporating stickiness of prices into modern macroeconomic models in an influential paper in the early 1980s: Julio J. Rotemberg, 1982, "Sticky Prices in the United States," *Journal of Political Economy* 90: 1187–1211.

4. Whether nominal prices are as sticky on the downward side as on the upward side is clearly an assumption we can question. Introspection about the world likely suggests that customer "anger" over a given magnitude price decrease (if, after all, this quadratic specification is meant to capture effects such as that) is a lot smaller (or perhaps altogether absent) than a given magnitude price increase. Our Rotemberg-inspired price-adjustment cost specification clearly cannot account for this.

As a brief reminder of the basics, then, once again a retail firm uses the Dixit–Stiglitz aggregator,

$$y_t = \left[\int_0^1 y_{it}^{1/\varepsilon} di \right]^\varepsilon,$$

which takes as inputs the various wholesale products y_{it}'s, $i \in [0,1]$, and yields as output the retail good y_t. As before, the period-t nominal profit function of the representative retail firm is

$$P_t y_t - \int_0^1 P_{it} y_{it} di,$$

which is simply its total revenue net of its total costs (recall our assumption that purchases of wholesale goods are the only cost items for a retail firm). Again as before, inserting the aggregator technology from above, we can re-express the profit function as

$$P_t \left[\int_0^1 y_{it}^{1/\varepsilon} di \right] - \int_0^1 P_{it} y_{it} di.$$

Profit maximization by the retail firm leads to a demand function for any wholesale good j:

$$y_{jt} = \left(\frac{P_{jt}}{P_t} \right)^{\varepsilon/(1-\varepsilon)} \cdot y_t,$$

once again exactly as before.

Thus, because costs of price adjustment do not impinge directly on retail firms, absolutely nothing regarding either the retail firm's optimization problem or solution is new.

Wholesale Firms

Where things are different is at the level of wholesale producers. We continue to focus on just the activities and decisions of one particular wholesale producer, producer j (recall that we have a continuum $[0, 1]$ of wholesale producers). We continue to maintain two assumptions from earlier: first, there are zero fixed costs of production; second, the production cost of each unit of intermediate output is identical regardless of the scale of production. Thus, just as before, these assumptions imply that the wholesale firm's *marginal cost of production is invariant to the quantity that it chooses to produce.*

Wholesale firms now also face a second type of cost, separate from costs associated with physical production; namely the quadratic menu costs. Given this, the nominal profit function of wholesale firm j in period t can be expressed as

$$P_{jt} \cdot y_{jt} - P_t \cdot mc_{jt} \cdot y_{jt} - \frac{\psi}{2} \cdot \left(\frac{P_{jt}}{P_{jt-1}} - 1 \right)^2 \cdot P_t,$$

which is nothing more than total (nominal) revenues minus total (nominal) costs. As before, from here on we will assume that the marginal production cost function is identical across wholesale firms, which allows us to drop the index j from mc.

We know from our study of the basic, flexible-price monopolistic competition model that we ultimately want to solve for the wholesale firm's optimal pricing decision regarding P_{jt}. In the flexible-price model it was sufficient to simply maximize (after appropriately substituting in the firm's demand function) the expression above, which is the *period-t* nominal profits of wholesale firm j. However, the menu cost introduces a dynamic element into the wholesale firm's profit-maximization problem, an aspect completely absent in the flexible-price benchmark. Indeed this dynamic element to a wholesale firm's optimal pricing decision should be thought of as *the* fundamental difference between any sticky-price view of the world and a flexible-price view of the world.

As usual, we want to analyze things from the perspective of the very beginning of period t. The term above is period-t nominal profits. However, consider also the wholesale firm's nominal profits in period $t + 1$:

$$P_{jt+1} \cdot y_{jt+1} - P_{t+1} \cdot mc_{t+1} \cdot y_{jt+1} - \frac{\psi}{2} \cdot \left(\frac{P_{jt+1}}{P_{jt}} - 1 \right)^2 \cdot P_{t+1}.$$

Notice that nominal profits in period $t + 1$ *depend in part on the nominal price P_{jt} charged in period t*. This is due to the presence of P_{jt} as part of the period $t + 1$ cost of price adjustment: apart from any direct physical costs of production, a particular price P_{jt} chosen for period t has consequences, all else equal, for both the menu costs the wholesale firm will incur in period t as well as the menu costs the firm will have to incur in period $t + 1$. This is why a sticky-price view of the world introduces a dynamic—that is, across multiple time periods—element into firms' profit-maximization problems.

Thus, in deciding its optimal period-t nominal price P_{jt}, wholesale firm j must take into account not only its period-t profits but also its *discounted* profits across both period t and $t + 1$. Specifically, the relevant objective it must maximize is

$$P_{jt} \cdot y_{jt} - P_t \cdot mc_t \cdot y_{jt} - \frac{\psi}{2} \cdot \left(\frac{P_{jt}}{P_{jt-1}} - 1 \right)^2 \cdot P_t$$

$$+ \frac{\beta}{1 + \pi_{t+1}} \cdot \left[P_{jt+1} \cdot y_{jt+1} - P_{t+1} \cdot mc_{t+1} \cdot y_{jt+1} - \frac{\psi}{2} \cdot \left(\frac{P_{jt+1}}{P_{jt}} - 1 \right)^2 \cdot P_{t+1} \right],$$

in which, note, we have applied a modified form of the subjective discount factor β to period $t + 1$ profits. Specifically, the discount factor required here is a *nominal* discount factor rather than a *real* discount factor. The discount factor β we used in our study of the representative consumer is a real discount factor—it discounts one-period-ahead utils and goods.

The profit function in the analysis here is instead specified in nominal terms. Thus, in addition to just β, we must also discount by the one-period-ahead nominal discount factor, P_t/P_{t+1}, which by our standard definitions, is simply $1/(1 + \pi_{t+1})$.[5]

Next recall that a monopolist (in our analysis, monopolistic competitor j) takes as given the demand function it faces when making its profit-maximizing choices. Thus we must make use of the demand function for wholesale good j that emerges from the retail firm's profit-maximization problem. Substituting in the demand function for wholesale good j in both period t and in period $t + 1$, we can re-express wholesale firm j's now-dynamic profit function as

$$P_{jt} \cdot \left(\frac{P_{jt}}{P_t}\right)^{\varepsilon/(1-\varepsilon)} y_t - P_t \cdot mc_t \cdot \left(\frac{P_{jt}}{P_t}\right)^{\varepsilon/(1-\varepsilon)} \cdot y_t - \frac{\psi}{2} \cdot \left(\frac{P_{jt}}{P_{jt-1}} - 1\right)^2 \cdot P_t$$

$$+ \frac{\beta}{1+\pi_{t+1}} \cdot \left[P_{jt+1} \cdot \left(\frac{P_{jt+1}}{P_{t+1}}\right)^{\varepsilon/(1-\varepsilon)} \cdot y_{t+1} - P_{t+1} \cdot mc_{t+1} \cdot \left(\frac{P_{jt+1}}{P_{t+1}}\right)^{\varepsilon/(1-\varepsilon)} \cdot y_{t+1} - \frac{\psi}{2} \cdot \left(\frac{P_{jt+1}}{P_{jt}} - 1\right)^2 \cdot P_{t+1}\right].$$

This is the dynamic profit function that wholesale firm j seeks to maximize, and it must set its period-t price in order to do so.

As before, to make our algebra a bit more transparent, we can combine some of the P_{jt} terms; specifically, rewrite the dynamic profit function as

$$P_{jt}^{1/(1-\varepsilon)} \cdot P_t^{\varepsilon/(\varepsilon-1)} \cdot y_t - P_{jt}^{\varepsilon/(1-\varepsilon)} \cdot P_t^{(2\varepsilon-1)/(\varepsilon-1)} \cdot mc_t \cdot y_t - \frac{\psi}{2} \cdot \left(\frac{P_{jt}}{P_{jt-1}} - 1\right)^2 \cdot P_t$$

$$+ \frac{\beta}{1+\pi_{t+1}} \cdot \left[P_{jt+1} \cdot \left(\frac{P_{jt+1}}{P_{t+1}}\right)^{\varepsilon/(1-\varepsilon)} \cdot y_{t+1} - P_{t+1} \cdot mc_{t+1} \cdot \left(\frac{P_{jt+1}}{P_{t+1}}\right)^{\varepsilon/(1-\varepsilon)} \cdot y_{t+1} - \frac{\psi}{2} \cdot \left(\frac{P_{jt+1}}{P_{jt}} - 1\right)^2 \cdot P_{t+1}\right].$$

Proceeding by brute force, the first-order condition of this expression (which is, after all, still simply wholesale firm j's dynamic profit function) with respect to P_{jt} is

$$\frac{1}{1-\varepsilon} \cdot P_{jt}^{\varepsilon/(1-\varepsilon)} \cdot P_t^{\varepsilon/(\varepsilon-1)} \cdot y_t - \frac{\varepsilon}{1-\varepsilon} \cdot P_{jt}^{(2\varepsilon-1)/(1-\varepsilon)} \cdot P_t^{(2\varepsilon-1)/(\varepsilon-1)} \cdot mc_t \cdot y_t$$

$$- \psi \cdot \left(\frac{P_{jt}}{P_{jt-1}} - 1\right) \cdot \frac{P_t}{P_{jt-1}} + \frac{\beta \cdot \psi}{1+\pi_{t+1}} \cdot \left(\frac{P_{jt+1}}{P_{jt}} - 1\right) \cdot \frac{P_{t+1}}{P_{jt}} \cdot \frac{P_{jt+1}}{P_{jt}} = 0.$$

In this first-order condition, terms arise through the period $t + 1$ price-adjustment cost because a choice for P_{jt} has consequences for, among other things, the menu costs that will be incurred later (in period $t + 1$), an important point mentioned above.

---

5. Apart from this technical issue, we are thus in effect assuming here that wholesale firms discount profits at the same discount rate as the representative consumer. An underlying justification for this may be that, ultimately, it is "consumers/individuals" that own—via, say, stock markets—firms and thus own claims to their profits. As long as the intertemporal incentives of firm managers are aligned with those of the firm's shareholders (which can sometimes be a questionable assumption), this is a useful way of articulating such a linkage.

An observation to make about this first-order condition is that if $\psi = 0$, meaning there are no menu costs, we have exactly the same first-order condition as in the simple flexible-price Dixit–Stiglitz model.[6] This is the sense in which we meant above that it was convenient to allow for the scale parameter ψ in the first place—it allows us to capture as a special case the flexible-price environment by setting $\psi = 0$. The sticky-price case of course features $\psi > 0$.

This first-order condition is essentially the **heart of New Keynesian analysis**; however, there are a few more conceptual issues and technical details to step through before we can see it in a cleaner form.

Symmetric Equilibrium

In the first-order condition we just derived, the price of wholesale good j, P_{jt}, and the price of the retail good, P_t, obviously both appear. In laying out the Dixit–Stiglitz and now Rotemberg models, we obviously relied a great deal on the separation into wholesale and retail sectors. Indeed we have needed this separation in order to articulate first the idea of price-*setting* firms and now of price-setting firms that incur costs of nominal price adjustment.

Now we are going to once again blur the distinction between "wholesale goods" and "retail goods" and again just speak of "goods." The reason for doing so is that in the end, macroeconomic analysis is concerned mostly with aggregates. From the point of view of the GDP measurement that most countries perform, there is no distinction between "wholesale goods" and "retail goods"—it is just "baskets of goods" that are being measured. We can (re-)capture this idea by now imposing, in the first-order condition we just derived, **symmetry** between wholesale and retail goods. Mathematically, symmetry (which is a distinct concept from steady state) is achieved by now simply dropping all the j subscripts.[7] Dropping all the j subscripts blurs the distinction between wholesale goods and retails goods. So we will re-label all goods as just "baskets" or *the* good produced, consumed, invested, and so on, in the economy.

Imposing symmetry in the first-order condition we just derived, we have

$$\frac{1}{1-\varepsilon} \cdot P_t^{\varepsilon/(1-\varepsilon)} \cdot P_t^{\varepsilon/(\varepsilon-1)} \cdot y_t - \frac{\varepsilon}{1-\varepsilon} \cdot P_t^{(2\varepsilon-1)/(1-\varepsilon)} \cdot P_t^{(2\varepsilon-1)/(\varepsilon-1)} \cdot mc_t \cdot y_t$$

$$- \psi \cdot \left(\frac{P_t}{P_{t-1}} - 1\right) \cdot \frac{P_t}{P_{t-1}} + \frac{\beta \cdot \psi}{1+\pi_{t+1}} \cdot \left(\frac{P_{t+1}}{P_t} - 1\right) \cdot \frac{P_{t+1}}{P_t} \cdot \frac{P_{t+1}}{P_t} = 0.$$

---

6. Verify this yourself.

7. An *extremely* important technical point to understand is that we can eliminate the j subscripts *only after having computed the wholesale firm's first-order condition*. If we had dropped the subscript j before computing this first-order condition, the entire analysis would be rendered moot from the start. Thus symmetry must be essentially the "last" step of the analysis.

We can now collapse many terms in this expression. First, note that
$P_t^{\varepsilon/(1-\varepsilon)} \cdot P_t^{\varepsilon/(\varepsilon-1)} = P_t^{-\varepsilon/(\varepsilon-1)} \cdot P_t^{\varepsilon/(\varepsilon-1)} = P_t^0 = 1,$
and similarly

$$P_t^{(2\varepsilon-1)/(1-\varepsilon)} \cdot P_t^{(2\varepsilon-1)/(\varepsilon-1)} = P_t^{(1-2\varepsilon)/(\varepsilon-1)} \cdot P_t^{(2\varepsilon-1)/(\varepsilon-1)} = P_t^0 = 1.$$

Thus the expression above becomes

$$\frac{1}{1-\varepsilon} \cdot [1 - \varepsilon \cdot mc_t] \cdot y_t - \psi \cdot \left(\frac{P_t}{P_{t-1}} - 1\right) \cdot \frac{P_t}{P_{t-1}} + \frac{\beta \cdot \psi}{1 + \pi_{t+1}} \cdot \left(\frac{P_{t+1}}{P_t} - 1\right) \cdot \frac{P_{t+1}}{P_t} \cdot \frac{P_{t+1}}{P_t} = 0.$$

Next we use the definition of inflation to make the substitutions $1 + \pi_t = P_t / P_{t-1}$ and $1 + \pi_{t+1} = P_{t+1} / P_t$ to get

$$\frac{1}{1-\varepsilon} \cdot [1 - \varepsilon \cdot mc_t] \cdot y_t - \psi \cdot \pi_t \cdot (1 + \pi_t) + \frac{\beta \cdot \psi}{1 + \pi_{t+1}} \cdot \pi_{t+1} \cdot (1 + \pi_{t+1})^2 = 0,$$

which obviously simplifies a bit to

$$\frac{1}{1-\varepsilon} \cdot [1 - \varepsilon \cdot mc_t] \cdot y_t - \psi \cdot \pi_t \cdot (1 + \pi_t) + \beta \cdot \psi \cdot \pi_{t+1} \cdot (1 + \pi_{t+1}) = 0.$$

This expression is the **New Keynesian Phillips curve,** and it is the critical component of the modern New Keynesian framework.

Interpreting the New Keynesian Phillips Curve

What the New Keynesian Phillips curve (abbreviated NKPC) articulates is that when firms are making optimal pricing decisions (and, of course, if those pricing choices are subject to menu costs), the period-t inflation rate (which is a consequence of firms' settings for P_{jt}, which in our symmetric equilibrium is identical to P_t) is linked to the period-t marginal cost of production *as well as the rate of inflation that will occur in period $t + 1$, π_{t+1}.*[8]

Two aspects of the NKPC set it apart from the "classic" Phillips curve. First, the classic Phillips curve was a relationship between only period-t events—the period $t + 1$ inflation rate played no role in it. The inclusion of the future rate of inflation in the NKPC is due to the fact that—drawing on basic insights of the real business cycle view of macroeconomics— firms in New Keynesian theory are viewed to be explicitly *dynamic* institutions, and price-setting is viewed to be explicitly a *dynamic* act. As we have stressed in many ways, dynamically optimal (i.e., across multiple time periods) decision-making is at the heart of modern macroeconomic theory.

---

8. Or, introducing some more realism, if there is uncertainty about the future, the expected inflation rate in period $t + 1$.

Second, the classic Phillips curve was a relationship between the period-t inflation rate and the period-t *unemployment rate*. Thus, even ignoring for a moment the presence of π_{t+1} in the NKPC, what the NKPC articulates is not a contemporaneous relationship between inflation and unemployment but rather a relationship between inflation and the *marginal costs of production*. Specifically, the NKPC posits that there is, ceteris paribus, a positive relationship between mc_t and π_t.

Employment—labor input—is typically the most important input into firms' production processes. Hence the classic Phillips curve can be viewed as stating that the more intensively firms use labor, the higher are the prices they set (due to some "pass-through" of costs to prices), and hence the higher the inflation rate an economy (in essentially the same type of symmetric equilibrium we are considering here) experiences. That is, the classic Phillips curve can be stated as articulating a *positive* linkage between employment and inflation. Of course, because employment and unemployment are inversely related, the Phillips curve can also be stated, as it typically is, as articulating a *negative* linkage between *un*employment and inflation.

The NKPC takes a somewhat broader view of the relationship between the intensity of firms' input usage and the inflation rate. The marginal cost of production is a broader measure of the intensity of firms' input usage than is simply the employment rate. Firms' marginal costs, of course, include employment costs, but also include the costs of any and all other inputs, notably capital and raw materials. Thus cost pressures can stem from employment costs, capital costs, or the costs of raw materials. What the NKPC articulates is that, again ceteris paribus, a rise in firms' production costs *for any reason* will lead to inflationary pressure. The classic Phillips curve essentially only articulates that employment-cost pressures (and the unemployment rate is *one* measure of such pressures) have consequences for inflation.

Discussion

The fundamental economic forces that determine inflation are completely different in the New Keynesian view compared to the flexible-price (RBC-style) view. In the New Keynesian view, *purposeful* price-setting decisions on the part of firms, subject to the menu costs they face, is the basic determinant of inflation. In contrast, in the RBC view, there are fundamentally no price-*setters* to begin with. Rather, equilibrium prices simply "arise" out of the forces of supply and demand—prices "simply" clear markets, and all decision-makers, be they consumers or firms, take them as given.

The view of price-*setting* firms, of course, does not require a menu-cost view of the world. Indeed the basic Dixit–Stiglitz framework, not the Rotemberg framework, is what captures the idea of purposeful price-setting by firms. It is sticky prices, though, that potentially gives monetary policy some lever over the economy. Whether or not prices are sticky—or, a bit more deeply, the precise reasons why some prices are sticky—is still a quite unresolved issue.

Finally, you may be wondering where, in the end, the "stickiness" of prices lies in the Rotemberg model. After all, each wholesale firm *is* able to change the price that it charges in every period $t, t + 1, t + 2, \ldots$ —that is, it is never "forbidden" from changing its nominal price. The stickiness stems simply from the menu cost. Say, in the absence of any menu costs, a firm would have chosen to increase its price by 20 percent. With menu costs, it will be partially deterred from this pricing strategy because the costs of changing prices are a convex function of the magnitude of the price change. Thus, instead of changing its price by 20 percent in a given time period, it will prefer to "smooth out" the price change, raising it by some proportion (less than 20 percent) in one period and by some other proportion (again, less than 20 percent) in future periods. Loosely speaking, then, a Rotemberg-type menu cost makes it *sub*optimal for a firm to move around its price by large magnitudes; instead, it will prefer to gradually change its price over time—price stickiness.[9]

9. The Problem Set Questions at the end of chapter 24 cover the material included in this chapter.

24

Optimal Monetary Policy with Sticky Prices

We now reconsider the issue of optimal monetary policy, this time in the Rotemberg sticky-price framework we just finished developing. We will find that the policy advice that arises in a sticky-price view of the economy is qualitatively quite different from the policy advice that arises in a flexible-price view of the economy.

The work we do in this chapter builds on virtually all of the ideas and concepts we have laid out so far. We will rely on the Dixit–Stiglitz and Rotemberg models of price-setting firms subject to menu costs. Our mode of optimal policy analysis will be identical to the structure by which we analyzed the optimal policy problem in chapter 17. As in chapter 17, we must first specify the private-sector equilibrium for any arbitrary policy the government (the central bank) might choose. This in itself requires setting up and solving the optimization problems of the demand and supply sides of the economy; we have already done most of this work, but there are a couple of new elements we introduce. Then, as in chapter 17, in a second step we determine the policy that maximizes the representative consumer's utility. The final step is to compute the actual optimal policy, which is done by comparing the solution of the optimal policy problem with the outcome in the private-sector equilibrium; the result is the optimal policy recommendation. We once again—because, we continue to maintain, it seems very natural—adopt the representative consumer's utility as the welfare criterion according to which the central bank ranks various policies.

Thus, just as in our earlier analysis of optimal policy, we can think of the policy makers as sitting "above" the economy, watching how equilibrium unfolds. We need to make a slight refinement to this view here, however: we will think of the policy makers as watching how a *symmetric equilibrium* unfolds. Thus policy makers understand that for any given policy they choose, the private sector (consumers, retail firms, and wholesale firms) will make optimal choices that will result in *some* symmetric equilibrium. All of this by-now quite familiar machinery allows us to continue to think of the optimal policy problem as a problem of choosing the *best* equilibrium, where "best equilibrium" means the one that maximizes the utility of the representative consumer.

Retail Firms

The representative retail firm is again no different from the one we developed in the basic Dixit–Stiglitz and Rotemberg models: a retail firm simply "packages" the continuum [0, 1] of differentiated wholesale products and sells the retail consumption basket to consumers via perfectly competitive markets. As before, the price of retail goods is determined only through the invisible hand of the market, and the profit-maximizing choice of any arbitrary wholesale good j leads to the demand function for wholesale good j,

$$y_{jt} = \left(\frac{P_{jt}}{P_t} \right)^{\varepsilon/(1-\varepsilon)} y_t, \tag{1}$$

for, as always, any $j \in [0,1]$. In terms of setting things up for the description of the full equilibrium below, there are *no* equilibrium conditions stemming directly from profit maximization by retail firms that we need to keep independent track of. The demand function (1) is a sufficient summary of the profit-maximizing choices of retail firms; but, because it will be subsumed inside the analysis of wholesale firms, we inevitably will end up "keeping track" of it.[1]

Wholesale Firms

Wholesale firms are also no different from the ones we developed in the basic Rotemberg model: a particular wholesale firm, wholesaler j, produces one good that is imperfectly substitutable with any other wholesale good, and sells it to the retail sector. Because of imperfect substitutability between its good and the good of any other wholesaler, wholesale firm j enjoys some monopoly power, making it explicitly a price-setter. In (re-)setting its nominal price from one period to the next, however, the wholesale firm is subject to the *real* quadratic cost of price adjustment,

$$\frac{\psi}{2} \cdot \left(\frac{P_{jt}}{P_{jt-1}} - 1 \right)^2,$$

in which, as before, ψ is a parameter that governs the magnitude of menu costs. Even more so than in our analysis so far, the fact that we are adopting the view that menu costs are *real* costs will be critical; it will be the key force shaping the optimal policy prescription at which we eventually arrive.

Finally, profit maximization by wholesale firm j, taking into account the costs of price adjustment, leads *in a symmetric equilibrium* to the New Keynesian Phillips curve (NKPC),

---

1. In this sense the distinction between "retail firms" and "wholesale firms" can be thought of as nothing more than a theoretical artifice to keep our thinking straight between consumers and firms.

$$\frac{1}{1-\varepsilon} \cdot [1 - \varepsilon \cdot mc_t] \cdot y_t - \psi \cdot \pi_t \cdot (1 + \pi_t) + \beta \cdot \psi \cdot \pi_{t+1} \cdot (1 + \pi_{t+1}) = 0, \tag{2}$$

which links together period-t inflation, period-$(t + 1)$ inflation, and period-t marginal costs of production. The NKPC (2) is one of the (symmetric) equilibrium conditions of our model economy, stemming from optimal price-setting decisions on the part of firms subject to menu costs. Indeed, for our analysis in this chapter, the NKPC is the key equilibrium condition, the one on which we will load essentially all of our intuition.

An issue that we have so far left unanswered in our analysis of wholesale firms is the underlying determinants of the marginal cost of production. We simply asserted that wholesale firms operate a production technology that exhibits a marginal cost of production independent of the quantity that it produces. Because specifying an optimal policy problem requires fully specifying the nature of private-sector equilibrium outcomes, which in turn requires specifying how production actually occurs and hence its underlying costs, we no longer can be silent about the underlying determinants of the marginal costs of production.

We will assume here, as we did in our first look at optimal monetary policy with flexible prices, the simplest possible physical production technology for wholesale firms, linear in labor: $y_{jt} = f(n_{jt}) = n_{jt}$. In principle, each wholesale firm could hire a quantity of labor different from other wholesalers, which is why, in general, we might need the subscript j on labor. However, in keeping with the symmetric equilibrium analysis we wish to pursue, we drop this potential asymmetry and from here on simply assert that every wholesale firm will actually demand the same quantity of labor as every other wholesale firm, allowing us to write wholesale firm j's production technology as $y_{jt} = f(n_t) = n_t$.

This labor is hired in a perfectly competitive labor market. Thus, in the labor market, wholesale firms take as given the real wage rate w_t. Some simple logic will now allow us to conclude that given the quite simple production structure we have set up, the marginal cost of production for wholesale firm j in period t is simply the market real wage rate w_t. To understand this, note that by definition (real) marginal cost is the resources a firm must spend in order to produce one more (the marginal) unit of output. Given our linear-in-labor production technology, production of one more (the marginal) unit of output requires one more (a marginal) unit of labor. For the wholesale firm, the cost of hiring one more (marginal) unit of labor is simply the market real wage. In turn, due to perfect competition, the market real wage is independent of any input or output decisions made by wholesale firm j—this is nothing more than the assertion that wholesale firms are price-takers in the labor market.

In order to expand output by one unit, the firm must spend w_t, meaning the real wage *is* the firm's marginal cost of production.[2] Thus the simple relation

---

2. This is not a completely general conclusion, but rather one that follows from the specific production function we have adopted here. A more general production function, such as Cobb–Douglas, involving both labor and capital would render the link between marginal costs and wages, while still close, less one for one.

$$mc_t = w_t \tag{3}$$

is an equilibrium condition of the environment we are considering.

Consumers in a Cashless Economy

In the New Keynesian view of the economy and monetary policy, the object called "money" actually plays no *physical* role whatsoever. This may seem surprising because the New Keynesian framework has become the dominant theoretical framework for the analysis of *monetary* policy. This de-emphasis of the physical role of money is also a stark departure from the MIU and CIA frameworks, in which we spent considerable effort trying to articulate the medium-of-exchange role—the physical role—of money and monetary demand.

Recall that the benchmark policy prescription we arrived at in those flexible-price frameworks was that in the long run the optimal monetary policy entails implementing the Friedman rule of deflation at the rate of consumer impatience—or, in terms of nominal interest rates, setting $i = 0$. This policy recommendation followed from the desire of the optimal policy maker to avoid distorting the consumer's consumption–leisure optimality condition away from the economically efficient one; an $i > 0$ (equivalently, recall, a steady-state money growth rate $\mu > \beta$) is precisely what caused a distortion in this optimality condition. In turn this distortion stemmed fundamentally from the cash-in-advance constraint—a *physical,* medium-of-exchange, role for money demand.

The New Keynesian framework, in contrast, asserts that the medium-of-exchange role is *not* the most important role played by money in a developed economy. It thus simply ignores—completely—money's role as a medium of exchange. Thus in our analysis here we will have no CIA or MIU aspects whatsoever.

Instead, the New Keynesian framework emphasizes only the unit-of-account role of money—the simple fact that society, however it does so, generally agrees upon an accepted "language" or "standard" in which all (most?) prices will be quoted. *How* a society "agrees upon" a common unit of account is an open question in economics; the New Keynesian view has nothing novel to say about why intrinsically useless pieces of paper printed by a country's central bank are, in modern times, almost universally an economy's unit of account.

With this modified view of the role of money in the economy, the representative consumer's problem is a bit simpler to state and characterize than in our flexible-price consideration of optimal monetary policy in chapter 17. The representative consumer begins period t with nominal bond holdings B_{t-1} and stock (a real asset) holdings a_{t-1}. The period-t budget constraint of the consumer is

$$P_t c_t + P_t^b B_t + S_t a_t = W_t n_t + B_{t-1} + (S_t + D_t)a_{t-1}, \tag{4}$$

where the notation again is as in the MIU model of chapter 15 and the CIA model of chapter 17: S_t is the nominal price of a unit of stock, D_t is the nominal dividend paid by each unit of stock, and P_t^b is the nominal price of a one-period, zero coupon nominal bond with face value = $1.

Compared to the budget constraints analyzed previously, however, note the *absence* of nominal money M. In the New Keynesian "cashless" view of the economy, because the physical medium-of-exchange function of money is de-emphasized, we simply completely ignore it in the consumer's optimization problem. Notice that because we have dropped nominal money from the representative consumer's budget constraint, we also have dropped, compared to chapter 17, the term τ_t, which was the lump-sum means by which the monetary authority achieved changes in the (physical) money supply.

Denoting by λ_t the Lagrange multiplier on the period-t budget constraint, we write the sequential Lagrangian for this problem as

$$
\begin{aligned}
&u(c_t, 1 - n_t) + \beta u(c_{t+1}, 1 - n_{t+1}) + \beta^2 u(c_{t+2}, 1 - n_{t+2}) + \ldots \\
&+ \lambda_t \left[W_t n_t + B_{t-1} + (S_t + D_t) a_{t-1} - P_t c_t - P_t^b B_t - S_t a_t \right] \\
&+ \beta \lambda_{t+1} \left[W_{t+1} n_{t+1} + B_t + (S_{t+1} + D_{t+1}) a_t - P_{t+1} c_{t+1} - P_{t+1}^b B_{t+1} - S_{t+1} a_{t+1} \right] \\
&+ \ldots.
\end{aligned}
\tag{5}
$$

In terms of analyzing just the consumer optimization problem, the absence of the CIA constraint makes the "cashless" economy quite a bit simpler than in the CIA (or MIU) model.

In period t the consumer chooses (c_t, n_t, B_t, a_t)—note the absence of M_t from the list of objects over which to optimize. The first-order conditions with respect to each of these four choice variables, respectively, are

$$
u_1(c_t, 1 - n_t) - \lambda_t P_t = 0,
\tag{6}
$$

$$
-u_2(c_t, 1 - n_t) + \lambda_t W_t = 0,
\tag{7}
$$

$$
-\lambda_t P_t^b + \beta \lambda_{t+1} = 0,
\tag{8}
$$

$$
-\lambda_t S_t + \beta \lambda_{t+1}(S_{t+1} + D_{t+1}) = 0.
\tag{9}
$$

Analysis of the rest of this now-cashless structure, from the consumer optimization point of view, proceeds just as in chapter 17.

Combining conditions (6) and (7) immediately yields the familiar consumption–leisure optimality condition

$$
\frac{u_2(c_t, 1 - n_t)}{u_1(c_t, 1 - n_t)} = w_t.
\tag{10}
$$

In contrast to the consumption–leisure optimality condition derived in chapter 17, monetary policy does *not* potentially drive a wedge into consumers' optimal choices. Thus, in stark contrast to the forces driving optimal policy recommendations in a "cash-full" flexible-price view of the economy, in the cashless sticky-price view the forces driving optimal policy recommendations are, as we will see, something quite different.

Finally, just as in chapter 17, we can express a consumption–savings optimality condition. Due to the *lack* of a CIA constraint here, it is simple to express this in terms of the marginal utility of consumption, rather than in terms of the marginal utility of leisure as we did in chapter 17; here we simply have

$$\frac{u_1(c_t, 1-n_t)}{u_1(c_{t+1}, 1-n_{t+1})} = \beta(1+r_t), \tag{11}$$

which results from combining (6) and (9) and defining the gross real interest rate $1 + r$ as the real return on stock holdings.[3]

Conditions (10) and (11) are thus equilibrium conditions stemming from the consumer (demand) side of the economy.

Government

We can still say that the government "prints money," and thus we can still speak of the growth rate of money. However, because we are being much less explicit about the physical medium of exchange used in the economy, we can get away without actually articulating a government budget constraint that describes the printing of money. So, in New Keynesian tradition, this aspect of the economy is left in the background.

Resource Constraint

As usual, the resource constraint of the economy describes the transformation of inputs into total output (GDP) as well as all of the possible different uses of total output. In our Rotemberg sticky-price economy, there are *two* uses for final output: consumption (of "goods"—remember, in symmetric equilibrium we blur the distinction between "retail goods" and "wholesale goods," even though the distinction is crucial for the derivation of the NKPC) and the real, physical, costs associated with price adjustment. After all, firms must expend resources—whatever exactly the "menu costs" are—in order to change their prices. Thus the resource constraint, in a symmetric equilibrium (which allows us to drop the distinction between P_{jt} and P_t) is

$$c_t + \frac{\psi}{2} \cdot \left(\frac{P_t}{P_{t-1}} - 1 \right)^2 = y_t. \tag{12}$$

Using the definition of inflation, $1+\pi_t = P_t/P_{t-1}$, we can instead express the economy-wide resource constraint as

---

3. See the analysis in chapter 17 for a reminder of these details.

$$c_t + \frac{\psi}{2} \cdot (\pi_t)^2 = y_t. \tag{13}$$

Finally, because we are limiting ourselves to a symmetric equilibrium, *in equilibrium* we can speak interchangeably of "retail goods," "wholesale goods," and "consumption baskets." Properly speaking, what we care about for the resource constraint is how the consumption baskets of the economy are produced. Because of symmetry, though, this is equivalent to caring about how wholesale goods are produced. We have assumed that wholesale goods are produced according to a linear-in-labor production technology. We can thus substitute the simple relation $y_t = n_t$ into (13) and express the welfare-relevant resource constraint as

$$c_t + \frac{\psi}{2} \cdot (\pi_t)^2 = n_t. \tag{14}$$

Equilibrium and Steady-State Equilibrium

Before proceeding to consideration of the optimal policy problem, we must be clear about the precise nature of the private-sector equilibrium. As always, equilibrium is a collection of prices and quantities that in concert make all markets clear, given that both demand (consumer choices) and supply (firm choices) decisions in the economy are made optimally. In our model economy here, equilibrium is described by the NKPC (2), the relation (3) linking marginal costs with real wages, the consumer optimality conditions (10) and (11), and the resource constraint (14).

Because condition (3) is so simple, let's simply substitute it into the NKPC. Doing so leaves us with a description of equilibrium that is condition (10), condition (11), condition (14), and the NKPC,

$$\frac{1}{1-\varepsilon} \cdot [1 - \varepsilon \cdot w_t] \cdot n_t - \psi \cdot \pi_t (1 + \pi_t) + \beta \cdot \psi \cdot \pi_{t+1} \cdot (1 + \pi_{t+1}) = 0. \tag{15}$$

Next we impose steady state on these four equilibrium conditions.[4] Doing so leaves us with, respectively,

$$\frac{u_2(c, 1-n)}{u_1(c, 1-n)} = w, \tag{16}$$

$$\frac{1}{\beta} = 1 + r, \tag{17}$$

---

4. Thus, just as in chapter 17, we limit our analysis to steady-state optimal policy.

$$c + \frac{1}{\psi} \cdot \pi^2 = n, \tag{18}$$

and

$$\frac{1}{1-\varepsilon} \cdot [1 - \varepsilon \cdot w] \cdot n - (1-\beta) \cdot \psi \cdot (1+\pi) = 0. \tag{19}$$

Our task in what follows is to continue to simplify these expressions as far as possible.

As we did in chapter 17, let's use the resource constraint (18) to eliminate the n terms in the other equilibrium conditions; this leaves us with

$$\frac{u_2\left(c, 1-c-(\psi/2) \cdot \pi^2\right)}{u_1\left(c, 1-c-(\psi/2) \cdot \pi^2\right)} = w, \tag{20}$$

$$\frac{1}{\beta} = 1 + r, \tag{21}$$

and

$$\frac{1}{1-\varepsilon} \cdot [1 - \varepsilon \cdot w]\left(c + \frac{\psi}{2}\pi^2\right) - (1-\beta) \cdot \psi \cdot \pi \cdot (1+\pi) = 0. \tag{22}$$

Next let's substitute for w in the NKPC using condition (20), which yields the pair of equilibrium conditions

$$\frac{1}{\beta} = 1 + r \tag{23}$$

and the rather unfriendly looking condition

$$\frac{1}{1-\varepsilon} \cdot \left[1 - \frac{\varepsilon \cdot u_2\left(c, 1-c-(\psi/2) \cdot \pi^2\right)}{u_1\left(c, 1-c-(\psi/2) \cdot \pi^2\right)}\right] \cdot \left(c + \frac{\psi}{2}\pi^2\right) - (1-\beta) \cdot \psi \cdot \pi \cdot (1+\pi) = 0. \tag{24}$$

Despite its "cashless" nature, the New Keynesian view does affirm that in the long run (i.e., in the steady state), a simple monetarist link between the rate of inflation, π, and the rate of money growth, g, exists.[5] Thus imposing $g = \pi$ on the previous two expressions leaves us with

$$\frac{1}{\beta} = 1 + r \tag{25}$$

---

5. However, the fundamental source of such a long-run monetarist link between money growth and inflation is left unspecified in the New Keynesian view. In contrast, recall, the CIA and MIU frameworks clearly articulated the source of the long-run link—the steady state of a money demand condition is the source of the monetarist link in both the MIU and CIA frameworks.

and

$$\frac{1}{1-\varepsilon}\cdot\left[1-\frac{\varepsilon\cdot u_2\left(c,1-c-(\psi/2)\cdot g^2\right)}{u_1\left(c,1-c-(\psi/2)\cdot g^2\right)}\right]\cdot\left(c+\frac{\psi}{2}g^2\right)-(1-\beta)\cdot\psi\cdot g\cdot(1+g)=0 \qquad (26)$$

as the set of (still two) equilibrium conditions.

For the optimal policy analysis to follow, condition (25) can essentially be ignored. In the cashless view, condition (25) is only useful insofar as it pins down, in steady state, a nominal interest rate *once* a money growth rate (and hence inflation rate) has been decided upon by the central bank. That is, a completely standard Fisher relation does exist in the New Keynesian view, and it is essentially nothing more than condition (25). In steady state, as usual, we can open up the real interest rate as

$$1+\pi = \beta(1+i), \qquad (27)$$

or, on invoking the long-run monetarist link between money growth and inflation, as

$$1+g = \beta(1+i). \qquad (28)$$

Thus, in the ensuing optimal policy analysis, once the central bank has chosen the welfare-maximizing g, condition (28)—equivalently, condition (25)—simply tells it what i to set to achieve the chosen g; condition (25)—equivalently, condition (28)—does not play any direct role in the policy problem.[6] Rather, it is condition (26)—which, despite its now cumbersome form, is simply the NKPC—that is the essential equilibrium condition for the optimal policy problem.

As we did in chapter 17, let's take stock of where we've arrived before proceeding to the optimal policy problem. After setting up and solving both retail firms' and wholesale firms' profit-maximization problems, as well as consumers' (cashless) utility-maximization problem, we defined the full equilibrium. We then imposed steady state on these conditions and proceeded to condense them into a single (albeit seemingly not informatively) expression, condition (26). Condition (26)—which, we emphasize again, is nothing more than the NKPC—describes the steady-state equilibrium *of the entire private sector of the economy.* What condition (26) describes is *how the steady-state equilibrium level of consumption depends on the steady-state rate of growth of the nominal money supply.* As in chapter 17, we've managed to write the entire model economy (i.e., its setup *and* solution) into a single expression. There is no (reliable) shortcut for all the analysis we have done; one *must* go through the entire solution of the demand and supply sides, description of the equilibrium, and then (*and only then*) can one impose steady state.

---

6. Or, if we framed things in terms of the central bank choosing i directly, then condition (28) would pin down the appropriate g to set to hit the target i. In our steady-state analysis, choosing one or the other instrument, g or i, is completely equivalent.

Formulation and Solution of Optimal Policy Problem

From the point of view of the central bank, condition (26) describes how the private sector of the economy responds (in steady state) to its chosen monetary policy. Although generally not amenable to an analytic solution, condition (26) indeed *defines the steady-state equilibrium c as a function of g*. To emphasize this *functional* dependence, let's from here on write $c(g)$. As in chapter 17, the optimal policy maker takes this "private-sector equilibrium reaction function" as given when maximizing the (steady-state) utility of the representative consumer.

Referring back to chapter 17 for details, the representative consumer's lifetime (steady-state) utility is given by

$$\sum_{s=0}^{\infty} \beta^s u\left(c(g), 1-c(g)-(\psi/2)g^2\right) = \frac{u\left(c(g), 1-c(g)-(\psi/2)g^2\right)}{1-\beta}. \tag{29}$$

The optimal policy problem thus boils down to choosing a (steady-state) growth rate of money that maximizes (29). Mathematically no constraints are required on this optimization problem *because we have already built all constraints imposed by equilibrium into* (29). Except for the fact that the resource constraint and hence the substitution for c in the utility function is not as simple as in chapter 17, the policy maker's objective function (29) is identical to that in chapter 17.

Being careful to apply the chain rule, the first-order condition of (29) with respect to g is

$$u_1\left(c(g), 1-c(g)-\frac{\psi}{2}g^2\right) \cdot c'(g) - u_2\left(c(g), 1-c(g)-\frac{\psi}{2}g^2\right) \cdot (c'(g)+\psi \cdot g) = 0, \tag{30}$$

in which, as in chapter 17, $c'(g)$ is how steady-state equilibrium consumption responds to a marginal change in the money growth rate (i.e., it is the derivative of the function $c(g)$ with respect to g).[7]

Rearranging terms, we have

$$u_1\left(c(g), 1-c(g)-\frac{\psi}{2}g^2\right) \cdot c'(g) - u_2\left(c(g), 1-c(g)-\frac{\psi}{2}g^2\right) \cdot c'(g)$$

$$-u_2\left(c(g), 1-c(g)-\frac{\psi}{2}g^2\right) \cdot \psi \cdot g = 0. \tag{32}$$

If it were the case that $\psi = 0$, this first-order condition would simplify exactly as in chapter 17. In the case of $\psi = 0$, the $c'(g)$ terms would cancel, and we would be left with the conclusion that if policy were being conducted optimally,

---

7. Note that we've dropped the $1-\beta$ term from this first-order condition because it does not affect the solution of the policy problem—that is, we have multiplied through by a constant.

$$\frac{u_2(c(g),1-c(g))}{u_1(c(g),1-c(g))}=1$$

and

$$\frac{u_2(c(g),1-c(g))}{u_1(c(g),1-c(g))}=1, \tag{33}$$

exactly as we found in chapter 17.

However, with $\psi > 0$, matters are a bit more complicated. If we divide the condition (32) by $u_1\left(c(g),1-c(g)-(\psi/2)g^2\right)\cdot c'(g)$, we have

$$\frac{u_2\left(c(g),1-c(g)-(\psi/2)g^2\right)}{u_1\left(c(g),1-c(g)-(\psi/2)g^2\right)}\cdot\left[1+\frac{\psi\cdot g}{c'(g)}\right]=1, \tag{34}$$

or, putting the terms in square brackets over a common denominator,

$$\frac{u_2\left(c(g),1-c(g)-(\psi/2)g^2\right)}{u_1\left(c(g),1-c(g)-(\psi/2)g^2\right)}\cdot\left[\frac{c'(g)+\psi\cdot g}{c'(g)}\right]=1. \tag{35}$$

Solving for the MRS $u_2(.)/u_1(.)$, we have

$$\frac{u_2\left(c(g),1-c(g)-(\psi/2)g^2\right)}{u_1\left(c(g),1-c(g)-(\psi/2)g^2\right)}=\left[\frac{c'(g)}{c'(g)+\psi\cdot g}\right], \tag{36}$$

which states that *if policy is chosen optimally,* the representative consumer's MRS between consumption and leisure is equated to a complicated function that depends on the money growth rate, the degree of price-stickiness in the economy, and, most complicated of all, the private-sector reaction function c(g) itself. This conclusion seems to be quite a bit more complicated than the one that emerged in chapter 17![8]

Nonetheless, our next step is conceptually identical. We must translate condition (36) into an actual policy *recommendation* for g. Exactly as we proceeded in chapter 17, this final step requires comparing the condition that describes the implications of optimal policy—which is condition (36)—with the condition that describes the mapping between any given (whether optimal or not) policy and the private-sector equilibrium outcome—which in our model here is condition (26).

---

8. The reason that this conclusion is identical in the two seemingly very different frameworks is that—aside from the precise forms of the arguments inside the marginal utility function—the marginal rates of *transformation* between consumption and leisure are simply *one* in both our model here and the model considered of only optimal monetary policy—examine the resource constraints in the respective environments to see this. At the end of the day, optimal policy is about trying to achieve economic efficiency, and the condition that *defines* economic efficiency (as discussed in the topic of economic efficiency in chapter 18) is that marginal rates of substitution be equated to marginal rates of transformation. This basic underlying force behind optimal policy-setting has nothing to do with whether or not price adjustment is costly.

This is an extremely daunting task; the precise setting for g that would make condition (26) exactly coincide with condition (36) is an extremely complicated expression. Unless we make one small modification to the analysis—that is, a modification that New Keynesian analysis typically makes. Let's first make this modification, draw the policy implications that stem from it, and defer until below what the economic content or meaning of this modification might be.

In the NKPC, condition (26), suppose that an ε term were present in the denominator of the second term inside the large square brackets. That is, suppose that the NKPC were

$$\frac{1}{1-\varepsilon}\cdot\left[1-\frac{\varepsilon\cdot u_2\left(c,1-c-(\psi/2)\cdot g^2\right)}{\varepsilon\cdot u_1\left(c,1-c-(\psi/2)\cdot g^2\right)}\right]\cdot\left(c+\frac{\psi}{2}g^2\right)-(1-\beta)\cdot\psi\cdot g\cdot(1+g)=0.. \tag{37}$$

If this (somehow) were the form of the NKPC, the ε terms in the second term inside the large square brackets would obviously cancel out, leaving

$$\frac{1}{1-\varepsilon}\cdot\left[1-\frac{u_2\left(c,1-c-(\psi/2)\cdot g^2\right)}{u_1\left(c,1-c-(\psi/2)\cdot g^2\right)}\right]\cdot\left(c+\frac{\psi}{2}g^2\right)-(1-\beta)\cdot\psi\cdot g\cdot(1+g)=0 \tag{38}$$

as the NKPC.

Based on this now-modified NKPC, it actually is quite simple to determine what money growth rate g would make the (modified) NKPC coincide with condition (36). *Simple observation tells us that setting $g = 0$ makes condition (38) coincide with condition (36).* Moreover $g = 0$ is the unique steady-state money growth rate that does so. Thus, taking as given for a moment the "modification" we just made to the NKPC, the benchmark New Keynesian policy prescription is that a central bank ought to implement (in the steady state, technically—i.e., on average) a zero growth rate of money, which in turn achieves a zero inflation rate.

Alternatively, if we wish to think about the optimal policy in terms of a prescription for the nominal interest rate, condition (28) (recall we stated above that condition (28) would only be necessary to use if we wanted to map from g to i) tells us that $i = (1/\beta)-1 > 0$. The optimal policy recommendation in the sticky-price framework can thus equivalently be thought of in terms of this precise *strictly positive* nominal interest rate, or in terms of a zero money growth rate/zero inflation rate.[9] It is usually the latter feature of New Keynesian policy recommendations that anchors our thinking.

Zero inflation is the cornerstone New Keynesian policy prescription. The first observation to make is that this prescription is in marked contrast to the optimal *deflation* prescribed by the Friedman rule that we obtained in chapter 17. The economics behind the zero-inflation—or, more realistically, low-inflation—prescription are quite simple, which

---

9. For example, if $\beta = 0.95$, a commonly accepted value at an annual frequency, then we have that the optimal nominal interest rate associated with a zero-inflation rate is roughly $i = 0.05$.

is part of the reason why it has nearly universally captured the imagination of policy makers.

Thinking about the details of the Rotemberg model, the menu *costs* of price *adjustment* are, as the term implies, *costs* of price changes. These costs are social costs, which we know because they appear in the resource constraint of the economy. However, from the point of view of the economy as a whole (rather than from the point of view of a single individual firm), there are absolutely no benefits whatsoever of price adjustment. We can conclude this because, again, the resource constraint only contains *costs* of price adjustment.

Standard economic decision-making principles dictate that choices should balance marginal costs and marginal benefits. From the point of view of the social planner, however, there are no marginal benefits to price adjustment; there are only marginal costs. Hence simple logic would lead us to conclude that an activity—in our case, nominal price adjustment—that only entails costs and no benefits whatsoever ought to be completely eliminated.

Zero inflation achieves exactly this. If in symmetric equilibrium there is zero inflation, by definition, no firm is ever changing its prices. Zero nominal price adjustment means that there are zero menu costs of price adjustment being borne by the economy. In other language that should be familiar, there are zero *deadweight losses* being incurred by the economy if there is zero inflation. In the Rotemberg formulation, the menu costs of price adjustment are purely deadweight losses; optimal policy—indeed economic efficiency—requires eliminating deadweight losses.

A Helping Hand from Fiscal Policy

To arrive at the zero-inflation policy prescription, we introduced an ε into the NKPC; clearly, the economic fundamentals we have laid out did not warrant this. Introduction of the ε is a reflection of some (in our analysis, unmodeled) *fiscal policy intervention*.

From the point of view of economic efficiency, there are two distinct distortions in our Rotemberg view of the economy. First, monopolistic competition *in and of itself* causes a deadweight loss, even if all price adjustment is costless. On top of the deadweight loss stemming from monopolistic competition, the menu costs of price adjustment impose another deadweight loss, as discussed above.

In principle, there is no way for *one* policy tool—monetary policy's setting of a money growth rate—to simultaneously correct *two* inefficiencies. Correcting two independent (separate) deadweight losses, in general, requires two independent (separate) policy instruments. The predominant view in the modern New Keynesian tradition is that fiscal policy "should" be used to offset deadweight losses arising from monopolistic competition, which frees up monetary policy to deal with "just" the deadweight losses arising from menu costs of price adjustment.

The ε term we introduced in moving from equation (26) to equation (39) effectively inserts the required corrective fiscal policy.[10] Our subsequent analysis then led us to conclude that, *given the presence of this corrective fiscal policy,* the goal of monetary policy in helping deliver an economically efficient outcome is to target zero inflation, which in the steady state requires setting a zero money growth rate.

A broader lesson here is that achieving the mantra, often invoked by policy makers, of the desirability of "low and stable inflation" requires some fiscal preconditions. That is, it is difficult, if not impossible, for monetary policy to do its job without some appropriately complementary conduct of fiscal policy. Without a supportive fiscal framework, a given monetary policy can often be quite ineffective or even do the opposite of what it was originally intended to do. Indeed this latter idea was the underlying theme of our analyses of the joint effects of monetary policy and fiscal policy in chapter 16. Here we've seen that complementarity between fiscal and monetary policies also is important for the determination of optimal policy-setting.

Chapter 24 Problem Set Questions

1. **Sticky prices, price indexation, and optimal long-run inflation targets.** Consider a variation of the Rotemberg model of nominal rigidities. Suppose that the price adjustment cost that wholesale firm i must pay is given by

$$\frac{\psi}{2}\left(\frac{P_{it}}{P_{it-1}(1+\pi)^{\chi}}-1\right)^2,$$

with parameters $\psi \geq 0$ and $\chi \geq 0$. If $\chi = 0$, this is exactly the Rotemberg model we have been studying. However, if $\chi > 0$, then the adjustment cost is mitigated, and it is only price adjustments that are faster (or slower) than some "normal" rate of inflation π that incur ("customer anger" and other) costs. Formally, think of π (without a time subscript) as the steady-state (i.e., long-run) rate of price inflation,

As in our basic Rotemberg framework, the adjustment cost is a firm-wide real cost, independent of how many units of output are sold. Hence the period-t nominal profit function for wholesale firm i is

$$\left(P_{it}-P_t mc_t\right)y_{it}-\frac{\psi}{2}\left(\frac{P_{it}}{P_{it-1}(1+\pi)^{\chi}}-1\right)^2 P_t;$$

note the P_t term multiplying the adjustment cost term, which converts the real adjustment cost into aggregate nominal units.

---

10. Here we do not go into the details of how and why this modification can be thought of as an appropriate setting for fiscal policy.

The associated period-t resource constraint (in an equilibrium that is symmetric across all wholesale goods firms) in this economy is

$$c_t + \frac{\psi}{2}\left(\frac{1+\pi_t}{(1+\pi)^\chi} - 1\right)^2 = y_t,$$

which shows that price adjustment costs are a real resource use in the economy—they drive a gap between total production y and total absorption (here, just c), hence are a deadweight loss.[11]

The rest of the environment is exactly as presented in the chapter: each intermediate firm takes as given its period-t demand schedule, there is a representative final goods firm that produces final output according to the Dixit–Stiglitz aggregator $y_t = \left[\int_0^1 y_{it}^{1/\varepsilon} di\right]^\varepsilon$, with all the usual notation, and so forth.

a. Following the setup we develop for the basic Rotemberg framework, construct the dynamic profit-maximization problem of intermediate firm i.

b. Based on the dynamic profit-maximization problem constructed in part a, compute the firm's first-order condition with respect to P_{it}.

c. Using the FOC you constructed in part b, impose symmetric equilibrium (i.e., $P_t = P_{it}, \ \forall i, \forall t$) and then develop an expression in which the only possibly time-varying objects are inflation, marginal costs of production, output, and the stochastic discount factor (i.e., the intertemporal marginal rate of substitution). That is, construct the New Keynesian Phillips curve (NKPC) for this variant of the Rotemberg model.

d. Consider the deterministic steady state of the expression obtained in part c. Solve for the long-run level of mc.

e. If $\chi = 1$, which corresponds to the case of full indexation of prices to the long-run inflation rate, how does marginal cost of production compare with the implications of optimal price-setting in the baseline flexible-price Dixit–Stiglitz framework?

f. If $\chi < 1$, which corresponds to the case of partial indexation of prices to the long-run inflation rate (or no indexation at all for the case of $\chi = 0$), what is the optimal inflation rate presuming the goal of monetary policy is to replicate the flexible-price outcome?

g. If $\chi = 1$, what is the optimal inflation rate presuming the goal of monetary policy is to replicate the flexible-price outcome?

---

11. As always, the resource constraint can be derived by summing the consumer budget constraint and the government budget constraint (which here reads $0 = 0$), and then imposing all equilibrium conditions to substitute for prices and, in this case, the profits of the intermediate sector that consumers take as lump sum in their optimization.

2. **Cash goods, credit goods, interest on money, and the Friedman rule.** Consider a variation of the basic cash-in-advance (CIA) model we have studied. Suppose that there are two "types" of consumption goods, "cash goods" and "credit goods." Cash goods, denoted by c_{1t}, are goods whose purchase requires money, while credit goods, denoted by c_{2t}, are goods whose purchase does not require money (i.e., they can be bought "on credit."). The market nominal price of each type of good is the same, P_t.

   The representative consumer consumes both cash and credit goods (i.e., both goods are in the consumer's utility function). To simplify the analysis a bit, let's abstract from labor-supply issues. Specifically, suppose that the instantaneous (i.e., period-t) utility function is $u(c_{1t}, c_{2t})$, and rather than receiving labor income, the consumer simply receives a real endowment y_t in period t (i.e., income that "falls from the sky," as in some of our early analysis), whose nominal value of $P_t y_t$.

   Furthermore let's assume that money holdings may pay positive interest. Specifically, the consumer's period-t budget constraint is

   $$P_t c_{1t} + P_t c_{2t} + M_t + B_t = P_t y_t + (1 + i_{t-1}^M)M_{t-1} + (1 + i_{t-1}^B)B_{t-1} + T_t,$$

   with i^M denoting the net nominal interest rate on cash holdings and i^B denoting the net nominal interest rate on bond holdings. Otherwise, the notation and timing of events is the same as in the simpler cash-in-advance model (and note here that we've also dropped "stock holdings" a_t from the problem, since they are irrelevant for the issue in this problem). Also, as usual, changes in the aggregate nominal money stock are conducted via lump-sum transfers/taxes vis-à-vis the consumer sector, denoted here by T. Finally, all nominal interest rates (on both bonds and money) are known at time $t-1$.

   Besides the budget constraint, in period t the representative consumer faces the cash constraint on the subset c_1 of goods, hence

   $$P_t c_{1t} = M_t.$$

   (Note: In analyzing this problem, you may not substitute the cash-in-advance constraint into the budget constraint—because, in principle, it is an inequality constraint, even though you are only analyzing it holding with equality.) As always, suppose that the representative consumer's subjective discount factor is $\beta \in (0,1)$.

   In this economy, what is the statement of the Friedman rule, when stated in terms of a condition/restriction on interest rates in the economy? (Hint: What does the Friedman rule amount to when thinking about it in terms of the value of the Lagrange multiplier on the cash-in-advance constraint?)

3. **Optimal monetary policy in cash good/credit good model.** Consider a variation of the basic cash/credit model we have studied. As before, cash goods, denoted by c_{1t}, are goods whose purchase requires money, while credit goods, denoted by c_{2t}, are goods whose purchase does not require money (i.e., they can be bought "on credit").

The representative consumer wants to consume both cash and credit goods: his instantaneous utility function is $u(c_{1t}, c_{2t})$. The representative consumer lives forever and discounts future utility by the factor $\beta \in (0,1)$. Note that there is no leisure in this utility function: the economy is an endowment economy, in which the real endowment y_t in each period t is outside the control of anyone in the economy.

The nominal price of both cash goods and credit goods in any period t is P_t. The important difference compared to the cash/credit model we have previously studied is that the resource constraint of the economy is $1.2c_{1t} + c_{2t} = y_t$.

The only asset that consumers have to accumulate is money (no bonds, no stock), and let M_{t-1} be the nominal amount of money that consumers begin period t with. Hence the period-t budget constraint of the consumer is $P_t c_{1t} + P_t c_{2t} + M_t = P_t y_t + M_{t-1} + \tau_t$, where τ_t is a lump-sum transfer from (or to) the central bank. The cash-in-advance constraint in this economy applies only to c_{1t}: in period t the cash-in-advance constraint is $P_t c_{1t} = M_t$ (note the subscript!). Finally, the transfer depends on some growth rate of money, $\tau_t = g_t M_{t-1}$—that is, there is no consolidated government budget constraint here, so fiscal policy issues can safely be ignored.

In period t the consumer chooses c_{1t}, c_{2t}, and M_t.

a. Setting up an appropriate Lagrangian, obtain the consumer's first-order conditions with respect to c_{1t}, c_{2t}, and M_t.

b. From the perspective of the Social Planner, what is the marginal rate of transformation (MRT) between credit goods and cash goods? Express this MRT as the number of additional cash goods the economy could produce if it produced one less credit good. Explain your logic carefully/clearly.

c. Suppose you are given that in the steady state of this economy, the representative consumer's MRS between cash and credit goods depends on the steady-state money growth rate g according to the expression

$$\frac{u_2}{u_1} = \frac{1+g}{2+2g-\beta}.$$

In this economy the government (policy maker) is able to achieve economic efficiency (in steady state) by setting the steady-state money growth rate g appropriately. What is the value of g the policy maker should choose in order to bring about economic efficiency? Briefly explain your logic.

d. If the optimal policy you found in part c is the Friedman rule, discuss (in no more than three succinct sentences!) why the Friedman rule is desirable here. If the optimal policy you found in part c is not the Friedman rule, discuss (in no more than three succinct sentences!) why the Friedman rule is not desirable here.

VI
LONG-RUN GROWTH ANALYSIS

Much of our study has been devoted to business cycle ups and downs around the long-run steady-state of an economy. Part VI focuses squarely on how and why long-run economic steady-states emerge.

Chapter 25 describes the seminal Solow growth framework. Chapter 26 then sketches the neoclassical growth framework. An important distinction between the Solow model and the neoclassical model is described in chapter 26. Importantly, the neoclassical growth model essentially brings us back full circle to the beginning of our studies because it creates the foundation from which "modern macroeconomic" frameworks first developed in the late 1970s and early 1980s.

25

Solow Growth Framework

Most of our study focuses on short-run macroeconomic fluctuations, rather than long-run growth. The basic growth framework is important because the heart of modern business cycle study is tightly connected with growth analysis. The Solow growth model (and later offshoots) has shaped the way economists approach both long-run growth issues and shorter run business cycle fluctuations.

Long-run growth is concerned with how an economy develops over long periods of time. From a utility-maximizing, or welfare-maximizing, perspective, the metric of development, in principle, should be something akin to "utils." This concept of an economic standard of living is, of course, a fiction, so it cannot be measured empirically.

Although it can be criticized on several fronts, the main empirical metric used to judge economic standards of living in an economy is real GDP per capita (i.e., GDP per person). Thus **economic growth** is measured as growth over long stretches of time in real GDP per capita.

For much of history there was essentially zero economic growth. Over the past two to three centuries, however, economic growth has been positive. Several reasons (this list is admittedly short) seem to be the Industrial Revolution,[1] the invention of the printing press, refrigerators, the development of personal computers, the widespread use of the Internet, and the concomitant ease of worldwide communication. Nonetheless, growth rates still vary widely from one region of the world to another, as well from one country to another.

There has been much debate about whether growth rates should imply convergence of real GDP per capita across countries. The idea of **convergence** is that over long periods of time, per-capita GDP should equalize across even widely differing countries, due to eventual technological diffusion. Evidence on convergence, however, has been mixed. Qualitatively, it seems many industrialized nations have indeed more or less converged to similar

---

1. This led the originators of the theory of communism, Karl Marx and Friedrich Engels, upon seeing such progress in London alongside wealthy entrepreneurs and juxtaposed poor workers, to be convinced that the whole system of nascent "capitalism" would collapse.

"standards of living." Yet many developing countries are stuck at far lower standards of living, despite some periods of "catch-up."

A caveat before developing the Solow framework. It is sometimes informally referred to as the "neoclassical growth model." However, this is formally not true. In the neoclassical growth model, savings *decisions* are determined by consumers' (or firms') optimality conditions. In the Solow model, there is no decision-making or "optimal choice" of savings; rather, the savings in which the economy engages is strictly a parameter.

We proceed as follows. First, the exogenous sources of growth are described. Next up is the manner by which inputs are transformed into output in the growing economy and how resources are saved over time. To obtain a solution, we have to **de-trend** the model, which itself is an inherent connection between growth analysis and business cycle analysis. After de-trending, we compute an analytical result for the long-run capital stock, and how it depends in natural ways on, among other things, aggregate savings propensities and technological innovations of different societies.

Solow Growth Model

A foundational model of economic growth is commonly attributed to Robert Solow in the 1950s. Many other innovators further helped shape the basic framework—as among them have Trevor Swan and Nicholas Kaldor, to name two—but Solow's continued development of the framework and future Nobel Prize cast him in the spotlight.

The Solow model takes a production-function approach to explain how per-capita real GDP increases over time. Figure 25.1 displays the exponential growth of per-person real GDP in the US economy since the National Income and Product Accounts (which is the GDP accounting expression, $GDP = C + I + G + NX$) began during the Great Depression. The population growth rate over the past century has averaged about 1.3 percent, which emphasizes that figure 25.1 shows per-person real GDP growth.

Applied to long-run analysis, the Solow framework is fundamentally *about how, why, and how quickly an economy accumulates physical capital.* There are a number of assumptions the framework makes (as does any framework) in studying the dynamics and implications of this model. Some of these assumptions can be rightly criticized as being too unrealistic. However, the model is extremely valuable in that it provides a useful benchmark for the performance of both other models of long-run growth as well as short-run fluctuations. Moreover a framework that both performs better and simpler to use has not been fleshed out in the more than half century since Solow's model became prominent.

Exogenous Sources of Growth

The total physical capital stock of an economy K and the total number of people N are the productive factors that in tandem construct total goods and services in the economy. The

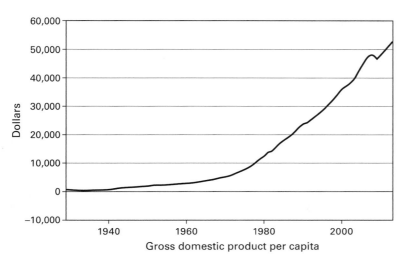

Figure 25.1
Real GDP per capita in the United States

total quantity of goods and services built in an economy *is* the definition of GDP, which is denoted by Y.[2]

The Solow framework asserts that *long-run growth factors are exogenous to the economy.* That is, they are *inputs* into the analysis, not *outputs* resulting from the analysis. There are various exogenous growth factors we could consider; we will focus on two.

One main exogenous source for economic growth is population growth gr_N, defined as

$$gr_N \equiv \frac{N_{t+1} - N_t}{N_t}\left(= \frac{N_{t+1}}{N_t} - 1\right),$$

in which N_t represents aggregate employment in period t.

Another input to economic growth is growth in the "productivity" of the economy. Broadly stated, "productivity" is how well or how easily the various factors of production mesh with each other in producing output. One example is that the knowledge and skills of employees are getting better over time. Another is that the quality of the physical machinery or computers or smartphones that one employee is working with to produce output is improving over time.

Based on these examples, productivity is fundamentally considered to be **labor-augmenting** or that the "effectiveness of labor" drives long-run growth. Because of

---

2. Two notes. First, K and Y are intentionally meant to be uppercase letters. Second, N can be interchangeably be interpreted as total number of people or total number of hours.

long-lasting improvements in technology or skills, one employee can produce more output as time marches on.

Whatever the various and many innovations over the decades have been, denote by X_t a worker's labor-augmenting productivity during time period t, and its growth rate gr_X, as

$$gr_X \equiv \frac{X_{t+1} - X_t}{X_t} \left(= \frac{X_{t+1}}{X_t} - 1 \right).$$

Both gr_N and gr_X are asserted to be constant for every time period, hence the lack of time subscripts. As mentioned above, in the US population growth rate has been roughly $gr_N = 0.013$ per year since 1900. In principle we could allow these percentage growth rates gr_N and gr_X to vary over time, but that would start to bring us into the realm of business cycle analysis, which is not necessary to study growth. Here our focus is on long-run growth, so we can purposely omit shorter run economic ups and downs.

Aggregate Production Function

The canonical production functional form for aggregate GDP is the Cobb–Douglas production function

$$Y_t = K_t^\alpha \left(X_t N_t \right)^{1-\alpha}$$

in which α, which is a number between 0 and 1, measures the "importance" of K in the production of GDP.[3] Consequently the number $1 - \alpha$, which also lies between 0 and 1, measures the "importance" of XN in the production of GDP.[4] The second argument XN is commonly known as **effective labor.** The Cobb–Douglas production function is a workhorse in both the study of long-run growth and business cycle fluctuations.

To understand the economic importance of α, consider the extreme case of $\alpha = 0$. In this case it is only worker's labor efforts that create GDP—an economy's production process is very **labor intensive** if α is close to zero. On the opposite extreme, $\alpha = 1$, labor efforts have virtually nothing to do with producing goods and services—this economy's GDP is essentially entirely produced with machines and factories and robots, thus the economy is very **capital intensive** because α is close to one.

Naturally, different economies display varying degrees of capital intensity. A widely accepted view is that the capital intensity of GDP production in advanced economies is $\alpha = 1/3$, which arises from econometric estimation for the United States and other developed economies. For the sake of generality, we will continue using the more general notation α.

---

3. Note that this is not at all the same concept of α as in the Keynesian macroeconometrics frameworks.

4. XN should not be confused with NX—the latter is the typical acronym for "net exports" (or, equivalently, the "trade balance").

This $Y_t = K_t^\alpha (X_t N_t)^{1-\alpha}$ form of writing the aggregate production function emphasizes a long-standing view that decades-long and centuries-long growth fundamentally occurs due to *labor-augmenting productivity*, which is the term X_t. Alternative terminology for X is *total factor productivity (TFP)* or the *Solow residual*.[5] We will use these three terms interchangeably.

Regardless of terminology, this constantly growing X_t is the centerpiece of Solow growth analysis. Difficult-to-measure changes in X_t over time could be thought of as a "measure of ignorance" about how various economies' inputs—which are K and N—yield output Y.[6]

Aggregate Savings and Aggregate Investment

The Solow model is a closed-economy structure, which implies that in the basic GDP accounting expression, we have $(GDP_t =) Y_t = C_t + I_t + G_t$. The GDP accounting equation is the resource frontier of the overall economy, which simply means that all goods produced—which is aggregate supply, the left-hand side of the accounting equation—are absorbed by one of the several expenditure components of aggregate demand (the right-hand side).

Government spending is not crucial for the analysis of the Solow framework, so let's simplify the resource constraint further to $Y_t = C_t + I_t$. Then, for ease of use below, let's rearrange it as

$$Y_t - C_t = I_t.$$

Next, using our definition of savings from the basic consumption–savings framework (recall the definition, $S_t = Y_t - C_t$), we have that economy-wide savings is the source of funding for economy-wide investment,

$$S_t = I_t,$$

which is simply due to accounting identities.

The Solow framework does *not* feature "optimizing" consumers or firms.[7] Thus *there is no "consumption–savings optimality condition" that pins down S_t.*

Instead, the Solow framework asserts that aggregate savings is a constant fraction s (be careful between uppercase S and lowercase s!) of GDP in each period. The relationship between the savings rate $s \in (0, 1)$ (the percentage of savings) and aggregate savings S_t is

---

5. An algebraic transformation allows us to equivalently express the production function as $Y_t = A_t \cdot K_t^\alpha N_t^{1-\alpha}$. The transformation to get from the X version to the A version is as follows: $Y_t = K_t^\alpha X_t^{1-\alpha} N_t^{1-\alpha} \rightarrow Y_t = X_t^{1-\alpha} \cdot K_t^\alpha N_t^{1-\alpha}$. Then define $A_t = X_t^{1-\alpha}$, which gets us to $Y_t = A_t \cdot K_t^\alpha N_t^{1-\alpha}$.

6. In *business cycle analysis*, this X term also arises and plays an important role, but Solow never intended for it to be a critical component of the study of short-run ups and downs.

7. Recall from our study of the history of macroeconomics, microeconomic-level optimization structures came into use for macroeconomic analysis after the Lucas critique of the late 1970s.

$S_t = s \cdot Y_t.$

Aggregate gross investment is defined as

$I_t = K_{t+1} - (1-\delta)K_t,$

in which $\delta \in (0, 1)$ stands for the rate of depreciation of capital K_t used in the period-t production process. It is natural that capital depreciates, or wears out, over time. Physical equipment, such as factories, engines, printers, and computer monitors, naturally wear down, or simply become obsolete, over time. This is the notion that is captured in the depreciation concept. The assumption of constant depreciation over time is a decent approximation to what empirical studies suggest is the annual rate of depreciation of the US capital stock, which is approximately 8 percent per year, hence $\delta = 0.08$ for the US economy at an annual frequency. The quantity of capital goods that depreciates during the production process of period t and thus can no longer be used in period $t + 1$ is δK_t.

Note the use of the word "gross" in the definition. If capital never depreciated—that is, if $\delta = 0$—then the definition above boils down to $I_t^{net} = K_{t+1} - K_t$, which is known as *aggregate net investment* (hence the superscript "net"). Thus $\delta = 0$ implies that $I_t = I_t^{net}$. Because capital gradually wears out during usage in the production process, $I_t > I_t^{net}$. Thus some portion of I_t is **replacement investment,** and the rest is directed toward accumulating the physical capital stock. Empirically it is gross investment I_t that is measured in the GDP accounts.

Equilibrium

To develop equilibrium for this model requires both using the relationships described in the previous section and normalizing, or **de-trending,** the framework in an appropriate manner.

First, using the relationship $S_t = s \cdot Y_t$, equating aggregate savings with aggregate gross investment gives

$I_t = s \cdot Y_t.$

Next, using the definition of aggregate gross investment to substitute for I_t, we have

$K_{t+1} - (1-\delta)K_t = s \cdot Y_t,$

an important expression to which we will soon return.

If the economy being analyzed displays nonnegative long-run growth (which is the perspective we adopt), $gr_N \geq 0$ and $gr_X \geq 0$ must both be true. In turn Y_t would grow explosively over the decades and centuries, as figure 25.1 suggests.

The Solow framework (indeed all of our macro frameworks) cannot handle "infinite" levels of GDP, or, for that matter, infinite quantities of consumption or savings or investment. The framework thus must be **normalized**, or scaled, in an appropriate manner. The appropriate scaling factor(s) is (are) the exogenous source(s) of growth. Referring to business cycle analysis, this process is exactly the de-trending procedure!

In our setup the two sources of growth are population and labor-augmenting productivity. Hence the appropriate scale factor in any given time period is $X \cdot N$. To perform the de-trending, let lowercase letters denote **per unit of effective labor** variables. Define

$$y_t \equiv \frac{Y_t}{X_t \cdot N_t} \text{ and } k_t \equiv \frac{K_t}{X_t \cdot N_t}$$

as GDP per unit of effective labor and capital per unit of effective labor, respectively. For ease of language from here on, we will refer interchangeably refer to "per unit of effective labor" as per capita.

Using the definitions of "per-capita" y_t and "per-capita" k_t, we can rewrite the GDP production function $Y_t = K_t^\alpha (X_t N_t)^{1-\alpha}$ in per-capita terms with a few algebraic steps. First, de-trend these variables, which gives us

$$\frac{Y_t}{X_t \cdot N_t} = \left(\frac{K_t}{X_t \cdot N_t}\right)^\alpha \left(\frac{X_t \cdot N_t}{X_t \cdot N_t}\right)^{1-\alpha}.$$

Next, use the definitions to rewrite as

$$y_t = k_t^\alpha \cdot 1^{1-\alpha}.$$

As in basic mathematics, $1^{1-\alpha} = 1$, so the aggregate production function is simply

$$y_t = k_t^\alpha.$$

This function expresses per-capita output as a function of the per-capita capital stock; it is illustrated in figure 25.2. A crucial point to notice is that because $\alpha < 1$, the production function displays diminishing marginal product in capital. Also illustrated in figure 25.2 is the per-capita savings function, which, in the Solow framework, is per-capita output times the savings rate $s \in (0, 1)$.

To analyze k in the Solow model, begin with $K_{t+1} - (1-\delta)K_t = s \cdot Y_t$, which first has to be stated in de-trended terms. Proceeding step by step with the algebra, first divide by $X_t N_t$, which gives

$$\frac{K_{t+1}}{X_t \cdot N_t} - (1-\delta)\frac{K_t}{X_t \cdot N_t} = s \cdot \frac{Y_t}{X_t \cdot N_t}.$$

Next substitute the y_t and k_t definitions into the right-hand side and the second term on the left-hand side, which leads to

$$\frac{K_{t+1}}{X_t \cdot N_t} - (1-\delta)k_t = s \cdot y_t,$$

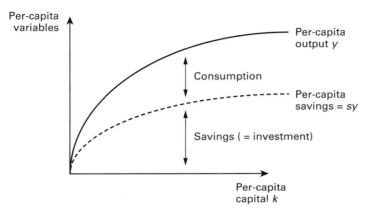

Figure 25.2
Decomposition of output y between savings for the future (the lower solid line) and immediate consumption.

or, if rewritten slightly using the per-capita production function $y_t = k_t^\alpha$,

$$\frac{K_{t+1}}{X_t \cdot N_t} - (1-\delta)k_t = s \cdot k_t^\alpha.$$

All of these terms are now normalized, with the important exception of the first expression on the left.

To de-trend $K_{t+1}/X_t \cdot N_t$, multiply and divide it by $X_{t+1} \cdot N_{t+1}$, so that the previous expression can be stated as

$$\left(\frac{K_{t+1}}{X_{t+1} \cdot N_{t+1}}\right) \cdot \left(\frac{X_{t+1} \cdot N_{t+1}}{X_t \cdot N_t}\right) - (1-\delta)k_t = s \cdot k_t^\alpha.$$

To continue proceeding, a couple of observations are required. First, the bracketed term $K_{t+1}/X_{t+1} \cdot N_{t+1}$ is simply k_{t+1} by definition! Second, notice that $N_{t+1}/N_t = 1 + gr_N$ reflects the population growth rate; similarly $X_{t+1}/X_t = 1 + gr_X$ reflects the growth rate of technology.

Inserting these definitions leads to

$$k_{t+1} \cdot (1 + gr_X) \cdot (1 + gr_N) - (1-\delta)k_t = s \cdot k_t^\alpha.$$

After two more steps of algebra, a final rewriting is

$$k_{t+1} = \frac{s \cdot k_t^\alpha}{(1 + gr_X) \cdot (1 + gr_N)} + \frac{(1-\delta)k_t}{(1 + gr_X) \cdot (1 + gr_N)},$$

which emphasizes k_{t+1} on the left-hand side. This expression is the **equilibrium law of motion for the (per-capita) capital stock k** in the Solow model.

The equilibrium law of motion is the heart of the framework. The law of motion states that for given values of s, α, gr_X, gr_N, and δ, the beginning of period-$t + 1$ capital stock k_{t+1} is completely determined by k_t. Figure 25.5, which we will consider at more length soon, plots the law of motion.

Long-Run Capital Stock

Figure 25.3 describes the steady-state equilibrium for the capital stock k. We can solve for steady-state $k*$ analytically, which is a powerfully sharp result of the Solow framework.[8] Several steps of algebra will get us there.

The most important step is to begin by imposing $k_{t+1} = k_t = k*$ in the law of motion. If the economy arrives at $k*$, then the equilibrium law of motion tells us that it will remain at $k*$ forever. Mathematically, a steady state is the condition at which an object stops evolving over time; dropping time subscripts is the way to operationalize a steady state.

Imposing steady state in the law of motion gives us

$$k^* = \frac{s \cdot \left(k^*\right)^{\alpha}}{(1 + gr_X) \cdot (1 + gr_N)} + \frac{(1 - \delta)k^*}{(1 + gr_X) \cdot (1 + gr_N)}.$$

The remainder of the algebra is to isolate the $k*$ term.

From this previous expression, subtract the second term on the right-hand side, which yields

$$k^* \cdot \left[1 - \frac{1 - \delta}{(1 + gr_X) \cdot (1 + gr_N)}\right] = \frac{s \cdot \left(k^*\right)^{\alpha}}{(1 + gr_X) \cdot (1 + gr_N)}.$$

The additive terms in square brackets can be combined, so we have

$$k^* \cdot \left[\frac{(1 + gr_X) \cdot (1 + gr_N) - (1 - \delta)}{(1 + gr_X) \cdot (1 + gr_N)}\right] = \frac{s \cdot \left(k^*\right)^{\alpha}}{(1 + gr_X) \cdot (1 + gr_N)}.$$

Next canceling the $(1 + gr_X) \cdot (1 + gr_N)$ terms allows us to simplify a bit to arrive at

$$k^* \cdot \left[(1 + gr_X) \cdot (1 + gr_N) - (1 - \delta)\right] = s \cdot \left(k^*\right)^{\alpha}.$$

Collecting the $k*$ terms on both the left-hand side and the right-hand side, and shifting the square-bracketed term to the right-hand side gives

$$\left(k^*\right)^{1-\alpha} = \frac{s}{(1 + gr_X) \cdot (1 + gr_N) - (1 - \delta)}.$$

8. The Solow framework in terms of growth analysis was impressive both in the 1950s and still today, and, since the 1980s, has been the foundation of modern business cycle analysis.

Box 25.1
Solow framework steady state k^*

$$k^* = \left[\frac{s}{(1+gr_X)\cdot(1+gr_N)-(1-\delta)}\right]^{1/(1-\alpha)}.$$

Finally, raise both sides of the expression to the power $1/(1-\alpha)$ to obtain the **analytic steady-state k^***, which is the main result of the Solow analysis, a result so crucial that it is highlighted in box 25.1.

This Solow steady-state expression for k^* contains several parts. To consider the basic economics, suppose that there is neither population growth nor technological growth, which means $gr_X = gr_N = 0$. Steady-state k^* in this case is

$$k^* = \left[\frac{s}{\delta}\right]^{1/(1-\alpha)},$$

which depends on the per-period savings rate s, the per-period depreciation rate δ, and the capital share α. It is clear from this expression that for a given capital share α, either an increase in s or a decrease in δ leads to a higher steady-state capital stock k^*.[9] In turn a larger value for steady-state GDP, $y^* = \left(k^*\right)^{\alpha}$, is achieved.

Stated in everyday terms, an increase in savings leads to an increase in wealth (wealth in this framework is the capital stock k). Left for you as exercises are further comparative statics of k^* (and hence of y^*, which, by definition of steady state, is also constant) with respect to the set of other parameters: $\{\alpha, gr_X, gr_N\}$.

Regardless of precise parameter values for $\{\alpha, gr_X, gr_N, s, \delta\}$, the phase diagram in figure 25.3 displays the steady-state equilibrium k^* as the intersection of the savings supply function and the **replacement investment demand function** (or, equivalently stated, the "break-even" investment demand function). In steady-state equilibrium, the quantity of replacement ("break-even") investment demanded is simply that required to replace depreciated capital (δk)—plus the additional per-capita resources for population growth ($gr_N k$), plus the additional per-capita resources for technological growth ($gr_X k$). If the economy achieves equilibrium k^*, there will be no further change in k.[10]

---

9. Stated mathematically, the steady-state elasticity of k^* with respect to s is strictly positive, and the steady-state elasticity of k^* with respect to δ is strictly negative.

10. In terms of differential equations (or the discrete time analogue we are considering here, which are difference equations), k^* is a stable steady state of the economy—once it reaches k^*, it will never depart from it. Unless, that is, some "shocks" cause it to, which is the point at which modern macroeconomic business cycle analysis begins.

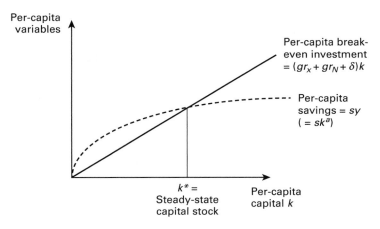

Figure 25.3
Intersection of savings function and break-even (alternatively, replacement) investment function determines the long-run (aka steady-state) level of physical capital.

Transitional Dynamics of Growth

The breakeven condition of the economy leads to a next natural question: If the economy is away from steady-state k^*, how, if at all, does it converge to k^*?

To consider convergence, we return to the full-fledged dynamic law of motion for the capital stock

$$k_{t+1} = \frac{s \cdot k_t^{\alpha}}{(1+gr_X)\cdot(1+gr_N)} + \frac{(1-\delta)k_t}{(1+gr_X)\cdot(1+gr_N)},$$

with time indexes explicitly included. The timeline in figure 25.4 is helpful for the analysis.

Consider an economy in period t—let's call it an "emerging economy"—that has $k_t < k^*$. The question to be answered is: Is k_{t+1} closer to k^* than k_t is, or is k_{t+1} further away from k^* than k_t is? In other words, is the economy moving **toward** its steady state or moving **away from** its steady state?

The mathematical details of the solution are left to a more advanced course.[11] In a nutshell, though, the law of motion answers the question: $k_{t+1} > k_t$; **thus k_{t+1} is closer to k^* than was k_t.** Repeating this logic forward, the law of motion informs us that $k_{t+2} > k_{t+1}$; **thus k_{t+2} is closer to k^* than was k_{t+1}.** Iterating the logic forward yet again, the law of motion tells us that $k_{t+3} > k_{t+2}$; **thus k_{t+3} is closer to k^* than was k_{t+2}.** And so on it goes **until the capital stock converges to k^*.**

---

11. The mathematics involves various stability theorems regarding difference equations.

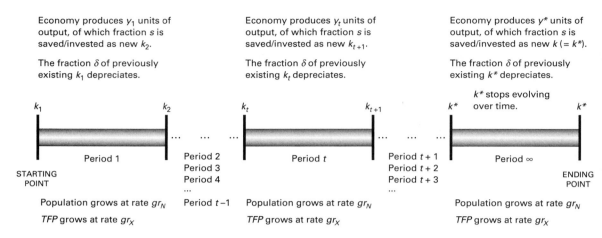

Figure 25.4
Timeline for dynamic long-run growth analysis. Eventually, the economy reaches the long-run (or steady-state) per-capita capital stock k^*.

The economics of convergence is due to the concavity of the production function (given that $\alpha \in (0, 1)$). The phase diagram in figure 25.5 conveys this point. Note carefully the axes in figure 25.5: k_t appears on the horizontal axis, and k_{t+1} appears on the vertical axis. Figure 25.5 is thus fundamentally about the **dynamic growth path** of the economy.

Figure 25.6 illustrates the same convergence idea in different coordinates. Figure 25.6 shows that if $k < k^*$, per-capita savings is larger than per-capita break-even investment. Hence the quantity of new capital produced is higher than that required for the break-even condition. The total stock of capital therefore rises. The mechanism by which the capital stock *decreases* until it hits steady state if it starts *above* k^* is analogous—the same logic simply operates in reverse.[12]

Shortcomings of the Solow Growth Model

One major shortcoming of the Solow model is that it predicts that each country eventually converges to steady state. If one believes that "mature" economies (United States, Western European economies, Japan, etc.) have all converged to their steady states, then we should observe identical per-capita capital stocks in all mature economies. But this is not what evidence shows.

One highly plausible modification to the theoretical model is to allow different countries to have different savings rates. That is, even if economies have the same production processes, perhaps one country has aggregate savings $= s_1 y$ and another has aggregate

12. You should work through this logic yourself.

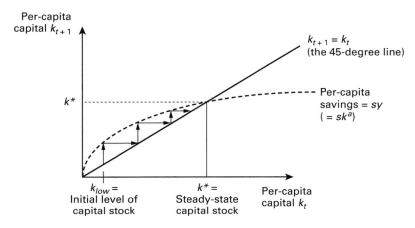

Figure 25.5
Dependence of k_{t+1} (vertical axis) on k_t (horizontal axis), as embodied in the equilibrium law of motion for capital k.

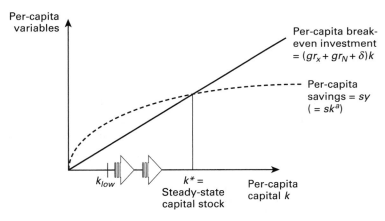

Figure 25.6
If k is below k^*, savings exceeds break-even investment, causing k to increase and converge toward k^*.

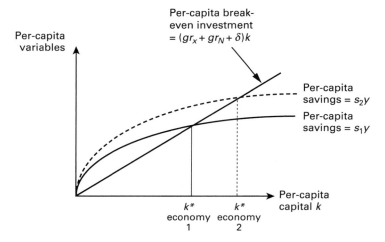

Figure 25.7
Different rates of savings. The economy with savings rate $s_2 > s_1$ converges to higher steady state per-capita k^*.

savings $= s_2 y$. As long as they both have the same depreciation rates (and growth rates of population and exogenous technological change), the steady-state levels of per-capita capital in the two economies will be different, as seen in figure 25.7. Referring back to figure 25.2, this implies different "propensities to consume" across economy 1 and economy 2. The economy with the lower propensity to consume—and hence the higher propensity to save—eventually reaches a higher value of steady-state per-capita capital and hence a higher value of per-capita GDP.

Another feature of the Solow model that could be extended is to allow for different depreciation rates of capital in different economies. It is left to you as an exercise to show that different values of δ across countries would imply different long-run capital stocks.[13]

Yet another seeming shortcoming of the model's predictions is the implication that economies eventually reach a state of zero growth. That is, once steady-state k^* is achieved, regardless of the precise savings rate s or other parameters $\{\alpha, gr_X, gr_N, \delta\}$, it seems there is no further economic growth: actual investment always equals break-even investment forever after convergence is achieved. Casual inspection of the diagrams in figure 25.5 or figure 25.6 confirms this.

The message, however, is more subtle. Diagrams such as figure 25.5 or figure 25.6 seem to show that growth eventually shrinks to zero. But recall that "per-capita" is a shorthand

---

13. Also left to you as an exercise is to show that different values across countries of either exogenous population growth gr_N or exogenous technological progress gr_X would imply different long-run per-capita capital stocks.

way of stating *per-effective units of labor*. In order to conduct our analysis, we de-trended the model by effective units of labor *XN*.

If we "reverse" the de-trending procedure that allowed for a finite value for *k**, we see that the overall, actual, economy being analyzed is experiencing positive growth as long as the population is growing or some relevant notion of productivity is growing.

Which of these two concepts of "growth" is more important—"per-capita growth," or "overall" growth—is left for the reader and future history to decide. But the universal consensus among economists is that *per-capita growth* is the notion that is of utmost importance.

Empirical consensus thus far indicates that most economists do not believe the United States has permanently stopped growing, despite the recent downturn. The population growth rate has been declining for several decades (i.e., gr_N, though positive, seems to be declining over the past several decades, which is not be confused with $gr_N < 0$).

The decline of the population growth rate implies that sustained long-run per-capita growth must be driven by the exogenous technological growth rate gr_X. The idea proposed by Solow was that there are some components of production, and hence economic growth, which are essentially impossible to quantify—a "measure of ignorance" of economists, if you will. One can, in principle, measure the quantity of machines, computers, trucks, airplanes, and so on, that are being put to productive purposes. Similarly one can measure the number of people employed.

Given these measures, if it turns out that k^α does not equal the measured quantity of goods and services *y,* then there is something else out there, some other valuable and productive "knowledge-based" input, that matters for sustainable growth.

What does this unknown productive input represent? Is it clean water supplies that are delivered unnoticed to your faucet? Is it the sudden emergence of refrigerators that allowed families to save food for the coming weeks? Is it the widespread use of automobiles that sprang up in the first half of the twentieth century? Is it the rapid adoption during the 1980s of the Microsoft Windows operating system? Or Apple's sheeny, have-to-have-it tech products? Or smartphones and smart-tablets? Perhaps it's the social networking that the smart-stuff enabled? Probably all of these.

But leaps in technology are hard to measure before they occur. Who could have predicted that Apple would make a big splash in the 1980s—and then would near bankruptcy in the 1990s—and then would a decade later magically take over a huge segment of the music industry and communications? Other than maybe Steve Jobs himself, probably very few.

Leaps in technology and innovation may be the prime "measure of ignorance" in the Solow model. But, once "technological advances" are input into the Solow model, these increases in productivity would rotate the production function up (in a nonparallel manner, because zero capital input would still yield zero output). An upward shift in the production function would then cause an upward shift in the savings function, *even if the savings RATE s does not change*. This can be seen in figure 25.8.

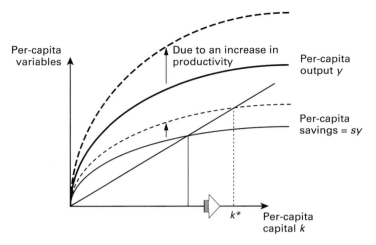

Figure 25.8
An increase in total factor productivity increases the total quantity of goods and services produced, holding fixed the break-even rate ($gr_X + gr_N + \delta$) and the savings rate s. In turn steady state k^* increases.

From the perspective of the Solow growth model, the primary reason for inexorable long-term economic growth, at least in mature economies, is continuing technological innovation. However, the Solow model does not have anything to say about *why* this ever-advancing technology occurs.

Endogenous growth theory attempts to address the "why" question. An overview of endogenous growth appears below. It is very brief, though, because the main thread of "macroeconomics"—which is business cycle analysis—is not based on endogenous growth.[14]

Endogenous Growth Theory (aka New Growth Theory)

The main focus of endogenous growth theory is to offer explanations to address the short-comings of the Solow model, namely that in the long run economic growth ceases—or, if growth continues, it occurs because of some unexplained change in the state of technology.

The main concept that endogenous growth theory applies to amend the Solow model is that there exist positive externalities[15] to innovation and research and development (R&D)

---

14. Indeed it has proved difficult so far for "mainstream" macroeconomic theory (in particular, when *shocks* are included in the framework) to be built on top of endogenous growth models. The profession still awaits an innovation on this.

15. You should be familiar with the notion of externalities from basic microeconomics.

activities. For example, when a firm develops a new method for writing software, it will benefit that firm directly because of increased sales and the customers of the firm will benefit because of the new product. However, other firms in the economy, simply by being exposed to the new ideas generated by the innovating firm, will also benefit. The exposure to new ideas will presumably enhance their design and manufacture, and so on, of new products—which in turn will help yet other consumers and lead to more ideas available for yet other firms to use.

The positive externalities stemming from knowledge accumulation will occur even if innovating firms are granted patents or copyrights for their inventions and development. A patent or copyright indeed grants certain rights to its holder—but it cannot prevent the dissemination of ideas through an economy, and it is ideas that fundamentally drive technological progress. Thus, in the language of the Solow growth model, the technology parameter X increases over time—implying positive economic growth even in the long run.

However, a firm, when deciding how much input to use in its R&D activities with the goal of creating new products or services, will not take into account the positive externalities of its innovations. In the language of the theory of externalities, the private (i.e., to the firm) marginal benefit from innovation is smaller than the social marginal benefit. Or, another way of stating this is that the private marginal cost of innovation is larger than the social marginal cost of innovation. Thus the amount of resources that a firm will use for research and development purposes will be smaller than the amount of resources that it *should* use *if* it cared about maximizing the welfare of the entire economy.[16]

The preceding discussion leads to a very important point: there is clearly a role for government intervention in promoting innovation. Provided that governments *do* care about maximizing the welfare of its citizens (even when private firms seek only to maximize their own profits), various policies can be implemented that encourage the socially optimal amount of innovation to occur. The most obvious in the context of the example above is for government to use public funds to subsidize research and development. Such a policy would have the effect of lowering the private marginal cost of research—which then induces the firm to engage in the socially optimal amount of research and development.

Because ideas can disseminate through the economy in the manner described, the original innovating firm cannot rest on its laurels. It will know that other firms will soon try to copy its products and enhance them—which will spur the original firm to continue developing new ideas. Thus, in this manner, the state of knowledge continually evolves.

---

16. Note that this does not imply that corporations are "evil"—they simply act to maximize their own private gain, which is what economics usually considers as the most rational goal.

Other ways that governments can encourage technical progress are through encouraging international trade and improving the quality and quantity of education. Again, both of these policies would expose domestic economic agents to more ideas (in the externality manner), which is the ultimate engine of economic growth.

Chapter 25 Problem Set Questions

1. **Comparative statics in the Solow model.** The steady-state (per-capita) equilibrium capital stock in the Solow model is

$$k^* = \left[\frac{s}{(1+gr_X)\cdot(1+gr_N)-(1-\delta)} \right]^{1/(1-\alpha)},$$

in which the exogenous parameters are the savings rate, $s \in (0,1)$, the capital deprecia-tion rate, $\delta \in (0,1)$, the elasticity of total per-capita output with respect to k, $\alpha \in (0,1)$, the net growth rate per period of population, gr_N, and the net growth rate per period of labor-augmenting technology, gr_X.

a. Compute the steady-state elasticity

$$\frac{\partial \ln k^*}{\partial \ln s}.$$

Is it strictly positive, strictly negative, strictly zero, or impossible to determine?

b. Compute the steady-state elasticity

$$\frac{\partial \ln k^*}{\partial \ln \delta}.$$

Is it strictly positive, strictly negative, strictly zero, or impossible to determine?

c. Compute the steady-state elasticity

$$\frac{\partial \ln k^*}{\partial \ln \alpha}.$$

Is it strictly positive, strictly negative, strictly zero, or impossible to determine?

d. Compute the steady-state elasticity

$$\frac{\partial \ln k^*}{\partial \ln gr_X}.$$

Is it strictly positive, strictly negative, strictly zero, or impossible to determine?

e. Compute the steady-state elasticity

$$\frac{\partial \ln k^*}{\partial \ln gr_N}.$$

Is it strictly positive, strictly negative, strictly zero, or impossible to determine?

2. **Growth and capital.** Suppose that two economies have completely identical s, δ, α, and gr_X, but economy 1 has a strictly larger gr_N than does economy 2. That is, $gr_N^{\text{economy } 1} > gr_N^{\text{economy } 2}$. Based on this information, which of the two economies has a larger steady-state (per-capita) equilibrium capital stock?

26

Neoclassical Growth

In the seminal Solow framework, the savings rate of the economy is an exogenous input parameter. While the *aggregate quantity of savings* of the economy is determined by the equilibrium condition that all savings are invested for the economy's future capital stock, the fraction of output that is devoted to savings (equivalently, investment) in the economy is not. The savings rate is determined neither by optimality conditions from consumers' utility maximization decisions nor by firms' profit maximization decisions.

In contrast, in the **neoclassical growth framework**, savings decisions are determined by consumers' optimality conditions. The savings rate is not an exogenous parameter of the economy; rather it is **endogenously** determined in the framework.

The notation is virtually identical to that in the Solow growth analysis, so, for the sake of brevity, is not described here. Also for the sake of brevity, we begin right away with de-trended variables, those that are denominated in "per effective units of labor." Thus, just as in the Solow framework, we can think of population growth or labor-augmenting productivity growth or any other source of exogenous growth "in the background" of our study here—"in the background" meaning it has been de-trended in all of the following analysis.

The timeline of events is the same as in the Solow model, with the important exception that the fraction s of output in any given time period is determined through a **consumption–savings optimality condition.** Indeed the following discussion has many connections with the basic consumptions–savings framework.

Neoclassical Growth Model

The neoclassical growth model is most often attributed to Ramsey (1928), Cass (1965), and Koopmans (1965). As stated above, all variables are denoted as per efficient units of labor, just as in our description of the Solow framework. Starting from the beginning of period 1, the objective function is to maximize present discounted value of lifetime utility,

$$\max_{\{c_t, k_{t+1}\}_{t=1}^{\infty}} \sum_{t=1}^{\infty} \beta^{t-1} u(c_t)$$

(in which the one-period-ahead subjective discount factor is $\beta \in (0,1)$), subject to the sequences of resource constraints of the economy

$$c_t + k_{t+1} - (1-\delta)k_t = k_t^\alpha,$$

for $t = 1, 2, 3, \ldots, \infty$. Constructing the Lagrange function should, at this stage of our studies, be straightforward.

The first-order conditions of the Lagrangian with respect to c_t and k_{t+1} are, respectively,

$$u'(c_t) - \lambda_t = 0$$

and

$$-\lambda_t + \beta\lambda_{t+1}(1 + \alpha k_{t+1}^{\alpha-1} - \delta) = 0,$$

for every time period $t = 1, 2, 3, \ldots, \infty$.

Inserting the expressions $u'(c_t) - \lambda_t = 0$ and $u'(c_{t+1}) - \lambda_{t+1} = 0$ (you should also recall from earlier the repeating, recursive patterns of the first-order conditions!) into the first-order condition with respect to k_{t+1} gives us

$$u'(c_t) = \beta u'(c_{t+1})(1 + \alpha k_{t+1}^{\alpha-1} - \delta).$$

Noticing that the term $\alpha k_{t+1}^{\alpha-1}$ is the marginal product of capital in period $t + 1$ (i.e., mpk_{t+1}), and dividing the entire expression through by $\beta u'(c_{t+1})$ gives us

$$\frac{u'(c_t)}{\beta u'(c_{t+1})} = 1 + \alpha k_{t+1}^{\alpha-1} - \delta.$$

This expression is the consumption–savings optimality condition across the two-period span of period t and period $t + 1$!

To remind ourselves, the left-hand side is the marginal rate of substitution (MRS) between period-t consumption and period-$(t + 1)$ consumption, and the right-hand side is the neoclassical growth model's appropriate $1 + r$ term. The appropriate $1 + r$ term here is the gross real return on physical capital, $1 + mpk_{t+1}$, net of the rate of wear and tear δ.

Equilibrium

Equilibrium (whether in the long run or the short run) occurs when aggregate savings equals aggregate investment, just as in the Solow growth framework. To obtain the long-run steady-state level of physical capital, all that is required is the steady-state expression of the consumption–savings optimality condition. Dropping time subscripts gives us

$$\frac{1}{\beta} = 1 + \alpha\left(k^*\right)^{\alpha-1} - \delta,$$

which must be solved for k^*. After a few steps of algebra (which, as always, you are encouraged to verify yourself), the *analytic steady-state k^* in the neoclassical growth framework* is

$$k_{neo}^* = \left[\frac{1}{\alpha} \cdot \left(\frac{1}{\beta} - (1 - \delta) \right) \right]^{1/(\alpha - 1)}.$$

How does this compare to the long run k^* that emerged from the Solow framework? To try to make the comparison as simple as possible, suppose that there is zero technology growth ($gr_X = 0$) and zero population growth ($gr_N = 0$). In this case the long-run Solow k^* is

$$k_{Solow}^* = \left[\frac{s}{\delta} \right]^{1/(1 - \alpha)},$$

in which the s term in the numerator of the right-hand side is the exogenous savings rate of the economy.

It is difficult to directly compare the k_{neo}^* and k_{Solow}^* expressions. The latter contains the savings rate s, whereas k_{neo}^* does not; the k_{neo}^* expression contains the subjective discount factor β, but the k_{Solow}^* expression doesn't. So let's instead proceed by considering the flip side of savings, which is consumption.

To obtain c^* in the neoclassical framework, insert the k_{neo}^* expression above into the steady-state resource constraint to arrive at

$$c^* + k^* - (1 - \delta)k^* = \left(k^* \right)^{\alpha}.$$

Solving for c^* from this expression (which admittedly takes several steps of algebra) gives

$$c_{neo}^* = \left[\frac{1}{\alpha} \cdot \left(\frac{1}{\beta} - (1 - \delta) \right) \right]^{\alpha/(\alpha - 1)} + \delta \cdot \left[\frac{1}{\alpha} \cdot \left(\frac{1}{\beta} - (1 - \delta) \right) \right]^{1/(\alpha - 1)}.$$

Obtaining c^* in the Solow model is quite a bit easier, due to the exogenous savings rate s. Start with the steady-state resource constraint, $c^* + \delta k^* = \left(k^* \right)^{\alpha}$. The aggregate quantity of savings in the Solow framework is $\delta k^* = s \cdot \left(k^* \right)^{\alpha} = s \cdot y^*$, which then allows us to rewrite the resource constraint as $c^* + s \cdot y^* = y^*$. Isolating steady-state c^* gives us

$$c_{Solow}^* = (1 - s) \cdot y^*.$$

This expression makes clear that if the savings rate were 100 percent ($s = 1$) in the Solow framework, all output produced in the economy would be saved for the future, which implies that *zero-consumption* activity occurs. The zero-consumption result also occurs for a savings rate of s that creeps down toward zero: if no resources are saved/invested for production purposes, then very little long-run consumption occurs. But for intermediate ranges of s between 0 and 100 percent, long-run consumption is positive.

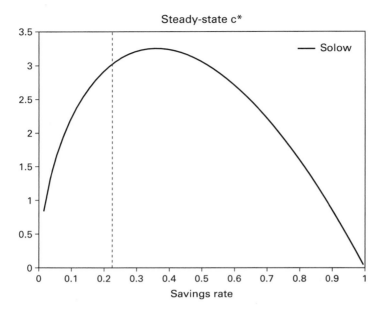

Figure 26.1
Long-run relationship between consumption and the savings rate in the Solow framework (curved) and in the neoclassical framework (vertical line). The underlying parameter values are $\delta = 0.08$, $\alpha = 0.36$, and $\beta = 0.96$.

Figure 26.1 illustrates the economics. The horizontal axis displays the savings rate of the economy, and the vertical axis displays steady-state c^*. An important takeaway point is that long-run consumption in the Solow framework is larger than long-run consumption in the neoclassical framework. Stated more precisely, the savings rate s, and hence the consumption rate $(1 - s)$ do not reflect any optimization on the part of the economy. Zooming in even further, there is no notion of a consumption–savings optimality condition in the Solow framework.

In contrast, the solid vertical line in figure 26.1 reflects the consumption–savings optimality condition that is inherent in the neoclassical growth model. For the numerical parameter values mentioned in the caption, the endogenous savings rate computed in the neoclassical setup turns out to be roughly $s = 0.24$, which in turn implies that $c^*_{neo} < c^*_{Solow}$. The long-run c^*_{neo} reflects **lifetime utility maximization**, whereas none of the c^*_{Solow} values do.

The Importance of "Impatience"

A next natural issue is that the endogenous long run c^*_{neo} depends on the numerical values of the depreciation rate δ, the importance of capital in the production process α, and the economy's "impatience" β across time periods.

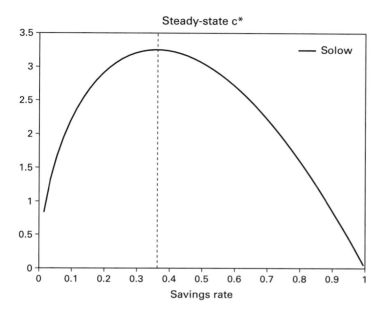

Figure 26.2
Long-run relationship between consumption and the savings rate in the Solow framework (curved) and in the neoclassical framework (vertical line). The underlying parameter values are $\delta = 0.08$, $\alpha = 0.36$, and $\beta \to 1$.

Of these three parameters, the most critical is the subjective discount factor β. If we allow β to tend toward one, then the neoclassical framework's optimal savings rate coincides with the Solow exogenous savings rate that maximizes c^*. This is illustrated in figure 26.2. The economics behind the $\beta \approx 1$ neoclassical case is that consumers do not care about the "time dimension" in their lifetime preferences.

Coming full circle, it is the neoclassical growth model that is the heart of modern macroeconomic analysis. For example, take a stark view of the neoclassical growth framework that lasts only "two periods." If we can swallow that, this *is exactly the two-period consumption–savings framework.*

VII
UNEMPLOYMENT

Part VII enriches the competitive labor-market structure by introducing a search-and-matching framework.

Chapter 27 extends the basic consumption–leisure framework and the firm profit-maximization analysis to include matching and probabilities of forming a job match, all within a one-period static framework.

Chapter 28 uses the optimality conditions from chapter 27 to consider how "markets clear" and shows that "wages" may not play as an important role as in competitive labor markets.

Chapter 29 extends the static search-and-matching framework to a multi-period framework to allow for both long-lasting jobs and a re-think about "how" wages are determined.

27

Search, Unemployment, and Vacancies

In the basic consumption–leisure framework, the representative individual is always employed. Stated in terms of probabilities, there is a 100 percent probability that the representative individual has a job. The concept of "labor supply" for the individual in chapter 2 is the **number of hours** during a given time period the individual optimally spends in market work. Optimal labor supply for the individual is characterized by the consumption–leisure optimality condition.

Similarly the baseline representative firm in chapter 6 is able to hire individuals for its jobs with 100 percent probability. The concept of "labor demand" for the firm is the **number of hours** during a given time period the firm optimally wants an individual to work. Optimal labor demand is characterized via firm profit maximization. However, there is no scope for unemployment in this "standard" framework.

The 2010 Nobel Prize in Economics was awarded to Peter Diamond, Dale Mortensen (who recently passed away), and Christopher Pissarides for their development (during the 1970s and 1980s) of **search-and-matching theory.** Search-and-matching theory is a framework especially suited for studying labor market issues. The search framework builds on, but is richer than, the basic concepts of "labor supply" and "labor demand." Search analysis can be applied to both the supply side of the labor market—building on the basic consumption–labor analysis—and the demand side of the labor market—building on basic firm analysis.

There are three basic ideas underlying search theory. First, search theory incorporates into basic supply-and-demand analysis the fact that when an individual chooses to spend time searching for a job (i.e., "supplies labor"), there is a chance that employment may not be found. That is, an individual "searching" for a job has a **probability less than one** that a suitable "match" will be found.

Second, as a direct consequence of the probabilistic nature of successfully finding a job, there is a **probability larger than zero** that an individual might end up "unemployed"— that is, having searched for work but not found anything. The usual outcome here is that he receives "unemployment benefits" from the government.

Third, search theory makes explicit the **costs associated with search activity.** As is realistic, when an individual wants a job, he/she does not simply "go to the market" as in basic supply-and-demand analysis. Rather, the individual must expend resources searching for a job (think of these costs as due to the time spent looking at recruiting advertisements through various web and networking channels, at career fairs, going through the interviewing process, etc.).

All of these ideas apply to firms as well. It takes time and effort for managers and the human resources departments of companies to, first, decide whether or not to try to hire somebody, and, second, go out and announce their job openings through various channels like Monster.com and promote their companies' fabulous jobs at job fairs, and so on.

We will incorporate these ideas into the one-period consumption–labor framework of chapter 2, thereby enriching the range of predictions that it can generate and policy or regulatory advice it may be able to offer. Likewise we will also introduce these concepts into basic firm profit theory.

Measuring Labor Markets

We saw figure 27.1 earlier, at the very end of the consumption–labor framework. The consumption–labor framework bundles together the categories of "unemployed" and "outside the labor force" in one category named "leisure."

The search-and-matching framework layers in a different, but crucial, "bundling," that of **individuals in the labor force** versus those that are outside the labor force. The labor force is defined as

Labor force ≡ (# of people employed)
           + (# of people unemployed AND actively searching for a job)

and, in turn, the **unemployment rate** is defined as

$$\text{Unemployment rate} \equiv \frac{\text{\# of people unemployed AND actively look for work}}{\text{Labor force}}.$$

More precisely, the standard definition of "unemployment" is individuals who are actively searching for work but are unsuccessful in finding a job. Figure 27.2 shows the US unemployment rate during the past forty years. As is clear, unemployment in the aggregate swings up and down quite a bit. The low point of roughly 4 percent unemployment was reached in the late 1990s and early 2000s. Unemployment highs were reached during the sharp recessions in the mid-1970s and early 1980s, and in the recent Great Recession.

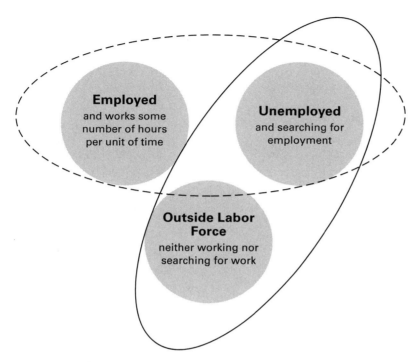

Figure 27.1
Three categories of people regarding labor market status. In the basic consumption–labor framework, unemployed individuals and individuals outside the labor force (the solid-circled categories) were considered to be in "leisure" activities. The search-and-matching framework considers employed individuals and unemployed individuals to be in the "labor force."

Representative Consumer

Recalling the definition of time spent in "leisure," it is the time an individual spends not working. There are many components of "nonwork." A few categories of "nonwork" are time spent visiting friends, time spent watching TV, time spent asleep, time spent cooking, time spent taking care of children, and time spent shopping.[1]

Another category is **time spent searching for a job.** This category is important for labor-market analysis. The goal of this section is to insert this category into the otherwise basic consumption–labor framework.

To do so, we will have to slightly re-think the utility function in order to include the idea of unemployment into our framework. Let's first define the following notation:

---

1. The ATUS (American Time Use Survey) conducted annually by the Bureau of Labor Statistics measures the amount of time people spend doing various activities, such as market work, childcare, volunteering, and socializing. Easy-to-read ATUS data are available at http://www.bls.gov/tus/.

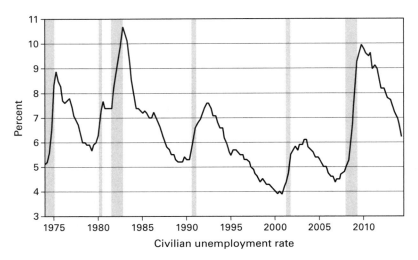

Figure 27.2
Unemployment rate in United States during past forty years

Notation	Definition
s	Amount of time spent searching for a job
p^{FIND}	Probability that a unit of time searching for a job finds suitable employment; by the definition of probability, $p^{FIND} \in [0, 1]$ (i.e., the probability is a number between zero and one). Hence the probability of not finding a job is $1 - p^{FIND}$. (Note: p^{FIND} does not denote a "price.")
n^s	Amount of time spent working in the market
$(1 - p^{FIND})s$	Unsuccessful searchers, who are classified as "unemployed"
ue	Unemployed searchers. (Note: $ue = (1 - p^{FIND})s$.)
lfp	Number of individuals in labor force. (Note: $lfp = (1 - p^{FIND})s + n^s$)

With this notation (some of which we will emphasize and define again as we proceed), the unemployed are $\left(1 - p^{FIND}\right) \cdot s$, which denotes **unsuccessful search time**, and the **unemployment rate** (due to the "one unit of time available" assertion back in the consumption–labor model, an assumption that is maintained here) in the framework is also $\left(1 - p^{FIND}\right) \cdot s$.

Next, asserting that "unemployment" leads to a decrease in individuals' utility in exactly the same way as "time spent in market work," n^h, does, the utility function can now be expressed as

$$u(c) - h\left(\left(1 - p^{FIND}\right)s + n^s\right),$$

which is a generalized version of the utility function considered in the standard consumption–labor model. In particular, the generalization is inside the $h(.)$ component of the utility function.[2]

Given this generalized utility function, a next natural and realistic idea is to suppose that the government provides unemployment benefits for each unemployed unit of time. The total quantity of unemployment benefits received would therefore be $(1 - p^{FIND}) \cdot s \cdot b$, in which b stands for the quantity (in terms of real goods) of benefits. We will temporarily include these government-provided unemployment benefits but soon will set them to $b = 0$ for two reasons. First, the "choice" of unemployment transfers is often a political economy or political science issue, not necessarily a direct economic issue. Second, when we begin considering "market clearing," $b = 0$ will simplify the algebra and more easily shed economic insight.

Including these unemployment benefits, the representative consumer's budget constraint is

$$c = (1-t)wn^s + (1 - p^{FIND})s \cdot b,$$

in which t is the labor income tax rate, and the relationship between n^s and s is

$$n^s = p^{FIND}s.$$

Observe that we could insert this $n^s = p^{FIND}s$ expression directly into the utility function stated above. If we did so, we have $u(c) - h((1 - p^{FIND})s + p^{FIND}s)$, which obviously simplifies to $u(c) - h(s)$.

However, let's not take this shortcut, because in a richer version of the search-and-matching framework considered in a couple of chapters, it will be helpful to consider $n^s = p^{FIND}s$ as a second constraint on the representative consumer's optimization. This second constraint is known as the **job-finding constraint.**

Given this, the next step is to construct the Lagrangian, in which two constraints appear, the budget constraint and the job-finding constraint, each with its own Lagrange multiplier. The Lagrangian is

$$u(c) - h((1 - p^{FIND})s + n^s) + \lambda^h[(1-t)wn^s + (1 - p^{FIND})s \cdot b - c] + \mu^h[p^{FIND}s - n^s],$$

in which λ^h is the Lagrange multiplier on the budget constraint and μ^h is the Lagrange multiplier on the job-finding constraint.

Based on the Lagrangian, the three first-order conditions with respect to c, n^s, and s are

$$u'(c) - \lambda^h = 0,$$

2. For simplicity of the mathematics below, this is an additively separable utility function between c and $(1 - p^{FIND}) \cdot s$. If we had considered the slightly more difficult to handle nonseparable functional form $u(c, (1 - p^{FIND}) \cdot s + n^s)$, all of the results described below would be identical.

$$-h'\left(\left(1-p^{FIND}\right)s+n^s\right)+\lambda^h(1-t)w-\mu^h=0,$$

$$-h'\left(\left(1-p^{FIND}\right)s+n^s\right)\cdot\left(1-p^{FIND}\right)+\lambda^h\left(1-p^{FIND}\right)b+\mu^h p^{FIND}=0.$$

After several steps of algebra (which you are encouraged to step through[3]) to eliminate the two multipliers λ^h and μ^h across all three of these conditions, we have a preliminary version of an optimality condition that is important in the framework,

$$\frac{h'\left(\left(1-p^{FIND}\right)s+n^s\right)}{u'(c)}=p^{FIND}\cdot(1-t)\cdot w+(1-p^{FIND})\cdot b.$$

As noted above, the standard empirical measure of the "labor force" is labor force = people unemployed and actively searching + people employed . Using our notation for s and p^{FIND}, we can thus define **labor force participation (LFP)** in our framework as

$$lfp\equiv\left(1-p^{FIND}\right)\cdot s+n^s.$$

Inserting this definition of lfp into the $h'(\cdot)$ marginal utility function on the left-hand side of the "preliminary version" above leads to a clean expression of the **consumption–LFP optimality condition**

$$\frac{h'(lfp)}{u'(c)}=p^{FIND}\cdot(1-t)\cdot w+(1-p^{FIND})\cdot b.$$

The economic interpretation of the consumption–LFP optimality condition is important. For every unit of time devoted to the labor force, there is a probability p^{FIND}, which is taken as given, that a job is found. In this case the benefit is the after-tax wage, $(1-t)\cdot w$. Alternatively, there is a probability $1-p^{FIND}$ that a job is not found, in which case the benefit is the unemployment payment b.

The consumption–LFP optimality condition is the matching framework's analog of the standard consumption–labor optimality condition. To recover the standard consumption–labor optimality condition, set $b=0$ (because there is no notion of "unemployment benefits" in our simpler framework) and set $p^{FIND}=1$ (because everyone trivially "finds a job" in that simpler framework). The consumption–LFP optimality condition then simplifies to $h'\left(n^s\right)/u'(c)=(1-t)\cdot w$, which is the standard consumption–labor optimality condition.

---

3. A sketch of the algebra is to take the second FOC and isolate the multiplier on the job-finding constraint, which gives $\mu^h=-h'(.)+\lambda^h(1-t)w$. Next, observe that multiplying this expression by p^{FIND} yields an intermediate expression $\mu^h p^{FIND}=-p^{FIND}h'(.)+p^{FIND}\lambda^h(1-t)w$, which is now highly comparable to the third FOC due to the $\mu^h p^{FIND}$ terms. Equating this intermediate expression with the third FOC gives us $-p^{FIND}h'(.)+p^{FIND}\lambda^h(1-t)w=h'(.)(1-p^{FIND})-\lambda^h(1-p^{FIND})b$. Simplifying slightly by adding $p^{FIND}h'(.)$ to both sides gives us $p^{FIND}\lambda^h(1-t)w=h'(.)-\lambda^h(1-p^{FIND})b$, and then adding the $\lambda^h(1-p^{FIND})b$ to both sides yields $p^{FIND}\lambda^h(1-t)w+\lambda^h(1-p^{FIND})b=h'(.)$. At this point, the final couple of steps of algebra should be apparent.

The consumption–LFP optimality condition thus **nests** the basic consumption–labor optimality condition. That is, the former is a more generalized concept of the latter. Given this generalization, the consumption–LFP optimality condition can be thought of as the **labor supply function** in the matching framework, highly analogous to the labor supply function in baseline consumption–leisure framework.

Representative Firm

On the other side of the labor market, firms have to pay a proportional **recruiting cost** for each "job advertisement" it posts. More broadly, this recruiting cost could be thought of as a "hiring cost." Depending on the particular categories and subcategories of hiring costs used to measure its prevalence in the overall economy, recruiting costs can comprise roughly 1 to 5 percent of total GDP, which is a sizable share.[4]

In our framework, each job advertisement—equivalently referred to as a **job vacancy** or a **job opening**—costs the firm ω (greek lowercase letter "omega") units. Thus total recruiting costs for the firm is $\omega \cdot vac$. The firm's operating profits are

$$A \cdot f\left(n^D\right) - w \cdot n^D - \omega \cdot vac,$$

in which A stands for productivity and $f(\cdot)$ denotes the production function. Each vacancy posted has a probability smaller than one of successfully attracting an applicant who is searching for a job. Denote this probability as q^{FIND}. Thus total labor actually hired by the firm is $n^D = q^{FIND} \cdot vac$, which is a constraint the firm faces in its profit maximization. This constraint is known as the **job-hiring constraint.**

The Lagrangian for firm profit maximization is thus

$$A \cdot f\left(n^D\right) - w \cdot n^f - \omega \cdot vac + \mu^f \left(q^{FIND} \cdot vac - n^D\right),$$

in which μ^f denotes the Lagrange multiplier on the representative firm's job-hiring constraint. The FOCs with respect to n^D and vac are, respectively,

$$A \cdot f'\left(n^D\right) - w - \mu^f = 0$$

and

$$-\omega + \mu^f \cdot q^{FIND} = 0.$$

Isolating the μ^f term from the FOC with respect to vac yields $\mu^f = \omega/q^{FIND}$. Inserting this expression for the multiplier into the FOC with respect to n^f gives the **job creation condition**

---

4. Some categories are managerial decisions on whether or not to hire a new person or several people to take over a job a previous senior employee had just stepped down from, informing the human resources department so that they can post the job openings in appropriate and visible locations, visiting college career fairs, interviewing potential job candidates, and so on. Each of these steps takes costly time and effort.

$$\frac{\omega}{q^{FIND}} = A \cdot f'\left(n^D\right) - w.$$

Slightly re-expressing this condition (after multiplying both sides by q^{FIND}), we have

$$\omega = q^{FIND} \cdot \left(A \cdot f'\left(n^D\right) - w\right),$$

which has a clear economic interpretation in terms of marginal costs and marginal benefits. Any given job advertisement costs ω units. Its probability of success in attracting an individual who would be hired is q^{FIND}. Then the firm's payoff is the employee's net payoff, $A \cdot f'\left(n^D\right) - w$, the employee's marginal productivity net of the wage paid to the employee. The job creation condition is the search-and-matching framework's analogue of the standard labor demand function.

Preview of "Market Clearing"

Summarizing, the labor supply function is described by $h'\left(lfp\right)/u'(c) = p^{FIND} \cdot (1-t) \cdot w + (1-p^{FIND}) \cdot b$ and labor demand is characterized by $\omega = q^{FIND} \cdot \left(A \cdot f'\left(n^D\right) - w\right)$.

As in a "standard" labor-market analysis, the real wage w appears in both of these expressions. The market probabilities p^{FIND} and q^{FIND} are also taken as given. The natural next step is to isolate the w terms from each expression and then hook them together. Let's proceed and see how much progress we make with this "standard" methodology.

To ease both the algebra and the economic interpretations somewhat, let's first suppose that unemployment benefits $b = 0$ and the tax rate $t = 0$. With these two simplifications, a couple of steps of algebra allow us to rewrite the consumption–LFP optimality condition as

$$\frac{h'(lfp)}{u'(c)} \cdot \frac{1}{p^{FIND}} = w$$

and the vacancy posting expression as

$$w = A \cdot f'\left(n^D\right) - \frac{\omega}{q^{FIND}}.$$

Observe that if recruiting costs were $\omega = 0$ and the probabilities were $p^{FIND} = q^{FIND} = 1$, equating these two expression provides us the market-clearing condition $h'(n)/u'(c) = A \cdot f'(n)$, which is identical to the standard $MRS_{c,n} = mpn$ labor-market equilibrium expression, in which the left-hand side describes labor supply and the right-hand side describes labor demand. Due to the market clearing, we can now use $n = n^s = n^D$.

If $\omega > 0$, equating the two expressions gives us

$$\frac{h'(ue+n)}{u'(c)} \cdot \frac{1}{p^{FIND}} = A \cdot f'(n) - \frac{\omega}{q^{FIND}}.$$

Once again, keep in mind that $n = n^s = n^D$, so this expression describes in effect **matching-market clearing**. That is, the quantity of **matched** labor supply equates with the quantity of **matched** labor demand. The term "matched" is important because the nature by which markets clear is somewhat different than in standard markets, to which we'll soon arrive.

Given $\omega > 0$, in order to continue to solve for equilibrium n based on the expression above, we will need functional forms for the production function $f(n)$ and for the utility function, the additively subcomponents of which are $u(c)$ and $h(lfp)$.

We can do all this but, as we will see next, there is another concept of "market-clearing" in the search-and-matching framework that does not necessarily have to do with "wage adjustments."

Chapter 27 Problem Set Questions

1. **Search, unemployment, and matching.** Continue to use the terminology:

    s: amount of time spent searching for a job

    p^{FIND}: probability that a unit of time spent searching for a job results in suitable employment. By definition, $p^{FIND} \in [0, 1]$ (i.e., the probability is a number between zero and one). Hence the probability of not finding a job is $1 - p^{FIND}$. (Note: p^{FIND} does not denote a "price.")

    b: "unemployment benefit" received by each unsuccessful searcher (refer to the budget constraint below to see this more clearly).

    The representative individual's utility function is

    $$\ln c - \ln\left(\left(1 - p^{FIND}\right) \cdot s + n^s\right),$$

    the budget constraint is

    $$c = p^{FIND} \cdot (1-t) \cdot w \cdot n^s + \left(1 - p^{FIND}\right) \cdot s \cdot b,$$

    and the job-finding constraint is

    $$n^s = p^{FIND} s.$$

    The job-finding constraint was not included in the chapter 2 framework but is important in describing the possibility of failing to find a job—that is, the possibility of unemployment.

    The Lagrangian for the consumer's optimization is

$$\ln c - \ln\left(\left(1 - p^{FIND}\right)s + n^s\right) + \lambda\left[p^{FIND} \cdot (1-t) \cdot w \cdot n^s + \left(1 - p^{FIND}\right) \cdot s \cdot b - c\right]$$
$$+ \mu\left[p^{FIND}s - n^s\right],$$

in which λ stands for the Lagrange multiplier on the budget constraint and μ stands for the Lagrange multiplier on the job-finding constraint (i.e., there are now two constraints on the representative consumer's best choices).

a. Based on the Lagrangian given above, compute the first-order condition (FOC) with respect to c.

b. Based on the Lagrangian given above, compute the first-order condition (FOC) with respect to n^s.

c. Based on the Lagrangian given above, compute the first-order condition (FOC) with respect to s.

d. Based on the three FOCs you computed above, construct this framework's "consumption–labor optimality condition." Your final solution *cannot* include any Lagrange multipliers in it (i.e., both λ and μ must be eliminated). Furthermore the final boxed expression should contain on the right-hand side only terms involving p^{FIND}, t, w, and b (i.e., there should be no terms involving c, n^s, or s on the right-hand side of this final boxed expression). Display fully the mathematical steps/algebraic procedure by which you obtained the final expression.

All the remaining parts of problem 1 are based on the optimality condition obtained in part d.

e. Starting from the "consumption–labor optimality condition" you obtained in part d, suppose for part e only that $p^{FIND} = 1$. With $p^{FIND} = 1$, how does your solution in part d compare to the "consumption–labor optimality condition" (aka, "consumption–leisure optimality condition") in chapter 2? Describe briefly in both mathematical terms and terms of economics. (Note: "Economics" does not mean restating verbally the mathematics.)

f. Return to the case that $p^{FIND} < 1$ but, for part f only, suppose that unemployment benefits are $b = 0$. With $p^{FIND} < 1$ and $b = 0$, how does your solution in part d compare to the "consumption–labor optimality condition" (aka, "consumption–leisure optimality condition") in chapter 2? Describe briefly in both mathematical terms and in terms of economics. (Note: "Economics" does not mean restating verbally the mathematics.)

For the remainder of problem 1, return to the case in which $p^{FIND} < 1$ and $b > 0$.

The US Bureau of Labor Statistics' (BLS) definition of "labor force participation" is

$$lfp = (1 - p^{FIND})s + n^s.$$

g. Substitute this BLS expression for *lfp* into the "consumption–labor optimality condition" you obtained in part d.

h. Using the expression you obtained in part g, qualitatively sketch a diagram that contains p^{FIND} on the vertical axis and *lfp* on the horizontal axis. (Note: All that matters for the qualitative diagram is whether the function is upward-sloping, downward-sloping, completely horizontal, or completely vertical.)

i. Provide a brief economic interpretation for the diagram drawn in part h. (Note: "Economic interpretation" does not mean restating verbally the mathematics.)

j. How does an increase in unemployment benefits *b* qualitatively affect the diagram drawn in part h? (Note: All that matters for this qualitative analysis is whether the function shifts outward, shifts inward, or doesn't shift at all.)

k. Provide a brief economic interpretation for your analysis in part j. (Note: "Economic interpretation" does not mean restating verbally the mathematics.)

2. Hiring, job openings, and matching. Let's reconsider the representative firm's profit-maximization framework chapter 6 in a few ways.

First, let's think in terms of one period, rather than the two-period analysis in chapter 6.

Second, suppose that the physical capital stock is $k = 1$. (Note: No time subscripts are needed because the analysis that follows is entirely within "one period" of time.)

Third, despite the seeming lack of importance of physical capital, there is still diminishing marginal product of labor in the representative firms' production function. The production function is

$$f\left(n^{D}\right)=\left(n^{D}\right)^{1-\alpha},$$

in which $\alpha \in (0, 1)$ and n^{D} denotes labor demand.

Fourth, in addition to the notation from chapter 6 (in which *c* denotes consumption, n^{s} denotes labor supply, *t* stands for the labor income tax rate, and *w* denotes the real wage), we now introduce the following:

vac: quantity of job openings (aka job vacancies)

q^{FIND} : probability that a job opening (aka job vacancy) delivers a suitable employee. By the definitions of probabilities, $q^{FIND} \in [0, 1]$ (i.e., the probability is a number between zero and one). Hence the probability of not finding a job is $1 - q^{FIND}$. (Note: q^{FIND} does not denote a "quantity.")

ω: (Greek lowercase letter "omega") cost incurred by the firm to "advertise" each job opening (aka job vacancy). Think of this as the time and money that managers and the human resources (HR) department would spend in an attempt to hire a new employee. (Refer to the profit function below to see this cost more clearly.)

The representative firm's profit function is

$$A \cdot f\left(n^{D}\right) - w \cdot n^{D} - \omega \cdot vac,$$

in which $A > 0$ represents "total factor productivity," w is the real wage, and the job-hiring constraint is

$$n^{D} = q^{FIND} vac.$$

The job-hiring constraint was not included in the chapter 6 framework, but it is important in describing the possibility of not being able to hire a new employee for a job.

The Lagrangian for the firm's optimization is

$$A \cdot \left(n^{D}\right)^{1-\alpha} - w \cdot n^{D} - \omega \cdot vac + \mu \cdot \left[q^{FIND} \cdot vac - n^{D}\right],$$

in which μ stands for the Lagrange multiplier on the job-hiring constraint.

a. Based on the Lagrangian given above, compute the first-order condition (FOC) with respect to n^{D}.

b. Based on the Lagrangian given above, compute the first-order condition (FOC) with respect to vac.

c. Based on the two FOCs you computed above, construct this framework's "labor demand function." The final boxed expression cannot include any Lagrange multipliers in it (i.e., μ must be eliminated). Furthermore the final boxed expression should contain ω only on the left-hand side. Display clearly the mathematical steps/algebraic procedure by which you obtain the final expression.

The remaining parts of the problem are based on the labor demand function obtained in part c.

d. Starting from the labor demand condition you obtained in part c, suppose for part d only that $q^{FIND} = 1$. With $q^{FIND} = 1$, how does your solution in part c compare to the "labor demand function" in chapter 6? Describe briefly in both mathematical terms and in terms of economics. (Note: "Economics" does not mean restating verbally the mathematics.)

e. Return to the case that $q^{FIND} < 1$ but, for part e only, suppose that the HR-related costs of advertising job openings is $\omega = 0$. With $q^{FIND} < 1$ and $\omega = 0$, how does your solution in part d compare to the "labor demand function" in chapter 6? Describe briefly in both mathematical terms and terms of economics. (Note: "Economics" does not mean restating verbally the mathematics.)

For the remainder of this problem, return to the case in which $q^{FIND} < 1$ and $\omega > 0$.

f. Using the expression you obtained in part c, qualitatively sketch a diagram that contains q^{FIND} on the vertical axis and n^D on the horizontal axis. (Note: All that matters for the qualitative diagram is whether the function is upward-sloping, downward-sloping, completely horizontal, or completely vertical.)

g. Provide a brief economic interpretation for the diagram drawn in part f. (Note: "Economic interpretation" does not mean restating verbally the mathematics.)

h. How does an increase in total factor productivity A qualitatively affect the diagram drawn in part f? (Note: All that matters for this qualitative analysis is whether the function shifts outward, shifts inward, or doesn't shift at all.)

i. Provide a brief economic interpretation for your analysis in part h. (Note: "Economic interpretation" does not mean restating verbally the mathematics.)

j. (Harder) Using the "perfectly competitive" diagram below, describe briefly and qualitatively "how" real wages are determined in the matching framework. (Note: This entire problem has nothing to do with labor supply, but it is possible to think in terms of this framework.)

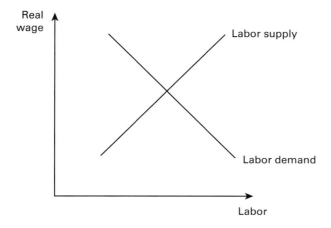

3. Consumption, labor, and unemployment: fiscal policy choices in a search framework. The 2010 Nobel Prize in Economics was awarded to Peter Diamond, Dale Mortensen (who recently passed away), and Christopher Pissarides for their development (in the 1970s and 1980s) of search theory. Search theory is a framework especially suited for studying labor market issues. The search framework builds on, but is richer than, the basic theory of supply and demand. Search theory can be applied to both the supply side of the labor market (building on the analysis of chapter 2) and the demand side of the labor market (building on the analysis of chapter 6). In what follows, you will study the application of search theory to the supply side of the labor market.

There are three basic ideas underlying search theory. First, search theory incorporates into basic supply-and-demand analysis the fact that when an individual wants to work (i.e., supplies labor), there is a chance that employment may not be found. That is, an individual "searching" for a job has a probability less than one that a suitable "match" will be found.

Second, as a direct consequence of the probabilistic nature of successfully finding a job, there is a probability larger than zero that an individual might end up "unemployed"—that is, having searched for work but not found anything. In this case he/she receives "unemployment benefits" from the government.

Third, search theory makes explicit the costs associated with search activity. As is realistic, when an individual wants a job, he/she does not simply "go to the market" as in basic supply-and-demand analysis. Rather, the individual must expend resources searching for a job (think of these costs as due to the time spent looking at recruiting advertisements through various web and networking channels, at career fairs, going through the interviewing process, etc.).

We will incorporate these three ideas into the one-period consumption–labor framework of chapter 2, thereby enriching the range of predictions that it can generate and policy advice it may be able to offer. To do so, first let's introduce some notation:

p^{FIND}: probability that an individual searching for a job finds suitable employment. By definitions, $p^{FIND} \in [0,1]$ (i.e., the probability is a number between zero and one). Hence the probability of not finding a job is $1 - p^{FIND}$. (Note: p does not denote a "price.")

s: "search cost," measured in real units (i.e., in units of consumption goods) that an individual incurs for each hour that he/she would like to work. For example, if the individual desires $n = 10$ hours of work during the week (i.e., "one" unit of time is one week), the total search cost is $10s$; if the individual desires $n = 20$ hours of work during the week, the total search cost is $20s$; and so on. The way to interpret this is that it is more costly (in search time) to find a "full-time" job because an individual has to send out more applications, go through more interviews, and so on. The search cost is $s \geq 0$.

b: "unemployment benefit," measured in real units (i.e., in units of consumption goods) that an individual receives for each hour that he/she does not work. For example, if the individual does not work (which is tantamount to "taking leisure") for $l = 0.3$ units of time, he/she receives a total of $0.3b$ in unemployment benefits;

if the individual does not work for $l = 0.6$ units of time, he/she receives a total of $0.6b$ in unemployment benefits; and so on. In principle, the unemployment benefit is $b \geq 0$. However, we will focus on the case in which $b = 0$ exactly, even though the term b does appear in the expressions below.

In quantitative and policy applications that use this framework, a commonly used utility function is

$$u(c,l) = \ln c - \frac{\theta}{1 + 1/\psi}(1-l)^{1+1/\psi},$$

in which ψ and θ (Greek lowercase letters "psi" and "theta," respectively) are constants (even though we will not assign any numerical value to them) in the utility function. The representative individual has no control over either ψ or θ, and both $\psi > 0$ and $\theta > 0$. You are to use this utility function throughout the analysis.

The budget constraint, expressed in real units (i.e., in units of consumption goods), is

$$c + sn = p^{FIND}(1-t)wn + \left(1 - p^{FIND}\right)bl,$$

in which, w denotes the real wage and t the labor income tax rate. The right-hand side (income side) of the budget constraint is expressed in "expected value form" because of the fact that two mutually exclusive things can occur: a job is found (which occurs with probability p^{FIND}), in which case income is after-tax wage earnings; or a job is not found (which occurs with probability $1 - p^{FIND}$), in which case income is the total unemployment benefits received from the government.[5] (Note: You should consider only the case of $b = 0$ exactly, even though it appears in the expression above.)

To complete the description of the (representative) individual's utility maximization problem:

- Just as in chapter 2, adopt the view that $n + l = 1$, with n denoting units of time that an individual works, and l the units of time spent not working.

- The variables taken as given by the individual are real wages, the probability of finding a suitable job, the search cost per hour (i.e., unit) of (desired) work, and the unemployment benefit per hour (i.e., unit) of nonwork. That is, the individual takes $\left(w, p^{FIND}, t, s, b\right)$ as given when solving his/her utility maximization problem.

---

5. The "expected value" form of the budget constraint arises from application of the probability and statistics concept of "expectations" of uncertain events (e.g., "getting a job" is an uncertain event). For our purposes, you can simply take the budget constraint as written as given, with no need to connect it to the underlying probability and statistics framework.

a. Using the setup of the problem, algebraically rearrange the given budget constraint so that, in your final expression, the variables c and l each appear only on the left-hand side, and the variable n does not directly appear at all. Fully present the steps and logic of your work. (Note: The correct expression for the budget constraint is critical for all of the analysis that follows, so you should make sure that your work here is absolutely correct!)

b. Based on the budget constraint in part a, construct the Lagrangian for the consumer's utility maximization problem. Fully present the steps and logic of your analysis.

c. Based on the Lagrangian constructed in part b, compute the first-order conditions with respect to both c and l. (Note: Your analysis is to be based on the utility function given above). Fully present the steps and logic of your analysis.

d. Based on the two first-order conditions computed in part c, construct the consumption–leisure optimality condition. The final expression must read

$$\frac{u_l(c, l)}{u_c(c, l)} = \dots$$

in which the right-hand side of the expression is for you to determine. Your final expression may not include any Lagrange multipliers in it. You should present very clearly the algebraic steps involved in constructing this expression.

e. Qualitatively sketch the consumption–leisure optimality condition obtained in part d in a graph with c on the vertical axis and l on the horizontal axis. Clearly label the slope of the budget line in the sketch.

Due to the economic downturn and associated sluggishness in employment, the government has been considering (and engaging in) various forms of interventions in labor markets aimed at increasing the welfare (the utility) of individuals. Based on the sketch in part e, you are to analyze various types of labor market interventions with a focus on determining whether or not they would increase the welfare (the utility) of the representative individual.

f. Based on and referring to the sketch in part e, would a reduction in the labor income tax rate t increase utility, decrease utility, or leave utility unchanged? Or is it impossible to determine? Provide a brief and clear economic interpretation (i.e., not simply a verbal restatement of the mathematical or graphical analysis) for your conclusion.

g. Based on and referring to the sketch in part e, would an increase in the unemployment benefit b increase utility, decrease utility, or leave utility unchanged? Or is it impossible to determine? Provide a brief and clear economic interpretation (i.e., not simply a verbal restatement of the mathematical or graphical analysis) for your conclusion.

h. Based on and referring to the sketch in part e, would policies aimed at reducing the search cost s incurred by individuals increase utility, decrease utility, or leave utility unchanged? Or is it impossible to determine? Provide a brief and clear economic interpretation (i.e, not simply a verbal restatement of the mathematical or graphical analysis) for your conclusion.

i. Based on and referring to the sketch in part e, would policies aimed at increasing the probability p^{FIND} that individuals can find suitable jobs increase utility, decrease utility, or leave utility unchanged? Or is it impossible to determine? Provide a brief and clear economic interpretation (i.e., not simply a verbal restatement of the mathematical or graphical analysis) for your conclusion.

28

Matching Equilibrium

The search and matching framework allows us to consider labor-market equilibrium in a different way than in classical markets. This new concept of market-determined equilibrium arises through adjustments in the probabilities of finding a job or hiring a worker, rather than the usual "wage-adjustment" process. In turn these probabilities that the representative consumer and the representative firm "take as given" are determined by an economy-wide matching function.

Matching Function

The centerpiece of the search and matching framework is the **aggregate matching function.** The matching function tractably describes how firms' attempts to hire new workers coordinate with individuals' labor search effort.

Define the aggregate matching function as

$$m(s, vac),$$

which is the number of newly hired individuals. As the arguments of $m(s, vac)$ emphasize, the number of employees hired depends on both how many job openings are available and how much "time" unemployed individuals spend actively searching for work.

The aggregate matching function coordinates firms' job creation activities—which, recall, is the notion of labor demand in the matching framework—and individuals' job search activities—which, recall, underpins the notion of labor supply in the matching framework. In the overall labor market, the **matching probabilities** are related to the matching function as

$$p^{FIND} = \frac{m(s, vac)}{s}$$

and

$$q^{FIND} = \frac{m(s, vac)}{vac}.$$

A typically used functional form for the matching function is the Cobb–Douglas function,

$$m(s, vac) = a \cdot s^{\gamma} vac^{1-\gamma}.$$

The lowercase a is a scale parameter, and for the sake of clarity of the analysis below, it can be thought of as $a = 1$. The parameter $\gamma \in (0,1)$ measures the sensitivity of aggregate matching—that is, the economy-wide creation of new employer–employee jobs—with respect to the number of individuals searching. Analogously, $1 - \gamma$ measures the sensitivity of aggregate matching with respect to the number of job vacancies to be filled.[1]

With Cobb–Douglas matching, the probabilities can be expressed as

$$p^{FIND} = \frac{s^{\gamma} vac^{1-\gamma}}{s}$$

$$= \left(\frac{vac}{s} \right)^{1-\gamma}$$

and

$$q^{FIND} = \frac{s^{\gamma} vac^{1-\gamma}}{vac}$$

$$= \left(\frac{s}{vac} \right)^{\gamma}$$

$$= \left(\frac{vac}{s} \right)^{-\gamma}.$$

Notice that the ratio (vac/s) appears in these now re-expressed probabilities p^{FIND} and q^{FIND}. This ratio is *crucial* for understanding equilibrium in search-and-matching markets.

Labor-Market Tightness

Denote by θ (Greek lowercase letter "theta") **labor-market tightness**. The definition of labor-market tightness is

$$\theta \equiv \frac{vac}{s}.$$

---

1. Stated more formally, γ is the elasticity of aggregate matches with respect to the number of people searching for jobs. Similarly $1 - \gamma$ is the elasticity of aggregate matches with respect to the number of job openings.

Labor-market tightness captures the idea of the relative number of traders on the two sides of a market: the numerator is the aggregate quantity of job openings looking for ("trading for") a new employee, and the denominator is the aggregate number of individuals searching for ("trading for") a new job.

With this definition of market tightness, we can recast our understanding of p^{FIND} and q^{FIND}. Using the Cobb–Douglas matching function, we see that p^{FIND} is strictly increasing in θ, and q^{FIND} is strictly decreasing in θ.[2] These dependencies of labor-market matching probabilities on aggregate labor-market tightness sheds economic insight on how search and matching markets operate.

Recalling that p^{FIND} describes the chance that an individual unit of time spent searching for a job, if there are more open jobs—meaning, higher *vac*—then an individual has a *higher* likelihood of finding a job. Similarly, recalling that q^{FIND} measures the chance that any given job advertisement results in successful recruitment of a worker, if there are more searching individuals—meaning, high *s*—then each job opening has a *smaller* likelihood of finding a suitable employee. This dependence of p^{FIND} and q^{FIND} on labor-market tightness θ often goes under the name **congestion effects.**

To describe equilibrium, we insert the matching market-determined p^{FIND} and q^{FIND} into the labor-force participation condition and the job-creation condition obtained earlier in chapter 27.

Dependence of Labor Supply on Market Tightness θ

Recall the labor-force participation condition (in which, for simplicity, unemployment benefits are set to $b = 0$ and labor income taxes are set to $t = 0$):

$$\frac{h'(lfp)}{u'(c)} = p^{FIND} \cdot w.$$

Given that $p^{FIND} = \theta^{1-\gamma}$, we can rewrite the LFP condition as

$$\frac{h'(lfp)}{u'(c)} = \theta^{1-\gamma} \cdot w \ .$$

Notice that in viewing the market-determined forces as means of inducing "optimal labor supply" places market tightness (and hence the likelihood of finding a job p^{FIND}) on an even footing with wages.[3] In other words, this brings market-based "congestion effects" into the analysis of labor supply.

2. More precisely, we have $p^{FIND} = (vac/s)^{1-\gamma} = \theta^{1-\gamma}$, which, because $\gamma > 0$, implies that p^{FIND} increases if market tightness θ increases. Analogously, $q^{FIND} = (vac/s)^{-\gamma} = \theta^{-\gamma}$, which, because $\gamma > 0$, implies that q^{FIND} decreases if market tightness θ increases.

3. Both θ and w appear on the right-hand side, and, as a reminder, both p^{FIND} and w are taken as given by the representative consumer.

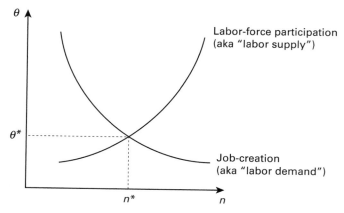

Figure 28.1

Market tightness θ that adjusts to clear matching-based labor markets. The functional forms and exogenous parameter values underlying this diagram are the production function $A \cdot f(n) = A \cdot n^{a}$; the utility function components $u(c) = c$ and $h(lfp) = -[\psi / (1 + 1 / \varphi)] \cdot lfp^{1+(1/\varphi)}$; the aggregate matching function $m(s, vac) = s^{\gamma} vac^{1-\gamma}$; and parameter values A = 1, α = 0.7, γ = 0.5, ω = 0.1, ψ = 4, and φ = 0.3. The assumption in this diagram is that the real wage w = 0.9.

Two steps of algebra allow us to isolate the tightness term on the left-hand side, which gives us

$$\theta = \left[\frac{h'(lfp)}{u'(c)} \cdot \frac{1}{w} \right]^{1/(1-\gamma)}.$$

This expression, which takes as given the real wage w, is the upward-sloping labor-force participation (aka "labor supply") function plotted in figure 28.1.

Dependence of Labor Demand on Market Tightness θ

Let's recall the job-creation expression we obtained earlier

$$\omega = q^{FIND} \cdot \left(A \cdot f'\left(n^{D}\right) - w \right).$$

Using the expression $q^{FIND} = \theta^{\gamma}$, we can re-express it as

$$\omega = \theta^{-\gamma} \cdot \left(A \cdot f'\left(n^{D}\right) - w \right).$$

This view of the market-determined forces that induce "optimal labor demand" places market tightness (and hence the likelihood of hiring an employee q^{FIND}) on an even footing with wages.[4] In other words, it brings market-based "congestion effects" into the analysis of labor demand.

---

4. Both θ and w appear on the right-hand side, and, as a reminder, both q^{FIND} and w are taken as given by the representative firm.

Two steps of algebra allow us to isolate the tightness term on the left-hand side, which gives us

$$\theta = \left[\frac{\omega}{A \cdot f'(n^D) - w} \right]^{-1/\gamma}.$$

This expression, which takes as given the real wage w, is the downward-sloping job-creation (aka "labor demand") function plotted in figure 28.1.

Labor-Market Equilibrium

In the search-and-matching framework, labor-market clearing occurs when

$$q^{FIND} \cdot vac = p^{FIND} \cdot s,$$

which states that the total quantity of employees hired by firms (the left-hand side) equates with the total quantity of individuals searching for a job that successfully find employment (the right-hand side). In turn the equilibrium quantity of hired workers (or, equivalently stated, filled jobs openings) n is

$$n = q^{FIND} \cdot vac = p^{FIND} \cdot s.$$

In figure 28.1, the intersection n^* is the quantity of new jobs created that clears the market at market tightness θ^*. The matching-market equilibrium quantity of n^* is due to the probabilities that arise from the aggregate matching function.

In order to precisely plot in (n, θ) space the labor-force participation function $\theta = [(h'(lfp)/u'(c)) \cdot (1/w)]^{1/(1-\gamma)}$ and the job-creation function $\theta = [\omega/(A \cdot f'(n) - w)]^{-1/\gamma}$, we require functional forms for utility and production, various exogenous parameters of the economy, and a value for the real wage w. Standard macroeconomic utility functions and parameters (along with, for the moment, a somewhat arbitrarily selected real wage w) are chosen for the diagram in figure 28.1.[5] The precise functional forms for utility, production of output goods, and matching markets, along with the parameter values listed in the caption of figure 28.1, are all exogenous to the matching framework, and furthermore macroeconomists would nearly universally consider them to be "uncontroversial."

However, "wages" are typically considered to be the clearing price for labor. In figure 28.1, though, a value of $w = 0.9$ seems to have been pulled out of thin air. If that wage turns out to be valid (a point we return to below), then let's pull another value of w out of thin air.

Suppose that the real wage increases to $w = 0.95$, and all other values described in the caption in figure 28.1 remain the same. Figure 28.2 shows that firms would advertise fewer job openings if wages were higher, and figure 28.3 shows that individuals would be willing to spend more time searching for jobs if wages were higher.

---

5. All of these are stated in the caption of figure 28.1.

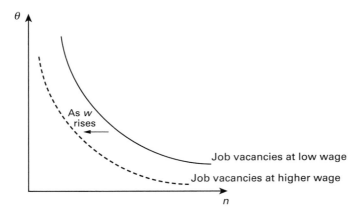

Figure 28.2
Job-creation condition shifts inward if real wage *w* rises

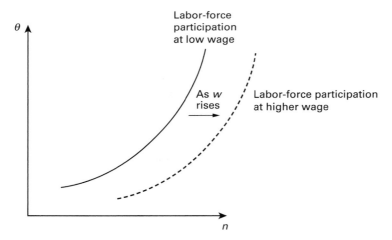

Figure 28.3
Labor-force participation shifts outward if real wage *w* rises

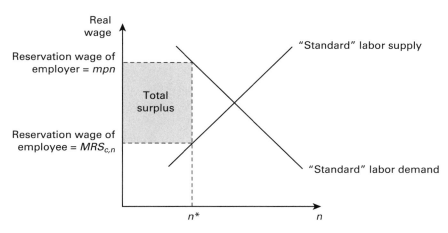

Figure 28.4
Market clearing that occurs at a higher quantity than n^* in the standard supply-and-demand view. In the search-and-matching framework, the matching-based equilibrium n^* creates a "surplus" between a successfully matched pair of a job vacancy and a job seeker. In the total surplus region, this surplus permits any real wage w to be an equilibrium wage.

Both figure 28.2 and figure 28.3 are clear to understand in economic terms. In a ceteris paribus analysis, firms' profits would decrease if wages were higher, which dis-incentivizes them from creating and advertising new job openings because each job posting has a positive cost ω. Analogously, individuals' wage earnings would increase if wages were higher, which induces them to spend more time searching for a job.

But the question still remains: How can it be economically meaningful that we seem to be simply "making up" the real wage w?

Wages and the Surplus Set

Let's return to the standard competitive framework of labor markets to understand the role that real wages play (or don't play) in the search-and-matching framework. Figure 28.4 considers the matching equilibrium outcome n^* depicted in figure 28.1, but through the classical view of labor supply from chapter 2 and labor demand from chapter 6, rather than in a search-and-matching framework. Because of the costs associated with searching—vacancy advertisement costs ω for firms and the disutility from time spent searching for individuals—n^* in figure 28.4 is smaller than the market-clearing n that would otherwise arise at the intersection of the classic concepts of supply and demand.

Think back to the starting point of our consumption–labor analysis. An important result that emerged was that the marginal rate of substitution between consumption and leisure (or, equivalently, consumption and labor) was the foundation for the classic labor supply as a function of real wages. Figure 28.4 marks a particular value of this $MRS_{c,n}$ on the labor supply function at the quantity n^*.

Similarly an important result that emerged from our analysis of the basic firm profit-maximization model was that firms hire workers up to the point that the real wage equates with the marginal product of labor. Figure 28.4 marks a particular value of this mpn on the classic labor demand function at the quantity n^*.

The $MRS_{c,n}$ represents the reservation wage of the newly matched employee. The reservation wage represents the minimum wage that the individual would be willing to agree on and begin his/her new job.[6] Similarly for a potential new employer the mpn represents the reservation wage of the company. This reservation wage represents the maximum wage the company would be willing to agree on and actually hire the candidate. The difference between these two reservation wages is commonly referred as the **total surplus** between the pair and is shaded in gray in figure 28.4.

Figure 28.4 reveals that *any wage* that lies below the reservation wage of the potential employer (mpn) and above the reservation wage of the potential new employee $MRS_{c,n}$ is agreeable to both parties. As the top graph of figure 28.5 shows, a wage that is closer to the reservation wage of the employer provides the new employee a larger percentage of the total surplus, whereas a wage closer to the reservation wage of the new employee provides a larger share of the surplus to the employer.

However, any real wage between a low of $MRS_{c,n}$ and a high of mpn would be acceptable to both parties. The lower graph of figure 28.5 shows a different wage outcome than in the top panel. Viewing wage payments in this "sharing-the-surplus" light, wages seem to play more of just a "fairness" role instead of just a "labor-market clearing" role.

So we still have lingering the question of how wages are determined. "How" wages are determined in "modern macroeconomic" frameworks that align with wage payments observed in the data has been a puzzling issue for the profession for decades. Although "long-term employer–employee relationships" do not solve this puzzle, it allows us to think about wages in a different light, which is the topic of chapter 29.

Chapter 28 Problem Set Questions

1.   **Matching-market clearing.** In all of the following questions, start from the matching-market-clearing diagram in which labor-market tightness θ equates labor force participation (LFP or "labor supply") with new job creation ("labor demand").

     a.   If labor productivity A rises above $A = 1$, does the job-creation function shift? If so, briefly describe whether inward or outward and its underlying economic rationale. If not, briefly show mathematically why not.

---

6. The "minimum wage" phrase is unrelated to legislatively mandated "minimum wage laws."

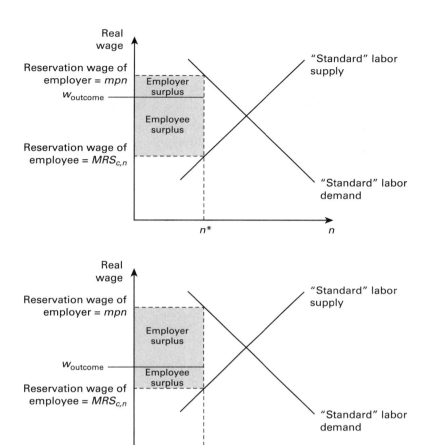

Figure 28.5
Split of the surplus that could favor employees over employers (top diagram) or employers over employees (bottom diagram) as determined by the agreed-upon wage.

b. If labor productivity A rises above $A = 1$, does the LFP function shift? If so, briefly describe whether inward or outward and its underlying economic rationale. If not, briefly show mathematically why not.

c. Based on your responses in parts a and b, does equilibrium labor-market tightness θ^* increase or decrease? And what about equilibrium n^*? Briefly explain why.

d. If labor productivity A decreases below $A = 1$, does the job-creation function shift? If so, briefly describe whether inward or outward and its underlying economic rationale. If not, briefly show mathematically why not.

e. If labor productivity A decreases below $A = 1$, does the LFP function shift? If so, briefly describe whether inward or outward and its underlying economic rationale. If not, briefly show mathematically why not.

f. Based on your responses in parts d and e, does equilibrium labor-market tightness θ^* increase or decrease? And what about equilibrium n^*? Briefly explain why.

g. If the recruiting cost ω rises, does the job-creation function shift? If so, briefly describe whether inward or outward and its underlying economic rationale. If not, briefly show mathematically why not.

h. If the recruiting cost ω rises, does the LFP function shift? If so, briefly describe whether inward or outward and its underlying economic rationale. If not, briefly show mathematically why not.

i. Based on your responses in parts g and h, does equilibrium labor-market tightness θ^* increase or decrease? And what about equilibrium n^*? Briefly explain why.

29

Long-Lasting Jobs

Out of the three main macro markets (goods markets, labor markets, and savings markets), it is labor markets in which we typically think of "long-lasting relationships." A person who is employed typically works at only one job and typically works at that one job for many time periods. Of course, we can also consider this idea in goods markets and savings markets too. For example, if a person enjoys shopping at a particular brand-name store, he or she may be inclined to be a repeat customer at that shop. If the store closes, the repeat customer may not like it, but for that customer, it may be easy and not very time-consuming to find another store or other varieties of those goods that are no longer available. In contrast, if a person who was working at a particular company or in a certain industry is all of a sudden laid off, it would likely take much more time and considerably more search effort to find a job than it would to find a new brand-name store.

Thus far we haven't discussed wages much. The *total surplus* that arises between a matched employer and employee can potentially describe both long-term job relationships and the nature by which wages can be set over long stretches of time. To get a good grasp of this concept, we should first extend the one-period search and matching framework to a "many, many, many period" framework. We have studied such infinite-period frameworks before, so we will not, except where needed, define notation or ideas that we have by this point used numerous times. Long-lasting jobs arise through the **sequence of job-finding constraints** for the representative consumer, the **sequence of job-hiring constraints** for the representative firm, and the **sequence of aggregate matching functions** and its implied probabilities of successfully finding a job and of successfully hiring a worker.

Figure 29.1 conveys much of the foundations and messages of not only the infinite-horizon search and matching framework but also of the "static" one-period matching analysis. The two key innovations in moving from the static framework to the now dynamic framework are (1) the introduction of the probability ρ (Greek lowercase letter "rho") that any preexisting employment relationship can be terminated, and relatedly (2) the "asset" or "stock variable" nature of employment. More precisely, the exogenous probability $\rho \in (0, 1]$ captures the fraction of previously existing jobs at the beginning of period t (which is labeled n_{t-1} on the timeline) that, for various reasons, end at the beginning

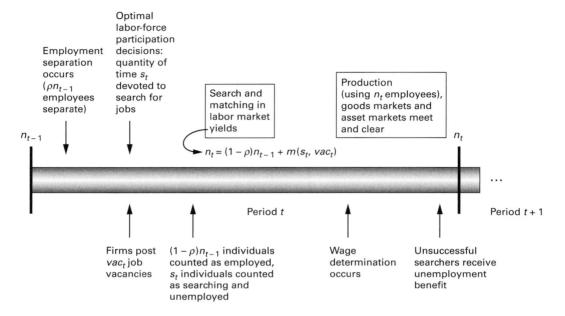

NOTE: Economic planning occurs for the ENTIRE remaining lifetime

Figure 29.1
Timing of aggregate events in the search-and-matching framework

of period t. In the previous static analysis, "separation" was never mentioned, but now we can see that it was implicitly $\rho = 1$. The reason that $\rho < 1$ is permissible in the search and matching framework is the total surpluses that arise from a successful match between job openings and unemployed individuals searching for a new job.

Representative Consumer

The lifetime present-discounted utility function for the representative consumer starting from the beginning of period t is

$$u(c_t) - h\left((1 - p_t^{FIND})s_t + n_t^s\right) + \beta\left[u(c_{t+1}) - h\left((1 - p_{t+1}^{FIND})s_{t+1} + n_{t+1}^s\right)\right]$$
$$+ \beta^2\left[u(c_{t+2}) - h\left((1 - p_{t+2}^{FIND})s_{t+2} + n_{t+2}^s\right)\right] + \beta^3\left[u(c_{t+3}) - h\left((1 - p_{t+3}^{FIND})s_{t+3} + n_{t+3}^s\right)\right] + \ldots$$
$$= \sum_{s=0}^{\infty} \beta^s\left[u(c_{t+s}) - h\left((1 - p_{t+s}^{FIND})s_{t+s} + n_{t+s}^s\right)\right].$$

The period-t flow budget constraint is

$$c_t = (1-t_t)w_t n_t^s + \left(1 - p_t^{FIND}\right)s_t \cdot b.$$

Long-term employment arises through the **job-finding constraint**

$$n_t^s = (1-\rho)n_{t-1}^s + p_t^{FIND}s_t,$$

which is the representative consumer's analogue of the aggregate $n_t = (1-\rho)n_{t-1} + m(s_t, vac_t)$ (which we discuss further below) displayed in figure 29.1. If $\rho = 1$, the static job-finding constraint $n_t^s = p_t^{FIND}s_t$ re-emerges.

Following the notation from our static analysis, denote by λ_t^h the period-t Lagrange multiplier on the period-t flow budget constraint[1] and by μ_t^h the period-t Lagrange multiplier on the period-t job-finding constraint. After constructing the sequential Lagrangian (which you should build on your own), the period-t first-order conditions with respect to c_t, n_t^s, and s_t are, respectively,

$$u'(c_t) - \lambda_t^h = 0,$$

$$-h'\left(\left(1 - p_t^{FIND}\right)s_t + n_t^s\right) + \lambda_t^h(1-t_t)w_t - \mu_t^h + \beta(1-\rho)\mu_{t+1}^h = 0,$$

and

$$-h'\left(\left(1 - p_t^{FIND}\right)s_t + n_t^s\right)\cdot\left(1 - p_t^{FIND}\right) + \lambda_t^h\left(1 - p_t^{FIND}\right)b + \mu_t^h p_t^{FIND} = 0.$$

Aside from the time subscripts, these first-order conditions are identical to those in the static framework, with one important exception: the first-order condition with respect to n_t^s now includes the **job-retention probability** $(1 - \rho)$. The job-retention probability is the likelihood that a newly hired employee in period t will continue to be an employee in period $t+1$. Figure 29.1 indicates this idea by placing n_t on the borderline between the very end of period t and the very beginning of period $t+1$, which conveys the notion that employment is a long-lived "asset." On average, once an individual successfully finds a job, the employment relationship—which one could interpret as an "employment contract," whether an explicit contract or an implicit contract—lasts at least for several time periods.

Constructing the consumption–LFP condition for a given period t requires many steps of algebra based on the period-t first-order conditions and their period-$(t+1)$ counterparts, which we will not go through here.[2] After numerous algebraic steps and rearrangements, the consumption–LFP condition for period t turns out to be

---

1. A question that perhaps has already occurred to you: Where in the flow budget constraint are the financial assets such as stocks, bonds, money, and so on? We could place all of them and more into the budget constraint here; in addition we could include these job-finding rates and constraints in all of our previous frameworks, too. But the focus in this unit is on search and matching, so we're trying to keep the framework as simple as possible.

2. You are welcome to give it a shot.

$$\frac{h'(\mathit{lfp}_t)}{u'(c_t)} = p_t^{FIND} \cdot \left[(1-t_t)\cdot w_t + (1-\rho)\left(\frac{\beta u'(c_{t+1})}{u'(c_t)}\right)\cdot\left(\frac{h'(\mathit{lfp}_{t+1})}{u'(c_{t+1})}\right)\right] + (1-p_t^{FIND})\cdot b,$$

which is extremely informative on two fronts. First, notice that if the separation probability $\rho = 1$ (equivalently stated, if the retention probability $1 - \rho = 0$), this expression is identical to the static consumption–LFP condition.

Second, if $\rho < 1$, note the second term inside the square brackets on the right-hand side, which is copied here for clarity

$$(1-\rho)\left(\frac{\beta u'(c_{t+1})}{u'(c_t)}\right)\cdot\left(\frac{h'(\mathit{lfp}_{t+1})}{u'(c_{t+1})}\right),$$

contains $\beta u'(c_{t+1})/u'(c_t)$, which *is* the pricing kernel for financial-market analysis that we have been studying! Its appearance indicates that there is some type of **asset value** for individuals who have a job, and its economic insight is clear: once one has a job, its long-lasting nature implies that the person does not have to spend the time and effort, at least while the job lasts, to search yet again for another job. Search effort incurs disutility, and the "asset value" of long-lasting employment is captured in the $h'(\mathit{lfp}_{t+1})/u'(c_{t+1})$ term. Note the time subscripts carefully: this $h'(\mathit{lfp}_{t+1})/u'(c_{t+1})$ is the *MRS* in period $t+1$ that describes (in units of goods) the (un)willingness to search again in period $t + 1$.[3]

The avoidance of disutility of search in the future, or, even more precisely, the disutility of search and the probability that one may not find another job quickly, is what makes a job an asset for an employed individual. A similar economic concept arises for firms, to which we now turn.

Representative Firm

In period t, the average firm produces output using the technology $A_t f\left(n_t^D\right)$, pays all of its workers $w_t n_t^D$, and must pay $\omega\cdot vac_t$ recruiting costs to hire new workers due to natural turnover of its employees.

Its lifetime profits are

$$A_t \cdot f\left(n_t^D\right) - w_t\cdot n_t^D - \omega\cdot vac_t + \frac{A_{t+1}\cdot f\left(n_{t+1}^D\right) - w_{t+1}\cdot n_{t+1}^D - \omega\cdot vac_{t+1}}{1+r_t}$$
$$+ \frac{A_{t+2}\cdot f\left(n_{t+2}^D\right) - w_t\cdot n_{t+2}^D - \omega\cdot vac_{t+2}}{(1+r_t)\cdot(1+r_{t+1})} + \ldots.$$

3. An equivalent interpretation of this *MRS* is the (un)willingness to *work* in period $t + 1$, but the interpretation stated above better highlights the disutility of search versus the disutility of work. In the framework they are essentially the same given the disutility function $-h((1 - p^{FIND})s + n^h)$.

in which $(1 + r_t)$ is the gross real interest rate between period t and period $t + 1$, $(1 + r_{t+1})$ is the gross real interest rate between period $t + 1$ and period $t + 2$, $(1 + r_{t+2})$ is the gross real interest rate between period $t + 2$ and period $t + 3$, and so on.

The firm's total number of employees that work to produce output in period t is described by the **job-hiring constraint**

$$n_t^D = (1 - \rho)n_{t-1}^D + q_t^{FIND} vac_t.$$

As per the experiment in the representative consumer discussion above, if $\rho = 1$, the static job-hiring constraint $n_t^D = q_t^{FIND} vac_t$ re-emerges. In this case the **job-turnover rate,** or **employee turnover rate,** both of which are often-used jargon, is 100 percent ($\rho = 1$).

Following the notation from our static analysis, denote by μ_t^f the period-t Lagrange multiplier on the period-t job-hiring constraint. After constructing the lifetime Lagrangian (which you should build on your own), the period-t first-order conditions with respect to n_t^D and vac_t are

$$A_t \cdot f'\left(n_t^D\right) - w_t - \mu_t^f + \left(\frac{1-\rho}{1+r_t}\right) \cdot \mu_{t+1}^f = 0$$

and

$$-\omega + \mu_t^f \cdot q_t^{FIND} = 0.$$

Aside from the time subscripts, these first-order conditions are identical to those in the static framework, with an important exception: the first-order condition with respect to n_t^D now includes the job-retention probability $(1 - \rho)$.

The job-retention probability is similar to that discussed in the consumer setup above: it is the likelihood that an individual employee in period t will continue to be an employee in period $t + 1$. The one caveat that distinguishes the economic interpretation of retention for firms versus for workers is that in the former case it is with respect to all of its employees, whereas for the latter it is tilted more toward newly hired individuals.

Nonetheless, figure 29.1 again indicates this idea by placing n_t on the borderline between the very end of period t and the very beginning of period $t + 1$, which conveys the notion that employment is a long-lived asset. It's not uncommon to hear CEOs or managers of companies to say "Our employees are our most valuable assets."

Constructing the job-creation condition for a given period t requires many steps of algebra based on the period-t first-order conditions and their period-$(t + 1)$ counterparts, which we will not go through here. After the required algebraic steps and rearrangements, the period-t job-creation condition is

$$\frac{\omega}{q_t^{FIND}} = A_t \cdot f'\left(n_t^D\right) - w_t + \left(\frac{1-\rho}{1+r_t}\right) \cdot \frac{\omega}{q_{t+1}^{FIND}},$$

or rewritten slightly,

$$\omega = q_t^{FIND} \left[A_t f'\left(n_t^D\right) - w_t \right] + q_t^{FIND} \cdot \left(\frac{1-\rho}{1+r_t} \right) \cdot \frac{\omega}{q_{t+1}^{FIND}}.$$

Based on our discussion of the "asset value" nature of a job for individuals, you should see parallels for the "asset value" nature of an employee for firms through the job-creation condition. First, if the employee turnover rate is $\rho = 1$, this expression is identical to the static job-creation condition.

Second, if $\rho < 1$, the second term on the right-hand side contains a (discounted by $1 + r_t$) future (i.e., period $t + 1$) cost of hiring ω. From earlier discussions of the intersection of macroeconomic theory and finance theory, or (now in hindsight) even more simply, the basic consumption–savings optimality condition, you should recall the important result regarding the pricing kernel

$$\frac{\beta u'(c_{t+1})}{u'(c_t)} = \frac{1}{1+r_t}.$$

Rewriting the job creation condition using this consumption–savings result, we have

$$\omega = q_t^{FIND} \left[A_t f'\left(n_t^D\right) - w_t \right] + q_t^{FIND} \cdot (1-\rho) \cdot \left(\frac{\beta u'(c_{t+1})}{u'(c_t)} \right) \cdot \left(\frac{\omega}{q_{t+1}^{FIND}} \right),$$

which perhaps more clearly displays the asset value for firms of their employees. The economic interpretation is that once a firm has gone through the costly job-advertising and interviewing process and has successfully hired a suitable applicant, it would be, ceteris paribus, unprofitable and potentially time-consuming to recruit a replacement worker, which is captured in the term ω/q_{t+1}^{FIND}.

Labor-Market Equilibrium and Intangible Capital

Defining equilibrium in the multi-period matching framework requires a slight generalization compared to the static framework. With the asset-like nature of the economy's pool of employees, the aggregate quantity of employment in period t relates to the aggregate quantity of employment in period $t - 1$ in the following manner:

$$n_t = (1-\rho)n_{t-1} + m(s_t, vac_t).$$

This period-by-period transition of an economy's stock of workers is shown in figure 29.1.

As in the static case, *clearing in matching markets* requires that

$$q_t^{FIND} \cdot vac_t = p_t^{FIND} \cdot s_t,$$

but, with $\rho < 1$, this is *distinct* from "market clearing" in terms of economy-wide n. This distinction is apparent from the $n_t = (1 - \rho)n_{t-1} + m(s_t, vac_t)$ expression above. If we understand this distinction, then we can continue to think about **clearing in matching markets** via adjustments in θ_t just as in the static matching framework.

Furthermore, if we understand the distinction between the **stock variable** n and the **flow variable** $m(s, vac)$, then we can broadly think of $m(s, vac)$ as the economy's investment in the **intangible capital** of job relationships between employers and employees because no job match (or, at least, not the average job match) is going to last forever. There is natural and inevitable turnover, or separation, in jobs due to quitting, firing, relocation to another city or state or country, switching career tracks, and so on, all which is captured by ρ. By analogy, the economy's **tangible capital** (manufacturing plants, network servers, roads, bridges, computers, etc.) doesn't last forever due to inevitable wear and tear, and needs to be replenished by construction of new roads, factories, machines, and other infrastructure.

Equilibrium Wages?

An important question still remains: How can it be economically meaningful that we still, despite the extension of the static matching framework to a multi-period framework, seem to be simply "making up" the real wage w_t in any or every time period?

Perhaps it's due to the surplus set described in the static scenario in combination with the long-lived asset-nature of jobs. Figure 29.2 provides an example by supposing that a job lasts for only two periods.

Figure 29.2 views labor markets across the two consecutive time periods through the classical labor supply and labor demand lens, but the different equilibrium n^* outcomes in each of the two consecutive periods arise from clearing in matching markets (i.e., via adjustment in market tightness θ_t in each time period) in addition to the retained workers from the previous time period.. These outcomes are based on the same logic in the static equilibrium matching case.

We also know from the static model that the real wage must lie somewhere lower than the reservation wage of the employer and somewhere above the reservation wage of the employee. This continues to hold true in the multi-period matching model.

Due to an exogenous shock (a positive labor productivity shock to A is the best candidate) that occurs in period $t + 1$, the representative firm's (and hence the aggregate) labor demand function shifts outward in period $t + 1$ compared to period t. The equilibrium number of employees increase from the n^* marked in the diagram on the left to the n^* marked in the diagram on the right.

What about the real wage in period t and in period $t + 1$?

Figure 29.2 proposes *one* pair of real wages across the two time periods that lie inside each period's surplus set. As sketched, the "pair" of real wages is actually just one wage,

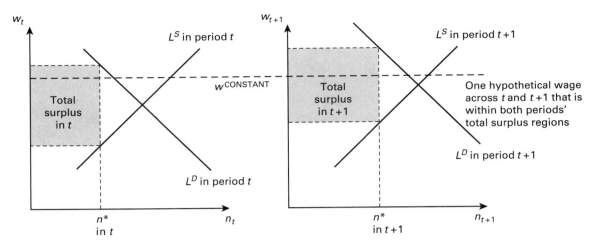

Figure 29.2
Classical labor supply and labor demand across time periods, with real wage on vertical axis. In each diagram, $n*$ is characterized by that particular time period's clearing of matching markets through adjustments in that particular period's market tightness θ. One possible real wage that lies within the total surplus regions of every time period is the constant real wage $w^{CONSTANT}$.

$w^{CONSTANT}$, in both time periods. Whether or not these wages are "fair" in either or both period t or $t+1$ doesn't play a role in this analysis—all that matters is that this *one* proposed pair of wages satisfies the reservation wages of employees and employers in *all* (the two) time periods.[4]

Are there other real wage scenarios that lie within the surplus set of both periods?

Here's one: suppose that the period-t real wage is exactly equal to the marginal product of labor in period t (i.e., the real wage is exactly on the classic labor demand function in period t at the point $n*$), and that the period-$(t+1)$ real wage is exactly equal to the $MRS_{c,n}$ in period $t+1$ (i.e., the real wage is exactly on the classic labor supply function in period $t+1$).

Is this pair of wages agreeable to both employees and employers? It certainly is because they both lie within the surplus regions of both period t and period $t+1$.

Here is another wage scenario: suppose that the period-t real wage is exactly equal to the $MRS_{c,n}$ in period t (i.e., the real wage is exactly on the classic labor supply function in period t at the quantity $n*$), and that the period-$(t+1)$ real wage is exactly equal to the marginal product of labor in period $t+1$(i.e., the real wage is exactly on the classic labor demand function in period $t+1$ at the point $n*$).

Is this pair of wages agreeable to both employees and employers? It certainly is because they both lie within the surplus regions of both period t and period $t+1$.

---

4. If we wanted to think about "fairness" considerations, it could be natural to think that the wage $w^{CONSTANT}$ is "extremely fair" to employees in period t, but that this wage is "less fair" to employees in period $t+1$.

Here is yet another wage scenario: suppose that the period-t real wage is exactly halfway between the reservation wage of the employer and the reservation wage of the employee (i.e., at the midpoint of the dashed vertical line between labor demand and labor supply at n^* in period t), and the period-$(t + 1)$ real wage is exactly halfway between the reservation wage of the employer and the reservation wage of the employee (i.e., at the midpoint of the dashed vertical line between labor demand and labor supply at n^* in period $t + 1$).

Is this pair of wages agreeable to both employees and employers? It certainly is because they both lie within the surplus regions of both period t and period $t + 1$.

How many more pairs of real wages would be agreeable to both employees and employers? An infinite number of pairs, as long as both are inside the particular period's surplus interval!

Where does this leave us regarding "how" wages are determined? It leads us to think about how "long-term employment relationships" can potentially heavily influence wages, or, more broadly, salaries and other forms of compensation. Returning to the $w^{CONSTANT}$ in figure 29.2, it could be that employees and employers are agreeing to share unexpected events and "shocks" that occur over time. These shocks could shift labor demand outward (as diagrammed in figure 29.2) or inward, could shift labor supply outward or inward, or both labor demand and labor supply at the same time in the same or opposite directions. Such agreements could arise implicitly ("I love this job, I would never want to leave"), or even explicitly by, for example, signing contracts that keep a worker's salary fixed for a year regardless of any economic shocks that might arise during the length of the contract.

Policy makers and academic researchers have been struggling with this topic of wage determination over the last several years because search-and-matching analysis has become widespread in macroeconomic thinking, especially during and since the Great Recession. There are several ways to describe real wages, but none has become conventional in "macro-labor" analysis.

The clear benefit, though, of the widespread incorporation of the search-and-matching model in macroeconomic frameworks is that it articulates precise reasons and mechanisms for why unemployment can arise in the first place, which the classic labor supply and demand framework cannot.

Chapter 29 Problem Set Questions

1. **Steady-state analysis: LFP.** Begin with the dynamic consumption–LFP optimality condition

$$\frac{h'(lfp_t)}{u'(c_t)} = p_t^{FIND} \cdot \left[(1-t_t) \cdot w_t + (1-\rho) \left(\frac{\beta u'(c_{t+1})}{u'(c_t)} \right) \cdot \left(\frac{h'(lfp_{t+1})}{u'(c_{t+1})} \right) \right] + (1 - p_t^{FIND}) \cdot b.$$

   a. Impose steady state on the expression above. Your final expression should contain only

$$\frac{h'(lfp)}{u'(c)} = ...$$

on the left-hand side.

b. Based on your steady-state consumption–LFP optimality condition in part a, what is the mathematical expression for the reservation wage of a unit of time spent searching for a job without knowing whether or not a job match will successfully be found?

2. Steady-state analysis: job creation. Begin with the dynamic job-creation condition

$$\frac{\omega}{q_t^{FIND}} = A_t \cdot f'\left(n_t^D\right) - w_t + \left(\frac{1-\rho}{1+r_t}\right) \cdot \frac{\omega}{q_{t+1}^{FIND}}.$$

a. Impose steady state on the expression above. Your final expression should contain only

$$\frac{\omega}{q^{FIND}} = ...$$

on the left-hand side.

b. Based on your steady-state job-creation condition in part a, what is the mathematical expression for the firm's reservation wage of a unit of costly recruiting for a job vacancy without knowing whether or not a new employee will successfully be hired?

3. Firms, capital, and labor-market turnover. Consider a slightly different version of the representative firm in the search and matching framework.

Basic notation and definitions:

q_{t+1}^{FIND}: probability, in period t, that a firm searching to fill a particular job opening finds a suitable worker. By the definitions of probabilities, $q_{t+1}^{FIND} \in [0,1]$. (Define in an analogous way q_{t+1}^{FIND}, q_{t+2}^{FIND}, q_{t+3}^{FIND}, etc.)

ω: "recruiting cost," in period t, measured in real terms, that is associated with each job opening that a firm is trying to fill; the recruiting cost is $\omega \geq 0$.

ρ: probability that a worker employed in a particular job in period t will not be employed at that same job in period $t + 1$ (whether due to quitting or being fired, each of which is a form of worker "turnover"). By definition, $\rho \in [0,1]$.

v_t: number of job vacancies in period t that a firm is attempting to fill (i.e., the number of job openings the firm has and is actively recruiting for). The cost of "setting up" each vacancy (the administrative cost associated with recruiting) is the cost ω described above. (Define in an analogous way v_{t+1}, v_{t+2}, v_{t+3}, etc.)

Supposing that the (representative) firm has "many" employees, the way in which the total number of employees that it has on its payroll changes from period t to period $t + 1$ is

$$n_{t+1} = (1-\rho)n_t + v_t q_t^{FIND},$$

which is to be understood as follows: the number of employees that work at the firm in period t is n_t, and then, because some new workers are hired in period t and some existing workers turn over between period t and $t + 1$, the firm has a (possibly different) number of employees in period $t+1$, n_{t+1}. Similarly the way in which the total number of employees that the firm has on its payroll changes from period $t + 1$ to period $t + 2$ is $n_{t+2} = (1-\rho)n_{t+1} + v_{t+1}q_{t+1}^{FIND}$, and the way in which the total number of employees that the firm has on its payroll changes from period $t + 2$ to period $t + 3$ is $n_{t+3} = (1-\rho)n_{t+2} + v_t q_{t+2}^{FIND}$, and so on. These previous three expressions (along with their analogues in periods $t + 3$, $t + 4$, etc.) are the firm's job-hiring constraints.

The complete description of the (representative) firm's (dynamic) profit-maximization problem, starting from the beginning of period t, is as follows:

- In period t, total output and hence total revenue of the firm (denominated in real terms) is $A_t f(k_t, n_t)$, in which A_t denotes total factor productivity (TFP) in period t, k_t is the amount of capital ("machines and equipment") the firm has at the start of period t (recall from chapter 6 that capital is a stock variable that "takes one period to build"), and $f(k_t, n_t)$ is the firm's production function. Similarly, for period $t + 1$, total output and hence total revenue of the firm (denominated in real terms) is $A_{t+1}f(k_{t+1}, n_{t+1})$, and so on.

- The real interest rate between any two consecutive time periods is always $r > 0$ (i.e., the real interest does not change over time, which is indicated by the lack of a time subscript).

- The real wage the firm must pay each worker in period t is w_t, which is taken as given by the firm. Similarly the real wage the firm must pay each worker in period $t + 1$ is w_{t+1}, in period $t + 2$ is w_{t+2}, and so on.

- The variables taken as given by the firm are real wages, the probabilities of finding workers, and the probabilities of worker turnover. That is, the firm takes (w_t, q_t^{FIND}, ρ) as given in period t, takes $(w_{t+1}, q_{t+1}^{FIND}, \rho)$ as given in period $t + 1$, takes $(w_{t+2}, q_{t+2}^{FIND}, \rho)$ as given in period $t + 2$, and so on.

- In period t the firm's profit function (in real terms) is

  $$A_t f(k_t, n_t) + k_t - w_t n_t - k_{t+1} - \omega v_t,$$

which, except for the inclusion of "total recruiting costs" ωv_t, is identical to the analysis in chapter 6. Thus the firm's profit function (in real terms) in period $t + 1$ is $A_{t+1} f(k_{t+1}, n_{t+1}) + k_{t+1} - w_{t+1} n_{t+1} - k_{t+2} - \omega v_{t+1}$, and so on for periods $t + 2$, $t + 3$, and so on.

With this background in place, your analysis is to proceed as follows:

a. Construct an infinite-period Lagrangian (starting from the beginning of period t) for the representative firm's (infinite-period) profit-maximization problem. This Lagrangian must take into account the employment constraints described above, along with correctly incorporating all of the other pieces of the theory described above. Use λ_t as your notation for the Lagrange multiplier on the period-t employment constraint, λ_{t+1} as the Lagrange multiplier on the period-$(t + 1)$ employment constraint, and so on. Because the Lagrangian has an infinite number of terms, write out the first several terms to make clear the nature of the Lagrangian, and provide any explanation needed in constructing the Lagrangian. (Note: Use the two-period analysis of firm theory in chapter 6 as your intuitive basis for constructing the Lagrangian. The Lagrangian is critical for all of the analysis that follows, so you should make sure that your work here is absolutely correct! If your Lagrangian here is incorrect, we will not necessarily "carry through the error" all the way through the remainder of your analysis when reviewing solutions.)

b. Based on the Lagrangian in part a, compute the first-order condition with respect to k_{t+1} (i.e., with respect to how much capital the firm would optimally like to use in its production process in period $t + 1$).

c. Based on the first-order condition computed in part b, explain (using any appropriate combination of mathematical analysis, graphical analysis, and logic) how the "search" aspects of labor markets affect the firm's capital demand decisions. For this part of the problem, you may (but do not need to) suppose that the production function is Cobb–Douglas: $f(k_t, n_t) = k_t^\alpha n_t^{1-\alpha}$, with $\alpha \in (0, 1)$.

d. Based on the Lagrangian in part a, compute the following three first-order conditions: with respect to v_t, with respect to n_{t+1}, and with respect to v_{t+1} (i.e., with respect to how many job openings ("vacancies") the firm optimally chooses in period t and period $t + 1$, and how many employees the firm would optimally like to have on its payroll at the beginning of period $t + 1$).

e. Based on the three first-order conditions computed in part d, construct an expression that reads

$$\frac{\omega}{q_t^{FIND}} = \dots,$$

in which the right-hand side of the expression is for you to determine. Your final expression may NOT include any Lagrange multipliers in it. (You should make very clear the algebraic steps involved in constructing this expression.)

The expression you obtained in part e is the job-creation condition. In the remainder of the analysis, you will compare and contrast the job-creation condition with the "labor demand" condition studied in chapter 6. For the remainder of the analysis, you may (but do not need to) suppose that the production function is Cobb–Douglas: $f(k_t, n_t) = k_t^\alpha n_t^{1-\alpha}$, with $\alpha \in (0, 1)$.

f. Consider the job-creation condition in part e. Suppose that all workers turn over every period:

$\rho = 1$.

With this assumption, what does the job creation condition simplify to? Briefly, but carefully, describe the economic interpretation of the job creation condition in this case?

g. Consider the job-creation condition in part e. As in part f, suppose that all workers turn over every period—that is, suppose $\rho = 1$. In addition suppose that a firm can always find a suitable worker:

$$q_t^{FIND} = q_{t+1}^{FIND} = q_{t+2}^{FIND} = q_{t+3}^{FIND} = \ldots 1 \, .$$

With these assumptions, what does the job creation condition simplify to? Briefly, but carefully, describe the economic interpretation of the job creation condition in this case?

h. Analytically, can the job creation condition in part e be simplified so that it becomes identical to the labor demand condition studied in chapter 6? If so, describe the entire set of assumptions needed to make the two identical (these assumptions would be of the form "variable x must have the numerical value y"). If not, describe why there is no set of assumptions that makes the job creation condition identical to the labor demand condition. In either case, briefly and qualitatively describe the economics of why (or why not) the two conditions can be made to coincide. (Hint: Your analysis here may build on your analysis in part f and/or part g; if you do so, carefully explain how your analysis builds on part f and/or part g.)

VIII
INTERNATIONAL MACROECONOMICS

Part VIII applies the tools, methods, and techniques that we have learned to "open-economy," or international, macroeconomics. An important connection between chapter 30 and chapter 31 is the concept of purchasing power parity (PPP).

Chapter 30 introduces us to international trade in goods and services, using a simple two-period analysis, which, by now, you are likely comfortable with.

Chapter 31 introduces the concepts of nominal exchange rates and real exchange rates and applies the concepts to a case study of a collapse of a fixed exchange rate regime.

30

Open-Economy Trade

The starting point for all of our dynamic macroeconomic analysis was the two-period consumption–savings framework. We learned the basic concepts of savings and net wealth through though the two-period model, we learned how to extend the analysis beyond two periods, how to apply multi-period frameworks to stock markets and bonds markets, how governments' taxation and spending policies can be viewed through a two-period or multi-period lens, how to apply it to both considerations of long-run growth as well as business cycles that are driven by "economic shocks," and so on.

The two-period model is a workhorse. We're now going to apply the workhorse two-period framework to yet another important topic in macroeconomic analysis: international trade of goods and services between countries.

There is a lot of "new" terminology that appears as we discuss the starting point of **open-economy** analysis, as opposed to the **closed-economy** study we've gone through so far. There already is the first of the "new" phrases to understand: **open-economy macroeconomics** refers to the consideration of trading goods and services across countries, whereas **closed-economy macroeconomics** refers to trades made inside a given country, ignoring the international sector.

Thankfully, the rest of the "new" terminology that will be presented and defined as we go along isn't actually all that new. As we will see, most, if not all, of the concepts embedded in "open-economy" language are clear analogues of the "closed-economy" language we have already been studying. What follows is an introduction to the international sector of an economy; more advanced topics and frameworks are properly left to a full course on international macroeconomics.

A Small Open Economy (SOE)

The simplest case of open-economy macroeconomics will get us started. Suppose there is one small open economy that we wish to analyze. A **small open economy** is one that takes the **world real interest rate as given.** It also takes other international prices as given, but the main focus is typically on real interests in global markets. The economic activities in a small open economy (typically abbreviated as SOE) cannot, in the usual ceteris paribus manner, affect world financial market prices or goods market prices because it is so tiny vis-à-vis the rest of the world (the rest of the world is typically abbreviated as ROW). A SOE has little or no economic might to shift either supply functions in international markets or demand functions in international markets all by itself.

There is no country in the world that is truly a small open economy; similarly there is no economy in the world that is a completely closed economy. But to keep things in perspective as we proceed, classic examples of SOE countries are Canada, Australia, Argentina, Mexico, Denmark, and Ireland.

Utility Function in SOE

You may already be recalling some similarities between the descriptions of an SOE and the "small" (relative to the entire market) consumers that were the starting point of the representative-consumer frameworks we have been discussing. For the SOE, we can think in terms of exactly the representative-consumer—or if we prefer, the representative-SOE—lens! Why? Because an SOE takes the real world interest rate, denoted as r_{ROW}, as given.

Just as in the closed-economy two period consumption–savings, let's consider the representative consumer (living in the representative SOE) first in terms of preferences across time and, soon, in budget constraint terms. Because we already know the two-period framework so well, we need not go into as much detail as when we first encountered it. Nonetheless, there are important differences.

For starters, the representative consumer living in a two-period SOE country has preferences across period-1 consumption and period-2 consumption captured by the lifetime (recall that "lifetime" means two periods) utility function $u(c_1, c_2)$. If we wish, we can include the β "subjective impatience factor" as well.

Here's where the first important difference comes in, which is entirely due to the open-economy nature of the analysis.

The "bundle" of goods in period 1, c_1, is itself a bundle of goods purchased from domestic firms and goods purchased from firms in the "rest of the world." Denote by $c_{1,H}$ goods produced by "domestic" firms (often interchangeably referred to as "home country" firms, hence the H subscript) and by $c_{1,ROW}$ goods produced by companies in the "rest of the world."[1]

---

1. In our modern, Internet, Amazon, speed of light delivery across the globe of Facebook pictures from family members that live 10 hours away blurs the "distinction" between "home goods and services" and "ROW goods and services." Despite the fact that the speed of and hence the cost of transportation, communication, and transmission has shrunk incredibly over the decades, a basic motivation for these leaps in technology was the desires of people in one country being able to purchase goods originally built or created in another country.

This bundle that composes c_1 can be written as

$$c_1 = \omega(c_{1,H}, c_{1,ROW}).$$

The $\omega(.)$ term is a function that takes both home-produced goods $c_{1,H}$ and foreign-produced goods $c_{1,ROW}$ and "packages" them into the period-1 bundle of goods c_1 that delivers utility to domestic consumers in period one.[2]

Similarly, for the second period, we have

$$c_2 = \omega(c_{2,H}, c_{2,ROW}).$$

If we insert these period-1 and period-2 bundled goods aggregators in the utility function from which we began, we have a utility function that sort of looks enormous:

$$u\left(\omega(c_{1,H}, c_{1,ROW}), \omega(c_{2,H}, c_{2,ROW})\right).$$

But keep in mind this is the same intertemporal utility function as above, except now each time period's c has an intratemporal, or static, component to it.

More precisely, there are preferences for consumption baskets c_1 and c_2 that are across time, just like in our two-period framework in the closed-economy case. Furthermore we can analyze the SOE's consumption–savings optimality condition. However, now with the open-economy dimension, we need to extend this consumption–savings idea to include the aggregator function ω. Inserting these aggregator functions is easy, but this admittedly requires a bit more writing.

A commonly used functional form for the consumption aggregator, used in both policy analysis and academic research, is

$$(c_1 =) \quad \omega(c_{1,H}, c_{1,ROW}) = \left[\sigma \cdot c_{1,H}^{\rho} + (1-\sigma) \cdot c_{1,ROW}^{\rho}\right]^{1/\rho}.$$

Similarly for period 2, the aggregator is

$$(c_2 =) \quad \omega(c_{2,H}, c_{2,ROW}) = \left[\sigma \cdot c_{2,H}^{\rho} + (1-\sigma) \cdot c_{2,ROW}^{\rho}\right]^{1/\rho}.$$

If the framework had more than two periods, the period-three consumption aggregator would look similar, as well as for period four, and so on. In the consumption aggregator, the parameters $\sigma \in (0, 1)$ (Greek lowercase letter "sigma") and $\rho > 0$ (Greek lowercase letter "rho") are under no control of the consumer—that is, they are exogenous.

If it were the case that $\sigma = 1$, then the aggregator is meaningless. Inserting $\sigma = 1$ in the expression above yields $c_1 = c_{1,H}$, the implication of which is that there is no

---

2. Broadly, one could describe the "preference" to have both domestically produced goods and services and goods and services produced abroad as a "love of variety." This sort of idea also appeared in the monopolistic competition analysis and the New Keynesian analysis earlier, in which we referred to it as "differentiated" products. Very generally speaking, the two concepts are similar; but don't worry, you don't need to recall monopolistic theory to understand the "love of variety" concept here.

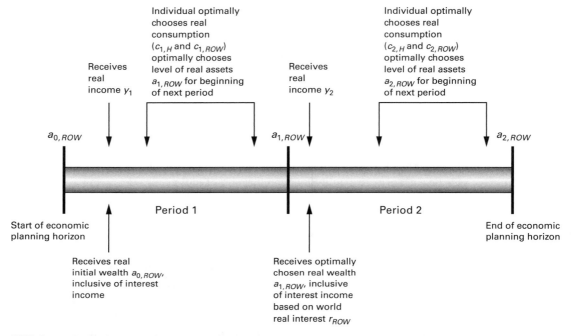

Figure 30.1
Timing of events in two-period SOE consumption–savings framework stated in real terms

international trade.[3] Supposing instead that the parameters are $\sigma = 0.5$ (the representative consumer cares equally about domestic goods and foreign goods) and $\rho = 2$, we have $c_1 = \sqrt{(c_{1,H}^2/2) + (c_{1,ROW}^2/2)}$. (Be careful with all the subscripts and superscripts here!) This utility functional form and parameterization is used to create the contour map displayed in figure 30.2, which describes the manner in which home goods and foreign goods combine into (aggregate up to) the period-1 consumption basket the SOE consumer enjoys.

Contour maps should be familiar by now. But we should *not* think of figure 30.2 as displaying indifference curves. Rather, figure 30.2 depicts how domestic goods and foreign goods "combine" into the c_1 consumption basket. It is c_1 (analogously, c_2) that the SOE consumer ultimately cares about.

Thus from here on, despite how cumbersome it appears, let's write the lifetime utility function as $u(\omega(c_{1,H}, c_{1,ROW}), \omega(c_{2,H}, c_{2,ROW}))$. A hint to remember for what's coming soon: we'll have to use the chain rule when computing the SOE consumer's optimality conditions.

---

3. You should be able to easily verify this for period 2, as well.

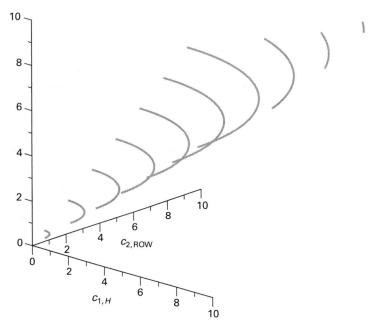

Figure 30.2
Contour map describing consumption in a given time period, which is an aggregate between domestic goods and goods from the rest of the world. Vertical axis is c_1. Parameter values are $\rho = 2$ and $\sigma = 0.5$.

Budget Constraints in SOE

Now let's turn to the expenditure side. The period-1 budget constraint is

$$c_{1,H} + e_1 \cdot c_{1,ROW} + a_{1,ROW} = y_1 + (1 + r_{ROW})a_{0,ROW},$$

and the period-2 budget constraint is similar,

$$c_{2,H} + e_2 \cdot c_{2,ROW} + a_{2,ROW} = y_2 + (1 + r_{ROW})a_{1,ROW}.$$

The $a_{2,ROW}$ and $a_{1,ROW}$ terms are the net wealth the SOE holds at different moments in time. As written in the budget constraints, the net wealth of an SOE (be it zero, negative, or positive) is entirely in foreign assets, rather than in domestic assets. We could include domestic assets as well, but it wouldn't change the main results and economic insights of our analysis, precisely because we are analyzing a *small* and *open* economy. In the framework studied here, **open** means there are no government regulations that prevent either the ROW purchasing SOE assets or SOE consumers purchasing ROW assets. With perfectly competitive financial markets between the SOE and ROW, domestic interest rates would simply equal r_{ROW}.[4]

The beginning-of-period-1 net wealth position is $a_{0,ROW}$, and just as in the closed-economy framework, suppose that $a_{2,ROW} = 0$. The net wealth position at the end of period 1 (and hence at the very start of period 2) emerges from the optimization of the representative individual, as a consequence of the savings decisions on the part of the SOE.

The y_1 and y_2 income terms "fall out of the sky" into the representative SOE consumer's wallet, and the individual has no control over it (i.e., y_1 and y_2 are endowments that are taken as given). This endowment income concept is exactly the same as in our closed-economy two-period analysis.

The e terms in the budget constraints are exchange rates. Specifically, e_1 is the *real exchange rate* in period 1, and e_2 is the *real exchange rate* in period 2. The reason that exchange rates arise is that *ROW* goods are denominated in "foreign goods" units, whereas *H* goods are denominated in "domestic goods" units. To be able to coherently add up $c_{1,H}$ and $c_{1,ROW}$ requires use of e_1, as the underbraces in the following shows:

$$\underbrace{\text{Domestic goods}}_{c_{1,H}} + \underbrace{\frac{\text{Domestic goods}}{\text{Foreign goods}}}_{e_1} \cdot \underbrace{\text{Foreign goods}}_{c_{1,ROW}}$$

The "foreign goods" units cancel out in the numerator and the denominator in the second term above. The same exact idea holds for period 2.[5]

Optimal Choice in SOE

Once again, just as in the closed-economy case, we can think in terms of the sequential approach or in terms of the lifetime analysis. We'll go through this quickly because by now this is a rehash of everything we've already covered in the book. But some important new terminology appears as we conduct the analysis.

Sequential Lagrange Analysis

Using the sequential Lagrangian approach,[6] the Lagrange function is

---

4. Furthermore, just as we extended the closed-economy two-period analysis to eventually many different types of assets, we could do the same here. Again, it would not change the main results of this framework.

5. We could also apply e to the stock of "foreign assets" a_{ROW}. But, because that would entail even more algebra, we avoid it and assume that "foreign"-based assets are already denominated in domestic goods units.

6. We could instead use a lifetime Lagrangian approach; just as in the basic two-period closed-economy framework, the two approaches lead to exactly the same results.

$$L(c_{1,H}, c_{1,ROW}, c_{2,H}, c_{2,ROW}, a_{1,ROW}, \lambda_1, \lambda_2) = u\big(\omega(c_{1,H}, c_{1,ROW}), \omega(c_{2,H}, c_{2,ROW})\big)$$
$$+ \lambda_1 \big[y_1 + (1 + r_{ROW})a_{0,ROW} - c_{1,H} - e_1 \cdot c_{1,ROW} - a_{1,ROW} \big]$$
$$+ \lambda_2 \big[y_2 + (1 + r_{ROW})a_{1,ROW} - c_{2,H} - e_2 \cdot c_{2,ROW} - a_{2,ROW} \big].$$

The first-order conditions are with respect to $c_{1,H}$, $c_{1,ROW}$, $c_{2,H}$, $c_{2,ROW}$, and $a_{1,ROW}$ (we'll leave out the FOCs with respect to the two multipliers because, by this point in our studies, we know what they are). Proceeding in order, we have

$$u_{c_1}\big(\omega(c_{1,H}, c_{1,ROW}), \omega(c_{2,H}, c_{2,ROW})\big) \cdot \omega_{c_{1,H}}(c_{1,H}, c_{1,ROW}) - \lambda_1 = 0,$$

$$u_{c_1}\big(\omega(c_{1,H}, c_{1,ROW}), \omega(c_{2,H}, c_{2,ROW})\big) \cdot \omega_{c_{1,ROW}}(c_{1,H}, c_{1,ROW}) - \lambda_1 \cdot e_1 = 0,$$

$$u_{c_2}\big(\omega(c_{1,H}, c_{1,ROW}), \omega(c_{2,H}, c_{2,ROW})\big) \cdot \omega_{c_{2,H}}(c_{2,H}, c_{2,ROW}) - \lambda_2 = 0,$$

$$u_{c_2}\big(\omega(c_{1,H}, c_{1,ROW}), \omega(c_{2,H}, c_{2,ROW})\big) \cdot \omega_{c_{2,ROW}}(c_{2,H}, c_{2,ROW}) - \lambda_2 \cdot e_2 = 0,$$

and

$-\lambda_1 + \lambda_2 \cdot (1 + r_{ROW}) = 0$. A lot of mathematics, for sure! But, it sheds good economic insight. Part of this good economic insight arises from an important point to observe: all of the FOCs with respect to goods (whether home goods or foreign goods) required use of the chain rule.

Optimality within Period 1

Eliminating the Lagrange multiplier λ_1 between the FOCs with respect to $c_{1,H}$ and $c_{1,ROW}$ gives us

$$\frac{\omega_{c_{1,ROW}}(c_{1,H}, c_{1,ROW})}{\omega_{c_{1,H}}(c_{1,H}, c_{1,ROW})} = e_1,$$

which, by this point in our studies, conveys a familiar economic result: at the representative SOE's optimal choice, the marginal rate of substitution between period-1 domestic goods and period-1 ROW goods equals some appropriate notion of relative price. The appropriate relative price in period 1 is the real exchange rate e_1, which is the quantity of the SOE's domestic baskets of goods that are required to purchase one basket of ROW goods.

Optimality within Period 2

Similarly eliminating the Lagrange multiplier λ_2 between the FOCs with respect to $c_{2,H}$ and $c_{2,ROW}$ gives us

$$\frac{\omega_{c_{2,ROW}}(c_{2,H}, c_{2,ROW})}{\omega_{c_{2,H}}(c_{2,H}, c_{2,ROW})} = e_2,$$

which conveys the same economic result as in period 1. The representative SOE consumer chooses the bundle $c_{2,H}$ and $c_{2,ROW}$ so that the marginal rate of substitution between period-2 domestic goods and period-2 ROW goods equals the real exchange rate in period 2, e_2.

Optimality across Period 1 and Period 2

How about the "consumption–savings optimality condition?" It is clear that the FOC with respect to ROW assets $a_{1,ROW}$ informs us that

$$\frac{\lambda_1}{\lambda_2} = 1 + r_{ROW} .$$

This expression already begins to imply that optimal savings and borrowing decisions by the representative SOE are conducted vis-à-vis the rest of the world. Keep this in mind when we define and discuss the "current account" below.

If we want to eliminate the λ_1 and λ_2 terms on the left-hand side so that we can see marginal utility terms, we apparently have, due to the several FOCs above, a few different ways to proceed. Regardless of which way we decide to continue, they all describe the same economic result. The only "differences" that may seem to arise are entirely due to real exchange rates and their movement across time periods.

One way to proceed is by using the FOCs with respect to $c_{1,H}$ and $c_{2,H}$ to eliminate both λ_1 and λ_2, which gives us a "consumption-savings optimality condition" of

$$\frac{u_{c_1}\left(\omega(c_{1,H}, c_{1,ROW}), \omega(c_{2,H}, c_{2,ROW})\right)}{u_{c_2}\left(\omega(c_{1,H}, c_{1,ROW}), \omega(c_{2,H}, c_{2,ROW})\right)} \cdot \frac{\omega_{c_{1,H}}(c_{1,H}, c_{1,ROW})}{\omega_{c_{2,H}}(c_{2,H}, c_{2,ROW})} = 1 + r_{ROW}.$$

The $u_{c1}(.)/u_{c2}(.)$ on the left-hand side should seem familiar from our closed-economy two-period consumption–savings framework.

Yet another way to proceed is using the FOCs with respect to $c_{1,ROW}$ and $c_{2,ROW}$ to eliminate both λ_1 and λ_2, which gives us a "consumption–savings optimality condition" of

$$\frac{u_{c_1}\left(\omega(c_{1,H}, c_{1,ROW}), \omega(c_{2,H}, c_{2,ROW})\right)}{u_{c_2}\left(\omega(c_{1,H}, c_{1,ROW}), \omega(c_{2,H}, c_{2,ROW})\right)} \cdot \frac{\omega_{c_{1,ROW}}(c_{1,H}, c_{1,ROW})}{\omega_{c_{2,ROW}}(c_{2,H}, c_{2,ROW})} \cdot \frac{e_2}{e_1} = 1 + r_{ROW},$$

in which **real exchange rates** appear. An alternative way of writing this is

$$\frac{u_{c_1}\left(\omega(c_{1,H}, c_{1,ROW}), \omega(c_{2,H}, c_{2,ROW})\right)}{u_{c_2}\left(\omega(c_{1,H}, c_{1,ROW}), \omega(c_{2,H}, c_{2,ROW})\right)} \cdot \frac{\omega_{c_{1,ROW}}(c_{1,H}, c_{1,ROW})}{\omega_{c_{2,ROW}}(c_{2,H}, c_{2,ROW})} = (1 + r_{ROW}) \cdot \frac{e_1}{e_2} .$$

Whichever of these two ways we prefer to write it, once again the $u_{c1}(.)/u_{c2}(.)$ on the left-hand side should look familiar from our closed-economy two-period consumption–savings framework.

Trade across Countries and the Current Account

Let's zoom out a bit. Unless domestic SOE consumers do not care at all about foreign ROW goods in their preferences,[7] an obvious result the framework conveys is that nations trade among each other.

Similar to the closed-economy two-period analysis, an important concept is the difference between **accumulation variables** and **flow variables.** Due to the "small" nature of the SOE, the accumulation variable is a_{ROW}, and changes of a_{ROW} across time are flow variables.

Let's rewrite the period-1 and period-2 budget constraints stated above,

$$c_{1,H} + e_1 \cdot c_{1,ROW} + a_{1,ROW} = y_1 + (1 + r_{ROW})a_{0,ROW}$$

and

$$c_{2,H} + e_2 \cdot c_{2,ROW} = y_2 + (1 + r_{ROW})a_{1,ROW},$$

in which, note, we have now set $a_{2,ROW} = 0$ in the period-2 budget for exactly the same reasons as in the closed-economy two-period framework.

Following the same procedure as in the closed-economy two-period analysis, isolate from the period-1 budget the difference in a_{ROW} between the end of period 1 and the beginning of period 1. Doing so gives us

$$\underbrace{a_{1,ROW} - a_{0,ROW}}_{\substack{\text{Capital account} \\ \text{in period 1}}} = \underbrace{\overbrace{y_1 - c_{1,H} - e_1 \cdot c_{1,ROW}}^{\text{Trade balance in period 1}} + \overbrace{r_{ROW}\, a_{0,ROW}}^{\substack{\text{Net factor payments} \\ \text{in period 1}}}}_{\text{Current account in period 1}},$$

in which the left-hand side, in open-economy terminology, is the **capital account** during period 1. The capital account measures the change of the SOE's foreign asset holdings during a given time period.

The first underbraced term on the right-hand side is the open economy's **trade balance** during period 1, and the second underbraced term on the right-hand side is the economy's **net factor payments** received at the very beginning of period 1. In turn the sum of the trade balance and net factor payments is known as the economy's **current account.**

An open economy's trade balance during a period could be positive, negative, or zero, and its net factor payments at the very beginning of that period could be positive, negative, or zero. In the trade balance expression above, the quantity of foreign ROW goods imported stated in units of domestic SOE goods is $e_1 c_{1,ROW}$, whereas the $c_{1,H}$ goods are produced and consumed domestically—that is, $c_{1,H}$ is *not* imported.

---

7. Which would occur if the consumption aggregator $\omega(.)$ in any and every time period did not include ROW goods at all, in which the economy has completely closed borders.

If we understand this terminology, it all applies to period 2, as well. If we were to extend the SOE framework to three periods, or four periods, or twelve periods, or more, all of this terminology remains.

Real Exchange Rates and Purchasing Power Parity (PPP)

To preview a part of the next chapter, let's simplify the framework and now suppose that domestic goods and foreign goods are perfect substitutes in utility. To describe this, recall the consumption aggregator example from earlier, $(c_1 =)$ $\omega(c_{1,H}, c_{1,ROW}) = \left[\sigma \cdot c_{1,H}^{\rho} + (1-\sigma) \cdot c_{1,ROW}^{\rho} \right]^{1/\rho}$. If $\rho = 1$, then it does not matter at all for SOE consumers whether they are enjoying SOE goods or ROW goods. All that matters is the relative price between the two goods. An analogous argument holds for period 2.

Turning to the relative price, the trade balance in period 1 is

$$tb_1 = y_1 - e_1 \cdot c_{1,ROW}$$

and similarly for period 2 is

$$tb_2 = y_2 - e_2 \cdot c_{2,ROW}.$$

These two expressions make clear that the real exchange rate e, which is the relative price between SOE and ROW goods, plays a central role in determining an economy's trade balance (regardless of whether it's a positive or negative trade balance).[8] Even more precisely, changes in e across time can heavily influence a SOE's trade balance.

A long-run empirical observation is that if cross-country trade barriers are low, then $e = 1$ on average. This idea of $e = 1$ is known as **purchasing power parity (PPP).** Trade across countries, though, almost always requires as an intermediate step an exchange of nominal currencies. The concept of PPP plays an important role in the analysis of nominal currency regimes, as chapter 31 discusses.

Chapter 30 Problem Set Questions

1. **Optimal SOE choices with and without foreign credit constraints: a numerical analysis.** Suppose for the period-1 consumption aggregator, $\omega(c_{1,H}, c_{1,ROW}) = \left[\sigma \cdot c_{1,H}^{\rho} + (1-\sigma) \cdot c_{1,ROW}^{\rho} \right]^{1/\rho}$, that $\sigma = 0$, which implies that $c_1 = c_{1,ROW}$. Similarly, for the period-2 consumption aggregator, $\omega(c_{2,H}, c_{2,ROW}) = \left[\sigma \cdot c_{2,H}^{\rho} + (1-\sigma) \cdot c_{2,ROW}^{\rho} \right]^{1/\rho}$, if $\sigma = 0$, then $c_2 = c_{2,ROW}$.

   Lifetime preferences of the representative SOE consumer are described by the utility function

---

8. The real exchange rate is defined as the quantity of domestic SOE baskets required to obtain one basket of foreign ROW goods.

$$u(c_1, c_2) = \sqrt{c_1} + \beta\sqrt{c_2},$$

where c_1 denotes consumption in period 1 and c_2 denotes consumption in period 2. The parameter β is known, and it is the subjective discount factor that measures the SOE consumer's degree of impatience: the smaller is β, the higher the weight the SOE consumer assigns to present consumption compared to future consumption.

Suppose that $\beta = 1/1.1$. The representative SOE household has initial real net foreign wealth of $(1 + r_{ROW})a_{0,ROW} = 1$, and has endowment $y_1 = 5$ units of goods in period 1 and endowment $y_2 = 10$ units of goods in period 2. The real interest rate paid on foreign assets held from period 1 to period 2 is $r_{ROW} = 0.1$, and the real exchange rate $e_1 = 1$ and $e_2 = 1$.

a. For the given utility function, calculate the equilibrium levels of consumption in periods 1 and 2. (Hint: Set up the Lagrangian and solve.)

b. Starting from your solutions in part a, calculate the SOE's trade balance in period 1 (tb_1) and current account in period 1.

c. Suppose now that foreign lenders to this SOE economy impose credit constraints on domestic SOE consumers. Specifically, foreign lenders impose the tightest possible credit constraint—SOE consumers are not allowed to be in debt at the end of period 1, which implies that the SOE consumer's real wealth at the end of period 1 must be nonnegative ($a_{1,ROW} \geq 0$). What is the SOE's optimal choices of period-1 and period-2 consumption under this cross-country credit restriction? Briefly explain, either logically or graphically or both.

d. Does the credit constraint described in part c enhance or diminish the welfare of the SOE economy (i.e., does it increase or decrease lifetime utility)?

2. **SOE government sovereignty and the consequences of sanctions.** Consider a two-period model of the SOE government, with g_1 and g_2 denoting real government spending in periods 1 and 2, and t_1 and t_2 denoting real lump-sum taxes collected by the government in periods 1 and 2.

The consideration of the government's "utility" function likely involves more than simple economic considerations. Nonetheless, one can study what a government (whether SOE or not) would choose to do if it had some particular some utility function.

Suppose that the SOE government's lifetime utility function is $g_1 - t_1$. That is, the government only cares (in terms of utils) about period-1 government spending net of tax collections. However, due to political considerations, there is an upper limit of 100 on how large a fiscal surplus can be run in period 2.

The government's lifetime budget constraint is

$$g_1 + \frac{g_2}{1+r} = t_1 + \frac{t_2}{1+r} + (1+r)b_0,$$

with r denoting the real interest rate. For simplicity, suppose throughout this problem that $r = 0$. The government's real asset position at the start of period one is b_0, at the end of period 1 is b_1, and (as usual in the two-period analysis of the government) at the end of period 2 is $b_2 = 0$.

Suppose that the SOE government begins period 1 with a negative asset position—that is, suppose $b_0 < 0$.

a. If $b_0 < 0$, is the government in debt at the beginning of period one? Or is it impossible to determine? Justify/explain in no more than two phrases/sentences.

b. Suppose that he government can possibly choose to reset b_0 to zero. That is, by sovereign right of being a government, suppose that it can simply "announce" $b_0 = 0$ even though, absent any such announcement, $b_0 < 0$. Would resetting b_0 to zero possibly allow the government to reach higher lifetime utility? Or would it necessarily decrease the lifetime utility the government could reach? Or would it leave the lifetime utility the government could reach unchanged? Or is it impossible to determine? Briefly, but thoroughly, justify/explain.

c. Suppose that the government can not only possibly choose to reset b_0 to zero (as in part b above), but it could also choose to reset b_0 to a strictly positive value (i.e., it could choose to set some $b_0 > 0$). However, if it does set b_0 to a strictly positive value, the rest of the world imposes "sanctions" on this country's government, which the government is fully aware of. These sanctions cause two things to happen:

i. Any positive b_0 that the government decides it has are removed by the sanctions; that is, the sanctions cause b_0 to fall back to exactly zero.

ii. The world's financial markets prohibit this particular government from borrowing at all during period 1.

Taking into account the consequences of the sanctions, would resetting b_0 to a strictly positive value possibly allow the government to reach higher lifetime utility? Or would it necessarily decrease the lifetime utility the government could reach? Or would it leave the lifetime utility the government could reach unchanged? Or is it impossible to determine? In answering this question, the policy choice of comparison should be the utility consequences of resetting b_0 to zero that was analyzed in part b. Briefly, but thoroughly, justify/explain

d. If the goal of the government is to maximize its lifetime utility, answer two related questions:

    i. What should it choose to do regarding b_0 (i.e., should it leave the $b_0 < 0$ as is; should it choose to reset b_0 to zero as in part b; or should it choose to reset b_0 to a strictly positive value as in part c)?

    ii. What value for $g_1 - t_1$ should it set in period 1?

(Note: You are to answer both of these questions, and keep in mind the setup of the question described above.) Briefly, but thoroughly, justify/explain

31

Fiscal Theory of Exchange Rates

We now turn to the subject of international monetary economics. Specifically, we will consider the interaction of a fixed exchange rate system with fiscal policy. Exchange rate management is typically thought to be in the domain of monetary, not fiscal, policy. However, we will learn that fiscal policy considerations also impact exchange rates. We will build a small theoretical model that allows us to study this interaction. Our theoretical model will consist of four building blocks:

1. Money demand function
2. Purchasing power parity (PPP)
3. Interest parity condition
4. Government budget constraint

Before we describe these four building blocks, we will discuss the timing of the model. Specifically, rather than a two-period economy we have considered in much of our study, we will consider an infinite-period economy. Then, after laying out the four building blocks, we consider the workings of the model, paying close attention to the influence of fiscal policy on nominal exchange rates.

Infinite-Period Economy

By now you are comfortable with the idea of the two-period economy we used in studying the representative consumer's consumption–savings decision. The two-period economy served our purposes in that task, but turns out to be insufficient in our present study of the interaction between fiscal policy and exchange rates. Thus we now generalize our model economy to allow for an infinite number of time periods. The reasons why we need an arbitrarily large number of time periods will become clearer as we proceed.[1]

In the two-period economy, the "names" of each of the two periods was fairly natural—we named them period 1 and period 2. We could analogously name the time periods in our

---

1. But you should recall that we've used the infinite-period framework for many applications already.

present infinite-period economy as period 1, period 2, period 3, period 4, period 5, and so on, without end. However, again as will become clearer below, the specific "name" of a given time period will have no relevance—all that will matter is how far (in time) a given time period is from any other given time period and whether it comes before or after it. For example, period 2 is two time periods earlier than period 4. But period 11 is also two time periods earlier than period 13. And period 134 is two time periods earlier than time period 136. Because all we will need to care about is how time periods relate to each other, rather than any absolute sense of time, we will name the time periods in a more general fashion, specifically by calling them t, $t+1$, $t+2$, $t+3$, $t+4$, ... With this notation, t can take on any value: we could have $t = 0$, in which case $t+1 = 1$ and $t+2 = 2$. Or we could have t =11, in which case $t+1 = 12$, $t+2 = 13$, and so on. With this notation, obviously period t is two time periods earlier than period $t+2$, and that is as specific as we will need to be for our upcoming analysis.

Money Demand Function

Consumers are assumed to need money in order to purchase their consumption in every period. That is, all consumption purchases require the use of cash, which implies that "checks" drawn against bank deposits do not exist in this economy. This need for cash gives rise to a money demand function that has the usual properties we have associated with a money demand function. Specifically, we will denote the **nominal money demand function** as

$$M_t = P_t \cdot \phi(c_t, i_t)$$

in which P_t denotes, as usual, the nominal price level (also the nominal price of consumption) in period t, the function $\phi(.)$ is the real money demand function, c_t denotes consumption in period t, and i_t denotes the nominal interest rate on bank deposits held by consumers between period t and $t+1$. The reason that $\phi(.)$ is **real** money demand is that if we divide both sides of the expression above by the price level P_t, we have real money demand M_t / P_t equals $\phi(c_t, i_t)$.

In general, consumption may be different in each period, hence the time subscript t. However, to focus our attention on the important issues, we will assume for simplicity that $c_t = \overline{c}$ in every period, where $\overline{c}$ is simply some constant (aka, steady-state) quantity of consumption. All this says is that in period t, consumption equals $\overline{c}$, in period $t+1$ consumption equals the same value $\overline{c}$, in period $t+2$ consumption equals the same value $\overline{c}$, and so on and on.[2]

---

2. In terms of the two-period consumption–savings model, you should be able to convince yourself that it is possible for an individual's optimal choice (i.e., the tangency between an indifference curve and the lifetime budget constraint) to occur at a point such that consumption is equal in the two periods. Our assumption here that consumption is constant in each of the infinite number of periods is simply the infinite-period analogue of that outcome. Equivalently, we can think of the economy being in long-run steady-state conditions.

Purchasing Power Parity (PPP)

We will follow a long-standing tradition in international economics and denote foreign country variables using a superscripted asterisk. Domestic country variables are thus denoted without an asterisk. With this convention, we define P_t^* as the foreign country price level in period t, P_t as the domestic country price level in period t, and E_t as the nominal exchange rate between the currencies of the two countries.

It is very important to be clear about the units associated with these variables, especially those of the nominal exchange rate. The units associated with the foreign price level P_t^* is foreign currency per one basket of foreign goods. The units associated with the domestic price level P_t is domestic currency per one basket of domestic goods.

The units of the nominal exchange rate is domestic currency per unit of foreign currency. For example, if we call the US the domestic country and Australia the foreign country, then we have P_t is the dollar price of one basket of US goods (i.e., think of the CPI basket here), P_t^* is the Australian dollar price of one basket of Australian goods, and E_t is the number of US dollars needed to buy one Australian dollar. It is, of course, possible to define E_t in the inverse way, as the number of Australian dollars needed to buy one US dollar. Thus our convention here is simply a matter of preference. However, it is crucial that once we adopt a convention (and our convention is domestic currency needed to buy one unit of foreign currency), we must be consistent throughout our analysis.

With this notation clear, we can proceed to describe the second fundamental building block of our model, purchasing power parity, abbreviated PPP. Simply put, the concept of PPP states that when prices of goods in any two different countries are converted into the same currency units (using the nominal exchange rate), they are the same.

Consider a simple recent (and recurring) example: *The Economist* newspaper's frequent "Big Mac Index" currency comparison reported that in the United States a 2014 McDonald's Big Mac cost $4.80 (USD), while in Australia a 2014 McDonalds's Big Mac[3] cost 270 Australian dollars (AUD). In 2014, the nominal exchange rate between the US dollar and the Australian dollar was 1.05 AUD per one USD (equivalently, $1/1.05 = 0.95$ USD per AUD). If we convert the AUD price of a Big Mac in Australia into USD terms, we find that the dollar price of a Big Mac in Australia was

$$\left(\frac{5.07 \text{ AUD}}{\text{Big Mac}} \right) \left(\frac{0.95 \text{ USD}}{1 \text{ AUD}} \right) = \frac{4.82 \text{ USD}}{\text{Big Mac}},$$

which is exactly the same as the dollar price of a Big Mac in the United States.

The notion of purchasing power parity (PPP) is the macroeconomic analogue of the idea this example illustrates. PPP states that identical baskets of goods in different countries

---

3. Let's ignore any regional variation (i.e., Australian burgers may have more "shrimp on the bahbie" than American burgers) and suppose that the Australian Big Mac is exactly the same product as the US Big Mac.

have the same price level when converted into a common currency. To extend our example, if the average basket of goods consumed by US consumers is the same as the average basket of goods consumed by Australian consumers, then PPP dictates that the price levels of the two economies are the same once converted into a common currency.[4]

Recall our notation: P_t^* denotes the foreign country price level, P_t denotes the domestic country price level, and E_t denotes the nominal exchange rate in units of domestic currency per one unit of foreign currency. By this notation, PPP is the condition[5]

$$P_t = E_t P_t^*.$$

This expression is the algebraic definition of PPP. We will assume throughout the analysis that PPP always holds in our model economy.

An important question that should naturally arise is: does PPP hold in reality? The answer, as the answer to most questions about the validity of assumptions in economics, is not exactly. In fact PPP does not hold between any two given countries at every point in time (i.e., every year). However, data suggest that PPP does seem to hold in the long run. That is, if we take averages of price levels and exchange rates over several or many years, the condition immediately above is more often satisfied. PPP is thus a long-run phenomenon. We are making the stronger assumption that PPP is also a short-run phenomenon because we will assume that it holds at every time period t.

Finally, we will make one further auxiliary assumption associated with PPP. This second assumption is simply to make our subsequent mathematical analysis simpler, and none of the general economic results we will derive depend on it. We will assume that the foreign country price level is constant and equal to one in every period. That is, $P_t^* = 1$ in every period. Imposing this assumption on the PPP condition above gives us

$$P_t = E_t,$$

which states that the domestic price level equals the nominal exchange rate in every period t. Note that if the domestic price level rises for any reason, it must be accompanied by a rise in E_t. A rise in E_t means that the domestic currency becomes weaker relative to the foreign currency, since it now takes more units of domestic currency to purchase one unit of the foreign currency. Such a weakening of one currency versus another is called a **depreciation.** Thus, again referring to the expression $P_t = E_t$, we can conclude that domestic price inflation implies, and is implied by, depreciation of the exchange rate. Similarly nominal price deflation (a fall in the domestic price level) implies, and is implied by, **appreciation**

---

4. The assumption that US consumers and Australian consumers consume exactly the same basket of goods is obviously a simplification. For example, it's likely that a good such as shrimp is a more important component of the Australian basket of goods than of the US basket of goods. But to the extent that Australian consumers and US consumers generally consume the same types of things (food, TV's, cars, etc.), it's perhaps not such a bad approximation to reality.

5. Convince yourself that this expression is essentially what we used in our Big Mac example.

of the exchange rate, which is a strengthening of the domestic currency versus the foreign currency.

Finally, notice that using the condition above ($P_t = E_t$) into the money demand function displayed earlier, we can rewrite the money demand function as

$$\frac{M_t}{E_t} = \phi(c_t, i_t).$$

Interest Parity Condition

The third building block of our model is the interest parity condition. To build this element of the model, we must introduce a concept known as **arbitrage.** When investors are faced with the option of investing in the nominal assets of different countries, not surprisingly, all other things equal, they will invest in those country's assets that yield the highest returns. Specifically, they will invest in those country's assets that yield the highest real, as opposed to nominal, returns, even though assets typically have only nominal returns associated with them. As a result of the typically (but, as we have seen, not necessarily always) highly competitive nature of global financial markets, the real returns of different countries' assets are equalized.[6] This does not mean, however, that real interest rates across countries are equalized. In fact the condition that describes this equalization of real returns is more subtle, as we now discuss.

Different countries' assets are denominated in different currencies. US assets are denominated in dollars and Australian assets are denominated in Australian dollars. Because of the different currency units associated with different countries' assets, comparing their relative attractiveness requires converting their returns into the same currency units. For example, a US investor presumably cares about the total dollar return on his investment regardless of whether he invests in the US or Australia.

Denote by i_t the domestic (in this example, the US) nominal interest rate, i_t^* the foreign (in this example, Australia) nominal interest rate, r_t^* the foreign real interest rate, and π_t^* the foreign inflation rate. If a US investor invests \$1 in a US bond, after the bond matures (e.g., at time $t+1$) he clearly will get back $1+i_t$ dollars. Consider his thought process about investing \$1 in a Australian bond, however. First, he would have to convert that \$1 into AUD at time t, which he can do at the exchange rate E_t USD per AUD. After the currency exchange, he has $1/E_t$ AUD which he can invest in the Australian asset. If he holds the Australian bond until maturity (also in period $t+1$), he will earn interest so that at maturity he will have $(1+i_t^*)(1/E_t)$ AUD. Because he lives in the United States, however, he needs to convert these AUD back into USD, which at time $t+1$ he can do at

---

6. Recall from basic microeconomics that in perfect competition, firms do not set prices but rather simply take the market price as given. Because of this, the price of each firm's output is the same.

the exchange rate E_{t+1} USD per AUD. Completing this final transaction would leave him with a total of $(1+i_t^*)(E_{t+1}/E_t)$ USD.

However, the exchange rate in the future is obviously not known. All the investor can base his decision on is what he expects the future exchange rate to be. Denote this expectation of the future exchange rate by E_{t+1}^e. He thus expects that by investing \$1 in a Australian bond he will get back a total of $(1+i_t)(E_{t+1}^e/E_t)$ in the future.

If arbitrage holds, as is generally the case in global financial markets, then the expected returns of investing in the United States should be the same as investing in Australia. From the analysis above, this implies that

$$1+i_t = (1+i_t^*)\frac{E_{t+1}^e}{E_t},$$

which is known as the **interest parity condition.** Because of our earlier assumption that the foreign price level is always $P_t^* = 1$, foreign inflation is always $\pi_t^* = 0$. This implies, by the Fisher equation, that the foreign nominal interest rate equals the foreign real interest rate in every period of the economy, $i_t^* = r_t^*$. Substituting this result into the interest parity condition allows us to rewrite it as

$$1+i_t = (1+r_t^*)\frac{E_{t+1}^e}{E_t}.$$

Again, you are probably questioning how accurate interest rate parity is in reality. Because of the highly competitive nature of global financial markets, it actually is a very good approximation. Most deviations that do occur from interest rate parity[7] last for only a short time. So we will take in our model that interest rate parity holds all the time.

Government Budget Constraint

Finally, we describe the most important building block of our model, the government budget constraint. This budget constraint is not a lifetime budget constraint, but rather a period-by-period budget constraint.

In each period t the government has three sources of income: nominal tax revenues T_t, money creation $M_t - M_{t-1}$, and interest earnings on foreign reserves. Foreign reserves are foreign countries' assets that a central bank holds for the purposes of official international financial transactions. Foreign reserves is a stock variable, similar to the net assets of the representative consumer that we encountered in our study of the consumption–savings model.

---

7. Deviations occur because of activities such as currency trading and bond trading by investors and financial institutions.

Denote by B_t^G the foreign reserves held by the central bank at the end of period t. Foreign reserves are usually not held in the form of hard currency but rather in the form of government bonds. For example, Argentina's central bank's reserves of dollars are not held as US currency but instead as US bonds. Thus foreign reserves pay interest. We will denominate interest earnings on foreign reserves in terms of domestic currency. To do this, we need three pieces: the nominal exchange rate, the foreign interest rate, and foreign reserve holdings at the end of the previous period. In period t, interest earnings on foreign reserves are then given by $E_t i_t^* B_{t-1}^G$. Again, because of our assumption of zero foreign inflation, we can replace i_t^* by r_t^* in this last expression. Thus we have algebraic expressions for the three sources of government revenue in each period t. The two expenditure items for the government are nominal government purchases G_t and additions (or subtractions) to its holdings of foreign reserves, which are represented by $E_t \left(B_t^G - B_{t-1}^G \right)$. We can now write the government budget constraint as

$$E_t \left(B_t^G - B_{t-1}^G \right) + G_t = T_t + \left(M_t - M_{t-1} \right) + E_t r_t^* B_{t-1}^G.$$

After a couple of further algebraic manipulations, we can again rewrite this expression in the following useful way,

$$B_t^G - B_{t-1}^G = \frac{M_t - M_{t-1}}{P_t} - \left[\frac{G_t}{P_t} - \frac{T_t}{P_t} - r_t^* B_{t-1}^G \right].$$

To get to the expression immediately above, we have used the fact that the price level equals the nominal exchange rate (the $P_t = E_t$ expression described earlier). The left-hand side of expression immediately above is the change in foreign reserve holdings during period t.

The first term on the right-hand side of the expression is real government seignorage revenue, which is the government's revenue from money creation (in real terms because it is divided by the nominal price level). And the second term on the right-hand side is the difference between government expenditure and income from the collection of taxes and the receipt of interest payments on foreign reserve holdings. This term is called the **real secondary deficit**, and we will denote it by DEF_t,

$$DEF_t = \frac{G_t}{P_t} - \frac{T_t}{P_t} - r_t^* B_{t-1}^G.$$

Using this definition and the fact that $P_t = E_t$ allows us to rewrite yet again the expression as

$$B_t^G - B_{t-1}^G = \frac{M_t - M_{t-1}}{E_t} - DEF_t.$$

This expression makes clear that a fiscal deficit $\left(DEF_t > 0 \right)$ must be associated with money creation $\left(M_t - M_{t-1} > 0 \right)$ or with a decline in the government's foreign reserves

$\left(B_t^G - B_{t-1}^G < 0\right)$, or both. This expression for the government budget constraint (abbreviated by GBC) will be the workhorse of our analysis of fixed exchange rate systems, to which we now turn.

Analyzing a Fixed Exchange Rate System

We now use the model we have just built to analyze the interaction of a fixed exchange rate system with fiscal policy.[8] To further focus our attention on the most important issues, we add one more assumption, that the foreign real interest rate is constant in every time period. Algebraically, $r_t^* = \bar{r}^*$, where $\bar{r}^*$ is simply some constant.

Suppose that a country is currently maintaining a fixed nominal exchange rate vis-à-vis a foreign country, which means that E_t is a constant. Even more specifically, the public expects the exchange rate to always be constant. Let E with no subscript denote this constant value of the nominal exchange rate. Because the public expects the exchange rate to continue to be pegged, $E_{t+1}^e = E_t = E$, meaning that the interest parity condition yields $i_t = \bar{r}^*$. Qualitatively, if a fixed exchange rate system is in place and is expected to remain in place, the domestic nominal interest rate equals the constant foreign real interest rate.[9]

Next insert this constant value for the domestic nominal interest rate into the money demand function. With a constant nominal interest rate and consumption constant at $c_t = \bar{c}$ every period, real money demand M_t / P_t must be a constant every period. But the domestic price level P_t is itself a constant during the fixed exchange rate system because $P_t = E_t$.

This implies that nominal money M_t must also be constant—that is, $M_t = M_{t-1}$ always. With constant nominal money in the economy, the GBC reveals that seignorage revenue is zero. This is the first important result obtained in this model: under a fixed exchange rate system, the government earns zero seignorage revenue because the money supply of the economy must be constant. The government is unable to print money under a fixed exchange rate system. Recall from our study of domestic (aka, closed-economy) macroeconomics that increasing the money supply usually leads to a short-term boost in GDP but leads, in the long-run, to inflation. Under a fixed exchange rate system, the central bank loses this channel of boosting GDP. But the potential benefit is that by tying their hands, the central bank avoids creating inflation in the economy.

Now, because seignorage revenue is zero, the GBC becomes

$$B_t^G - B_{t-1}^G = -DEF_t..$$

This expression shows that under a fixed exchange rate system, a fiscal deficit necessarily implies a loss of foreign reserves. As a simple example, suppose that a country has a fixed

---

8. The analysis of a floating exchange rate system using this model is more complicated, and we leave this topic for a more advanced course in International Economics.

9. More generally, it equals the foreign nominal interest rate. But we have $i_t = r_t$ always here in our model.

exchange rate system in place and the government has \$20 billion of US foreign reserves at the end of period $t-1$ (e.g., the year 1999). During period t the exchange rate peg continues in force, meaning seignorage revenue is zero. The government simultaneously runs a real secondary deficit, so that $DEF > 0$ in period t. By the expression above, this necessarily means that foreign reserves at the end of period t are smaller than foreign reserves at the end of period $t-1$. Essentially the government had to use some of its stock of foreign reserves to pay for its deficit.

The Collapse of a Fixed Exchange Rate System

The natural lower limit on foreign reserves is zero. When a country runs out of foreign reserves ($B^G = 0$), that's it.[10] Thus, if a country is running a fixed exchange rate system simultaneous with a real secondary deficit, eventually foreign reserves will be completely drained. Once the country runs out of foreign reserves, it has two options. One option is to reverse its secondary deficit and preserve its fixed exchange rate. The other option, if it doesn't have the political will to reverse the deficit, is to abandon the fixed exchange rate by beginning to print money. We briefly analyze these two alternatives using the model we have laid out.

When foreign reserves run out (and they cannot go negative), no further depletion of foreign reserves can occur. Suppose at the end of period $t-1$, foreign reserves have been depleted down to $B_{t-1}^G = 0$. The government must decide how to manage its finances in period t. The GBC must hold in period t (as it must in every period!)—that is, the government must somehow make it hold. If the government wishes to maintain the fixed exchange rate in period t, that automatically means the money supply will not change, so that $M_t = M_{t-1}$. Seignorage revenue is zero. With no more foreign reserves to use, the GBC shows that DEF cannot be strictly negative in period t.

If the government somehow balances its budget so that $DEF = 0$, foreign reserves continue to be zero but at least the situation is sustainable. Alternatively, the government may somehow find the political will to turn the deficit into a surplus, $DEF > 0$ in period t, which would mean that foreign reserves would once again begin to accumulate.

If the government is unable to reverse the deficit, however, the only available recourse is to devalue the currency (i.e., purposely weaken the domestic currency versus the foreign currency). The devaluation may be either anticipated or unanticipated by the public.

Suppose first that the devaluation is unanticipated, meaning that $E_t^e = E_{t-1}$, but the actual exchange rate turns out to be $E_t > E_{t-1}$. By instituting a one-time surprise devaluation, the central bank is able to raise seignorage revenue in period t. To see this, first note that a

10. This is not technically true. It is possible for a country to have "negative" foreign reserves, through arrangements known as central banks' special drawing rights. Essentially, such arrangements allow central banks to borrow foreign reserves from each other. We leave this more technical aspect to a more advanced course on international economics and simply suppose that the lower limit on foreign reserves is zero.

devaluation in period t necessarily means $P_t > P_{t-1}$. If the public expects there to never be a devaluation again, then $c_t = \bar{c}$ continues to hold and $i_t = \bar{r}^*$ continues to hold (the latter follows from the interest parity condition). Thus real money demand remains unchanged in period t and the entire rise of the price level must be met with increased nominal money in period t. The fact that $M_t > M_{t-1}$ means seignorage revenue becomes strictly positive in period t. The amount of seignorage revenue needed is at least that required to pay off the deficit in period t, because the left-hand side of the GBC cannot be negative in period t.

Yet the devaluation could have been anticipated by the public. An anticipated devaluation manifests itself in period $t-1$ as $E_t^e > E_{t-1}$. By the interest parity condition, the anticipated devaluation means that the domestic nominal interest rate in period $t-1$ rises compared to its usual level. The money demand function then shows us that real money demand in period $t-1$ falls relative to that in period $t-2$. The price level in period $t-1$ has not yet risen, which necessarily implies that nominal money in period t -1 is smaller than nominal money in period t -2.

With $M_{t-1} < M_{t-2}$, seignorage revenue is negative in the period preceding the fall of the nominal exchange rate peg. Inspecting the government budget constraint shows that the negative seignorage revenue coupled with the fiscal deficit means foreign reserves drain even more quickly in period $t-1$ than if the devaluation were not anticipated. This situation is termed a **balance of payments crisis.** What is going on is that domestic residents, fearing an impending devaluation of their currency, rush to the central bank to exchange their domestic currency for foreign currency. When they do so, the exchange rate is still pegged. In order to honor the commitment to the fixed exchange rate, the central bank must cash in some of its stockpile of foreign reserves to give its residents foreign currency. This cashing in of foreign reserves represents a second drain in addition to the fiscal deficit. The end result is that the fixed exchange rate must be abandoned even sooner than period $t+1$ (call it "period t and a half" if you like).

We consider below how to model a balance of payments crisis in more detail. First, however, we consider the equilibrium of the model we have set up under a floating exchange rate system.

Equilibrium under a Floating Exchange Rate Regime[11]

Under a floating exchange rate regime, the nominal exchange rate is market-determined (i.e., set by the forces of supply and demand). In order to consider nominal exchange rate determination in such an environment, we must take a stand on what type of monetary policy the central bank follows. For simplicity, and because it serves to illustrate the main issues, we will assume the central bank simply determines how much money

---

11. This and the subsequent sections are adapted from *International Macroeconomics* by Stephanie Schmitt-Grohe and Martin Uribe.

is in circulation each period—that is, we will assume the central bank follows a money growth rule.

Specifically, suppose the central bank expands the money supply at the constant rate μ between any two consecutive periods, so that

$$M_{t+1} = (1+\mu)M_t;$$

for example, if the central bank expands the money supply by 5 percent between any two periods t and $t+1$, we would have $\mu = 0.05$. Our goal is to determine how the nominal exchange rate, the price level, real balances, and the domestic nominal interest rate evolve over time when the central bank is following this money supply rule. To do this, we will guess, and then verify, that in equilibrium the nominal exchange rate depreciates at the rate μ. Thus we guess that the nominal exchange rate evolves over time according to

$$E_{t+1} = (1+\mu)E_t.$$

Because in our model PPP holds and the foreign price level equals one in every period, we know that $P_t = E_t$ in every period; this means that the domestic price level evolves over time according to

$$P_{t+1} = (1+\mu)P_t.$$

This expression says that given our guess for how the nominal exchange rate moves over time, the rate of inflation equals the rate of money growth chosen by the central bank. There is a lot of empirical evidence across countries that shows that on average a country's inflation rate is very closely related to the money growth rate; furthermore evidence also shows that for currencies that have floating exchange rates, the rate of depreciation of the nominal exchange rate is also very closely related to the money growth rate.[12] Our model formalizes these relationships.

Next, to determine the domestic nominal interest rate i_t, we use the interest parity condition

$$1+i_t = (1+r^*)\frac{E_{t+1}^e}{E_t} = (1+r^*)\frac{(1+\mu)E_t}{E_t} = (1+r^*)(1+\mu).$$

We can solve this expression for the domestic nominal interest rate,

$$i_t = (1+r^*)(1+\mu)-1,$$

which shows that i_t depends on μ. Let's compactly denote this functional dependence by writing $i_t = i(\mu)$, where the functional notation $i(\mu)$ on the right-hand side

---

12. The observation that inflation and money growth are highly correlated is the foundation of the *quantity theory of money,* a theory of how monetary policy affects inflation that owes much of its original articulation to the late Nobel Prize-winning economist Milton Friedman.

abstractly captures the relationship. If $\mu = 0$, clearly $i_t = r^*$. If $\mu > 0$, then the domestic nominal interest rate exceeds the foreign interest rate. The economic intuition behind this is that expansion of the domestic money supply makes it less valuable; the resulting depreciation of the domestic currency requires that bonds denominated in domestic currency must carry a higher interest return in order to induce investors to purchase it. Note that if the function $i(\mu)$ is increasing in μ, the higher is the domestic money growth rate, and the higher is the domestic nominal interest rate. Mathematically, $i'(\mu) > 0$.

Substituting the relationship $i_t = i(\mu)$ into the money demand function yields

$$\frac{M_t}{E_t} = \phi(\overline{c}, i(\mu)).$$

Consumption $\overline{c}$ is as before constant over time; with a time-invariant money growth rate μ, the nominal interest rate is also constant over time. Hence the right-hand side of the previous expression is constant over time. For the money market to be in equilibrium, the left-hand side of the previous expression must therefore also be constant over time. We already know—because of the assumed money growth rule—that M grows at the rate μ every period. The only way the left-hand side can be constant is for E to grow at the rate μ every period, as well. This is indeed true under our initial guess that $E_{t+1} = (1 + \mu)E_t$. Thus we have verified our original guess and have determined how the nominal exchange rate, the domestic price level, and the domestic nominal interest rate all evolve over time if the central bank is following a constant money growth rule with a flexible nominal exchange rate.

Balance of Payments (BOP) Crises

A balance of payments (BOP) crisis is a situation in which the government is unable or unwilling to meets its international financial obligations. These difficulties may manifest themselves in a variety of ways, such as the failure to honor the domestic and/or foreign public debt or the suspension of currency convertibility.

Often the root cause of a BOP crisis is an unsustainable mix of fiscal policy and monetary policy. A classic example of such an unsustainable policy mix is a situation in which the government pegs the nominal exchange rate at a level stronger than under the floating rate and the government simultaneously runs a fiscal deficit. As we saw earlier, under a fixed exchange rate system, the government must finance any fiscal deficit by running down its foreign reserves because it cannot change the nominal money supply—that is, when the nominal exchange rate is pegged, $\mu = 0$.

As we alluded to above, however, in the days or weeks immediately **before** a peg collapses, the equilibrium money supply **shrinks** because holders of domestic currency, fearing the coming devaluation of their nominal assets, rush to rid themselves of their domestic currency holdings. In this rest of this chapter we will study in detail the most popular model used to study the dynamics of a collapse of a fixed exchange rate system.

Consider a country that is running a constant fiscal deficit $DEF > 0$ every period. Also suppose that the government has fixed the nominal exchange rate at E units of domestic currency per unit of foreign currency. The government has positive foreign reserves, but its foreign reserves can never go below zero. Based on our earlier discussion, it is thus clear that as long as the fixed exchange rate is in place, the fiscal deficit causes a continuous drain on foreign reserves, which at some point will be completely depleted. Put differently, if the fiscal deficit is not eliminated, at some point the government will be forced to abandon the currency peg and start printing money in order to cover the deficit.

Let T denote the period in which, as a result of having run out of foreign reserves, the government abandons the peg and begins printing money to pay for its fiscal deficit. The dynamics of the currency crisis can be characterized by three distinct phases:

1. *Pre-collapse phase* During this phase, which lasts until (and including) period $T - 2$, the currency peg is in place.

2. *BOP crisis* This crisis takes place in period $T - 1$ and is the period in which the domestic central bank faces a run against the domestic currency, resulting in massive losses of foreign reserves.

3. *Post-collapse phase* In this phase the nominal exchange rate floats freely and the central bank expands the money supply at a rate consistent with paying for the fiscal deficit.

Pre-Collapse Phase

From some point in the past through period $T - 2$, the nominal exchange rate is pegged, so the variables of interest behave just as described earlier. To recap, the nominal exchange rate is constant and equal to E, that is, $E_t = E$ for $t = T - 4, T - 3, T - 2$. By PPP and our assumption $P_t^* = 1$, the domestic price level is also constant over time and equal to E ($P_t = E$ for $t = ..., T - 4, T - 3, T - 2$). Because the exchange rate is fixed, the devaluation rate $(E_t - E_{t-1})/E_{t-1}$ is equal to zero. The nominal interest rate i_t, which by the interest parity condition satisfies $1 + i_t = (1 + r^*)E_{t+1}^e / E_t$, is equal to r^*. Note, in particular, that the nominal interest rate in period $T - 2$ is equal to r^* because the fixed exchange rate is still in place in period $T - 1$—thus $i_t = r^*$ for $t = T - 4, T - 3, T - 2$.

Also as discussed earlier, by pegging the nominal exchange rate, the government relinquishes the ability to change the nominal money supply. Also as before, the fact that seigniorage revenue equals zero under the peg means that the dynamics of foreign reserves are governed by

$$B_t^G - B_{t-1}^G = -DEF$$

for $t = T - 4$, $T - 3$, $T - 2$. The central bank loses the quantity DEF units of foreign reserves every period during the pre-collapse phase. The continuous loss of foreign reserves in combination with the zero lower bound on the central bank's foreign reserve holdings makes it clear that a currency peg is unsustainable in the long run in the presence of persistent fiscal deficits.

Post-Collapse Phase

At the beginning of period T, the government has zero foreign reserves $\left(B_T^G = 0\right)$. Given that B^G cannot go below zero and that government cannot (or does not) eliminate the fiscal deficit, it follows than in period T the monetary authority is forced to abandon the currency peg and to print money in order to finance the fiscal deficit. Thus, in the post-collapse phase, the government lets the nominal exchange rate float. Consequently the behavior of all variables is as we discussed above when we studied equilibrium under a floating exchange rate. In particular, the central bank must choose a money growth rate μ in order to generate enough seignorage revenue to finance the fiscal deficit, implying, just as above, that the nominal exchange rate depreciates each period at the rate μ, the domestic price level grows each period at the rate μ (i.e., the domestic inflation rate is μ), and the domestic nominal interest is higher than the foreign interest rate r^* by an amount that depends on μ.

Let's compare the economy's dynamics pre- and post-crisis. The first thing to note is that with the demise of the fixed exchange rate, price stability disappears as inflation sets in. In the pre-collapse phase, the rate of money growth, the rate of devaluation, and the rate of inflation are all zero. In contrast, in the post-collapse phase, these variables are all constant at the positive rate μ. Second, the sources used to finance the government's fiscal deficit are very different in the two phases. In the pre-crisis phase, the deficit is financed entirely with foreign reserves. As a result foreign reserves display a steady decline during the pre-collapse phase. Still, in the post-collapse phase the fiscal deficit is financed through seignorage income and foreign reserves are constant (and equal to zero in our example). Finally, in the post-collapse phase, real money balances are lower than in the pre-collapse phase because the domestic nominal interest rate is higher ($i_t > r^*$ during the post-collapse phase, while $i_t = r^*$ during the pre-collapse phase).

BOP Crisis: Period $T - 1$

In period $T - 1$, the fixed exchange rate has not yet collapsed. Thus the nominal exchange rate and the domestic price level are still equal to their values during the pre-collapse phase: $E_{T-1} = E$ and $P_{T-1} = E$. However, the important difference is that the domestic nominal interest rate is no longer equal to r^*. In period $T - 1$, the public expects a depreciation of the domestic currency to occur in period T.

Supposing that markets' expectations are rational (which means, in statistics terminology, that they will, on average, be correct), the expected rate of depreciation between period $T - 1$ and period T is μ: the same μ we have already been considering. That is,

$$\frac{E_T^e - E_{T-1}}{E_{T-1}} = \mu.$$

Therefore the nominal interest rate in period $T - 1$ jumps up to its post-crisis level, $i_{T-1} = (1 + r^*)(1 + \mu) - 1$ even though the depreciation hasn't yet happened.

As a result of the increase in the nominal interest rate, real balances fall in period $T - 1$ to their post-collapse level; that is,

$$\frac{M_{T-1}}{E} = \phi(\overline{c}, i(\mu)).$$

Because the nominal exchange rate in period $T - 1$ is still E, the fall in **real** money balances in period $T - 1$ (the right-hand side of the previous expression) must be brought about entirely through a fall in **nominal** money balances.

In period $T - 1$, fearing the imminent collapse of the domestic currency, the public runs to the central bank to exchange domestic currency for foreign currency. In period $T - 1$, the government still honors its commitment to exchange currency at the rate E, so it must dip into its foreign reserves (which, after all, represent claims to foreign currency) in order to do so. Thus, in period $T - 1$, foreign reserves at the central bank fall by more than DEF.

To see this more formally, the government budget constraint in period $T - 1$ tells us that

$$B_{T-1}^G - B_{T-2}^G = \frac{M_{T-1} - M_{T-2}}{E} - DEF$$

$$= \phi(\overline{c}, i(\mu)) - \phi(\overline{c}, r^*) - DEF$$

$$< -DEF.$$

The equality in the second line follows from the fact that $M_{T-1} / E = \phi(\overline{c}, i(\mu))$ and $M_{T-2} / E = \phi(\overline{c}, r^*)$. The inequality in the third line follows from the fact that $i(\mu) = (1 + r^*)(1 + \mu) - 1 > r^*$ and the fact that the money demand function is decreasing in the nominal interest rate: the higher is the nominal interest rate, the lower is the value of $\phi(.)$ (for a given value of $\overline{c}$).

The government budget in period $T - 1$ formalizes the reason for the demise of currency pegs is typically preceded by a speculative run against the domestic currency and large losses of foreign reserves by the central bank: even though the exchange rate is still fixed in period $T - 1$, the nominal interest rate rises in anticipation of a devaluation in period T, which in turn causes a contraction of the demand for real money balances in period $T - 1$. Because in period $T - 1$ the domestic currency is still convertible at the fixed rate E, the central bank must absorb the entire decline in the real demand for money by surrendering foreign reserves, which accelerates the onset of the crisis.

Chapter 31 Problem Set Questions

1. **Hazards of fixed exchange rates.** In this question you will use the fiscal theory of exchange rates to analyze the collapse of Argentina's fixed exchange rate in early 2002. The model is just as we have studied in class—in particular, consumption is constant at $\bar{c}$ in every period, real money demand is described by the function, $M_t / P_t = \phi(\bar{c}, i_t)$, PPP holds, and the foreign price level is equal to one in every period (i.e., $P_t^* = 1$ in every period t). Argentina runs a fiscal deficit of $DEF = 5.5$ every period, and there is no political will to ever reduce this deficit. The real money demand function is given by $\phi(\bar{c}, i_t) = \bar{c} - 10 \cdot i_t$, with $\bar{c} = 11$, and the exchange rate that Argentina is pegging (for as long as it can) is $E = 1$ peso per US dollar. Finally, the foreign real interest rate is $r^* = 0.10$, the government starts period 1 with foreign reserves of $B_0^G = 22$, and foreign reserves can never go below zero.

   a. As long as the fixed exchange rate is in place and is expected to remain in place, what is the numerical value of Argentina's nominal interest rate? Briefly justify your answer.

   b. As long as the fixed exchange rate is in place and is expected to remain in place, what is the numerical value of seignorage revenue for Argentina? Briefly justify your answer.

   c. As long as the fixed exchange rate is in place and is expected to remain in place, what is the numerical value of Argentina's BOP surplus or BOP deficit? Briefly justify your answer.

   d. If Argentine residents for some reason never expect a devaluation of the peso, how many periods will the fixed exchange rate last? Briefly justify your answer.

   e. If Argentine residents expect a 50 percent devaluation of the peso (i.e., in terms of our notation from class $\mu = 0.50$) in the very next period, what is the numerical value of the nominal interest rate in Argentina in the current period? Briefly justify your answer, and provide economic intuition for what you find.

   f. If Argentine residents do eventually come to expect a devaluation of the peso of 50 percent (as in part e), how many periods will the fixed exchange rate last? Carefully justify your answer, and also discuss the economic reason why there is (or is not) any difference between what you find here and what you found in part d.

2. **Fiscal theory of exchange rates.** In this question you will use the fiscal theory of exchange rates to analyze some consequences of a fixed exchange rate system. The

model is just as we have studied in class—in particular, consumption is constant at $\overline{c} = 11$ in every period, real money demand is described by the function, $M_t / P_t = \phi(\overline{c}, i_t)$, PPP holds, and the foreign price level is equal to one in every period (i.e., $P_t^* = 1$ in every period t). The domestic country runs a fiscal deficit of $DEF = -5.5$ (a negative deficit is a surplus...) every period, and there is no political will to ever change this deficit. The real money demand function is given by $\phi(\overline{c}, i_t) = \overline{c} - 10 \cdot i_t$, and the exchange rate that the country is pegging (for as long as it can) is $E = 2$ units of domestic currency per unit of foreign currency. Finally, the foreign real interest rate is $r^* = 0.10$, the government starts period 1 with foreign reserves of $B_0^G = 22$, and foreign reserves can never go below zero.

a. As long as the fixed exchange rate is in place and is expected to remain in place, what is the numerical value of the domestic nominal interest rate? Briefly justify your answer.

b. As long as the fixed exchange rate is in place and is expected to remain in place, what is the numerical value of the domestic country's BOP surplus or BOP deficit? Briefly justify your answer.

c. Based on your answer in part b, is the floating exchange rate higher than, lower than, or equal to $E = 2$? Briefly justify your answer. (Note: You do not need to compute any numerical values here.)

d. If markets/investors for some reason never expect a change in the nominal exchange rate, how many periods will the fixed exchange rate last? Briefly justify your answer.

The following applies to the remainder of this question: suppose that the government of the domestic country announces in period $T-1$ that in period T and forever beyond, the nominal exchange rate will be 1.9 units of domestic currency per unit of foreign currency, and markets/investors believe this announcement. For reference, note that $1.9/2 = 0.95$.

e. How does the domestic nominal interest rate in period $T - 1$ compare to the domestic nominal interest rate in period $T - 2$ (i.e., is it smaller than, larger than, or equal)? Briefly justify your answer, and provide economic intuition for what you find, including a brief economic explanation for why i_{T-1} differs from r^* if it does. (Note: You do not need to compute any numerical values here.)

f. Based on what you found in part e, is the domestic government's seignorage revenue in period $T - 1$ larger than, smaller than, or equal to its seignorage revenue in period $T - 2$? Briefly justify your answer, and provide economic intuition for what you find, including a brief economic explanation for why seignorage revenue differs from zero if it does. (Note: You do not need to compute any numerical values here.)

g. Based on what you found in part f, is the domestic country's BOP in period $T - 1$ larger than, smaller than, or equal to its BOP in period $T - 2$? Explain precisely your logic.

h. Does the expectation of a change in the exchange rate (from 2 units of domestic currency per unit of foreign currency to 1.9 units of domestic currency per unit of foreign currency, as described above) mean that the exchange rate system will last longer than without this change in expectations, shorter than without this change in expectations, or is it impossible to tell? Explain precisely your logic.

3. **BOP crises.** Consider the fiscal theory of exchange rates. Assume that consumption is constant at $\bar{c}$ in every period, real money demand is described by the money demand function, $M_t / P_t = \phi(\bar{c}, i_t)$, PPP holds, and the foreign price level is equal to one in every period (i.e., $P_t^* = 1$ in every period t). Also assume that interest rate parity holds throughout, and that the world real interest rate is $r^* = 0.10$. The government currently has net foreign bonds (net foreign reserves) of $B_0^G = 10$ (i.e., at the end of period zero—equivalently, at the beginning of period 1—the government has foreign reserves of 10), and is running a secondary deficit of 1 every period (i.e., $DEF = 1$ every period).

a. Suppose that there is a fixed exchange rate regime in place. Compute the domestic nominal interest rate as well as seignorage revenue for the government each period while the fixed exchange rate is in place.

b. If foreign creditors will not allow the government to have a negative net foreign reserve position (i.e., $B^G < 0$ can never occur), how many periods does it take for the fixed exchange rate to collapse, assuming that the eventual devaluation is a complete surprise to people?

Suppose that foreign reserves have now fallen to $B^G = 2$ (i.e., at the very beginning of the current period foreign reserve holdings are 2), and that the fiscal deficit remains as above. Suppose also that domestic residents now anticipate a devaluation of the domestic currency in the next period, and that the expected rate of depreciation between the current period and the next period is 10 percent. Call this expected rate of depreciation μ, so that $\mu = 0.10$.

c. What is the domestic nominal interest rate in the current period? Explain how you arrive at your answer and also provide brief economic intuition for your answer. (Hint: As in the chapter, the units of the exchange rate should be units of domestic currency per unit of foreign currency. Note that you do not need any numerical values for the exchange rate in order to solve this question.)

d. Based on your answer in part c, is seignorage revenue positive, negative, or zero in the current period? Briefly explain the economic intuition.

e. Now you will quantitatively determine how many periods it will actually take for the exchange rate to collapse, assuming that the devaluation does not come as a complete surprise to people and given the following circumstances:

  - The exchange rate set by the government (until the collapse) every period is $E = 1$.

  - The government has $DEF = 1$ every period.

  - The government starts with $B_0^G = 10$.

  - $r^* = 0.10$.

  - When the devaluation happens, people expect the currency to devalue by 10 percent (i.e., $\mu = 0.10$).

  - The money demand function is

    $$\phi(i_t) = 100 - 9.0909 i_t.$$

How many periods does it now take for the fixed exchange rate to collapse? How does your answer compare to what you found in part b above? Briefly explain economically why your answer here is the same or why it is different. (Hint: Use the intuition you gained in part c and part d.)

Mathematical Appendix: Refreshers, Reviews, and Reminders

This appendix provides a basic toolkit of mathematics that is often used in economic and macroeconomic analysis. The toolkit is not meant to be comprehensive, but rather as a reference point for the theory-based and empirically grounded applications in our discussions in this text.

Virtually all of the mathematical tools for economic applications revolve around the concept of **mathematical functions.** The concept of a function is a very general and powerful one. A function is a mathematical object that serves as a fundamental tool in many fields of analysis. We will not here give a rigorous or comprehensive treatment of the mathematical notion of a function. The purpose here is to (re)familiarize you with the basic concepts and the most important ways in which we will use functions as we develop tools of economic analysis in this course.

Abstract Functions and Functional Forms

A **function** transforms an **input** into an **output.** More specifically, a function is a rule that specifies how an input is to be transformed into some output. At its simplest level, the level with which we will be concerned, the inputs and outputs will all be numbers. In general, any function can have multiple inputs and multiple outputs. Every function that we will use will have only one output—that is, a function whose operation results in only one numeric value as its output. However, we will regularly encounter functions that have multiple inputs, in addition to functions that have simply a single input.

A function can be written and used in abstract form, as when we simply write and use the function $f(x)$ without specifying anything further about what the function actually does. Sometimes, however, in order to do something useful with a function, we need to specify a particular **functional form**—that is, we sometimes need to specify what a function actually does (i.e., what the rule is). Some examples of common functional forms will help illustrate the concept:

$$f(x) = x^2,$$

$$f(x) = 2x + 8,$$

$$f(x) = \sqrt{x},$$

$$f(x) = \ln(x),$$

$$f(x, y) = \ln(x) + 0.8\ln(y).$$

In these simple functions (functional forms) note that each function returns only one number as its output (as promised). Also note that the fifth function presented, and as displayed again here,

$$f(x, y) = \ln(x) + 0.8\ln(y),$$

is **a function of two inputs,** while the others are all functions of one input.

Arguments of Functions

To be a bit more formal mathematically, an input(s) to a function is commonly known as its **argument(s),** and the output of a function is commonly known as its **result** or **value.** Using the functions defined above, we see that each of the first four functions take one argument named x. The fifth function, $f(x, y)$, takes two arguments named x and y.

When actually performing numerical calculations using functions, the x in each case of the first four functions above would be replaced with an actual number because it is meaningless to *square the letter x,* because only *numbers* can be squared. This leads to the distinction between **formal arguments** and **actual arguments.**

Think of a formal argument as a placeholder in an abstract function. In each of the first four functions, the formal argument is x. In contrast, the $f(x, y)$ function contains **two formal arguments,** named x and y. More will be said about replacing formal arguments with actual arguments, but first let's examine the components of a function definition.

Dissecting the Components of a Function Definition

Examining the components of a function definition will help illuminate what a function actually represents. Consider the simple function given above:

$$f(x) = x^2.$$

There is much to understand about this function definition. Proceeding left to right:

- The name of the function is f. There is nothing particularly special about the name given to a function—f is a popular choice when trying to be as abstract as possible. Sometimes, the letter used to name a function is chosen so that it somehow represents a memorable aspect of the function. For example, the money demand function in maroeconomics is often named M^D. But any name is perfectly valid. In the example under consideration, we could have written $g(x) = x^2$ or $F(x) = x^2$ or $h(x) = x^2$ or *ExampleFunction*$(x) = x^2$. In short, we could have given *any* name to the function, not only f.

- The parentheses () contain the formal argument(s) of the function. In this case, the formal argument to the function f is x. In a function such as $f(x, y)$ above, the parentheses contain two arguments. An important point to note, similar to the point immediately above, is that the name of the formal argument is unimportant. In the functional form $f(x) = x^2$, the name of the formal argument is x. But it could have just as easily been named y, in which case the function definition would be $f(y) = y^2$. It could also have just as easily been named *argument,* in which case the function definition would then be $f(\text{argument}) = \text{argument}^2$. There would be absolutely no material change to the function definition if this were the case—precisely because the formal argument is simply a placeholder and does not itself mean anything.

- One the right-hand side of the equals sign is the **body** of the function. The body uses the formal argument(s) of the function and specifies what calculation should be performed. In our simple example above, the body specifies that the result should be the square of the argument. In the function $f(x) = 2x + 8$ above, the body specifies that the return value of the function should be two times the argument plus eight. Similarly for the other functions above.

Replacing Formal Arguments with Actual Arguments

As alluded to above, the usefulness of a function is in its ability to substitute actual numeric values for the formal arguments of the functions and thereby generate numeric results. Table A1 computes the results of two simple inputs for two of our example functions. All that has been done is to substitute actual arguments (10 and 20 in these particular cases) for the formal arguments x in the first two functions above. Specifically, what has been done is that the actual arguments have been substituted for the formal arguments in the *body* of the functions. The body of the function is then numerically computed, and the resulting numeric value is the return value of the function.

Table A1
Examples of functions

Functional form	Input	Calculation	Output/value
$f(x) = x^2$	10	10^2	100
$f(x) = x^2$	20	20^2	400
$f(x) = 2x + 8$	10	$2(10) + 8$	28
$f(x) = 2x + 8$	20	$2(20) + 8$	48

Note that in the absence of specifying actual arguments, the return value of the function is simply the body of the function itself—which *includes* the formal arguments. That is, if you are not given a numerical input for the argument x but are asked what $f(x)$ "is," it is simply (using the first row of table A1 as an example) x^2, which is the body of the function.

Using Abstract Functions in Algebraic Manipulations

A very important concept to understand is that functions can be manipulated algebraically just as "ordinary" variables and numbers are manipulated algebraically. The following visual illustrates this concept:

$x + 7 = 12$ $f(x) + 7 = 12$
⇓ **subtract 7 from both sides**   ⇓ **subtract 7 from both sides**
$x = 5$ $f(x) = 5$

In the simple expression $x + 7 = 12$, in order to solve for x, the value 7 is subtracted from both sides of the equality, which yields the solution $x = 5$. Completely analogously, if the expression $f(x) + 7 = 12$ is to be solved for $f(x)$, simply subtract 7 from both sides of the equality, which yields the solution $f(x) = 5$. If a particular functional form for f is not specified, then this is as far as we can take the calculation. That is, when no functional form is given, $f(x) = 5$ is a perfectly valid solution!

However, if a functional form *is* specified, then we can proceed a bit further. Continuing with our example from the preceding paragraph, if the function specified were $f(x) = 2x + 8$, then we can solve for x as follows:

$f(x) = 5$
⇓ **replace** $f(x)$ by the given functional form
$2x + 8$
⇓ **solve for** x
$x = -3 / 2$

Trying for yourself the other functional forms we have encountered would be a good exercise at this point.

The main point to understand is that performing algebraic manipulations with (abstract or particular) functions is just like performing algebraic manipulations with "ordinary" variables and numbers. There is nothing mysterious here, and you should make yourself comfortable with this concept and its mechanics because we will use it repeatedly throughout our study.

Key Concepts

- A function takes (numeric) inputs and results in (numeric) outputs.

- When provided with a specific functional form for a function, computations can be carried further then if no functional form is specified.

- When performing numerical calculations, if actual arguments are provided, the actual arguments replace the formal argument in the body of the function definition.

- Abstract functions can be manipulated algebraically just like ordinary variables and numbers.

Lagrange Optimization

With the concept of a function in hand, we now provide a brief overview of **constrained optimization.** The starting point in any economic analysis is to optimize the use of limited resources. Hence we often want to *maximize a function given some feasibility or affordability constraints.*

Formally, a constrained optimization problem is one in which the goal is to find numerical values for the arguments of a function in such a way that the numerical value of that function is maximized (or minimized) and that satisfy some pre-specified relationship(s) between the arguments being chosen.

Many of our economic applications of constrained optimization will involve functions of two arguments, so we first illustrate the method of **Lagrange optimization,** which is the standard mathematical tool used to solve constrained optimization problems, using a problem with two variables. Note, however, that the Lagrange method readily applies to functions of one, three, four, or any number of variables.

Consider the following mathematical constrained optimization problem. There is a function $f(x, y)$, and the goal is to find the numerical values of x and y that, when used simultaneously in f, maximize the numerical value of f *and* satisfy the relationship $g(x, y) = 0$. That is, g is some other function that the two variables x and y satisfy—but the goal is not to maximize (or minimize) g, the goal is to maximize f.

The Lagrange method in this problem proceeds as follows. Define an auxiliary variable λ (Greek lowercase letter "lambda"). The variable λ is the **Lagrange multiplier.** With the Lagrange multiplier, construct the following function, called the **Lagrange function:**

$$L(x, y, \lambda) = f(x, y) + \lambda g(x, y).$$

That is, the Lagrange function L is a function of **three** variables: x, y, and the newly constructed variable λ. The Lagrange function is made up of two components summed together: the **objective function** f that is to be maximized and λ times the **constraint function** g.

The next step in the procedure is to compute the partial derivatives of L with respect to each of its three arguments and set each resulting expression to zero. Using general notation, these three expressions are:

$$\frac{\partial L}{\partial x} = \frac{\partial f}{\partial x} + \lambda \frac{\partial g}{\partial x} = 0,$$

$$\frac{\partial L}{\partial y} = \frac{\partial f}{\partial y} + \lambda \frac{\partial g}{\partial y} = 0,$$

$$\frac{\partial L}{\partial \lambda} = g(x, y) = 0.$$

These three equations are the **first-order conditions** of the optimization problem under consideration. These three expressions are three equations in the three unknowns, x, y, and λ, which typically can be solved for unique values of the three unknowns once we specify particular functional forms for the functions $f(x, y)$ and $g(x, y)$ (recall our discussion of functions above). Note that the third expression is in fact just the constraint on the optimization problem. This is a general principle: the first-order condition of the Lagrangian with respect to the Lagrange multiplier always delivers back the constraint function.

Remember the goal here is to ultimately solve for x and y (and the Lagrange multiplier λ). We can solve each of the first two equations above for λ:

$$\lambda = -\frac{\partial f / \partial x}{\partial g / \partial x},$$

$$\lambda = -\frac{\partial f / \partial y}{\partial g / \partial y}.$$

Setting these two equal to each other, we find that

$$\frac{\partial f / \partial x}{\partial g / \partial x} = \frac{\partial f / \partial y}{\partial g / \partial y},$$

Or, equivalently,

$$\frac{\partial f / \partial y}{\partial f / \partial x} = \frac{\partial g / \partial y}{\partial g / \partial x}.$$

This expression literally states that *at the optimal solution*, the ratio of partial derivatives of the objective function f is equal to the ratio of partial derivatives of the constraint function g. At this point this is a completely abstract mathematical idea, but the basic result—that at the optimal solution, the ratio of partials of the objective function is equal to the ratio of partials of the constraint function—will be critical for many of the economic ideas we study, so it is well worth it to understand this idea as well as possible now.

The **optimality condition** (a term we will encounter in more precise instances) captured by the previous expression is one that *must* be satisfied *at the optimal solution*. Away from the optimal solution, however, this expression need not be satisfied (and in general will not be). Note well the content of these last two statements.

The multiplier λ has been eliminated from the optimality condition. This optimality condition coupled with the first-order condition of the Lagrangian with respect to λ, now comprise two equations in the two unknowns x and y. Given functional forms for f and g, we would be able to compute the required partial derivatives and thus solve for the optimal values of x and y (i.e., that combination of x and y that yields the maximum value of f and satisfies the constraint $g(x,y) = 0$).

To take a concrete example to see how the Lagrange technique yields a numerical solution, suppose $f(x,y) = \ln x + \ln y$ and $g(x,y) = x + y - 5 = 0$. The necessary partial derivatives are: $\partial f / \partial x = 1 / x$, $\partial f / \partial y = 1 / y$, $\partial g / \partial x = 1$, and $\partial g / \partial y = 1$. With these partials, the optimality condition becomes

$$\frac{\partial f / \partial y}{\partial f / \partial x} = \frac{\partial g / \partial y}{\partial g / \partial x} \Rightarrow \frac{1 / y}{1 / x} = \frac{1}{1},$$

which easily simplifies to $x = y$. Thus we now know that for this example, at the optimal solution (but not away from the optimal solution), $x = y$. Use this relationship in the constraint function (which, recall, is simply the first-order condition of the Lagrangian with respect to the multiplier), giving us $x + x - 5 = 0$. Clearly, the solution is $x = 2.5$, which then also implies that $y = x = 2.5$. The optimization problem is now solved: the values of x and y that sum to 5 and maximize the given function $\ln x + \ln y$ are $x = 2.5, y = 2.5$.

We have illustrated the Lagrange method using one constraint function. The method readily generalizes to handle two, three, four, or any arbitrary number of constraints on a given optimization problem. We will encounter economic applications in which there are multiple constraint functions on an optimization problem. To start simply, consider an example in which there are two constraint functions, $g(x,y) = 0$ as well as $h(x,y) = 0$, that must be satisfied in the optimization of the function $f(x,y)$. In order to handle two constraints, we need two Lagrange multipliers—let's name them λ_1 and λ_2. The Lagrange function in this case would be

$$L(x, y, \lambda_1, \lambda_2) = f(x,y) + \lambda_1 g(x,y) + \lambda_2 h(x,y).$$

The Lagrange function L here is a function of the **four** variables x, y, λ_1, and λ_2, and we must compute the partial derivatives of L with respect to each of its four arguments and set each resulting expression to zero. Again using general notation, the four first-order conditions are

$$\frac{\partial L}{\partial x} = \frac{\partial f}{\partial x} + \lambda_1 \frac{\partial g}{\partial x} + \lambda_2 \frac{\partial h}{\partial x} = 0,$$

$$\frac{\partial L}{\partial y} = \frac{\partial f}{\partial y} + \lambda_1 \frac{\partial g}{\partial y} + \lambda_2 \frac{\partial h}{\partial y} = 0,$$

$$\frac{\partial L}{\partial \lambda_1} = g(x, y) = 0,$$

$$\frac{\partial L}{\partial \lambda_2} = h(x, y) = 0,$$

which are four equations in four unknowns. In general, the system of equations can be solved to yield a unique solution for each of the four variables. Of course, the algebra here is a bit more tedious because there are more equations to work through.

Implicit Function Theorem

Although we will use this concept sparingly, the implicit function theorem (IFT) is a clever way of obtaining a derivative of one argument in a function with respect to another argument of that function *in a way that maintains the output value.*

As a simple warm-up illustration, suppose that $f(x, y) = x + y$. If $x = 5$ and $y = 3$, then obviously the output value is $f(x, y) = 8$. If we wanted to maintain the output value $f(x, y) = 8$ but want to change the **mix** between x and y, there are clearly an infinite number of combinations. One combination is $x = 3$ and $y = 5$. Another combination is $x = 4$ and $y = 4$. Yet another combination is $x = 1.235$ and $y = 6.765$. And so on. Thus, for every one unit change in the input argument x, there must be a one unit change in the argument y in **the equal and opposite direction** in order to maintain $f(x, y) = x + y = 8$.

Thus, if we seek to maintain the output value at $f(x, y) = 8$, but want to change the combination of x and y, the IFT tells us how.

More formally, given a function $f(x, y)$, the derivative of y (which, note, is one of the arguments of the f function) with respect to x (which, note, is also one of the arguments of the f function) is given by

$$\frac{dy}{dx} = -\frac{\partial f / \partial x}{\partial f / \partial y}.$$

Referring to the warm-up example above, for every one unit increase in x, a one unit decrease in y is needed in order to maintain $f(x, y) = x + y = 8$.

To use the IFT in a more interesting example, suppose $f(x, y) = xy^2$. To compute the partial derivative of f with respect to x, we treat y as a constant, in which case we obtain $\partial f / \partial x = y^2$, and to compute the partial derivative of f with respect to y, we treat x as a constant, in which case we obtain $\partial f / \partial y = 2xy$. The IFT then tells us that

$$\frac{dy}{dx} = -\frac{y^2}{2xy}$$

$$= -\frac{y}{2x}.$$

Thus, for every one unit change in the argument x, there must be a change in the argument y of $-y/2x$ units in order to maintain a particular value of $f(x, y)$.

Elasticity

Very often important in economic analysis—so now we are moving away from abstract mathematics basics—is the sensitivity of one variable to a change in another variable. That is, when one variable changes, how much impact does it have on another variable. Note that elasticity is not the same concept as the implicit function theorem.

A classic example is the sensitivity of quantity demanded for a particular good when a change has occurred in its market price. This sensitivity is defined as the elasticity of quantity demand with respect to the market prices

$$\varepsilon_{q^d, p} = \frac{\% \text{ change in quantity demanded of a good}}{\% \text{ change in market price of that good}}.$$

The notation ε (Greek lowercase letter "epsilon") is often used to describe elasticity. In this example, it is the elasticity of quantity demanded with respect to its price, hence the two subscripts q^d and p. Implicit in being able to compute an elasticity is that we already know the functional relationship between the two variables. In our example, consider it to be the **market demand function $q^d(p)$.**[1]

There are two major elasticity concepts in economics: the **arc elasticity** and the **point elasticity.** As you may recall from basic microeconomics, an arc elasticity averages between two potentially widely varying points on the known functional relationship. If the gap between these two points turns out to be very small, the arc elasticity is effectively the same as the point elasticity. For macroeconomic purposes, because changes that occur are typically "small," the important one is the point elasticity. Thus the point elasticity should be thought of as *the percentage by which one variable changes when a different variable changes by one percent, starting from a particular pair of those variables.*

The point elasticity is mathematically defined as

$$\varepsilon_{q^d, p} = \frac{\partial \ln q^d(p^{known})}{\partial \ln p^{known}} = \frac{\partial q^d(p^{known})}{\partial p^{known}} \cdot \frac{p^{known}}{q^d(p^{known})}.$$

---

1. Based on what we described above, the name of the function is q^d, the argument of the function is p, and the body is left unspecified.

This expression understandably seems very complicated, but it is for the sake of clarity. Suppose we know, based on the demand function, the starting pair (p^{known}, $q^d(p^{known})$), which is one single point on the demand function. Obtaining the point elasticity then requires computing the derivative of quantity demand with respect to price, *evaluated at the point* (p^{known}, $q^d(p^{known})$). Multiplying this by $p^{known}/q^d p^{known}$ yields the point elasticity of quantity demanded around the starting pair.

An example illustrates this. Suppose $q^d(p) = p^\psi$ (ψ is the lowercase Greek letter "psi"). This implies that $\partial q^d/\partial p = \psi p^{\psi-1}$, and hence the point elasticity, after several steps of algebra, is

$$\varepsilon_{q^d,p} = \frac{\partial \ln q^d}{\partial \ln p} = \frac{\partial q^d}{\partial p} \cdot \frac{p}{q^d}$$

$$= \frac{\psi p^{\psi-1} \cdot p}{q^d}$$

$$= \frac{\psi p^\psi}{q^d}$$

$$= \frac{\psi p^\psi}{p^\psi}$$

$$= \psi.$$

Notice that in the fourth step, the known functional relationship $q^d(p) = p^\psi$ was substituted in, which is perfectly valid to do.

Math Appendix Problem Set Questions

1. **Partial derivatives.** For each of the following multi-variable functions, compute the partial derivatives with respect to both x and y.

   a. $f(x,y) = xy$

   b. $f(x,y) = 2x + 3y$

   c. $f(x,y) = x^2 y^4$

   d. $f(x,y) = \ln x + 2 \ln y$

   e. $f(x,y) = 2\sqrt{x} + 2\sqrt{y}$

   f. $f(x,y) = x/y$

   g. $f(x,y) = y/x$

2. Implicit function theorem and the marginal rate of substitution. An important result from multivariable calculus is the implicit function theorem, which states that given a function $f(x, y)$, the derivative of y with respect to x is given by

$$\frac{dy}{dx} = -\frac{\partial f / \partial x}{\partial f / \partial y},$$

where $\partial f / \partial x$ denotes the partial derivative of f with respect to x and $\partial f / \partial y$ denotes the partial derivative of f with respect to y. Simply stated, a partial derivative of a multivariable function is the derivative of that function with respect to one particular variable, treating all other variables as constant. For example, suppose $f(x, y) = xy^2$. To compute the partial derivative of f with respect to x, we treat y as a constant, in which case we obtain $\partial f / \partial x = y^2$, and to compute the partial derivative of f with respect to y, we treat x as a constant, in which case we obtain $\partial f / \partial y = 2xy$.

We have described the slope of an indifference curve as the marginal rate of substitution between the two goods. Imagining that c_2 is plotted on the vertical axis and c_1 plotted on the horizontal axis, compute the marginal rate of substitution for the following utility functions:

a. $u(c_1, c_2) = \ln(c_1) + \ln(c_2)$

b. $u(c_1, c_2) = \sqrt{c_1} + \sqrt{c_2}$

c. $u(c_1, c_2) = c_1^a c_2^{1-a}$, where $a \in (0, 1)$ is some constant

Index